REGULATION OF TAX PRACTICE

LexisNexis
GRADUATE TAX SERIES

REGULATION OF TAX PRACTICE

LINDA GALLER
Professor of Law
Hofstra University School of Law

MICHAEL B. LANG
Professor of Law
Chapman University School of Law

Library of Congress Cataloging-in-Publication Data

Galler, Linda.
   Regulation of tax practice / Linda Galler, Michael B. Lang.
      p. cm. — (Graduate tax series)
   Includes index.
   ISBN 978-0-8205-6248-3 (hardbound)
   1. Tax lawyers—United States. 2. Tax consultants—United States. 3. Legal ethics—United States.
I. Lang, Michael B. II. Title.
   KF299.T3G35 2010
   343.7305'2044–dc22

                                                        2010002753

NOTE TO USERS
To ensure that you are using the latest materials available in this area, please be sure to periodically check the LexisNexis Law School web site for downloadable updates and supplements at www.lexisnexis.com/lawschool.

Editorial Offices
121 Chanlon Rd., New Providence, NJ 07974 (908) 464-6800
201 Mission St., San Francisco, CA 94105-1831 (415) 908-3200
www.lexisnexis.com

                                             (Pub. 3209)

PREFACE

The Lexis Graduate Tax Series grew out of the recognition that the goals of a graduate tax program are different than those of J.D. tax courses. J.D. tax courses are introductory in nature. Although many J.D. tax courses provide a good overview of their targeted areas of law, time rarely permits either in-depth analysis of complicated Code or Regulation provisions, or the application of those provisions to real life problems. In essence, J.D. tax courses provide students a foundation in the core statutory and judicial concepts.

LL.M. programs build on, and significantly expand, students' knowledge of the Code, Regulations, and judicial doctrines, and enhance their Code and Regulations reading skills. LL.M. programs require students to concentrate on the primary sources of the law, the Code and Regulations. Students are expected to improve their ability to read, comprehend, and apply the Code and Regulations, and they do so by working on complex fact patterns that raise difficult legal issues.

The different goals of graduate tax programs and J.D. tax courses suggest that the course materials used in those programs should also be different. Students in LL.M. programs need to move away from the standard, J.D., "author tells all," casebooks, which contain extensive quotations from cases and other secondary sources, and toward emphasis on the primary sources of the law. By applying the Code and Regulations to real-life fact patterns, students gain the confidence necessary to rely on the Code and Regulations as their main source of information.

An important, but different, driving force behind the development of specially-designed course materials for LL.M. programs is the dramatic expansion of the quantity and complexity of tax law over the past forty or fifty years. The current commercially available versions of the Code and Regulations are roughly four times as large as their 1970 predecessors. Over that period, class time dedicated to tax has grown very little. Covering much more material in the same period of time has led authors to write longer J.D. textbooks, many of which exceed one thousand pages. Such comprehensive coverage leads to extended textbook assignments. This both forces and permits the students to bypass the assigned Code and Regulations provisions and spend their available time answering problems by reference solely to the author's explanation of the law in the textbook. Tax casebooks written primarily for the larger J.D. market that purport to be suitable for both J.D. and LL.M. tax courses, also lean towards comprehensive explanations of the Code and Regulations, which tend to deflect students away from the primary sources.

Books in the Graduate Tax Series are designed to be read with, and complement, the study of the Code and Regulations. Although some chapters of books in the Series provide detailed explanation of the topic, more frequently the chapters provide a general, normally brief, overview of the topic together with more complete explanations of the applicable portions of the Code and Regulations that are particularly difficult to understand. Also, many of the problems are based on situations encountered in practice or found in decided cases. Although some of the questions either state or disclose the issues and even the applicable statutes, many of them require analysis of a given set of facts to first determine and then resolve the critical issues.

This book differs from others in the Graduate Tax Series by focusing on primary source materials other than the Code, Regulations and judicial decisions rendered by federal judges. Perusal of the list of Appendices reflects that wide array of sources governing the practice of tax law. State ethics rules and opinions, rules of court, and state judicial opinions are as significant in the regulation of tax practice as provisions of the Code (*e.g.*, return preparer penalties in Section 6694) and Regulations. In addition, ethics rules governing accountants who provide tax services are relevant to those who concurrently maintain professional licenses as lawyers and accountants, and also serve as nonbinding guidance to non-accountant lawyers who practice in the tax area.

Linda Galler would like to express her appreciation for the summer research grants provided by the Hofstra University School of Law that helped to make this book possible. She thanks her husband, Murray E. Singer, for his never-ending assistance and support, and for the example he sets of good moral character and wise judgment.

Michael Lang thanks Chapman University School of Law for providing summer research funding and research assistance to support his work on this book. He also appreciates the efforts of his research assistants, Michael Gates, Robert Thompson, Sharona Keshrim, and Van Ha, all of whom contributed to making the book a better work.

This book is supplemented by a LexisNexis "Web Course" that contains links to the lexis.com version of the Internal Revenue code and the Regulations. To access the Web Course:

1. Go to http://www.lexisnexis.com/lawschool/webcourses
2. Enter your LexisNexis Custom ID and Password (please call the LexisNexis Law School Support Line at 800-455-3947 [800-45LEXIS] if you have misplaced your Custom ID or Password)
3. Click the red "Courses" tab
4. Click on "National Web Courses" under the Course Catalog
5. Scroll down the list to find "Graduate Tax Series"
6. Click on "Enroll"

TABLE OF CONTENTS

Introduction

THE TAX LAWYER'S DUTY TO THE SYSTEM[1]

A fundamental, underlying issue in the field of lawyers' ethics, reflected in each of the tax practice-related topics covered in this text, is the conflict between a lawyer's duty to her client and her "duty to the system." Oddly, while "duty to the system" is a commonly used — perhaps overly used — phrase, it is virtually impossible to find a clear or concise definition of the "system" to which the duty relates! This definitional imprecision makes it difficult for students to conceptualize the lawyer's competing obligations and to appreciate the policy considerations that apply in reaching an ethically sound result. The notion of zealous representation of client interests is intuitive to law students; offsetting responsibilities, all too often, are not. Thus, our study begins with a modest attempt to define the tax lawyer's "duty to the system" in the hopes that such a discussion will afford context to the specific matters covered throughout this text.

The tax lawyer's "duty to the system" can mean one or more of four distinct obligations, only some of which apply to lawyers who practice in fields other than tax. First, "duty to the system" can refer to a series of limitations under the American Bar Association (ABA) Model Rules of Professional Conduct (Model Rules) on lawyers' zealous representation of clients. Second, "duty to the system" serves as a surrogate for the sentiment that lawyers should act honestly and ethically. Third, in some contexts the term "system" refers specifically to the set of laws and system of administration that comprise our nation's revenue raising process. Finally, the duty may not be to a system as such, but rather to a particular participant in the tax collection process, namely the IRS, which administers and enforces the tax laws on behalf of the federal government.

A. Limitations on Zealous Representation

In its broadest sense, the concept of a duty to the system derives from the principle of zealous regard for a client's interests. Under the ABA Model Code of Professional Responsibility (Model Code), the predecessor to the current Model Rules, lawyers were explicitly bound to represent clients "zealously within the bounds of the law."[2] This paramount duty of "warm zeal" was described in the 1908 Canons of Professional Ethics:

> The lawyer owes "entire devotion to the interest of the client, warm zeal in the maintenance and defense of his rights and the exertion of his utmost learning and ability," to the end that nothing be taken or be withheld from him save by the rules of law, legally applied. No fear of judicial disfavor or

---

[1] This Introduction is based on Linda Galler, *The Tax Lawyer's Duty to the System*, 16 VA. TAX REV. 681 (1997). The authors wish to thank the Virginia Tax Review, which has kindly granted permission for its use.

[2] Model Code Canon 7. Although the duty of a lawyer to represent her client zealously may be thought of as a duty to the client, it is described in the Model Code as a duty both to the client and to the legal system. Model Code EC 7-1; Model Code EC 7-19. Indeed, EC 7-19 is the first Ethical Consideration under the heading "Duty of the Lawyer to the Adversary System of Justice."

public unpopularity should restrain him from the full discharge of his duty. In the judicial forum the client is entitled to the benefit of any and every remedy and defense that is authorized by the law of the land, and he may expect his lawyer to assert every such remedy and defense.

Canons of Professional Ethics Canon 15 (1908 Canons). Although the Model Rules state the principle of zealous representation only in a comment[3] and substitute "reasonable diligence and promptness" for "zeal," the comment makes clear that Model Rule 1.3 carries forward interpretations of "zealous representation" under the Model Code.

A lawyer's duty to zealously represent her clients is not unrestrained, however. As "an officer of the legal system and a public citizen having special responsibility for the quality of justice,"[4] the lawyer must abide by a series of limitations stated in the Model Rules. For example, lawyers have a duty of candor toward tribunals and of fairness to opposing parties and their counsel; lawyers must disclose adverse authority to the court; lawyers may not advise or assist clients in criminal or fraudulent conduct, etc. These limits on zeal, which apply primarily but not exclusively to lawyers engaged in litigation, are often described as duties to the system of justice or to the court, which override a lawyer's duty to her client when a conflict arises.

Limitations on zealous representation exist in many areas of tax practice. As a return preparer, for example, the adviser's reporting standard (currently "substantial authority" for nondisclosed positions, under Section 6694 of the Internal Revenue Code[5]) reflects an attempt to restrain lawyers from assisting clients in playing "the audit lottery." Regarding a lawyer's duty to maintain client confidences, relatively recent changes to Model Rule 1.6(b) permit lawyers to disclose confidential client information in certain circumstances involving substantial injury to the financial interests of another, e.g., the federal government or IRS. In the context of the tax lawyer's role as tax planner and adviser, Circular 230 prescribes detailed rules on the degree of analysis required in rendering written tax opinions and extent to which a lawyer may rely on others. These examples are merely teasers for what will be covered in this text. The overriding point for the moment, however, is that in each of these settings, the tax lawyer, like her counterparts in other areas of law practice, must carefully weigh the obligation to zealously represent her client against the restraints imposed by the Model Rules and other professional regulations.

---

[3] Comment [1] to Model Rule 1.3 states:

> A lawyer should pursue a matter on behalf of a client despite opposition, obstruction or personal inconvenience to the lawyer, and may take whatever lawful and ethical measures are required to vindicate a client's cause or endeavor. A lawyer should act with commitment and dedication to the interests of the client and with zeal in advocacy upon the client's behalf.

The obligation of zeal as stated in the Model Code was subject to three criticisms. First, "zealousness" might be interpreted to mean "zealotry," justifying wrongful conduct on behalf of a client. Second, "zeal" might imply personal involvement by the lawyer rather than detached professional commitment. Third, there is a lack of fit between the concept of "zealousness" and the appropriate quality of representation in nonadversarial contexts.

[4] Model Rules, Preamble.

[5] Unless otherwise indicated, all references to "Code" in this text are to the Internal Revenue Code of 1986, as amended from time to time. Unless otherwise indicated, all references to "Section" are to sections of the Code.

B. The Duty to Act Honestly and Ethically

The tax lawyer's duty to the system has been described as a responsibility to act fairly and honestly and to represent one's clients with integrity:[6] "The tax practitioner has the responsibility, above all, to walk upright."[7] Former Commissioner of Internal Revenue Margaret Richardson has said:

> [T]he confidence of the American people in our tax system, which is still the standard for the rest of the world ..., ultimately ... rests on the integrity and professional conduct of those of us who are charged with administering the system, as well as those of you whose livelihoods depend upon the system.[8]

That the responsibility to act ethically extends beyond the client to the legal system is reflected in the standards of ethics adopted by the profession. The Preamble to the Model Code, for example, admonishes that "it is the desire for the respect and confidence of the members of his profession and of the society which he serves that should provide to a lawyer the incentive for the highest possible degree of ethical conduct." Ethical rules that impose a duty of candor to the court or fairness to an adversary, for example, are premised upon maintenance of public confidence in a concept of justice that is both fair and impartial. Likewise, in order to obtain effective legal assistance, a client must be able to trust her lawyer. It is not enough that the lawyer be skilled and act diligently; she also must be worthy of her client's confidence.

The duty to act with honesty and integrity permeates each of the tax lawyer's roles. The lawyer's personal integrity is particularly significant in tax planning, where the lawyer assists her client in making or creating facts, rather than in characterizing events that have already occurred. Some cases are easy: a lawyer may never participate in perpetrating a lie. Other situations are more difficult. Where the tax consequences of a transaction depend upon the taxpayer's purpose or motive, for example, what degree of assurance must the lawyer have that the client's state of mind is in fact that which is most favorable from a tax standpoint? If a lawyer believes that her client's state of mind is otherwise, may she assist in creating evidence to support the desired tax treatment? Surely, the first consideration in answering questions like these — before consulting professional regulations — must be the lawyer's own sense of honesty and integrity.

C. Duty to the Revenue System

Despite the seemingly generic nature of the phrase "duty to the system," most commentators on tax ethics mean to refer to the tax lawyer's responsibilities to the nation's revenue raising apparatus — "a set of laws and a system of

---

[6] Randolph W. Thrower, *Preserving the Integrity of the Federal Tax System*, 33 N.Y.U. INST. ON FED. TAX'N 707, 709–11 (1975); Milton Young, *Does the Tax Practitioner Owe a Dual Responsibility to His Client and to the Government?–The Practice*, 15 S. CAL. TAX INST. 39, 49 (1963).

[7] Young, *supra*, at 49. Mr. Young similarly stated, "It seems to me that we have a continuing responsibility to our clients and to all citizenry, hence the Government, to maintain a dignity and a decency in our professional conduct." *Id*. at 41.

[8] Margaret Milner Richardson, Remarks at the Invitational Conference on Professionalism in Tax Practice (Oct. 1993), *quoted in* Michael Mulroney, *Report on the Invitational Conference on Professionalism in Tax Practice, Washington, D.C., October 1993*, 11 AM. J. TAX POL'Y 369, 373 (1994).

administration."[9] Tax attorneys, they say, are obliged "to protect the revenue"[10] and "to see that the tax system is functioning honestly, fairly and smoothly."[11] Under this view, lawyers advising clients in tax matters must balance the immediate demands of their clients against the public's interest in a sound tax system that operates in accord with policy judgments reached through a democratic process. The duty to the revenue laws, of course, overlaps with the lawyer's duty to act honestly and with integrity: "When you are fair and honest and able in your controversies with the Service, you contribute to the system."[12]

The duty to the revenue system may be conceptualized as a duty to third parties, not in the sense of investors or other non-clients who could rely upon a lawyer's written opinion, but of "unrepresented citizens who ascribe value to a well-functioning tax system."[13] The public, after all, has an abiding interest in protecting the government's ability to fund itself and in ensuring that each taxpayer pays her fair share of governmental costs as allocated by democratic processes.

Tax practice differs from other areas because the client's adversary is always the government. The question has long been debated whether this distinction implies that attorneys engaging in tax practice are subject to different standards than attorneys who practice in other areas of law. On one side, it is argued that ethical issues encountered in dealing with the government are largely the same as those presented in dealing with any adversary. On the other side, proponents of separate (or additional) standards for tax practitioners argue that a tax system based on voluntary compliance and self-assessment necessitates dual responsibilities to the client and to the tax laws.

In ordinary situations, lawyers or their clients can be expected to review documents received from adversary parties; where differences cannot be resolved, courts are called upon to make determinations. The IRS, however, receives approximately 250 million tax returns annually and cannot possibly be expected to scrutinize each return to assure its accuracy. Lawyers advising clients in the preparation of tax returns, therefore, may have a special duty to the tax system to see that client returns are as accurate and truthful as possible, without regard to whether they will ever be examined. Certain restrictions are necessary to discourage the taking of return positions designed to exploit the audit selection process. Circular 230's standard for advising tax return positions and its limitations on contingent fees may be thus explained.

The duty to the revenue raising system arises in the controversy setting as well. An age-old issue that remains controversial today is the dilemma confronted by an attorney who receives a settlement document from the IRS that contains a mathematical error in favor of the client. Does the lawyer's duty to the system trump her duty to the client if the client instructs her not to call the

---

[9] Thrower, *supra* note 6, at 707.

[10] Michael C. Durst, *The Tax Lawyer's Professional Responsibility*, 39 U. FLA. L. REV. 1027, 1051 n.81 (1987).

[11] Mortimer M. Caplin, *Responsibilities of the Tax Advisor—A Perspective*, TAXES (CCH) 1030, 1032 (Dec. 1962).

[12] Thrower, *supra* note 6, at 711.

[13] Ann Southworth, Note, *Redefining the Attorney's Role in Abusive Tax Shelters*, 37 STAN. L. REV. 889, 912 (1985).

error to the attention of the IRS? Must she consult with the client in the first instance, before notifying the IRS of the error?

D. Duty to the Government

Finally, tax lawyers have a duty to the government itself. The rules here vary with role or context. At the return preparation stage, the lawyer acts as both an advocate and an adviser. As an adviser, the lawyer's role is to advise her client how to comply with the legal obligation to file an annual return, not to engage the government as an opponent. ABA Formal Op. 85-352, however, regards the filing of a tax return as a possible first step in an adversary proceeding. Therefore, the lawyer has an ethical duty not to mislead the IRS by misstatement, silence, or through her client, but has no ethical duty to disclose the weaknesses of her client's case. She may advise the statement of positions most favorable to the client, even if she believes that the positions probably will not prevail, so long as she has a good faith belief that those positions are warranted in existing law or can be supported by a good faith argument for an extension, modification, or reversal of existing law. As students will learn shortly, the principle articulated in the preceding sentence may be inconsistent with the provisions of the Code, in particular the preparer penalty rules in Section 6694. (Under that section, advisers could be subject to a hefty penalty for advising taxpayers to take positions that lack "substantial authority.") Thus, the precise contours of a tax lawyer's ethical duties, at the moment, are unclear. The basic point, however, remains: while a tax adviser may ethically advise her client to take a return position that she believes could lose in court, there are clear limits on how aggressive tax advice may be.

On the other hand, where an audit or litigation is underway, the IRS is on notice that the lawyer is an adversary and her primary duty is to the client. Thus, the lawyer's obligations to the IRS in this context are those of one litigator to another. She may make any nonfrivolous argument that could win for the client and need not act in the government's interest.

Chapter 1

SOURCES OF PROFESSIONAL REGULATION

A study of the professional regulation of tax advisers must begin with an introduction to the various sources of rules and guidance that regulate the conduct of such professionals. These rules are promulgated at both the state and the federal level. It is assumed for purposes of this study that students are familiar generally with the ethics rules that apply to all members of their professions (law and accounting). Therefore, the discussion below focuses specifically on regulation of tax practice.

I. STATE REGULATION

A. Introduction

Like their counterparts in other areas of law practice, tax attorneys are subject to rules of professional conduct adopted in the states in which they practice. Most of these rules or codes emanate from one of several sets of model rules prepared by the ABA. The ABA, however, has amended its models from time to time, and states have adopted their own variations. Thus, while this text generally utilizes the Model Rules when it addresses obligations and duties arising under state ethics rules, students are cautioned to consult their own states' rules in actual situations.

Violations of ethical rules may result in professional discipline by the states, e.g., suspension or disbarment from practice. Although the rules are drafted with an eye towards discipline within the profession, courts increasingly look to ethical rules in litigation. In legal malpractice actions, it is not unusual to see lawyers accused of breaching professional duties by failing to comply with prescribed ethical standards. Or, in a fee dispute, a client might be excused from paying a legal fee because a lawyer or law firm has violated a state's ethical code. (State ethics rules usually provide explicitly that violation of an ethical rule should not, in and of itself, give rise to a cause of action or create a presumption that a legal duty has been breached. *See* Model Rules Scope [20].) Finally, motions to disqualify a lawyer or law firm are sometimes premised on violations of state ethical rules, for example (and perhaps most notably), those prohibiting conflicts of interest.

Bar associations at all levels issue advisory opinions on discrete ethical questions. While these are never binding, they are both helpful and instructive. In the area of tax practice, two ABA opinions, ABA Formal Op. 314 (1965) and ABA Formal Op. 85-352, are and have been particularly influential. (ABA Formal Op. 314 is reproduced in full later in this chapter. ABA Formal Op. 85-352 is referred to throughout this text and can be found at Appendix B.) The ABA Section of Taxation Committee on Standards of Tax Practice has occasionally issued Statements of Standards of Tax Practice, which offer ethical guidance to practitioners in tax practice specific situations.

Unlike the ABA, the American Institute of Certified Public Accountants (AICPA)[1] has the power to discipline its members. Thus, violations of the AICPA Code of Professional Conduct may result in expulsion or suspension from the AICPA, admonishment, or receipt of a letter of required corrective action. The AICPA has issued a series of Statements on Standards for Tax Services (SSTSs), which are considered part of the AICPA Code of Professional Conduct and are enforceable rules. (The full text of the AICPA SSTSs and Interpretations can be found at Appendix C. Interpretation No. 1-2, "Tax Planning," was issued separately and can be found at Appendix D.) Courts, moreover, sometimes refer to the SSTSs (and their predecessors, the AICPA Statements of Responsibilities in Tax Practice) in litigation, in defining an appropriate standard of care. The Council of the AICPA designates bodies to interpret the AICPA Code of Professional Conduct, often resulting in ethical rulings. In the tax area, interpretations are issued by the Tax Executive Committee.

Since individual states license accountants to practice, each state's Board of Accountancy also may issue its own rules. A number of states have adopted the AICPA SSTSs as enforceable standards. State boards of accountancy may issue ethics opinions or other guidance.

PROBLEM 1-1

Preparation of an income tax return does not constitute the practice of law in the sense that non-lawyers may lawfully prepare returns. If an attorney prepares tax returns for clients, should her services be subject to her state's professional conduct rules? *See* Libarian v. State Bar of California, 21 Cal. 2d 862, 136 P.2d 321 (1943).   Yes

PROBLEM 1-2

Many tax attorneys are also CPAs, who hold themselves out as dual professionals and whose practices consist of providing both legal and accounting services. If the ethical rules of each profession differ, for example, as to referrals or as to solicitation of clients, which profession's rules must the individual follow? May such a practitioner choose to follow the rule that is least restrictive? Why or why not? *See* Pa. Bar Ass'n Comm. on Legal Ethics and Prof'l Responsibility, Informal Op. 90-157 (Dec. 11, 1990); ABA Formal Op. 328 (1972).

No - Follow more restrictive

B. The Relationship Between Tax Lawyers and the IRS

ABA Formal Op. 314 addresses the relationship between the IRS and lawyers who practice before it, and sets out the basic duties owed by such lawyers to the agency. Opinion 314 has been superseded as to the "reasonable basis" reporting standard[2] but otherwise accurately describes the guiding principles.

---

[1] Not all accountants are CPAs and the AICPA rules are binding only on its members. As to others, however, AICPA materials serve as a guide to ethical behavior.

[2] ABA Formal Op. 85-352, which is discussed at several points in this text, superseded ABA Formal Op. 314 with respect to the "reasonable basis" standard for advising on tax return positions. Under ABA Formal Op. 85-352:

ABA Formal Opinion 65-314 *— Reasonable Basis*
(Apr. 27, 1965)[3]

The Committee has received a number of specific inquiries regarding the ethical relationship between the Internal Revenue Service and lawyers practicing before it. Rather than answer each of these separately, the Committee believing this to be a matter of general interest, has formulated the following general principles governing this relationship.

Canon 1 says: "It is the duty of the lawyer to maintain towards the Courts a respectful attitude." Canon 15 says that the lawyer owes "warm zeal" to his client and that "The office of attorney does not permit, much less does it demand of him for any client, violation of law or any manner of fraud or chicane." Canon 16 says: "A lawyer should use his best efforts to prevent his clients from doing those things which the lawyer himself ought not to do, particularly with reference to their conduct towards Courts . . .". Canon 22 says: "The conduct of the lawyer before the Court and with other lawyers should be characterized by candor and fairness."

All of these canons are pertinent to the subject here under consideration, for Canon 26 provides: "A lawyer openly, and in his true character, may render professional services . . . in advocacy of claims before departments of government, upon the same principles of ethics which justify his appearance before the Courts . . .".

Certainly a lawyer's advocacy before the Internal Revenue Service must be governed by "the same principles of ethics which justify his appearance before the Courts". But since the service, however fair and impartial it may try to be, is the representative of one of the parties, does the lawyer owe it the same duty of disclosure which is owed to the courts? Or is his duty to it more nearly analogous to that which he owes his brother attorneys in the conduct of cases which should be conducted in an atmosphere of candor and fairness but are admittedly adversary in nature? An analysis of the nature of the Internal Revenue Service will serve to throw some light upon the answer to these questions.

The Internal Revenue Service is neither a true tribunal, nor even a quasijudicial institution. It has no machinery or procedure for adversary proceedings before impartial judges or arbiters, involving the weighing of conflicting testimony of witnesses examined and cross-examined by opposing counsel and the consideration of arguments of counsel for both sides of a dispute. While its procedures provide for "fresh looks" through departmental reviews and informal and formal conferences procedures, few will contend that the service

---

A lawyer may advise reporting a position on a tax return so long as the lawyer believes in good faith that the position is warranted in existing law or can be supported by a good faith argument for an extension, modification or reversal of existing law and there is some realistic possibility of success if the matter is litigated.

As will be discussed later in this text, in light of changes to Section 6694(a) (preparer penalty rules), ABA Formal Op. 85-352 itself is in need of revision.

provides any truly dispassionate and unbiased consideration to the taxpayer. Although willing to listen to taxpayers and their representatives and obviously intending to be fair, the service is not designed and does not purport to be unprejudiced and unbiased in the judicial sense.

It by no means follows that a lawyer is relieved of all ethical responsibility when he practices before this agency. There are certain things which he clearly cannot do, and they are set forth explicitly in the canons of ethics.

Canon 15 scorns the false claim that it is the duty of the lawyer to do whatever may enable him to succeed in winning his client's cause no matter how unscrupulous, and after making it clear that the lawyer owes entire devotion to the interest of his client, Canon 15 concludes as follows:

> . . . But it is steadfastly to be borne in mind that the great trust of the lawyer is to be performed within and not without the bounds of the law. The office of attorney *does not permit*, much less does it *demand* of him for any client, violation of law or any manner of fraud or chicane. He must obey his own conscience and not that of his client [emphasis supplied].

Canon 22 relating to candor and fairness, states that

> It is unprofessional and dishonorable to deal other than candidly with the facts . . . in the presentation of causes.

These and all kindred practices are unprofessional and unworthy of an officer of the law charged, as is the lawyer, with the duty of aiding in the administration of justice.

Canon 29 provides in part that a lawyer should strive at all times to uphold the honor and to maintain the dignity of the profession and to improve not only the law but the administration of justice.

Canon 32 states that

> No client . . . is entitled to receive nor should any lawyer render . . . any advice involving disloyalty to the law whose ministers we are . . .

> [He] advances the honor of his profession and the best interests of his client when he . . . gives advice tending to impress upon the client and his undertaking exact compliance with the strictest principles of moral law . . . [A] lawyer will find his highest honor in a deserved reputation for fidelity to private trust and to public duty, as an honest man and as a patriotic and loyal citizen.

In addition, the preamble to the canons concludes as follows:

> No code or set of rules can be framed which will particularize all the duties of the lawyer . . . in all the relations of professional life. The following canons of ethics are adopted by the American Bar Association as a general guide, yet the enumeration of particular duties should not be construed as a denial of the existence of others equally imperative, though not specifically mentioned.

The problem arises when, in the course of his professional employment, the attorney acquires information bearing upon the strength of his client's claim. Although a number of canons have general bearing on the problem (Canons 15, 16,

22 and 26), Canon 37 regarding client confidences and Canons 29, 41 and 44 regarding perjury, fraud and deception and the withdrawal of an attorney are most relevant.

For example, what is the duty of a lawyer in regard to disclosure of the weaknesses in his client's case in the course of negotiations for the settlement of a tax case?

Negotiation and settlement procedures of the tax system do not carry with them the guarantee that a correct tax result necessarily occurs. The latter happens, if at all, solely by reason of chance in settlement of tax controversies just as it might happen with regard to other civil disputes. In the absence of either judicial determination or of a hypothetical exchange of files by adversaries, counsel will always urge in aid of settlement of a controversy the strong points of his case and minimize the weak; this is in keeping with Canon 15, which does require "warm zeal" on behalf of the client. Nor does the absolute duty not to make false assertions of fact require the disclosure of weaknesses in the client's case and in no event does it require the disclosure of his confidences, unless the facts in the attorney's possession indicate beyond reasonable doubt that a crime will be committed. A wrong, or indeed sometimes an unjust, tax result in the settlement of a controversy is not a crime.

Similarly, a lawyer who is asked to advise his client in the course of the preparation of the client's tax returns may freely urge the statement of positions most favorable to the client just as long as there is reasonable basis for those positions. Thus where the lawyer believes there is a reasonable basis for a position that a particular transaction does not result in taxable income, or that certain expenditures are properly deductible as expenses, the lawyer has no duty to advise that riders be attached to the client's tax return explaining the circumstances surrounding the transaction or the expenditures.

The foregoing principle necessarily relates to the lawyer's ethical obligations — what he is required to do. Prudence may recommend procedures not required by ethical considerations. Thus, even where the lawyer believes that there is no obligation to reflect a transaction in or with his client's return, nevertheless he may, as a tactical matter, advise his client to disclose the transaction in reasonable detail by way of a rider to the return. This occurs when it is to the client's advantage to be free from either a claim of fraud (albeit unfounded) or to have the protection of a shorter statute of limitations (which might be available by the full disclosure of such a transaction in detail by way of a rider to the return).

In all cases, with regard both to the preparation of returns and negotiating administrative settlements, the lawyer is under a duty not to mislead the Internal Revenue Service deliberately and affirmatively, either by misstatements or by silence or by permitting his client to mislead. The difficult problem arises where the client has in fact misled but without the lawyer's knowledge or participation. In that situation, upon discovery of the misrepresentation, the lawyer must advise the client to correct the statement; if the client refuses, the lawyer's obligation depends on all the circumstances.

Fundamentally, subject to the restrictions of the attorney-client privilege imposed by Canon 37, the lawyer may have the duty to withdraw from the matter. If for example, under all the circumstances, the lawyer believes that the service relies on him as corroborating statements of his client which he knows to be false, then he is under a duty to disassociate himself from any such reliance unless it is obvious that the very act of disassociation would have the effect of violating Canon 37. Even then, however, if a direct question is put to the lawyer, he must at least advise the service that he is not in a position to answer.

But as an advocate before a service which itself represents the adversary point of view, where his client's case is fairly arguable, a lawyer is under no duty to disclose its weaknesses, any more than he would be to make such a disclosure to a brother lawyer. The limitations within which he must operate are best expressed in Canon 22:

> It is not candid or fair for the lawyer knowingly to misquote the contents of a paper, the testimony of a witness, the language or the argument of opposing counsel, or the language of a decision or a textbook; or with knowledge of its invalidity, to cite as authority a decision that has been overruled, or a statute that has been repealed; or in argument to assert as a fact that which has not been proved, or in those jurisdictions where a side has the opening and closing arguments to mislead his opponent by concealing or withholding positions in his opening argument upon which his side then intends to rely.

It is unprofessional and dishonorable to deal other than candidly with the facts in taking the statements of witnesses, in drawing affidavits and other documents, and in the presentation of causes.

So long as a lawyer remains within these limitations, and so long as his duty is "performed within and not without the bounds of the law", he "owes 'entire devotion to the interest of the client, warm zeal in the maintenance and defense of his rights and the exertion of his utmost learning and ability', to the end that nothing be taken or be withheld from him, save by the rules of law, legally applied" in his practice before the Internal Revenue Service, as elsewhere (Canon 15).

The AICPA has not explicitly addressed the relationship between the IRS and accountants who practice before it or defined the basic duties owed by CPAs to the IRS. However, the AICPA SSTSs, which provide guidance as to specific circumstances, are meant both to reflect the AICPA's standards of tax practice and to delineate accountants' responsibilities to taxpayers, the public, the government, and the profession.

PROBLEM 1-3

Is filing a tax return an adversarial process? If it is, then a lawyer arguably acts as an advocate in rendering advice in connection with positions taken on a return. As an advocate, ethics rules permit a lawyer to advise her client not to volunteer information to the IRS and the lawyer herself is not obligated to disclose weaknesses in her client's position. Indeed, a lawyer in an advocacy role is prohibited, with only narrow exceptions, from disclosing client confidences without express permission from the client. *See* Model Rule 1.6; ABA Formal Op. 85-352. On the other hand, advice rendered to a client in connection with return preparation may be characterized as merely helping a client to satisfy the legal obligation to file a tax return. In advising a taxpayer how to comply with the law, duties as an advocate arguably do not come into play at all. But see Section 6694(a), which imposes a steep penalty on tax return preparers who advise return positions that do not satisfy specific statutory standards. (Section 6694 will be examined in considerable detail in Chapter 2.)

PROBLEM 1-4

Tax practice differs from other practice areas because the client's adversary is always the government. Does this distinction imply that attorneys engaging in tax practice are or should be subject to different standards than attorneys who practice in other areas of law? On one hand, it can be argued that ethical issues encountered in dealing with the government are largely the same as those presented in dealing with any adversary. On the other, however, a tax system based on voluntary compliance and self-assessment may necessitate dual responsibilities to the client and to the tax laws. The Introduction to this text posits that tax lawyers are indeed subject to special duties — to the nation's revenue raising process and to the government agency that administers it, i.e., the IRS.

C.   Jurisdictional Questions

Multijurisdictional practice ("MJP") refers to law practice in a host state by a lawyer who is licensed in a different state. MJP raises two principal issues: (1) does the out-of-state lawyer violate a host state's unauthorized practice of law ("UPL") rules; and (2) if an out-of-state lawyer is permitted to practice in a host state, what ethical rules must that lawyer follow while carrying out work in the host state?[4] These issues are particularly relevant in tax practice, which largely concerns matters of federal law, not state law. However, many attorneys are asked to render advice as to state tax law, as well, and often are called upon to advise with respect to state tax laws in states in which they are not licensed. MJP and other matters related to state regulation of tax practice will be taken up in Chapter 5.

PROBLEM 1-5

Lawyer has been licensed to practice law in Washington, D.C., for many years and has had a federal tax law practice there for most of that time. He has gotten tired of the "beltway" rat race and has decided to move to pristine Bend, Oregon, and open a practice limited to representing clients on federal tax matters such as federal income, corporate and estate tax filings. Can Lawyer do this without taking and passing the Oregon bar examination? *See* Model Rule 5.5. Even before amendments were proposed to Model Rule 5.5, some states allowed out-of-state lawyers to give advice regarding federal law. *See, e.g.,* State Bar of Arizona No 00-08 (practice restricted to claims against the federal Social Security Administration and appeals of Social Security cases before the Federal Courts in Arizona).

---

[4] A third question, which is not addressed here, is: If an out-of-state lawyer is permitted to practice in a host state and does so, which state has the right to discipline the lawyer for failing to meet the relevant ethical standard?

PROBLEM 1-6

Lawyer is a tax partner in a Seattle law firm. Lawyer represents a large corporation that is under audit. The revenue agent and Lawyer agree to send certain issues to IRS Appeals, and the case is assigned to the IRS Appeals office in San Francisco. Lawyer is unable to resolve the matter through e-mail and telephone conversations and it becomes necessary to hold a hearing. Lawyer travels to San Francisco for the hearing. Would California be justified in asserting that Lawyer has engaged in UPL in California? *See* Sperry v. Florida, 373 U.S. 379 (1963) (holding that federal patent regulations preempted state regulations that prohibited non-lawyers from prosecuting patents in the United States Patent Office).

No limited purpose

PROBLEM 1-7

OH

Lawyer is a tax associate at a Cincinnati law firm and is licensed to practice in Ohio. She often works in her home office in Kentucky on weekends. In which state is Lawyer practicing law on the weekends? *See* Zelinsky v. Tax Appeals Tribunal, 769 N.Y.S.2d 464 (Ct. App. 2003), *cert. denied*, 541 U.S. 1009 (2004) (upholding New York's right to tax a law professor's income attributable to services performed at his home in Connecticut).

II.   FEDERAL REGULATION: CIRCULAR 230

The Secretary of the Treasury is statutorily authorized to regulate the practice of representatives before the Treasury Department (Treasury), as well as the admission, suspension, and disbarment from such practice. 31 U.S.C. § 330. Under that authority, the Secretary has issued regulations that are commonly referred to as "Circular 230." Circular 230 is most easily accessed on the IRS's website, http://www.irs.gov/pub/irs-pdf/pcir230.pdf, but its official citation is 31 C.F.R. part 10. (The latest version of Circular 230 can also be found in Appendix A.)

Circular 230 consists of five parts. The first part of Circular 230 establishes the Office of Professional Responsibility (OPR), which administers and enforces the provisions of Circular 230 and sets out rules on eligibility to practice before the IRS. That is followed by the "guts" of Circular 230 — the rules, i.e., duties, responsibilities, and restrictions applicable to practitioners when they engage in practice before the IRS. (As will be discussed shortly, what constitutes practice before the IRS is broadly construed to include tax-related services in which the IRS is not directly involved.) Part three encompasses the sanctions that can be imposed for violations of Circular 230 and part four contains the rules and procedures applicable in disciplinary proceedings in which practitioners are accused of violating Circular 230. The last part of Circular 230 contains several rules that don't fit anywhere else.

A.   Practicing Before the IRS

Circular 230 §§ 10.2, 10.3 and 10.7

Members of five professions are permitted to represent taxpayers before the IRS. By virtue of their professional licenses, attorneys and CPAs have the right to practice before the IRS. "Enrolled agents" are neither lawyers nor CPAs, but persons who are former IRS employees or who have enough knowledge of tax law and practice to pass an examination administered by OPR and who maintain those skills through required continuing professional education. "Enrolled actuaries" are licensed actuaries who are permitted to practice before the IRS only with respect to certain issues pertaining to employee retirement plans. Likewise, "enrolled retirement plan agents" may practice before the IRS only with respect to employee retirement plan matters; such individuals must either have worked for the IRS or pass an OPR-administered examination. All such professionals are referred to as "practitioners" in Circular 230. In limited circumstances, for example, representing immediate family members, others are permitted to practice before the IRS.

"Practice before the IRS" comprehends all matters connected with a presentation to the IRS or any of its officers or employees relating to a taxpayer's rights, privileges, or liabilities under laws or regulations administered by the IRS. Not surprisingly, such presentations include preparing and filing documents, corresponding and communicating with the IRS, and representing a client at conferences, hearings and meetings. Several years ago, the definition of practice was expanded to include the rendering of written advice with respect to any entity, transaction, plan or arrangement, having a potential for tax avoidance or evasion. Thus, office practice can constitute practice before the IRS, and failure to comply with Circular 230 in that setting may result in disciplinary sanctions.

Noticeably absent from the list of activities constituting practice before the IRS, and therefore not subject to the provisions of Circular and oversight by OPR, is the preparation and filing of federal tax returns for clients.[5] A person needs no particular training or professional credential to prepare tax returns for others. (This may explain why so many used car dealerships are listed in the Yellow Pages under both Used Cars and Tax Return Preparation. We imagine that the dealers permit clients of the return preparation business to use their anticipated tax refunds as down payments!) The omission was intentional, however, largely because of (1) a desire to make tax return filing easy as a means of encouraging taxpayers to file and (2) the cost and administrative burden any governmental oversight or regulation would entail. From time to time, the IRS considers whether to regulate return preparers but no such proposals have been acted upon.[6]

PROBLEM 1-8

A friend of yours knows that you took a lot of tax courses at law school. At some point before you are admitted to the bar, your friend asks you to prepare her federal income tax return for 2009. Can you do it? Why or why not?

PROBLEM 1-9

(You are still not admitted!) A friend receives a letter from the IRS concerning an income tax return that she filed last year. She asks for your help and

---

[5] Some argue that return preparation *is* covered by the general definition of "Practice before the IRS" in Circular 230 § 10.2(a)(4) but that, since Circular 230 § 10.7(e) permits any individual to prepare returns, merely preparing returns does not bring a person within the jurisdiction of Circular 230.

[6] For a discussion of the latest proposals to regulate return preparers, see Jeremiah Coder, *Will Self-Regulation of Preparers Take Root?*, 124 TAX NOTES 10 (2009).

No — can't practice before IRS

advice. At this point, it looks as if all you'll have to do is write a letter to the IRS clarifying a few facts. Can you write the letter on your friend's behalf? Why or why not? If a face-to-face meeting is called for, can you represent your friend? Why or why not?

Yes, immediate family member?

PROBLEM 1-10

(You are still not admitted!) Your parents receive a letter from the IRS notifying them that their joint federal income tax return for 2007 has been selected for audit. Wishing to get their money's worth from all of the tuition bills that they have paid on your behalf, they ask you to represent them. Can you? Why or why not?

B. Duties and Restrictions Relating to Practice Before the IRS

Circular 230 §§ 10.22, 10.23 and § 10.33
Model Rule 1.3 and Comments *? Where is this (ask)*

The individual rules and restrictions comprising the second part of Circular 230 will be covered in context throughout this text. At this point, however, two specific rules are noted; these rules apply in all practice contexts and permeate all practice before the IRS.

Due diligence. Section 10.22 imposes a duty to exercise "due diligence." Circular 230 does not define due diligence but, based on other rules in Circular 230, the concept probably means that while a practitioner is not required to "audit" her client, she must make reasonable inquiries when a client provides information that suggests a need for further inquiry; that a practitioner may rely on information provided to her by her client but may not ignore implications learned from the information provided; and that a practitioner must make reasonable inquiries if information provided by or on behalf of a client seems incorrect, incomplete or inconsistent with other information in the possession of the practitioner.

The concept of due diligence does not appear anywhere in the Model Rules. While Model Rule 1.3 is titled "Diligence," that rule does not embody the substance of "due diligence" in Circular 230. Students should review Model Rule 1.3. The Comments under Model Rule 1.3 focus on competence, meeting deadlines, zealous representation, and completing all work related to a client matter. Promptly meeting deadlines is consistent with Circular 230 § 10.23, which imposes a duty not to unreasonably delay the prompt disposition of any matter before the IRS. The *Sykes* opinion, *infra* Section II.D., reflects an unsuccessful attempt by OPR to discipline an attorney for failing to exercise due diligence by issuing tax opinion letters that did not analyze relevant facts, law, and regulations that could have had an effect on the basis issue opined on in the letters.

Circular 230 § 10.22 also addresses reliance on other professionals. Except as provided Circular 230 §§ 10.34, 10.35 and 10.37, a practitioner is presumed to have exercised due diligence if she relies on the work product of another person and the practitioner used reasonable care in engaging, supervising, training, and evaluating that other person, taking account of the nature of the relationship between the two.

Best Practices. Circular 230 § 10.33 delineates what Treasury considers are best practices in the context of IRS practice. These best practices are aspirational only and cannot form the basis for discipline.

C. Sanctions for Violating Circular 230

Circular 230 §§ 10.50, 10.51 and § 10.52
OPR Guide to Sanctions (Appendix E)

Violations of Circular 230 may result in one or more of four sanctions: censure (i.e., public reprimand), suspension from practice before the IRS, disbarment from practice before the IRS, or monetary penalty. Suspension and disbarment from practice before the IRS are the most commonly imposed sanctions.

Congress gave the IRS authority to impose monetary penalties for Circular 230 violations in 2004. A monetary penalty may be imposed on a firm as well as on an individual violator of Circular 230 if the practitioner whose actions violated Circular 230 was acting on behalf of an employer or firm and the employer or firm knew or reasonably should have known of the conduct. A monetary penalty may be imposed in addition to other sanctions, and a penalty may be imposed on both the individual and her employer or firm.[7] A monetary penalty will not exceed the gross income derived (or to be derived) by the individual and the firm or entity from the conduct giving rise to the penalty.

Although Circular 230 § 10.50(c) calls for imposition of such penalties, and the IRS has issued additional guidance on how it would implement its authority, Notice 2007-39, 2007-1 C.B. 1243, to date OPR has refrained from initiating any proceedings to collect monetary penalties ostensibly because of ambiguities in the rules and procedures applicable to firms. It is anticipated, however, that such rules will be issued shortly and that OPR will begin to use its authority.

Three categories of act or omissions are sanctionable under Circular 230:

1. incompetent and disreputable conduct,
2. willful violations of Circular 230, and
3. violations of certain provisions of Circular 230 through recklessness or gross incompetence.

Incompetence and disreputable conduct includes any of fifteen specific acts or omissions listed in Circular 230 § 10.51. (Oddly, Section 10.50 refers to conduct that is incompetent *or* disreputable while Section 10.51(a) uses the terms conjunctively. It is unclear whether this difference has or has had any practical effect.) The level of intent (e.g., reckless, willfulness, etc.) is indicated in each of the items in the list. For example, under Circular 230 § 10.51(a)(14), failure to sign a client's return, where the practitioner's signature is required by federal tax law, is not considered incompetent and disreputable conduct if the failure is due to reasonable cause and not to willful neglect. Students are cautioned that willfully failing to file one's own federal income tax return is considered incompetent and disreputable conduct, which may result in

---

[7] It is anticipated that Circular 230 will be revised to preclude the IRS from "stacking" monetary penalties and preparer penalties imposed and collected under Section 6694 with respect to the same conduct.

sanction even if a practitioner's representation of clients is impeccable.[8] Circular 230 § 10.51(a)(6).

Willful violations of *any* section of Circular 230 (except for Section 10.33, which sets forth aspirational best practices) are sanctionable. According to the opinion in *Sykes, infra* Section II.D., the term "willful" for Circular 230 purposes means the same thing that it does in civil and criminal tax contexts — "the voluntary, intentional violation of a known legal duty." Consequently, OPR does not have to show that a practitioner acted with malicious intent or bad purpose, only that he purposefully disregarded or was indifferent to his obligations.

Violations of Circular 230 §§ 10.34, 10.35, 10.36 or 10.37 (standards with respect to tax returns and other documents, covered opinions, and other written advice) are sanctionable only if they result from recklessness or gross incompetence. It is unclear what recklessness and gross incompetence (as opposed to mere incompetence) encompass, but Circular 230 § 10.52(a)(13) might be helpful in this regard. (That section considers as incompetent and disreputable conduct within Section 10.51 the giving of a false opinion, knowingly, recklessly or through gross incompetence, or engaging in a pattern of providing incompetent opinions on questions arising under the federal tax laws.)

> For purposes of this paragraph (a)(13), reckless conduct is a highly unreasonable omission or misrepresentation involving an extreme departure from the standards of ordinary care that a practitioner should observe under the circumstances. A pattern of conduct is a factor that will be taken into account in determining whether a practitioner acted knowingly, recklessly, or through gross incompetence. Gross incompetence includes conduct that reflects gross indifference, preparation which is grossly inadequate under the circumstances, and a consistent failure to perform obligations to the client.

The process for deciding which sanction or sanctions to impose has long been a source of mystery to the practicing tax bar. Recently, however, OPR released a Guide to Sanctions outlining the circumstances under which particular sanctions will be imposed, and setting forth mitigating and aggravating factors. This Guide will become part of the Internal Revenue Manual at some point; at present, it can be found on the IRS web site at http://www.irs.gov/pub/irs-utl/newly_revised_final_tax-non_compliance_sanction_guidelines_3.pdf. (It is also reproduced at Appendix E.) The Guide ranks sanctions from censure through increasing periods of suspension to disbarment based on a list of factors, the number of violations, and OPR's perceptions of a practitioner's current fitness to practice. The Guide contains the following characterization of the circumstances under which each of the sanctions might be appropriate:

---

[8] OPR regularly publishes, in the Internal Revenue Bulletin, a list of practitioners who have been subjects of OPR disciplinary proceedings. (Yes, the listing includes names and states of residence.) Taking one recent list as an example, Announcement 2009-46, 2009-21 I.R.B 1040 (which covers no particular period of time), reported that two attorneys and four CPAs had been suspended from practice before the IRS for failing to file several federal tax returns and one attorney had been disbarred from practice before the IRS for willful failure to file a federal tax return.

In general, a reprimand or censure is appropriate where that sanction is all that is necessary to correct the behavior. Where the determination of suspension is 6 months or less, reprimand or censure may be appropriate. Suspensions up to 24 months are appropriate where a suspension is necessary to bring home to the practitioner the severity of his or her violation of Circular 230. Suspensions in excess of 24 months are appropriate where the misconduct indicates that the practitioner may be perpetrating an on-going harm to the taxpaying community or where the misconduct, for instance, multiple instances of violations, indicates a current lack of fitness to practice that would not be rectified by a shorter suspension. The suggested suspensions are for each individual violation. Disbarment will be sought for any violation where the determination of suspension is at least 5 years.

Oddly, all of the examples in the Guide involve practitioners' failures to timely file their own federal income tax returns. One comes away with the impression that OPR has elevated such practitioner lapses to an enforcement priority. Whether or not this is so, the examples (and the Guide as a whole) do provide a glimpse into the process that OPR follows in determining the severity of sanctions.

D. Disciplinary Proceedings

Circular 230 §§ 10.60, 10.61 and 10.76(b)

A practitioner charged with violating Circular 230 is entitled to a hearing before an Administrative Law Judge (ALJ).[9] Many, if not most, charges, however, are resolved by settlement between the practitioner and OPR. Circular 230 § 10.61(b) permits OPR to agree to a voluntary sanction, presumably including both a unilateral consent to a sanction initially proposed by OPR and a sanction negotiated between a practitioner and OPR.

While it is beyond the scope of this text to outline the specific procedures followed by OPR during the disciplinary process, several points will be made after students have studied the opinion below. The opinion was issued by an ALJ in a Circular 230 disciplinary proceeding involving one of the taxpayers' attorneys in the infamous Long-Term Capital tax shelter transaction. Students might wish to review the district and appellate court opinions in that case in conjunction with the ALJ's disciplinary opinion below to fully appreciate the role of the tax attorney and his advice. *Long-Term Capital Holdings v. United States,* 330 F. Supp. 2d 122 (D. Ct. 2004), *aff'd,* 150 Fed. Appx. 40 (2d. Cir. 2005). (*Long-Term Capital* is referred to later in this text, at Chapter 4, in connection with an issue relating to attorney-client privilege.)

---

[9] Disciplinary proceedings under Circular 230 are presided over by ALJs. Circular 230 § 10.70. Because the IRS does not maintain its own corps of ALJs, those presiding in Circular 230 disciplinary proceedings are borrowed from other agencies and typically have little or no tax practice experience or expertise. The ABA Section of Taxation has commented that this arrangement is acceptable or even, perhaps, optimal, and should not be changed. *ABA Tax Section Submits Comments on Disciplinary Procedures of IRS Office of Professional Responsibility,* 2005 TNT 236-18 (Dec. 8, 2005).

Director, Office of Professional Responsibility
v. John M. Sykes, III
Complaint No. 2006-1
www.irs.gov/pub/irs-utl/sykes_alj_dec_redacted.pdf

This matter arises from a complaint issued on January 19, 2006, by the Director, Office of Professional Responsibility, Department of the Treasury, Internal Revenue Service (OPR), pursuant to 31 C.F.R. 10.60 and 10.91, issued under the authority of 31 U.S.C. 330 (1986), seeking to have Respondent, John M. Sykes, III, an attorney engaged in practice before the Internal Revenue Service, suspended from such practice for a period of one year. The complaint alleges that Respondent failed to exercise due diligence in connection with certain opinions he issued to the investment firm comprised of Large Hedge Fund LP #1, Large Hedge Fund LP #2 and Large Hedge Fund LP #3,[10] on or about Date 1 and Date 2, and that he willfully engaged in disreputable conduct within the meaning of 31 C.F.R. Part 10, when he issued those opinions.

Respondent filed a timely answer denying that he engaged in any misconduct and/or that he has engaged in any disreputable conduct and asserting that this proceeding is time-barred under the statute of limitations provided in 28 U.S.C. 2462 because the alleged misconduct occurred more than five years prior to issuance of the complaint.

A hearing was held in Washington, DC, on September 18 through 20, 2007, at which the parties were given a full opportunity to examine and cross-examine witnesses and to present other evidence and argument. Proposed findings of fact, conclusions of law, and supporting reasons submitted by the parties have been given due consideration. Upon the entire record and my observation of the demeanor of the witnesses, I make the following

Findings of Fact

Respondent is a tax attorney who has been associated with the State #1 office of the law firm of Attorney & Attorney (A&A) since Date 4 and has been a partner in that firm since Date 3. He has an LL.M. degree in tax from NYU Law School and has over 30 years of experience in a practice specializing in the tax aspects of leasing transactions. Partner 1, a retired A&A partner who also specialized in the tax aspects of leasing transactions and who worked with Respondent for many years, described him as one of the brightest tax attorneys he has ever met. Tax Attorney 1, a tax attorney and financial advisor with extensive experience in private practice, Government, and academia, testified that he regarded Respondent "as one of the best tax lawyers I've worked with." In its post-hearing brief, OPR states that "Respondent is an acknowledged expert in the area of the tax law at issue in the underlying case," which gave rise to the complaint in this proceeding. Respondent first became involved with what led to the underlying case when he was part of an A&A team that worked on a series of leasing transactions known as Leasing Transactions #1 and Leasing Transactions #2.[11]

---

[10] [1] These entities were related limited partnerships and will be referred to collectively as Large Hedge Fund.

[11] [2] The Leasing Transactions #1 involved leases of Corporation #1 computer equipment and the Leasing Transactions #2 transaction involved truck leases.

The Leasing Transactions #1 were designed by Tax Attorney 1 and the financial advisory firm of Advisory Firm #1 for its client Corporation #1 and involved Corporation #1's computer leasing business. In Date 5, Corporation #1 sought the assistance of Advisory Firm #1 to improve its competitive position in the computer leasing industry. Previously, Corporation #1 had leased computer equipment it owned to end-users for approximately 36 months. Under the leasing structure devised by Advisory Firm #1 in the Leasing Transactions #1, Corporation #1 entered a master lease, leasing the computer equipment to Offshore Entity #1 for a period of 60 months, subject to the end-user leases. Offshore Entity #1, in turn, subleased the computer equipment, also subject to the end-user leases for a period of approximately 48 months to Limited Partnership #1, a limited partnership comprised of Advisory Firm #1 and the investment firm Investment Company #1. Under the sublease Limited Partnership #1 was to pay rent to Offshore Entity #1 for the term of the sublease. Limited Partnership #1 prepaid a portion of its rent under the sublease in an amount equal to about 92 percent of the rents due it under the end-user leases. To do this Limited Partnership #1 borrowed money from Bank #1, securing the loan with the rents it anticipated receiving under the end-user leases. Offshore Entity #1 used the prepayment to purchase U.S. Treasury securities which served as security for Offshore Entity #1's rental payments to Corporation #1 under the master lease. In addition to the economic benefits flowing to Corporation #1 and others in these transactions, they were designed to create substantial tax benefits for various investors by shifting otherwise taxable income to Offshore Entity #1, which was not subject to taxation by the United States, and shifting deductions and losses related to that income to entities that were U.S. taxpayers.

In order for the transactions to have the desired effects, it was essential that the leases be considered "true leases" for U.S. tax purposes. If Corporation #1, as the owner of the computer equipment, did not retain sufficient burdens and benefits of ownership at the end of the lease terms the leases could be considered sales of the property rather than leases. Among the factors to be considered in determining a "true lease" are the value of the equipment at various times during the lease term and the expected remaining useful life of the leased property at the end of the lease.

As the Leasing Transactions #1 were being formulated in early Date 5, A&A was retained by Advisory Firm #1 to advise it on structuring the transactions and to provide opinions on the "true lease" status of the leases. The A&A team was under the direction of firm Partner 1[12] and Respondent, at that time an associate attorney of the firm, was part of that team.[13] The credited testimony of Partner 1 and Respondent and the documentation in the record establishes that the A&A team and its co-counsel sought to identify all of the legal issues likely to be involved and that they conducted extensive legal research and analyses of the tax statutes and common law doctrines reasonably expected to have an impact on the lease transactions before A&A issued any opinions. These included Internal Revenue Code (Code) Sections 269, 446, and 482, and

---

[12] [3] Partner 1 estimated that, as of Date 5, he had worked on between 50 and 100 tax opinions involving the subject of "true leases."

[13] [4] The law firm of Law Firm #3 served as co-counsel and assisted in putting these transactions together.

the common law doctrines of business purpose, economic substance, substance-over-form, step transactions and sham transactions.

One of the important factors in the analysis done by A&A was an appraisal of the computer equipment. If the equipment had insufficient value and remaining useful life, it could result in the lease transactions being treated as sales for tax purposes. Partner 1 and Respondent were involved in selecting the appraiser of the computer equipment. After interviewing four appraisal firms, the firm of Appraisal Firm #1 was chosen and Appraiser #1 did the appraisal of the computer equipment. Partner 1 testified that they closely examined all of the appraisal firms and concluded that Appraisal Firm #1 had the needed experience in the computer equipment area. Respondent testified that he reviewed a draft of Appraiser #1's appraisal to assure that it was internally consistent and that it provided the answers needed to evaluate the tax consequences of the lease transactions. He also discussed the appraisal with Appraiser #1 and had him explain any parts that were unclear. Partner 1 testified that because he had not dealt with leases of computer equipment before he wanted someone else with experience in that area to review the Appraisal Firm #1 appraisal to give him "some level of comfort" that the approach used and the value determined by Appraisal Firm #1 were correct and that its conclusions were reasonable. The firm of Accounting Firm #1, with whom Partner 1 had previously dealt, was selected to review the Appraisal Firm #1 appraisal. Accounting Firm #1 concluded that the Appraisal Firm #1 appraisal followed generally accepted appraisal procedures, the conclusions in the appraisal were reasonable, and that the methodology used to determine residual values of the computer equipment was reasonable.[14]

Ultimately, A&A issued five written opinions signed by Partner 1 concerning the federal tax consequences of the subject lease transactions which closed between August Date 5 and July Date 6. Those opinions concluded that the master leases and subleases were "true leases" and that the rent prepayment under the subleases was income to Offshore Entity #1.

These opinions were issued as "short form" opinions, meaning that they contained a detailed recitation of the facts and conclusions relating to the particular transaction but did not contain a written legal analysis. Partner 1 testified that in his experience clients in leasing transactions preferred to have, and A&A always issued, short form opinions. He said that much of the legal analysis in the firm's leasing practice was similar and cumulative and involved a collection of materials in the firm's files which were developed in connection with other leasing transactions, sometimes, dating back several years.

These true lease opinions were issued at the "more likely than not level," which Partner 1 testified means that there is at least a 51 percent chance that the conclusions in a tax opinion given to a client are correct and that if the case went to court, was properly tried, and all of the facts and law were understood by the tribunal, that is what the result would be. This is contrasted with a "reasonable basis" opinion which has a 25 percent chance that it is correct, a "substantial authority" opinion which has about a 40 percent chance, a "should"

---

[14] [5] Respondent testified that the Leasing Transactions #2 involving trucks was simpler and A&A did not feel a need for a review of that appraisal.

opinion which has a 75 to 80 percent chance, and a "will" opinion which has about a 95 percent chance.[15]

The next steps in these lease transactions were the "exchange transactions" in which during Date 5 and Date 6 Offshore Entity #1 transferred its lease-hold interests and the U. S. Treasury securities to a number of U.S. corporate investors in exchange for preferred stock in those corporations.[16] These exchanges were structured to be tax-free exchanges under Section 351 of the Code and were intended to provide tax benefits to the U.S. corporations by separating the income received by Offshore Entity #1, which was not subject to U.S. taxation, from the deductions for the rent paid to Corporation #1 under the leases by the U.S. corporate taxpayers. The process is referred to as "lease stripping."

On October 13, 1995, the IRS had issued Notice 95-53 in which it announced its intention to challenge losses claimed as a result of lease stripping transactions. The notice indicated that new regulations might be issued and also stated that the IRS may apply various specified sections of the Code and corresponding regulations to such transactions, as well as, common law principles, including, the business-purpose doctrine, the substance-over-form doctrine, and the step and sham transaction doctrines, to existing transactions.

A&A had acted as counsel to Advisory Firm #1 on the five Leasing Transactions #1 exchange transactions which closed between October Date 5 and August Date 6. It provided the corporate investors with the true lease opinions signed by Partner 1 which were based on the work done in connection with the lease transactions. Other counsel for the corporate investors used these true lease opinions in issuing their own opinions advising the clients concerning the deductibility of their rental payments under the master leases and whether the exchange transactions met the requirements of Section 351 of the Code.[17]

The tax opinions authored by the Respondent which led to the complaint in this matter concern the basis for tax purposes of the preferred stock held by Offshore Entity #1 as a result of the exchange transactions. Some of that stock was acquired by Large Hedge Fund which in Date 3 requested that A&A provide it with opinions as to the basis of the stock in order to claim substantial losses on its partnership tax returns when the stock was sold and to insulate it from penalties that might be asserted by the IRS. Respondent authored and signed those tax basis opinions and OPR alleges that in doing so he failed to exercise due diligence and engaged in disreputable conduct.

The basis opinions authored by Respondent were short form opinions. They opined that (a) the exchange transactions met the requirements for a tax-free exchange under Section 351 of the Code, (b) the stock received by Offshore Entity #1 would have a basis equal to the amount specified therein, and (c) if Offshore Entity #1 were to sell that stock for cash in a bona fide arms-length

---

[15] [Eds. note: There is no apparent basis for the ALJ's descriptions, in percentage terms, of the various opinion standards. Tax opinion standards are discussed in Chapter 3, *infra*.]

[16] [6] Those corporations were Corporation #3, Corporation #4, Corporation #5, Corporation #6, and Corporation #7.

[17] [7] The firms were Law Firm #5, Law Firm #4, and Accounting Firm #2.

transaction with economic substance, its gain or loss from that sale would be determined by reference to the basis specified in the opinion.

In Date 7, Large Hedge Fund sold some of the stock it had received from Offshore Entity #1 for approximately one million dollars. On its Federal partnership tax returns, relying [on] a tax opinion from the firm of Law Firm #2 as to the tax consequences of the acquisition and sale of the stock and on the basis opinion provided by Respondent as to the tax basis of that stock, Large Hedge Fund claimed a basis which purportedly gave it net capital losses of over $100 million. After an examination of those returns, the IRS disallowed the losses claimed by Large Hedge Fund on the grounds that the transactions between Offshore Entity #1 and Large Hedge Fund were sham transactions which lacked a non-tax business purpose and did not have reasonable expectations of profit apart from the benefits accruing to Large Hedge Fund from the purported losses for tax purposes. Substantial penalties were also imposed on Large Hedge Fund for understatement of income.

Large Hedge Fund challenged the IRS's determinations in the U.S. District Court for the District of State #2 and lost. The court held that the sale of the high basis preferred stock lacked economic substance beyond the creation of tax benefits, that the transfer of the stock to Large Hedge Fund in exchange for a partnership interest and the subsequent sale of that interest back to Large Hedge Fund constituted a single sham transaction not having a reasonable expectation of profit and lacking in any business purpose other than tax avoidance. The court also held that Large Hedge Fund was subject to the understatement of income penalties asserted against it because it did not establish that it could reasonably rely on the Law Firm #2 opinion regarding tax treatment of the partnership transactions. Because of that, the court did not reach the question of whether Large Hedge Fund could have reasonably relied on the A&A opinions concerning the basis of the stock. (Redacted opinions concerning third party.) Following the trial and decision in the district court in the Large Hedge Fund tax case, the Department of Justice, which had represented the IRS in that proceeding, referred this matter to OPR which subsequently issued the complaint against Respondent.

Analysis and Conclusions

While the Respondent admits to having engaged in "limited practice" before the IRS, he does not concede that the matters involved here constitute practice before the IRS or make him subject to the federal statute, 31 C.F.R. U.S.C. 330, and the regulations at 31 C.F.R. Part 10 governing such practice.[18] However, he has not pursued this contention in his post-trial brief. Section 10.2(d) of 31 C.F.R. broadly defines practice before the IRS to include all matters connected to a presentation to the IRS or any of its officers and employees relating to a taxpayer's rights, privileges, or liabilities under the federal tax laws. The ultimate purpose of the basis opinions prepared by Respondent which are the

---

[18] [8] The regulations are contained in what is known as Treasury Department Circular No. 230. The current version of Circular No. 230 was last revised in 2005 and contains the procedural rules applicable to this proceeding. The 1996 version was in effect when Respondent's basis opinions were issued and govern this proceeding.

subject matter of this proceeding was to convince the IRS that the basis of the stock in question for tax purposes was what the opinions said it was and to shield the taxpayer from penalties that might be asserted if the IRS disagreed with the basis being claimed. I find that the opinions were intended and were reasonably expected to be a part of the taxpayer's presentation to the IRS in support of its position with respect to the basis of the stock and that Respondent's preparation of those opinions constituted practice before the IRS. Consequently, I find that Respondent is subject to the law and regulations governing such practice.

Inasmuch as OPR seeks to suspend Respondent from practice before the IRS for a period of one year, 31 C.F.R. 10.76(a) requires that "an allegation of fact that is necessary for a finding against the practitioner must be proven by clear and convincing evidence in the record." While not defined in Circular No. 230, a generally accepted definition of clear and convincing evidence is that it requires a degree of proof which will produce in the mind of the trier of fact a firm belief as to the allegations sought to be established. It is more than a mere preponderance but less than proof beyond a reasonable doubt. *Jove Engineering, Inc., v. IRS.* 92 F.3d 1539, 1545 (11th Cir. 1996); *Hobson v. Eaton,* 399 F.2d 781, 784 fn. 2 (6th Cir.1968). The allegations must be proven to a "high probability." *Waits v. Frito-Lay, Inc.,* 978 F.2d 1093, 1105 (9th Cir. 1992).

The complaint alleges that Respondent failed to exercise due diligence in violation of 31 C.F.R. 10.22(a) and (c) when he authored the five basis opinions addressed to Large Hedge Fund in which he failed to analyze, and advise his clients of, relevant facts, law, and regulations that could have had an effect on the basis of the stock. Specifically, it alleges that (1) the opinions contained no analysis of the possible effect of IRS Notice 95-93 which advised that the IRS would challenge lease stripping transactions under current law and regulations and by applying the "business purpose" doctrine and the "substance-over-form" doctrine, including the "sham transaction and "step transaction" doctrines; (2) the opinions contained no analysis of the substance-over-form doctrine, including the sham transaction and step transaction doctrines; (3) the opinions contained no analysis of the economic substance of the lease stripping transactions; (4) Respondent did not make sufficient inquiries to determine whether the assumptions contained in the opinions were correct; and (5) Respondent did not make sufficient inquiries to determine whether the lease stripping transactions had a valid and reasonable expectation of a pre-tax profit and whether the parties to the transactions had complied with the contractual terms of the transactions. The complaint also alleges that when Respondent authored the basis opinions without performing due diligence he willfully engaged in disreputable conduct within the meaning of 31 C.F.R. 51.

Section 10.22 of 31 C.F.R., Diligence as to accuracy, provides:

Each attorney, certified public accountant, enrolled agent, or enrolled actuary shall exercise due diligence

(a) In preparing or assisting in the preparation of, approving, and filing returns, documents, affidavits, and other papers relating to Internal Revenue Service matters;

. . . .

(c) In determining the correctness of oral or written representations made by him to clients with reference to any matter administered by the Internal Revenue Service.

Section 10.52 of 31 C.F.R., Violation of regulations, provides:

A practitioner may be disbarred or suspended from practice before the Internal Revenue Service for any of the following:

(a) Willfully violating any part of the regulations contained in this part.

While the term "willful" is not defined in the regulations, its use in the Treasury laws has consistently been held to mean, in both civil and criminal contexts, the "voluntary, intentional violation of a known legal duty." E.g., *United States v. Pomponio,* 429 U.S. 10, 12 (1976); *Thibodeau v. United States,* 828 F. 2d 1499, 1505 (11th Cir. 1987). Consequently, OPR does not have to show that Respondent acted with malicious intent or bad purpose, only that he purposefully disregarded or was indifferent to his obligations.

OPR has established that Respondent was aware of his client's purpose in seeking the basis opinions, i.e., to establish a tax basis for use in claiming substantial deductions, that he was aware of Notice 95-53, which gave notice that the IRS intended to challenge lease stripping transactions when he authored those opinions, and that he was familiar with the requirements of Treasury Regulation 1-6664-4, which provide standards as to when a taxpayer may rely on the advice of tax advisors as evidence of reasonable cause and good faith for purposes of avoiding substantial understatement of income penalties with respect to tax shelter items. The regulation requires that the advice take into account all relevant facts and circumstances, including the taxpayer's purpose in entering into and structuring the transaction, and must not be based on any unreasonable factual or legal assumptions or representations. OPR asserts that in preparing and issuing the basis opinions Respondent willfully failed to meet the duty of due diligence owed to its client Large Hedge Fund and to the Internal Revenue Service and by so doing he engaged in disreputable conduct.

Specifically, OPR asserts that using the short form opinions, which contained "facts, assumptions and conclusions without setting forth any analysis," put Large Hedge Fund at risk because they did not show that all relevant information had been taken into account and they did not provide adequate documentation to justify Large Hedge Fund's tax position or provide it with penalty protection. It asserts that Respondent failed to exercise due diligence because he knew that the IRS had issued Notice 95-53 and that the tax losses Large Hedge Fund sought to take advantage of had been generated by lease stripping transactions before he issued the basis opinions, but the opinions he issued did not indicate that the high basis of the stock was the result of lease stripping transactions. The opinions failed to mention Notice 95-53 and did not discuss the various statutes and common law doctrines mentioned therein or their applicability to these lease stripping transactions or how they might affect the basis of the stock. They did not show the due diligence performed in arriving at the conclusions as to basis or provide Large Hedge Fund with protection from penalties that might be asserted if the claimed losses were disallowed. This deprived Large Hedge Fund of the opportunity to make an informed decision whether or not to acquire the stock from Offshore Entity #1 and to evaluate its chances for success should the IRS question the asserted basis of the stock and disallow the claimed losses.

Respondent credibly testified as to the due diligence he performed in connection with the basis opinions he issued to Large Hedge Fund and introduced numerous documents on which he relied in arriving at his opinions, which were not included a *[sic]* part of those "short form" opinions. These opinions dealt with the basis of the preferred stock in the hands of Offshore Entity #1 after the exchange transactions with the U.S. companies. He said that prior to the issuance of those opinions he needed to consider several things to reach his conclusions as to basis, i.e., whether the leases were true leases, whether the prepayment of rent by Limited Partnership #1 to Offshore Entity #1 constituted taxable income for federal tax purposes, and whether the exchange of assets by Offshore Entity #1 for the preferred stock constituted tax-free exchanges under Section 351 of the Code.

OPR asserts that Respondent failed to exercise due diligence because he failed to make sufficient inquiries concerning the correctness of certain of the assumptions contained in the opinions. In addressing the issue of whether the transactions between Offshore Entity #1 and the corporations whose stock it acquired constituted valid tax-free exchanges under Section 351 of the Code, he included two assumptions that had not been contained in the earlier "true lease" opinions issued by A&A, i.e., "Assumption (S)" which stated that the U.S. corporate investor had a reasonable expectation of realizing a significant profit from the exchange transaction and "Assumption (V)" which stated that "the exchange transaction was entered into for substantial bona fide non-tax business purposes." However, he did not explain why these assumptions were reasonable and he did not secure such representations from the corporate investors but relied on representations from Advisory Firm #1 which was not a disinterested party but one with a considerable interest in the outcome of the transactions. It asserts that Respondent failed to reconsider and update the legal analysis underlying the "true lease" opinions he relied on and that he failed to resolve questions about the reliability of the appraisals done by Appraisal Firm #1 in connection with those opinions.

OPR did not present any witnesses with any direct knowledge of the lease stripping transactions involved here, the interaction between Respondent and his client Large Hedge Fund, or the preparation of the basis opinions it alleges constitute disreputable conduct. Rather, it chose to rely on the opinions, which it apparently contends speak for themselves and establish misconduct on Respondent's part. First, OPR asserts that Respondent's use of "short form" opinions with respect to the basis of the stock Large Hedge Fund acquired was inappropriate and shows a lack of due diligence on his part, or at least constitutes evidence of a lack of due diligence. The evidence in the record does not support that view. On the contrary, it establishes that use of the short form opinion at that time was the accepted norm.

Respondent testified that prior to making partner at A&A and issuing the opinions in question in Date 3; he had assisted other firm partners in the preparation of dozens of tax opinions, the vast majority of which were short form. No client had ever rejected the use of the short form and he was aware that other members of the tax bar used short form opinions. He knew of no IRS guidelines prohibiting the use of short form opinions until Circular 230 was amended some years after 2000 to require that "covered" opinions be in writing and set forth the reasoning underlying the opinion. Since the amendment, he has not used the short form for the opinions he has issued in order to comply with those requirements.

Respondent also presented the testimony of Larry Langdon, whom I find was qualified as an expert witness. Langdon has extensive tax law experience with the IRS, corporations, private practice, and professional associations. This experience included 22 years as the chief tax officer of Hewlett-Packard Corporation where he had the opportunity and responsibility to review tax opinions prepared by a number of the leading U.S. and international law firms. His IRS experience included serving as its Commissioner of the Large and Midsized Business Division dealing with corporate tax shelter activity. In that position, he was involved in drafting guidelines for practitioners which were issued by the IRS. He established his familiarity with the use of opinions provided to taxpayers by outside counsel and with the published requirements of the IRS with respect to such opinions, including those in Circular 230.

Langdon testified that while, ideally, a taxpayer might prefer to receive a long form opinion detailing all of the facts, all of the possible contingencies, and all of the legal issues, as a practical matter, when A&A provided the basis opinions to Large Hedge Fund it was typical and an accepted practice for outside counsel to use the short form. He described the short form opinion as the "gold standard of opinion writing at that point in time." He said that several factors drove tax practitioners to favor the short form, including, the time and expense involved in preparing a long form opinion and the need for reasonably quick guidance as whether to go ahead with a transaction or not. This led the opinion authors to concentrate on the key issues of strategic importance, "rather than in effect writing a law review article about issues that might arise at some later point. He testified that a short form opinion did not fail to meet the requirements in Circular 230 which did not require an opinion to set forth a law firm's legal analysis underlying the opinion. He also testified that he reviewed opinions issued by the law firms of Law Firm #3, Law Firm #4, and Law Firm #5 concerning aspects of the lease stripping transactions in issue here and that those opinions were short form opinions. There is no evidence that any of those opinions were alleged to be inappropriate or inadequate.

Langdon testified that, in addition to the opinions of the above-mentioned law firms, he reviewed the basis opinions Respondent prepared, background memos and files, draft memos and notes, and valuation reports relating to the transactions. He said that, in his opinion, the quality of the work underlying the basis opinions issued by Respondent to Large Hedge Fund was very thoughtfully done, it did a good job of analyzing the underlying facts, and it met an acceptable standard of legal efficacy for the positions that the basis opinions were supporting, at either the "should" or "more likely than not" level. He said that the basis opinions were "clearly within the top tier, clearly within the top 15, 20 percent of all the opinions" he saw while serving as counsel at Corporation #2.

Partner 1, another experienced tax attorney, testified that he had authored between 50 and 100 short form opinions in his practice before the basis opinions were issued. He said that, in his experience, clients preferred short form opinions which contained a description of the facts, any assumptions that were made, and the conclusions. The detailed legal analysis of a transaction contained in the issuing firm's files was not made a part of the short form opinion; consequently, such an analysis, discussing not only the pros but also the cons of a transaction, would not be accessible by a taxing authority examining the transaction. Technical Advisor #1, an IRS technical advisor for tax shelters, called as a witness by OPR, testified that she was aware that prior to the year 2002, short form opinions were commonly issued by law firms on tax issues and she was not aware of any rules prohibiting their use. The regulations in Circular 230 were revised, effective December 20, 2004, to require that opinions "relate the applicable law (including potentially applicable judicial doctrines) to the relevant facts." 31 C.F.R. 10.35(c)(2). As Respondent's brief points out, such a revision would have been unnecessary if this were already required by the due diligence standard in Circular 230. Moreover, Treasury Reg. 1-6664-4(c), concerning the standards for reliance by a taxpayer on professional advice for penalty protection, states that such advice "does not have to be in any particular form." I find that OPR has failed to establish that Respondent's use of short form opinions was inappropriate or is evidence of a lack of due diligence.[19]

It is with this in mind that OPR's other contentions must be considered. OPR contends that Respondent failed to exercise due diligence because he failed to mention in his basis opinions that the purported high basis in the stock acquired by Large Hedge Fund came from lease stripping transactions and because he was aware of but did not discuss in those opinions Notice 95-53, in which the IRS announced its intent to challenge lease stripping transactions. This, it asserts, deprived Large Hedge Fund of the opportunity to make an informed decision regarding whether to enter the transactions with Offshore Entity #1 and make a reasonable evaluation of its potential for success if it subsequently attempted to rely on the basis of the stocks set forth in Respondent's opinions. I find there is no factual basis for this assertion in this record. As noted, OPR did not call any representative of Large Hedge Fund as a witness or present any other evidence tending to establish that Large Hedge Fund was not aware that the stock it was to acquire in these transactions involved lease stripping, that it did not have knowledge of Notice 95-53, or that the information available to it was not sufficient to make an informed decision about whether to acquire it. Respondent's credible and uncontradicted testimony was that during his first meeting with representatives of Large Hedge Fund to discuss the possibility of representation, he discussed Notice 95-53 with Accountant #1, an accountant and tax attorney who served as Large Hedge Fund's Tax Director. Aside from this, it is simply unreasonable to assume that Large Hedge Fund, which was investing millions of dollars in these transactions, did not know that lease stripping was involved. That knowledge was no doubt one of the reasons why Large Hedge Fund sought the basis opinions in the first place. Further evidence that Large Hedge Fund was made aware of Notice 95-53 is contained in a memo Respondent caused to be sent to Accountant #1, dated October 30, Date 3, which had an attached copy of a portion of an opinion letter A&A had issued to another taxpayer in November Date 6, "which discusses the potential impact of the IRS notice on so-called 'lease stripping' transactions."

---

[19] [9] I find that the comments of the judge in the Large Hedge Fund case about Respondent's opinions to be of little persuasive value since there is no indication that she was aware of the due diligence undertaken by Respondent but not a part of the short form opinions.

More importantly, the evidence shows that Respondent was aware of Notice 95-53 and had analyzed the statutes and legal doctrines referenced therein before he issued the basis opinions. The documentation in the record and testimony of Respondent and Partner 1 establishes that they and other members of A&A had worked together closely in doing the extensive research and analysis leading to the true lease opinions that Partner 1 issued to Advisory Firm #1 in Date 5 and Date 6, which concluded that the master leases and subleases were "true leases" and that the rent prepayment under the subleases was income to Offshore Entity #1. Neither the extent nor the quality of the due diligence underlying these opinions is questioned here. The evidence shows that in the course of their research and analysis they recognized the possible applicability and considered each of the following statutes and common law doctrines which were delineated in Notice 95-53 when it was subsequently issued in October Date 6: Code Sections 269, 446(b), and 482; business purpose doctrine; economic substance doctrine; and substance-over-form doctrine, including the step and sham transaction doctrines.

Although obviously pertinent to the some of the issues Respondent would later address in his basis opinions, OPR dismisses this work as not relevant to whether Respondent engaged in due diligence in preparing those opinions and says that, even if it was relevant, that due diligence "needed to reconsidered and updated to ensure that the legal analysis was still valid at the time of the exchanges between Long Term and Offshore Entity #1." It does not say why. Notice 95-53 did not change the law applicable to lease stripping transactions, it merely said that the IRS might be issuing new regulations which would apply to future transactions lease stripping transactions [sic] and that it would be examining past transactions using various statutes and legal doctrines. The evidence shows that A&A had already considered those statutes and legal doctrines and concluded that they did not apply or, as in the case of the step transaction theory, specifically structured the transactions so that it did not apply. Respondent has also established that the basis of the stock in question was established as of the date of the exchange transactions and that subsequent events had no effect on it or required further consideration before he reached the conclusions set forth in the basis opinions. Respondent testified that this was the case, as did an expert witness Expert Witness #1, a tax attorney with over 30 years of experience primarily in the area of finance and leasing, who said that "the things that defined basis were done upon the completion of the exchange." OPR's witness Technical Advisor #1 also agreed with that proposition. OPR asserts that this argument is "unpersuasive," but it presented no evidence or authority to the contrary.

As a part of its argument that Respondent needed to reconsider the due diligence performed in connection with the true lease opinions, OPR asserts that Respondent failed to make sufficient inquiries to determine the correctness of two of the assumptions contained in his basis opinions which were not part of the previous opinions. It contends that these assumptions concerning the parties' expectations of profits were not reasonable. It asserts that he failed to contact the appropriate parties to confirm that they expected a profit from the transactions, but accepted, without question, the representations of Advisory Firm #1, which had a financial interest in the transactions which it had promoted, as to their profit motives. It also asserts that the appraisal of the computer equipment on which the computations of potential profits were based was deficient and that it was unreasonable to rely on it.

I find that the evidence fails to establish that Respondent's reliance on representations of Advisory Firm #1 was unreasonable as *[sic]* matter of law because it had a financial interest in these transactions. On the contrary, the credible and uncontradicted evidence was that Advisory Firm #1 was a leading firm in the leasing field with a reputation for professionalism and integrity. Expert Witness #1 testified that he was familiar with the firm and its personnel and described it as "absolutely first rate," and having an excellent reputation as a firm that would get a job done right and would have more knowledge about the transactions involved than most of the participating parties. He was asked if he would rely on a representation from Advisory Firm #1 in a leasing transaction in which he represented one of the parties and said that he "would rely on their representation regarding financial matters." Partner 1 testified that Advisory Firm #1 was the pre-eminent firm in its field and that he "felt very comfortable relying on any representation they made." He said that Advisory Firm #1's position in the leasing field was "so exalted" that it could not afford to provide anything but "an accurate and thorough representation." Respondent, likewise, testified that he was aware of Advisory Firm #1's standing in the industry. He said that when he was given the representation that Advisory Firm #1 had provided one of the corporations involved in the exchange transactions he felt that he could reasonably rely on it in reaching his opinion because it would not make a statement as to a fact or a financial analysis it did not believe it could stand behind. The evidence here indicates that a representation made by Advisory Firm #1 would be at least as reliable as a representation by a party who stood to gain by establishing that it had an expectation of a nontax benefit from the transaction. The cases cited by OPR as purportedly establishing the unreasonableness of reliance on representations by the promoters of a transaction or their agents are all factually distinguishable from the situation presented here. But in any event, Respondent has shown that he did not than uncritically accept representations from Advisory Firm #1.

Respondent testified that he had reviewed the written representations from Offshore Entity #1 in the record that it had entered into the transactions with the expectation of making a meaningful pre-tax profit from its interest in the transactions. For each transaction, he had examined and analyzed a detailed spreadsheet showing Offshore Entity #1's expected pre-tax return from the transaction and, in turn, that of the U.S. corporation issuing the exchanged stock which took over Offshore Entity #1's position in the leasing transaction and determined that it also had a substantial non-tax economic benefit from the transaction. The transaction he discussed in detail in his testimony involving Subsidiary #1, a subsidiary of Corporation #3, projected a 21 percent rate of return. He said he was also aware of due diligence Subsidiary #1 had done before entering the exchange transaction which included an opinion obtained from the law firm of Law Firm #5 concerning the exchange transaction and he drew on his own knowledge of the transactions.

Key to the question of whether the parties had an expectation of a non-tax profit from these transactions was the residual value of the subject computer equipment. According to Partner 1, the appraisal of that value was "the fundamental factual reference point" from which the tax opinions issued by A&A flowed. OPR contends that A&A did not investigate the appraiser's qualifications and had "reservations" about the appraisal obtained from Appraisal Firm #1. Therefore, Respondent should have done something more to assure that the appraised values were accurate before he issued his basis opinions. The evidence does not support that contention. In fact, there is no evidence that any of the numerous parties or attorneys involved in these transactions ever questioned the accuracy of the appraisals. Respondent and Partner 1 credibly testified that they interviewed four appraisal firms and according to Partner 1 made an "extensive" examination of their qualifications before selecting Appraisal Firm #1. OPR's contention is apparently based on the fact that after A&A received and analyzed the Appraisal Firm #1 appraisal it engaged Accounting Firm #1 to review it as well. Partner 1 credibly testified that he did this because he had not used Appraisal Firm #1 before, he had not done lease financing involving computer hardware before, and he wanted assurance that the approach used and the value determined by Appraisal Firm #1 was reasonable. There is no evidence that A&A believed that the Appraisal Firm #1 appraisal was not accurate or that its methodology was flawed in any way. Contrary to the assertion by OPR, it does not appear that A&A placed significant restrictions on Accounting Firm #1's review of the appraisal. That is what it got. It appears that OPR now faults Respondent for not doing the same kind of due diligence that A&A had already done. I find that OPR has failed to prove by clear and convincing evidence that Respondent's use of the assumptions it questions in his basis opinions was unreasonable or amounted to a lack of due diligence on his part.

Conclusions of Law

I find that OPR initiated this disciplinary proceeding based on the fact that Respondent used short form opinions in advising Large Hedge Fund concerning the basis of the stock it obtained in the exchange transactions with Offshore Entity #1. It has provided little more than that fact as the evidence in support of its complaint allegations and has failed to prove any of those allegations by clear and convincing evidence, as required by Circular No. 230.[20] Respondent's evidence establishes that use of the short form opinions was an accepted practice at the time they were issued, and more important, that he had done the due diligence necessary to support the conclusions contained in those opinions. Accordingly, I find that OPR has not proved that Respondent failed to meet the requirements of the regulations or that he willfully engaged in disreputable conduct when he issued those the basis opinions to Large Hedge Fund. I find that the complaint should be dismissed.[21]

On these findings of fact and conclusions of law and on the entire record, I issue the following

---

[20] [10] Respondent has repeatedly questioned OPR's good faith in bringing this proceeding. However, it appears that if he had been more forthcoming during OPR's investigation of his conduct in preparing the basis opinions, this complaint might not have been issued.

[21] [11] Having found that Respondent did not engage in any misconduct, I find it unnecessary to reach the question of whether or not the statute of limitations in 28 U.S.C. 2462 is applicable to this proceeding.

ORDER

The complaint is dismissed in its entirety.

Dated, Washington, D.C. January 29, 2009

NOTES

1. OPR initiated proceedings against Mr. Sykes upon referral from the Department of Justice, which represented the government in the Long-Term Capital litigation. All OPR cases stem from referral; practitioners are never selected for professional discipline at random. Referrals come primarily from personnel in other parts of the IRS, but OPR receives many referrals from outside the agency as well (e.g., from the Department of Justice, disgruntled clients, private practitioners who have observed the professional conduct of other practitioners, state licensing authorities, etc.). Therefore, if a practitioner is contacted by OPR, she can safely conclude that someone has reported specific conduct about her to OPR and should treat the OPR communication with appropriate care and attention. Indeed, footnote 10 implies that Mr. Sykes was not forthcoming during OPR's investigation of his conduct and, had he been more accommodating, the complaint might never have been issued. Commenting on the *Sykes* case, the current Director of OPR has suggested that had Mr. Sykes presented mitigating evidence to OPR at the investigatory phase, perhaps the disciplinary proceeding could have been avoided. She also called attention, generally, to the duty under Circular 230 § 10.20(b) to respond to OPR's queries and requests for nonprivileged information, and threatened to charge uncooperative practitioners under that section in addition to filing other charges.[22]

2. The ALJ appears not to have understood the role of opinion letters in tax practice. He found that the ultimate purpose of the basis opinions prepared by Mr. Sykes was "to convince the IRS that the basis of the stock in question for tax purposes was what the opinions said it was and to shield the taxpayer from penalties that might be asserted if the IRS disagreed with the basis being claimed." He therefore found that "the opinions were intended and were reasonably expected to be a part of the taxpayer's presentation to the IRS in support of its position with respect to the basis of the stock."[23] As is discussed in Chapter 3, penalty protection is often a primary purpose of tax opinion letters. However, opinions are rarely used to convince the IRS regarding substantive tax positions and likewise are rarely part of a taxpayer's presentation to the IRS to support its position. A better conclusion would have been that the opinion letter was intended to assist the taxpayer in taking a reporting position on its return and, thus, was connected indirectly to a presentation before the IRS. *See* Circular 230 § 10.2(a)(4).

3. Mr. Sykes raised a statute of limitations defense. By statute, the federal government generally has five years to pursue "an action, suit or proceeding for

---

[22] Jeremiah Coder, *OPR Plans to Impose Monetary Sanctions, Director Says*, 123 TAX NOTES 1178 (2009).

[23] The purpose of the ALJ's findings in this regard was to support his conclusion that Mr. Sykes had engaged in practice before the IRS by rendering opinion advice to the taxpayer. As noted by the ALJ, that issue has been resolved by statutory changes and amendments to Circular 230.

the enforcement of any civil fine, penalty, or forfeiture, pecuniary or otherwise." 28 U.S.C. § 2462. It is unclear, however, precisely when the statute begins to run. It is generally understood that OPR's (unarticulated) policy is not to pursue allegations that the IRS knew of, or should have known of, if the misconduct occurred more than five years prior to the date on which OPR can reasonably expect to institute a proceeding. ("Instituting a proceeding" refers to the formal commencement of the disciplinary process, by filing a complaint in accordance with Circular 230 procedures. Circular 230 § 10.60(a). Thus, informal communications may have the effect of extending the five year period.) The ALJ in *Sykes* never reached the issue, having concluded that Mr. Sykes did not engage in any misconduct.

4. Under Circular 230 § 10.76(b), the standard of proof varies with the proffered sanction. If OPR seeks censure or a suspension of less than six months, an allegation of fact is proven by "a preponderance of the evidence in the record." If OPR seeks a monetary penalty, disbarment, or a suspension of six months or longer, an allegation of fact must be proven by "clear and convincing evidence in the record." According to the ALJ in *Sykes*, a generally accepted definition of "clear and convincing evidence" is "that it requires a degree of proof which will produce in the mind of the trier of fact a firm belief as to the allegations sought to be established. It is more than a mere preponderance but less than proof beyond a reasonable doubt. . . . The allegations must be proven to a 'high probability.'"

III. FEDERAL REGULATION: PREPARER PENALTIES

Code Sections 6694 and 7701(a)(36)
Treas. Reg. § 301.7701-15

A. Brief Overview

Section 6694 imposes civil (i.e., not criminal) penalties on "tax return preparers." For returns or claims for refund that reflect an understatement of tax liability due to an unreasonable position, the penalty is the greater of $1,000 or 50% of the income derived (or to be derived) by the tax return preparer for each return or refund claim; this is referred to as the Section 6694(a) penalty. For returns or refund claims that reflect an understatement due to willful or reckless conduct by the tax return preparer, the penalty is the greater of $5,000 or 50% of the income received (or to be received) by the tax return preparer for each return or refund claim; this is referred to as the Section 6694(b) penalty. Whether imposed under Section 6694(a) or (b), the penalty covers preparers of income tax returns as well as preparers of estate, gift, employment and excise tax returns, and returns of exempt organizations.

Preparer penalties will be studied in some detail in Chapter 2. Several general comments are relevant at this point, however.

"Tax return preparer." A "tax return preparer" can be the person who signed a return — a "signing preparer" — or a person who did not — a "nonsigning preparer." Basically, a return preparer is a person who prepares for compensation, or who employs one or more other persons to prepare for compensation, all or a substantial portion of any tax return or refund claim.

Treas. Reg. § 301.7701-15(a). Attorneys who do not physically prepare or review client returns may be surprised to learn that preparer penalties can be assessed against them. Such attorneys, as well as other tax professionals, are considered nonsigning preparers if they offer written or oral advice to a taxpayer or to another preparer and that advice leads to a position or entry that constitutes a substantial portion of a taxpayer's return. A nonsigning professional, however, can be a preparer only as to advice given with respect to events that have already occurred; thus, typical pre-transactional planning advice is not covered by the preparer penalty. (Where advice is given both before and after a transaction, practitioners are advised to carefully review the regulations.)

Three separate standards. The Section 6694(a) penalty can be avoided if the position meets one of three standards: one that applies only as to positions that are not disclosed on the taxpayer/client's return, a second that applies only as to positions that are disclosed on the taxpayer/client's return, and a third that applies when a return position relates to a tax shelter in which the taxpayer/client has participated.

1. Nondisclosed positions. No penalty will be imposed with respect to an undisclosed position if there was substantial authority for the position. "Substantial authority" will be discussed in some detail in Chapter 2. For present purposes, it is enough to point out that "substantial authority" is also the basic standard for avoidance of penalties by taxpayers so that the basic taxpayer and professional reporting standards are the same.

2. Disclosed positions. No penalty will be imposed with respect to a position that is disclosed on the client taxpayer's return if there was a reasonable basis for the position disclosed. Since avoidance of the penalty by disclosure involves persuading the taxpayer/client to disclose, practical obstacles often result from a taxpayer's unwillingness to disclose. In such a circumstance, the IRS considers the disclosure requirement to have been met where the practitioner advises the client to disclose and maintains documentation of such advice in her own files.

3. Tax shelter positions. If the position is with respect to a tax shelter (as defined in Section 6662(d)(2)(C)(ii)) or a reportable transaction (to which Section 6662A applies), no penalty will be imposed if it is reasonable to believe that the position would more likely than not be sustained on its merits.

None of these standards apply with respect to the Section 6694(b) preparer penalty (for willful or reckless conduct). The only way to avoid that penalty is to show that the position or advice was neither willful, defined as willfully attempting in any manner to understate the liability for tax on the return or claim, nor reckless, defined as involving a reckless or intentional disregard of rules or regulations.

Reasonable cause and good faith exception. No Section 6694(a) penalty will be imposed if it is shown that there was reasonable cause for the understatement and the tax return preparer acted in good faith. Factors considered include the nature of the error, the materiality of the error, the frequency of the error, the preparer's normal office practice, and the preparer's reliance on the advice of another preparer. There is no reasonable cause and good faith defense to the Section 6694(b) penalty.

B. Relationship to Professional Standards

As will be explained in some detail in Chapter 2, the "substantial authority" standard in Section 6694(a) was adopted in 2008 after an earlier Congressional attempt, in 2007, to impose a "more likely than not standard." Treasury began the process of amending Circular 230 § 10.34(a)[24] to conform to the 2007 standard but curtailed its efforts when the statute was amended in 2008. Thus, the preparer penalty standards and the professional standards set forth in Circular 230 are inconsistent. It is anticipated that Circular 230 § 10.34(a) will be amended to conform to Section 6694. The ABA has not announced plans to change its professional standards.

The AICPA recently amended its standard in a revision of SSTS No. 1 (reproduced in Appendix C). Under the new standard, a CPA is required to follow standards imposed by the applicable taxing authority with respect to recommending a tax return position or signing a tax return. If the applicable taxing authority has no such written standards, or if those standards are lower than the standards sets forth in SSTS No. 1, then:

1. A CPA should not recommend a position or sign a tax return taking a position unless the CPA has a good faith belief that the position has at least a realistic possibility of being sustained administratively or judicially on its merits if challenged.

2. Notwithstanding the preceding rule, a CPA may recommend a tax return position if she (i) concludes that there is a reasonable basis for the position and (ii) advises the taxpayer to appropriately disclose that position; and a CPA may prepare or sign a tax return that reflects a position if (i) she concludes there is a reasonable basis for the position and (ii) the position is appropriately disclosed.

According to the Internal Revenue Manual, referral to OPR is mandatory when Section 6694(a) or (b) penalties are asserted at the audit level or by IRS Appeals. IRM ¶ 20.1.6.2.1.

---

[24] You will notice that the current version of Circular 230 indicates that Section 10.34(a) is "reserved." The prior version, which was consistent with Section 6694(a) as it existed prior to amendment in 2007, read as follows:

(a) Realistic possibility standard. A practitioner may not sign a tax return as a preparer if the practitioner determines that the tax return contains a position that does not have a realistic possibility of being sustained on its merits (the realistic possibility standard) unless the position is not frivolous and is adequately disclosed to the Internal Revenue Service. A practitioner may not advise a client to take a position on a tax return, or prepare the portion of a tax return on which a position is taken, unless —

(1) The practitioner determines that the position satisfies the realistic possibility standard; or

(2) The position is not frivolous and the practitioner advises the client of any opportunity to avoid the accuracy-related penalty in section 6662 of the Internal Revenue Code by adequately disclosing the position and of the requirements for adequate disclosure.

C.   Other Statutory Preparer Penalties

Return preparers should bear in mind other Code sections under which penalties can be imposed, in addition to Section 6694(a) and (b): Section 6695 (failure to furnish a copy of the tax return to the taxpayer; failure to sign a required return; failure to furnish a required taxpayer's identifying number; failure to retain a completed copy of the return or a record of the taxpayer's name, identification number, tax year, and type of return prepared; failure to comply with due diligence requirements with respect to determining a taxpayer's eligibility for, or amount of, the earned income credit), Section 6701 (aiding and abetting the understatement of a tax liability), and Section 6713(a) (disclosing or using any tax return information other than to prepare or assist in preparing the taxpayer's return).

Where a practitioner's conduct warrants, the government may also seek criminal sanctions under Section 7206(1) (making a false statement), Section 7206(2) (aiding and abetting preparation or presentation of false returns or documents), and/or Section 7207 (submitting false documents).

Under Section 7407(a), the government may seek to enjoin an income tax return preparer from engaging in specific abusive practices or from acting as an income tax return preparer altogether. An injunction may be issued if a court determines that the preparer has engaged in conduct subject to a preparer penalty under Section 6694, engaged in conduct subject to a criminal penalty under the Code, misrepresented her eligibility to practice before the IRS, misrepresented her experience or education as a preparer, guaranteed the payment of any tax refund or the allowance of any tax credit, or engaged in any other fraudulent or deceptive conduct that substantially interferes with the proper administration of the tax law, and that injunctive relief is appropriate to prevent the recurrence of that conduct.

IV.   FEDERAL REGULATION: UNITED STATES TAX COURT RULES

Tax Court Rules 200, 201 and 202 (Appendix F)

Attorneys and nonattorneys are permitted to represent taxpayers in proceedings before the United States Tax Court (Tax Court) although they must be admitted to practice before the court. For attorneys, admission requires proof of admission to practice before, and membership in good standing of, the Bar of the Supreme Court of the United States or of the highest or appropriate court of any state, the District of Columbia, or any U.S. commonwealth, territory, or possession. Nonattorneys are admitted to practice before the Tax Court upon passing a written examination administered by the court; the exam shows that the applicant possesses the requisite qualifications to provide competent representation. It is rare for nonattorneys to represent taxpayers in Tax Court beyond initial filing of a petition.

Both attorneys and nonattorneys practicing before the Tax Court are required to conduct themselves in accordance with letter and spirit of the Model Rules, which the Tax Court has specifically adopted. Violations of the letter and spirit of the Model Rules are grounds for discipline by the Tax Court as are certain other behaviors listed in Tax Court Rule 202. Discipline may consist of disbarment, suspension from practice before the court, reprimand, admonition, or any other sanction that the court may deem appropriate.

PROBLEM 1-11

Despite their eligibility to practice before the Tax Court, one rarely sees nonattorneys representing clients there. Why?

Examination too much of hassel,
Client wants real attorney,
Co. Preparer works for has their own attorneys?

TP's prevail in Taxcourt only 20% of time.
Reputation is core of not representing.

Chapter 2

TAX RETURN PREPARATION AND ADVICE

I. INTRODUCTION

Code §§ 6694 and 7701(a)(36)

Much of the advice provided by tax professionals relates to how items of income, deduction, loss and credit should or should not be reported on tax returns. The principal focus of this chapter is on the standards of practice applicable to those involved in preparing tax returns, including many tax professionals who provide advice that is ultimately reflected on a tax return, but who are not generally regarded by the general public as preparers of the return. Historically, the return preparer standards have formed a patchwork of confusion, mixing ethical standards of the legal and accounting professions, Circular 230, and a number of provisions of the Code. Furthermore, in exceptional cases, a return preparer's deficient performance could trigger malpractice liability, but we will leave that subject to Chapter 6 since it appears that the other return preparer standards are both more demanding than the malpractice standard and far more likely to be the subject of enforcement. Because recent statutory changes impose far more rigorous standards than the professional ethical standards and have, as of this writing, yet to be reflected in amendments to Circular 230, this chapter will focus on the statutory standards and accompanying regulations.

The Code provides the accuracy standards that "tax return preparers"[1] must satisfy in Section 6694. The other sources alluded to above, although out of date, still provide useful guidance on a number of subsidiary issues that inform the preparer's behavior. In addition, the Code sets forth recordkeeping, filing and related requirements for return preparers.

Looking at the statutory standards, one immediately notices their dependence on the quality of the position advised on the taxpayer/client's tax return. This might lead one to believe that the return preparer standards with respect to the accuracy of tax returns parallel the accuracy standards applicable to taxpayers themselves. While this is true to a large extent today, this congruence is a very recent phenomenon. Until 2008, the taxpayer accuracy standards and the return preparer accuracy standards, although at points related or using parallel terminology, diverged in one way or another for decades. The current happy (although not perfect) convergence of the two sets of standards is the result of the last two of four major pieces of pertinent legislation, the Tax Extenders and Alternative Minimum Tax Relief Act of 2008, Div. C of Pub. L. 110–343, 122 Stat. 3765 ("the 2008 Act"), and the Small Business and Work

---

[1] The term "tax return preparer" is defined in Section 7701(a)(36), as augmented by extensive regulations, discussed *infra*. For present purposes, it is important to note that a tax practitioner does not have to actually prepare the return in order to be included within the definition of a "tax return preparer."

Opportunity Tax Act of 2007, Pub. L. 110–28, 121 Stat. 190 ("the 2007 Act"). Each of the four relevant pieces of legislation discussed in this section has been accompanied by subsequent regulatory activity. At this writing, the most recent guidance package included final regulations issued under the 2007 Act[2] (still applicable to the extent not inconsistent with the 2008 Act), accompanied by additional nonregulatory guidance on other provisions of the 2008 Act.[3]

In the remainder of this section, we will briefly review the legislative activity, with an occasional bow to the regulatory activity, beginning with the Tax Reform Act of 1976, Pub. L. 94–455, 90 Stat. 1521 ("the 1976 Act"). The next section of this chapter will address the current taxpayer accuracy standards. Following that, we will take up return preparer standards, first providing more background about the return preparation process. We will then examine who qualifies as a "tax return preparer" and is therefore subject to the return preparer accuracy standards and obligations. We will then discuss the obligations and standards imposed on return preparers. In discussing the standards, we will focus on current rules, imposed to some degree retroactively by the 2008 Act. We will allude to the earlier standards at various points because they will help us to understand the current standards and because the application of the earlier standards will be relevant in the audit and administrative context for some time to come. In addition, the current regulations draw on the earlier regulations in many respects. We will also refer to Circular 230 and professional ethics rules where their application is significant.

The initial return preparer provisions of the Code appeared as part of the 1976 Act. The 1976 version of Section 7701(a)(36) defined the term "income tax return preparer" for purposes of several sections of the Code: Section 6107, which requires an income tax return preparer to provide a copy of the return to the taxpayer and to retain a copy of the return for three years after the close of the "return period;"[4] Section 6109, which requires the preparer's identifying number to be included on the return; Section 6694(a), which, for documents prepared after 1976, imposed a modest penalty ($100) if any part of an understatement was due to the preparer's negligence or intentional disregard of the rules and regulations; and Section 6694(b), which, for documents prepared after 1976, imposed a larger penalty ($500) where part of the understatement was due to a willful attempt to understate the taxpayer's tax liability. These return preparer provisions reflected Congressional concern about abusive practices by preparers, fraudulent returns, and difficulty in determining which returns were prepared by preparers rather than by taxpayers, making it difficult to identify preparers with a pattern of abusive practices.[5]

The 1976 provisions were implemented with regulations issued in 1977.[6] The regulatory definition of "income tax return preparer" went beyond those who physically prepared returns to expressly include persons who rendered advice (for compensation) that "is directly relevant to the determination of the

---

[2] T.D. 9436, 73 Fed. Reg. 78430 (Dec. 22, 2008), *as corrected*, 74 Fed. Reg. 5103 (Jan. 29, 2009).

[3] Notice 2009-5, 2009-3 I.R.B. 309; Rev. Proc. 2009-11, 2009-3 I.R.B. 313 (returns covered by penalty provisions).

[4] The "return period" is a June 30 fiscal year. IRC § 6060(c).

[5] S. Rep. No. 94–938 at 350–51 (1976).

[6] T.D. 7519, 42 Fed. Reg. 17452 (Apr. 1, 1977).

existence, characterization, or amount of an entry on a return or a claim for refund," provided such a person prepared a "substantial portion" of the return or claim within the meaning of then Section 7701(a)(36)(A).[7] The inclusion of these "nonsigning preparers" in the preparer definition "reflected the considered view that excluding nonsigning tax professionals from the reach of Section 6694 would result in a lack of accountability for a position taken on a return, with taxpayers pleading reliance on return preparers to avoid penalties, return preparers pleading reliance on nonsigning tax advisors to avoid penalties, and nonsigning advisors avoiding penalties because not defined as 'preparers.'"[8]

In 1989, Section 6694(a) was amended to penalize a preparer $250, but only for an understatement due to a position for which there was not a "realistic possibility of [the position] being sustained on its merits," provided the preparer knew or had reason to know of the position, and the position was either not disclosed on the return or was frivolous.[9] The Section 6694(b) penalty was expanded to cover understatements due to the preparer's reckless or intentional disregard of rules or regulations. The 1989 legislation also rationalized the other preparer penalties under Section 6695, including those for failing to furnish a copy of a return or claim for refund to the taxpayer, failing to sign the return, failing to include the preparer's identification number on the return, and failing to file a correct information return. Finally, the 1989 Act included the current Section 6662 penalty structure for taxpayers, thereby subjecting taxpayers to a different accuracy standard for undisclosed positions — the substantial authority standard — than the standard then imposed on preparers — the realistic possibility of success standard. For disclosed positions, the taxpayer was required to have a reasonable basis for the position, also somewhat different and somewhat higher than the then preparer standard. The differences between the preparer and taxpayer standards created an unhealthy tension, in some instances confronting the preparer with a conflict of interest. The only reason this conflict was not more problematic was the lack of significant enforcement of the Section 6694 standard and the modest amount of the penalty. In any event, extensive regulations were issued following the enactment of the 1989 legislation, both to spell out the application of the taxpayer standards in Section 6662 and to reflect the 1989 return preparer standards.

---

[7] See Treas. Reg. § 301.7701-15(b)(2), as in effect before the effective date of the 2007 Act. The general definition in Section 7701(a)(36) defined the term to include any person who prepares all or a substantial portion of a return or claim for refund for compensation or employs one or more others to do so. While "substantial portion" was not defined in the statute, the Committee reports provided guidance, which was ultimately reflected in the regulations. See Treas. Reg. § 301.7701-15, as in effect prior to the effective date of the 2007 Act.

[8] Notice of Proposed Rulemaking, 73 Fed. Reg. 34560, 34561–34562, (June 27, 2008), also noting that there was concern that the 1976 rules would subject preparers of less complex returns to the new rules, but possibly exempt tax attorneys and other professionals who might play an important role in the preparation of more complex returns.

[9] Pub. L. 101–239, 103 Stat. 2106 ("the 1989 Act"). Both the ABA and AICPA ultimately adopted versions of the "realistic possibility" standard as professional standards, as well. ABA Formal Op. 85–352; AICPA SSTS No. 1. The "realistic possibility" standard was generally viewed as requiring the position to have at least a one in three chance of success on the merits, although the different formulations of the standard stated this in slightly different terms. Michael B. Lang, *Commentary on Return Preparer Obligations,* 3 FLA. TAX REV. 128, 132–34 (1996).

In 2007, Congress again revisited Section 6694, this time to broaden the application of Section 6694 to all "tax return preparers" (expanding the penalty provisions to preparers of other types of returns, e.g., estate tax returns), to raise the standards for both undisclosed positions and disclosed positions, and to increase the penalty amounts. For undisclosed positions, the 2007 Act provided that the preparer could avoid a penalty only if there was a "reasonable belief that the position would more likely than not be sustained on its merits," a standard generally regarded as higher than the substantial authority standard applicable to taxpayers themselves. For disclosed positions, however, Congress chose to conform the preparer standard to the reasonable basis standard that already applied to taxpayers. The Section 6694(a) penalty was raised to the greater of $1,000 or 50 percent of the income derived (or to be derived) from preparing the return or claim, while the Section 6694(b) penalty was raised to the greater of $5,000 or 50 percent of the income derived (or to be derived) from the return or claim. These changes were supposed to be effective after the date of enactment (May 25, 2007). However, since the 2007 changes were a surprise to Treasury — there is no legislative history explanation of why the change was enacted and there were no hearings on the subject — Treasury's first response was to defer the application of the new Section 6694(a) standards generally until 2008.[10]

Subsequently, the IRS issued Notice 2008-13, 2008-3 I.R.B 282, providing interim guidance on the application of the 2007 Act rules for the period preceding the effective date of final regulations reflecting the new standards. Proposed regulations were then issued in June 2008, not only addressing the new standards, but revisiting the earlier definition of a "return preparer" and related matters. Congress, however, stepped in once again with the 2008 Act. The 2008 Act reduced the preparer standard for undisclosed positions to the "substantial authority" standard applicable to taxpayers; this change was made retroactive to the effective date of the 2007 Act. However, the 2008 Act retained a version of the "more likely than not" standard for positions with respect to tax shelters, as defined in Section 6662(d)(2)(c)(ii), and reportable transactions to which Section 6662A applies. The latter (tax shelter) provision applies with respect to taxable years ending after October 3, 2008, regardless of whether the position is disclosed.[11]

II. TAXPAYER ACCURACY STANDARDS

Code §§ 6662 and 6664
Treas. Reg. §§ 1.6662-2(a)-(c), 1.6662-3(a)-(c), 1.6662-4(a), (b), (d)-(g) and 1.6664-4(a)-(d)

The return preparer standards are defined under Section 6694 in terms of the viability of the position advised by the practitioner, which in turn depends

---

[10] Notice 2007–54, 2007–27 I.R.B. 12. This Notice is somewhat more complex than described in the text. No relief was provided with respect to the increased level of penalties. This was true under both Section 6694(a) and (b). *See also* Notice 2008–11, 2008-3 I.R.B. 279 (pre-2008 advice by non-signing preparers subject to pre-2007 Act standards).

[11] The government's view on the treatment of positions with respect to tax shelters and reportable transactions during the period between the effective dates of the 2007 and 2008 Acts apparently is that the 2007 Act standards apply, in effect allowing a disclosed position for which there is a reasonable basis to be taken on the return without risk of a penalty. *See* Notice 2009-5, *supra* note 3.

up to a point on whether the taxpayer/client can take the advised position on a return without risking a penalty if the position is challenged and ultimately rejected by the IRS (and judicially, if the taxpayer ends up in court). We say "up to a point" because under current law, the taxpayer can escape a penalty in some cases with a position that could nonetheless lead to the return preparer being subject to a penalty.[12] Despite this, we still think it best to first familiarize ourselves with the taxpayer accuracy standards, the standards that determine whether a position taken by a taxpayer could subject that taxpayer to a penalty.

Section 6662 sets forth the taxpayer accuracy standards. It does not, however, state them directly. Instead, Section 6662(a) and (b) provide generally that the portion of an underpayment of tax that is attributable to a defined category of substandard behavior is subject to a taxpayer penalty (20 percent of the portion of the underpayment involved). The crucial categories of substandard behavior for most taxpayers are "negligence or disregard of rules or regulations" and "any substantial understatement of income tax." Section 6662(b)(1) and (2).[13]

Section 6662(c) defines "negligence" to include "any failure to make a reasonable attempt to comply" with the tax law and "disregard" to include "any careless, reckless or intentional disregard." The regulations provide considerable elaboration in both cases, making it clear, for example, that a failure to keep adequate books and records or to substantiate items properly constitutes negligence, and that disregard is "careless" if the taxpayer "does not exercise reasonable diligence to determine the correctness of a return position that is contrary to a rule or regulation." Of particular importance is a statement that "a return position that has a reasonable basis" is not "attributable to negligence." Treas. Reg. § 1.6662-3(b)(1), third sentence. "Reasonable basis" is then defined as "a relatively high standard of tax reporting, that is significantly higher than not frivolous or not patently improper," a return position, for example, reasonably based on authorities spelled out in the regulations, even though the return position "may not satisfy the substantial authority standard." Treas. Reg. § 1.6662-3(b)(3). The regulations do not provide a specific probability of success threshold for the reasonable basis standard, thus leaving practitioners to argue whether a position that has only a 5 percent chance of being sustained on the merits meets the standard or whether a position must instead have as much as a 20 percent chance of success to pass muster. This, of course, assumes that the strength of a reporting position can be determined with such precision, a dubious assumption to be sure. There is no minimum threshold of underpayment that must be satisfied to trigger the negligence/disregard penalty.

By contrast, no particular defined behavior triggers the substantial understatement penalty; this penalty is triggered when an understatement exceeds

---

[12] For example, the taxpayer may be able to rely on the preparer's advice and qualify for the "good faith and reasonable cause" exception even though the preparer's advice was so clearly wrong that the preparer could be subject to a penalty for giving the advice.

[13] Section 6662(b) includes several other penalty categories, including for substantial valuation misstatement, substantial overstatement of pension liabilities, and substantial estate or gift tax valuation understatement. Although the IRS can assert penalties in the alternative, there is no stacking of penalties. Treas. Reg. § 1.6662-2(c).

a certain threshold amount.[14] (Thus, some practitioners and commentators refer to the substantial understatement penalty as a "no-fault penalty." Of course, the availability of the reasonable cause and good faith exception, discussed *infra*, does bring fault, or lack thereof, into the calculus.) In general, the penalty does not apply to any portion of an understatement attributable to an item for which (1) there is or was substantial authority for the taxpayer's treatment of the item, or (2) for which there is adequate disclosure of the relevant facts *and* there is a "reasonable basis" for the taxpayer's treatment of the item.[15] However, items attributable to defined "tax shelters" are excepted from this provision by Section 6662(d)(2)(C), although the regulations provide that in the case of a noncorporate taxpayer, a tax shelter item is treated as properly shown on the return if its tax treatment is supported by substantial authority *and* the taxpayer reasonably believed the treatment was more likely than not the proper treatment. Treas. Reg. § 1.6662-4(g)(1). (This regulation has no apparent basis in the statute.)

Even if a position on the return does not satisfy one of the requisite standards, the taxpayer may still be protected by Section 6664(c)(1), the so-called "reasonable cause and good faith exception," which protects the taxpayer from a penalty under Section 6662 "if it is shown that there was reasonable cause [for the portion of the underpayment involved and] the taxpayer acted in good faith with respect to such portion." The application of this exception, although elaborated on in the regulations under Section 6664, is confusing at best. For example, although it applies by its terms even if the negligence or disregard penalty might otherwise apply, there seems to be some inherent contradiction in allowing it to apply in such cases. Furthermore, its potential application in the context of items attributable to defined "tax shelters" or "reportable transactions" has been reduced by the inclusion of special conditions in the regulations that have the effect in some cases of requiring that an accuracy or disclosure standard be satisfied as a prerequisite. Thus, in the case of items attributable to a defined "tax shelter," a corporate taxpayer can be treated as satisfying the reasonable cause and good faith standard only if the position (1) is supported by substantial authority and (2) the taxpayer reasonably believed that the tax treatment of the item was more likely than not the proper treatment.[16]

The substantial authority standard, unlike other taxpayer and practitioner accuracy standards (including the now rejected "realistic possibility" standard), does not focus on the merits of the taxpayer's position or the likelihood that the taxpayer would prevail were the position challenged. Instead, it focuses on whether the weight of legal authorities supporting the taxpayer's position is substantial in relation to the weight of the contrary authorities, a determination for which the regulations provide considerable guidance,

---

[14] *See* Section 6662(d)(1) (generally the greater of 10 percent of the correct amount of tax or $5,000, with a special rule for corporations).

[15] Section 6662(d)(2)(B), adding that a corporation is not treated as having a reasonable basis for its tax treatment of an item attributable to a multiple-party financing transaction unless such treatment clearly reflects income. For "adequate disclosure," see Treas. Reg. § 1.6662-3(c).

[16] Treas. Reg. § 1.6664-4(f). (This parallels the regulatory standard for noncorporate taxpayers.) *See also* Treas. Reg. § 1.6664-4(d) (failure to disclose reportable transaction is "strong indication" of lack of good faith with respect to items attributable to the reportable transaction).

including a list of authorities that can be taken into account. Treas. Reg. § 1.6662-4(d). Students should examine this section of the regulations with care, noting that non-primary authorities, such as treatises, do not count at all and remembering that often there are no relevant authorities. However, the regulations do provide that a well-reasoned construction of the statute can count as an authority; hence, a well-reasoned construction of the statute that supports a statement in a non-primary authority may qualify as an authority on its own merits.[17]

Because the substantial authority standard focuses on legal authorities, it is unclear how it should be applied where the issue is entirely one of fact.[18] If a substantial understatement is the result of a taxpayer's mistake or misjudgment as to the facts, the taxpayer might be protected against a penalty by the reasonable cause and good faith exception, but the application of the substantial authority provision itself in a factual context remains puzzling.

PROBLEM 2-1

a. Claudia is an independent contractor solving emergency problems for electrical utilities, and travels extensively for her work. When she prepared her federal income tax return last year, she deducted 100 percent of her expenses for meals and lodging while away from home in pursuit of her trade or business, but she kept no receipts and has very little in the way of records. If she is audited and some or all of her expenses are ultimately disallowed, could she be subject to a penalty under Section 6662? Assume that if deductions are disallowed, the understatement will be substantial within the meaning of Section 6662(d)(1).

b. Same facts as (a), above, except that a CPA prepared Claudia's return, but never asked Claudia if she had any receipts or records.

c. Same facts as (a), above, except that Claudia has detailed receipts and records.

d. Same facts as (c), above, except that a CPA prepared Claudia's return and never asked her about her receipts and records. The CPA simply accepted what she told him without further inquiry.

e. Same facts as (d), above, except that the CPA told Claudia that only 50 percent of her expenses for meals were deductible and asked her if she had receipts for her expenses. She replied that she had receipts and had actually spent twice the amount she had told the CPA to deduct for meals.

f. Same facts as (d), above, except that she provided the CPA complete receipts and records.

---

[17] Treas. Reg. 1.6662-4(d)(3)((ii) (last sentence). One should pause here to reflect on the irony that non-primary authorities, such as the classic corporate tax treatise by Boris Bittker and James Eustice, are not authorities, but an argument that the IRS deems "well-reasoned" is an authority.

[18] The courts have made some effort to apply the standard to fact issues anyway. *See* Kluener v. Commissioner, 154 F.3d 630 (6th Cir. 1998) (reviewing prior cases with regard to both the application of the substantial authority standard to fact issues and the standard of appellate review of trial court holdings on such issues; reversing imposition of penalty because "substantial evidence" supported the taxpayer's position).

[handwritten margin notes: "212 - Exp. for production of income", "3(c) Bus. & b exp. subject to", "274(h)", "Yes 6662(a)(1)", "20% of portion of underpayment", "doesn't matter"]

g. Same facts as (a), above, except that in addition to her usual travel, Claudia likes to see her mother, who lives in Honolulu, a couple of times a year, but the airfare is pretty high. Claudia read in an industry news-letter about an all-day conference on emergency readiness training for the electric utility industry scheduled for Honolulu on a Friday in November. Claudia decided to go, flying to Honolulu on Thursday night, staying with her mother, spending all day Friday at the conference, and then visiting with her mother on Saturday before flying home after a nice brunch with her mother and her mother's friends on Sunday. Claudia deducted her airfare, airport transportation costs, and the cost of meals on Friday and Saturday on her income tax return. If she is audited and some or all of these expenses are ultimately disallowed, will she be subject to a penalty under Section 6662 for these deductions and, if so, to what extent? Is her case better or worse than if she had stayed in a hotel (at a substantial cost — does this matter?) instead of with her mother?

h. Same facts as (a), above, except that Claudia attached a complete list of her expenses to the return. *[handwritten: →There would need to be reasonable basis 6662(i)(d)(2)(B)(ii)(II)]*

PROBLEM 2-2

This problem requires close attention to Treas. Reg. § 1.6662-4(d). *[handwritten: (3) iii A]*

a. A position on Bill's federal income tax return is supported by two private letter rulings, but a case from the United States District Court for the District of Montana has held to the contrary. Bill lives in San Diego. *[handwritten: Maybe, No]* Is there substantial authority for his position? If the situation were reversed — that is, Bill's position is supported by the District Court case, but there are two private letter rulings to the contrary — is there sub- *[handwritten: Yes]* stantial authority for his position? Suppose the case from Montana is 20 years old, but the private letter rulings were issued last year? *[handwritten: Yes]*

b. Bill's return from five years ago was audited. Bill took the same position in that return as the position taken in this year's return. The Revenue Agent never commented on the position. Is there substantial authority for the position taken in this year's return? *[handwritten: Yes No]*

c. Same facts as (b), above, except that the Revenue Agent issued a written report at the completion of the audit. The report specifically approved of the position. Is there substantial authority for the position taken in this year's return? *[handwritten: → yes E 6662-4d 5)iii A]*

d. Same facts as (c), above, except that, last year, the IRS issued a revenue ruling taking a contrary position. *[handwritten: Yes No 6662-4d 5)ii A iiiii]*

e. Same facts as (c), above, except that a recent United States District Court decision from the Southern District of New York held to the contrary. *[handwritten: → yes]*

f. Same facts as (c), above, except that the Tax Court recently held to the contrary. *[handwritten: → No yes]*

g. Bill's position on his return is contrary to the express language of the statute, but a statement in the reports of both the House Ways & Means Committee and the Senate Finance Committee indicates that Congress *[handwritten: yes No]* expected the Treasury to issue regulations that are consistent with Bill's position. Is there substantial authority for Bill's position?

h. Bill's position is contrary to the express language of a regulation, but is supported by a decision of the Tax Court that was issued before the regulation was promulgated. Is there substantial authority for Bill's position? Does it matter whether Bill's position represents a good faith challenge to the regulation's validity?

i. Bill's position is supported by a statement in the most authoritative treatise on the subject, but is contrary to a revenue ruling. Is there substantial authority for Bill's position? Does it matter whether the treatise provides a well-reasoned argument in support of the statement that it makes?

j. Bill's position has been rejected by three Circuit Courts of Appeals but the Court of Appeals for the Ninth Circuit has ruled the other way, supporting Bill's position. Is there substantial authority for Bill's position?

k. Same facts as (j), above, except that the position is with respect to a defined "tax shelter" item. If Bill's position is not adequately disclosed on his return, is he subject to a penalty? Can he avoid the penalty by disclosing the position?

l. If you concluded in any of parts (a) through (k), above, that a position was not supported by substantial authority, did the position nonetheless have a reasonable basis?

III. PRACTITIONER ACCURACY STANDARDS

A. Background

Taxpayers often live complex economic lives and cannot reasonably be expected to readily determine which provisions of the tax law apply to them and to properly apply those provisions to their personal situations. The immensity and complexity of the tax law and the difficulty of applying even apparently clear legal provisions to complex sets of facts (perhaps the most difficult lesson to learn in law school for the law student) leads many taxpayers to seek the assistance of tax professionals in preparing their returns.

Tax professionals generally fall into one or more of four groups: (1) lawyers licensed to practice law in at least one state or the District of Columbia (lawyers); (2) CPAs; (3) persons admitted to practice before the IRS under the provisions of Circular 230;[19] and (4) "tax return preparers," as defined in Section

---

[19] The most significant members of this group are enrolled agents, most of whom must take a special examination to qualify to practice before the IRS, and lawyers and CPAs admitted to practice before the IRS. As discussed in Chapter 1, *supra*, enrolled actuaries and enrolled retirement plan agents are also eligible to practice before the IRS, but only in particular areas involving employee benefit plans or retirement plans, respectively. Nothing precludes an enrolled actuary or an enrolled retirement plan agent from preparing tax returns, however. The enrolled actuary or retirement plan agent might then be subject to the same standards as "enrolled agents" with regard to the preparation of tax returns, although it is not clear that Circular 230 envisions this possibility. A variety of other persons may practice before the IRS in limited circumstances. *See* Circular 230 § 10.7. Amending Circular 230 to bring commercial return preparers within its jurisdiction has been discussed from time to time. Indeed, on June 4, 2009, IRS Commissioner Douglas Shulman announced a comprehensive review of return preparers with the goal of making recommendations that will enhance taxpayer compliance and insure that high ethical standards are followed by preparers, so change may be in the works. *See* Jeremiah Coder, *IRS to Address Regulation of Return Preparers by Year's End*, 123 TAX NOTES 1200 (2009).

7701(a)(36). As explained in Chapter 1, professionals in each category are subject to their own practice standards. Professionals in the tax field often are members of more than one group and thus are subject to multiple sets of standards. For example, lawyers or CPAs are subject to their respective state regulatory authorities, Circular 230, and the statutory provisions affecting return preparers.

When a taxpayer seeks the help of a professional, several difficulties inevitably mar the return preparation process. First, although the professional should be more skilled than the taxpayer at finding the law that is relevant to the taxpayer's situation, the professional's knowledge of the facts underlying the taxpayer's situation depends entirely on the information known to and conveyed by the taxpayer. The way in which the professional inquires about the facts may influence how the taxpayer reports the facts. Moreover, the taxpayer might deliberately slant the facts in the hope of reducing her tax, or simply fail to report all of the relevant facts due to misunderstanding, misperception, or forgetfulness. These considerations raise the prospect that a return prepared by even the most assiduous professional may be less accurate than what a well-informed, well-intentioned taxpayer might have prepared independently.[20]

Inevitably, the precision of the return preparation process also suffers because the taxpayer must pay for the professional's services, a factor that significantly limits the amount of time and effort that the professional can commit to the taxpayer's return. While the taxpayer might be willing to spend his own time establishing exact amounts for various return entries and satisfying substantiation requirements, resort to estimates and less rigorous review of supporting documentation are bound to follow when a professional's time (and fees) are involved. Similarly, the legal research and analysis necessary to determine the proper treatment of various items may prove more costly than is justified by the amount at stake for the taxpayer.[21]

In theory, the taxpayer and the professional are both interested in preparing an accurate return, but in some cases, the taxpayer's interest in reducing the tax shown on the return conflicts with the professional's responsibility to assure that the return meets some minimum standard. The taxpayer might simply fail to cooperate or refuse to follow the advice of the professional in the preparation of the return. How professionals respond to such taxpayers can have major consequences for the viability of the self-assessment system.

The foregoing issues define the environment in which the accuracy standards applicable to tax professionals must apply. These standards are designed to assure that returns prepared by tax professionals are basically accurate and

[20] There is some empirical evidence that noncompliance is greater on returns prepared by return preparers than on returns prepared by taxpayers themselves. *See, e.g.*, Brian Erard, *The Impact of Tax Practitioners on Tax Compliance: A Research Summary*, 90 TNT 237–47 (Nov. 21, 1990).

[21] The ABA Section of Taxation at one time tried to respond to this problem by proposing that taxpayers be permitted to request low-cost limited scope tax advice the provision of which would be subject to reduced due diligence and competence standards. This well thought out proposal was ultimately rejected by the ABA. The Model Rules now allow the lawyer and client to agree to limit the scope of the representation, but not to the extent that the tax bar had hoped. *See* Model Rule 1.1 Comment [5], Model Rule 1.2(c), Comments [6] and [7].

complete. The standards may also have the salutary effect of offering the scrupulous tax professional shelter against the entreaties of the unscrupulous taxpayer/client. In general, the standards represent an accommodation between the practical concerns discussed above and the need for integrity in the filing of tax returns.

Given the diverse sources of the standards, it is somewhat surprising that until the 2007 Act, all of the sources applied similar rules in similar contexts, regardless of the professional status of the practitioner. Indeed, despite differences in wording, emphasis, and, in some cases, important substantive results, the pre-2007 Act rules could be largely discussed as a whole. In addition to facilitating efficient, intelligent discussion of an otherwise unmanageable morass, this approach offered the additional benefit of suggesting how the morass could be transformed into a body of uniform standards. The regulations, Circular 230 and ethical strictures of the legal and accounting professions must now be modified to reflect the 2008 version of Section 6694. It remains to be seen whether the various standards will fuse into a single standard or reflect multiple variations on a single theme.

The multiple sets of standards, although now at odds with the standards of Section 6694, are still useful in providing guidance in two major problem areas: (1) the evaluation of facts and the application of the law to the facts, and (2) whether there is an obligation to amend a return subsequently found to be erroneous. In both of these contexts, the role of the taxpayer is preeminent, and the integrity of the return may ultimately be beyond the control of even the most conscientious tax professional.

In addition, once the facts and applicable law have been established, there may be choices about how to report some items on the return. The professional should discuss alternative positions that may be taken on the return (and the disclosures that some positions may require) and explain the risks associated with those positions (including the possibility of a successful challenge by the IRS, penalties, and other costs, such as legal and accounting fees, of pursuing a dispute with the IRS). Failure to provide this advice to the taxpayer might, in a worst case scenario, be the first step in the direction of being on the wrong side of a malpractice action. Ultimately, however, it is the taxpayer's decision how to report items on the return. If the taxpayer, after being properly informed about the risks and rewards of taking alternative positions on a return, takes a position that leads to the imposition of a penalty, the professional should not be penalized or subject to malpractice liability, except where the professional is a return preparer with respect to the return and has failed to satisfy the standards of Section 6694. Similarly, as discussed below, it is ultimately the taxpayer's decision whether to amend an erroneous return.

Although the taxpayer's greater knowledge of and access to the facts affecting the taxpayer's tax liability has played a major role in the development of the practice standards, the standards also reflect the concerns of those with different stakes in both the tax system and the interests of their clients. Thus, the statutory return preparer rules of Section 6694 and the provisions of Circular 230 regarding return preparation by those admitted to practice before the IRS (including both general due diligence standards and provisions historically reflecting the standards of Section 6694) all reflect a governmental concern with receiving accurate tax returns. The taxpayer accuracy standards discussed in the first part of this chapter also reflect this concern. To varying degrees, all of these standards limit the aggressive advocate's ability to assist a taxpayer/client in making a nonfrivolous challenge to a government tax position.

Lawyers on the other hand, have always viewed loyalty to the client, who is to be represented zealously within the bounds of the law, as the base line for ethical analysis. That the taxpayer/client may at some point be represented by the lawyer in an adversarial proceeding involving the client's tax return has long colored the development of ethical standards governing the provision of tax advice by lawyers.[22] Even the Supreme Court has drawn a sharp contrast between the lawyer's training as an advocate and the CPA's role in audit and attest functions, where independence from the client is essential.[23] Although the Court noted this distinction in the context of the First Amendment protection accorded commercial speech in the form of in-person uninvited solicitations of business, the distinction must be borne in mind in understanding the historical underpinnings of both professions' approaches to the ethical standards applicable to return preparation. This is true despite the fact that lawyers and CPAs perform essentially the same roles in advising about and preparing tax returns and representing the taxpayers on audit, roles which are also performed by enrolled agents and, to a lesser extent, other return preparers.

B. Tax Return Preparers Generally

Code §§ 7701(a)(36), 6695, 6695A and 6696 *Need to look up!*.
Treas. Reg. §§ 301.7701-15, 1.6695-1 and 1.6695-2 *Need to Look Up!*

After the 2007 Act, the term "tax return preparer" is defined as a person who prepares a return or claim for refund (expanded to "a substantial portion" of a return or claim for refund by the regulations) for compensation or employs one or more others to do so. Exceptions are provided for a person who (1) merely furnishes mechanical assistance such as typing or copying, (2) prepares a return or refund claim for an employer (or an officer or employee of the employer) by whom the person is regularly and continuously employed, (3) prepares a return or refund claim as a fiduciary, or (4) prepares a refund claim in response to a notice of deficiency issued to the taxpayer or in response to a waiver of restriction after commencement of an audit of the taxpayer or, in certain circumstances, an audit of another taxpayer which affects the tax liability of the taxpayer for whom the refund claim is prepared. Section 7701(a)(36)(B). This list of exceptions has been considerably elaborated and expanded in the regulations, which now except, among others: IRS employees performing official duties, individuals preparing returns as part of a Volunteer Income Tax Assistance (VITA) program or as part of an elderly tax counseling program established under Section 163 of the Revenue Act of 1978 and organizations sponsoring or administering such programs, individuals preparing returns as

301.7701-15

---

[22] See ABA Formal Op. 85–352 ("In many cases a lawyer must realistically anticipate that the filing of the tax return may be the first step in a process that may result in an adversary relationship between the client and the IRS.").

[23] Edenfield v. Fane, 507 U.S. 761 (1993).

part of a qualified Low-Income Taxpayer Clinic (LITC) program and such LITC programs, and persons who prepare returns with "no explicit or implicit agreement for compensation." Treas. Reg. § 301.7701-15(f).

The regulations distinguish between a "signing preparer" and a "nonsigning preparer," a distinction that is not found in the statute. A "signing tax return preparer" is "the individual tax return preparer who has the primary responsibility for the overall substantive accuracy of the preparation" of the return. Treas. Reg. § 301.7701-15(b)(1). In many cases, a return preparer provides advice to a taxpayer with respect to only one or a few individual issues on the return; such a return preparer would not have primary responsibility for the overall substantive accuracy of the return and would not be a signing tax return preparer with respect to the return. A signing tax return preparer is required to sign the return. *See* Treas. Reg. § 1.6695-1(b)(3) (implementing Section 6695's penalty for failure to sign).

Any tax return preparer who is not a signing tax return preparer but prepares all or a "substantial portion" of a return or refund claim "with respect to events that have occurred at the time the advice is rendered" is a "nonsigning tax return preparer" and thus subject to the preparer penalty provisions in Section 6694 with respect to the return or substantial portion thereof as to which the person provided written or oral advice to either the taxpayer or to another tax return preparer.[24] It is not at all clear why a tax professional, usually a planner at a law or CPA firm, who provides tax advice before a transaction takes place is not subject to the Code's accuracy standards with respect to such advice, while a perhaps far less knowledgeable preparer of a return (maybe a seasonal employee of a return preparer firm) whose advice comes after the fact is subject to the rigorous standards of Section 6694. Regardless of the merits of this line-drawing, the regulations include a special de minimis rule to allow planners to provide a modest amount of post-transaction advice without being treated as nonsigning tax return preparers for purposes of Section 7701(a)(36).[25]

The regulations elaborate on the "substantial portion" concept by providing that a person "who renders tax advice on a position that is directly relevant to the determination of the existence, characterization, or amount of an entry on a return or claim for refund" is regarded as preparing the entry. Determining whether something is a substantial portion depends on whether the person has actual or constructive knowledge that the tax attributable to the entry or other portion is "a substantial portion of the tax required to be shown on the return or claim for refund." The regulations indicate the size and complexity of the item relative to the taxpayer's gross income and the size of the understatement attributable to the item compared to the taxpayer's reported tax liability are

---

[24] Treas. Reg. § 301.7701-15(b)(2)(i). The IRS has decided that preparers of information returns, such as Forms 1099 and W-2, are not preparers of the income tax returns on which the items reported on the information returns are entered for purposes of Section 6694 (a), but only for purposes of Section 6694(b). *See* Rev. Proc. 2009–11, 2009-3 I.R.B. 313. It seems doubtful that Congress intended this distinction.

[25] Treas. Reg. § 301.7701-15(b)(2)(i) (second sentence). This is followed by a peculiar anti-abuse rule designed to prevent tax return preparers from disguising themselves as transaction planners to avoid the rigors of Section 6694! See Example (3) following the de minimis rule, which illustrates both the de minimis rule and the anti-abuse exception.

among the factors to consider in determining whether the item is a substantial portion. Treas. Reg. § 301.7701-15(b)(3)(i). They then provide de minimis rules precluding "substantial portion" treatment where the portion involves less than specified amounts of gross income, deductions, or basis for which credits are determined.[26]

PROBLEM 2-3

Cindy CPA provides return preparation guidance, but she rarely actually prepares returns. Bill teaches kindergarten and knows how to handle most of the items on his return, but he received a Schedule K-1 from an S corporation *his portion* controlled by his sister. The Schedule K-1 shows his share of the S corpora- *$9,600* tion's nonseparately stated taxable income as $9,600, as well as small amounts of separately stated credits, a capital gain of $570 and Section 179 expenses of $800. He sends Cindy the Schedule K-1 as well as other information about his investment and asks her how he should handle the Schedule K-1 data. She sends him a short letter explaining which forms he needs to file and where the items on the Schedule K-1 should be reported on those forms, but she incorrectly advises him that he doesn't have to report the income because it is less than his basis in the S corporation stock. He follows her instructions and files the return.

yes ← *If her advise was substantial portion of return yes*

a. Is Cindy a tax return preparer under Section 6694?

No *fits w/in scope of de minimus exception*

b. Would your answer to (a), above, be the same if the capital gain were $370 instead of $570? ~~(possibly, depending on Bill's yrly inc)~~

c. Would your answer to (a), above, be the same if Cindy provided instructions with respect to filling out the remainder of entire tax return? *See* Treas. Reg. §301.7701-15(c). *yes → Then it is definitely substantial portion*

d. Would your answers be different if Bill were a successful ophthalmologist?[27] *yes* *b/c most likely 1 K-1 wouldn't be substantial (de minis rule would apply)*

PROBLEM 2-4

No b/c this does not make up substantial portion of b/c de minimis < $10,000 cannot hold Kim accountable

Kim is a tax lawyer. She prepared the return and Schedules K-1 for a 23-partner partnership. Bob's percentage interest (1 percent) is the smallest of all of the partners' interests. The nonseparately stated taxable income figure for the partnership is $200,000, which reflects large deductions for repairs to a building owned by the partnership and depreciation. Bob's pro rata share of these deductions, if separately stated, would have been more than $51,000, but his nonseparately stated taxable income share is only $2,000. Kim is vaguely aware that Bob was at some point a "starving artist." Is Kim a tax return preparer with respect to Bob's income tax return? With respect to the other partners' income tax returns? *See* Goulding v. United States, 717 F. Supp. 545 (N.D. Ill. 1989).

↳ *Depends on their individual situations, most likely not.*

---

[26] Treas. Reg. § 301.7701-15(b)(3)(ii). The de minimis rules, which do not apply to a signing preparer, represent an expansion of the de minimis rules of the prior regulations.

[27] *See also* ROBERT FULGHUM, ALL I REALLY NEED TO KNOW I LEARNED IN KINDERGARTEN (1990) (e.g., share everything, play fair, don't hit people, put things back where you found them, clean up your own mess, don't take things that aren't yours, say you're sorry when you hurt somebody, wash your hands before you eat, flush, warm cookies and cold milk are good for you, etc.).

PROBLEM 2-5

a. Harper, a member of the Model State Bar, spent 100 billable hours during Year One advising Client Claude how to trade his appreciated apartment building for two other rental properties in a Section 1031 like kind exchange and then reviewed documentation for the transaction to be sure it complied with the Section 1031 requirements. The transaction was completed in September of Year One. In February of Year Two, Claude called Harper and asked for a detailed written explanation of the tax consequences of the transaction to provide to his CPA who was preparing Claude's Year One income tax return. Harper spent all day the following Saturday (nine billable hours) drafting the requested document. The Section 1031 exchange itself will not result in any gross income to be included on Claude's Year One income tax return, although the gain realized on the sale exceeds Claude's total includible gross income for the year. However, the document prepared by Harper details how the transaction qualifies for like kind exchange treatment and provides the basis and depreciation computations that need to be used for reporting the rental income and expenses from the properties received in the exchange. Is Harper a tax return preparer with respect to Claude's Year One income tax return?

9/109_ 50/0
→ yes)
(non signing)

b. The CPA takes the basis and depreciation computations provided by Harper and enters them on Claude's return. Is the CPA a tax return preparer with respect to these entries? (Anticipating the next section of this chapter, can CPA rely on Harper's conclusions regarding the application of Section 1031?)

→ yes
(signing)
6694-2e5
He can rely

c. Same facts as (a), above, except that, instead of the detailed document, Harper sent Claude an outline of the same issues that took him only two billable hours to prepare.

No < 50/0 [.7701-15 b2i

d. Same facts as (a), above, except that Claude asks Harper for "the files" instead of for the written advice. Harper has his assistant copy the files and forward them to Claude. Claude then turns the files over to the CPA for his review. The files do not contain a memo or other analysis of the transaction with a conclusion that the requirements of Section 1031 are met but, rather, contain transactional documents reflecting a transaction designed to comply with Section 1031. On the basis of his review of the files and his assumption that the transaction qualified under Section 1031, CPA calculates the basis and depreciation figures needed to prepare Claude's Year One return. He then prepares that part of the return (twelve billable hours). Is the CPA a tax return preparer with respect to the positions reflected in the depreciation deductions on the return? With respect to the underlying conclusion that the exchange was tax-free under Section 1031? If not, is Harper a tax return preparer with respect to this position?

→yes
→ yes
→No only rendered
planning advice

e. Same facts as (a), above. Early in Year Three, Claude again contacts Harper for the basis and depreciation computations needed for Claude's Year Two income tax return. Harper sends an outline document with this information; the process of refreshing his memory regarding the transaction and preparing an outline to send to Claude takes him four billable hours. Is Harper a tax return preparer with respect to Claude's Year Two income tax return? Would the answer be different if the work took Harper seven billable hours?

No good answer
could go either way.

→ then, yes.

PROBLEM 2-6

A, B and C work for the same law firm. A is a CPA who prepares both income and transfer tax returns for firm clients. B is a partner in the firm who is an expert on tax-exempt bonds and rarely handles other tax matters. C is an experienced associate with a strong general tax background. One of C's responsibilities is to review income tax returns prepared for firm clients by CPAs who are employed by the firm. A prepares an income tax return for Client, a long-standing client of B. C then reviews the return and forwards it to B for transmittal to the client, who will file the return. Who should sign the return as the signing preparer? Are either of the other two nonsigning preparers? Is this arrangement satisfactory? *See* Model Rule 5.3; *cf.* Circular 230 § 10.36(a).

[handwritten: A should sign B+C do not constitute non-signing preparers]

[handwritten: C → Signing   B should probably not deliver return   A → non signing]

PROBLEM 2-7

What is the purpose of Treas. Reg. §301.7701-15(e)? How likely is it to be enforced?

[handwritten: ? Need to print reg Sec. 301.7701-15(e)]

Section 6695 imposes penalties on signing return preparers for failing to sign the return, failing to provide a copy of the return to the taxpayer, failing to provide an identification number on a completed return presented to the taxpayer, failing to retain a copy or record of a prepared return, negotiating a refund check issued to a taxpayer or failing to satisfy the earned income tax credit due diligence requirements. The regulations address each of these penalties and cross reference the provisions that impose the underlying duties. Treas. Reg. § 1.6695-1 and -2.

C. Return Preparer Substantive Standards

Code § 6694
Treas. Reg. §§ 1.6694-1 and 1.6694-2
Circular 230 §§ 10.22 and 10.34

A return preparer must, above all, prepare returns in conformity with the law; that law is stated in Section 6694. As discussed previously, Section 6694's standards were amended in both 2007 and 2008. Our focus in this section will be on the strengthened standards that resulted from the combination of those two amendments — "more likely than not" for "tax shelter"[28] positions or positions with respect to "reportable transactions," "substantial authority" for other nondisclosed positions, and "reasonable basis" for other disclosed positions. It is worth noting at this point, however, that practitioners subject to Circular 230 must also satisfy Circular 230's return preparer standards and due diligence requirements, requirements that resemble both those applied in malpractice litigation against professionals and professional ethical standards. Indeed, if a preparer fails to satisfy the standards of Section 6694 and the taxpayer, as a result, ends up liable for significant amounts of penalties and interest, the preparer is likely to be on the wrong end of a malpractice action.

---

[28] For which among several preparers of a return may be subject to a penalty for a particular position, see Treas. Reg. § 1.6694-1(b). For the possibility that both the individual who prepared the return position and the firm employing the individual or of which the individual is a partner, member, shareholder or other equity holder may both be subject to penalty, see Treas. Reg. § 1.6694-1(b)(5).

In any event, all of the statutory standards use terms of art, the general application of which is discussed below.

Section 6694 imposes civil (i.e., not criminal) penalties on "tax return preparers." For returns or claims for refund that reflect an understatement of tax liability due to an unreasonable position, the penalty is the greater of $1,000 or 50 percent of the income derived (or to be derived) by the tax return preparer from the return or refund claim (the Section 6694(a) penalty). For returns or refund claims that reflect an understatement of tax liability due to willful or reckless conduct by the tax return preparer, the penalty is the greater of $5,000 or 50 percent of the income derived (or to be derived) by the tax return preparer from the return or refund claim (the Section 6694(b) penalty). The regulations indicate that all compensation that the preparer receives or expects to receive for preparing the return or claim for refund or providing advice with respect to the position on the return or claim for refund giving rise to the understatement is taken into account in computing the penalty.[29] A refund of part of the fee does not reduce the amount of the penalty. When a penalty is imposed on both the individual preparer and the preparer's firm, the total amount of the penalties may not exceed 50 percent of the income derived by the firm from the engagement.

1. Positions with Respect to a Tax Shelter or a Reportable Transaction

A position with respect to a tax shelter (as defined in Section 6662(d)(2)(C)(ii)) or a reportable transaction to which Section 6662A applies is subject to the Section 6694(a) penalty unless "it is reasonable to believe that the position would more likely than not be sustained on its merits." Section 6694(a)(2)(C). Section 6662(d)(2)(C) defines the term "tax shelter" to mean a partnership or other entity, any investment plan or arrangement, or any other plan or arrangement if a significant purpose of the partnership, entity, plan or arrangement is the avoidance or evasion of Federal *income* tax. This definition excludes non-income tax planning from the definition of "tax shelter," thus leaving positions attributable to non-income tax (e.g., estate tax) planning governed by the more liberal "substantial authority" (nondisclosed positions) and reasonable basis (disclosed positions) standards discussed below, unless such positions are also with respect to a reportable transaction. However, this "loophole" is inconsistent with the trend of subjecting estate planning and other non-income tax planning to the same standards as income tax planning,[30] and may be addressed in future legislation.

The "more likely than not" standard is satisfied if the preparer, in reliance on an analysis of all of the pertinent facts and authorities, reasonably concludes in good faith that the position has a greater than 50 percent chance of being sustained on its merits. Treas. Reg. § 1.6694-2(b)(1). The preparer's analysis may not take into account the possibility that the position will not be

---

[29] Treas. Reg. § 1.6694-1(f)(1). The preparer or the preparer's firm may be able establish that less than all of the compensation associated with an engagement is attributable to the position giving rise to the understatement. Treas. Reg. § 1.6694-1(f)(2)(iv). The principal regulations on the return preparer penalties are contained in the income tax regulations; however, regulations applicable to other taxes generally incorporate the income tax regulations by reference. *See, e.g.,* Treas. Reg. § 20.6694-1 (estate tax returns).

[30] *Cf.* Circular 230 § 10.35.

challenged, but should use the analysis of authorities set forth in the regulations under Section 6662, discussed earlier in this chapter. As noted earlier, such authorities are generally limited to those that are binding on the IRS (such as statutory and regulatory provisions, treaties, and judicial decisions) and a variety of other official documents, such as Blue Books, congressional committee reports, administrative pronouncements, and official explanations of treaties.[31]

The real difficulty with this approach to analyzing whether the substantial authority or the more likely than not standard is met is that weighing authorities to evaluate the strength of a return position on a fairly well-defined legal issue is rarely the difficult part of assisting a client in the preparation of a return. The preparer must first ascertain the facts from a client who may be ignorant, inarticulate, unable or unwilling to cooperate, or lacking the crucial information. Often, the client's ability to substantiate the facts raises questions. Once the facts are ascertained, the preparer must determine how the applicable law applies to the facts. These factors must all be weighed in evaluating whether the return position satisfies the applicable standard, yet the ability to research, evaluate, and weigh various legal authorities is frequently of little help in dealing with them. Furthermore, how the preparer deals with a particular client's tax return depends in large part on the economics of the situation and the preparer's judgment about the client. The regulations recognize these considerations to some extent, providing that the preparer's required diligence depends on the particular situation, the preparer's experience with the federal tax law and the taxpayer's affairs and the complexity of the issues and facts, and permitting the preparer to rely in good faith without verification on information provided by the taxpayer, and information and advice provided by another advisor, another preparer or another party.[32]

Because there is no statutory taxpayer standard for positions with respect to a tax shelter that parallels the preparer standard of Section 6694 (as noted earlier, a taxpayer is considered under the regulations to have reported a tax shelter item properly if it is supported by substantial authority and the taxpayer reasonably believed that the tax treatment is more likely than not the proper treatment), temporary guidance provides that for purposes of Section 6694(a), a position with respect to a tax shelter will not be deemed unreasonable (and hence not subject to a penalty) if the preparer advises the taxpayer of the two-part regulatory standard and that disclosure will not protect the taxpayer from assessment of a penalty under Section 6662 if both parts of the standard are not satisfied, and contemporaneously documents this advice in the preparer's files.[33] Unless the taxpayer standard is changed, these rules are likely to be reflected in future regulations.

---

[31] A limited special provision allows consideration of certain written determinations issued to or naming the taxpayer, such as private rulings, determination letters, and technical advice memorandums, but it is not likely to be of much help in this context. *See* Treas Reg. §§ 1.6662-4(d)(3)(iv), 1.6694-2(b)(4). The preparer may rely on such a "written determination" to avoid a penalty with respect to an item otherwise subject to the more likely than not standard. Treas. Reg. § 1.6694-2(b)(3).

[32] Treas. Reg. § 1.6694-2(b)(1), referring to Treas. Reg. § 1.6694-1(e) and -2(e)(5).

[33] Notice 2009-5, *supra* note 3. A parallel rule is provided for advice by a nonsigning tax return preparer to another tax return preparer.

2. Substantial Authority for Nondisclosed Positions

If an undisclosed position is not with respect to either a tax shelter or a reportable transaction, the position satisfies the Section 6694 standard if it is supported by substantial authority. As described in the preceding discussion of the more likely than not standard, the definition of "substantial authority" and evaluation of authorities for this purpose closely parallels the definition of "substantial authority" and evaluation process in Treas. Reg. § 1.6662-4(d)(2), discussed earlier in this chapter, subject to a few modifications in temporary guidance.[34] In particular, in the case of a return preparer, a written determination with a misstatement or omission of material fact is only substantial authority if the return preparer did not know and should not have known of the misstatement or omission when the return or claim for refund was filed. Also, there is substantial authority for a position only if there is substantial authority on the date the return or claim for refund was prepared (or deemed prepared) or on the last day of the taxable year reflected on the return.

3. Reasonable Basis for Disclosed Positions

If a position is not with respect to a tax shelter or a reportable transaction, but is also not supported by substantial authority, the preparer can nonetheless avoid a penalty under Section 6694 if there is a "reasonable basis" for the position and it is adequately disclosed. "Reasonable basis" carries the same meaning as in Treas. Reg. § 1.6662-3(b)(3), discussed earlier. In determining whether a return preparer has a reasonable basis for a position in the context of the Section 6694 penalty, the return preparer may rely in good faith without verification on information provided by the taxpayer and information and advice provided by others. Treas. Reg. § 1.6694-2(d)(2). Even if a return preparer does not have a reasonable basis for a position and might therefore be subject to a penalty, the taxpayer who relies on the return preparer and files a return with the position appropriately disclosed may still be able to avoid a Section 6662 penalty for negligence or a substantial understatement because the reliance on the preparer might qualify as reasonable cause if the taxpayer acted in good faith. See Section 6664(c)(1).

The regulatory definition of "adequate disclosure" for this purpose is somewhat at odds with the statute. See Treas. Reg. § 1.6694-2(d)(3). In easy cases, of course, a position is adequately disclosed if it is disclosed on a properly completed and filed Form 8275 or Form 8275-R, or on the return in the manner provided in an annual revenue procedure. The regulations permit the disclosure requirement to be satisfied in other ways to deal with fact that a taxpayer might reject the preparer's advice to disclose. In that event, a signing preparer can satisfy the disclosure requirement by providing the taxpayer a prepared tax return that includes the required disclosure;[35] it does not matter for purposes of Section 6694 whether the taxpayer actually files the return with the disclosure. Nonsigning preparers can also satisfy the disclosure requirement by advising the taxpayer of any opportunity to avoid penalties under Section 6662 by disclosure, provided

---

[34] Notice 2009-5, *supra* note 3.

[35] Treas. Reg. § 1.6694-2(d)(3)(i)(B). Of course, the preparer should retain a copy of the return. If the taxpayer could be subject to a penalty under Section 6662 other than the substantial understatement of income penalty, the signing return preparer can make disclosure by advising the taxpayer of the applicable penalty standards under Section 6662, provided the preparer also documents the advice contemporaneously in the preparer's files.

the advice is documented contemporaneously in the preparer's files. While the regulations elaborate at some length about the contents of the advice provided by either a signing or a nonsigning preparer, the bottom line is that there is no requirement that a position actually be disclosed on the return as the statute appears to require.

4. Reasonable Cause and Good Faith

Even if a return position does not satisfy any of the accuracy standards of Section 6694(a), the preparer may still be able to avoid a penalty if the understatement was due to reasonable cause and the preparer acted in good faith. The regulations indicate that whether this exception applies requires consideration of all the facts and circumstances; they discuss several relevant factors — the nature of the error causing the understatement (was it complex, uncommon or highly technical, or something that would have been apparent from a general review of the return?), the frequency of errors (the exception does not apply if there is a pattern of errors), materiality of the error, the preparer's normal office practice, reliance on information or advice of others (reliance is okay unless the information or advice was unreasonable on its face, the preparer knew or should have known that the other party was not aware of all relevant facts, or the preparer knew or should have known that the advice or information was no longer reliable due to developments in the law), and reliance on generally accepted administrative or industry practice.[36] This reasonable cause and good faith exception largely parallels the similar exception for taxpayers in Section 6664 except that the preparer is held to a much higher standard, as seems appropriate.

PROBLEM 2-8

Minerva prepares income tax returns for Filing Are Us (FAU), a commercial return preparation firm. Smith is a real estate investor. Minerva prepared Smith's 2009 federal income tax return for a total fee of $10,000. FAU guarantees that its filings are within 1 percent of the correct tax amount or the taxpayer's fee is refunded. Minerva made an error on Smith's return that resulted in the entire fee being refunded. Minerva spent three weeks of her 50-week work year preparing the return; her annual salary is $50,000. Assuming that the IRS determines that both Minerva and FAU should be penalized under Section 6694(a), how much will each of them be fined? See Treas. Reg. § 6694-1(f). Would your answer be the same if the fee had not been refunded? Is there something wrong here?

PROBLEM 2-9

a. On a highly technical tax issue attributable to a tax shelter, two lawyers in the same law firm disagree on a reporting position that affects two unrelated clients' tax returns. Both lawyers are well-qualified, recognized experts in this area of tax law. Lawyer A believes that it is more likely than not that the type of transaction qualifies for nonrecognition. Lawyer B, on the other hand, believes that it is more likely than not that the type of transaction is taxable. Both lawyers' arguments for their respective positions are well-reasoned. Assuming that the lawyers are signing preparers for their respective clients, can they sign returns on behalf of the firm with contrary positions for their respective clients?

[36] Treas. Reg. § 1.6694-2(e). For some comments on the role of office procedures, see James R. Hamill, *Proper Procedures Can Help to Avoid Preparer Penalties*, 55 TAX'N ACCT. 294 (1995).

b. Lawyer A and Lawyer B are members of two different firms, but represent the same client. Both lawyers are well-qualified, recognized experts in tax law. Lawyer A has provided the client a written opinion to the effect that a reporting position with respect to a tax shelter satisfies the more likely than not standard. Lawyer B is preparing the client's return. Client provides Lawyer A's opinion to Lawyer B, who does not agree that the position satisfies the more likely than not standard. Can Lawyer B prepare the return treating the item as nontaxable without disclosure (and without advising the client about penalty exposure), relying on Lawyer A's more likely than not opinion? *→ No*

Not advisable to rely on memo.

c. Same facts as (a), above, except that the issue does not involve a tax shelter or a reportable transaction, and Lawyer A concludes that nonrecognition treatment is supported by substantial authority while Lawyer B believes taxable treatment is supported by substantial authority. Can they sign returns on behalf of the firm with the contrary nondisclosed positions for their respective clients? *→ Yes, but may incur penalties*

PROBLEM 2-10

If a preparer is unable, after a reasonable amount of research and analysis, to determine whether she believes a position attributable to a tax shelter item is more likely than not to be sustained on its merits, can she advise the taxpayer to take the position on the return without risking a penalty under Section 6694? If not, how should the preparer advise the client to report the item attributable to a tax shelter on his return? *→ As taxable* ~~Redisclose~~

Advice consultant preparer does not preparer.

No tax shelter

→ No, cannot sign return, non signing preparer & thus no liability as distanced themselves.

PROBLEM 2-11

a. Client sold an asset in 2006 in exchange for a note payable over 5 years. Although treating the sale as an installment sale was not supported by substantial authority (but did meet the reasonable basis standard), Preparer X nonetheless prepared the client's income tax returns in accordance with the installment sale rules for 2006, 2007 and 2008 without disclosing the position, perhaps out of ignorance at the time. In preparing the client's 2009 calendar year tax return, is Preparer X required to prepare a disclosure with respect to the treatment of the portion of the gain reported on the 2009 return? *→ Yes if they want to avoid the Penalty*

If there is ~~reasonable basis~~

b. Same facts as (a), above, except that Preparer Y, another preparer who is neither affiliated with nor knows Preparer X, is preparing Client's 2009 return. If Preparer Y receives copies of the earlier returns from Client and otherwise knows nothing about the 2006 transaction, may Preparer Y rely on the earlier returns to continue reporting the gain from the transaction on the installment method on the 2009 return? *→ No*

c. Same facts as (b), above, except that Preparer Y's review of the earlier returns leads her to suspect that the transaction was not eligible for installment sale treatment. *→ No*

PROBLEM 2-12

a. F, a lawyer, has prepared Client's federal income tax returns for many years. In preparing Client's 2009 return, F notices that Client did not provide a Form 1099-INT from Bank, which had produced significant interest income in prior years, including 2008. F does not ask Client about the missing form and prepares the return without reporting any interest from Bank. The return is filed as prepared by F. A couple of years later, when Client is under IRS audit, it becomes clear that Client did receive a large amount of interest from Bank in 2009, leading to a substantial understatement of income tax. What are the possible consequences to F of this understatement?

b. Same facts as (a), above, except that F asked client whether she had any other interest income and client responded by providing a Form 1099-INT from another bank, but did not provide one from Bank. What are the possible consequences to F in this situation?

D. Consequences if Client Rejects Advice on Return Position

*Model Rule 1.16 and Comments
ABA Formal Op. 85-352 (Appendix B)
AICPA SSTS No. 1 (Appendix C)
AICPA Interpretation No. 1-2, "Tax Planning" (Appendix D)

The peculiar approach of the regulations in defining what constitutes adequate disclosure of a position on a return so as to protect the preparer against imposition of a penalty eliminates a puzzling problem under prior law. If, under prior law, the taxpayer did not want to disclose a position on the return, but the position was one that a signing preparer could not advise not disclosing without risking a penalty, the preparer had to refuse to sign the return to avoid incurring a preparer penalty. (This situation was aggravated by the fact that the taxpayer and preparer standards were often different.) The preparer might also have had to advise the taxpayer of any other penalties that the taxpayer's return position might trigger. The current situation, with largely parallel accuracy standards for preparers and taxpayers and special "disclosure" options for preparers is much more manageable.

In discussing the risks of aggressive return positions with a client, the preparer should not suggest that the risks are lessened by the improbability of an audit. Nonetheless, if asked directly, many practitioners consider it appropriate for the preparer to indicate the likelihood of an audit.[37] In all

---

[37] In the case of a lawyer, once the taxpayer/client has decided to file a return asserting a position that the lawyer is not permitted to recommend, the lawyer, in the opinion of one of the authors, is obligated to withdraw from the engagement (of preparing the return) and hence may not subsequently answer questions about the likelihood of an audit. A vigorous discussion at the January 20, 1996 Meeting of the ABA Tax Section Committee on Standards of Tax Practice indicated that many tax lawyers do not agree with the author's view. Others may agree that responding to such an inquiry is inappropriate, but for different reasons. Professor David M. Richardson has argued, for example, that lawyers do not have enough knowledge about the possibility of an audit to answer such a question.

If the client has not yet made a decision about the position to be taken on her return or if the preparer is not a lawyer, the propriety of responding to the client's inquiry about the audit lottery is likely to be even more controversial. Full discussion of this issue is beyond the scope of this text. For two views, see ALI RESTATEMENT OF THE LAW GOVERNING LAWYERS § 151, Draft Comments (Preliminary Draft No. 10, 1994); *A Gathering of Legal Scholars to Discuss "Professional Responsibility and the Model Rules of Professional Conduct" — Panel Discussion*, 35 U. MIAMI L. REV. 639, 659 (1981) (statement of Professor Geoffrey Hazard, Jr.). See also AICPA SSTS No. 1, ¶ 8, allowing a CPA to discuss the "likelihood that each [of two positions meeting the then AICPA realistic possibility of success standard] might or might not cause the taxpayer's return to be examined," perhaps implying that the likelihood of an audit should not be discussed in other circumstances.

cases where a preparer has advised taxpayers about the risks of aggressive return positions, the preparer should, for his own protection, maintain records of the advice. *Cf.* Treas. Reg. § 1.6694-2(d)(3)(i)(C), (ii)(B) & (iii). A lawyer should take care in maintaining such records to preserve the confidentiality of communications with a taxpayer whose relationship with the lawyer is an attorney-client relationship. A federally authorized tax practitioner should take similar precautions to preserve the confidentiality of communications in circumstances where the communications could be protected by the Section 7525 privilege.

CPAs under pre-2008 Act standards apparently did not have an option to provide the client a return with disclosure and then let the client decide what to do with it. When a CPA concluded that a position did not meet the AICPA version of the prior law realistic possibility of success standard, the CPA was supposed to prepare and sign a return including the position only if the position was not frivolous and was adequately disclosed on the return.[38] If these requirements were not met, the CPA apparently was supposed to neither prepare nor sign the return, although the SSTS did not explicitly state this. In recommending certain tax return positions and signing a return, the CPA was supposed to, where relevant, advise the client of potential penalty consequences of the recommended positions and the opportunities, if any, to avoid penalties through disclosure. Whether and, if so, how to disclose, were the client's decisions.

The AICPA recently updated its SSTSs, effective January 1, 2010. The new version of SSTS No. 1 requires a CPA to follow standards imposed by the applicable taxing authority with respect to recommending a tax return position or signing a tax return. If the applicable taxing authority has no such written standards, or if those standards are lower than the standards sets forth in SSTS No. 1, then:

1. A CPA should not recommend a position or sign a tax return taking a position unless the CPA has a good faith belief that the position has at least a realistic possibility of being sustained administratively or judicially on its merits if challenged.

2. Notwithstanding the preceding rule, a CPA may recommend a tax return position if she (i) concludes that there is a reasonable basis for the position and (ii) advises the taxpayer to appropriately disclose that position; and a CPA may prepare or sign a tax return that reflects a position if (i) she concludes there is a reasonable basis for the position and (ii) the position is appropriately disclosed.

Because the standards in Section 6694 are higher than those in the SSTS, a CPA advising with respect to, preparing, or signing a federal tax return must comply with Section 6694.

The pre-2008 Act ethical obligations imposed on lawyers who prepare returns were not as clearly defined as one might have hoped, in part because return preparation may be a small part of the lawyer's representation of the client. If

---

[38] AICPA SSTS No. 1, ¶ 2c (prior to revision in November 2009). This was consistent with the prior version of Section 6694, except that the AICPA took the rather lenient view that a "frivolous" position is one that is "knowingly advanced in bad faith and is patently improper." *Id.* ¶ 9.

a position on the taxpayer's return did not meet the realistic possibility of success standard of ABA Formal Op. 85-352, the lawyer was generally not supposed to prepare the return, regardless of whether the lawyer signed the return or simply forwarded it (without his signature) to the taxpayer.[39] This general rule raised two major questions: (1) Could a lawyer recommend a nonfrivolous, or perhaps somewhat more promising, return position that did not satisfy the realistic possibility of success standard without risking professional discipline? *No* (2) If the client insisted on asserting a return position that the lawyer was ethically precluded from recommending, was the lawyer required to withdraw from *Yes* representing the client? Although the realistic possibility of success standard has been superseded in the Code by the substantial authority standard and, for tax shelter or reportable transaction items, the more likely than not standard, the same question arises under the new standards. To put the matter somewhat differently, is it ethical for a lawyer to provide a client tax advice with *Not ethical* respect to a possible return position where the advice is neither false nor misleading but the advice could subject the lawyer to a penalty under the Code?

ABA Formal Op. 85-352 does not expressly provide a disclosure exception for return positions that do not meet the realistic possibility of success standard. Nonetheless, a leading treatise in this area, after a full canvas of the issue, concluded that, pre-2008 Act, lawyers should have been permitted to recommend a disclosed nonfrivolous return position.[40] The authors noted both that adequate disclosure put the IRS on notice of the position (thus preventing the taxpayer from playing the audit lottery with the issue) and that the Section 6694(a) penalty on preparers for substandard return positions did not apply to a nonfrivolous position that was adequately disclosed. Despite the changes effected by the 2008 Act, the first rationale for this view still makes sense. This suggests that the lawyer may ethically provide a client advice in a way that results in the lawyer voluntarily subjecting herself to a penalty since Section 6694(a) now penalizes a preparer for a disclosed position that lacks a reasonable basis even if it is nonfrivolous. Nonetheless, the authors believe that if the lawyer fully apprises the client of the risk in taking such a position on the return, the lawyer has acted ethically and that, furthermore, this can be done in a way that is consistent with the existing regime. The lawyer may not sign the return and should probably document the advice provided contemporaneously in her records. Since the lawyer cannot sign the return, the lawyer should consider withdrawing from the engagement to the extent of advising as to the position taken on the return. *See* Model Rule 1.16; *cf. Report of the Special Task Force on Formal Opinion 85-352*, 39 TAX LAW. 635, 639 (1986). Of course, under the current Section 6694 regulations, if the position has a reasonable basis, the lawyer could first satisfy the disclosure requirement to protect herself against a penalty under Section 6694. As a result, it is a little difficult to say whether the actual withdrawal is mandatory since the lawyer is not otherwise being asked to violate an ethical rule or do something that is illegal. The lawyer could presumably continue to represent the client in other matters, such as a child custody dispute.

---

[39] *See* BERNARD WOLFMAN, JAMES P. HOLDEN & KENNETH L. HARRIS, STANDARDS OF TAX PRACTICE ¶ 207.2.1 (6th ed. 2004) ("inappropriate" for lawyer to prepare return and send it to client with "note attached indicating that the position should not be taken," referring to Paul J. Sax, *Ethics in Tax Practice: Current Issues*, 38 TUL. TAX INST. ch. 18 (1988)).

[40] WOLFMAN, et al., *supra*, at ¶ 204.2.4.2.

Suppose, however, that preparation of the return is part of an engagement involving a larger transaction or one of many ongoing client matters involving tax planning and advice. Must the lawyer withdraw from the entire engagement or "fire" the client? This seems to depend on the circumstances. The lawyer should weigh a variety of factors, including the importance of the return position to the overall transaction or relationship with the client (for example, whether a transaction's viability depends on the questionable return position or the position is a peripheral matter), the proportion of the lawyer's work on the engagement or for the client with respect to tax work represented by the return, the potential harm to the client that the lawyer's withdrawal might occasion, and whether the client's refusal to follow the lawyer's advice has raised serious concerns in the lawyer's mind about her comfort level in continuing to work with the client. Even if the lawyer does withdraw, the lawyer does not appear to be precluded from representing the client subsequently when the return position is raised on audit, provided, of course, that the client does not claim to have relied on the lawyer's advice in taking the position on the return.

E. Due Diligence and Care
*Treas. Reg. §§ 1.6694-1(e) and 1.6695-2
Circular 230 § 10.22

Circular 230 and principles of tort and contract law provide guidance on the degree of skill, care, and diligence a preparer must exercise in preparing a return. Circular 230 § 10.22 requires those admitted to practice before the IRS to exercise due diligence in preparing, assisting, approving, and filing returns with the IRS. Professionals have similar duties under both tort and contract principles, as well as under professional ethical standards. Finally, the Code and regulations provide special due diligence standards applicable to preparers of returns and claims for refund involving claims for the earned income tax credit. Treas. Reg. § 1.6695-2. These various due diligence standards may at times diverge in practical application, given their varied sources, the parties called upon to apply them (e.g., juries, judges, OPR, and state bar and accounting licensing authorities), and the kinds of penalties or other costs occasioned by their breach. Nonetheless, the proper level of practitioner skill, care, and diligence is measured in such terms.

Clearly, the preparer is not required to guarantee every fact underlying the return or to audit the taxpayer's records. Treas. Reg. § 1.6694-1(e)(1). This would not be economical or, in some cases, possible. On the other hand, the preparer should make a reasonable effort to obtain all relevant information from the taxpayer. Prior years' returns should be reviewed, where appropriate, because they may be helpful in avoiding omissions or duplications of items and may provide a basis for the treatment of similar or related items in the current

---

[41] Treas. Reg. § 1.6694-1(e)(1); *see* Rev. Rul. 80-266, 1980-2 C.B. 378 (negligence penalty applied to preparer who failed to ask whether taxpayer had sufficient records to satisfy Section 274(d) substantiation requirements for travel and entertainment expenses deducted on return and failed to show adequate normal office practices).

return. In gathering information, the preparer may in good faith without verification rely on information provided by the taxpayer and information and advice provided by third parties. Treas. Reg. § 1.6694-1(e)(1). However, the preparer cannot rely on information that appears either on its face or from other facts known to the preparer to be incorrect, incomplete, or inconsistent. Similarly, the preparer may rely in good faith without verification on tax returns previously prepared by the taxpayer or another preparer and filed with the IRS. Treas. Reg. § 1.6694-1(e)(2). In such cases, the preparer must make whatever further inquiry seems reasonable under the circumstances.

Reasonable efforts should be made to confirm the adequacy of the taxpayer's recordkeeping procedures and to inquire about the adequacy of substantiation where substantiation of return items is an issue. Often, it is probably sufficient if, in response to such an inquiry, the taxpayer represents that adequate records or other kinds of sufficient evidence exist.[41] Other facts or the nature of the taxpayer's response may, however, indicate that further inquiry is necessary. For example, if a taxpayer residing in a suburban area tells the preparer that all automobile use is business-related and claims to have adequate records to support the claim, the preparer should probably pursue the issue further. Also, if the preparer knows that the taxpayer could not substantiate similar deductions when audited with respect to a prior tax year, the preparer may have a duty to explore the matter further, despite the taxpayer's statement that he has sufficient records.

The preparer should make a reasonable effort to obtain from the taxpayer appropriate answers to all questions on the return that apply to the taxpayer. Reasonable grounds may exist for the return to omit an answer to a question, such as when the information regarding a relatively insignificant item (in terms of taxable income or loss or in terms of the tax liability shown) is unavailable, when there is genuine uncertainty regarding the meaning of the question, or when the answer is voluminous (although the return should then provide assurance that the information will be supplied upon request).[42]

PROBLEM 2-13

a. Karen is a tax lawyer and is preparing a return for Charlie, who is in the business of buying and selling antiques. This is the first time Karen has handled his tax return. Among the deductions claimed by Charlie is a deduction for a $30,000 loss from a fire that destroyed a storage bin where Charlie says he stored books and antiques. Charlie generally does business in cash, but he has provided a list of the antiques he says were destroyed and his recollection of their cost. He also says he spent $4,568 traveling to flea markets and the like to buy and sell antiques. Can Karen rely on this information in preparing his return? If not, what should she do before preparing the return?

[handwritten: preparer is allowed to be objective, professional skepticism]

[handwritten: She will need further info. or ask if records are kept since this is 1st yr. of return + business owin cash]

---

[42] The subject of responding to return questions is addressed by AICPA SSTS No. 2, which states that a CPA is not required to explain the reasonable grounds that justify omitting an answer to an applicable question. The prior version of SSTS No. 2 stated that the CPA "should consider whether the omission of an answer to a question may cause the return to be deemed incomplete." This could prove damaging to the client (e.g., by attracting an audit or by tolling the statute of limitations), a factor that must always be weighed and should be discussed with the client.

b.   Same facts as (a), above, except that Karen has been preparing Charlie's returns for years and she knows that he keeps meticulous, detailed records of all his business expenses. *Yes she can rely on info then*

PROBLEM 2-14

Docb/ignre 1.4695-2

A 20 year-old college student with $4,000 in earned income and a 2 year-old daughter states that she lives with her parents. She wants to treat her daughter as a qualifying child for purposes of the earned income tax credit. What must the preparer do before preparing a return for the student? *see if she is claimed as dependent on parents return*

IV.   VALUATION AND ESTIMATES

AICPA SSTS No. 4 (Appendix C)

Often, the exact amount to be entered on a return is uncertain because (1) it is impossible or impracticable to obtain all of the data needed to determine the amount or (2) the amount is not susceptible to exact determination. In the first situation, the use of estimates may be necessary; however, the taxpayer or the tax professional is often in a position to make an estimate that is reasonable under the circumstances. In the second situation, generally involving a question of valuation, the tax professional should often defer to someone with appropriate expertise. In both situations, the figure entered on the return should not be presented in a manner that is misleading. For example, if the estimated amount is $5,000, it should not be entered on the return as $5,021.43.

AICPA SSTS No. 4 provides helpful guidance on the use of estimates. It discusses the appropriateness of using estimates for transactions involving small expenditures, for cases where accuracy in recording data may be difficult to achieve, and when records are missing or precise information is not available on the return's due date. The SSTS indicates that although specific disclosure that an estimate has been used is ordinarily not required, disclosure may be necessary in unusual circumstances to avoid misleading the IRS. Examples of such unusual circumstances include the death or illness of the taxpayer, the failure of the taxpayer to receive a Form K-1 from a flow-through entity, pending litigation bearing on the return, or the destruction of relevant records by fire or computer failure.

How a preparer should deal with a valuation issue may depend on the value of the property and the potential tax liability involved as well as what legal provision controls. Often, particularly when relatively small amounts of property are involved, the preparer should be able to rely on the taxpayer's valuation of property. A brief inquiry to be sure that the taxpayer's valuation is not without foundation should suffice. Where the property is more substantial, an appraisal is likely to be necessary, although special factors, such as arm's length bargaining over the property's value, may obviate the need for an appraisal.

In some instances, however, an appraisal is required by law.[43] Also, obtaining a "qualified appraisal" from a "qualified appraiser" may insure against penalties for overvaluation or undervaluation of property. *See* Section 6664(c)(2).

---

[43] *See, e.g.,* Treas. Reg. § 1.170A-13(c)(2)(i)(A) (requiring a "qualified appraisal" for a charitable gift of more than $5,000 in the form of property other than money or publicly traded securities).

If the taxpayer does not wish to bear the cost of obtaining a professional appraisal when an appraisal is appropriate, the preparer has a duty to advise the taxpayer of the operative law and the risks involved in not obtaining the appraisal. If a required appraisal is not obtained, a preparer who nonetheless signs the return subjects himself to a penalty. The preparer should assure himself that any valuation, whether by an appraiser, the taxpayer, or another person, is responsibly done, makes sense, is well-reasoned, and is internally consistent.

Ordinarily, because of ethical limitations on a lawyer serving as a witness and advocate in the same proceeding, a lawyer who may later represent the taxpayer as an advocate against the IRS should refrain from serving as appraiser of the taxpayer's property. *See* Model Rule 3.7; Tax Court Rule 24(g) (in Appendix G). However, following an appropriate explanation of the lawyer's ethical concerns about possibly being unable to serve as both witness and advocate for the client if the valuation issue ultimately ends up litigated, and assuming the lawyer adheres to the ethical requirements for engaging in a business transaction with a client (*e.g.,* Model Rule 1.8), the lawyer, if qualified, may serve as appraiser. Of course, the lawyer might later be unable to represent the taxpayer as an advocate with respect to the issues involved. A preparer who is not a lawyer should consider whether any subsequent representation of the taxpayer before the IRS would lessen the credibility or weight of her appraisal. The preparer should generally discuss this issue with the taxpayer before agreeing to serve as appraiser.

PROBLEM 2-15

Harry is lawyer and the owner of an art gallery. His friend, Petula, has donated a painting by an artist represented by Harry to the local museum. Harry believes the painting is worth $100,000. Assuming Harry is qualified to appraise the painting, he wants your advice about whether he can appraise the painting for charitable contribution deduction purposes, charge Petula a fee for the appraisal, and then prepare Petula's tax return, for which he will also charge a fee. If he needs to take any other action first, please also advise him of that.

V.   ERRORS AND AMENDED RETURNS

Circular 230 § 10.21

AICPA SSTS No. 6 (Appendix C)

Under Circular 230 § 10.21, a practitioner who knows that her client has not complied with the revenue laws of the United States or has made an error in or

---

[44] Treas. Reg. § 1.451-1(a); Treas. Reg. § 1.461-1(a)(3) (taxpayer *should* file an amended return). *See also* Badaracco v. Commissioner, 464 US 386, 393 (1984) ("Internal Revenue Code does not explicitly provide either for a taxpayer's filing, or for the Commissioner's acceptance, of an amended return").

[45] AICPA SSTS No. 6 discusses this subject at length, including the possibility that (1) an erroneous method of accounting might have significant cumulative effects in future years, (2) the taxpayer's refusal to file an amended return might predict future behavior that could require termination of the relationship, (3) the taxpayer might need to consult legal counsel if fraud or criminal charges are considered a possibility, and (4) the practitioner might have to consult counsel herself before deciding how to proceed. Most of this thinking is useful to non-CPA practitioners, as well. One drawback of this SSTS is that it states that most of the advice suggested may be given orally, which is not sufficient to protect to practitioner against an unscrupulous client.

omission from any return, is required to "advise the client promptly of the fact of such noncompliance, error, or omission." The practitioner must also advise the client of the consequences of the noncompliance, error, or omission. *See also* AICPA SSTS No. 6, ¶ 4. The practitioner should advise the taxpayer that the law does not require the filing of an amended return to correct the error,[44] but if the error, omission or noncompliance has a significant effect on the taxpayer's tax liability, the practitioner should recommend corrective measures, including the filing of an amended return to correct the error.[45] Correction of the error, of course, is the proper ethical action on the part of the taxpayer and is often the most practical action. In explaining this to the taxpayer, the practitioner should note why it may be important to correct the return because of future return filing requirements, the possibility of an audit, or any possible inquiry to the taxpayer's attorney from an independent auditor about the presence of contingent liabilities that should be disclosed on a financial statement.

The taxpayer should also be advised of the risk that filing an amended return could lead to the imposition of penalties or charges of fraud or criminal misconduct.[46] If the preparer is not a lawyer (or, if a lawyer, is not sufficiently familiar with tax fraud and criminal tax issues), the taxpayer should be advised to consult with experienced legal counsel before acting, particularly in situations presenting a risk of criminal charges. Such counsel should fully apprise the client of the various options to consider when faced with a potential criminal indictment, including assertion of any applicable constitutional rights.[47]

When the error is on a return prepared by the adviser, particularly if the error is the professional adviser/preparer's fault, the preparer's interest in having the error corrected may conflict with the taxpayer's interest in not filing an amended return. Accordingly, in such cases, one commentator has advised that the preparer — after explaining the potential conflict — should advise the taxpayer to seek other advice about correcting the error.[48] If the preparer was responsible for the error, the preparer might consider preparing the amended return at no expense to the taxpayer and paying any interest or penalties that resulted from the error.

The final decision whether to amend a return is the taxpayer's alone. Nonetheless, if a client chooses not to amend a return, the adviser must consider whether to continue in the professional relationship. Each category of professional must make this decision in light of relevant ethical principles. Clearly, the professional should not represent the taxpayer in an audit of the uncorrected return if the taxpayer refuses to have the error disclosed on audit.[49] Some degree of withdrawal from the relationship with the taxpayer is also likely to be appropriate where the return was prepared by the preparer. If the preparer chooses to continue the professional relationship with a noncorrect-

---

[46] *See Badaracco*, 464 U.S. 386 (filing an amended return does not start the running of the statute of limitations where the earlier return was fraudulent).

[47] *See* Frederic G. Corneel, *Guidelines to Tax Practice Second,* 43 TAX LAW. 297, 307 (1990).

[48] Corneel, *supra*, at 307. In most cases, simply advising the taxpayer of the conflict of interest should suffice. The taxpayer should be free to decide not to seek other advice. In some cases, however, the conflict of interest may be such that the client must seek independent advice. Although this analysis derives from the conflict of interest rules applicable to lawyers, the practical conclusions should apply with equal force to other preparers.

[49] *See* ABA Formal Op. 85-352; AICPA SSTS No. 6 ¶ 6.

ing taxpayer, the preparer should take reasonable steps to assure that the error is not repeated or compounded in a return for a subsequent year.

PROBLEM 2-16

Your client, for whom you have implemented various transactions and provided tax advice over several years, consults you on a reporting position with regard to a transaction. You advise your client that the transaction must be reported on his income tax return in a certain way. Later, your client sends you a copy of the return, as filed, for your records and you notice that the client did not report the transaction as you advised. When you raise the issue with the client, he tells you that he got a second opinion that was contrary to your advice. How should you respond?

[handwritten: Wldraw?]
[handwritten: OK → ensure if audited, you don't represent him on position you provided, since he didn't use it.]

PROBLEM 2-17

Ariana is representing Tommy Tycoon in a bitterly contested divorce. In reviewing Tommy's financial records, including his 2007 and 2008 federal income tax returns and a variety of financial statements from his employer and investment advisors, Ariana discovers that Tommy received a stock bonus (worth $150,000) in 2008 that should have been included in his income, but was not.

[handwritten: Notify TP + discuss remedial action]

a. What action or actions is she required to take following her discovery of this omission? *[handwritten: → Notify Tommy to discuss error w/ preparer]*

b. Does your answer change if Tommy tells her he just sold the stock (in 2009) for $126,000? *[handwritten: No → Gain for stock bonus needs to be reported in '09. need to amend full disclosure]*

c. If Tommy decides not to file an amended 2008 return, will Ariana be able to prepare his return for 2009? Will she be able to continue representing him in the divorce litigation? *[handwritten: → Yes No, she can't against legal obligation wld from representation. preparer may come across so an abetter]*

[handwritten left margin: Yes, but shouldn't make same mistakes as done in '08. ← Should report + sale]

QUESTIONS FOR THOUGHT *[handwritten: + perpetuator]*

1. Are there good reasons to subject different groups of tax practitioners to different sets of regulatory rules with regard to the preparation of tax returns? For example, the attorney-client privilege and the lawyer's role as advocate may call for special regulatory rules for lawyers engaged in tax practice in some contexts, but is return preparation such a context? *[handwritten: No]*

2. What reforms would improve the overall regulation of this area? Should the Code, the ethical rules applicable to lawyers or CPAs, and Circular 230 more clearly reflect the non-adversarial nature of return preparation? *[handwritten: No then would manifest a diffused less strict system]*

3. What are the best arguments for and against requiring the filing of amended returns to correct at least material errors? *[handwritten: Discovery + penalties]*

4. Should the regulations under Section 6662 (and by cross reference, under Section 6694) be amended to reflect a more realistic view of relevant authorities to consider in applying the substantial authority and other accuracy standards? Why or why not? *[handwritten: No leave it vague to practicioner to interpret]*

Chapter 3

TRANSACTIONAL PLANNING AND ADVICE

I. CLIENT CONFLICTS

Circular 230 §§ 10.20 and 10.29
Tax Court Rule 24(g) (Appendix G)
Model Rules 1.7, 1.8, 1.9 and 1.13(a) *Need to look up
AICPA ET § 102.03 and Interpretation 102-2 (Appendix H)

A. Introduction

The point of conflicts of interest rules is to protect clients' reasonable expectations that legal advisors and representatives will act on their behalf free from compromising loyalties and influences. Thus, the basic principle embodied in the Model Rules' conflict provisions is that a lawyer may not represent anyone where the interests of another person — a current or former client, perhaps, or the lawyer's own interests — could impair the lawyer's ability to zealously and impartially act on a client's behalf. Resolution of a conflict might entail declining to undertake representation, withdrawing from an existing representation, or obtaining a client or clients' written consent to proceed despite a conflict.

The basic rules governing conflicts of interest are contained in Model Rule 1.7. This rule sets out the general conflicts of interest principles on which all other conflicts rules rely. Model Rule 1.7(a) provides that a lawyer may not represent a client if that representation involves a concurrent conflict, meaning that either:

1. the representation of one client will be directly adverse to another client, or

2. there is a significant risk that representation of one or more clients will be materially limited by the lawyer's responsibility to another client, a former client, or a third person, or by the lawyer's own personal interest.

Notwithstanding a concurrent conflict, however, Model Rule 1.7(b) permits a lawyer to represent a client if:

1. the lawyer believes that she will be able to competently and diligently represent each affected client,

2. the representation is not prohibited by law,

3. the representation does not involve the assertion of a claim by one client against another client represented by the lawyer in the same litigation or other proceeding, and

4. each affected client gives informed consent, confirmed in writing.

AICPA conflicts of interest rules are set forth at AICPA Code of Professional Conduct ET Section 102.03 and Interpretation 102–2, which are reproduced at Appendix H. Conflicts of interest for accountants are defined in terms of relationships that could be viewed by a client, employer, or another party as impairing a CPA's objectivity. If a CPA believes that a professional service can be performed with objectivity, however, and the relationship is disclosed to and consent is obtained from the client, employer, or other appropriate party, then the CPA is permitted to perform the professional service. Conflicts cannot be waived with respect to engagements that require independence, e.g., audits, reviews and other attest services.

B. Differences Among the Guiding Principles

The conflicts of interest rules in Circular 230 § 10.29 are very similar to those in Model Rule 1.7. Circular 230 § 10.29, however, imposes three additional requirements. First, while both the Model Rules and Circular 230 require that conflict waivers be confirmed in writing, Circular 230 mandates that confirmation be obtained within a reasonable period of time, but in no event later than 30 days after the client has consented to the representation. (The AICPA standards do not require written consent.) Second, unlike Model Rule 1.7, which permits affected clients to provide informed consent verbally if the consent is contemporaneously documented by the practitioner in writing, a verbal consent followed by a confirmatory letter authored by the practitioner will not satisfy Circular 230 § 10.29 unless the confirmatory letter is countersigned by the client. Finally, under Circular 230, practitioners are required to retain copies of written consents for at least 36 months from the date on which representation of the client concludes.

Practitioners must provide copies of written consents to IRS officers or employees, including those from OPR, upon request. Although the requirement to turn over copies of written consents is explicitly stated in Circular 230 § 10.29(c), it is consistent with the practitioner's duty, as a general matter under Circular 230 § 10.20, to provide documents and information to the IRS upon proper and lawful request. Unlike Circular 230 § 10.29(c), however, Circular 230 § 10.20 explicitly provides that information and documents need not be turned over if the practitioner believes in good faith and on reasonable grounds that the records or information are privileged. Perhaps the very fact that Circular 230 § 10.29 requires that written consents be obtained and held for 36 months should the IRS or OPR request them is meant to negate privilege as to such written consents because there could be no realistic expectation of privacy. Of course, this argument presumes that the client understands at the time of signing that the consent must be turned over by the practitioner to the IRS upon request. It is the client's expectation of privacy, and not the attorney or tax adviser's, that matters for privilege purposes.

Alternatively, it is possible that OPR regards written consents as ineligible for protection by the attorney-client or Section 7525 privilege in the first instance. Such a position may often be incorrect, particularly if a written consent document includes or reflects privileged communications. Therefore, where a practitioner chooses to explain the nature of a conflict to her client in writing, it would be prudent to have the client consent, or confirm consent, in a separate document, which could be turned over to the IRS or OPR without worry. It is generally understood that OPR considers failure to retain or turn over a written consent a violation of Circular 230 regardless of the quality of the underlying representation.

Practitioners representing clients in Tax Court proceedings must comply with the Tax Court's own rule on conflicts of interest:[1] Tax Court Rule 24(g) provides that if any counsel of record "represents more than one person with differing interests with respect to any issue in the case," she must secure the clients' informed consent to the representation, withdraw from the case, or take whatever other steps are necessary to obviate the conflict of interest. Tax Court Rule 24(g) imposes the same obligations on any counsel who "was involved in planning or promoting a transaction or operating an entity that is connected to any issue in a case." Counsel who is a potential witness in a case must withdraw or take other steps necessary to obviate a conflict; obtaining the client's informed consent is not an option in this situation.

PROBLEM 3-1

X is the president and chief executive officer of Family-Run Corp., a small, family-run business. Family-Run engages Practitioner to prepare tax returns for the company, its officers and its shareholders (all family members). As Practitioner prepares Family-Run's return, there is a question as to whether a payment the company made to X is a deductible payment of compensation or a nondeductible return of capital. Does Practitioner have a conflict of interest? If so, can it be cured, and how?

PROBLEM 3-2

Q, A and B, all individuals, are partners in LP, a limited partnership. Q is the general partner. Q engages Practitioner to prepare LP's return (Form 1065) and the partners' Schedules K-1. Practitioner is separately engaged by Q, A and B to prepare their individual income tax returns. While preparing LP's return, Practitioner identifies an issue as to the meaning of a provision in the partnership agreement that will affect the allocation of partnership items to the partners. This provision could be interpreted to provide an allocation of certain tax benefits to Q, to the detriment of A and B. Does Practitioner have a conflict of interest? If so, can it be cured, and how?

PROBLEM 3-3

Jon and Kate were married for all of 2009. In June 2009, Kate initiated divorce proceedings. In early 2010, Jon engages Practitioner to prepare the couple's joint tax return for 2009. Not long after, Kate (through her attorney) asks Practitioner to prepare her 2009 tax return as married filing separately. When Practitioner informs Kate's attorney that he was already engaged by Jon to prepare a joint return for the couple, the attorney informs Practitioner that Kate has no intention of signing a joint return. Does Practitioner have a conflict of interest? If so, can it be cured, and how?

---

[1] Practitioners representing clients in Tax Court must comply with all of the Model Rules, which have been adopted as rules of practice before the court. Tax Court Rule 201(a). Differences between the Model Rules and the rules adopted by one's own state of admission or practice, therefore, should be carefully monitored.

C. Business Planning

Most Corporate Tax classes begin with a study of the tax consequences of corporate formation, "Section 351 exchanges." Inevitably, students are asked to consider a hypothetical set of facts involving several unrelated persons who, together, desire to incorporate a new entity, with each person transferring previously-owned property, cash and/or services to the newly-formed entity in exchange for stock and, perhaps, other property ("boot"). Students are routinely asked to consider whether each transferor recognizes gain or loss, and what each transferor's basis in her newly acquired stock and boot will be. On the corporate side, students learn that the corporation itself recognizes no gain or loss on the issuance of shares, and master the increasingly complicated rules governing a corporation's basis in property received from transferors. Professors go to great lengths to assist students in divining those situations in which nonrecognition is a benefit and those in which it is not. Students brainstorm solutions to assist the various players in, e.g., recognizing losses but not gains, preserving or protecting unrecognized losses, and maximizing corporate basis in depreciable assets. Corresponding concepts are covered in Partnership Tax classes in connection with formation of partnerships and limited liability companies.

What typically is omitted from such instruction, however, is an examination of the ethical situation in which an attorney hired by all of the transferors finds herself. While individuals entering into a new business venture might view their interests as common, that is not necessarily so. Particularly in the case of small businesses founded by individuals, one attorney is often hired by the entire group to handle the corporate formation.

depends on individual Transfers

If a lawyer agrees to accept representation, who is the client, the individual transferors (separately or as a group) or the corporation that results from the representation? Does the answer depend upon whether the attorney will continue to work professionally with the corporation? *yes*

State Bar of Arizona Opinion No. 02-06
(Sept. 2002)[2]

Summary

A lawyer may form a business entity for various individuals and be counsel only for the yet-to-be-formed entity, if appropriate disclosures and consents occur. Alternatively, a lawyer may represent all of the incorporators, collectively, with appropriate disclosures.

Facts

Lawyer is a business law practitioner who currently represents several businessmen in various matters. The existing clients ask the lawyer to form a new entity corporation for them and to be counsel only for the entity.

Questions Presented

1. May a lawyer represent a yet-to-be-formed entity during formation? *Yes*
2. Can a lawyer represent the prospective entity without being deemed to *No conflict* also represent the incorporators? *interest need written consent*
3. If so, what disclosures must the lawyer make to the constituents to clarify who is the client? ✓

* * *

Opinion

1. Can a lawyer represent an entity that does not yet exist?

Yes, as long as the incorporators understand that they are retaining counsel on behalf of the yet-to-be-formed entity and will need to ratify this corporate action, *nunc pro tunc*, once the entity is formed. According to [Rule] 1.13(a), a lawyer may represent an "organization." The Comments to the Rule explain that an "organizational client is a legal entity, but it cannot act except through its officers, directors, employees, shareholders and other constituents. ... The duties defined in this comment apply equally to unincorporated associations."

An "organizational client" or "entity" can be a separate client. For purposes of the ethical analysis, this Opinion will refer to "corporations" as the entity at issue, but the analysis also is applicable to other legal entities.

To determine whether a lawyer ethically may represent a yet-to-be-formed corporation, the analysis must include a review of Arizona corporate and partnership statutes. A.R.S. § 10-203 provides:

A. Unless a delayed effective date is specified in the articles of incorporation, incorporation occurs and the corporate existence begins when the articles of incorporation and certificate of disclosure are delivered to the commission for filing.

Under this statute, a corporation does not exist as a separate legal entity until its articles of incorporation are filed with the Corporation Commission.[3] Section 10-204 of the Arizona Revised Statutes further cautions that individuals who attempt to transact business as a corporation, knowing that no corporation exists, will be jointly liable for their actions. Presumably, however, a newly formed corporation may ratify pre-incorporation acts of the corporation, *nunc pro tunc*.

A decision from Wisconsin specifically holds that a lawyer hired to form an entity can represent the to-be-formed entity, not the incorporators, and the "entity" rule applies retroactively. Jesse v. Danforth, 485 N.W.2d 63 (Wis. 1992). This view would be consistent with the "entity" theory of representation, under [Rule] 1.13(a). The "entity" theory holds that a lawyer may represent the corporation and does not, necessarily, represent any of the constituents that act on behalf of the entity — even if it is a closely held corporation. See, e.g., Skarbrevik v. Cohen, England & Whitfield, 282 Cal. Rptr. 627 (Cal. App. 1991); Bowen v. Smith, 838 P.2d 186 (Wyo. 1992).

---

[3] [1] Partnerships, however, are not required to make a filing to establish their existence; a partnership exists once there is an "association of two or more persons to carry on as co-owners [of] a business for profit... whether or not the persons intend to form a partnership." A.R.S. § 29-1012.A.

An alternative view is the "aggregate" theory in which the lawyer is found to represent the incorporators/constituents collectively as joint clients. See Griva v. Davison, 637 A.2d 830 (D.C. 1994). Under the aggregate theory, a lawyer represents multiple co-clients during formation of the corporation and then once the entity is formed, the clients must determine whether the lawyer will continue to represent all of the constituents and the entity, or just the entity. Who a lawyer may represent depends upon whether the lawyer's independent professional judgment would be materially limited because of the lawyer's duties to another client or third person. See [Rule] 1.7(b); Matter of Shannon, 179 Ariz. 52, 876 P.2d 548 (1994). As discussed below in Section 3, there are specific disclosures that a lawyer must make to co-clients, in order for them to consent to a joint representation.

Thus, a lawyer may represent an entity during the formation process, as long as the constituents who are acting on behalf of the yet-to-be-formed entity understand and agree to the entity being the client.

2. Can a lawyer represent *only* the yet-to-be-formed entity and not the constituents?

Who a lawyer represents depends upon the reasonable perceptions of those who have consulted with the lawyer. In re Petrie, 154 Ariz. 295 (1987). When two or more individuals consult with a lawyer about forming an entity, it is the responsibility of the lawyer at that initial meeting to clarify who the lawyer will represent. [Rule] 1.13 provides that a lawyer may represent an entity and the Rule suggests that the lawyer will not automatically be considered counsel for the constituents because paragraph (e) of the Rule provides:

A lawyer representing an organization may also represent any of its directors, officers, employees, members, shareholders or other constituents, subject to the provisions of [Rule] 1.7. If the organization's consent to the dual representation is required by [Rule] 1.7, the consent shall be given by an appropriate official of the organization other than the individual who is to be represented, or by the shareholders.

In Samaritan v. Goodfarb, 176 Ariz. 497, 508, 862 P.2d 870 (1993), the Arizona Supreme Court confirmed that a lawyer representing an entity does not automatically represent the constituents. Therefore, unless a lawyer wants to be counsel to all of the incorporators and the entity, the lawyer should specify that the lawyer does not represent the constituents collectively — the lawyer only represents the entity. If an engagement letter or oral representation by the lawyer suggests that the constituents are represented as an aggregate, then the lawyer will have ethical obligations to each constituent. Aggregate representation also is ethically proper if the disclosure to each client includes an explanation that the lawyer may have to withdraw from representing each client if a conflict arises among the clients.

3. What disclosures should a lawyer make to the incorporating constituents to obtain their informed consent to the limited representation of the entity?

The underlying premise of the conflict Rules is loyalty to clients. Where a lawyer's independent professional judgment for a client is materially limited due to anything or anyone, a conflict may exist. Thus, in order to avoid inadvertent conflicts caused by misunderstandings of constituents in corporate representations, it is crucial for lawyers to specify exactly who they represent, who they do not represent, and how information conveyed to the lawyer by constituents of an entity client will be treated, for confidentiality purposes. The Restatement Third, The Law Governing Lawyers, Comment b to § 14 provides in part: "A lawyer may be held to responsibility of representation when the client reasonably relies on the existence of the relationship. ..."

See also Comment f: "[A] lawyer's failure to clarify whom the lawyer represents in circumstances calling for such a result might lead a lawyer to have entered into client-lawyer representations not intended by the lawyer."

Therefore, it is crucial that a lawyer specify in the engagement agreement if the lawyer is not representing the constituents of an entity client.

Even if the engagement letter specifies that the constituents are not clients, lawyers still should regularly caution constituents that they are not clients — particularly when they consult with counsel. Lawyers who represent entities also must be aware of the entity's potential fiduciary duties to the constituents, so that the lawyer does not run afoul of those statutory or common law obligations. For instance, there are cases that have held that lawyers may have fiduciary duties to non-clients, depending upon whether the entity represented had fiduciary duties to the third parties. See Fickett v. Superior Ct. of Pima Cty, 27 Ariz. App. 793, 558 P.2d 988 (1976); Matter of Estate of Shano, 177 Ariz. 550, 869 P.2d 1203 (App. 1993) (lawyer disqualified as counsel to administrator for an estate because of prior representation of one beneficiary and derivative duty of neutrality to all beneficiaries). Accordingly, lawyers for entities should be mindful of this potential responsibility and that a derivative fiduciary duty to constituents may cause a conflict of interest for the lawyer.

The engagement letter also should explain that once the entity is created, the constituents agree to ratify the lawyer's services, *nunc pro tunc* on behalf of the entity.

With respect to confidentiality obligations, lawyers should specify how information conveyed to the lawyer will be treated for confidentiality purposes. If the firm is representing only the entity, constituents must be advised that their communications to the lawyer will be conveyed to the other decision-makers for the entity and are not confidential as to the entity. The information is confidential, however, according to Rule 1.6(a), to the "outside world." Similarly, information shared by one co-client that is necessary for the representation of the other joint clients will be shared with the other co-clients because there is no individual confidentiality when a joint representation exists.

Finally, if the lawyer has chosen to represent multiple clients, including the constituents and the entity, the lawyer should explain, at the beginning of the joint representation, that in the event that a conflict arises among the clients, the lawyer most likely will need to withdraw from representing all of the co-clients. However, some commentators, including the Restatement Third, note that the engagement agreement may provide that in the event of a conflict, the lawyer may withdraw from representing one of the co-clients and continue to represent the remaining clients. The usefulness of such provisions was recently demonstrated in In re Rite Aid Corp. Securities Litigation v. Grass, 139 F. Supp. 2d 649 (E.D. Pa. April 17, 2001), where the court permitted the law firm to withdraw as counsel for one of the executives of Rite Aid and continue as counsel for the entity in a class action suit, primarily because the engagement agreement provided for such action.

In *Jesse v. Danforth*, 485 N.W.2d 63 (Wis. 1992), a case referred to in the State Bar of Arizona opinion, *supra,* the Wisconsin Supreme Court held that the client is the corporation, not the corporation's constituents. This is referred to as "the entity theory." The court stated:

> We thus provide the following guideline: where (1) a person retains a lawyer for the purpose of organizing an entity and (2) the lawyer's involvement with that person is directly related to that incorporation and (3) such entity is eventually incorporated, the entity rule applies retroactively such that the lawyer's pre-incorporation involvement with the person is deemed to be representation of the entity, not the person.
>
> In essence, the retroactive application of the entity rule simply gives the person who retained the lawyer the status of being a corporate constituent during the period before actual incorporation, as long as actual incorporation eventually occurred.

Id. at 67. Under the "entity theory" of representation, a corporate lawyer typically is not disqualified from representing the corporation in litigation between the corporation and one or more of its constituents. It also means that the corporate lawyer generally is not liable to shareholders, officers, or directors for malpractice or breach of fiduciary duty. Moreover, as specifically noted by the court in *Jesse v. Danforth*, the identity of the client has implications with respect to the attorney-client privilege. The corporation, and not the constituents, holds the privilege as to communications pertaining to the organization of the entity. Individual constituents, however, hold the privilege where a communication does not relate directly to the purpose of organizing the entity.

If the lawyer's dealings with constituent individuals become so extensive and personal that the individuals reasonably believe that the lawyer represents them personally, a court or disciplinary authority might conclude that, despite the "entity theory," a lawyer-client relationship has nonetheless been formed between the lawyer and the individual constituent. Attorneys should be familiar with their own states' corporate laws when evaluating possible conflicts of interest questions in the context of business representation.

Samples of conflicts language for engagement letters often are available on the web sites of state bars. For example, the Georgia Bar web site includes a lengthy "Report on Engagement Letters in Transactional Practice." That report is available at http://www.gabar.org/public/pdf/sections/buslaw/eltp. pdf. The Colorado state bar web site also contains an interesting example, at http://www.cobar.org/repository/LPM%20Dept/FeeAgmts/EngageLtr ConflictofInterestASparkman.pdf?ID=260. The American College of Trust and Estate Counsel offers samples, as well, at http://www.actec.org/public/ EngagementLettersPublic.asp.

PROBLEM 3-4

Three prospective clients meet with Lawyer to discuss a new business venture. A, who has experience in the business, would contribute his management skills, B would contribute a substantial amount of cash, and C would contribute assets that could be used in the business. Each person would receive one-third of the stock in a newly formed corporation. A, B and C have asked Lawyer to create the corporation and to advise them with respect to tax and other issues related to forming and operating the business.

a. May Lawyer represent all three individuals seeking to form the business? Whom should Lawyer represent in the case? How would you advise Lawyer to proceed?

b. Would your answer to (a), above, change if A, B and C brought in another "partner," D, who would contribute property with an adjusted basis in excess of value?

c. If a dispute were to arise among the three "partners," and one of them decided to hire her own lawyer, could Lawyer continue to represent the remaining "partners"?

d. Suppose that you accept the representation in full compliance with your ethical obligations and that several years later, A calls you to discuss renegotiating her salary. How should you handle her call?

PROBLEM 3-5

You recently filed a letter ruling request with the IRS on behalf of Smithco, Inc. to the effect that a series of contemplated transactions should, with application of the step transaction doctrine, be treated as a tax-free reorganization. Jonesco, Inc. has asked you to represent it in Tax Court litigation in which its position will be that a similar series of transactions should not to be stepped together, but should instead be treated as separate steps, with the result that there is no reorganization. Can you take the case? Would your answer be different if you are representing Smithco in Tax Court rather than in the ruling process? What is the answer if you are representing Smithco in connection with an audit, after the transaction has already been reported as a reorganization on a filed tax return?

D.   When Business or Personal Relationships Fail

Human nature being what it is, disputes often develop between or among business "partners" once business operations have commenced. Whether a lawyer previously worked with all of the co-venturers or merely represented the entity, questions arise as to whether the attorney may continue in the representation and whom the attorney may represent. Among the concerns is the possibility that the attorney received confidential information that may not be used against a former client. While the case below arose out of a personal, not a business, relationship, the ethical considerations are well exemplified.

DEVORE v. COMMISSIONER
United States Court of Appeals, Ninth Circuit
963 F.2d 280 (1992)

PER CURIAM:

Gary Devore appeals from the United States Tax Court's denials of his motions to vacate deficiency judgments for the tax years 1970-1975. Devore contends that dual representation of himself and his ex-wife in the tax proceedings resulted in a conflict of interest that prevented their joint counsel from raising defenses on his behalf. We have jurisdiction under 26 U.S.C. §§ 7482(a), 7483. We reverse the orders of the tax court and remand for an evidentiary hearing to determine whether Devore was prejudiced by his former counsel's conflict of interest and whether Devore had reasonable grounds for failing to seek independent counsel.

Background

For many years, Maria Cole and her former husband, Nat King Cole, had been represented by attorney Harry Margolis. Margolis continued to represent Maria Cole after Nat King Cole's death. Maria Cole and Gary Devore were married in 1969. For the year 1970, Devore filed an individual return. Joint returns were prepared for all other years during the marriage. Until June 1987, Harry Margolis was the sole counsel of Cole and Devore. Leo Branton, Jr., became co-counsel with Margolis in June 1987. Margolis died on or about July 15, 1987 and Branton became the sole counsel of record on behalf of Cole and Devore in connection with the instant actions. The tax proceedings culminated in the entry of two judgments against Devore.

Cole and Devore were separated in 1976, and were divorced in 1978. The tax court did not render judgments in the instant cases until 1989. Despite their divorce, joint counsel continued to represent Cole and Devore throughout the tax proceedings.

After a four day trial, the tax court determined that Devore was individually liable for a federal tax deficiency of $135,302, and for a negligent return penalty of $6,765. The tax court found that Devore failed to carry his burden of proof in establishing that certain checks totaling $210,000 did not constitute reportable income to him. Two checks had been issued to Devore by a company controlled by Margolis. These checks were received by Devore, but were immediately endorsed over to Margolis. Devore alleges that these funds were then used to purchase a home in the name of Maria Cole. The tax court found that the $210,000 represented by the two checks was income attributable to Devore.

In a second judgment entered pursuant to stipulations of settlement, Devore and Cole were held jointly and severally liable for deficiencies totaling over $300,000 for the years 1971-1975.

Devore states that he entered and left his marriage to Cole with a net worth of less than $10,000 and that he lacks the money to satisfy the judgments. He further states that he was unsophisticated in tax matters and that he was continually excluded from the financial affairs of Maria Cole.

Devore moved, through new counsel, to vacate the tax court's deficiency judgments. He asserted that when counsel represented him and Cole jointly, a conflict of interest resulted. This conflict, argues Devore, prevented joint counsel from bringing innocent spouse and agency defenses which would have diminished his tax liability. The tax court denied these motions.

Discussion

A tax court's decision not to reopen a record for the submission of new evidence "is not subject to review except upon a demonstration of extraordinary circumstances which reveal a clear abuse of discretion." *Nor-Cal Adjusters v. Commissioner*, 503 F.2d 359, 363 (9th Cir. 1974).

The facts of Devore's case constitute "extraordinary circumstances." One spouse was in a substantially weaker position with reference to the other. Devore earned a negligible income while his wife controlled a significant sum of money. Devore was unsophisticated in tax matters and was excluded from the financial affairs of his wife.

Our research uncovered only one case that is directly on point. In *Wilson v. Commissioner*, 500 F.2d 645 (2nd Cir.1974), a husband and wife had filed joint tax returns. The husband earned a much larger income than his wife. A deficiency judgment was entered against the couple. Throughout the tax proceedings, they were jointly represented by the same attorney. However, they were also engaged in a simultaneous annulment action. In the annulment action, the husband was represented by the same attorney who represented the couple in the tax proceedings.

The Second Circuit held that it could "reverse a discretionary denial by the Tax Court of post-opinion motions only if there are shown to be 'extraordinary circumstances.'" *Wilson*[,] 500 F.2d at 648, quoting *Pepi, Inc. v. C.I.R.*, 448 F.2d 141, 148 (2nd Cir. 1971). The court held that the facts in Wilson were sufficiently compelling to constitute "extraordinary circumstances." The attorney could not competently advance the interests of the wife in the tax proceedings while representing the husband in a separate annulment action. It thus reversed the tax court's denial of Mrs. Wilson's post-opinion motions. It remanded the case to the tax court, allowing Mrs. Wilson to present evidence explaining her failure to seek the advice of independent counsel and to raise the annulment issue.

The facts supporting Devore's claim of "extraordinary circumstances" are at least as compelling as those of Wilson. In Wilson, the attorney represented both the husband and wife in tax proceedings while representing the husband in a simultaneous annulment litigation. However, the couple was still married at the time of the tax proceedings. In the instant case, the parties were separated in 1976 and divorced in 1978. The trial did not take place until 1989. By this time, the marriage was clearly over. Arguably, Devore's interests were compromised by counsel's simultaneous representation of Devore and Cole.

Accordingly, we remand to the tax court for an evidentiary hearing to determine if Devore was prejudiced by his former counsel's conflict of interest and to establish the reasonableness of his failure to retain independent counsel. If Devore satisfies these burdens, he should be granted a new trial at which innocent spouse and agency defenses may be asserted.

The *Devore* case is somewhat unique in that the aggrieved spouse was the ex-husband. Most often, innocent spouse claims are made by an ex-wife. Why? What special responsibilities does this impose on a lawyer who perhaps has a preexisting professional relationship with the ex-husband? *Moral, duty*

Many law firms are loathe to provide legal services at the same time to individuals (e.g., estate planning) and businesses entities in which those individuals own interests because disagreements often arise between or among the individuals, creating painful conflicts of interest problems for lawyers. For an example of such a conflict, see *Pascale v. Pascale*, 549 A.2d 782 (NJ 1988), *infra*, Section I.F.

Typically not involved Fin. affairs.

PROBLEM 3-6

You have represented Mr. and Mrs. Mildew in connection with an audit of their joint federal income tax return. Following the audit, the IRS issues them a joint notice of deficiency. You prepare a petition, which they both sign, and which is then filed in the Tax Court. Two weeks before the case is scheduled to go to trial, Mrs. Mildew calls, says they are getting divorced and tells you that her divorce lawyer has discovered that her husband was skimming cash receipts out of their jointly owned restaurant without reporting them on the couple's tax returns. What are your ethical and other obligations to each of the Mildews, IRS counsel, and the Tax Court? → *Possibly w/draw*

→ Compel Mr. Mildew to properly
↳ Make Mr. aware   report earning, possibly
PROBLEM 3-7   w/draw

May accept case as int'l or mutual interest is invoking innocent spouse

Practitioner prepared a joint return filed by a married couple. The couple later divorced. May Practitioner represent both spouses in connection with an IRS challenge to expenses that were claimed on the joint return? Note that Section 6013(e) (innocent spouse relief provision that applied at the time *Devore* was decided) has been replaced by Section 6015. Does your analysis change because of the statutory change? What must Practitioner do if she decides to accept representation? *→ Disclose / get consent / Make Election under 6015 (c)(3)*

No
↳ No, b/c they have burden of proof to prove against other spouse (client)

Privilege w/ husband + business

PROBLEM 3-8

Several years ago, before Husband married Wife, Lawyer represented Husband in connection with the formation of a business venture. Recently, Wife approached Lawyer to request representation in divorce proceedings against Husband. Can Lawyer accept the representation? What are Lawyer's ethical obligations? *intellectual property of business venture*   *Yes ≠ No*   *Not convey any prior dealings to husband business*
Get consent from wife

E.   Tax Shelters

During the last several years, taxpayers and the IRS have been actively engaged in litigating over the tax consequences of transactions that the IRS has labeled "tax shelters." For tax benefits generated from a purported tax shelter transaction to be upheld, courts have consistently held that the transaction or series of transactions at issue must have economic substance. In an often-quoted articulation of the economic substance doctrine, the Court of Appeals for the Fourth Circuit stated:

> To treat a transaction as a sham, the court must find [1] that the taxpayer was motivated by no business purposes other than obtaining tax benefits in entering the transaction, and [2] that the transaction has no economic substance because no reasonable possibility of a profit exists.

Rice's Toyota World v. Commissioner, 752 F.2d 89, 91 (4th Cir. 1985).

The Circuit Courts of Appeals that have considered the economic substance doctrine agree generally on the articulation of its two parts as set forth in *Rice's Toyota*, but differ on how to apply the test. Some circuits have required that a transaction satisfy both the business purpose and economic profit standards to validate a transaction (conjunctive test). Other circuits require satisfaction of only one of the standards to validate a transaction (disjunctive test). Some *[handwritten margin note: Economic substance 7701 (a)]*

courts give more weight to one prong than the other, in some cases disregarding one or the other of the two prongs altogether. In some cases, courts will consider both prongs as merely factors, among others, in determining whether a transaction has any practical economic effects other than the creation of tax benefits.

The following problems exemplify conflicts of interest issues arising in the context of the economic substance doctrine.

PROBLEM 3-9

Your law firm represents eighteen different clients who invested in a transaction sold by the same accounting firm. For each client, you must prove that the client had a profit motive for investing in the transaction, which the IRS has called a tax shelter. Can you offer the same profit motive for each client (e.g., expectation of a specific return on a series of hedging transactions)? *[handwritten: consistency motivation for same reason]* *[handwritten: Yes depends on individual]*

PROBLEM 3-10

If profit motive or business purpose is an essential element of proof to obtain a deduction from a tax shelter investment, does representation of multiple clients who invested in essentially the same transaction (1) dilute any single client's chances of obtaining a favorable settlement or (2) impose ethical constraints on the lawyer when additional clients are added to the representation roster? *[handwritten: yes + yes no if consistent motivation. More clients may un diminish pos of initial client.]*

PROBLEM 3-11

With the informed consent of the parties, your law firm has undertaken representation of investors in a tax shelter in proceedings before the Tax Court in which the tax benefits of the shelter are being challenged. During the pendency of the proceeding, a separate class action is brought against the shelter promoters on behalf of a putative class consisting of the investors in the shelter, including some of your firm's clients. Your firm does not anticipate participating as counsel in the class action on behalf of either side. Can your firm continue in the Tax Court representation? *See* D.C. Opinion No. 165 (Jan. 21, 1986). Would it matter whether the promoters have agreed to pay all of your professional fees incurred by the investors in the Tax Court proceeding? *[handwritten: No]* *[handwritten: No]*

PROBLEM 3-12

An accounting firm developed and promoted a tax shelter in which your firm's client invested. Can your firm represent that client at the same time that it represents the accounting firm in malpractice cases that do not involve tax shelters? Can your firm represent that client at the same time that it represents the accounting firm in malpractice cases that do involve tax shelters? *[handwritten: yes]* *[handwritten: →No seems dubius + deceitful]*

PROBLEM 3-13

Your law firm's banking department does loan documentation work for a bank that provided financing for a tax shelter transaction. A tax department client invested in one such tax shelter transaction. Can the firm represent both the bank and the investor? *[handwritten: →No similar but seperate suits if opposing]*

PROBLEM 3-14

Your law firm represents a large insurance company on general corporate and regulatory matters. The insurance company sold a transaction, which the IRS alleges is substantially similar to a listed transaction but which the insurance company claims was substantially different than the listed transaction, to Investor. Can you represent Investor in connection with an IRS audit?

F. Estate Planning

Conflicts of interest generally arise in estate planning in one of four situations.

Spouses. First, and most commonly thought of, are conflicts involving concurrent representation of spouses. (Many, but not all, of the same issues arise, as well, when representing unmarried cohabitants.) Children from prior marriages or large disparities in wealth between spouses might be a reason to suggest separate representation. Spouses of substantially different ages may have conflicts in their planning goals. In addition, when one spouse dies, the surviving spouse and the estate could have differing interests. For example, the surviving spouse may wish to make an election against the estate or the executor may wish to make an election that increases the surviving spouse's share of the estate while decreasing the interests of other beneficiaries.

Nonetheless, and despite all of the possible conflicts, spouses frequently visit attorneys together for the purpose of preparing their wills. Often, these are reciprocal wills — wills that are essentially mirror images of each other, in which each spouse leaves his or her residuary estate to the other. Under Model Rule 1.7, a lawyer should, in most cases, be able to represent and plan for both spouses jointly. However, the lawyer should require each spouse to sign a written waiver of confidentiality as to the other so that any information provided to the lawyer by either spouse must be revealed to the other spouse. All information provided to the lawyer, of course, would still be protected against disclosure to third parties. The reluctance of a spouse to sign a waiver should alert the lawyer to the possible existence of a non-waivable conflict of interest.

The lawyer must explain to both spouses that their interests could conflict, particularly where they do not agree on the identity of beneficiaries or fiduciaries. Under Model Rule 1.7, each spouse must sign this statement, agreeing to allow the lawyer to use his or her best efforts and judgment to represent each of them, despite these possible conflicts. It would be wise for the lawyer and spouses to agree that both spouses must be present whenever either wishes to change any of his or her estate planning documents.

The American College of Trust and Estate Counsel offers samples of conflicts language for engagement letters in estate planning, at http://www.actec.org/public/EngagementLettersPublic.asp. The Colorado state bar web site also contains a good example, at http://www.cobar.org/repository/Inside_Bar/Trust Estate/OrangeBook_Dec2007_EngagementLetter.pdf?ID=2841.

Families. Second, conflicts may arise where parents and children seek representation or advice. A parent and child might have different ideas about the use or disposition of a trust fund benefitting the child, or an adult child and an infirm parent might disagree about transfers of the parent's property. Conflicts also often arise when adult children are involved in a family-owned business, which forms a substantial portion of a parent's estate.

Particularly where the lawyer is approached by an adult child or children in connection with estate planning for a parent, care should be given to the question of who is the client — the adult child(ren) or the parent? Surprisingly, intentions in this regard are often unclear: is the purpose of the representation to plan for the disposition of the parent's assets as he or she intends or to protect the interests of a particular beneficiary? If the attorney previously represented either the parent or the child, the attorney might possess confidential information, gained through the course of that representation that would be inconsistent with representing the other.[4]

Once it is determined who the client is, it is important to make sure that everyone understands and agrees. Even where such an understanding is reached, however, maintaining confidentiality between lawyer and client often presents challenges. For example, elderly clients may feel more comfortable meeting with the lawyer in the company of their children. Significant decisions are made at these meetings and it is the attorney's responsibility to establish a clear and confidential line of communication without the presence or undue influence of family members. Attorneys are strongly advised to talk to the client alone to make sure that problems of conflicts of interest and undue influence do not exist, and to explain confidentiality concerns.

Businesses and their Constituents. Third, a conflict may arise when a lawyer represents a business entity and a majority or controlling owner, as was discussed earlier in this chapter. Additional issues arise where business and estate planning overlap. For example, an estate plan of a majority shareholder of a closely-held corporation could affect the business plans or ownership of the corporation as well as the relationship between the corporation and other shareholders.

PASCALE v. PASCALE
New Jersey Supreme Court
549 A.2d 782 (1988)

POLLOCK, J.

Plaintiff, John J. Pascale (Pascale), seeks to set aside a transfer of stock and real estate to his son David P. Pascale (David). Pascale contends that a confidential relationship existed between him and David and that the same attorney advised both of them in connection with the transfer. The issue is whether the transfers are invalid because David exercised undue influence over Pascale.

* * *

Nearly fifty years ago, in 1939, Pascale founded a machine tool and die business, which was later incorporated under the name Quality Tool & Die Company Inc. (Quality). In 1952, plaintiff established a second, smaller machine tool company, Majoda Tool and Die Company (Majoda), which operated out of

[4] Moreover, if the parent is incapacitated or appears to suffer from a diminished capacity, particular issues pertaining to such a representation must be considered. Discussion of such matters is beyond the scope of this book.

Quality's premises in Hoboken. By 1960, both businesses had become quite profitable.

In the 1960s, Pascale introduced his older son, John, Jr., into the businesses, and six years later, Pascale gave all the stock in Majoda to John, Jr. David began full-time employment with Quality in 1971. Sometime before 1972, John, Jr. left Majoda and assigned all of his stock to Pascale and David.

In March 1972, Pascale's wife instituted a divorce action, and the two sons chose sides: John, Jr. sided with his mother, and David with Pascale. Consequently, Pascale did not see John, Jr. again until their apparent reconciliation in 1978. In 1973, to minimize his net worth and thereby to reduce his wife's share in an equitable distribution of his assets, Pascale signed a stock certificate, which purported to transfer ownership of his Quality shares to David. The certificate, however, was backdated to 1968, four years before the institution of the divorce action.

Initially, the fraud worked. An accounting firm, which was appointed by the matrimonial court to investigate Pascale's assets, reported on June 7, 1973, that Pascale was "essentially responsible" for the operations of Quality and Majoda, but that he had transferred his stock in both corporations to David on October 16, 1968. The matrimonial court approved the property settlement based on this false information. Although Pascale claims that the stock certificate and corporate books are lost, David produced at the trial of the within matter a photocopy of a signed copy of the backdated October 16, 1968, stock certificate.

Consistent with the certificate, David claimed in his deposition that Pascale transferred all the Quality stock to him in 1968. David denied that any transfer of stock from his father to him occurred between 1970 and 1976. When asked at trial who owned the Quality stock in 1976, however, David testified, "my father did." The foregoing facts led the trial court to find that Pascale signed the backdated certificate in 1973 as part of "a scheme to defraud [Pascale's] wife and the matrimonial court."

Following the transfer, Pascale and David continued in their respective roles at Quality. Until 1979, Pascale remained in control, with David managing accounts and performing other office work. From 1971 until late 1981, Pascale and David enjoyed a close personal relationship. Pascale lavished expensive gifts on David and his wife, including cars, real estate, a sable coat, jewelry, and large amounts of cash. David handled Pascale's personal financial affairs, such as check writing, personal bills, safe deposit boxes, and securities.

Late in 1975, however, the Internal Revenue Service asserted a tax deficiency claim against Pascale personally and also against Quality. On the advice of his personal and business accountant, J. Bennett Schwartz, Pascale retained a tax attorney, Bernard Berkowitz, who resolved the IRS matter in January 1979. In the interim, Pascale asked Berkowitz to prepare an estate plan for him.

Early in his representation on both matters, Berkowitz communicated exclusively with Pascale. Pascale, however, directed Berkowitz to "deal directly with David Pascale or Ben Schwartz, but primarily David." According to Berkowitz, Pascale instructed him to develop an estate plan that left "everything to David" while incurring as little tax liability as possible. David confirmed Berkowitz's testimony by acknowledging that he served as an agent for Pascale in dealing with Berkowitz.

As early as 1977, Berkowitz and his associate, Stephen C. Levitt, discussed with David and Schwartz an estate plan that would have left Pascale in control of Quality. For tax purposes, Berkowitz recommended that Pascale transfer to Quality land he owned in Hoboken and that Pascale convert his common stock in Quality into three classes: preferred stock, voting common stock, and non-voting common stock. The then-existing value of Quality would be ascribed to the preferred stock, which Pascale would retain along with all the voting common stock. David would receive the nonvoting common stock to which all future growth would be attributed.

In May 1978, Berkowitz worked out the details of the recapitalization with David and Schwartz, who in turn informed Pascale of the plan. Although Pascale approved the recapitalization, the plan was never executed.

A year later, on May 9, 1979, Berkowitz, Levitt, and Schwartz met with David. At this meeting, while reading the 1973 accountant's report from the matrimonial action, Berkowitz first learned that Pascale apparently had transferred the Quality shares to David in 1968. It became apparent to Berkowitz that there was a conflict between David and Pascale about the ownership of the Quality stock. As Berkowitz testified, "David Pascale thought he owned the stock; John Pascale thought that he owned the stock." Because the recapitalization plan was premised on Pascale's ownership of the Quality stock, the confusion about stock ownership caused Berkowitz to abandon this plan.

Berkowitz also ascertained that no gift tax had been paid on the backdated transaction. Confronted with this information, Berkowitz devised an alternate plan to fulfill Pascale's intention of leaving, with a minimal tax impact, all of his business assets to David. The plan was for Pascale to give the Hoboken properties and the Quality stock to David, with David paying the gift taxes of $ 54,947. That proposal was consistent with the will prepared by a different attorney and executed by Pascale on December 10, 1975, in which Pascale left his entire estate to David. Berkowitz further believed that the gift to David would reduce the problems inherent in the fraudulent matrimonial scheme, which was evidenced by the backdated stock certificate.

The trial court found that Berkowitz discussed the alternate plan with David and Schwartz, and that each of them in turn discussed it with Pascale. Both David and Schwartz claimed that Pascale understood that by agreeing with this plan, he would be yielding control of Quality to David. Indeed, Schwartz testified that he spoke with Pascale on May 24, 1979, the day Pascale executed the alternate plan, and specifically admonished him that by executing the plan, "he was giving the company away, he could be thrown out in a week."

On that date, Berkowitz, David, and Pascale met at Pascale's office in Hoboken to execute the plan. According to Levitt, with the exception of several letters that his law firm had mailed to Pascale, this meeting was the first time since January 11, 1978, that the firm "had any contact or has any records that reflect any contact with John Pascale." At the meeting, Pascale signed various documents, including two stock certificates of Quality: one that described Pascale as the owner of 310 shares, and the other that described David as the owner of 310 shares. Pascale also signed an assignment transferring his 310 shares of Quality to David, a deed from Pascale and Quality conveying the Quality premises in Hoboken to David, and an affidavit of consideration.

The main dispute in this case is whether Pascale understood that these documents effected an outright transfer of the Quality stock and real estate to David. On this point, as on others, the testimony at trial was in sharp conflict.

According to Pascale, before the May 24, 1979, meeting, he had not received any of the documents. He contends that he had no opportunity to read the documents before signing them, that neither Berkowitz nor David explained the documents to him, and that he relied on them in signing the documents. Pascale testified that he thought he "was to have control [of Quality] to the day I died or was incapable of handling the business."

David and Berkowitz testified, however, that Berkowitz reviewed the documents in detail with Pascale before he signed them. Berkowitz did not remember whether he discussed with Pascale the implications of transferring the Quality stock and the Hoboken properties to David, but he believed that the implications were so obvious that such a discussion was unnecessary. David, however, testified that Berkowitz explained to Pascale that the effect of signing the documents would be to relinquish control of Quality to David. Pascale signed the documents.

On the same day, David executed a will prepared by Berkowitz, in which David bequeathed all his Quality stock to a testamentary stock trust, of which Pascale was the trustee. The beneficiaries of the trust were Pascale and David's wife, and all income was payable to Pascale during his lifetime. In the following year, on October 7, 1980, however, David executed another will, which eliminated the trust and provided that the Quality stock and land would pass to his wife, if she survived, and if she predeceased him, to his mother-in-law.

After the May 24, 1979, meeting, David assumed greater responsibility in managing Quality. Pascale remained active in the business, and continued to receive his $3,500 weekly salary, plus approximately $700 in travel and entertainment expenses. In January 1980, however, David attempted to reduce Pascale's salary to $3,000 per week, but Pascale responded by retroactively reinstating his salary to $3,500.

Relations between David and Pascale cooled when David learned that Pascale was helping John, Jr. in a competing machine and tool business. According to Pascale, he first learned that he was no longer in control of Quality in October 1981 following a dispute with David over Pascale's assistance to John, Jr. David ordered Pascale to leave the Quality premises and to consult with a lawyer to confirm that David now controlled Quality and had the right to terminate Pascale's employment. Notwithstanding their dispute, Pascale remained on Quality's payroll until October 1982, two months after he filed the within action. In the interim, during the spring of 1982, Pascale consulted with Levitt, who told him that the effect of the May 24, 1979, transfers was to place David in control of Quality.

* * *

[T]he trial court found that Pascale's attorney, Berkowitz, was not in a position of conflict when he prepared Pascale's estate plan and advised him to execute it, stating, "[a]t all times Berkowitz was Pascale's rather than David's attorney."

The Appellate Division reversed. 216 N.J. Super. 133. It found that a confidential relationship existed between Pascale and David, and that Berkowitz was in a position of conflict when he advised Pascale to execute the transfers.

* * *

We now turn to the question of the conflict of interest on the part of the attorney, Berkowitz, in representing both David and Pascale at the time of the challenged transfer. Here, we also agree with the Appellate Division's assessment that Berkowitz was in a position of conflict in representing both parties. Berkowitz and his associate, Levitt, admitted that there was a conflict in the positions of David and Pascale concerning the ownership of the Quality stock prior to May 24, 1979. Moreover, David admitted Pascale was never informed of the services rendered by Berkowitz in preparing David's estate plan. Despite the fact that David told Berkowitz that he, not Pascale, owned the Quality stock on May 9, 1979, Berkowitz simultaneously represented David and Pascale. Neither Berkowitz nor David ever informed Pascale, however, of David's claim to the stock or that Berkowitz was now representing David. Nonetheless, the trial court found that "[a]t all times Berkowitz was Pascale's rather than David's attorney." The Appellate Division rejected that finding and found that Berkowitz was in a position of conflict because of his simultaneous representation of the parties. 216 N.J. Super. at 142. We agree.

As we have previously stated, "[a] lawyer cannot serve two masters in the same subject matter if their interests are or may became *[sic]* actually or potentially in conflict." *In re Chase*, 68 N.J. 392, 396 (1975). Disciplinary Rule 5-105(A), which was in effect at the time of the transaction, like present Rule of Professional Conduct 1.7, prohibited a lawyer from accepting or continuing employment "if the exercise of his professional judgment in behalf of a client will be or is likely to be adversely affected by the acceptance of" or continuance of the employment.

A conflict arises when an attorney represents in separate matters multiple clients who have adverse interests in at least one of those matters. "Developments in the Law — Conflicts of Interest in the Legal Profession," 94 Harv. L. Rev. 1244, 1296-1306 (1981). The attorney has divided loyalties that can prevent faithful representation of both clients in the matter in which the conflict arises. *Ibid*. For example, an attorney may not, without making appropriate disclosure, simultaneously represent the testator and the beneficiaries of a will. *Haynes, supra*, 87 N.J. at 181-85. Similarly, here, Berkowitz should not have represented Pascale on the transfer of real estate and stock to David without disclosing that he was simultaneously representing David on an independent matter. Even if Berkowitz believed he could adequately represent the interests of both Pascale and David, he failed to comply with the requirement of Disciplinary Rule 5-105(C) that he fully disclose the conflict.

Consequently, we agree with the Appellate Division that the conflicting claims to ownership of the Quality stock placed Berkowitz in a position of conflict arising from his dual representation of David and Pascale. On the same day, Berkowitz represented Pascale in the transfer of substantial assets to David and also represented David in the drafting and execution of his will. The conflicting claims of stock ownership, as the Appellate Division found, "raised an immediate conflict having the clear potential to raise in the mind of legal counsel the question as to which of the two masters was to be served and protected." 216 N.J. Super. at 142.

Referrals. Finally, an attorney is often asked to recommend a particular bank, trust company or person to serve as a trustee or executor knowing that the company or person will hire the attorney who drafted the will as attorney for the estate. Because this situation potentially creates a conflict between the client and the lawyer's own interest, it should be analyzed under Model Rule 1.7(a)(2) and Circular 230 § 10.29(a)(2).

Illinois State Bar Association Advisory Opinion 99-06
(Nov. 1999)[5]

Facts

An Illinois trust company has developed a lawyer/trust administrator program in which licensed Illinois lawyers, who practice substantially in the area of estate planning, enter into an agency relationship with the trust company. The agency agreement provides that the lawyers will furnish trust administrator services for trusts in which the trust company has been named trustee. The lawyers perform the administrative services for the trust from their law offices and may continue to render legal services to the clients in matters related to the trust or otherwise, for which they bill separately. Once accepted as a trust administrator, the lawyers may refer clients and other persons as potential customers for the trust company's services. The lawyer will bill his clients for legal services in preparing trust instruments and other documents. The trust company does not prepare the trust documents or otherwise practice law.

Assets of the trusts are deposited with the trust company and administered by the trust company's investment advisors or, at the option of the client, in self-directed accounts. Services of the trust company personnel are paid from the trust assets pursuant to an established fee schedule, and the lawyer/trust administrator is paid a fee by the trust company, again under a published fee schedule, from the fee paid to the trust company from the client's trust.

The lawyer/trust administrator acts as a conduit of information between the trust company and its customers, directs payments from the trust, forwards customer investment directives, and responds on behalf of the trust company to customer inquiries. The lawyer/trust administrator offers no investment advice with respect to the trusts. The lawyer's relationship with the trust company, his compensation as trust administrator, and other relevant information are set out in an extensive written disclosure and consent form which the client must sign as a part of the trust agreement.

Inquiry is made as to whether the arrangement described violates any provision of the Rules of Professional Conduct.

Opinion

A variety of issues created by relationships involving lawyers, their clients and fiduciary institutions have been considered by this Committee.

We have stated, for example, that a lawyer who is both a director and lawyer for a bank may not insist that his client designate the bank as a fiduciary, even where the relationship is disclosed to the client. See Opinion No. 90-02 (1990).

[5] Reprinted with permission of the Illinois State Bar Association. Copyright by the ISBA; on the web at www.isba.org. ISBA Advisory Opinions on Professional Conduct are prepared as an educational service to members of the ISBA. While the Opinions express the ISBA interpretation of the Illinois Rules of Professional Conduct and other relevant materials in response to a specific hypothesized fact situation, they do not have the weight of law and should not be relied upon as a substitute for individual legal advice.

We have also opined that it is professionally improper for a lawyer employed by an institution marketing revocable living trusts to prepare or review such documents for possible use by his clients. Such an arrangement, we felt, posed significant conflict of interest problems that would prevent the lawyer from fairly representing the consumer/client and acting in his best interests. In addition, the lawyer violated Rule 5.5(b) by aiding the unauthorized practice of law by the institution in connection with its preparation of the trust documents. See Opinion No. 90-20 (1991).

Finally, we have held that the referral of clients to an investment advisor or securities broker, whereby the referring lawyer is paid a fee from the funds being managed for the client, may be permissible provided that appropriate disclosures are made. See Opinion No. 97-04 (1998).

The Committee considers the arrangement outlined above sufficient to satisfy the concerns expressed in our prior opinions, provided that appropriate safeguards are employed to satisfy the rules regarding conflicts of interest.

Where a lawyer's representation of a client may be limited by the lawyer's responsibilities to a third person or by the lawyer's own interests, the lawyer may undertake or continue the representation only if he reasonably believes that the representation will not be adversely affected and the client consents after disclosure. Rule 1.7(b) states the general rule:

> A lawyer shall not represent a client if the representation of that client may be materially limited by the lawyer's responsibilities to another client or to a third person, or by the lawyer's own interest, unless:
>
>> (1) the lawyer reasonably believes the representation will not be adversely affected; and
>>
>> (2) the client consents after disclosure.

Here, the lawyer as an agent of the trust company is expected to develop business for the trust company by recommending the trust company's services to the lawyer's clients and others. Where the trust company is selected by the client, the lawyer is paid a fee for his services as trust administrator by the trust company based upon the fee for trust services paid by the client/customer. The lawyer accordingly has an incentive to recommend the trust company's services over those of a competing fiduciary. The relationship between the lawyer and the trust company, and the compensation generated by that relationship, involve "responsibilities to a third person" and "the lawyer's own interests," as described in the rule.

Nonetheless, the lawyer may, in the Committee's judgment, reasonably believe that his representation of the client may not be adversely affected by his relationship with the trust company. Since the client may disagree, however, it is incumbent upon the lawyer, pursuant to Rule 1.7(b) of the Rules of Professional Conduct, to disclose his relationship with the trust company, the fee arrangement and method of calculation (including the source of payment to him), and all other aspects of the relationship. Although the rule does not by its terms require that the disclosure be in writing, the Committee has noted that that is the more prudent practice.

In our Opinion No. 97-04, supra, the Committee had occasion to consider two slightly different referral arrangements involving lawyers, their clients, and an investment adviser and securities broker. In each case, the referring lawyer was paid a portion of the management fee generated by the investment of the client's funds. We pointed out that such an arrangement constituted a business transaction with a client, governed by Rule 1.8 of the Rules of Professional Conduct, which provides:

> Unless the client has consented after disclosure, a lawyer shall not enter into a transaction with the client if:
>
> (1) the lawyer knows or reasonably should know that the lawyer and client have or may have conflicting interests therein; or
>
> (2) the client expects the lawyer to exercise the lawyer's professional judgment therein for the protection of the client.

We stated that, under pertinent Illinois case law, a presumption of undue influence arises where a lawyer benefits from a business transaction with a client. The presumption may be rebutted only by clear and convincing evidence. Generally, this requires a showing of full disclosure of all relevant information, a transaction that was fair and reasonable, and that the client had the advice of independent counsel, or the opportunity for such advice, before entering into the transaction. In re Anderson, 52 Ill. 2d 202, 287 N.E.2d 682, 682 (1972); In re Schuyler, 91 Ill. 2d 6, 61 Ill. Dec. 540, 424 N.E.2d 1137 (1982); Franciscan Sisters Health Care v. Dean, 95 Ill. 2d 452, 69 Ill. Dec. 960, 448 N.E.2d 872 (1982).

As in Opinion No. 97-04, the investment of the client's trust assets in the case at hand is clearly a business transaction. The profits realized from the investment program are the basis for the trust company's fees from which, in turn, the lawyer/trust administrator's fees are paid. As in Opinion No. 97-04, these fees are not for legal services performed; they emanate from a business transaction in which the lawyer and the client are jointly interested.

Since the amount of the lawyer/trust administrator's fee is affected by the performance of the trust being administered, there is at least the potential for a conflict of interest between the lawyer and his client. The client's objectives with respect to the trust program may dictate a relatively conservative investment approach, which may generate lesser fees to the trust administrator (and the trust company) than would a more aggressive approach. Disclosure must therefore be made and the client's consent obtained in the same manner as prescribed with respect to Rule 1.7(b). It should also be remembered that a conflict of interest problem, although initially addressed by appropriate disclosure and consent, imposes a continuing duty on the part of the lawyer to make supplemental disclosures as developing circumstances warrant.

For the reasons given, the Committee believes that the arrangement described is not professionally improper.

* * *

Illinois' version of Rule 1.8(a) is based on the Model Code DR 5-104 rather than the Model Rule. The case law relied on in the Opinion, however, is more or less consistent with Model Rule 1.8(a): the transaction must be fair and reasonable to the client, the lawyer must fully disclose all relevant information, and the client must obtain the advice of independent counsel or have opportunity to obtain such advice before entering into the transaction. Moreover, the Opinion notes that prudent practice entails obtaining the client's written consent to the essential terms of, and the lawyer's role in, the transaction, as is required by Model Rule 1.8(a).

PROBLEM 3-15

You are asked to do estate planning and will drafting for Bill, the majority shareholder and CEO of Widgets, Inc. (a regular firm client), and Bill's wife, Mary.

a. What must you initially advise Bill and Mary before agreeing to take on their estate planning? *Possibility of CoI, need consent + disclosure* *Company, Bill + Mary*

b. Assume that after having heard your initial advice, Bill and Mary still prefer to have you handle all of their estate planning. They provide you with the appropriate informed consent. What would that be? *Written consent*

c. You do the planning and draft the wills, which Bill and Mary execute, but you notice that Bill does not have a buy-sell agreement with Fred, the CFO of Widgets, who is also the minority shareholder. What should you do now? *→ Advise the Co. once disussing w/ Bill, Draft + let fred know*

d. The buy-sell agreement is drafted to provide that on the occurrence of certain events (death, divorce, or bankruptcy of a shareholder), the company will buy back the shareholder's shares in the company, with the valuation determined on a formula basis. When the agreement is ready, Bill offers to set up a meeting for the two of you and Fred in order to get the agreement signed. At that meeting, you ask how Widgets will fund the share repurchase, particularly in the case of Bill's death. Bill says, "Don't worry. It won't be a problem." Fred is concerned, but doesn't pursue the issue. Are you ready to let Bill and Fred sign the agreement? *No* *fred needs his own counsel + needs to know Bill's lawyer does not represent him.*

e. The buy-sell agreement is signed. As you sit at your son's soccer game two years later, you hear from another parent (who works for Widgets) that Bill has been having an affair with Widgets' sales manager, Melody, for "months." What should you do? *Nothing, Client privilege bill + lawyer speak w/ Bill inquire if true*

f. Mary calls you later that fall, notes that she and Bill are getting a divorce, and asks you to draft a new will for her. Can you do this? Can your firm continue to represent Widgets? *Maybe? or W/draw? probably want Co. as client over Mary.* *cannot draft new will w/o Bill's permission must for eventual event w/ widgets*

PROBLEM 3-16

Lawyer has represented Husband and Wife for many years in a range of personal matters, including estate planning. Husband and Wife have substantial individual assets, and they also own substantial jointly-held property. Recently, Lawyer prepared new updated wills that Husband and Wife signed. Like their previous wills, the new wills primarily benefit the surviving spouse for his or her life, with beneficial disposition at the death of the survivor being made equally to their children (none of whom were from a prior marriage).

Husband, Wife, and Lawyer have always shared all relevant asset and financial information. Consistent with previous practice, Lawyer met with Husband and Wife together to confer regarding the changes to be made in updating their wills.

Several months after the execution of the new wills, Husband confers separately with Lawyer. Husband reveals to Lawyer that he has just executed a codicil (prepared by another law firm) that makes a substantial beneficial disposition to a woman with whom Husband has been having an extra-marital relationship. Husband tells Lawyer that Wife does not know about the relationship or the new codicil, as to which Husband asks Lawyer to advise him regarding Wife's rights of election in the event she were to survive Husband. What are Lawyer's ethical obligations? *→ Wldraw or convince Husband to admit discuss wl wife.*

Suppose that Lawyer tells Husband that Lawyer cannot advise him regarding Wife's rights and that Lawyer is withdrawing from representation of both Husband and Wife. What are Lawyer's obligations with respect to informing or not informing Wife of the substance of Husband's revelation if Husband does not do so himself? *See* Florida Bar Opinion 95-4 (May 30, 1997, *revised,* June 23, 2009). *Lawyer ethically precluded from disclosure to spouse upon withdrawal → May have obligation (co-clients) discuss btw them, but not 3rd parties*

PROBLEM 3-17

Your law firm regularly engages an appraisal firm to prepare appraisal reports for use in family limited partnership transactions and as litigation support for valuation issues. The appraisal firm did a valuation of corporate stock that was an integral part of a tax shelter. Can you represent an investor in the tax shelter in connection with an IRS audit or Tax Court litigation? *Yes. Realtor, atty, sellers realter + Huntington all referrals. supposed to be client confidentiality*

II. CONFLICTS BETWEEN LAWYERS AND CLIENTS

Circular 230 §§ 10.27 and 10.29
Internal Revenue Manual ¶ 4.11.55.4.2 (Appendix I)
Model Rules 1.5, 1.7 and 1.8
AICPA ET § 302 and Interpretation 302-1 (Appendix J)

Among the circumstances described in the general rule governing conflicts of interest, Model Rule 1.7, is one that bans a lawyer from representing a client if there is a significant risk that the representation will be materially limited by a personal interest of the lawyer. Circular 230 § 10.29(a)(2) contains a similar rule. Model Rule 1.8 identifies specific instances of such conflicts and prescribes rules and procedures for dealing with them; in some instances, the client may waive a conflict while, in others, representation is strictly prohibited. (Situations that are not specifically addressed in Model Rule 1.8. remain subject to the more general strictures of Model Rule 1.7.)

PROBLEM 3-18

A brokerage house performed all of the option trades at issue in tax shelter transactions entered into by your Client. The same firm manages all of the 401(k) accounts of your law firm. Do you have a conflict of interest? *Yes, stude manipulation if post suit may be COI. may arize after suit* *No, COI now*

PROBLEM 3-19

Lawyer has a number of estate planning clients who could benefit from financial planning advice. She is considering establishing a relationship with Financial Planner, who would pay her a referral fee for each client she refers to him. Can Lawyer accept the referral fee? *Yes confidential relationship, integrity of lawyers prohibited! CPAs yes can acct accountant Planner*

Suppose that Lawyer and Financial Planner wish to enter into a reciprocal arrangement under which Lawyer would refer clients to Financial Planner for

[handwritten margin note: No COI if w/ in scope limits of law. cannot be exclusive to eachother]

financial planning services and Financial Planner would refer clients to Lawyer for legal services. *See* Model Rule 7.2(b)(4); Philadelphia and Pennsylvania Bar Associations Joint Opinion 2000-100 (May 2000); Supreme Court of Ohio Opinion 2000-1 (Feb. 11, 2000).

PROBLEM 3-20

[handwritten margin note: ✓ No, COL exists, independent personal gain to atty. Alter ego client needs independent counsil. No]

Lawyer holds a patent on an estate planning strategy that might be useful to Client. Can Lawyer ethically recommend the strategy to Client? If so, can Lawyer charge Client a license fee (for use of the patent) in addition to her customary fee for estate planning services?

PROBLEM 3-21

[handwritten margin note: COL exists both need separate council]

Lawyer has provided tax and other legal advice to a limited liability company (LLC) in a traditional fee-for-service relationship. LLC's business has grown over time and its members believe that it should have a general counsel. They have asked Lawyer to take on this responsibility, on a part-time basis. In lieu of fees for this work, the LLC members have proposed to give Lawyer a 20 percent ownership interest in LLC and a percentage of the company's profits, if any. If Lawyer accepts this position, she would continue her private practice representing other clients. Under what circumstances is Lawyer ethically permitted to enter into the proposed arrangement? *[handwritten: written consent + declaration]*

A. Contingent Fees

Circular 230 § 10.27[6] contains a general rule barring unconscionable fees in matters before the IRS. No guidance is provided on what unconscionability means in this context; presumably, the principles in Model Rule 1.5 would govern. Under Model Rule 1.5, factors considered in determining the reasonableness of a fee include:

1. the time and labor required, the novelty and difficulty of the questions involved, and the skill requisite to perform the legal service properly;

2. the likelihood, if apparent to the client, that acceptance of the particular employment will preclude other employment by the lawyer;

3. the fee customarily charged in the locality for similar legal services;

4. the amount involved and the results obtained;

5. the time limitations imposed by the client or by the circumstances;

6. the nature and length of the professional relationship with the client;

7. the experience, reputation, and ability of the lawyer or lawyers performing the services; and

8. whether the fee is fixed or contingent.

---

[6] Circular 230 § 10.27(b) permits practitioners to collect contingent fees in three specific situations (which are discussed in the text). On March 26, 2008, the IRS issued Notice 2008-43, 2008-15 I.R.B. 748, adding a fourth situation in which contingent fees are permitted and announcing its intention to amend certain language in Section 10.27(b). The text assumes that the changes announced in Notice 2008-43 have been incorporated into Circular 230. Students should make sure to refer to Notice 2008-43 until such time as Circular 230 is formally amended.

Model Rule 1.5(c) permits contingent fee arrangements — except in domestic relations and criminal matters — so long as they are documented in a writing signed by the client and stating the method by which the fee will be calculated.

The AICPA prohibits contingent fee arrangements in connection with the preparation of an original or amended tax return, or a claim for refund. AICPA ET Section 302 (together with AICPA Interpretation 302-1, reproduced at Appendix J). AICPA Interpretation 302-1 provides several examples of circumstances in which contingent fees are permitted in connection with tax matters:

1. representing a client in an examination by a revenue agent of the client's federal or state income tax return,

2. filing an amended federal or state income tax return claiming a tax refund based on a tax issue that is either the subject of a test case (involving a different taxpayer) or with respect to which the taxing authority is developing a position,

3. filing an amended federal or state income tax return (or refund claim) claiming a tax refund in an amount greater than the threshold for review by the Joint Committee on Internal Revenue Taxation ($2 million) or state taxing authority,

4. requesting a refund of either overpayments of interest or penalties charged to a client's account or deposits of taxes improperly accounted for by the federal or state taxing authority in circumstances where the taxing authority has established procedures for the substantive review of such refund requests,

5. requesting, by means of "protest" or similar document, consideration by the state or local taxing authority of a reduction in the "assessed value" of property under an established taxing authority review process for hearing all taxpayer arguments relating to assessed value., and

6. representing a client in connection with obtaining a private letter ruling or influencing the drafting of a regulation or statute.

Circular 230's guidance on the use of contingent fees in tax matters is similar, but not identical, to the AICPA rules. A contingent fee is defined for Circular 230 purposes as:

any fee that is based, in whole or in part, on whether or not a position taken on a tax return or other filing avoids challenge by the Internal Revenue Service or is sustained either by the Internal Revenue Service or in litigation. A contingent fee includes a fee that is based on a percentage of the refund reported on a return, that is based on a percentage of the taxes saved, or that otherwise depends on the specific result attained. A contingent fee also includes any fee arrangement in which the practitioner will reimburse the client for all or a portion of the client's fee in the event that a position taken on a tax return or other filing is challenged by the Internal Revenue Service or is not sustained, whether pursuant to an indemnity agreement, a guarantee, rescission rights, or any other arrangement with a similar effect.

Circular 230 § 10.27(c)(1). Contingent fees are prohibited generally for services rendered in connection with any matter before the IRS. Thus, practitioners may not charge contingent fees in connection with preparing or filing of an original tax return, amended tax return, or claim for refund. Restricting contingent fees in this context is thought to discourage return positions that exploit the "audit lottery." Circular 230 does permit contingent fee arrangements, however, in four specific situations.

First, a practitioner may charge a contingent fee for services rendered in connection with an IRS examination of, or challenge to, an original tax return, amended return, or claim for refund where the amended return or claim for refund is filed (1) before the taxpayer receives a written notice of examination of, or a written challenge to, the original tax return or (2) no later than 120 days after receipt of such written notice or challenge. Contingent fees are permitted in this situation because unlike, e.g., an original return, substantive review by the IRS of the taxpayer's position here is a certainty. Therefore, the rule does not encourage practitioners to encourage frivolous positions that exploit the audit lottery. The 120-day limit addresses governmental concerns over the use of contingent fee arrangements in connection with claims for refund or amended returns that are filed very late in the process of an examination (audit) in the hope that an IRS officer or employee will not look closely at the claims.

Second, a practitioner is permitted to charge a contingent fee for services rendered in connection with a claim for refund filed solely in connection with the determination of statutory interest or penalties assessed by the IRS. This exception is meant to address services provided by "account review practitioners" who retroactively evaluate corporate taxpayers' IRS accounts to determine whether they have overpaid interest or penalties. Typically, account review practitioners' fees are based on a percentage of the savings uncovered. Because the interest or penalties have already been paid, a claim for refund is necessary, assuring substantive review by an IRS employee or officer.

Third, a practitioner may charge a contingent fee for services rendered in connection with a whistleblower claim under Section 7623. That section establishes a program under which the IRS may pay rewards to persons who report underpayments of tax by others. Such persons ("whistleblowers") may be entitled to receive a percentage of the taxes recovered by the IRS.

Fourth, a practitioner may charge a contingent fee for services rendered in connection with any judicial proceeding arising under the Code.

PROBLEM 3-22

Lawyer has been asked by Client for advice in connection with Client's investment in a series of financial transactions, which Client hopes will result in substantial tax savings to Client. Among the services to be provided by Lawyer, Lawyer will issue an opinion letter describing the tax consequences of the investment. May Lawyer's fee reflect a portion of the projected tax savings? Would it matter if Lawyer agreed to (perhaps retroactively) reduce her fee if the tax savings did not hold up under audit or litigation?

B. Tax Return Accuracy Standards

Differences between the income tax return accuracy standards for taxpayers and for the professionals who advise them could result in conflicts of interest. Specifically, with respect to the same position on a taxpayer's return, a tax adviser might face the imposition of a penalty if such position is not disclosed (i.e., flagged) on the return while, at the same time, the taxpayer faces no penalty risk for nondisclosure. In other words, it could be in the adviser's interest, but not in the taxpayer/client's interest, to disclose a position. Thankfully, Congress significantly reduced the potential for such conflicts by amending Section 6694 (the preparer penalty rules) in 2008 to conform the preparer and taxpayer standards. As is discussed in Chapter 2, *supra*, the basic standard is now "substantial authority" for both groups: return positions that are supported by substantial authority generally will not subject anyone to penalties; positions that lack substantial authority could subject both the taxpayer and her professional adviser to penalties unless the positions are disclosed on the return. *See* Sections 6694(a)(2), 6662(d)(2)(B).

The professional standard articulated in ABA Formal Op. 85-352 differs from the taxpayer standard. That difference creates the potential for conflicts of interest. *See* ABA Section of Taxation Committee on Standards of Tax Practice, Standards of Tax Practice Statement 2000-1 (Dec. 4, 2000), http://www.abanet.org/tax/groups/stp/stmt00-1.html. ABA Formal Op. 85-352 concludes that "[a] lawyer may advise reporting a position on a tax return so long as the lawyer believes in good faith that the position is warranted in existing law or can be supported by a good faith argument for an extension, modification or reversal of existing law and there is some realistic possibility of success if the matter is litigated" (the "realistic possibility of success" standard). A "realistic possibility of success" has been quantified as a likelihood of success approximating one-third. The realistic possibility of success standard also applies to CPAs, but only where the applicable taxing authority has no written standards or if its standards are lower than the AICPA standards. *See* AICPA SSTS No. 1 & Interpretation No. 1-1, "Realistic Possibility Standard" (in Appendix C). The realistic possibility of success standard is inconsistent with Section 6694, as amended, and should be revised or withdrawn.[7] Until revision, however, attorneys are strongly advised to follow the higher standard in Section 6694.

C. Referrals to OPR

The Internal Revenue Manual lists circumstances in which a Revenue Agent *must* or *may* refer a practitioner to OPR. Referral is mandatory in the following situations:

1. when cases in which understatements due to unrealistic positions (Section 6694(a)) are closed (should be "unreasonable positions" in light of 2008 amendments);[8]
2. when cases in which understatements due to willful or reckless conduct (Section 6694(b)) are closed;

---

[7] No efforts to revise ABA Formal Op. 85-352 are underway as of the date of publication of this text. The AICPA recently revised its SSTSs effective January 1, 2010. The new standard retains the realistic possibility of success standard but requires CPAs to follow a higher standard if one is adopted by the relevant taxing authority. Therefore, CPAs are subject to the higher substantial authority standard in preparing federal returns.

[8] Although Directors of OPR from time to time have indicated that referrals to OPR by Revenue Agents would not be automatic in the case of Section 6694(a) penalties, the Internal Revenue Manual is clear in mandating referrals in these situations.

3. when a penalty for negotiation of a refund check (Section 6694(f)) is assessed;

4. when a penalty for aiding and abetting (Section 6701) is assessed (Revenue Agents should consider referrals to OPR where the Section 6701 penalty was considered but not imposed);.

5. when a penalty for promoting abusive tax shelters (Section 6700) is assessed against an attorney, CPA or enrolled agent;

6. when an injunctive action (Section 7407 or Section 7408) is taken against promoters of abusive tax shelters; and

7. when injunctive action (Section 7408) is taken against an attorney, CPA or enrolled agent.

IRM ¶ 4.11.55.4.2.2.1 (2005).

The following situations *may* warrant a referral to OPR:

1. when return preparer referrals are made to the IRS Criminal Investigation Division (Section 7206);

2. when an appraiser who aids or assists in the preparation or presentation of an appraisal in connection with the tax laws will be subject to disciplinary action if the appraiser knows that the appraisal will be used in connection with the tax laws and will result in an understatement of the tax liability of another person;

3. when a by-pass of representative letter was issued to a tax practitioner;

4. when a practitioner engages in disreputable conduct or incompetence as described in Circular 230 § 10.51;

5. when a tax practitioner is implicated in a frivolous tax return matter (Section 6702);

6. when an accuracy-related penalty (Section 6662(d)) for a substantial understatement is asserted and the facts of the case suggest the practitioner did not exercise due diligence in the preparation of the return;

7. when a practitioner fails to comply with the tax shelter registration requirement (Section 6111) or characterizes such registration as an IRS endorsement of the shelter and takes a position on a tax return that reflects the purported endorsement;

8. when opinions rendered by tax practitioners are used or referred to in the marketing of tax shelters (abusive or otherwise); and

9. when an examination report is written with respect to any tax return of an attorney, CPA, or enrolled agent, or a return prepared by an attorney, CPA or enrolled agent where a Pre-filing Notification Letter was issued in connection with a tax shelter and the loss and/or credit from the promotion was nevertheless claimed on the tax return.

IRM ¶ 4.11.55.4.2.2.2 (2005).

PROBLEM 3-23

Several years ago, Lawyer gave tax advice to a long-time client (Client) with respect to an investment that Client was then considering. Client made the investment. Client's income tax return for the year in which the investment was made is now under audit by the IRS. Because Lawyer is Client's regular tax counsel, Lawyer is representing Client in the proceeding. From comments made by the IRS Revenue Agent during the course of discussions, Lawyer has the impression that the Revenue Agent believes that Lawyer gave Client bad advice at the time of the investment. What, if anything, should Lawyer do? What, if anything, must Lawyer do? *Lawyer must advise client + IRS, reccommend new counsel to client, + withdraw.*

PROBLEM 3-24

Lawyer represents Client during what Lawyer originally thought was a routine audit. During the course of the proceeding, Lawyer realizes that the Revenue Agent may have grounds for referring her to OPR. Is there automatically a conflict of interest? How should Lawyer decide whether or not to withdraw from the representation? *Yes, Lawyer is concerned with themselves + no longer has client's best interest as priority. Both need new counsel. Atty must advise Client.*

III. OPINION LETTERS AND WRITTEN ADVICE

Circular 230 §§ 10.22, 10.35, 10.36 and 10.37
Model Rule 2.3
AICPA SSTS No. 1 and Interpretation No. 1-2 (Appendix C and Appendix D)

A. Opinion Letters

Clients frequently ask their tax advisers for written opinion letters stating the lawyers' or accountants' views on the tax treatment or consequences of transactions or investments described in the letters. The letters typically begin with a detailed description of the transaction or investment with respect to which opinions are rendered (these are the facts on which the opinions are based), continue with a statement of the relevant legal principles and authorities and an analysis of how those principles and authorities apply to the facts at issue, and conclude by stating opinions on the tax treatment or consequences. For a variety of reasons, many of which are discussed in this section, opinion letters usually contain a variety of embellishments, as well, e.g., the identity of the person or persons from whom the facts were obtained, the extent to which an opinion relies on representations of others, etc.

Tax opinion letters can be useful in a variety of circumstances. Sometimes, a client merely seeks written comfort that her advisors have thought carefully through the relevant issues and have confidence in their advice. With the adoption and implementation of FASB FIN 48,[9] tax lawyers anticipate being asked

---

[9] Financial Accounting Standards Board (FASB) Interpretation (FIN) No. 48, "Accounting for Uncertainty in Income Taxes." For tax years beginning after December 15, 2006 (with some exceptions), FIN 48 governs the evaluation by CPAs of material positions taken in any income tax return, for purposes of financial accounting. According to the FASB:

> [FIN 48] clarifies the accounting for uncertainty in income taxes recognized in an enterprise's financial statements in accordance with FASB Statement No. 109, Accounting for Income Taxes. This Interpretation prescribes a recognition threshold and measurement attribute for the financial statement recognition and measurement of a tax position taken or expected to be taken in a tax return.

www.fasb.org/cs/BlobServer?blobcol=urldata&blobtable=MungoBlobs&blobkey=id&blob where=1175818746949&blobheader=application%2Fpdf. The full text of FIN 48 is available through links on the FASB and AICPA websites.

for written opinions to influence auditors in creating tax accruals. Clients seek opinion letters as a means of defending against the possible imposition of tax penalties by the IRS; such opinion letters are casually referred to as "penalty protection." Some clients seek tax opinions in order to influence others to participate or invest in a transaction. Finally, sometimes opinions are required by law. For example, federal securities laws may require that transactions involving issuance of securities to the public include an opinion to support discussions of tax consequences included in the offering materials.

Tax opinion letters predict the likelihood of a position being sustained on its merits if challenged by the IRS. In other words, they predict how a court would rule if called upon to decide the issue or issues opined upon, assuming that the court were familiar with all of the relevant facts. In reality, the likelihood of any particular outcome is difficult to quantify; nonetheless, clients ask for, and receive, greater or lesser degrees of assurance depending on the purpose or context of the letter. Although there are neither formal definitions of relevant terminology nor any real agreement on the strength of the various levels, tax opinion letters typically give assurance at one of five levels.[10]

1. <u>Reasonable basis</u> has been quantified by some to be as low as 5% and by others as high as the 20 to 25% range. According to Treas. Reg. § 1.6662-3(b)(3):

> The reasonable basis standard is not satisfied by a return position that is merely arguable or that is merely a colorable claim. If a return position is reasonably based on one or more of the authorities set forth in the [substantial authority regulations,] the return position will generally satisfy the reasonable basis standard even though it may not satisfy the substantial authority standard.

A position having a reasonable basis avoids a negligence penalty. Treas. Reg. § 1.6662-3(b)(1). Moreover, a return position must have at least a reasonable basis in order to avoid, through disclosure,[11] a penalty for substantial understatement of income tax or a preparer penalty under Section 6694(a). Sections 6662(d)(2)(B)(ii), 6694(a)(2)(B).

2. <u>Substantial authority</u> is difficult to quantify numerically but it certainly may be less than 50%. "Substantial authority" is more stringent than the reasonable basis standard but less stringent than the more likely than not (i.e., greater than 50%) standard. Treas. Reg. § 1.6662-4(d)(2).

> There is substantial authority for the tax treatment of any item only if the weight of the authorities supporting the treatment is substantial in relation to the weight of authorities supporting contrary treatment.

---

[10] There could be other standards for opinions, e.g., "not frivolous." The text addresses only the standards that are most commonly utilized. For a tongue-in-cheek breakdown of tax opinion standards, see *A Detailed Guide to Tax Opinion Standards*, 106 TAX NOTES 1469-71 (2005).

[11] Form 8275 is attached to a return whenever a taxpayer or tax return preparer wishes to disclose items or positions in order to avoid certain penalties. Form 8275 is filed, for example, to avoid the portions of the accuracy-related penalty due to disregard of rules or to a substantial understatement of income tax for nontax shelter items if the return position has a reasonable basis. It can also be used for disclosures relating to preparer penalties for understatements due to unreasonable positions or disregard of rules. (Where disclosure is made of return positions that are contrary to a regulation, Form 8275-R is used.)

> All authorities relevant to the tax treatment of an item, including the authorities contrary to the treatment, are taken into account in determining whether substantial authority exists. The weight of authorities is determined in light of the pertinent facts and circumstances in the manner prescribed in [Treas. Reg. § 1.6662-4(d)(3)(ii)].

Treas. Reg. § 1.6662-4(d)(3)(i). (Students should be quite comfortable with the meaning of "substantial authority" after having studied Chapter 2 of this text.)

Because this standard can be satisfied at less than 50% certainty, it is possible that there could be substantial authority for more than one position. Moreover, unlike any of the other levels of assurance, substantial authority is not stated in the regulations in terms of how likely a particular outcome will be but focuses instead on the strength, or relative strength, of the authority or authorities supporting a position.

A position must have substantial authority in order to avoid the penalty for substantial understatement of income tax without disclosure or a preparer penalty under Sections 6694(a).[12] Sections 6662(d)(2)(B)(i), 6694(a)(2)(A).

3. <u>More likely than not</u> means having a greater than 50% likelihood of being sustained on the merits. Treas. Reg. §§ 1.6662-4(g)(4)(i)(B), 1.6694-2(b)(1).[13] For tax years beginning after December 15, 2006 (with some exceptions), "more likely than not" is the standard or threshold that must be used by CPAs in assessing all material positions taken in any income tax return.[14] FIN 48 requires a company to undertake and retain a detailed analysis of tax positions that may be uncertain and to document whether each such position can be recognized as more likely than not. While tax opinions are not required to meet the FIN 48 threshold, companies routinely engage outside tax counsel or advisers to prepare tax opinions on significant positions to determine whether such positions meet the "more likely than not" standard.

4. <u>Should</u> is not quantified or defined in either the Code or the regulations, but is generally considered to mean a likelihood of success of more than 70%. Thus, a "should" opinion opines at a level greater than "more likely than not" but less than "will." Although some attorneys use the phrases "weak should" and "strong should" to describe the strength of their opinions, such terminology rarely is reflected in the opinion letters themselves. Because the level of "should" is uncertain, these letters typically include reasoning or analysis so that the reader can assess the degree of certainty or uncertainty for herself. (Not surprisingly, an opinion letter that includes a lengthy analysis is referred to as a "reasoned opinion.").

---

[12] In addition, substantial authority is required in order to qualify for the reasonable cause exception to the penalty for reportable transaction understatements. Section 6664(d)(2)(B).

[13] A position must meet the more likely that not standard to avoid certain penalties related to tax shelters and reportable transactions. Sections 6664(d)(3)(C), 6694(a)(2)(C).

[14] The "more likely than not" threshold, for FIN 48 purposes, means that: (1) a benefit related to an uncertain tax position may not be recognized in financial statements unless it is "more likely than not" that the position will be sustained based on its technical merits; and (2) there must be more than a 50 percent likelihood that the position would be sustained if challenged and considered by the highest court in the relevant jurisdiction.

5. <u>Will</u> means 95 to 100%. A "will" opinion is considered a "clean" or "unqualified" opinion of near certainty. "Will" opinions may be subject to exceptions, limitations, and/or assumptions, so long as they are customary and are stated in the letter.

B. Ethical Considerations
1. Ethical Rules

In drafting an opinion, lawyers must be mindful of traditional ethical standards. For example, under ABA Formal Op. 85-352, a lawyer is prohibited from advising tax return positions that fall short of a "realistic possibility of success" standard. The same standard is generally thought to govern any tax advice given to a client to the extent that tax return positions are or will be involved (e.g., advice in the course of structuring transactions that will involve tax return positions), including tax advice in the course of preparing legal documents. Opinion 85-352 states:

> [A] lawyer, in representing a client in the course of the preparation of the client's tax return, may advise the statement of positions most favorable to the client if the lawyer has a good faith belief that those positions are warranted in existing law or can be supported by a good faith argument for an extension, modification or reversal of existing law. A lawyer can have a good faith belief in this context even if the lawyer believes the client's position probably will not prevail. However, good faith requires that there be some realistic possibility of success if the matter is litigated.

> * * *

> Thus, where a lawyer has a good faith belief in the validity of a position in accordance with the standard stated above that a particular transaction does not result in taxable income or that certain expenditures are properly deductible as expenses, the lawyer has no duty to require as a condition of his or her continued representation that riders be attached to the client's tax return explaining the circumstances surrounding the transaction or the expenditures.

> In the role of advisor, the lawyer should counsel the client as to whether the position is likely to be sustained by a court if challenged by the IRS, as well as of the potential penalty consequences to the client if the position is taken on the tax return without disclosure. Section 6661 [now Section 6662] of the Internal Revenue Code imposes a penalty for substantial understatement of tax liability which can be avoided if the facts are adequately disclosed or if there is or was substantial authority for the position taken by the taxpayer. Competent representation of the client would require the lawyer to advise the client fully as to whether there is or was substantial authority for the position taken in the tax return. If the lawyer is unable to conclude that the position is supported by substantial authority, the lawyer should advise the client of the penalty the client may suffer and of the opportunity to avoid such penalty by adequately disclosing the facts in the return or in a statement attached to the return. If after receiving such advice the client decides to risk the penalty by making no disclosure and to take

the position initially advised by the lawyer in accordance with the standard stated above, the lawyer has met his or her ethical responsibility with respect to the advice.

In all cases, however, with regard both to the preparation of returns and negotiating administrative settlements, the lawyer is under a duty not to mislead the Internal Revenue Service deliberately, either by misstatements or by silence or by permitting the client to mislead.

In summary, a lawyer may advise reporting a position on a return even where the lawyer believes the position probably will not prevail, there is no 'substantial authority' in support of the position, and there will be no disclosure of the position in the return. However, the position to be asserted must be one which the lawyer in good faith believes is warranted in existing law or can be supported by a good faith argument for an extension, modification or reversal of existing law. *This requires that there is some realistic possibility of success if the matter is litigated.* In addition, in his role as advisor, the lawyer should refer to potential penalties and other legal consequences should the client take the position advised.

The realistic possibility of success standard has been quantified as a one in three, or greater, likelihood of being sustained on the merits. Treas. Reg. § 1.6694-2(b)(1) (as in effect prior to Dec. 15, 2008); Circular 230 § 10.34(d)(1) (as in effect prior to Apr. 4, 2008). Prior to 2008, Circular 230 mandated the same realistic possibility of success standard with respect to tax return positions, and the preparer penalty rule under Section 6694(a) incorporated that standard, as well. The AICPA rule was the same. Thus, all tax professionals were governed by the same reporting standards in all contexts. (The tax professional was governed by a different reporting standard than her client, however — realistic possibility of success versus substantial authority.[15])

In 2008, Section 6694(a) was amended to require that, with respect to tax advice, a return preparer must meet the substantial authority standard (as described in Chapter 2). The realistic possibility of success standard was removed from Circular 230 § 10.34(a) because it was inconsistent with the statutory amendments.[16] Therefore, while the tax practitioner's statutory reporting (i.e., penalty) standard now conforms to her client's (i.e., both are now substantial authority), the attorney's ethical standard is now inconsistent with both, and Circular 230 is silent on the matter. As of this writing, ABA Formal Op. 85-352 has not been revised to reflect the incongruities and no efforts to make the appropriate revisions are underway. The ethical standard set forth in Opinion 85-352, therefore, must be revised to conform the ethical standard to Section 6694(a), or withdrawn.

---

[15] Ethical issues arising out of this conflict were addressed by the ABA Section of Taxation Committee on Standards of Tax Practice in its Standards of Tax Practice Statement 2001-1 (Dec. 4, 2000), http://www.abanet.org/tax/groups/stp/stmt00-1.html. Specifically, this Statement explores whether the benefits of adequately disclosing return positions, which might have affected taxpayers and advisers differently, generated conflicts of interest.

[16] As of the date of publication of this text, the substantial authority standard has not been added to Circular 230. While the Director of OPR has indicated that an amendment to Circular 230 § 10.34(a) will be proposed shortly, it is not clear that the forthcoming standard will mirror Section 6694(a).

Opinion letters that may be used or relied upon by third parties (other than the client), e.g., prospective investors in a transaction organized and promoted by a client, must comport with Model Rule 2.3, under which (1) the rendering lawyer must reasonably believe that making an evaluation for the benefit of third parties is compatible with other aspects of the lawyer's relationship with the client and (2) if the lawyer knows or reasonably should know that the evaluation is likely to affect the client's interests materially and adversely, the lawyer may not provide the evaluation unless the client gives informed consent. According to the Comments to Model Rule 2.3, when a question about the legal situation of a client arises at the instance of the client's financial auditor, the lawyer's response may be made in accordance with procedures recognized in the legal profession, such as the so-called "treaty" entered into between the ABA and AICPA. *See* ABA Comm. on Audit Inquiry Responses, *Statement of Policy Regarding Lawyers' Responses to Auditors' Requests for Information,* 31 BUS. LAW. 1709 (1975).[17]

2.   AICPA Standards

According to the AICPA SSTSs and interpretations (Appendix C), the same standard that applies to tax return preparation applies to professional services involving tax planning. Interpretation No. 1-2 to SSTS No. 1 (Appendix D). Tax planning, for this purpose, includes any oral or written recommendation or expression of an opinion in a prospective or completed transaction on either a return position or on a specific tax plan by the member, the taxpayer or a third party. Interpretation No. 1-2 provides guidelines for issuing opinions and for reviewing opinions given to the client by other tax professionals.

Under the AICPA standard, "[a] member should not recommend that a tax return [or tax planning] position be taken with respect to any item unless the member has a good faith belief that the position has a realistic possibility of being sustained administratively or judicially on its merits if challenged." The AICPA recently revised this standard, which was at odds with both Circular 230 and Section 6694(a). The new standard retains the realistic possibility of success standard in situations where the applicable taxing authority has no written standards or where such written standards are lower than the AICPA's standards; otherwise, members would be required to comply with standards imposed by such an authority. Thus, in the case of a federal tax return, the preparer penalty standard in Section 6694 (i.e., substantial authority) would govern.

C.   Circular 230

In 2004, Treasury issued final regulations prescribing opinion standards and rules that were aimed primarily at opinions rendered in tax shelter transactions. The regulations, however, cover other written opinions, as well. Please review Circular 230 §§ 10.35, 10.36, and 10.37. Circular 230 § 10.35 provides standards and rules applicable when rendering a "covered opinion." Circular 230 § 10.37 provides standards and rules that apply when Circular 230 § 10.35

---

[17] The treaty is currently under revision in light of statutory and other changes, including FIN 48. The ABA's position paper on responding to auditor responses in light of FIN 48 is available at http://meetings.abanet.org/webupload/commupload/CL965000/otherlinks_files/fin48statement.pdf.

does not. Thus, the first hurdle to overcome is whether any particular written advice is or will be considered a "covered opinion." Although the definition of a "covered opinion" is elaborate, the standards and rules that apply to "covered opinions" are straightforward.

As a preliminary matter, Circular 230 § 10.35 applies only to "written advice," including electronic communications. Oral advice is not affected. The inclusion of electronic communications means that relatively innocuous e-mails covering tax topics may constitute "written advice" within the regulations. If they do, then the requirements of Circular 230 § 10.35 apply unless the e-mail explicitly disclaims that its contents may be relied upon by the recipient for certain purposes. *See, e.g.*, Circular 230 § 10.35(b)(5)(iii). This explains the ubiquitous Circular 230 disclaimers that are now prominent at the end of e-mails sent from many law and accounting firms.[18]

1. Covered Opinions

A "covered opinion" is written advice (including electronic communications) that concerns one or more federal tax issues arising from of the following:

1. A transaction that is the same as or substantially similar to a "listed transaction." These are transactions that the IRS identifies as tax avoidance transactions, typically in a Notice. (The IRS web site contains a listing of listed transactions, e.g., "Recognized Abusive and Listed Transactions — LMSB Tier I Issues in Alphabetical Order," http://www.irs.gov/businesses/corporations/article/0,,id=204155,00.html.) Listed transactions are a type of reportable transaction, participation in which must be disclosed in an investor's tax return. Treas. Reg. § 1.6011-4.

2. An entity, plan or arrangement, the principal purpose of which is federal tax avoidance or evasion. The fact that "principal purpose" is not defined is a source of frustration to practitioners. But see Treas. Reg. § 1.6662-4(g)(ii), which defines "principal purpose" in the context of the substantial understatement penalty as it applies to tax shelters.

3. An entity, plan or arrangement, a significant purpose of which is federal tax avoidance or evasion, but only if the written advice is:

   a. a reliance opinion,

   b. a marketed opinion,

   c. subject to conditions of confidentiality, or

   d. subject to contractual protection.

These four subcategories, (a)-(d), are expounded upon in Circular 230 § 10.35. In practice, it may be difficult to conclude that a transaction *does not* have a significant purpose where tax consequences were considered in making structuring decisions. Therefore, many tax practitioners rely on falling outside of the four subcategories to avoid having to comply with the Circular 230 § 10.35(c) rules, or include in their written advice or opinion letters the disclaimer language discussed below.

[18] An example: "Any statements regarding federal tax law contained herein are not intended or written to be used, and cannot be used, for the purposes of avoiding penalties that may be imposed under federal tax law or to market any entity, investment plan or arrangement."

A "covered opinion" does not include preliminary written advice if a practitioner reasonably expects to provide the client with more extensive written advice later in the representation. Moreover, written advice that would be a "covered opinion" under the significant purpose category is not considered a "covered opinion" if the advice (1) concerns the qualification of a qualified plan, (2) is a state or local bond opinion,[19] or (3) is included in documents required to be filed with the SEC. (Query whether documents that are typically filed with the SEC, but which are not explicitly required to be filed, are "covered opinions.")

a. Significant Purpose Transactions

Of the three categories of written advice that can be covered opinions, the third, the significant purpose transaction, poses the most issues for practitioners because these transactions are not necessarily overtly tax-motivated and because practitioners must determine which of the four subcategories, if any, within the significant purpose category the written advice falls into. The most significant and potentially troubling of the four is the "reliance opinion," which is the type of opinion that clients use or attempt to use to defend against imposition of penalties; hence, reliance opinions conclude at a confidence level of at least more likely than not that one or more significant federal tax issues would be resolved in favor of the taxpayer. The regulation permits clients and tax advisers to opt out of Circular 230 § 10.35 by prominently disclosing in the written advice that it was not intended or written by the practitioner to be used, and that it cannot be used, for the purpose of avoiding penalties. Thus, the taxpayer cannot use the opinion letter to establish the reasonable cause and good faith defense to the accuracy-related penalty. *See* Section 6664(c); Treas. Reg. § 1.6664-4.

Written advice constitutes a marketed opinion if the practitioner knows or has reason to know that the written advice will be used or referred to by a person other than the practitioner or her firm in promoting, marketing, or recommending an entity, investment plan, or arrangement. A disclaimer can take the written advice out of the category. While the drafters of the regulation probably had in mind marketed tax shelter opinions, the regulatory language is broad enough to apply to private offerings in the capital markets (in which filing with the SEC is not required). Such transactions probably meet the "significant purpose" test where the investments themselves offer tax advantages. For example, preferred stock bears a lower tax cost than straight debt because dividends are taxed at capital gains rates. *See* Section 1(h). For foreigners, straight debt often offers tax advantages because, e.g., the interest might be exempt under the portfolio interest rules. *See* Section 871(h).

The remaining two categories pose fewer issues for practitioners.

b. Requirements for Covered Opinions

Circular 230 § 10.35(c) sets forth specific requirements that must be met in giving a covered opinion. While most good practitioners have, in the past,

---

[19] State and local bond opinions are addressed separately in Circular 230.

followed similar practices to those in the regulation in rendering tax opinions, the regulation exceeds prior practice in several significant ways. First, the requirements apply to what practitioners might otherwise think of as casual advice, e.g., e-mails. Under Circular 230 § 10.35, if an e-mail constitutes a covered opinion, then all of the requirements must be followed. Second, the regulations require that the practitioner's analysis be set forth in the opinion itself. In the past, opinions might have contained a detailed analysis (a "long-form opinion") or might have simply stated the practitioner's opinions and conclusions (a "short-form opinion'). In some cases, analysis underlying short-form opinions was provided separately to clients and/or maintained in the practitioner's file. (A short-form opinion was the basis for OPR's unsuccessful disciplinary proceeding in the *Sykes* case discussed in Chapter 1.) Third, the regulation requires that certain information be set forth in separate sections, as prescribed, rather than in a format selected by the rendering practitioner.

The regulation requires that conclusions be stated with respect to each significant federal tax issue considered in the opinion. In the past, practitioners might have rendered opinions on some, but not all, tax issues. Perhaps clients' motives were nefarious but, in many cases, clients asked for opinions only on issues which they anticipated the IRS would be likely to examine. Under the current rules, practitioners may provide an opinion that considers less than all of the significant federal tax issues only if (1) the practitioner and client agree that the client may rely on the opinion for penalty protection only with respect to issues addressed in the opinion, (2) the opinion does not pertain to a listed transaction or a principal purpose transaction, and (3) the opinion includes certain required disclosures.

Students should review the requirements of Circular 230 § 10.35(c) at this time. An opinion that meets the requirements of Circular 230 § 10.35 satisfies the practitioner's responsibilities under that section. However, the persuasiveness of the opinion and the taxpayer's good faith reliance on the opinion will be determined separately should the need arise (e.g., if the taxpayer uses the opinion to satisfy the reasonable cause and good faith exception to the accuracy-related penalty). In broad stroke, Circular 230 § 10.35(c) mandates that practitioners consider all relevant facts, relate the law to the facts, evaluate the significant federal tax issues, and provide a conclusion.

1. <u>Factual matters.</u> The practitioner must make reasonable efforts to identify and ascertain the facts and is prohibited from basing her opinion on unreasonable factual assumptions or representations. The opinion must contain a section identifying all relevant facts, all factual assumptions, and all representations, statements, or findings of the taxpayer relied on in the opinion.

2. <u>Relate law to facts.</u> The opinion must relate the applicable law to the relevant facts. The practitioner may not assume a favorable conclusion with respect to any significant federal tax issue or otherwise base an opinion on unreasonable assumptions or representations. The opinion may not contain any internally inconsistent legal analyses or conclusions.

3. <u>Evaluation of significant federal tax issues.</u> The opinion must consider all significant federal tax issues and provide conclusions as to the likelihood that the taxpayer will prevail on the merits of each. The opinion must provide a

conclusion, and indicate the confidence level of the conclusion, as to each of the issues and explain and describe the reasons for all conclusions. A covered opinion that fails to conclude at a confidence level of at least more likely than not that a significant federal tax issue would be sustained on its merits if challenged must prominently disclose that the opinion does not reach that confidence level and that the taxpayer may not use the opinion to avoid penalties. Moreover, none of the following possibilities may be taken into account in evaluating the taxpayer's chances of success on the merits: that a tax return will not be audited, that an issue will not be raised on audit, or that an issue will be resolved through settlement if raised.

4. <u>Overall conclusion.</u> A covered opinion must state an overall conclusion or explain why an overall conclusion could not be reached.

In rendering an opinion, a practitioner is permitted to rely on the opinion or opinions of another practitioner with respect to one or more significant federal tax issues unless the practitioner knows or should know that the opinion or opinions of the other practitioner should not be relied upon. If a practitioner relies on the opinion of another practitioner, however, the relying practitioner's opinion must identify the other opinion and set forth the conclusions reached in that other opinion.

2. Best Practices

Circular 230 § 10.36 requires that individuals rendering written advice and their firms take reasonable steps to ensure that the firm has adequate procedures for complying with Circular 230 § 10.35. Failure to maintain adequate procedures could result in discipline under Circular 230 as to both the firm and the individual. While the IRS has not ruled on the matter, it would seem that the traditional practice of requiring approval by at least two partners before rendering a formal tax opinion (the so-called "two partner rule") would constitute a reasonable practice.

3. Other Written Advice

Written advice that does not constitute a "covered opinion" must be rendered in accordance with the rules in Circular 230 § 10.37, which are less detailed than those in Circular 230 § 10.35. The rules in Circular 230 § 10.37 are essentially procedural; practitioners are permitted to give written advice regardless of whether the practitioner concludes that any particular issue will be resolved in favor of the taxpayer and regardless of the confidence level the practitioner has with respect to any particular issue's resolution. It seems clear under general ethical principles, however, that a practitioner's reservations about the strength her advice should be communicated to the client.

Under Circular 230 § 10.37, a practitioner is prohibited from giving written advice only under four circumstances:

1. the practitioner bases the written advice on unreasonable factual or legal assumptions, including assumptions as to future events;

2. the practitioner unreasonably relies on representations, statements, findings or agreements of the taxpayer or any other person;

3. the practitioner does not consider all relevant facts that the practitioner know or should know; or

4. in evaluating a federal tax issue, the tax practitioner takes into account the possibility that a tax return will not be audited, that an issue will not be raised on audit, or that an issue will be resolved through settlement if raised.

In evaluating whether a practitioner has failed to comply with Circular 230 § 10.37, all facts and circumstances will be considered. A heightened standard of care is expected of a practitioner who gives written advice that she knows or has reason to know will be used or referred to by a person other than the practitioner in promoting, marketing or recommending to others an entity, plan or arrangement with a significant tax avoidance or evasion purpose. This is written advice that satisfies the first part of the definition of "marketed opinion" in Circular 230 § 10.35 but which otherwise does not quality as a "covered opinion." Thus, the heightened standard applies to written advice that otherwise looks like a marketed opinion but which contains the required disclaimers.

PROBLEM 3-25

Are the following "covered opinions"? If so, what advice would you give to the practitioners about the preparation and content of the advice? In the alternative, how can the practitioners in each case alter the advice to avoid the "covered opinion" rules? If the "covered opinion" rules do not apply, what standards should the advice meet?

a. A corporate lawyer receives the following question by e-mail from a long-time client: "I'm buying a machine for $10,000. I'm paying $1,000 cash and financing the rest. I'll get to take depreciation deductions from a $10,000 basis, right?" The corporate lawyer responds: "Yes."

b. In discussing with her client whether to accept a settlement in a tort suit involving personal physical injury, a trial lawyer reminds her client (in writing) that "the settlement won't be taxable to you."

c. In (a) and (b) above, would it matter if the advice were given orally? Why or why not?

PROBLEM 3-26

a. Practitioner advised client prior to the commencement of negotiations for a transaction. Alternative structures were discussed and different assumptions were made regarding future circumstances as a means of determining the strategy for negotiations. After the transaction is completed, the taxpayer checks with the practitioner, by e-mail, to confirm the tax treatment of a particular item associated with the transaction. Is the practitioner's reply, if in writing, subject to the covered opinion rules?

b. Suppose that several years later, the client is notified that the IRS intends to examine its return for the year in which the transaction occurred. The practitioner advises the client in writing about the possible likelihood or grounds for an IRS challenge, and discusses the possible range of settlement outcomes under various dispute resolution alternatives, speculating or opining on the likely outcomes under each alternative. Does the discussion constitute a "covered opinion" or "other written advice"? How can the practitioner answer if the client asks whether she had a reasonable basis for any of the positions?

PROBLEM 3-27

Do the following e-mail communications constitute covered opinions? Why or why not?

a. Lawyer has advised Client, a group of investors, regarding an acquisition of Target, an S corporation organized in Delaware. Client has formed Purchaser, a Delaware corporation, to make the purchase. The purchase is intended to be a "qualified stock purchase" with respect to which a Section 338 election will be made. Client sends an e-mail to Lawyer: "Lawyer — The largest shareholder in Target would like the opportunity (but not the obligation) to invest in Purchaser at some point after Purchaser acquires Target. Will that have any effect on the basis step-up that we are expecting?" Lawyer responds: "As long as he isn't obligated to reinvest, I believe that should be ok, although the answer isn't entirely clear-cut."

b. Client, a U.S. citizen, is an employee of an Italian corporation the stock of which is traded on the New York Stock Exchange. Client e-mails Lawyer: "My employer is offering me the opportunity to purchase stock. However, they are requiring that I contractually agree not to sell the stock for three years. Will I still be entitled to a 15 percent rate on the dividends if I agree to that?" Lawyer: "Yes, I believe that you will still be entitled to the 15 percent rate. To get that rate, the stock must be 'readily tradable' on a U.S. exchange. But, I believe that that requirement applies based on the class of stock that you own, such that individual contractual arrangements with respect to the stock don't matter."

c. Lawyer has been advising Client regarding a divisive tax-free reorganization of one of its businesses. Client's in-house tax counsel sends Lawyer the following e-mail: "Lawyer — I know you said that Parent needs to use 100% of the cash it receives from Subsidiary in the reorganization to pay down third-party debt of Parent under Section 361(b)(3). Parent plans to invest the $1 million it receives from Subsidiary in certificates of deposit, then six months later, pay $1 million to third-party creditors of Parent, but Parent will keep the interest it earns on the $1 million through the certificate of deposit. Ok?" Lawyer responds: "Your proposal probably works. We should talk."

d. Lawyer has been advising Acquiror regarding the negotiation of Acquiror's merger with Target throughout the past three months. The merger is intended to qualify as a reorganization of Target into Acquiror under Section 368(a)(1)(A). Shortly before the merger agreement is to be signed, Acquiror sends an e-mail to Lawyer that states: "Lawyer — Target is skeptical when we say that our proposed consideration of 60% stock/40% cash will satisfy the continuity of interest requirement. Could you confirm that this consideration mix will not pose a continuity problem? I would like to forward your e-mail to Target's CEO." Lawyer quickly responds by email: "As we have discussed many times, the consideration mix will satisfy the continuity of interest requirement."

e. Lawyer has advised Client, a Delaware corporation, for years regarding corporate transactions. Client sends Lawyer the following e-mail: "Lawyer — Quick question, if we own stock in a corporation and a large number of options to purchase stock in that corporation, and the corporation redeems all of our stock (but we still hold the options), is it possible that we would receive dividend treatment on the redemption (qualifying for the dividends received deduction)?" Lawyer responds by e-mail: "Obviously I need more facts to reach a firm conclusion, but generally, when a person owns an option to purchase stock, the tax law treats the person as owning the stock for purposes of testing a redemption. So, in a situation where you owned enough options, you would qualify for dividend treatment (and the dividends received deduction) when the corporation redeems your stock. However, there would be collateral consequences, including possible gain recognition under the extraordinary dividend rules of Section 1059, which we need to discuss."

PROBLEM 3-28

Taxpayer intends to issue a debt instrument that has a variety of equity characteristics. Taxpayer requests that Lawyer provide a formal written opinion that Section 163(l) should not prevent deductibility of interest on the instrument. Lawyer is willing to deliver such opinion. Can she? *Yes if confidence level is more likely than not std.*

Chapter 4

CLIENT CONFIDENTIALITY AND EVIDENTIARY PRIVILEGES

I. INTRODUCTION

Code § 7525 — *Client Confidentiality*

Model Rule 1.6

This chapter addresses the protection of confidential client information under ethical standards and rules of evidence. These two sources of regulation overlap to some degree but they each are designed to protect different categories of client information. It is essential that every attorney and nonattorney "federally authorized tax practitioner" (within the coverage of the Section 7525 privilege) understand how the two kinds of protection differ.

Ethical rules such as Model Rule 1.6 generally preclude a lawyer from disclosing any information relating to the representation of a client without the client's informed consent, except in narrowly drawn circumstances.[1] This protection of client confidential information applies whenever a lawyer is not being compelled to produce evidence for a judicial or other proceeding. It applies to all information relating to the representation, whatever the source, not only to matters communicated by the client to the lawyer. Disclosure of protected information could subject the lawyer to discipline by the state bar of the jurisdiction in which she is admitted or practices; sanctions may include suspension or disbarment.

The rules of evidence generally prohibit compelled disclosure of certain kinds of otherwise relevant, probative evidence in an administrative or a judicial proceeding. The first of these rules, attorney-client privilege, protects the client from having his lawyer compelled to disclose confidential communications between the client and the lawyer. Unlike the class of confidential information protected by Model Rule 1.6, the attorney-client privilege protects only communications between the client and the lawyer, not other information learned by the lawyer in the course of representing a client. The attorney-client privilege is subject to very limited exceptions, although inadvertent disclosure by the client of the information involved could constitute a waiver of the privilege.

Drawing on the attorney-client privilege concept, Congress enacted a limited privilege for communications between a client and a federally authorized tax practitioner. The Section 7525 privilege mimics the attorney-client privilege in that it applies to the same sorts of communications, i.e., communications between a client and a federally authorized tax practitioner, but Section 7525 applies only in very limited circumstances, as discussed below.

---

[1] The AICPA also has a rule, discussed in Section II below, that generally prohibits a CPA from disclosing confidential client information.

The other important rule of evidence that may prevent disclosure of client-related information in a judicial or other proceeding is the work product doctrine, designed to prevent opposing counsel from learning about a lawyer's analysis, theories and thought processes that are developed in anticipation of litigation. While the work product doctrine, like the attorney-client privilege, may be waived by disclosure, even absent waiver, it is only a conditional privilege: If the party seeking disclosure makes a sufficient showing of need for the protected evidence, the court may order disclosure.

In this chapter, we will first take up the ethical rule protecting confidential client communications, initially focusing on what is protected, then discussing the circumstances in which disclosure is nonetheless permitted or even required, with a particular focus on issues that may arise in tax practice. We will then look at the more limited protection afforded information learned from a prospective client who discusses with a lawyer the possibility of engaging the lawyer to handle a matter. Finally, we will explore the contours of the attorney-client privilege, the federally authorized tax practitioner privilege, and the work product doctrine, again with emphasis on particular issues that arise in the tax field.

II. CONFIDENTIALITY UNDER THE ETHICAL RULES

A.   General Rule

Model Rule 1.6 and Comment [4]
AICPA ET § 301.01 (Appendix K)

Model Rule 1.6 generally prohibits the lawyer from disclosing information relating to the representation of the client regardless of whether it was provided to the lawyer in confidence or whether it was provided by the client. Comment [4] notes that the prohibition applies not only to a disclosure of the protected information itself, but also to any disclosure that "could reasonably lead to the discovery of such information by a third person."

AICPA ET § 301 prohibits CPAs from disclosing any confidential client information without the client's specific consent. The rule expressly states that it does not prohibit disclosure to comply with a validly issued and enforceable subpoena or summons. In addition, the AICPA rule may not be construed to relieve a CPA from professional obligations under Rule 201 (ET § 202.01) and Rule 203 (ET § 203.01) (compliance with accounting standards and principles). The client, not the CPA, has ultimate control over the disclosure of confidential information. When a CPA determines, for example, that financial statements have not been prepared in accordance with generally accepted accounting principles (GAAP), the CPA may not disclose that knowledge or any confidential information; she must inform the client that she will have to resign or issue a qualified statement unless the client discloses the information. (Of course, news of withdrawal by an auditor from a major account spreads, cluing in outsiders that there may be a problem.) In the tax context, however, the CPA's relationship with a client is not a public matter, so withdrawal can be a private affair.

PROBLEM 4-1

Holly is a business lawyer who handles tax planning and related transactional matters for both Miracle Ventures, an S Corporation engaged in organizing travel adventures for religious groups, and the sole owner of Miracle Ventures, Penelope. During a recent meeting in which Holly suggested transferring some of the stock of Miracle Ventures to trusts for Penelope's children (who are 9 and 11), Penelope mentioned that she recently met with a divorce lawyer because she is thinking about whether to file for divorce. Holly asked who Penelope had consulted. Penelope said, "Harry Smith in Redwood City. He's supposed to be tough, but sensible and reasonable. I think he gave me some good advice." Holly had never heard of Harry Smith before Penelope mentioned him and has done no follow-up research on Harry.

a. The following week, a business associate of Holly and Penelope, Bill, says to Holly at a cocktail party, "Have you heard that Penelope and Travis (Penelope's husband) are having problems?" What can Holly say in response to this question? *no comment.*

b. Instead, suppose that Bill approaches Holly at the cocktail party and asks if she can recommend a tough but reasonable divorce lawyer. Can Penelope recommend Harry Smith? Assuming that she does recommend Harry, what can Penelope say if Bill asks Penelope what she knows about him? *yes if consulted by Bill. No confidential relationship must speak truth*

PROBLEM 4-2

Jan and Earl are having lunch at the local pub. Myra, a waitress at the pub, knows both of them and knows that Jan is a tax lawyer because she represented her in an audit last year. (Earl is a plumber.) She saunters up to the pair and, after an exchange of greetings, says, "Jan, a couple of the girls said the IRS says we need to report our tips. Is that right?" Jan responds: "Sure is." Myra then asks: "Do they really audit this kind of stuff? I mean, how likely is it that I will get in trouble if I don't report my cash tips?" Jan tells Myra she doesn't know.

a. Can Jan disclose this conversation to anyone? *yes general questions no confidentiality*

b. Assuming Myra says she's going to report her tips, can Jan tell the IRS that the other waitresses are not reporting theirs? *No client, practitioner privilege.*

PROBLEM 4-3

Jose represents the Estate of Flyer, an airline pilot who flew and showed a World War II era fighter plane at air shows for a number of years before the plane crashed with Flyer in it. Flyer won a number of substantial prizes at the air shows and treated his air show activities as a trade or business. The IRS, after audit, denied the related deductions on the ground that the activities did not constitute either a trade or business or a profit-motivated activity, but rather amounted merely to a hobby. In building the case for the Estate, Jose has obtained a number of magazines relating to flying and air shows, some of which include pictures of Flyer and his plane and text about Flyer's flying. All of the magazines include information about the prizes that can be won at air shows. Can Jose let his son Timmy, who builds and flies model airplanes, see the magazines? Can Jose share the magazines with Timmy's teacher, a long-time fan of air shows? *yes, magazines are public matter, publishing. yes.*

PROBLEM 4-4

Michelle is representing Tommy on audit. The IRS has taken the position that a series of trips from New York to Miami were for personal rather than business purposes, noting that most of them occurred between November and May. Tommy provides Michelle with detailed information about business conducted on each trip, including the names of some of his business contacts. In checking on some of the information provided, Michelle inadvertently learns from one of the business contacts that Tommy's significant other lives in Coral Gables, near the University of Miami. Can this information be disclosed to the IRS? If so, under what circumstances? *No, business reason may still be legitimate.*

client confidentiality.

B.   Exception Where Disclosure is Required

Model Rule 3.3
ABA Opinion 314 (in Chapter 1)

Model Rule 3.3(a)(2) requires a lawyer to disclose to "the tribunal legal authority in the controlling jurisdiction known to the lawyer to be directly adverse to the position of the client and not disclosed by opposing counsel." Disclosure is required under Model Rule 3.3 even though the lawyer's duty of confidentiality under Model Rule 1.6 may be breached. The application of this provision in tax practice is not nearly as clear as it might seem, as the problems below indicate.

PROBLEM 4-5

Larry Lawyer is representing Alpha and Beta, the two shareholders of an S corporation, in a case raising questions about the S corporation's gross income, which is allocated 50/50 between the two. The case is now before the Tax Court but, since Alpha and Beta live in different regions, Alpha's case would be appealable to the Ninth Circuit Court of Appeals while Beta's would be appealable to the Second Circuit. Assume that the Ninth Circuit has a rule stating that its unpublished opinions issued prior to January 1, 2007 may not be cited as precedent, but the Second Circuit does not.

a. It so happens that there is a 2005 unpublished Ninth Circuit opinion that is directly adverse to the position of Alpha and Beta that has not been cited or mentioned by IRS counsel. Should Larry disclose this to the court? See ABA Informal Op. 84-1505, suggesting that Model Rule 3.3 (a)(2) would apply even though the decision is not from a court with reviewing authority over the trial court. Is this a fair reading of the rule?

Yes to the 2nd circuit, yes may bring Fin. model rule "tribunal legal authority"!

b. Suppose that there is an unpublished Second Circuit opinion that is directly adverse to the IRS position that has not been cited or mentioned by Larry. Must IRS counsel disclose the opinion to the court? (Presumably, students studying this text have already received training in legal research for tax practitioners. These problems underscore the importance of good and thorough research.)

yes all evidence possibly incriminating opposing party must be disclosed.

PROBLEM 4-6

if not subst. auth yes, yes, yes

Does the disclosure obligation of Model Rule 3.3(a)(2) apply when a tax return is filed? When a lawyer represents a taxpayer on audit? When a lawyer represents a taxpayer before the Appeals division of the IRS? See Model Rule 1.0(m); ABA Opinion 314 (reproduced in Chapter 1). Does it make sense to apply a different rule at an earlier stage of the process of resolving a tax dispute than at a later stage? *Yes as preceding rule has been over-ruled.*

C. Exception Where Disclosure is Permitted but Not Required

Model Rules 1.6(b), Comment [7], and 4.1(b)

Model Rule 1.6(b) spells out several exceptions to the protection of client confidential information in Model Rule 1.6(a). Of particular significance to tax lawyers are Model Rule 1.6(b)(2) and (3). The first permits a lawyer to reveal information relating to the representation of the client "to the extent the lawyer reasonably believes necessary" to "prevent the client from committing a crime or fraud that is reasonably certain to result in substantial injury to the financial interests or property of another [i.e., the IRS] and in furtherance of which the client has used the lawyer's services." The goal here is to allow the lawyer to provide information to enable "affected persons or appropriate authorities to prevent the client from committing a crime or fraud." Model Rule 1.6 Comment [7]. Rule 1.6(b)(3), by contrast, addresses the situation where the lawyer only learns of the client's crime or fraud after the fact, and therefore permits disclosure of information "to the extent the lawyer reasonably believes necessary" to "prevent, mitigate or rectify substantial injury to the financial interests or property of another that is reasonably certain to result or has resulted from the client's commission of a crime or fraud in furtherance of which the client has used the lawyer's services." By their terms, both rules permit disclosure only where the client used or is using the lawyer's services to further the commission of the crime or fraud at issue. Thus, these exceptions do not apply where a lawyer learns of the crime or fraud in a context that is protected from disclosure under Model Rule 1.6(a) and the lawyer's services are not involved.

Model Rule 1.6(b)(2) and (3) do not themselves actually require the lawyer to do anything. However, Model Rule 4.1(b) requires disclosure in situations in which the only way a lawyer can avoid assisting a client's crime or fraud is by disclosing confidential client information. (Ordinarily, a lawyer is able to avoid assisting a client's crime or fraud by quietly withdrawing from the representation.) Model Rule 4.1(b) prohibits a lawyer, in the course of representing a client, from knowingly failing "to disclose a material fact when disclosure is necessary to avoid assisting a criminal or fraudulent act by a client, *unless disclosure is prohibited by Rule 1.6*" (emphasis added). It appears that the effect of Model Rule 1.6(b)(2) in conjunction with Model Rule 4.1(b) is to require disclosure in cases subject to Model Rule 4.1(b) for which Model Rule 1.6(b)(2) permits disclosure. Model Rule 4.1(b), however, has no effect on disclosure under Model Rule 1.6(b)(3) if the crime or fraud has already occurred.

Model Rule 1.6(b)(2) and (3) were added to the Model Rules in 2001. These exceptions to the principle of client confidentiality are among the most controversial of all legal ethics rules. How the issues are treated varies considerably from state to state, from disclosure being mandated in some contexts to disclosure not being permitted at all in the situations addressed by Rule 1.6(b)(2) and (3).[2] Some jurisdictions, in fact, also require the lawyer to attempt either to dissuade the client from committing the crime or fraud or to persuade the client to take corrective action after the fact.[3] The careful lawyer should check what the rules provide in his or her jurisdiction.

PROBLEM 4-7

a. Danny, a tax lawyer, is preparing 2009 federal and state income tax returns for his longtime client, Barbara. He tells her that the $800,000 gain she realized from the sale of her vacation home in Costa Rica must be reported on her tax return. She frowns and asks how likely it is that the IRS will find out about the sale if she leaves the money in a bank in Costa Rica. Danny says he doesn't know. Barbara says leave it off. Danny says he can't do that, so Barbara says she'll do the return herself. Danny withdraws from preparing the return. May Danny disclose to the IRS and the state revenue authorities that Barbara plans to file income tax returns that do not include the gain from the sale of the vacation home? If not, if Barbara tells him a month later that she has filed the returns without reporting the gain, may he then report this to the IRS and state tax authorities? Is he required to do so under the ethics rules?

b. Same as facts as (a), above, except that Danny told Barbara in response to her question that the IRS would probably never find out about the sale if she left the money in Costa Rica.

c. Same facts as (a), above, except that Barbara never told Danny about the sale of the vacation home. He prepared the returns and signed them as preparer. Barbara filed her federal return with the IRS in March 2010, well before the filing deadline. On April 2, 2010, at a cocktail reception at the local art museum, Barbara mentioned that she made "a killing on selling my vacation place in Costa Rica last summer." Danny says, "What?" Barbara says, "Oh, Danny, don't worry about it. The IRS will never know." May Danny disclose the contents of this conversation? Must he disclose this conversation? What else might he think about doing? *See* Model Rule 1.16.

PROBLEM 4-8

You are a member of the bar in a state, such as California,[4] that neither permits nor requires disclosure of information in the circumstances addressed by Model Rule 1.6(b)(2) and (3). You are in house counsel for a publicly traded corporation and have been actively involved in reviewing all of the company's proxy materials and registration statements for its stock. You have now learned for the first time that last year the company invested in a questionable tax shelter in

---

[2] For example, compare New Jersey Rule 1.6(b)(1), which mandates disclosure of information to "proper authorities" to prevent the client from committing a "criminal, illegal or fraudulent" act that the lawyer reasonably believes is likely to result in substantial injury to the financial interests or property of another, with California Rule 3-100, which has no permissive disclosure in the circumstances described in Model Rule 1.6(b)(2) or (3); *see also* Cal. Bus. & Prof. Code § 6068(e).

[3] *See* Okla. Rule 1.6(b)(3); Tex. Rule 1.02(d) and (e).

[4] Cal. Rule 3-600 is the California approach to this problem. Is it satisfactory?

connection with which the company booked a substantial gain for financial reporting purposes, but a sizable loss for tax purposes. You have reason to believe that the company management will not disclose this voluntarily. A regulation of the Securities and Exchange Commission, 17 C.F.R. § 205.3(d)(2), provides that:

> An attorney appearing and practicing before the Commission in the representation of an issuer may reveal to the Commission, without the issuer's consent, confidential information related to the representation to the extent the attorney reasonably believes necessary:
>
> (i)   To prevent the issuer from committing a material violation that is likely to cause substantial injury to the financial interest or property of the issuer or investors;
>
> (ii) To prevent the issuer, in a Commission investigation or administrative proceeding from committing perjury, proscribed in 18 U.S.C. 1621; suborning perjury, proscribed in 18 U.S.C. 1622; or committing any act proscribed in 18 U.S.C. 1001 that is likely to perpetrate a fraud upon the Commission; or
>
> (iii) To rectify the consequences of a material violation by the issuer that caused, or may cause, substantial injury to the financial interest or property of the issuer or investors in the furtherance of which the attorney's services were used.

Can you reveal this information to the SEC? Cf. Model Rule 1.13. If you can, *[handwritten: Yes, consider resigning from Co.]* what considerations would you weigh in deciding whether or not to do so?

D. Prospective Clients

Model Rules 1.18(b) and 1.9(c)

PROBLEM 4-9

You have just had an initial meeting with Possible New Client ("PNC"). PNC is under audit by the IRS with respect to his 2006 income tax return. PNC tells you that some questions have been raised about business travel expenses and other matters. PNC seems nervous. You ask whether PNC has any specific concerns beyond the questioned issues. PNC says: "I did not answer the question about foreign bank accounts accurately because I had $45,000 in interest from foreign accounts that I didn't want to pay tax on. I haven't ever reported interest from my foreign accounts." You and PNC agree that you are not the lawyer PNC needs. You suggest that PNC contact a criminal tax lawyer and you provide him with the names of several skilled attorneys. Can you disclose anything about this conversation to the IRS or to your tennis partner?

[handwritten margin note: COI, may disclose to IRS, not tennis partner.]

III. ATTORNEY-CLIENT AND FEDERALLY AUTHORIZED TAX PRACTITIONER PRIVILEGES

Code §§ 7525 and 6662(d)(2)(C)(ii)

The attorney-client privilege is a rule of evidence that protects communications, but not underlying facts,[5] between a client and her lawyer. The classic formulation of the privilege is set forth in Wigmore on Evidence:

---

[5] *See* Upjohn Co. v. United States, 449 U.S. 383, 395–96 (1981).

(1) Where legal advice of any kind is sought (2) from a professional legal adviser in his capacity as such, (3) the communications relating to that purpose, (4) made in confidence (5) by the client, (6) are at his instance permanently protected (7) from disclosure by himself or by the legal adviser, (8) except the protection be waived.

JOHN HENRY WIGMORE, 8 WIGMORE ON EVIDENCE §2292 (McNaughton rev. 1961).[6] The privilege attaches to confidential communications made by a client to a lawyer and to communications from a lawyer to her client to the extent they reflect the client's confidential communications to her. In the tax field, communications by clients with attorneys often raise questions about whether a communication was really made in confidence, especially where the intention was to have the information reported to the IRS, for example on a tax return, and about whether the attorney was providing legal services or advice (privileged) or accounting services or business advice (not privileged). The cases below illustrate these and other aspects of the attorney-client privilege in a tax practice context, although students should be aware that the case law in this area is neither clear nor consistent.

In response to claims that the attorney-client privilege unreasonably bestowed on lawyers an advantage over other tax professionals, Congress created the federally authorized tax practitioner privilege in 1998. Section 7525 was meant to provide clients of nonlawyers with similar protections to those conferred on clients of lawyers. Leveling the proverbial playing field entirely would have entailed amending the Federal Rules of Evidence, which are outside the jurisdiction of Congress's tax writing committees. Thus, the next best alternative was to grant parity, in privilege terms, to practitioners admitted to practice before the IRS in matters or proceedings before the IRS. (Section 7525 applies also to tax proceedings in federal courts brought by or against the United States.) For policy reasons, Section 7525 does not provide privilege protection in criminal proceedings or with respect to written communications in connection with the promotion of a tax shelter (as defined in Section 6662(d)(2)(C)(ii)).

Because Section 7525 is meant to provide the same protections with respect to "tax advice" as the attorney-client privilege,[7] cases, particularly tax cases, involving the limits of either privilege are carefully monitored by lawyers and nonlawyers alike. The following case, *United States v. Frederick*, underscores two points of importance to all tax professionals. First, communications made by a client to assist her adviser in preparing a return are not privileged, primarily because the client cannot be said to have an expectation of confidentiality where the subject of the communication will be disclosed on her tax return. Second, the case casts doubt on the wisdom, from the perspective of privilege, of an attorney or federally authorized tax practitioner preparing returns or representing clients at audit where other services, such as tax planning, are

---

[6] For a nice summary of the general principles of the attorney-client privilege, see RESTATEMENT OF THE LAW (THIRD): THE LAW GOVERNING LAWYERS §§ 68 to 86 (2000). Fed. R. Evid. 501 has the effect of leaving the attorney-client privilege entirely to case law development.

[7] The federally authorized tax practitioner privilege incorporates all of the limitations applicable to the attorney-client privilege regarding subject matter, potential waiver, the intent that the communication be confidential and the like. For example, the crime-fraud exception to the attorney-client privilege also applies to the tax practitioner privilege. *See* United States v. BDO Seidman, LLP, 2005 U.S. Dist. LEXIS 5555 (N.D. Ill. 2005).

provided to the same client on the same matter. As you will read shortly, in *Frederick*, an attorney-accountant claimed the attorney-client privilege for work papers that he had prepared in the process of preparing tax returns for his individual clients and their closely-held corporation. The court held that the lawyer's "legal cogitations born out of his legal representation of them" that ultimately appeared in the worksheets for preparation of the tax return would not be privileged because of their use in tax return preparation. Under this view, which is probably less sympathetic to the application of attorney-client privilege than the view taken in many circuits, disclosures made by a client during tax planning might lose their privileged status if incorporated in any way into workpapers leading to the preparation of a tax return by the same representative.

UNITED STATES v. FREDERICK
United States Court of Appeals, Seventh Circuit
182 F.3d 496 (1999), *cert. denied*, 582 U.S. 1154 (2000)

POSNER, CHIEF JUDGE.

These appeals challenge an order enforcing summonses that the Internal Revenue Service issued to Richard Frederick. Frederick is both a lawyer and an accountant, and he both provides legal representation to, and prepares the tax returns of, Randolph and Karin Lenz and their company, KCS Industries, Inc. The IRS is investigating the Lenzes and their company, and the summonses directed Frederick to hand over hundreds of documents that may be germane to the investigation. Frederick balked at handing over all of them, claiming that some were protected by either the attorney-client privilege or the work product privilege (or both). His refusal precipitated this enforcement proceeding. 26 U.S.C. § 7604(b). The district judge examined the documents in camera and ruled that some were privileged but others were not. The appeals challenge the latter ruling.

As is generally though not always the case when an appeal challenges the application of a legal rule to the facts (sometimes called a ruling on a "mixed question of fact and law," our review of the judge's ruling on the privilege claims is deferential; we ask not whether the ruling was erroneous but whether it was clearly erroneous. Whether a particular document is privileged is a fact-specific and case-specific issue, the sort of issue that district judges are particularly experienced in resolving. It is not the sort of issue that lends itself to governance by a uniform rule that a court of appeals might prescribe and enforce. In these circumstances, a light appellate touch is best.

* * *

Most of the documents in issue were created in connection with Frederick's preparation of the Lenzes' tax returns. They are drafts of the returns (including schedules), worksheets containing the financial data and computations required to fill in the returns, and correspondence relating to the returns. These are the kinds of document that accountants and other preparers generate as an incident to preparing their clients' returns, or that the taxpayers themselves generate if they prepare their own returns, though in the latter case there is unlikely to be correspondence. The materiality of the documents to the IRS's investigation of the Lenzes is not in issue.

There is no common law accountant's or tax preparer's privilege, and a taxpayer must not be allowed, by hiring a lawyer to do the work that an accountant, or other tax preparer, or the taxpayer himself or herself, normally would do, to obtain greater protection from government investigators than a taxpayer who did not use a lawyer as his tax preparer would be entitled to. To rule otherwise would be to impede tax investigations, reward lawyers for doing non-lawyers' work, and create a privileged position for lawyers in competition with other tax preparers—and to do all this without promoting the legitimate aims of the attorney-client and work product privileges. The attorney-client privilege is intended to encourage people who find themselves involved in actual or potential legal disputes to be candid with any lawyer they retain to advise them. The hope is that this will assist the lawyer in giving the client good advice (which may head off litigation, bring the client's conduct into conformity with law, or dispel legal concerns that are causing the client unnecessary anxiety or inhibiting him from engaging in lawful, socially productive activity) and will also avoid the disruption of the lawyer-client relationship that is brought about when a lawyer is sought to be used as a witness against his client. The work product privilege is intended to prevent a litigant from taking a free ride on the research and thinking of his opponent's lawyer and to avoid the resulting deterrent to a lawyer's committing his thoughts to paper.

Communications from a client that neither reflect the lawyer's thinking nor are made for the purpose of eliciting the lawyer's professional advice or other legal assistance are not privileged. The information that a person furnishes the preparer of his tax return is furnished for the purpose of enabling the preparation of the return, not the preparation of a brief or an opinion letter. Such information therefore is not privileged.

We do not, however, accept the government's argument that there is no issue of privilege here because the information was transmitted to a tax preparer with the expectation of its being relayed to a third party, namely the IRS. It is true that "if the client transmitted the information so that it might be used on the tax return, such a transmission destroys any expectation of confidentiality." *United States v. Lawless,* [709 F. 2d 485, 487 (7th Cir. 1983)]. That is, the transmittal operates as a waiver of the privilege. But the tax preparer here was also the taxpayers' lawyer, and it cannot be assumed that everything transmitted to him by the taxpayer was intended to assist him in his tax-preparation function and thus might be conveyed to the IRS, rather than in his legal-representation function.

We also reject the government's argument that numerical information can never fall within the attorney-client or work product privilege. Such cases are rare, but they can be imagined. Suppose a lawyer prepared an estimate of his client's damages; the estimate would be numerical, but insofar as it reflected the lawyer's professional assessment of what to ask the jury for it would be attorney work product. Similarly, if the lawyer asked his client how much he had obtained in the theft for which he was being prosecuted and the client answered, "$10,000," the answer would be protected by the attorney-client privilege. But we do not agree with the appellants that the district judge based his ruling on the erroneous view that numbers can never be privileged. He found no basis for privileging these numbers, remarking, rightly, "It cannot be argued that numbers in the hands of the accountant are different from numbers in the hands of a lawyer."

Besides the information supplied to Frederick by the Lenzes, there are the worksheets, which Frederick prepared and which doubtless reflect some of his own thinking. But the Supreme Court has held that an accountant's worksheets are not privileged, [*United States v. Arthur Young & Co.*, 465 U.S. 805, 817–19 (1984)], and a lawyer's privilege, as we explained earlier, is no greater when he is doing accountant's work. A complicating factor is that when Frederick was doing these worksheets and filling out the Lenzes' tax returns, he knew that the IRS was investigating the Lenzes and their company, albeit in connection with different tax years, and he was representing them in that investigation. But people who are under investigation and represented by a lawyer have the same duty as anyone else to file tax returns. They should not be permitted, by using a lawyer in lieu of another form of tax preparer, to obtain greater confidentiality than other taxpayers. By using Frederick as their tax preparer, the Lenzes ran the risk that his legal cogitations born out of his legal representation of them would creep into his worksheets and so become discoverable by the government. The Lenzes undoubtedly benefited from having their lawyer do their returns, but they must take the bad with the good; if his legal thinking infects his worksheets, that does not cast the cloak of privilege over the worksheets; they are still accountants' worksheets, unprotected no matter who prepares them.

Put differently, a dual-purpose document — a document prepared for use in preparing tax returns and for use in litigation — is not privileged; otherwise, people in or contemplating litigation would be able to invoke, in effect, an accountant's privilege, provided that they used their lawyer to fill out their tax returns. And likewise if a taxpayer involved in or contemplating litigation sat down with his lawyer (who was also his tax preparer) to discuss both legal strategy and the preparation of his tax returns, and in the course of the discussion bandied about numbers related to both consultations: the taxpayer could not shield these numbers from the Internal Revenue Service. This would be not because they were numbers, but because, being intended (though that was not the only intention) for use in connection with the preparation of tax returns, they were an unprivileged category of numbers.

The most difficult question presented by this appeal, and one on which we cannot find any precedent, relates to documents, numerical and otherwise, prepared in connection with audits of the taxpayers' returns. An example is a memo from Frederick to a paralegal asking her for the amount that Mr. Lenz and his corporation had paid Frederick for legal services rendered personally to Lenz in 1992. The memo was prepared to help Frederick respond to questions raised in an audit of the Lenzes' and the corporation's tax returns. An audit is both a stage in the determination of tax liability, often leading to the submission of revised tax returns, and a possible antechamber to litigation. When a revenue agent is merely verifying the accuracy of a return, often with the assistance of the taxpayer's accountant, this is accountants' work and it remains such even if the person rendering the assistance is a lawyer rather than an accountant. Throwing the cloak of privilege over this type of audit-related work of the taxpayer's representative would create an accountant's privilege usable only by lawyers. If, however, the taxpayer is accompanied to the audit by a lawyer who is there to deal with issues of statutory interpretation or case law that the revenue agent may have raised in connection with his examination of the taxpayer's return, the lawyer is doing lawyer's work and the attorney-client privilege may attach. But the documents in issue do not, so far as we are able to determine, relate to such representation.

We should consider the possible bearing of a new statute, 26 U.S.C. § 7525, which extends the attorney-client privilege to "a federally authorized tax practitioner," that is, a nonlawyer who is nevertheless authorized to practice before the Internal Revenue Service. § 7525(a)(3)(A). Nonlawyers (including tax preparers, many of them accountants) have long been allowed to practice before it. 5 U.S.C. § 500(c); 31 C.F.R. §§ 10.3, 10.7(c)(viii). The new statute protects communications between a taxpayer and a federally authorized tax practitioner "to the extent the communication would be considered a privileged communication if it were between a taxpayer and an attorney." § 7525(a)(1). (It does not protect work product.) Nothing in the new statute suggests that these nonlawyer practitioners are entitled to privilege when they are doing other than lawyers' work; and so the statute would not change our analysis even if it were applicable to this case, which it is not, because it is applicable only to communications made on or after July 22, 1998, the date the statute was enacted . . . .

The discussion in *Frederick* of the distinction between lawyer's work and accountant's work at best reflects an outdated view of the tax practice world. Nonetheless, many courts seem to regard return preparation as accountant's work, with the result that communications to a lawyer in this context are not protected by privilege. *Frederick* is typical of such cases. Other circuits may be more willing to focus on the client's intent, perhaps accepting the view that an intent that a communication be treated as confidential be presumed, absent evidence to the contrary. *See generally* Claudine Pease-Wingerter, *Does Attorney-Client Privilege Apply to Tax Lawyers? An Examination of the Return Preparation Exception to Define the Parameters of Privilege in the Tax Context,* 47 WASHBURN L.J. 699, 721–23 (2008).

PROBLEM 4-10

No, 7525 pertains to tax advice

Are documents prepared by a lawyer or federally authorized tax practitioner in connection with an IRS audit protected by privilege?

What constitutes a "confidential communication" is not at all clear when a client communicates with a transactional tax lawyer prior to consummation of a transaction. The substance of pre-transaction communications does not necessarily end up on a tax return nor are such communications necessarily made with the tax return in mind. Nonetheless, some courts have held that pre-transaction communications are not privileged if the taxpayer expects her participation in the transaction to be disclosed on a tax return or even because the taxpayer could be legally compelled in an audit to disclose her participation! *See, e.g.,* John Doe 1 v. KPMG, 325 F. Supp. 2d 746 (N.D. Tex. 2004). *Long-Term Capital Holdings v. United States,* excerpted below, determined that a written tax opinion, which the taxpayer intended would be disclosed and/or used in the preparation of its tax return, was not protected by the attorney-client privilege. The fact that this opinion was not privileged, however, did not affect the privileged status of a second opinion, rendered by a second law firm, that covered other tax aspects of the same transaction.

LONG-TERM CAPITAL HOLDINGS
v. UNITED STATES
United States District Court, District of Connecticut
2003 U.S. Dist. LEXIS 7826 (2003)

MARGOLIS, UNITED STATES MAGISTRATE JUDGE.

[The procedural history of this decision is convoluted but can be distilled as follows for purposes of the following excerpt. The parties were arguing over the disclosure of an opinion letter rendered by the law firm of "K&S" (the "K&S opinion"). In the text of the K&S opinion, K&S referred to an opinion letter rendered by another law firm, "S&S" (the "S&S opinion" or the "Shearman opinion"). Whereas the K&S opinion opined as to the tax consequences of the rather complicated series of transactions that were the subject of the underlying dispute with the government, the S&S opinion opined merely as to the basis of certain assets acquired through the transactions at issue.[8]

The main issue in the excerpt below is whether the taxpayer was required to disclose the K&S opinion to the government. One legal basis for requiring such disclosure might be that, by sharing the S&S opinion (i.e., a privileged document) with K&S, the taxpayer waived the attorney-client privilege with respect to the S&S opinion and, since the two opinions addressed the same subject, a subject-matter waiver occurred with respect to the K&S opinion, as well. The taxpayer argued, *inter alia*, that the S&S opinion was not protected by the attorney-client privilege in the first instance so that disclosing the S&S opinion to K&S could not have constituted a waiver.]

Petitioners seek reconsideration on the following four grounds: (1) the S&S opinion and the K&S opinion do not address the same subject matter; [and] (2) the S&S opinion is not protected by the attorney client privilege, so that there can be no waiver thereof.

As to Petitioner's [two] legal arguments, Respondent responds that: (1) Petitioners waived attorney-client privilege by disclosing the substance of the K&S opinion; (2) Petitioners waived attorney-client privilege by voluntarily disclosing the S&S opinion and subject matter waiver cannot be avoided because the two documents relate to different aspects of the same legal issue; (3) Petitioners waived attorney-client privilege by placing the legal advice received in issue; and (4) Petitioners' attorney-client privilege and work product privilege were waived with respect to underlying and related documents.

* * *

A. PETITIONER'S MOTION FOR RECONSIDERATION — REEVALUATION IN LIGHT OF IN CAMERA REVIEW

   1. SUBJECT MATTER OF THE S&S OPINION AND THE K&S OPINION

Petitioners assert that this Court's in camera review will reveal that the K&S opinion and the S&S opinion address materially distinct legal and factual issues. According to Petitioners, the S&S opinion was the "means by which the

---

[8] This appears to be the same opinion letter that gave rise to the *Sykes* disciplinary proceeding addressed in Chapter 1. — Eds.

partnerships complied with their regulatory duty to determine the tax basis of contributed property in the hands of a contributing partner," while the K&S opinion is a "separate consideration of the tax consequence of a subsequent transaction involving some of the contributed property," thus not "directly related to" or an "underlying communication" of the S&S opinion. After a careful in camera review of the K&S opinion, this Court finds that in fact, the K&S opinion is separate from the S&S opinion, as the former does state the consideration of possible tax consequences that may have resulted from a subsequent transaction.

2. APPLICABILITY OF THE ATTORNEY-CLIENT PRIVILEGE TO S&S OPINION AND SUBJECT MATTER WAIVER

Petitioners assert that the S&S opinion was not privileged and thus disclosure does not effect a waiver. In its brief, Petitioners listed four reasons why the S&S opinion was not protected by the attorney-client privilege: (1) "there was no indication from Shearman that the tax basis information in the opinion[ ] was being conveyed in confidence"; (2) "the Shearman Opinion [itself], do[es] not, on [its] face assert that [it is] subject to an attorney-client privilege"; (3) the "Shearman Opinion[ ] [was] the source for the tax basis that the accountants for the Partnerships used in preparing their tax returns;" and (4) "while the Shearman Opinion[ ] [was] rendered in connection with an attorney-client relationship, the advice concerned transactions in which the Partnerships did not participate," so that "Shearman did not rely on confidential communications from the Partnerships in rendering its opinion[ ]."

* * *

In their current briefs, Petitioners rely on their third argument asserted in their brief in opposition to Respondent's Motion to Compel, namely that the S&S opinion is not subject to the attorney-client privilege because the "Shearman opinion[] [was] the source for the tax basis that the accountants for the Partnerships used in preparing their tax returns", and offer, for the first time, substantiation for their argument. Petitioners assert that the reason that the S&S opinion was not protected by the attorney-client privilege is that the S&S opinion was the "sole means by which the partnerships determined the tax basis of the contributed property and as such constituted a component of the partnerships' books and records."

Petitioners further contend that "an understanding of tax law is required in order to report any item on a tax return." However, an assertion of that tautology does not end the discussion. The inherent tension in determining whether communications to tax attorneys regarding tax matters are privileged was summarized well by U.S. District Judge Droney last year as follows:

> There can, of course be no question that the giving of tax advice and the preparation of tax returns . . . are basically matters sufficiently within the professional competence of an attorney to make them prima facie subject to the attorney-client privilege. A tax attorney cannot assert a blanket privilege for documents relating to the representation of a client, however, because much of the information transmitted to an attorney by a client is not intended to be confidential, but instead is given for transmittal by the attorney to others, for example, for inclusion

in a tax return. But [when] the tax preparer . . . was also the taxpayers' lawyer, . . . it cannot be assumed that everything transmitted to him by the taxpayer was intended to assist him in his tax-preparation function. . . .

Bria v. United States of America, 2002 U.S. Dist. LEXIS 7306, at 5–6 (D. Conn. March 20, 2002) (multiple citations omitted).

Petitioners argue that the S&S opinion was issued in accordance with the "applicable Federal Treasury regulations [which] provide that 'for purposes of its books and records,' [which must be made] available for inspection by the Internal Revenue Service whenever the contents thereof become material in the administration of any Internal Revenue law, 'or for purposes of furnishing information to a partner, the partnership needs to determine . . . the basis to the partnership of contributed property.'" See 26 C.F.R. § 301.6231(a)(3)-1(c)(2); 26 C.F.R. § 1.6001-1. Thus, according to Petitioners, the opinion is the result of the government's "requirement" that has been "imposed . . . on partnerships to document the means by which they determine the tax basis of contributed property." Accordingly, Petitioners assert that the October Ruling's finding of a waiver of the attorney-client privilege essentially results in a "global[] waiver [of] any claim to the attorney-client privilege" merely because Petitioners complied with the regulatory requirement of determining the tax basis of contributed property.

Having now provided, for the first time, appropriate citations to the Court, Petitioners have demonstrated that the subject matter of the August 1996 S&S opinion complies with regulatory requirements. Although the substance of the opinion includes more than just a conclusion as to the tax basis of particular stock, the August 1996 S&S opinion does analyze the tax basis of a contributing party's property in the hands of the contributor. See 26 U.S.C. § 723. Although at the time Petitioners sought this advice Petitioners did not hold the property whose basis was the subject of the S&S opinion, the opinion was issued on or about the date that Onslow acquired its partnership interest in LTCP by contributing the property at issue in the S&S opinion. Thus, the opinion was used for Petitioners to ascertain, in accordance with 26 U.S.C. §§ 722 & 723 and 26 C.F.R. § 301.6231(a)(3)-(1)(c)(2), the tax basis in the property that was contributed to the partnership. Petitioners could have complied with the regulations by independently ascertaining the tax basis of the stock upon contribution, though because Petitioners were not parties to the transactions that originated the stock, they likely did not possess enough information to do so, or Petitioners could have accepted Onslow's representations as to the basis of the stock. However, Petitioners chose to engage the law firm of Shearman & Sterling to establish the basis of the stock and to document that basis in an opinion that would necessarily be made available to the IRS upon demand should the contents thereof ever become "material in the administration of any internal revenue law." See 26 C.F.R. § 1.600-1.

Therefore, in light of the additional information that was provided in Petitioner's briefs in support of their Motion for Reconsideration, the Magistrate Judge finds, contrary to the October Ruling, that the S&S opinion was not privileged as it was not intended to be kept confidential because it was solicited so that Petitioners would have a record of the tax basis of the stock that Onslow contributed shortly thereafter, a record which would be furnished to the IRS upon demand. See 26 C.F.R. § 1.6001.1.

* * *

[I]n light of the evidence now before the Court, the Court has now found, contrary to the October Ruling, that the S&S opinion was not subject to the attorney-client privilege and thus the privilege was not waived upon disclosure of the opinion. Consequently, the disclosure of the opinion could not effectuate a subject matter waiver.

* * *

3. APPLICABILITY OF THE ADVICE-OF-COUNSEL DEFENSE

[The next part of the opinion addresses the question of whether the taxpayer waived attorney-client privilege with respect to the K&S opinion when it notified the IRS that it intended to rely on an opinion of counsel regarding basis of stock acquired in the transactions, i.e., the S&S opinion. What the court refers to as the "advice-of-counsel defense" is better known among tax practitioners as an example of the "reasonable cause and good faith" exception to the imposition of accuracy related penalties under Code Section 6662 and Code Section 6664, the "reasonable cause" being the reliance on counsel's advice. See Chapter 2.

[The government argued, *inter alia*, that the taxpayer had made a subject matter waiver with respect to both law firm opinions when it referred to only one of them.]

* * *

Whether the advice of counsel defense may be asserted in this proceeding and what defenses Petitioners may assert are not issues pending before the Court at this time. Rather, the issue is whether Petitioners have asserted good-faith reliance upon the legal advice given in the K&S opinion. Petitioners' memorandum, dated January 26, 2000, represented that the partnerships had acted with "reasonable cause and good faith" based upon the partnerships "good faith reliance on the opinions of reputable and well-informed outside tax counsel as to the basis of the Stock." This disclosure of the advice-of-counsel defense referred to the S&S opinion, which the Court now has concluded is not privileged. After reviewing the K&S opinion in camera, no subject matter waiver is found, as the subject matter of the K&S opinion differs from that of the S&S opinion. Additionally, although Petitioners have relied on the legal advice it received from S&S and have asserted the defense relating to this opinion, the S&S opinion was not protected by the attorney-client privilege, and a broad waiver of the privilege cannot therefore exist, let alone extend to the K&S opinion.

In house counsel are, and should be, treated the same as outside counsel for purposes of determining whether privilege applies. (The client is the attorney's employer or a related corporation.) However, especially when an attorney is a member of a department other than the general counsel's office, which is typical in the case of tax lawyers, who rarely report to the general counsel, it may be difficult to convince a court that communications were privileged because the court might presume that advice given outside of the general counsel's office is business advice (not privileged) rather than legal advice (privileged).

As is reflected in the *Boca Investerings* opinion that follows, the taxpayer must make a clear showing that in house counsel's advice was given in a professional legal capacity. It is advisable, therefore, that written communications from in house counsel be clearly marked "privileged and confidential" and that attorneys in departments other than the general counsel's office use titles indicating their legal capacity, e.g., "Tax Counsel."

BOCA INVESTERINGS PARTNERSHIP v. UNITED STATES
United States District Court, District of D.C.
31 F. Supp. 2d 9 (1998)

FRIEDMAN, UNITED STATES DISTRICT JUDGE.

In a Memorandum Opinion and Order entered on June 9, 1998, Magistrate Judge Facciola considered plaintiffs' claim of attorney-client privilege with respect to eleven documents and defendant's motion to compel production of those documents. He granted the motion in part and denied it in part, requiring that Document Nos. 1, 3, 4, 7, 8, 9 and 10 be produced in their entirety and that Document Nos. 2, 5 and 11 be produced in redacted form; he concluded that Document No. 6 was privileged and need not be produced at all. . . . The matter is now before this Court on defendant's motion for reconsideration of the Magistrate Judge's rulings. Specifically, defendant seeks those portions of Document Nos. 5 and 11 that were redacted by the Magistrate Judge and production of Document No. 6 in its entirety.

* * *

Having carefully reviewed Magistrate Judge Facciola's opinion and orders, the Court cannot conclude that his determinations with respect to the applicability of the attorney-client privilege to the redacted portions of Document Nos. 5 and 11 and the entirety of Document No. 6 are either clearly erroneous or contrary to law.

The author of Document No. 5 is Thomas M. Nee, whom plaintiffs identify as "Vice President for Taxes for AHP." Mr. Nee is a lawyer (although not a member of the New York Bar) who does not work in the Legal Department or for the General Counsel of AHP but rather for the Tax Department, a corporate component within AHP's Financial Group. The defendant argues that because Mr. Nee's position was not organizationally within AHP's Legal Department, because he was not under the direction and control of the General Counsel, and because he was not a member of the bar of the jurisdiction in which he was purporting to practice law, he may not invoke the attorney-client privilege. All of these factors, defendant suggests, indicate that Mr. Nee was not engaged in the practice of law or in providing legal advice but, rather, that he was providing some sort of business advice. Since the burden of demonstrating the right to protect material as privileged rests with the party asserting the privilege, the defendant concludes that Magistrate Judge Facciola was wrong not to require disclosure of Document No. 5 in its entirety.

Communications made by and to in-house lawyers in connection with representatives of the corporation seeking and obtaining legal advice may be protected by the attorney-client privilege just as much as communications with outside counsel. By contrast, communications made by and to the same in-house lawyer with respect to business matters, management decisions or business advice are not protected by the privilege. "The possession of a law degree and admission to the bar is [sic] not enough to establish a person as an attorney for purposes of determining whether the attorney-client privilege applies. . . . the lawyer must not only be functioning as an advisor, but the advice given must be predominately legal, as opposed to business, in nature." North Am. Mortgage Investors v. First Wisconsin Nat'l Bank, 69 F.R.D. 9, 11 (E.D. Wisc. 1975). When a lawyer acts merely to implement a business transaction or provides accounting services, the lawyer is like any other agent of the corporation whose communications are not privileged.

A corporation can protect material as privileged only upon a "clear showing" that the lawyer acted "in a professional legal capacity." Because an in-house lawyer often has other functions in addition to providing legal advice, the lawyer's role on a particular occasion will not be self-evident as it usually is in the case of outside counsel. A court must examine the circumstances to determine whether the lawyer was acting as a lawyer rather than as business advisor or management decision-maker. One important indicator of whether a lawyer is involved in giving legal advice or in some other activity is his or her place on the corporation's organizational chart. There is a presumption that a lawyer in the legal department or working for the general counsel is most often giving legal advice, while the opposite presumption applies to a lawyer such as Mr. Nee who works for the Financial Group or some other seemingly management or business side of the house. A lawyer's place on the organizational chart is not always dispositive, and the relevant presumption therefore may be rebutted by the party asserting the privilege.

At his deposition, Mr. Nee described his responsibilities as follows:

> I was responsible for the corporation's worldwide tax matters, which included providing tax counsel on all transactions the company might enter into; as well as responsibility for filing all the corporation's tax returns both in the United States — federal, state and local returns — as well as making sure that the laws of all the foreign countries we operated in were adhered to from a tax standpoint, and that the proper filings would be made; handling all of the company's tax audits; possible litigation that might come up on tax issues, whether they be state or federal or foreign.

With respect to Document No. 5, the memorandum in question, Mr. Nee testified that "the purpose of the memorandum was to give tax advice to American Home Products Corporation.. . . They requested that I advise them on the tax consequences of entering the Investerings Partnership." Finally, in response to the question whether "any business justifications, aside from tax considerations" were contained in the memorandum, Mr. Nee testified that the memorandum dealt "exclusively with giving tax advice with respect to financial transactions.. . . Business justifications were not set out.. . . The memorandum does not discuss motivation. It gives tax advice on the consequences of certain transactions."

While preparation of tax returns and handling tax audits are functions that may or may not be performed by a lawyer and memoranda and conversations in connection therewith generally should not be considered privileged, Mr. Nee gave "tax advice with respect to [the] financial transactions discussed in the memorandum" and "on the consequences of certain transactions." Magistrate Judge Facciola distinguished portions of the memorandum relating to such advice from other portions of the memorandum that "do not discuss the transaction as contemplated . . . [but instead] communicate either the lawyer's opinion as to the technical soundness of the contemplated transactions and information for a third party, Merrill Lynch." He found the former privileged and therefore protected, and he required production of the latter. This Court cannot say that Magistrate Judge Facciola's opinion on this score is either clearly erroneous or contrary to law.

Document No. 6, which Magistrate Judge Facciola found privileged in its entirety, is a memorandum prepared by two lawyers from the law firm of Lee Toomey & Kent and sent to Thomas Nee. Defendant concedes that if the confidential factual information contained in the memorandum was received by the law firm from American Home Products it is privileged. Defendant argues, however, that plaintiffs do not state this as a fact and Magistrate Judge Facciola did not so find. In fact, American Home Products did state in its brief to the Magistrate Judge, "So there can be no confusion . . . AHP hereby asserts that the factual information contained in the Lee Toomey memorandum was provided to AHP's outside tax lawyers by AHP." Against this background, Magistrate Judge Facciola reviewed Document No. 6 *in camera* and determined that because the document consisted of communications concerning "the transactions as contemplated by AHP and its lawyers" the document was privileged. The Court cannot find that this determination is clearly erroneous.

Finally, with respect to Document No. 11, an opinion letter prepared by Lee Toomey & Kent, Magistrate Judge Facciola, having reviewed the document *in camera,* found it to be a formal opinion letter as to the tax consequences of the transaction. He redacted portions of the opinion that disclosed the transaction as contemplated but made available to the defendant information that is publicly known, the attorney's opinion as to such information and any and all references to already completed financial transactions. He directed that Document No. 11 be produced in redacted form. Again, this Court cannot say that the Magistrate Judge's decision was erroneous or contrary to law. Accordingly, it is hereby ORDERED that the defendant's motion for reconsideration of Magistrate Judge Facciola's ruling on the attorney-client privilege claims is DENIED.

PROBLEM 4-11

Revisit Problems 4-1 through 4-4. To what extent would the facts involved in each situation, or the magazines in Problem 4-3, be protected from compelled disclosure by the attorney-client privilege? Would the actual conversations in Problems 4-1 and 4-2 be protected from disclosure by the attorney-client privilege?

PROBLEM 4-12

Taxpayer received a substantial authority opinion from Lawyer that the sale of certain patent rights for $400,000 was reportable on his 2009 tax return as a capital gain. The position was not with respect to an item attributable to a tax shelter. During audit, it becomes clear that the Revenue Agent believes that the gain should have been reported as ordinary income and that the Agent is considering assessing a substantial understatement penalty. What should the Taxpayer do vis-à-vis the opinion letter that she has received? Does the Revenue Agent have the right to demand that Taxpayer turn over any written opinion that she might have received? If the Taxpayer announces her intention to offer a reasonable cause and good faith defense, has she waived the privilege, even if she never specifically mentions the existence of a written opinion?

[handwritten left margin: should seek counsel. No, protected under 7525. No, b/c legal advice is not a concern this is just business advice.]

PROBLEM 4-13

Largeco is a public traded corporation whose books are audited annually as required by federal securities laws. During an annual financial audit by Big Four Accounting Firm, the engagement team obtained a memo prepared in house at Largeco regarding a potential contingent liability. The memo, which documented the company's conclusions regarding the loss contingency, indicated that Largeco's conclusion that an accrual was not required was based on the written advice of counsel. Big Four has asked Largeco for a copy of counsel's advice, which it intends to file in its workpapers. Would you advise Largeco to turn over the written advice? What do you suppose would be the consequences to Largeco if it refused to turn over the advice?

[handwritten left margin: Auditor cannot give an unqualified opinion. Once turned over confidentiality waived. IRS still cannot access work product doctrine. Memo Drafted in anticipation of litigation. May prevail under other authority.]

By its very terms, Section 7525 provides "the same common law protections of confidentiality" with respect to "tax advice" as the attorney-client privilege. Two significant shortcomings of Section 7525 are highlighted in the following case. First, while there are cases denying privilege where a lawyer provides nonlegal advice, e.g., business advice, the circumstances under which the Section 7525 privilege will not apply because the services are not legal are likely to be more frequent since nonlawyers, of course, generally (1) provide many services that are not legal services and (2) do not, except within limits, generally provide legal services.

Second, Section 7525 protection does not apply to any written communication between a Section 7525 practicer and any person, any representative of such person or anyone holding a capital or profits interest in such person "in connection with the promotion of the direct or indirect participation of that person in any tax shelter as defined in Section 6662(d)(2)(C)(ii)." A tax shelter is defined in Section 6662(d)(2)(C)(ii) as a partnership or other entity, any investment plan or arrangement, or any other plan or arrangement, "if a significant purpose of such partnership, entity, plan, or arrangement is the avoidance or evasion of Federal income tax." The term "significant purpose" is not defined in Section 6662 or regulations. As the *Valero Energy* opinion below suggests, it may be difficult to conclude that any more-or-less routine transaction (e.g., a corporate acquisition) *does not* have such a "significant purpose" if tax consequences were considered and tax advice was sought in making structuring decisions. Therefore, many practitioners and commentators have focused on the word "promotion" in Section 7525 arguing that the exception to privilege should be applied narrowly to communications in the context of marketing investments in tax-motivated transactions. The court in *Valero Energy* rejected that argument.

VALERO ENERGY CORP. v. UNITED STATES

United States Court of Appeals, Seventh Circuit

569 F.3d 626 (2009)

EVANS, CIRCUIT JUDGE.

In this appeal, Valero Energy Corporation asks us to take a close look at the tax practitioner-client privilege. Valero sought to protect several documents under this privilege, and the result was a mixed bag — some documents were shielded from the Internal Revenue Service, while others were not. Valero now contends that by reaching this decision, the district court misconstrued not only the privilege, but also an exception to the privilege, which grants the government access to certain documents when tax shelters are promoted.

Valero is a large company involved in crude oil refining (it's the largest refiner in the United States according to its Web site) and oil-product marketing. The Texas-based giant got even bigger in December 2001, when it acquired Ultramar Diamond Shamrock Corporation (UDS), an oil company with Canadian subsidiaries. This acquisition not only expanded Valero's reach northward, it also resulted in some pretty hefty tax savings. Before the deal took place, UDS consulted with Ernst & Young about restructuring and refinancing its Canadian operations. Valero, in turn, called on its long-time advisors at Arthur Anderson to review Ernst & Young's plan and provide further tax advice. At this time, the Canadian currency was in a slump vis-à-vis the United States dollar, and Valero took advantage. In 2002, shortly after the acquisition was completed, Valero realized $105 million in tax-deductible foreign currency losses (under 26 U.S.C. §§ 987, 988) through a complicated series of transactions implemented with Arthur Anderson's help. The transactions included the creation of spinoff entities, several same-day wire transfers of cash, a large distribution from one of the Canadian subsidiaries to a United-States-based parent, reclassification of a separate foreign subsidiary as a branch of Valero for tax purposes, and the extinguishment of debt.

This loss was big enough to catch the government's eye, and the IRS began investigating. The IRS eventually issued a summons to Arthur Andersen, seeking all documents related to

> tax planning, tax research, or tax analysis, by or for, Ultramar Diamond Shamrock (including any of its subsidiaries or partnerships, both domestic and foreign) and Valero Energy Corporation (including any of its subsidiaries or partnerships, both domestic and foreign) in connection with their 2001, 2002 and 2003 Canadian and U.S. income taxes.…

Valero, as a third party, asked the district court to quash the summons. See 26 U.S.C. § 7609(b). It argued that the summons was overbroad and that many documents were protected by either the work product doctrine or the tax practitioner-client privilege. The privilege shields communications between a federally authorized tax practitioner and her client "to the extent the communication would be considered a privileged communication if it were between a taxpayer and an attorney." 26 U.S.C. § 7525(a)(1). The government countered by arguing that the scope of the summons was appropriate and that even if the tax practitioner-client privilege applied, the documents were discoverable since they were made in connection with the promotion of a tax shelter, a statutory exception to the privilege. Id. at § 7525(b).

* * *

We begin by noting that there is no general accountant-client privilege. *United States v. Frederick*, 182 F.3d 496, 500 (7th Cir. 1999). In 1998, Congress provided a limited shield of confidentiality between a federally authorized tax practitioner and her client. This privilege is no broader than the existing attorney-client privilege. It merely extends the veil of confidentiality to federally authorized tax practitioners who have long been able to practice before the IRS, see 5 U.S.C. § 500(c); 31 C.F.R. § 10.3, to the same extent communications would be privileged if they were between a taxpayer and an attorney. 26 U.S.C. § 7525(a)(1) (privilege does not apply in criminal proceedings). Nothing in the statute "suggests that these nonlawyer practitioners are entitled to privilege when they are doing other than lawyers' work. . . ." *Frederick*, 182 F.3d at 502; *see also United States v. BDO Seidman*, 337 F.3d 802, 810 (7th Cir. 2003) (BDO II). Accounting advice, even if given by an attorney, is not privileged.

This means that the success of a claim of privilege depends on whether the advice given was general accounting advice or legal advice. Admittedly, the line between a lawyer's work and that of an accountant can be blurry, especially when it involves a large corporation like Valero seeking advice from a broad-based accounting firm like Arthur Anderson. But we have set some guideposts to help distinguish between the two. For starters, the preparation of tax returns is an accounting, not a legal service, therefore information transmitted so that it might be used on a tax return is not privileged. On the other side of the spectrum, communications about legal questions raised in litigation (or in anticipation of litigation) are privileged. Of course, there is a grey area between these two extremes, but to the extent documents are used for both preparing tax returns and litigation, they are not protected from the government's grasp. *Frederick*, 182 F.3d at 501. This circumscribed reading of the tax practitioner-client privilege is in sync with our general take on privileges, which we construe narrowly because they are in derogation of the search for truth.

On top of that, our review of the district court's ruling is deferential, and we will reverse only if it is clearly erroneous. Findings regarding privilege are fact-intensive, case-specific questions that fall within the district court's expertise, and, under these circumstances, "a light appellate touch is best." And as is the case with any privilege, the one seeking its protection must carry the burden of showing that it applies. The narrowness of the tax practitioner-client privilege, our deferential standard of review, and the allocation of the burden of proof all pose high hurdles for Valero. Obstacles, as it turns out, Valero is unable to overcome.

Valero's contention that the documents consist of federal tax advice misses the mark. As we've noted, there is no general privilege between a federal tax practitioner and her client — it's not enough that the communications raised federal tax topics. Many of these documents consist of worksheets containing financial data and estimates of tax liability, while others discuss deductions and the calculations of gains and losses. These documents contain the type of information generally gathered to facilitate the filing of a tax return, and such accounting advice is not covered by the privilege, whether or not the information made it on the tax returns filed by Valero. Still other documents raise issues about Valero's inventory methods, compensation packages, or general structure, and analyze how they affect tax computations. While these documents contain some legal analysis, it comes part and parcel with accounting advice, and is therefore also open to the government. Simply asserting that the documents discuss federal tax issues does not convince us that the district court clearly erred in finding them discoverable.

* * *

The more interesting question raised by this appeal concerns an exception to the tax practitioner-client privilege. As we've noted, Valero's claim of privilege wasn't a complete bust. The district court agreed that Valero met its initial burden as to some of the documents but ordered a subset to be released after it concluded that they fell into a statutory exception to the privilege. The privilege does not cover any written communications with a corporate representative or agent "in connection with the promotion of the direct or indirect participation of the person in any tax shelter. . . ." *Id.* at § 7525(b)(2) (emphasis added). Valero disputes the court's finding by attacking its interpretation of the statutory exception. Few courts have examined this exception and none have squarely addressed the question that Valero raises here: namely, what exactly does it mean to promote a tax shelter?

[handwritten margin note: "Promotion" usually more than 1.]

The parties have plucked two different definitions of promotion out of the dictionary. Valero, seeking to narrow the application of the tax shelter exception, contends that promotion means the "active furtherance of sale of merchandise through advertising or other publicity." Valero takes it a step further and urges us to consider the tax practitioner's merchandise to be prepackaged, tax-shelter products. Since Arthur Anderson provided Valero with an individualized tax reduction plan, not a one-size-fits-all scheme, Valero contends that the documents are beyond the government's reach. The government, unsurprisingly, reads promotion more expansively to mean "furtherance" or "encouragement" and asks us to affirm the district court's decision to release the documents under the tax-shelter exception.

A statute is not ambiguous simply because one of its words is susceptible to two meanings. When interpreting a statute we must read it as a whole, as opposed to looking at single words in isolation, and doing so here goes a long way to resolving this controversy. Valero's reading of the statute creates an unnecessary conflict. While Congress left promotion up to judicial interpretation, it took care to define tax shelter by explicit reference to another section of the tax code. For purposes of the exception, a tax shelter is "(I) a partnership or other entity, (II) any investment plan or arrangement, or (III) any other plan or arrangement, if a significant purpose of such partnership, entity, plan, or arrangement is the avoidance or evasion of Federal income tax." 26 U.S.C. § 6662(d)(2)(C)(ii). Nothing in this definition limits tax shelters to cookie-cutter products peddled by shady practitioners or distinguishes tax shelters from individualized tax advice. Instead, the language is broad and encompasses any plan or arrangement whose significant purpose is to avoid or evade federal taxes. By advocating such a narrow definition of promotion, Valero is, through the back door, proposing a definition of tax shelters at odds with the text of the statute. We decline to read such a contradiction into the statute. This definition of tax shelter is broad and could, as Valero points out, include some legitimate attempts by a company to reduce its tax burden. But it is not our place to tinker with the unambiguous definition provided by Congress. And even under this definition, tax shelters are not boundless. Only plans and arrangements with a significant — as opposed to an ancillary — goal of avoiding or evading taxes count. *focus is tax reduction driven w/o a good business deal.*

But Valero goes further and argues that accepting the definition of promotion put forth by the district court would effectively read the word out of the statute by granting the government access to any documents connected to a tax shelter. And if that's the case, Valero urges, the exception will swallow the privilege. We disagree. Promotion, even under the broader reading, limits the exception to written communications encouraging participation in a tax shelter, rather than documents that merely inform a company about such schemes, assess such plans in a neutral fashion, or evaluate the soft spots in tax shelters that a company has used in the past. In fact, the district court's ruling here belies Valero's alarmist argument. Even operating under a broad definition of promotion, the court sustained some of Valero's claims of privilege. The district court's understanding of promotion does place limits on the exception, just not the limits that Valero wants.

This same observation also undermines Valero's reliance on *United States v. Textron Inc. and Subsidiaries*, 507 F. Supp. 2d 138 (D. R.I. 2007). The *Textron* court is among the few to have examined the scope of the tax-shelter exception, and thus, even though *Textron* is not binding authority, it deserves a close look. In that case, the IRS sought tax accrual work papers prepared by Textron's in-house accountants and lawyers. Those papers identified items on tax returns susceptible to challenge by the IRS and estimated, in percentage terms, Textron's chances of prevailing in any litigation over those issues. Textron refused to release the work papers, arguing that they were protected by the tax practitioner-client privilege (among others). The government countered by contending that the work papers were fair game under the tax-shelter exception. The district court, however, disagreed with the government, reasoning that the work papers reflected opinions "regarding the foreseeable tax consequences of transactions that, already, had taken place, not future transactions they were seeking to promote." *Id.* at 148.[9] *Textron* thus stands for the rather uncontroversial principle that you can't promote participation in something once the deed is already done. While the court did mention that the Textron accountants were not "peddlers of corporate tax shelters," id., that dicta does Valero little good since there is a fundamental difference between the documents Textron sought to shield from the government and those that Valero seeks to protect. Valero's documents concern the structure of (what was then) future transactions, not those that have already taken place.

* * *

Perhaps anticipating this conclusion, Valero turns to the legislative history of the tax-shelter exception to bolster its argument. For starters, since the

---

[9] [1] The district court went on to find that Textron waived the privilege by releasing the work papers to its outside accountants, and the First Circuit reviewed the case without discussing the tax practitioner-client privilege. *United States v. Textron Inc. and Subsidiaries*, 553 F.3d 87 (1st Cir. 2009) (addressing claims regarding work product doctrine). The First Circuit has since vacated this decision and will rehear the case en banc. *United States v. Textron*, 560 F.3d 513 (1st Cir. 2009). [The *en banc* opinion in *Textron* is reproduced *infra*. — Eds.]

statute is unambiguous we need not turn to the legislative history to interpret its meaning. But even if we were to consider it, it would do little to support Valero's position. The strongest endorsement for Valero's argument comes from Senator Connie Mack, who stated during a conference committee that the exception should be "narrow" and target "written promotional and solicitation materials used by the peddlers of corporate tax shelters." 144 Cong. Rec. S7667 (1998). But the view of one senator cannot trump the unambiguous statutory text. . . . Valero also points to Senator Daniel Moynihan's comments expressing dismay at the confusion that would, in his view, arise from the privilege and its exception. Senator Moynihan thought that the privilege would be "a right that most taxpayers will never be eligible to assert, and many will be surprised to learn about [its] limitations." 144 Cong. Rec. S7621 (1998). Senator Moynihan, although implying support for a broader privilege, highlighted the narrowness of the privilege as written in the statute. His statement does Valero more harm than good.

Finally, Valero points to the conference report which clarifies that "the promotion of tax shelters [is not a] part of the routine relationship between a tax practitioner and a client," and should not "adversely affect such routine relationships." H.R. Rep. No. 105-199 at 269 (1998). A conference report, unlike the words of a single senator, is often a good record of Congress's intent . . . but the report does not go nearly as far as Valero contends. The report does nothing to confine the exception to actively marketed tax shelters or prepackaged products. In fact, in the same paragraph relied upon by Valero, the report reiterates the breadth of the definition of tax shelters to include "any partnership, entity, plan, or arrangement a significant purpose of which is the avoidance or evasion of income tax." H.R. Rep. No. 105-599 (1998).

We close by noting what this opinion does not do. At this early stage, we are *IRS prevails* not evaluating the propriety of Valero's tax-reduction plan. The IRS only wants access to documents, it is not (in this appeal) asking Valero to pay anything. It is not pointing any fingers. The government's burden to overcome the privilege is relatively light — it need only show that there is some foundation in fact that a particular document falls within the tax-shelter exception. We affirm the district court's holding that the IRS has met this burden and leave for another day any other issues which may percolate out of this squabble between Valero and the government.

PROBLEM 4-14

Congress no longer permits patents of tax shelters

a. Can the IRS require that a lawyer who holds a patent on an income tax *clients buying* planning strategy reveal the names of all persons who have contacted *shelters is business* the lawyer about the strategy? *Business not legal advice* *not client list buying* *patent not privilege*

b. Can the IRS require that the lawyer reveal whether each such person or, in the case of a person who requested information on behalf of an entity, *if known to the* such entity, actually implemented the strategy? *See* United States *atty yes.* v. BDO Seidman, LLP, 337 F.3d 802 (7th Cir. 2003), *cert denied*, 540 U.S. 1178 (2004). (because participation in potentially abusive tax shelters is information ordinarily subject to full disclosure under federal tax law, participants had no expectation of confidentiality about being identified as participants in tax shelters otherwise subject to list maintenance and registration requirements); *cf*. Vingelli v. United States, 992 F.2d 449, 452 *[handwritten top margin:]* "Listed transaction" provider is supposed to maintain a list.

[handwritten left margin:] Lawyer could invoke atty client privelege if not a listed transaction. also if not 7525 could be employed b/c whether or not a taxshelter has not been determined.

(2d Cir. 1993) ("in the absence of special circumstances client identity and fee arrangements do not fall within the attorney-client privilege because they are not the kinds of disclosures that would not have been made absent the privilege and their disclosure does not incapacitate the attorney from rendering legal advice"). Does it matter, as to any person who requested information, whether the holder/lawyer actually served as the taxpayer's lawyer in implementing the strategy or simply licensed the patent to the taxpayer or the taxpayer's lawyer or CPA?

[handwritten left margin:] "exception" 7525 does not extend to estate planning only income tax planning. Thus tax shelters are protected in estate planning but not in income tax.

c. Same facts as (a) and (b), above, except that the holder of the patent is a federally authorized tax practitioner under IRC Section 7525, but not a lawyer.

d. Same facts as (c), above, except that the patented strategy involves estate planning.

PROBLEM 4-15

Bob and Linda filed joint federal and state income tax returns for 2008. A year later, Bob filed for divorce. During the divorce process, their 2008 federal tax return was audited. Bob had received $200,000 from the sale of some patent rights in 2008. At the time, he sought advice from CPA, who advised him in writing that there was a reasonable basis for treating the $200,000 as a capital gain, but that he should disclose the position on his return to avoid incurring a penalty. CPA also prepared a document showing the difference in overall tax that would result from treating the sale proceeds as a capital gain rather than as ordinary income. Bob did not discuss the advice or the comparison with Linda, and reported the $200,000 as a capital gain without disclosure.

[handwritten left margin:] NPPs in prep of tax return are not protected. Just legal advise + should be priviledged.

a. The IRS requested any documents related to the 2008 joint income tax return. Bob acknowledged the existence of CPA's opinion and the comparison document but refused to provide them. If the IRS issues a summons for production of the documents, can they be withheld as privileged from disclosure under Section 7525?

[handwritten left margin:] -privelidge waived if disclosed to a 3rd party.

b. If the CPA's opinion is disclosed to Linda and her lawyer in the divorce proceeding, is it still privileged from disclosure in response to an IRS summons under Section 7525?

[handwritten left margin:] No state issue. Voluntarily or involuntarily once waived remains waived IRS can request this.

c. If the state revenue agency by summons requests any documents related to the 2008 state joint income tax return, can CPA's opinion be withheld on the authority of Section 7525? If Bob complies with the state revenue agency's summons, is CPA's opinion privileged from disclosure to the IRS? If the state revenue agency receives the documents and then sends copies of the opinion to the IRS, can the IRS look at the opinion?

d. To test your recollections from Chapter 3: Can the same attorney represent both Bob and Linda when their 2008 federal income tax returns are audited? Why or why not? *[handwritten:]* NO COI

PROBLEM 4-16

The IRS will sometimes request a copy of the engagement letter and/or fee agreement between a Circular 230 practitioner and the practitioner's client, perhaps to determine the intended use of money deposited with the practitioner

or to determine if there is something improper about the engagement. When a
practitioner receives such a request, how should she respond? *See* Circular 230,
§ 10.20. Under what circumstances could an engagement letter or fee agreement be privileged? Might it matter whether the practitioner is a lawyer?

[handwritten margin note: Only if tailored + gave legal advice otherwise must be furnished.]

IV. WORK PRODUCT DOCTRINE

   Simply stated, the work product doctrine protects from discovery documents
prepared in anticipation of litigation. The doctrine derives from a decision by
the United States Supreme Court, *Hickman, v. Taylor*, 329 U.S. 495 (1947),
which granted to the work product of an attorney a qualified immunity from
discovery in judicial proceedings. The *Hickman* rule is codified in Federal Rule
of Civil Procedure 26(b)(3). This protection applies to written statements, private memoranda and personal recollections, prepared or formed by an adverse
party's counsel in the course of his legal duties, which are not protected by the
attorney-client privilege. The work product doctrine is intended to prevent a
litigant from having free access to the reasoning and thinking of his opponent's
lawyer and, thus, to avoid deterring a lawyer from committing her thoughts to
paper. Litigation need not have commenced, or even be imminent, for the doctrine to apply. Rather, litigation or administrative adversarial proceedings
must only be a real possibility at the time the documents at issue are
prepared.

   Unlike the attorney-client privilege, the work product privilege is a qualified
privilege, meaning that it can be overcome by a showing of substantial need by
the party seeking to overcome the privilege. When opinion work product, consisting of an attorney's mental impressions, conclusions, opinions, or legal theories, is involved, the burden of establishing substantial need is greater than it
is with respect to facts or documents that are merely obtained by the party who
possesses them.

   The work product doctrine protects items that are not protected by the
attorney-client privilege in the first instance and items with respect to which
the attorney-client privilege has been waived. Thus, the *Long-Term Capital*
court held[10] that the taxpayer's disclosure to its tax accountant of the gist of a
written tax opinion received from a law firm (which waived the attorney-client
privilege with respect to the opinion) did not waive the work product protection afforded to the opinion. Because the opinion contained mental impressions, conclusions, opinions and legal theories concerning the litigation, work
product protection applied as to the entire opinion, barring the IRS from
examining any of it.

   The work product doctrine is a headline issue at the moment, as the question of whether tax accrual workpapers are protected wends its way through
the courts. This issue will be discussed after the following case, which raises
many of the same issues.

---

[10] The portion of the opinion excerpted earlier in this chapter does not include the court's discussion of the work product doctrine. Interested students should read the full opinion.

UNITED STATES v. ADLMAN
United States Court of Appeals, Second Circuit
134 F.3d 1194 (1998)

LEVAL, CIRCUIT JUDGE.

This appeal concerns the proper interpretation of Federal Rule of Civil Procedure 26(b)(3) ("the Rule"), which grants limited protection against discovery to documents and materials prepared "in anticipation of litigation."[11] Specifically, we must address whether a study prepared for an attorney assessing the likely result of an expected litigation is ineligible for protection under the Rule if the primary or ultimate purpose of making the study was to assess the desirability of a business transaction, which, if undertaken, would give rise to the litigation. We hold that a document created because of anticipated litigation, which tends to reveal mental impressions, conclusions, opinions or theories concerning the litigation, does not lose work product protection merely because it is intended to assist in the making of a business decision influenced by the likely outcome of the anticipated litigation. Where a document was created because of anticipated litigation, and would not have been prepared in substantially similar form but for the prospect of that litigation, it falls within Rule 26(b)(3).

The district court ruled that the document sought by the IRS in this case did not fall within the scope of Rule 26(b)(3) and ordered its production. Because we cannot determine whether the district court used the correct standard in reaching its decision, we vacate the judgment and remand for reconsideration.

Background

Sequa Corporation is an aerospace manufacturer with annual revenues of nearly $ 2 billion. Prior to 1989, Atlantic Research Corporation ("ARC") and Chromalloy Gas Turbine Corporation ("Chromalloy") were wholly-owned Sequa subsidiaries. Appellant Monroe Adlman is an attorney and Vice President for Taxes at Sequa.

In the spring of 1989, Sequa contemplated merging Chromalloy and ARC. The contemplated merger was expected to produce an enormous loss and tax refund, which Adlman expected would be challenged by the IRS and would result in litigation. Adlman asked Paul Sheahen, an accountant and lawyer at Arthur Andersen & Co. ("Arthur Andersen"), to evaluate the tax implications of the proposed restructuring. Sheahen did so and set forth his study in a memorandum (the "Memorandum"). He submitted the Memorandum in draft form to Adlman in August 1989. After further consultation, on September 5, 1989,

---

[11] [1] Fed. R. Civ. P. 26(b)(3) provides in relevant part that "a party may obtain discovery of documents and tangible things otherwise discoverable . . . and prepared in anticipation of litigation or for trial by or for another party or by or for that other party's representative (including the other party's attorney, consultant, surety, indemnitor, insurer, or agent) only upon a showing that the party seeking discovery has substantial need of the materials in the preparation of the party's case and that the party is unable without undue hardship to obtain the substantial equivalent of the materials by other means. In ordering discovery of such materials when the required showing has been made, the court shall protect against disclosure of the mental impressions, conclusions, opinions, or legal theories of an attorney or other representative of a party concerning the litigation."

[handwritten annotation: IRS prevails in lower court to get access to the memorandum]

Sheahen sent Adlman the final version. The Memorandum was a 58-page detailed legal analysis of likely IRS challenges to the reorganization and the resulting tax refund claim; it contained discussion of statutory provisions, IRS regulations, legislative history, and prior judicial and IRS rulings relevant to the claim. It proposed possible legal theories or strategies for Sequa to adopt in response, recommended preferred methods of structuring the transaction, and made predictions about the likely outcome of litigation.

Sequa decided to go ahead with the restructuring, which was completed in December 1989 in essentially the form recommended by Arthur Andersen. Sequa sold 93% of its stock in ARC to Chromalloy for $ 167.4 million, and the remaining 7% to Bankers Trust for $ 12.6 million. The reorganization resulted in a $ 289 million loss. Sequa claimed the loss on its 1989 return and carried it back to offset 1986 capital gains, thereby generating a claim for a refund of $ 35 million.

In an ensuing audit of Sequa's 1986–1989 tax returns, the IRS requested a number of documents concerning the restructuring transaction. Sequa acknowledged the existence of the Memorandum, but cited work product privilege as grounds for declining to produce it.[12] On September 23, 1993, the IRS served a summons on Adlman for production of the Memorandum.

When Adlman declined to comply, the IRS instituted an action in the United States District Court for the Southern District of New York to enforce the subpoena. Adlman defended on the grounds that the Memorandum was protected by both the attorney-client and work product privileges. The district court (Knapp, J.) in its first decision rejected Adlman's claim that the Memorandum was protected by attorney-client privilege, finding that Adlman had not consulted Arthur Andersen in order to obtain assistance in furnishing legal advice to Sequa. It rejected Adlman's claim of work product privilege because the Memorandum was prepared for litigation based on actions or events that had not yet occurred at the time of its creation. The court granted the IRS's petition to enforce the summons.

On appeal, we affirmed denial of Adlman's claim of attorney-client privilege. We vacated the district court's enforcement order, however, because the district court had evaluated Adlman's claim of work product privilege under the wrong standard. Although the non-occurrence of events giving rise to litigation prior to preparation of the documents is a factor to be considered, we explained, it does not necessarily preclude application of work product privilege. For example, where a party faces the choice of whether to engage in a particular course of conduct virtually certain to result in litigation and prepares documents analyzing whether to engage in the conduct based on its assessment of the likely result of the anticipated litigation, we concluded that the preparatory documents should receive protection under Rule 26(b)(3). We therefore remanded for reconsideration whether the Memorandum was protected work product.

---

[12] [2] IRS summonses are "subject to the traditional privileges and limitations," United States v. Euge, 444 U.S. 707, 714, 100 S. Ct. 874, 879, 63 L. Ed. 2d 141 (1980), including the work product doctrine codified at Rule 26(b)(3). Upjohn Co. v. United States, 449 U.S. 383, 398–99, 101 S. Ct. 677, 687, 66 L. Ed. 2d 584 (1981).

District used wrong std of work product doctrine. If you know it will be litigated it's protected.

140   CLIENT CONFIDENTIALITY AND EVIDENTIARY PRIVILEGES   CH. 4

On remand, Adlman argued that the Memorandum was protected by Rule 26(b)(3) because it included legal opinions prepared in reasonable anticipation of litigation. Litigation was virtually certain to result from the reorganization and Sequa's consequent claim of tax losses. Sequa's tax returns had been surveyed or audited annually for at least 30 years. In addition, the size of the capital loss to be generated by the proposed restructuring would result in a refund so large that the Commissioner of Internal Revenue would be required by federal law to submit a report to the Joint Congressional Committee on Taxation. See 26 U.S.C.A. § 6405(a). Finally, Sequa's tax treatment of the restructuring was based on an interpretation of the tax code without a case or IRS ruling directly on point. In light of the circumstances of the transaction, Adlman asserted there was "no doubt that Sequa would end up in litigation with the IRS." Sequa's accountant at Arthur Andersen concurred, opining that "any corporate tax executive would have realistically predicted that this capital loss would be disputed by the IRS" because of the "unprecedented and creative nature of the reorganization, the fact that Sequa was continually under close scrutiny by the IRS and the size of the refund resulting from the capital loss."

The district court again rejected the claim of work product privilege, concluding that the Memorandum was not prepared in anticipation of litigation. Adlman appeals.

Discussion

The work product doctrine, codified for the federal courts in Fed. R. Civ. P. 26(b)(3), is intended to preserve a zone of privacy in which a lawyer can prepare and develop legal theories and strategy "with an eye toward litigation," free from unnecessary intrusion by his adversaries. Hickman v. Taylor, 329 U.S. 495, 510–11 (1947). Analysis of one's case "in anticipation of litigation" is a classic example of work product . . . and receives heightened protection under Fed. R. Civ. P. 26(b)(3).

This case involves a question of first impression in this circuit: whether Rule 26(b)(3) is inapplicable to a litigation analysis prepared by a party or its representative in order to inform a business decision which turns on the party's assessment of the likely outcome of litigation expected to result from the transaction. Answering that question requires that we determine the proper interpretation of Rule 26(b)(3)'s requirement that documents be prepared "in anticipation of litigation" in order to qualify for work product protection.

I.

In Hickman v. Taylor, the Supreme Court held that notes taken by the defendant's attorney during interviews with witnesses to the event that eventually gave rise to the lawsuit in the case were not discoverable by the plaintiff. As the Court explained,

> In performing his various duties, . . . it is essential that a lawyer work with a certain degree of privacy, free from unnecessary intrusion by opposing parties and their counsel. Proper preparation of a client's case demands that he . . . prepare his legal theories and plan his strategy without undue and needless interference.

[*Id.*] at 510–11.

Were the attorney's work accessible to an adversary, the Hickman court cautioned, "much of what is now put down in writing would remain unwritten" for fear that the attorney's work would redound to the benefit of the opposing party. Id. at 511. Legal advice might be marred by "inefficiency, unfairness and sharp practices," and the "effect on the legal profession would be demoralizing." Id. at 511. Neither the interests of clients nor the cause of justice would be served, the court observed, if work product were freely discoverable.

The Supreme Court has reaffirmed the "strong public policy" underlying the work-product privilege in the decades since *Hickman*. . . . It has also made clear that documents that "tend[ ] to reveal the attorney's mental process" — described by commentators as "opinion work product," *see Special Project, The Work Product Doctrine*, 68 Cornell L. Rev. 760, 817 (1983) — receive special protection not accorded to factual material. Upjohn, 449 U.S. at 399, 101 S. Ct. at 687. Special treatment for opinion work product is justified because, "at its core, the work-product doctrine shelters the mental processes of the attorney, providing a privileged area within which he can analyze and prepare his client's case." Nobles, 422 U.S. at 238, 95 S. Ct. at 2170.

Rule 26(b)(3) codifies the principles articulated in Hickman. The Rule states that documents "prepared in anticipation of litigation or for trial" are discoverable only upon a showing of substantial need of the materials and inability, without undue hardship, to obtain their substantial equivalent elsewhere. Even where this showing has been made, however, the Rule provides that the court "shall protect against disclosure of the mental impressions, conclusions, opinions, or legal theories of an attorney or other representative of a party concerning the litigation."

II.

The first problem we face is to determine the meaning of the phrase prepared "in anticipation of litigation." The phrase has never been interpreted by our circuit; furthermore, courts and commentators have expressed a range of views as to its meaning. It is universally agreed that a document whose purpose is to assist in preparation for litigation is within the scope of the Rule and thus eligible to receive protection if the other conditions of protection prescribed by the Rule are met. The issue is less clear, however, as to documents which, although prepared because of expected litigation, are intended to inform a business decision influenced by the prospects of the litigation. The formulation applied by some courts in determining whether documents are protected by work product privilege is whether they are ① prepared "primarily or exclusively to assist in litigation" — a formulation that would potentially exclude documents containing analysis of expected litigation, if their primary, ultimate, or exclusive purpose is to assist in making the business decision. Others ask whether the documents were prepared "because of" existing or expected litigation — a formulation that would ② *Broader std.* include such documents, despite the fact that their purpose is not to "assist in" litigation. Because we believe that protection of documents of this type is more consistent with both the literal terms and the purposes of the Rule, we adopt the latter formulation.

1.   "Primarily to assist in" litigation.

The "primarily to assist in litigation" formulation is exemplified by a line of cases from the United States Court of Appeals for the Fifth Circuit. In United States v. Davis, 636 F.2d 1028 (5th Cir.), cert. denied, 454 U.S. 862 (1981), the Fifth Circuit denied protection to documents made in the course of preparation of a tax return. This result was well justified as there was no showing whatsoever of anticipation of litigation. In what might be characterized as a dictum, or in any event a statement going far beyond the issues raised in the case, the court asserted that the Rule applies only if the "primary motivating purpose behind the creation of the document was to aid in possible future litigation." 636 F.2d at 1040.

Then, in United States v. El Paso Co., 682 F.2d 530 (5th Cir. 1982), cert. denied, 466 U.S. 944 (1984), a large public corporation sought to shield documents that analyzed prospective liabilities that might result from litigation with the IRS over its tax returns. The documents were prepared not to assist in litigation but to establish and justify appropriate reserves in El Paso's financial statements. Treating the Davis dictum as law, the Fifth Circuit held that because the "primary motivating force [behind the preparation of the documents was] not to ready El Paso for litigation" but rather "to bring its financial books into conformity with generally accepted auditing principles," 682 F.2d at 543, and because the documents' liability analysis was "only a means to a business end," the documents were not prepared "in anticipation of litigation" within the meaning of the Rule and enjoyed no work product protection. The El Paso requirement that the document be prepared to aid in litigation was then applied by a Fifth Circuit judge writing for the Temporary Emergency Court of Appeals in United States v. Gulf Oil Corp., 760 F.2d 292, 296–97 (Temp. Emer. Ct. App. 1985).

We believe that a requirement that documents be produced primarily or exclusively to assist in litigation in order to be protected is at odds with the text and the policies of the Rule. Nowhere does Rule 26(b)(3) state that a document must have been prepared to aid in the conduct of litigation in order to constitute work product, much less primarily or exclusively to aid in litigation. Preparing a document "in anticipation of litigation" is sufficient.

The text of Rule 26(b)(3) does not limit its protection to materials prepared to assist at trial. To the contrary, the text of the Rule clearly sweeps more broadly. It expressly states that work product privilege applies not only to documents "prepared . . . for trial" but also to those prepared "in anticipation of litigation." If the drafters of the Rule intended to limit its protection to documents made to assist in preparation for litigation, this would have been adequately conveyed by the phrase "prepared . . . for trial." The fact that documents prepared "in anticipation of litigation" were also included confirms that the drafters considered this to be a different, and broader category. Nothing in the Rule states or suggests that documents prepared "in anticipation of litigation" with the purpose of assisting in the making of a business decision do not fall within its scope.

In addition, the Rule takes pains to grant special protection to the type of materials at issue in this case — documents setting forth legal analysis. While the Rule generally withholds protection for documents prepared in anticipation of litigation if the adverse party shows "substantial need" for their disclosure and inability to obtain their equivalent by other means, even where the party seeking disclosure has made such a showing the Rule directs that "the court shall protect against disclosure of the mental impressions, conclusions, opinions, or legal theories of . . . [a party or its representative] concerning the litigation." As the Advisory Committee notes indicate, Rule 26(b)(3) is intended to ratify the principles that "each side's informal evaluation of its case should be protected, that each side should be encouraged to prepare independently, and that one side should not automatically have the benefit of the detailed preparatory work of the other side." Where the Rule has explicitly established a special level of protection against disclosure for documents revealing an attorney's (or other representative's) opinions and legal theories concerning litigation, it would oddly undermine its purposes if such documents were excluded from protection merely because they were prepared to assist in the making of a business decision expected to result in the litigation.

* * *

In addition to the plain language of the Rule, the policies underlying the work product doctrine suggest strongly that work product protection should not be denied to a document that analyzes expected litigation merely because it is prepared to assist in a business decision. Framing the inquiry as whether the primary or exclusive purpose of the document was to assist in litigation threatens to deny protection to documents that implicate key concerns underlying the work product doctrine.

The problem is aptly illustrated by several hypothetical fact situations likely to recur:

(i) A company contemplating a transaction recognizes that the transaction will result in litigation; whether to undertake the transaction and, if so, how to proceed with the transaction, may well be influenced by the company's evaluation of the likelihood of success in litigation. Thus, a memorandum may be prepared in expectation of litigation with the primary purpose of helping the company decide whether to undertake the contemplated transaction. An example would be a publisher contemplating publication of a book where the publisher has received a threat of suit from a competitor purporting to hold exclusive publication rights. The publisher commissions its attorneys to prepare an evaluation of the likelihood of success in the litigation, which includes the attorneys' evaluation of various legal strategies that might be pursued. If the publisher decides to go ahead with publication and is sued, under the "primarily to assist in litigation" formulation the study will likely be disclosed to the opposing lawyers because its principal purpose was not to assist in litigation but to inform the business decision whether to publish. We can see no reason under the words or policies of the Rule why such a document should not be protected.

(ii) A company is engaged in, or contemplates, some kind of partnership, merger, joint undertaking, or business association with another company; the other company reasonably requests that the company furnish a candid assessment by the company's attorneys of its likelihood of success in existing litigations. For instance, the company's bank may request such a report from the company's attorneys concerning its likelihood of success in an important litigation to inform its lending policy toward the company. Or a securities underwriter contemplating a public offering of the company's securities may wish to see such a study to decide whether to go ahead with the offering without waiting for the termination of the litigation. Such a study would be created to inform the judgment of the business associate concerning its business decisions. No part of its purpose would be to aid in the conduct of the litigation. Nonetheless it would reveal the attorneys' most intimate strategies and assessments concerning the litigation. We can see no reason why, under the Rule, the litigation adversary should have access to it. But under the Fifth Circuit's "to assist" test, it would likely be discoverable by the litigation adversary.

(iii) A business entity prepares financial statements to assist its executives, stockholders, prospective investors, business partners, and others in evaluating future courses of action. Financial statements include reserves for projected litigation. The company's independent auditor requests a memorandum prepared by the company's attorneys estimating the likelihood of success in litigation and an accompanying analysis of the company's legal strategies and options to assist it in estimating what should be reserved for litigation losses.

In each scenario, the company involved would require legal analysis that falls squarely within Hickman's area of primary concern — analysis that candidly discusses the attorney's litigation strategies, appraisal of likelihood of success, and perhaps the feasibility of reasonable settlement. The interpretation of Rule 26(b)(3) advocated by the IRS imposes an untenable choice upon a company in these circumstances. If the company declines to make such analysis or scrimps on candor and completeness to avoid prejudicing its litigation prospects, it subjects itself and its co-venturers to ill-informed decisionmaking. On the other hand, a study reflecting the company's litigation strategy and its assessment of its strengths and weaknesses cannot be turned over to litigation adversaries without serious prejudice to the company's prospects in the litigation.

We perceive nothing in the policies underlying the work product doctrine or the text of the Rule itself that would justify subjecting a litigant to this array of undesirable choices. The protection of the Rule should be accorded to such studies in these circumstances. . . . We see no basis for adopting a test under which an attorney's assessment of the likely outcome of litigation is freely available to his litigation adversary merely because the document was created for a business purpose rather than for litigation assistance. The fact that a document's purpose is business-related appears irrelevant to the question whether it should be protected under Rule 26(b)(3).[13]

---

[13] [4] Judge Kearse argues in dissent that Rule 26(b)(3) has no application where the anticipated litigation will not occur unless the client makes a contemplated business decision. We believe this view writes a significant and unauthorized limitation into the Rule. The Rule extends limited protection to documents prepared "in anticipation of litigation." According to Judge Kearse's reading, it protects documents prepared "in anticipation of litigation, but not where the anticipated litigation would result from a business decision still in contemplation." We can find no justification in the Rule, the commentary, or the purposes underlying the Rule for adding such a limitation.

Judge Kearse also argues that work product protection is unnecessary because protection will generally be accorded by the attorney-client privilege. No doubt in many instances this will be true, but it is irrelevant. Where true, the issue is moot. In other circumstances, however, the attorney-client privilege may be unavailable for a number of reasons. For example, as suggested in hypothetical examples considered above, the document may have been shown to others simply because there was some good reason to show it. The attorney-client privilege and the work product rule serve different objectives. The fact that a document does not come within the attorney-client privilege should not result in the deprivation of the protection accorded by Rule 26(b)(3).

We note that in Delaney, Migdail & Young, Chartered v. IRS, 826 F.2d 124 (D.C. Cir. 1987), the IRS successfully argued against the very position it here advocates. The D.C. Circuit sustained the IRS's claim of work product privilege in circumstances where the claim would have failed under the test applied by the Fifth Circuit and advocated by the IRS on this appeal. The documents sought in Delaney were prepared by IRS attorneys for a business purpose — to help the IRS decide whether to adopt a proposed system of statistical sampling for its corporate audit program for large accounts. However, the study was prepared because of expected litigation which would result from adoption of the program; it analyzed expected legal challenges to the use of the proposed program, potential defenses available to the agency, and the likely outcome. Based on the preparatory study, the IRS concluded that the proposed statistical sampling program presented an acceptable legal risk and authorized it. The court refused discovery with the observation that the party requesting discovery was

> seeking the agency's attorneys' assessment of the program's legal vulnerabilities in order to make sure it does not miss anything in crafting its legal case against the program. *This is precisely the type of discovery the [Supreme] Court refused to permit in Hickman v. Taylor.*

826 F.2d at 127.

* * *

2. Prepared "because of" litigation.

The formulation of the work product rule used by the Wright & Miller treatise, and cited by the Third, Fourth, Seventh, Eighth and D.C. Circuits, is that documents should be deemed prepared "in anticipation of litigation," and thus within the scope of the Rule, if "in light of the nature of the document and the factual situation in the particular case, the document can fairly be said to have been prepared or obtained because of the prospect of litigation." Charles Alan Wright, Arthur R. Miller, and Richard L. Marcus, 8 Federal Practice & Procedure § 2024, at 343 (1994) (emphasis added).

The Wright & Miller "because of" formulation accords with the plain language of Rule 26(b)(3) and the purposes underlying the work product doctrine. Where a document is created because of the prospect of litigation, analyzing the likely outcome of that litigation, it does not lose protection under this formulation merely because it is created in order to assist with a business decision.

Conversely, it should be emphasized that the "because of" formulation that we adopt here withholds protection from documents that are prepared in the ordinary course of business or that would have been created in essentially similar form irrespective of the litigation. It is well established that work product privilege does not apply to such documents.

Furthermore, although a finding under this test that a document is prepared because of the prospect of litigation warrants application of Rule 26(b)(3), this does not necessarily mean that the document will be protected against discovery. Rather, it means that a document is eligible for work product privilege. The district court can then assess whether the party seeking discovery has made an adequate showing of substantial need for the document and an inability to obtain its contents elsewhere without undue hardship. The district court can order production of the portions of the document for which a litigant has made an adequate showing. The court can focus its attention on whether the document or any portion is the type of material that should be disclosed, while retaining the authority to protect against disclosure of the mental impressions, strategies, and analyses of the party or its representative concerning the litigation.

In short, we find that the Wright & Miller "because of" test appropriately focuses on both what should be eligible for the Rule's protection and what should not. We believe this is the proper test to determine whether a document was prepared "in anticipation of litigation" and is thus eligible for protection depending on the further findings required by the Rule.

III.

We cannot determine from the district court's opinion what test it followed in concluding that the Memorandum was ineligible for protection.

* * *

We remand with instructions to the district court to reconsider the issue under the Wright & Miller test of whether "the document can fairly be said to have been prepared . . . because of the prospect of litigation." There is little doubt under the evidence that Sequa had the prospect of litigation in mind when it directed the preparation of the Memorandum by Arthur Andersen. Whether it can fairly be said that the Memorandum was prepared because of that expected litigation really turns on whether it would have been prepared irrespective of the expected litigation with the IRS.

If the district court concludes that substantially the same Memorandum would have been prepared in any event — as part of the ordinary course of business of undertaking the restructuring — then the court should conclude the Memorandum was not prepared because of the expected litigation and should adhere to its prior ruling denying the protection of the Rule.

On the other hand, if the court finds the Memorandum would not have been prepared but for Sequa's anticipation of litigation with the IRS over the losses generated by the restructuring, then judgment should be entered in favor of Sequa.

The IRS contends that even if the Memorandum qualifies as work product, it has made a sufficient showing of substantial need and unavailability so as to overcome the qualified protection accorded by Rule 26(b)(3). We disagree. The Memorandum falls within the most protected category of work product — that which shows the "mental impressions, conclusions, opinions or legal theories of an attorney or other representative." The Rule makes clear that a showing of "substantial need" sufficient to compel disclosure of other work product is not necessarily sufficient to compel disclosure of such materials. We need not decide whether such opinion work product is ever discoverable upon a showing of necessity and unavailability by other means. The Rule is clear that, at a minimum, such material is to be protected unless a highly persuasive showing is made. The IRS has failed to meet that high standard.

The IRS claims necessity for the Memorandum on the ground that it will provide insight into Sequa's subjective motivation for engaging in corporate restructuring and is thus relevant to determining whether the transaction was motivated by a legitimate business purpose. In camera review of the

Memorandum shows that it does not reflect the motives of Sequa's executives, but rather the legal analysis of its accountants. The Memorandum, being the technical and legal analysis of outside accountants, and not the reflections of decisionmakers at Sequa, simply does not address or reflect Sequa's business reason for the proposed restructuring.

The IRS is currently engaged in a battle with corporate taxpayers over the discoverability of tax accrual workpapers, i.e., files prepared and compiled by publicly traded companies to support how they have reflected contingent tax liabilities on audited financial statements. Workpapers generally include candid assessments by (in house or outside) counsel of the likely outcome of anticipated disputes with the IRS regarding uncertain tax positions. Although companies usually share their tax accrual workpapers with their independent auditors (who might create their own workpapers), many practitioners and commentators argue that the IRS would secure unfair advantage by having access to a taxpayer's thought processes as reflected in the workpapers. Indeed, workpapers could be a road map to the weaknesses in a corporate taxpayer's reporting positions.

In 1984, the United States Supreme Court ruled in *Arthur Young & Co. v. United States*, 465 U.S. 805 (1984), that tax accrual workpapers prepared by a CPA firm are not protected by the work product doctrine. The Court explained that there was no privilege applicable to work product prepared by accountants, and it declined to establish such a privilege. *See also* United States v. El Paso Co., 682 F.2d 530 (5th Cir. 1982) (tax pool analysis prepared to support a financial balance sheet was not protected by the work product doctrine because it was prepared to comply with financial reporting standards required by securities laws, not in anticipation of litigation). Perhaps to appease the complaints of those who argued that the nation's financial markets could be affected if accountants had any incentives to do less than thorough objective analyses of companies under financial audit, the IRS celebrated its victory in *Arthur Young* by announcing a policy of restraint under which it agreed to seek tax accrual workpapers only in extraordinary circumstances.

In 2002, the IRS modified its policy of restraint by announcing that it would seek tax accrual workpapers from taxpayers that it believed had participated in questionable corporate tax shelters. At least two taxpayers, Textron Inc. and Regions Financial Corp., refused to comply when summoned by the IRS under the new policy. Both companies initially were successful in resisting the IRS summonses on work product grounds, in district court litigation. Unlike the *Arthur Young* case, however, the documents at issue in both of these cases were opinions or analyses prepared by legal counsel that were included in the workpaper files. In *United States v. Textron*, 507 F.Supp. 2d 138 (D.R.I. 2007), the court denied the IRS access to tax accrual workpapers prepared by Textron legal personnel. Textron successfully argued that its tax accrual workpapers contained information protected by the attorney work product doctrine (not the accountant work product doctrine rejected in *Arthur Young*). The court was satisfied that Textron's tax accrual workpapers were protected by the attorney work product doctrine even though they were also used for the nonlitigation purpose of supporting its accounting treatment with respect to uncertain tax positions. Moreover, the court held that Textron's disclosure of its tax accrual workpapers to its independent auditor did not waive work product protection because its auditor was neither an adversary in this context nor a likely conduit of this information to the IRS. In *Regions Financial Corp. v. United States*, 2008 U.S. Dist. LEXIS 41940 (N.D. Ala. 2008), another district court ruled in favor of the taxpayer on the same issue.

The government appealed both cases but withdrew its appeal in *Regions Financial* when the issues in the underlying audit were settled. In *Textron*, 553 F.3d 87 (1st Cir. 2009), a divided panel of the Court of Appeals for the First Circuit ruled that tax accrual workpapers may, in many instances, be protected from disclosure under the work product doctrine. Two months later, on March 25, 2009, the First Circuit court granted an IRS motion for rehearing *en banc* and vacated the panel decision, scheduling a rare *en banc* rehearing. *See also* Michelle M. Henkel, *Textron: The Debate Continues as to Whether Auditor Transparency Waives the Work Product Privilege*, 50 BNA Tax MANAGEMENT MEMORANDUM 251 (June 22, 2009).

In reviewing the *Textron* opinion, particular attention should be paid to the legal standard applied by the court; as in *Adlman*, protection under the work product doctrine could depend on whether the court follows the "primarily to assist in litigation" or the "because of" test. The courts that have decided the issue in favor of taxpayers have applied the "because of" test in interpreting Rule 26(b)(3); this test has been adopted by the vast majority of the Circuits in other contexts. However, the Fifth Circuit applied the "primarily to assist in litigation" test in deciding the *El Paso* case in favor of the government. Although the *El Paso* case on the facts is not directly at odds with the result in the more recent cases because it was not clear whether the workpapers involved were prepared by accountants or lawyers, the case would clearly have been decided the same way had it been clear that only lawyers were involved because the Fifth Circuit has adopted the "primarily in anticipation of litigation" test. As a result, *Textron* could ultimately be a vehicle — via a petition for certiorari to the Supreme Court by the taxpayer, which lost in the First Circuit — for not only resolving whether tax accrual workpapers prepared by lawyers are protected by work product privilege, but also the more general question about how Rule 26(b)(3) applies.

After the rehearing in *Textron*, but before the reversal by the First Circuit Court of Appeals, another federal district court sided with the taxpayer. In *United States v. Deloitte & Touche USA*, 623 F. Supp. 39 (D.D.C. 2009), the government, through the Department of Justice,[14] subpoenaed an internal Deloitte USA draft memorandum "recording the thoughts and impressions of Dow's attorneys concerning tax issues related to" a subsidiary of Dow Chemical Company. In a brief opinion that cited *Regions Financial* and both *Textron* decisions, the court reasoned that the memorandum was prepared "because of" the prospect of litigation with the IRS over the tax treatment of the subsidiary.

---

[14] Although the facts in the case are sparse, it appears that the Department of Justice's subpoena requested documents that would not have been requested by the IRS under its modified policy of restraint.

UNITED STATES v. TEXTRON INC. *TP loses*

United States Court of Appeals, First Circuit
577 F.3d 21 (2009)
OPINION EN BANC

BOUDIN, CIRCUIT JUDGE.

The question for the *en banc* court is whether the attorney work product doctrine shields from an IRS summons "tax accrual work papers" prepared by lawyers and others in Textron's Tax Department to support Textron's calculation of tax reserves for its audited corporate financial statements. Textron is a major aerospace and defense conglomerate, with well over a hundred subsidiaries, whose consolidated tax return is audited by the IRS on a regular basis. To understand the dispute, some background is required concerning financial statements, contingent tax reserves and tax audit work papers.

As a publicly traded corporation, Textron is required by federal securities law to have public financial statements certified by an independent auditor. *See* 15 U.S.C. §§ 78*l*, 78m (2006); 17 C.F.R. § 210 *et seq.* (2009). To prepare such financial statements, Textron must calculate reserves to be entered on the company books to account for contingent tax liabilities. Such liabilities, which affect the portrayal of assets and earnings, include estimates of potential liability if the IRS decides to challenge debatable positions taken by the taxpayer in its return.

The calculation of such reserves entails preparing work papers describing Textron's potential liabilities for further taxes; these underpin the tax reserve entries in its financial statement and explain the figures chosen to the independent auditor who certifies that statement as correct. By examining the work papers the accountant discharges its own duty to determine "the adequacy and reasonableness of the corporation's reserve account for contingent tax liabilities." *United States v. Arthur Young & Co.,* 465 U.S. 805, 812, 104 S.Ct. 1495, 79 L.Ed.2d 826 (1984) (rejecting claim of accountant work product privilege protecting such work papers).[15] The work papers are thus one step in a process whose outcome is a certified financial statement for the company.

In Textron's case, its Tax Department lists items in the tax return that, if identified and challenged by the IRS, could result in additional taxes being assessed. The final spreadsheets list each debatable item, including in each instance the dollar amount subject to possible dispute and a percentage estimate of the IRS' chances of success. Multiplying the amount by the percentage fixes the reserve entered on the books for that item. The spreadsheets reflecting these calculations may be supported by backup emails or notes.

A company's published financial statements do not normally identify the specific tax items on the return that may be debatable but incorporate or reflect only the total reserve figure. As the Supreme Court explained in Arthur *Young,* tax accrual work papers provide a resource for the IRS, if the IRS can get

---

[15] [1] The procedural requirement that auditors examine tax accrual work papers is based on a combination of Statement on Auditing Standards No. 96, Audit Documentation (2002), *superseded by* Auditing Standards No. 3, Audit Documentation (2004); Statement on Auditing Standards No. 326, Evidential Matter (1980); and Auditing Interpretation No. 9326, Evidential Matter: Auditing Interpretations of Section 326 (2003).

access to them, by "pinpoint[ing] the 'soft spots' on a corporation's tax return by highlighting those areas in which the corporate taxpayer has taken a position that may, at some later date, require the payment of additional taxes" and providing "an item-by-item analysis of the corporation's potential exposure to additional liability." 465 U.S. at 813, 104 S.Ct. 1495.

The IRS does not automatically request tax accrual work papers from taxpayers; rather, in the wake of Enron and other corporate scandals, the IRS began to seek companies' tax accrual work papers only where it concluded that the taxpayer had engaged in certain listed transactions "that [are] the same as or substantially similar to one of the types of transactions that the [IRS] has determined to be a tax avoidance transaction." 26 C.F.R. § 1.6011-4(b)(2) (2009). Only a limited number of transactions are so designated.[16]

The present case began with a 2003 IRS audit of Textron's corporate income tax liability for the years 1998–2001. In reviewing Textron's 2001 return, the IRS determined that a Textron subsidiary—Textron Financial Corp. ("Textron Financial")—had engaged in nine listed transactions. In each of the nine instances, Textron Financial had purchased equipment from a foreign utility or transit operator and leased it back to the seller on the same day. Although such transactions can be legitimate, the IRS determined that they were sale-in, lease-out ("SILO") transactions, which are listed as a potential tax shelter subject to abuse by taxpayers.

SILOs allow tax-exempt or tax-indifferent organizations—for example, a tax-exempt charity or a city-owned transit authority—to transfer depreciation and interest deductions, from which they cannot benefit, to other taxpayers who use them to shelter income from tax. Where the only motive of a sale and lease back is tax avoidance, it can be disregarded by the IRS and taxes assessed on the wrongly sheltered income.

Textron had shown the spreadsheets to its outside accountant, Ernst & Young, but refused to show them to the IRS. The IRS issued an administrative summons pursuant to 26 U.S.C. § 7602 (2006), which allows the IRS, in determining the accuracy of any return, to "examine any books, papers, records, or other data which may be relevant or material to such inquiry." *Id.* § 7602(a)(1). According to IRS policy, where the taxpayer claims benefits from only a single listed transaction, the IRS seeks only the workpapers for that transaction; but where (as in Textron's case) the taxpayer claims benefits from multiple listed transactions, the IRS seeks all of the workpapers for the tax year in question. I.R.S. Announcement 2002-63, 2002-27 I.R.B. 72 (July 8, 2002). The summons also sought related work papers created by Ernst & Young in determining the adequacy of Textron's reserves that Textron might possess or could obtain. Textron again refused.

The IRS brought an enforcement action in federal district court in Rhode Island. *See* 26 U.S.C. § 7604(a) (2006). Textron challenged the summons as lacking legitimate purpose and also asserted, as bars to the demand, the attorney-client and tax practitioner privileges and the qualified privilege

---

[16] [2] A current list of such transaction types, amounting to less than three dozen, appears at Internal Revenue Service, Recognized Abusive and Listed Transactions-LMSB Tier I Issues, http://www.irs.gov/businesses/corporations/article/0,id= 120633,00. html (visited July 7, 2009).

available for litigation materials under the work product doctrine. The IRS contested all of the privilege claims. Both the IRS and Textron filed affidavits and, in addition, the district court heard witnesses from both sides.

Textron agreed that it usually settled disputes with the IRS through negotiation or concession or at worst through the formal IRS administrative process; but it testified that sometimes it had litigated disputed tax issues in federal court. Its evidence also showed that the estimates for tax reserves and the supporting work papers were generated within its Tax Department but that tax lawyers in that department were centrally involved in their preparation and that Textron Financial also used an outside counsel to advise it on tax reserve requirements.

Textron described generically the contents of the work papers in question: these included (1) summary spreadsheets showing for each disputable item the amount in controversy, estimated probability of a successful challenge by the IRS, and resulting reserve amounts; and (2) back up e-mail and notes. In some instances the spreadsheet entries estimated the probability of IRS success at 100 percent. Textron said that the spreadsheets had been shown to and discussed with its independent auditor but physically retained by Textron.

Neither side disputed that the immediate purpose of the work papers was to establish and support the tax reserve figures for the audited financial statements. Textron's evidence was to the effect that litigation over specific items was always a possibility; the IRS did not deny that in certain cases litigation could result although it said that this was often unlikely. Whether Textron's evidence is materially different than that of the IRS remains to be considered.

Ultimately, the district court denied the petition for enforcement. *United States v. Textron Inc.,* 507 F.Supp.2d 138, 150, 155 (D.R.I.2007). The court agreed with the IRS that the agency had a legitimate purpose for seeking the work papers. It also ruled that insofar as the Textron-prepared work papers might otherwise be protected by attorney-client privilege, or the counterpart tax practitioner privilege for non-lawyers engaged in tax practice, *see* 26 U.S.C. § 7525 (2006), those privileges had been waived when Textron disclosed the work papers' content to Ernst & Young.

However, the district court concluded that the papers were protected by the work product privilege, which derived from *Hickman v. Taylor,* 329 U.S. 495, 67 S.Ct. 385, 91 L.Ed. 451 (1947), and is now embodied in Rule 26(b)(3) of the Federal Rules of Civil Procedure. This privilege, the district court held, had not been waived by disclosure of the work papers to the accountant. The district court's decision that the work papers were protected work product involved both a description of factual premises and a legal interpretation of applicable doctrine.

The district court first said (paraphrasing a Textron witness) the work papers were prepared to assure that Textron was "adequately reserved with respect to any potential disputes or litigation" over its returns; the court also said that, by fair inference, the work papers served "to satisfy an independent auditor that Textron's reserve for contingent liabilities satisfied the requirements of generally accepted accounting principles (GAAP) so that a 'clean' opinion would be given" for Textron financial statements.

Then, in its discussion of legal doctrine, the district court stated:

> As the IRS correctly observes, the work product privilege does not apply to "'documents that are prepared in the ordinary course of business or that would have been created in essentially similar form irrespective of the litigation.'" *Maine*, 298 F.3d at 70 (quoting [*United States v. Adlman*, 134 F.3d 1194, 1202 (2d Cir. 1998)]). However, it is clear that the opinions of Textron's counsel and accountants regarding items that might be challenged by the IRS, their estimated hazards of litigation percentages and their calculation of tax reserve amounts would not have been prepared at all "but for" the fact that Textron anticipated the possibility of litigation with the IRS. . . . Thus, while it may be accurate to say that the workpapers helped Textron determine what amount should be reserved to cover any potential tax liabilities and that the workpapers were useful in obtaining a "clean" opinion from E & Y regarding the adequacy of the reserve amount, there would have been no need to create a reserve in the first place, if Textron had not anticipated a dispute with the IRS that was likely to result in litigation or some other adversarial proceeding.

Textron, 507 F.Supp.2d at 150.

The court concluded that the work papers were therefore prepared "because of" the prospect of litigation, a phrase used in *Maine v. United States Dep't of Interior*, 298 F.3d 60, 68 (1st Cir. 2002). The court rejected the IRS' reliance on a Fifth Circuit decision rejecting work product protection for tax accrual work papers on the ground that the Fifth Circuit followed a different "primary purpose" test for work protect. *Textron*, 507 F.Supp.2d at 150 (discussing *United States v. El Paso Co.*, 682 F.2d 530, 543 (5th Cir. 1982), *cert. denied*, 466 U.S. 944, 104 S.Ct. 1927, 80 L.Ed.2d 473 (1984)).

On appeal, a divided panel upheld the district court's decision. The *en banc* court then granted the government's petition for rehearing *en banc*, vacated the panel decision, and obtained additional briefs from the parties and interested amici. We now conclude that under our own prior *Maine* precedent — which we reaffirm *en banc* — the Textron work papers were independently required by statutory and audit requirements and that the work product privilege does not apply.

The case presents two difficulties. One, which can readily be dispelled, stems from the mutability of language used in the governing rules and a confusion between issues of fact and issues of legal characterization. The other problem is more basic: how far work product protection extends turns on a balancing of policy concerns rather than application of abstract logic; here, two circuits have addressed tax accrual work papers in the work product context, but, apart from whatever light is cast by *Arthur Young*, the Supreme Court has not ruled on the issue before us, namely, one in which a document is not in any way prepared "for" litigation but relates to a subject that might or might not occasion litigation.

In origin, the work product privilege derives from the Supreme Court's decision in *Hickman v. Taylor*, 329 U.S. at 510-11, 67 S.Ct. 385, and focused at the outset on the materials that lawyers typically prepare for the purpose of litigating cases. *Hickman v. Taylor* concerned ongoing litigation in which one side filed interrogatories seeking from opposing counsel memoranda recording witness interviews that the latter had conducted after receiving notice of possible claims. Often such material and other items designed for use at trial (*e.g.,* draft briefs, outlines of cross examination) are not obtained from or shared with clients and are unprotected by the traditional attorney-client privilege.

Hickman v. Taylor addressed "the extent to which a party may inquire into oral and written statements of witnesses, or other information, secured by an adverse party's counsel in the course of preparation for possible litigation after a claim has arisen." The Court cited a privilege in English courts protecting

> [a]ll documents which are called into existence for the purpose-but not necessarily the sole purpose-of assisting the deponent or his legal advisers in any actual or anticipated litigation. . . . Reports . . . if made in the ordinary course of routine, are not privileged. . . .

Id. at 510 n. 9, 67 S.Ct. 385.

This history led the Court to practical considerations:

> Proper preparation of a client's case demands that he assemble information, sift what he considers to be the relevant from the irrelevant facts, prepare his legal theories and plan his strategy without undue and needless interference. . . . This work is reflected, of course, in interviews, statements, memoranda, correspondence, briefs, mental impressions, personal beliefs, and countless other tangible and intangible ways-aptly though roughly termed . . . as the "work product of the lawyer."

Id. at 511, 67 S.Ct. 385.

On this basis the Court declared that the interrogatories, which sought witness interviews conducted by opponent counsel in preparation for litigation, were protected by a qualified privilege. When in 1970 the Supreme Court through the rule-making process codified the work product privilege in Rule 26(b)(3), it described the privilege as extending to documents and other tangible things that "are prepared in anticipation of litigation or for trial." This phrase, as illuminated by *Hickman v. Taylor*'s reasoning, is the one to be applied in this case.

Turning back to the present case, the IRS is unquestionably right that the immediate motive of Textron in preparing the tax accrual work papers was to fix the amount of the tax reserve on Textron's books and to obtain a clean financial opinion from its auditor. And Textron may be correct that unless the IRS might dispute an item in the return, no reserve for that item might be necessary, so perhaps some of the items might be litigated. But in saying that Textron wanted to be "adequately reserved," the district judge did not say that the work papers were prepared *for use* in possible litigation — only that the reserves would cover liabilities that might be determined in litigation. If the judge had made a "for use" finding — which he did not — that finding would have been clearly erroneous.

That the purpose of the work papers was to make book entries, prepare financial statements and obtain a clean audit cannot be disputed. This was the testimony of IRS expert and former Chief Auditor of the Public Company Accounting Oversight Board Douglas Carmichael:

Q. . . . Would you please explain what tax accrual workpapers are?

A. . . . Tax accrual workpapers really include all the support for the tax assets and liabilities shown in the financial statements. . . .

A. Well, from the company's perspective, they're created because, for example, for a public company, the key officers of the company sign a certification saying that those financial statements are fairly presented, and they need support for that.

From the auditor's perspective, it's the same thing, the auditor needs to record in the workpapers what the auditor did to comply with generally accepted auditing standards. So the workpapers are the principal support for the auditor's opinion.

Q. And why do public companies prepare financial statements?

A. Usually, to meet requirements for raising capital. If they're a public company, they need to file annual financial statements on a form 10 K with the SEC and quarterly information on a 10Q.

The Textron witnesses, while using the word "litigation" as often as possible in their testimony, said the same thing. Textron's testimony differed from that of the IRS expert only in its further assertion that, without the possibility of litigation, no tax reserves or audit papers would have been necessary. For example, Roxanne Cassidy, Textron's director of tax reporting, testified as follows:

Q. . . . [W]hat was Textron's purpose in preparing those tax reserve papers?

A. The purpose primarily was to determine whether Textron was adequately reserved with respect to any potential disputes or litigations that would happen in the future. We would need to ensure that we were adequately reserved in the current year on Textron's financial statements.

. . .

Q. And as a publicly traded company, is Textron required to file its financial statements with the Securities and Exchange Commission?

A. Yes.

Q. And do those financial statements include tax reserves?

A. Yes. . . .

. . .

Q. And in having its tax reserves audited by an independent auditor, must Textron be able to support the determinations it has made regarding the adequacy of its tax reserves with some type of evidence?

A. Yes, the support needs to be to the satisfaction of the auditors.

As the IRS expert stated, even if litigation were "remote," the company would still have to prepare work papers to support its judgment. Textron's own witness acknowledged that it would "have to include in its . . . tax accrual work papers any new transactions that the company entered into that year that there might be some tax exposure on" regardless of whether it anticipated likely litigation. Judged by Textron's own experience, most — certainly those with high percentage estimates of IRS success — would never be litigated.

To complete the story, we note *one* suggestion by one Textron witness that, if litigation did occur, the work papers could be useful to Textron in that litigation.[17] This assertion was not supported by any detailed explanation, was *not* adopted by the district judge and is more than dubious: the main aim of audit work papers is to estimate the amount potentially in dispute and the percentage chance of winning or losing. Even an academic supporter of Textron's legal position conceded that "it is doubtful that tax accrual workpapers, which typically just identify and quantify vulnerable return positions, would be useful in the litigation anticipated with respect to those positions." Pease-Wingenter, *The Application of the Attorney-Client Privilege to Tax Accrual Workpapers: The Real Legacy of United States v. Textron*, 8 Houston Bus. & Tax L.J. 337, 346

Any experienced litigator would describe the tax accrual work papers as tax documents and not as case preparation materials. *Whether* work product protection should apply to such documents is a *legal* question informed by the language of rules and Supreme Court doctrine, direct precedent, and policy judgments. The first of these sources — Supreme Court doctrine and the wording of the rules — is helpful to the IRS; direct circuit precedent and the underlying policy of the doctrine and other prudential considerations are more helpful still. Legal commentators can be found on each side; the most persuasive of them favors the IRS.

From the outset, the focus of work product protection has been on materials prepared for use in litigation, whether the litigation was underway or merely anticipated. Thus, *Hickman v. Taylor* addressed "the extent to which a party may inquire into oral and written statements of witnesses, or other information, secured by an adverse party's counsel *in the course of preparation for possible litigation* after a claim has arisen." 329 U.S. at 497, 67 S.Ct. 385 (emphasis added). Similarly, the English privilege, invoked by *Hickman v. Taylor,* privileged "documents which are called into existence for *the purpose-but not necessarily the sole purpose-of assisting the deponent or his legal advisers in any actual or anticipated litigation.*" *Id.* at 510 n. 9, 67 S.Ct. 385 (emphasis added) (internal quotation marks omitted).

The phrase used in the codified rule — "prepared in anticipation of litigation or for trial" did not, in the reference to anticipation, mean prepared for some purpose other than litigation: it meant only that the work might be done *for* litigation but *in advance of* its institution. The English precedent, doubtless the source of the language in Rule 26, specified the purpose "of assisting

[17] [5] Textron Vice President of Taxes Norman Richter said that Textron would still prepare tax accrual workpapers absent GAAP requirements "[b]ecause it guides us-it's-the analysis is still-it would guide us in making litigation and settlement decisions later in the process." This assertion was not contained in Richter's affidavit, which instead said that Textron prepared the work papers "to comply with GAAP" as required for reporting taxes to the SEC, and was not supported by detail or explanation in the record.

the deponent or his legal advisers in any actual or anticipated litigation. . . ." The Advisory Committee's Note cited with approval a decision denying work product protection to a driver's accident report, made pursuant to Interstate Commerce Commission rules, even though it might well have become the subject of litigation. Fed.R.Civ.P. 26 advisory committee's note (1970).

It is not enough to trigger work product protection that the *subject matter* of a document relates to a subject that might conceivably be litigated. Rather, as the Supreme Court explained, "the literal language of [Rule 26(b)(3)] protects materials *prepared for* any litigation or trial as long as they were prepared by or for a party to the subsequent litigation." This distinction is well established in the case law.

Nor is it enough that the materials were prepared by lawyers or represent legal thinking. Much corporate material prepared in law offices or reviewed by lawyers falls in that vast category. It is only work done in anticipation of or for trial that is protected. Even if prepared by lawyers and reflecting legal thinking, "[m]aterials assembled in the ordinary course of business, or pursuant to public requirements unrelated to litigation, or for other nonlitigation purposes are not under the qualified immunity provided by this subdivision." Fed.R.Civ.P. 26 advisory committee's note (1970). *Accord Hickman v. Taylor,* 329 U.S. at 510 n. 9, 67 S.Ct. 385 (quoting English precedent that "[r]eports . . . if made in the ordinary course of routine, are not privileged").

Every lawyer who tries cases knows the touch and feel of materials prepared for a current or possible (*i.e.,* "in anticipation of") law suit. They are the very materials catalogued in *Hickman v. Taylor* and the English precedent with which the decision began. No one with experience of law suits would talk about tax accrual work papers in those terms. A set of tax reserve figures, calculated for purposes of accurately stating a company's financial figures, has in ordinary parlance only that purpose: to support a financial statement and the independent audit of it.

Focusing next on direct precedent, work product protection for tax audit work papers has been squarely addressed only in two circuits: this one and the Fifth. In *Maine,* we said that work product protection does not extend to "documents that are prepared in the ordinary course of business or that would have been created in essentially similar form irrespective of the litigation." *Maine,* 298 F.3d at 70 (quoting *United States v. Adlman,* 134 F.3d 1194, 1202 (2d Cir.1998)). *Maine* applies straightforwardly to Textron's tax audit work papers — which were prepared in the ordinary course of business — and it supports the IRS position.

Similarly, the Fifth Circuit in *El Paso* denied protection for the work papers because the court recognized that the company in question was conducting the relevant analysis because of a need to "bring its financial books into conformity with generally accepted auditing principles." 682 F.2d at 543. The Fifth Circuit, which employs a "primary purpose" test, found that the work papers' "sole function" was to back up financial statements. Here, too, the only purpose of Textron's papers was to prepare financial statements.

Other circuits have not passed on tax audit work papers and some might take a different view. But many of the debatable cases affording work product protection involve documents unquestionably prepared for potential use in litigation if and when it should arise.[18] There is no evidence in this case that the work papers were prepared for such a use or would in fact serve any useful purpose for Textron in conducting litigation if it arose.

Finally, the underlying prudential considerations squarely support the IRS' position in this case, and such considerations have special force because *Hickman v. Taylor* was the child of such considerations, as the quotations above make clear. The privilege aimed centrally at protecting the *litigation process*, specifically, work done by counsel to help him or her in *litigating* a case. It is not a privilege designed to help the lawyer prepare corporate documents or other materials prepared in the ordinary course of business. Where the rationale for a rule stops, so ordinarily does the rule.

Nor is there present here the concern that *Hickman v. Taylor* stressed about discouraging sound preparation for a law suit. That danger may exist in other kinds of cases, but it cannot be present where, as here, there is in substance a legal obligation to prepare such papers: the tax audit work papers not only have a different purpose but *have* to be prepared by exchange-listed companies to comply with the securities laws and accounting principles for certified financial statements. *Arthur Young* made this point in refusing to create an accountant's work product privilege for tax audit papers:

> [T]he auditor is ethically and professionally obligated to ascertain for himself as far as possible whether the corporation's contingent tax liabilities have been accurately stated. . . . Responsible corporate management would not risk a qualified evaluation of a corporate taxpayer's financial posture to afford cover for questionable positions reflected in a prior tax return.

465 U.S. at 818–19, 104 S.Ct. 1495.

Textron apparently thinks it is "unfair" for the government to have access to its spreadsheets, but tax collection is not a game. Underpaying taxes threatens the essential public interest in revenue collection. If a blueprint to Textron's possible improper deductions can be found in Textron's files, it is properly available to the government *unless* privileged. Virtually all discovery against a party *aims* at securing information that may assist an opponent in uncovering the truth. Unprivileged IRS information is equally subject to discovery.[19]

The practical problems confronting the IRS in discovering under-reporting of corporate taxes, which is likely endemic, are serious. Textron's return is massive — constituting more than 4,000 pages — and the IRS requested the work papers only after finding a specific type of transaction that had been shown to be abused by taxpayers. It is because the collection of revenues is

---

[18] [9] *See, e.g., Delaney, Migdail & Young, Chartered v. IRS*, 826 F.2d 124, 127 (D.C.Cir.1987) (protection for "attorneys' assessment of . . . legal vulnerabilities in order to make sure it does not miss anything in crafting its legal case"); *see also In re Sealed Case*, 146 F.3d 881, 885 (D.C.Cir.1998) (protection for documents to "protect the client from future litigation about a particular transaction").

[19] [10] *See Abel Inv. Co. v. United States*, 53 F.R.D. 485, 488 (D.Neb.1971) (holding that IRS documents created during an audit were not protected work product, despite containing attorneys' mental impression and legal theories, because an IRS audit is not litigation).

essential to government that administrative discovery, along with many other comparatively unusual tools, are furnished to the IRS.

As Bentham explained, all privileges limit access to the truth in aid of other objectives, 8 Wigmore, *Evidence* § 2291 (McNaughton Rev. 1961), but virtually all privileges are restricted — either (as here) by definition or (in many cases) through explicit exceptions — by countervailing limitations. The Fifth Amendment privilege against self-incrimination is qualified, among other doctrines, by the required records exception, *see Grosso v. United States,* 390 U.S. 62, 67-68, 88 S.Ct. 709, 19 L.Ed.2d 906 (1968), and the attorney client privilege, along with other limitations, by the crime-fraud exception, *see Clark v. United States,* 289 U.S. 1, 15, 53 S.Ct. 465, 77 L.Ed. 993 (1933).

To sum up, the work product privilege is aimed at protecting work done for litigation, not in preparing financial statements. Textron's work papers were prepared to support financial filings and gain auditor approval; the compulsion of the securities laws and auditing requirements assure that they will be carefully prepared, in their present form, even though not protected; and IRS access serves the legitimate, and important, function of detecting and disallowing abusive tax shelters.

The judgment of the district court is *vacated* and the case is *remanded* for further proceedings consistent with this decision. *It is so ordered.*

TORRUELLA, CIRCUIT JUDGE, with whom LIPEZ, CIRCUIT JUDGE, joins, dissenting.

To assist the IRS in its quest to compel taxpayers to reveal their own assessments of their tax returns, the majority abandons our "because of" test, which asks whether "'in light of the nature of the document and the factual situation in the particular case, the document can be fairly said to have been prepared or obtained *because of* the prospect of litigation.'" *Maine v. United States Dep't of the Interior,* 298 F.3d 60, 68 (1st Cir.2002) (emphasis in original) (quoting *United States v. Adlman,* 134 F.3d 1194, 1202 (2d Cir.1998)). The majority purports to follow this test, but never even cites it. Rather, in its place, the majority imposes a "prepared for" test, asking if the documents were "prepared for use in possible litigation." This test is an even narrower variant of the widely rejected "primary motivating purpose" test used in the Fifth Circuit and specifically repudiated by this court. In adopting its test, the majority ignores a tome of precedents from the circuit courts and contravenes much of the principles underlying the work-product doctrine. It also brushes aside the actual text of Rule 26(b)(3), which "[n]owhere . . . state[s] that a document must have been prepared *to aid* in the conduct of litigation in order to constitute work product." *Adlman,* 134 F.3d at 1198. Further, the majority misrepresents and ignores the findings of the district court. All while purporting to do just the opposite of what it actually does.

I.   The Majority Quietly Rejects Circuit Precedent

The majority claims allegiance to our prior decision in *Maine,* 298 F.3d at 70. Specifically, the majority seizes upon a single line from that decision: "the 'because of' standard does not protect from disclosure 'documents that are prepared in the ordinary course of business or that would have been created in essentially similar form irrespective of the litigation.'" *Id.* (quoting *Adlman,*

134 F.3d at 1202). This qualification is important to be sure, and I will address it *infra,* Section III.B.2. But I must start by addressing the rest of the *Maine* decision, which the majority is careful to ignore.

In that decision, Maine sought documents prepared by the Department of the Interior regarding its decision, made during pending related litigation, to classify salmon as a protected species. The district court found some of these administrative documents unprotected as the Department had not shown that litigation preparation was "'the primary motivating factor for the preparation of the documents.'" This formulation of the test for "anticipation of litigation" was based on the Fifth Circuit rule that the work-product doctrine did not protect documents that were "not primarily motivated *to assist in* future litigation." *United States v. El Paso,* 682 F.2d 530, 542–43 (5th Cir.1982) (emphasis added) (citing *United States v. Davis,* 636 F.2d 1028, 1040 (5th Cir.1981)). On appeal in *Maine,* we specifically repudiated this test and adopted the broader "because of" test, which had been thoughtfully and carefully explained by Judge Leval in the Second Circuit decision in *Adlman,* 134 F.3d at 1202–03. *See Maine,* 298 F.3d at 68 ("In light of the decisions of the Supreme Court, we therefore agree with the formulation of the work-product rule adopted in *Adlman* and by five other courts of appeals.").

In the present case, the majority purports to follow *Maine,* but really conducts a new analysis of the history of the work-product doctrine and concludes that documents must be "'*prepared for* any litigation or trial.'" Similarly, at another point, the majority suggests that documents must be "for use" in litigation in order to be protected. *Grolier* did not establish such a test and the majority can point to no court that has so ruled.[20] Rather, the majority of circuit courts, led by the Second Circuit's decision in *Adlman,* have rejected such a rule.

Adlman's articulation of the "because of" test is fatal to the majority's position. In that case, Judge Leval discussed the application of the work-product doctrine "to a litigation analysis prepared by a party or its representative in order to inform a business decision which turns on the party's assessment of the likely outcome of litigation expected to result from the transaction." *Adlman,* 134 F.3d at 1197. In other words, *Adlman* asked whether the work-product doctrine applies where a dual purpose exists for preparing the legal analysis, that is, where the dual purpose of anticipating litigation and a business purpose

---

[20] [11] To support its conclusion, the majority commits a plain logical error. The majority states that work-product protection must not be judged solely on its subject matter, but rather whether the documents's purpose is *for use* in litigation. In support of this proposition, the majority cites a number of cases that propound the uncontroversial proposition that a document must be judged according to its purpose, not solely its content. But those cases do not establish the majority's rule that the documents' purpose *must be limited to use in litigation.* Rather, one of the cases the majority cites adopts the test that the document must have been created "because of" litigation, which, as *Adlman* describes, is antithetical to the majority's new requirement. *United States v. Roxworthy,* 457 F.3d 590, 593–94 (6th Cir.2006) (adopting *Adlman*'s "because of" test). Another of the majority's citations is from the D.C. Circuit, which has also since adopted the "because of" test. *Senate of Puerto Rico v. United States Dep't of Justice,* 823 F.2d 574, 587 n. 42 (D.C.Cir.1987). The final decision cited by the majority, from the Northern District of California, deals with the deliberative process privilege, not the work-product doctrine. *Church of Scientology Int'l v. IRS,* 845 F.Supp. 714, 723 (C.D.Cal.1993). In any event, the Ninth Circuit also applies the "because of" test. *In re Grand Jury Subpoena,* 357 F.3d 900, 907-08 (9th Cir.2004) (praising and following *Adlman*).

co-exist. To answer that question, the *Adlman* court examined and rejected the "primary purpose" test adopted by the Fifth Circuit in *El Paso*, 682 F.2d at 542-43, which only grants work-product immunity to workpapers prepared "primarily motivated to assist in future litigation over the return," *id.* at 543:

> [Protection] is less clear, however, as to documents which, although prepared because of expected litigation, are intended to inform a business decision influenced by the prospects of the litigation. The formulation applied by some courts in determining whether documents are protected by work-product privilege is whether they are prepared "primarily or exclusively to assist in litigation"—a formulation that would potentially exclude documents containing analysis of expected litigation, if their primary, ultimate, or exclusive purpose is to assist in making the business decision. Others ask whether the documents were prepared "because of" existing or expected litigation—a formulation that would include such documents, despite the fact that their purpose is not to "assist in" litigation. Because we believe that protection of documents of this type is more consistent with both the literal terms and the purposes of the Rule, we adopt the latter formulation.

Adlman, 134 F.3d at 1197-98, *quoted in part in Maine,* 298 F.3d at 68. And if it needs to be spelled out any more clearly, *Adlman* makes it explicitly clear that the broader "because of" formulation is not limited to documents prepared *for use* in litigation:

> We believe that a requirement that documents be produced primarily or exclusively to assist in litigation in order to be protected is at odds with the text and the policies of the Rule. Nowhere does Rule 26(b)(3) state that a document must have been prepared *to aid* in the conduct of litigation in order to constitute work product, much less *primarily or exclusively* to aid in litigation. Preparing a document "in anticipation of litigation" is sufficient.
>
> The text of Rule 26(b)(3) does not limit its protection to materials prepared to assist at trial. To the contrary, the text of the Rule clearly sweeps more broadly. It expressly states that work-product privilege applies not only to documents "prepared . . . for trial" but also to those prepared "in anticipation of litigation." If the drafters of the Rule intended to limit its protection to documents made to assist in preparation for litigation, this would have been adequately conveyed by the phrase "prepared . . . for trial." The fact that documents prepared "in anticipation of litigation" were also included confirms that the drafters considered this to be a different, and broader category. Nothing in the Rule states or suggests that documents prepared "in anticipation of litigation" with the purpose of assisting in the making of a business decision do not fall within its scope.

Id. at 1198-99 (emphasis and alterations in original). Rather than confront this language, the majority resorts to simplistic generalizations. Using its novel "prepared for" test, the majority unhelpfully explains that "[e]very lawyer who tries cases knows the touch and feel of materials prepared for a current or possible . . . law suit." Maj. Op. at 30. Once the majority ignores decades of controlling precedent, the matter becomes so clear that "[n]o one with experience of law suits" could disagree. *Id.*

I need say little else; the majority's new "prepared for" rule is blatantly contrary to *Adlman,* a leading case interpreting the work-product doctrine that we specifically adopted in *Maine.* The majority's opinion is simply stunning in its failure to even acknowledge this language and its suggestion that it is respecting rather than overruling *Maine.*

II.   The Majority Announces a Bad Rule

The majority acts as if it is left to this court to draw a line from *Hickman* to the present case. In so doing, the majority ignores a host of cases which grapple with tough work product questions that go beyond the stuff that "[e]very lawyer who tries cases" would know is work product. Lower courts deserve more guidance than a simple reassurance that a bare majority of the en banc court knows work product when it sees it. Of course, since this is an en banc proceeding, the majority is free to create a new rule for the circuit — though it would be better if it admitted that it was doing so. But our new circuit rule is not even a good rule.

First, as Judge Leval observed in *Adlman,* a "prepared for" requirement is not consistent with the plain language of Federal Rule of Civil Procedure 26, which provides protection for documents "prepared in anticipation of litigation *or* for trial." There is no reason to believe that "anticipation of litigation" was meant as a synonym for "for trial." Claudine Pease-Wingenter, *Prophetic or Misguided? The Fifth Circuit's (Increasingly) Unpopular Approach to the Work Product Doctrine,* 29 Rev. Litig. (forthcoming 2009) (analyzing and rejecting many of the arguments advanced by the majority in favor of a narrow construction of the phrase "anticipation of litigation"). Since the terms are not synonymous, the term "anticipation of litigation" should not be read out of the rule by requiring a showing that documents be prepared for trial. *See Carcieri v. Salazar,* — U.S. —, 129 S.Ct. 1058, 1066, 172 L.Ed.2d 791 (2009) (discussing the basic principle that statutes should be construed to give effect to each word).

Second, though the majority goes into some depth describing the foundational case of *Hickman v. Taylor,* it misses the fundamental concern of that decision with protecting an attorney's "privacy, free from unnecessary intrusion by opposing parties and their counsel." Without such privacy, litigants would seek unfair advantage by free-riding off another's work, thus reducing lawyers' ability to write down their thoughts:

> Were the attorney's work accessible to an adversary, the *Hickman* court cautioned, "much of what is now put down in writing would remain unwritten" for fear that the attorney's work would redound to the benefit of the opposing party. Legal advice might be marred by "inefficiency, unfairness and sharp practices," and the "effect on the legal profession would be demoralizing." Neither the interests of clients nor the cause of justice would be served, the court observed, if work product were freely discoverable.

Adlman, 134 F.3d at 1197 (quoting *Hickman,* 329 U.S. at 511, 67 S.Ct. 385). The majority posits that these rationales do not apply to documents containing a lawyer's legal analysis of a potential litigation, if that analysis was prepared for a business purpose. This is both unpersuasive and directly contrary to the policy analysis in *Adlman,* which we adopted in *Maine. Adlman* identified an example of a protected document:

> A business entity prepares financial statements to assist its executives, stockholders, prospective investors, business partners, and others in evaluating future courses of action. Financial statements include reserves for projected litigation. The company's independent auditor requests a memorandum prepared by the company's attorneys estimating the likelihood of success in litigation and an accompanying analysis of the company's legal strategies and options to assist it in estimating what should be reserved for litigation losses.

Adlman, 134 F.3d at 1200. Discussing this example, the court concluded that in this scenario "the company involved would require legal analysis that falls squarely within *Hickman*'s area of primary concern-analysis that candidly discusses the attorney's litigation strategies, appraisal of likelihood of success, and perhaps the feasibility of reasonable settlement." *Id*. Further, there is "no basis for adopting a test under which an attorney's assessment of the likely outcome of litigation is freely available to his litigation adversary merely because the document was created for a business purpose rather than for litigation assistance." *Id*. In other words,

> [i]n addition to the plain language of the Rule, the policies underlying the work-product doctrine suggest strongly that work-product protection should not be denied to a document that analyzes expected litigation merely because it is prepared to assist in a business decision. Framing the inquiry as whether the primary or exclusive purpose of the document was to assist in litigation threatens to deny protection to documents that implicate key concerns underlying the work-product doctrine.

Id. at 1199; *see also Roxworthy*, 457 F.3d at 595 (stating "the IRS would appear to obtain an unfair advantage by gaining access to KPMG's detailed legal analysis of the strengths and weaknesses of [the taxpayer's] position. This factor weighs in favor of recognizing the documents as privileged.").

The majority offers no response to this sound policy analysis and no reason to doubt that inefficiency and "sharp practices" will result from its new rule allowing discovery of such dual purpose documents, which contain confidential assessments of litigation strategies and chances. Instead of addressing these concerns, the majority's policy analysis relies instead on case-specific rationales — namely the need to assist the IRS in its difficult task of reviewing Textron's complex return. Such outcome determinative reasoning is plainly unacceptable. Thus, properly framed, it is clear that the rationales underlying the work-product doctrine apply to documents prepared in anticipation of litigation, even if they are not also for use at trial.[21]

And these policy rationales are squarely implicated in this case. First, Textron's litigation hazard percentages contain exactly the sort of mental impressions about the case that *Hickman* sought to protect. In fact, these percentages contain

---

[21] [13] Perhaps because of these very same concerns about privacy and fairness, the IRS itself argued for the protection of its documents prepared for the dual purposes of helping the IRS understand the litigation risks that might result if the IRS made the administrative decision to adopt a new program. *Delaney, Migdail & Young, Chartered v. IRS*, 826 F.2d 124 (D.C.Cir.1987). This point was also noted by the *Adlman* court when it observed that "the IRS successfully argued against the very position it here advocates." *Adlman*, 134 F.3d at 1201.

counsel's ultimate impression of the value of the case. Revealing such impressions would have clear free-riding consequences. With this information, the IRS will be able to immediately identify weak spots and know exactly how much Textron should be willing to spend to settle each item. Indeed, the IRS explicitly admits that this is its purpose in seeking the documents.

Second, as argued to us by amici, the Chamber of Commerce of the United States and the Association of Corporate Counsel, if attorneys who identify good faith questions and uncertainties in their clients' tax returns know that putting such information in writing will result in discovery by the IRS, they will be more likely to avoid putting it in writing, thus diminishing the quality of representation. The majority dismisses such concerns, concluding that tax accrual workpapers are required by law. But the majority fails to cite the record for this conclusion, likely because the majority is simply wrong. As the majority opinion earlier admits, the law only requires that Textron prepare audited financial statements reporting total reserves based on contingent tax liabilities. Accounting standards require some evidential support before such statements can be certified, but do not explicitly require the form and detail of the documents prepared here by Textron's attorneys with respect to each potentially challenged tax item. *See also* Michelle M. Henkel, *Textron: The Debate Continues as to Whether Auditor Transparency Waives the Work Product Privilege,* 50 Tax Management Memorandum 251, 260 (2009) (distinguishing auditor's workpapers and corporate workpapers and explaining that the latter are not mandatory but serve to evaluate a company's litigation risks). Rather, all that must be actually reported is the final tax reserve liability amount. Thus, as amici worry, the majority's new rule will have ramifications that will affect the form and detail of documents attorneys prepare when working to convince auditors of the soundness of a corporation's reserves.

These concerns are even more clearly implicated in this case because the majority's decision will remove protection for Textron's "backup materials" as well as its actual workpapers. The district court found that these materials included "notes and memoranda written by Textron's in-house tax attorneys reflecting their opinions as to which items should be included on the spreadsheet and the hazard of litigation percentage that should apply to each item." *United States v. Textron Inc.,* 507 F.Supp.2d 138, 143 (D.R.I.2007). Thus, these documents thus go beyond the numbers used to compute a total reserve. Rather, they explain the legal rationale underpinning Textron's views of its litigation chances. The majority fails to acknowledge this subtlety, explain why it views such documents as required by regulatory rules, or explain why such mental impressions should go unprotected. Exposing such documentation to discovery is a significant expansion of the IRS's power and will likely reveal information far beyond the basic numbers that the IRS could discover through production of Textron's auditor's workpapers.

But more important are the ramifications beyond this case and beyond even the case of tax accrual workpapers in general. The scope of the work-product doctrine should not depend on what party is asserting it. Rather, the rule announced in this case will, if applied fairly, have wide ramifications that the majority fails to address.

For example, as the IRS explicitly conceded at oral argument, under the majority's rule one party in a litigation will be able to discover an opposing party's analysis of the business risks of the instant litigation, including the amount of money set aside in a litigation reserve fund, created in accordance with similar requirements as Textron's tax reserve fund. Though this consequence was a major concern of the argument in this case, the majority does not even consider this "sharp practice," which its new rule will surely permit.

And there are plenty more examples. Under the majority's rule, there is no protection for the kind of documents at issue in *Adlman,* namely "documents analyzing anticipated litigation, but prepared to assist in a business decision rather than to assist in the conduct of the litigation." 134 F.3d at 1201–02. Nearly every major business decision by a public company has a legal dimension that will require such analysis. Corporate attorneys preparing such analyses should now be aware that their work product is not protected in this circuit.

III.   The Workpapers Are Protected Under the Right Test

Applying the "because of" test thoughtfully adopted in *Adlman* and *Maine,* the majority should have concluded that Textron's workpapers are protected by the work-product doctrine. The proper starting point in reaching this legal conclusion should be the factual findings of the district court, which held an evidentiary hearing to understand the nature of the documents sought here by the IRS.

A.   Factual findings

After considering affidavits and testimony, the district court found that the tax accrual workpapers are:

1. A spreadsheet that contains:

(a) lists of items on Textron's tax returns, which, in the opinion of Textron's counsel, involve issues on which the tax laws are unclear, and, therefore, may be challenged by the IRS;

(b) *estimates by* Textron's *counsel expressing, in percentage terms, their judgments regarding Textron's chances of prevailing in any litigation over those issues (the "hazards of litigation percentages");* and

(c) the dollar amounts reserved to reflect the possibility that Textron might not prevail in such litigation (the "tax reserve amounts").

Textron, 507 F.Supp.2d at 142-143 (emphasis added). These workpapers do not contain any facts about the transactions that concerned the IRS.

The district court also found, "[a]s stated by Norman Richter, Vice President of Taxes at Textron and Roxanne Cassidy, Director, Tax Reporting at Textron, Textron's ultimate purpose in preparing the tax accrual workpapers was to ensure that Textron was 'adequately reserved with respect to any potential disputes or litigation that would happen in the future.'" *Id.* at 143. Further, "there would have been no need to create a reserve in the first place, if Textron had not anticipated a dispute with the IRS that was likely to result in litigation or some other adversarial proceeding." *Id.* at 150.

In addition to recognizing these litigation purposes, the district court also recognized the dual purposes driving the creation of these documents and found that the workpapers' creation "also was prompted, in part" by the need to satisfy Textron's auditors and get a "clean" opinion letter. The district court later clarified:

> Thus, while it may *be* accurate to say that the workpapers helped Textron determine what amount should be reserved to cover any potential tax liabilities and that the workpapers were useful in obtaining a "clean" opinion from [the auditor] regarding the adequacy of the reserve amount, there would have been no need to create a reserve in the first place, if Textron had not anticipated a dispute with the IRS that was likely to result in litigation or some other adversarial proceeding.

Id. at 150. Relatedly, the district court found that anticipation of litigation was the "but for" cause of the documents' creation. Thus, the district court clearly found two purposes leading to the creation of the workpapers.

The majority makes no effort to reject these factual findings, but simply recharacterizes the facts as suits its purposes. For example, the majority declares, without reference to the district court's more nuanced findings, that the "the IRS is unquestionably right that the immediate motive of Textron in preparing the tax accrual work papers was to fix the amount of the tax reserve on Textron's books and to obtain a clean financial opinion from its auditor." At another point, the majority boldly pronounces, "the only purpose of Textron's papers was to prepare financial statements." Of course, as explained above, the district court's factual findings about Textron's "ultimate purpose" were directly contrary to these pronouncements. Discarding a district court's factual finding on causation without any demonstration of clear error is not within this court's proper appellate function. *See* Fed.R.Civ.P. 52(a) ("Findings of fact, whether based on oral or other evidence, must not be set aside unless clearly erroneous, and the reviewing court must give due regard to the trial court's opportunity to judge the witnesses' credibility."); *see also Constructora Maza, Inc. v. Banco de Ponce,* 616 F.2d 573, 576 (1st Cir.1980) (noting that clear error review applies even when "much of the evidence is documentary and the challenged findings are factual inferences drawn from undisputed facts").

Instead, the majority exalts in the fact that the district court made no finding that the documents were "*for use* in possible litigation." That proposition is true. But, as described above, "for use" (i.e. "prepared for") is not and has never been the law of this circuit.

The majority does suggest that the documents business purpose "cannot be disputed." This is also uncontroversial. The district court found both a litigation and a business purpose. But, in straining to ignore the documents' litigation purposes, the majority proceeds to rely heavily on the IRS's expert. In so doing, the majority makes no effort to explain why the district court should have been required to adopt the view that the workpapers existed only for a non-litigation purpose. The majority claims that Textron's witnesses agreed with the IRS expert, but the majority fails to reconcile this proclamation with the competing view of Textron's witnesses, which the district court explicitly relied upon in its factual findings regarding Textron's "ultimate purpose." *Textron,* 507 F.Supp.2d at 143. This is another corruption of the proper role of an appellate court. *See Anderson v. Bessemer City,* 470 U.S. 564, 574, 105 S.Ct. 1504, 84 L.Ed.2d 518 (1985) ("Where there are two permissible views of the evidence, the factfinder's choice between them cannot be clearly erroneous.").

The majority does suggest that the district court's findings regarding the cause of the workpapers' creation was only stated in its legal analysis section. But the actual purpose of the documents' creators, or, in the words of the district court, "but-for" causation, is a factual issue, and the majority makes no effort to explain why such issue should be reviewed as a legal conclusion.

The majority also proclaims, without record support, that "[a]ny experienced litigator would describe the tax accrual work papers as tax documents and not as case preparation materials." As described above, this conclusion reverses, without any finding of clear error, the district court's factual findings. Further, this language dangerously suggests that this court can, from its general knowledge, offer an expert opinion as to how such documents are always seen by "experienced litigators." Another of the many errors of this approach is revealed by reference to undisputed record testimony. Namely, the majority's assumption that tax accrual workpapers are a uniform class from corporation to corporation is simply wrong. When the district court carefully and specifically defined what documents were actually at issue in this case, it explained that "there is no immutable definition of the term 'tax accrual papers,'" and that their content varies from case to case, *Textron,* 507 F.Supp.2d at 142, a conclusion that is consonant with the testimony of the government's expert. Thus, even were it not our rule that we defer to the district court's factfinding, such a rule would make good sense in handling the wide range of workpapers likely to confront district courts in the future as the IRS increasingly seeks their discovery.

Even if we looked at the purpose of tax accrual workpapers as a general matter, the district court's conclusion that Textron's anticipation of litigation drove its reporting obligations is not so outrageous as to leave us with a firm conviction of error. Rather, other courts reviewing similar kinds of documents have reached similar conclusions. *Regions Fin. Corp. & Subsidiaries v. United States,* No. 2:06-CV-00895-RDP, 2008 WL 2139008, at *6 (N.D.Ala. May 8, 2008) (concluding, in examining another company's workpapers that "[w]ere it not for anticipated litigation, Regions would not have to worry about contingent liabilities and would have no need to elicit opinions regarding the likely results of litigation"); *Comm'r of Revenue v. Comcast Corp.,* 453 Mass. 293, 901 N.E.2d 1185, 1191, 1205 (2009) (affirming a finding of work-product protection for a business memorandum analyzing the "pros and cons of the various planning opportunities and the attendant litigation risks" since the author "had 'the prospect of litigation in mind when it directed the preparation of the memorandum'" and would not have been prepared irrespective of that litigation (quoting *Adlman,* 134 F.3d at 1204)).

B. Analysis

This court should accept the district court's factual conclusion that Textron created these documents for the purpose of assessing its chances of prevailing in potential litigation over its tax return in order to assess risks and reserve funds. Under these facts, work-product protection should apply.

1. The "because of" test

First, the majority does not develop any analysis contesting the proposition that disputes with the IRS in an audit can constitute litigation, within the meaning of Fed.R.Civ.P. 26(b)(3)(A). Indeed, such a conclusion is clear. For these purposes, the touchstone of "litigation" is that it is adversarial. *See* Restatement (Third) of the Law Governing Lawyers § 87 cmt. h (2000). Though the initial stages of a tax audit may not be adversarial, the disputes themselves are essentially adversarial; the subject of these disputes will become the subject of litigation unless the dispute is resolved.

Applying the "because of" test as articulated in *Adlman* and *Maine,* the work-papers are protected. Under these precedents, a document is protected if, "'in light of the nature of the document and the factual situation in the particular case, the document can be fairly said to have been prepared or obtained *because of* the prospect of litigation.'" *Maine,* 298 F.3d at 68 (emphasis in original) (quoting *Adlman,* 134 F.3d at 1202). The "because of" test "really turns on whether [the document] would have been prepared irrespective of the expected litigation with the IRS." *Adlman,* 134 F.3d at 1204. As the district court found, the driving force behind the preparation of the documents was the need to reserve money in anticipation of disputes with the IRS. *Textron,* 507 F.Supp.2d at 143. Though other business needs also contributed to Textron's need to create the documents, those needs depended on Textron's anticipating litigation with the IRS. In other words, without the anticipation of litigation, there would be no need to estimate a reserve to fund payment of tax disputes. *Id.* at 150. In this way, the dual purposes leading to the documents' creation were intertwined, and work-product protection should apply. *See In re Grand Jury Subpoena,* 357 F.3d at 910 ("The documents are entitled to work product protection because, taking into account the facts surrounding their creation, their litigation purpose so permeates any non-litigation purpose that the two purposes cannot be discretely separated from the factual nexus as a whole."); *see also* Andrew Golodny, *Note: Lawyers versus Auditors: Disclosure to Auditors and Potential Waiver of Work-Product Privilege in United States v. Textron,* 61 Tax Law. 621, 629 (2008) ("As a commentator noted, 'in the case of tax contingency reserves, the prospect of future litigation and the business need for the documents are so intertwined that the prospect of future litigation itself creates the business need for the document.'" (quoting Terrence G. Perris, *Court Applies Work Product Privilege to Tax Accrual Workpapers,* 80 Prac. Tax. Strategies 4 (2008))).

The majority simply refuses to accept the district court's finding that the documents would not exist but for Textron's need to anticipate litigation. This rejection is essential to the majority's erroneous conclusion. Accepting the district court's findings regarding purpose compels a finding of work-product protection, since the precedents are clear that under the "because of" test, dual purpose documents are protected. In fact, that is one of the very reasons some courts have adopted the test. 8 Charles Alan Wright, Arthur R. Miller & Richard L. Marcus, *Federal Practice and Procedure,* § 2024 (2d ed. 2009) ("'Dual purpose' documents created because of the prospect of litigation are protected even though they were also prepared for a business purpose."); *see also Roxworthy,* 457 F.3d at 598-99 ("[D]ocuments do not lose their work product privilege 'merely because [they were] created in order to assist with a business decision,' unless the documents 'would have been created in essentially similar form irrespective of the litigation.'" (quoting *Adlman,* 134 F.3d at 1202)); *In re Grand Jury Subpoena,* 357 F.3d at 907 (adopting Wright and Miller's "because of" test in order to handle "dual purpose" documents); *Maine,* 298 F.3d at 68 (adopting *Adlman* after recounting the distinction between the "because of" test and the "primary purpose" test in their handling of dual purpose documents); *Adlman,* 134 F.3d at 1197-98, 1202 ("Where a document is created because of the prospect of litigation, analyzing the likely outcome of that litigation, it does not lose protection under this formulation merely because it is created in order to assist with a business decision."); *In re Special Sept. 1978 Grand Jury (II),* 640 F.2d 49, 61 (7th Cir.1980) ("We conclude that the materials . . . were indeed prepared in anticipation of litigation, even though they were prepared as well for the filing of the Board of Elections reports.").

2. The exception to the "because of" test

The majority reads too much into one sentence from *Maine* and *Adlman.* Specifically, it is true that "the 'because of' standard does not protect from disclosure 'documents that are prepared in the ordinary course of business or that would have been created in essentially similar form irrespective of the litigation.'" *Maine,* 298 F.3d at 70 (quoting *Adlman,* 134 F.3d at 1202). This proviso relates to the advisory notes to the rule, which excludes from protection "[m]aterials assembled in the ordinary course of business, or pursuant to public requirements unrelated to litigation, or for other nonlitigation purposes." Fed.R.Civ.P. 26 advisory committee's note (1970). Understood in light of the fact that the "because of" test unequivocally protects "dual purpose" documents, this proviso does not strip protection for dual purpose documents that have one business or regulatory purpose. Rather, the best reading of the advisory committee's note is simply that preparation for business or for public requirements is preparation for a nonlitigation purpose insufficient in itself to warrant protection. The note states that there is no protection for documents created for business, regulatory, or "other nonlitigation purposes." This language suggests the note is considering business and regulatory purposes as nonlitigation purposes, but does not suggest that the presence of such a purpose should somehow override a litigation purpose, should one exist. Thus, correctly formulated, this exception should be understood as simply clarifying the rule that dual purpose documents are protected, though "there is no work-product immunity for documents prepared in the regular course of business *rather than* for purposes of the litigation." Charles A. Wright & Arthur R. Miller, *supra,* § 2024 (emphasis added); *see also Roxworthy,* 457 F.3d at 599 ("[A] document can be created for both use in the ordinary course of business and in anticipation of litigation without losing its work-product privilege."). Under the majority's interpretation, the exception swallows the rule protecting dual purpose documents.

So understood, the exception does not control this case. After citing this exception, the district court concluded that the documents were not created irrespective of litigation because Textron would not have prepared the documents but for the anticipation of litigation. *Textron,* 507 F.Supp.2d at 150. The majority makes no effort to label this finding clearly erroneous. To the contrary, the finding is correct. The tax accrual workpapers identify specific tax line items, and then anticipate the likelihood that litigation over those items will result in Textron having to pay the IRS more money. That Textron will not ultimately litigate each position does not change the fact that when it *prepared* the documents, Textron was acting to anticipate and analyze the consequences of possible litigation, just like the memorandum example in *Adlman,* 134 F.3d at 1200. The documents would not be the same at all had Textron not anticipated litigation. So, under the "because of" test, as applied in *Adlman* and the many circuit courts that have followed it, these documents were not prepared "irrespective" of the prospect of litigation. They should be protected.

3. *Arthur Young* and *El Paso* do not control

Neither the Supreme Court's decision in *United States v. Arthur Young & Co.,* 465 U.S. 805, 104 S.Ct. 1495, 79 L.Ed.2d 826 (1984), nor the Fifth Circuit's decision in *El Paso,* 682 F.2d at 530, support a different result.

In *Arthur Young,* the Court declined to recognize an accountant's work-product doctrine, thus holding that tax accrual workpapers created by an independent auditor were not protected. *Arthur Young,* 465 U.S. at 815-21, 104 S.Ct. 1495. But unlike the Court in *Arthur Young,* we are not now confronted with the question of whether to recognize a new privilege. Here, the doctrinal decision we face is how to apply existing work-product doctrine to the present facts, in other words whether the "because of" test protects dual purpose documents, as the *Maine* and *Adlman* courts so held. This question was not at all presented in *Arthur Young*.

On the other hand, *El Paso* is clearly factually on point — there the Fifth circuit rejected work-product protection for similar tax accrual workpapers. *El Paso,* 682 F.2d at 542. But, as explained above, that court applied a different definition of the work-product doctrine, asking whether the "*primary motivating purpose* behind the creation of the document was to aid in possible future litigation." *Id*. at 542-44 (concluding that the document should not be protected as it "carries much more the aura of daily business than it does of courtroom combat"). Finding Textron's workpapers protected would not *create* a circuit split, but be merely an application of a widely acknowledged existing difference between our law and the law of the Fifth Circuit. It is precisely in these "dual purpose" situations that the "because of" test used in this circuit is meant to distinguish itself from the "primary purpose" test used in the Fifth Circuit. *Maine,* 298 F.3d at 68 (citing *Adlman* for the proposition that the primary purpose test "is at odds with the text and the policies of Rule 26 because nothing in it suggests that documents prepared for dual purposes of litigation and business or agency decisions do not fall within its scope"). Thus, unlike the Fifth Circuit, we need not assess whether the tax accrual workpapers carry more of one "aura" than another.

IV.   Conclusion

The majority's decision may please the IRS and some tax scholars who understandably see discovery of tax accrual workpapers as an important tool in combating fraud. But this decision will be viewed as a dangerous aberration in the law of a well-established and important evidentiary doctrine. Whatever else one may think about this case, the majority's assertion that it is following *Maine* is plainly erroneous. Rather, the majority's "prepared for" test is directly contrary to *Adlman,* a decision we explicitly adopted in *Maine*.

In straining to craft a rule favorable to the IRS as a matter of tax law, the majority has thrown the law of work-product protection into disarray. Circuits have already split interpreting the meaning of "anticipation of litigation," between the "primary purpose" and "because of" tests. Now this court has proceeded to further the split by purporting to apply the "because of" test while rejecting that test's protection for dual purpose documents. In reality, the majority applied a new test that requires that documents be actually "prepared for" use in litigation. The time is ripe for the Supreme Court to intervene and set the circuits straight on this issue which is essential to the daily practice of litigators across the country.

The correct test is that spelled out in *Adlman,* and adopted by most circuit courts. Applying that test to the facts actually found by the district court, these tax accrual workpapers should be protected. For these reasons, I respectfully dissent.

———————

Textron filed a petition of certiorari with the United States Supreme Court on December 24, 2009.

PROBLEM 4-17

Client is approached by CPA-1, who offers to provide Client a plan that will generate tax losses to offset client's large gain from selling Client's business. Client hears CPA-1 out. Client expresses some doubt about the plan. CPA-1 refers Client to CPA-2, who provides Client a written opinion about the tax consequences of the plan. Client agrees to move forward with the plan. Client retains Lawyer to implement the plan. In March of the following year, Client goes to Enrolled Agent for preparation of Client's income tax return. Enrolled Agent calls CPA-3 with Client's approval for advice about the tax consequences of the plan, which CPA-3 provides in writing; Enrolled Agent relies on this advice in preparing Client's return. Which, if any, of the communications with the CPAs, Enrolled Agent or Lawyer are privileged?

PROBLEM 4-18

Assuming that the district court decision in *Textron* is upheld, would the result be the same with respect to FIN 48 workpapers for a year to which FIN 48, discussed in Chapter 3, applies?

PROBLEM 4-19

If *Textron* is reversed on the ground that the tax accrual workpapers were not prepared "because of" the prospect of litigation, but rather to comply with SEC rules, would the result be the same for a privately held company, with no intention of "going public," that voluntarily undertakes a similar analysis to support its financial statements, perhaps to strengthen its application for an increased loan from its bank?

Chapter 5

STATE REGULATORY ISSUES

I. INTRODUCTION

Model Rule 5.7 and Comments

The tax professional community includes a range of people with different levels and kinds of experience, education and professional licenses. Members of this community include lawyers, CPAs, other accountants, enrolled agents, return preparers with limited expertise, enrolled actuaries, employee benefits and pension consultants who may or may not have law or accounting backgrounds and others, in environments ranging from bank trust departments to real estate offices and insurance companies. Virtually all of these people at one time or another give advice to their clients or customers about tax matters; such advising, no matter how modest, would probably be considered the practice of law if undertaken by a lawyer in a law firm for the benefit of a client.[1] The theory in such cases seems to be that because an attorney is licensed to practice law, any professional services performed by the attorney are performed in his capacity as an attorney.[2] This position is also reflected in Model Rule 5.7, often subjecting a lawyer to the provisions of the Model Rules with respect to the provision of "law-related services."[3] Indeed, ABA Formal Op. 328 (1972) (predating the Model Rules) stated that lawyers who engage in a second occupation that is so law-related as to involve some practice of law are held to the standards of the bar in the second occupation because, in carrying on a law-related profession, a lawyer "almost inevitably will engage to some extent in the practice of law, even though the activities are such that a layman can engage in them without being engaged in the unauthorized practice of law."

However, much of this activity, when engaged in by nonlawyers, is either not regarded as the practice of law or is tolerated, regardless of whether regarded as the practice of law, by state bars, state supreme courts and even some state statutes. For example, the preparation of a simple tax return by a salaried return preparer working for H & R Block would almost certainly not be treated as the practice of law by even the most protective state supreme court. However, once the return gets more complicated, how the states will respond is much less clear.[4] For this reason, although this chapter is principally about how the

---

[1] *See, e.g.*, Comm. on Prof'l Ethics & Conduct of the Iowa State Bar Ass'n v. Mahoney, 402 N.W. 2d 434 (Iowa 1987) (tax return preparation); Columbus Bar Ass'n v. Agee, 196 N.E.2d 98, 101 (Ohio 1964) (general statement about work in income tax field); *see also* ABA Formal Op. 85–352 (1985).

[2] *See* State v. Williamson, 123 N.W. 2d 452 (Wis. 1963); Librarian v. State Bar, 136 P.2d 321 (Cal. Super. Ct. 1943).

[3] Comment [9] to Model Rule 5.7(b) offers accounting and tax preparation services as examples of law-related services.

[4] *See Mahoney*, 402 N.W.2d at 436 (tax return preparation not always the practice of law); Gardner v. Conway, 48 N.W.2d 788,796–797 (preparation of returns by accountant not the practice of law, but is the practice of law if required to resolve "difficult or doubtful questions of law").

reach of regulation of the practice of law at the state level affects tax professionals generally, including lawyers, the chapter begins by looking at what activities of tax professionals may be regarded as the practice of law even when conducted by nonlawyers, such that these activities might be viewed by the state bars or courts as the unauthorized practice of law (UPL).

After examining the unauthorized practice of law issue as a matter of state bar regulation, we will turn to the impact of the authority conferred by the federal government on tax professionals to practice before the IRS, considering whether this may be said in effect to authorize some tax practitioners for all practical purposes to engage in the practice of law to some degree. We will next consider the degree to which tax lawyers may engage in multijurisdictional practice (MJP), either within the confines of state bar ethical rules that permit limited MJP or by virtue of the authority enjoyed to practice before the IRS.

The final section of the chapter will explore advertising and solicitation restrictions applicable to tax professionals, both under state bar ethics rules and under Circular 230. In this connection, we will also look at state bar programs that certify tax specialists, this being one qualification that can lawfully be advertised.

II. UNAUTHORIZED PRACTICE OF LAW BY NONLAWYERS

TP wins bcts, engaging in Law, unlikely event.

AGRAN v. SHAPIRO
California Superior Court, Appellate Department
273 P.2d 619 (1954)

PATROSSO, J.

Plaintiff instituted this action to recover the sum of $2,000 for what his complaint denominates as "accounting services" rendered to the defendants, and from a resulting judgment in favor of the plaintiff for the amount sued for, defendants appeal.

Plaintiff is a certified public accountant practicing his profession in the city of Los Angeles, and admitted to practice as an agent before the Treasury Department of the United States. He is not, however, a member of the bar, and the question presented is whether the services in question or some portion thereof constitute the practice of law and for which he is not entitled to recover. The evidence discloses that in 1948 plaintiff was retained by the defendants as an accountant and auditor for a corporation, Motor Sales of California, Inc., which was owned or controlled by them, and also for the preparation of defendants' individual income tax returns. We are not concerned with the services rendered by plaintiff to the corporation, but only with those performed for the defendants as individuals. These consisted of the preparation of their federal income tax returns for each of the years 1947 to 1950, inclusive, as well as their estimated return for 1951 and other services related thereto as hereinafter set forth.

In the preparation of the joint return of the defendants for the calendar year 1948 plaintiff claimed as a deduction a loss in the sum of $43,260.56. [The defendants had leased a building to a used car dealer and had agreed to guarantee a bank against losses on used cars financed by and contracts discounted with the bank by the lessee. The loss resulted from this guarantee after the bank fore-closed against the lessee.]

Following the preparation by plaintiff of the defendants' 1948 return, . . . plaintiff prepared and filed on behalf of each defendant a separate "application for tentative carry-back adjustment" of the excess loss shown by the 1948 return ($ 29,074.83) to the two preceding years, 1946 and 1947. . . . While the record is somewhat obscure on this point, it appears inferentially at least that such applications were granted and each of the defendants received [a refund for the two years together totaling $ 1,804.65].

For the preparation of the 1947 return plaintiff charged and was paid the sum of $30. Plaintiff, however, submitted no statement to the defendants for the preparation of the returns for the years subsequent to 1947 except insofar as a charge for such services may be included in the bill which he submitted to the defendants under date of March 31, 1952, to which reference will hereinaf-ter be made. In explanation of this plaintiff testified that early in 1949 he advised the defendants "that he could not state what his fee at that time would be because as a matter of ordinary practice in the Bureau of Internal Revenue all tentative tax refund claims and income tax returns related thereto would be audited and investigated within three years from the date thereof by a rev-enue agent from said bureau, and therefore plaintiff would not be able to fix his accounting fee now but would charge defendants at a later date for the time and work involved in preparing said tax returns, refund claim, subsequent returns related thereto and in conferring and discussing said problem regard-ing this net operating business loss with revenue agent, and also would base said fee on any tax savings accomplished thereby."

It does not appear that plaintiff performed any services in connection with income tax matters for the defendants other than as stated, and seemingly no "problem" arose in connection with any of the previous returns until August, 1951, at which time he received a call from Mr. Manson, a treasury agent, in regard to the 1949 return, in which there had been claimed as a deduction the unused por-tion ($ 7,776.01) of the [loss sustained in 1948]. Several meetings were held between plaintiff and Mr. Manson, in the course of which the latter stated that the . . . loss did not qualify as a "net operating loss" and that as a result in recom-puting the returns for 1946 to 1949, inclusive, the defendants were subject to an additional assessment in the sum of $ 15,000. Plaintiff disputed this contention of Mr. Manson, countering with the claim that the loss was a "net operating loss" which could be "carried back" and "that tax benefits and refunds could be secured for the years 1946 through 1950." Plaintiff further testified that in his several conferences with Mr. Manson he "cited him numerous cases" and "spent five days in the county law library and in his office reading tax services, cases, reports and decisions." Again he testified that "he spent approximately four days in reading and reviewing over one hundred cases on the proposition of law involved." As a final result of the conferences between himself and plaintiff, Mr. Manson stated that he would submit a report recommending an additional assessment of $6,280, and such report was thereafter filed by him. At a later date another treasury agent, Mr. Stewart, was assigned to the case, with whom plaintiff met upon at least one occasion and had at least two telephone conferences.

Following these conferences plaintiff was advised by Mr. Stewart that he was in agreement with plaintiff's contention but that he "wanted to talk to the defendant once more"; Mr. Stewart further stating that the assessment would be reduced from $ 6,280 as recommended by Mr. Manson to $200, which latter amount would be assessed because of certain errors in the return unrelated to the matter of the loss in question. Some time later, in January or February, 1952, plaintiff was advised by Mr. Shapiro that he no longer needed plaintiff's services, and at the same time was advised that Mr. Shapiro had signed an agreement with Mr. Stewart closing the matter. Following this, and under date of March 31, 1952, plaintiff submitted a bill to the defendants in the sum of $ 2,000 which reads as follows:

"To Professional Services Rendered: —

"Conferences with revenue agent Edgar Manson re his examination of the income tax returns of Morris and Helen Shapiro for the years 1946, 1947, 1948 and 1949.

"Research of the problems involved and preparation of arguments to overcome the following proposed assessments of income tax:

"1946 and 1947	Morris	$1,804.65
	Helen	1,804.65
"1949		2,671.29
	Total Proposed Assessment	$6,280.59

"Conference with conferee James A. Stewart and subsequent discussion of the questions involved by telephone, resulting in a reversal of all disputed items contained in revenue agent Manson's report.

"Report submitted by conferee James A. Stewart resulted in a tax saving in excess of $ 6,000.00 and was cleared to the Collector of Internal Revenue on February 5, 1952.

"Total due for services to date $ 2,000.00."

While courts have experienced difficulty in formulating a precise and all-embracing definition as to what constitutes the practice of law, the one generally accepted is that announced in *Eley* v. *Miller*, 7 Ind. App. 529, 535, and adopted by our Supreme Court in *People* v. *Merchants Protective Corp.* (1922), 189 Cal. 531, 535, as follows: "as the term is generally understood the practice of law is the doing and performing services in a court of justice in any matter depending therein throughout its various stages and in conformity with the adopted rules of procedure. But *in a larger sense it includes legal advice and counsel and the preparation of legal instruments and contracts by which legal rights are secured although such matter may or may not be depending* [sic] *in court.*" (Emphasis added.) However, whether a particular activity falls within this general definition is frequently a question of considerable difficulty, and particularly is this true in the field of taxation where questions of law and accounting are frequently inextricably intermingled as a result of which doubt arises as to where the functions of one profession end and those of the other begin. Specifically, whether practice before an administrative tribunal in tax matters constitutes the practice of law has been the subject of decisions elsewhere which appear to be in some conflict. The question, under the circumstances here, is a particularly perplexing one, and we acknowledge the aid and assistance which has been afforded us in our efforts to resolve it by the excellent briefs filed by counsel as amici curiae on behalf of The State Bar of California and the California Society of Certified Public Accountants, respectively.

It appears to be generally conceded that it is within the proper function of a public accountant, although not a member of the bar, to prepare federal income tax returns, except perhaps in those instances where substantial questions of law arise which may competently be determined only by a lawyer. In the case at hand we find no real difficulty in concluding that in the preparation of the income tax returns in question plaintiff did not engage in the practice of law. They are of such a simple character that an ordinary layman without legal or accounting training might have prepared them in the first instance. An inspection thereof discloses that the defendants had but three sources of taxable income: Mr. Shapiro's salary, the rental received from the building leased to Mr. Pritchard, and the rental from a two-flat building, one-half of which was occupied by the defendants as their residence, with the exception of the year 1950 in which the defendants in addition received interest from savings and loan associations in the total sum of $ 612.68. Likewise the deductions claimed therein, other than the portion of the Pritchard loss carried forward into the 1949 return were usual and ordinary expenses incident to the ownership and operation of income producing real property, the determination of the propriety of which required no particular legal knowledge.

A different and more serious question arises, however, with respect to the services rendered by the plaintiff in preparing the applications for a carry back adjustment and refund of taxes paid for the previous two years, and the preparation of the 1949 return wherein a deduction was claimed for a portion of the Pritchard loss, as well as his subsequent services in resisting the additional assessment proposed by the Treasury Department upon the ground that the Pritchard loss did not constitute a "net operating loss" within the meaning of the "carry back" provisions of the statute. At this stage no question of accounting was involved. Neither the fact that the loss had been sustained nor the manner in which it arose was questioned. The only question was whether, under the admitted facts, the loss was one which could be "carried back," the answer to which depended upon whether or not it was a loss "attributable to the operation of a trade or business regularly carried on by the taxpayer" within the meaning of that phrase as used in the Internal Revenue Code, section [172]. We see no escape from the conclusion that under the circumstances this question was purely one of law. . . . And in *Commissioner of Int. Rev.* v. *Smith* (U.S.C.A. 2 Cir., 1953), 203 F.2d 310, 311, rev. 17 T.C. 135, 142, cert. den., 346 U.S. 816, the court said: "Whether a particular loss or expense is incurred in a taxpayer's trade or business is a question of fact in each particular case. *Higgins* v. *Commissioner of Int. Rev.*, 312 U.S. 212; Treas. Reg. 111, sec. 29.23 (k)-6. But insofar as this determination involves interpretation of the statutory language, it raises an issue of law on which the Tax Court's decision is subject to review here. . . ."

Not only was the question which arose here one of law but a difficult and doubtful one as well, as evidenced by the many occasions upon which the courts and the Treasury Department have had occasion to consider it. Moreover, it is evident that the plaintiff himself fully appreciated this. He not only testified that "in his opinion it was a tough case because it was an isolated one" but he detailed at length the extensive research of the legal authorities which he was required to make in order to support his position that the loss was one which qualified as a "net operating loss" under a proper interpretation of the statutory definition.

Both parties place reliance upon the decision in the *Matter of New York County Lawyers Assn.* (1948), 273 App. Div. 524, commonly referred to as the Bercu case, which was affirmed without opinion in 299 N.Y. 728. There one Bercu, an accountant, not a member of the bar, was consulted by a corporation . . . as to whether or not certain sales taxes accrued but not paid in a preceding year could be deducted in the income tax return for a subsequent year. Thereafter he rendered an opinion to the effect that such taxes might be deducted in the year of their payment, for which services he submitted a bill for $500. This not being paid, he instituted suit in the municipal court and was denied recovery upon the ground that the services for which he sought payment constituted the practice of law. Thereafter the reported proceeding was instituted by the Lawyers' Association to have him adjudged guilty of contempt of court and to enjoin him from similar activities in the future. The court held that in undertaking to render an opinion upon the point in question Mr. Bercu was unlawfully undertaking to practice law. However, the court seems to have been influenced in reaching the conclusion which it did largely by reason of the fact that Mr. Bercu had not previously performed any accounting work for the corporation, nor was the advice given in connection with the preparation by him of an income tax return for the corporation. It must be admitted that, as contended by plaintiff here, the language of the opinion suggests that if Bercu had been the accountant of the corporation or engaged to prepare its income tax return, he might have advised it as he did in his opinion without subjecting himself to the charge of practicing law in so doing. In the course of the opinion it said (78 N.Y.S.2d 220): "Respondent is most persuasive when he challenges the consistency of recognizing an accountant's right to prepare income tax returns while denying him the right to give income tax advice. As respondent says, precisely the same question may at one time arise during the preparation of an income tax return and at another time serve as the subject of a request for advice by a client. The difference is that in the one case the accountant is dealing with a question of law which is only incidental to preparing a tax return and in the other case he is addressing himself to a question of law alone."

Thus it would appear that the New York court adopts, as the criterion for determining whether advice relative to tax matters constitutes the practice of law, whether or not it is given as an incident to accounting work or in the preparation of tax returns. While for reasons hereinafter stated we are not prepared to accept the view to its fullest extent, we do not believe that the court necessarily entertained the view that, as plaintiff here contends, having prepared the return, an accountant who is not a member of the bar may thereafter undertake to advise his client with respect to difficult or doubtful legal questions arising therefrom or undertake to seek a refund, the right to which depends wholly upon the interpretation of the taxing statutes. No such question was there presented, and we are not prepared to accept the decision as holding that a nonlawyer may properly perform services such as those last enumerated.

We believe, however, that the criterion formulated by the New York court for determining whether a particular activity does or does not constitute the practice of law is unsatisfactory for the reasons well stated by the Supreme Court of Minnesota in *Gardner* v. *Conway* (1951), 234 Minn. 468. There a nonlawyer had undertaken to prepare a federal income tax return which necessarily involved the determination by him of various questions of law. By reason of this a proceeding in contempt and to restrain him from similar practice in the future was instituted against him, and he defended upon the ground that, while the preparation of the tax return involved the determination of legal questions, this did not constitute the practice of law because the resolving of such questions was but incidental to the preparation of the return which was an act that any layman might perform. . . . In the course of an elaborate opinion, after pointing out the necessity, despite the difficulty involved, of establishing some criterion for distinguishing "that which is from that which is not law practice," the court said: "If we bear in mind that any choice of criterion must find its ultimate justification in the interest of the public and not in that of advantage for either lawyer or nonlawyer, we soon cease to look for an answer in any rule of thumb such as that based upon a distinction between the incidental and the primary. Any rule which holds that a layman who prepares legal papers or furnishes other services of a legal nature is not practicing law when such services are incidental to another business or profession completely ignores the public welfare. A service performed by one individual for another, even though it be incidental to some other occupation, may entail a difficult question of law which requires a determination by a trained legal mind. Are we to say that a real estate broker who examines an abstract of title and furnishes an opinion thereon may not be held to practice law because the examination of a title is ancillary to a sale and purchase of real estate? . . . The incidental test has no value except in the negative sense that if the furnishing of the legal service is the primary business of the actor such activity is the practice of law, even though such service is of an elementary nature. In other words, a layman's legal service activities are the practice of law unless they are incidental to his regular calling; but the mere fact that they are incidental is by no means decisive. In a positive sense, the incidental test ignores the interest of the public as the controlling determinant.

"In rejecting the incidental test, it follows that the distinction between law practice and that which is not may be determined only from a consideration of the nature of the acts of service performed in each case. No difficulty arises where such service is the primary business of the actor. We then have law practice. Difficulty comes, however, when the service furnished is incidental to the performance of other service of a nonlegal character in the pursuit of another calling such as that of accounting. In the field of income taxation, as in the instant case, we have an overlapping of both law and accounting. An accountant must adapt his accounting skill to the requirements of tax law, and therefore he must have a workable knowledge of law as applied to his field. By the same token, a lawyer must have some understanding of accounting. In the income tax area, they occupy much common ground where the skills of both professions may be required and where it is difficult to draw a precise line to separate their respective functions. The public interest does not permit an obliteration of all lines of demarcation. We cannot escape reality by hiding behind a facade of nomenclature and assume that 'taxation,' though composed of both law and accounting, is something *sui generis* and apart from the law. If taxation is a hybrid of law and accounting, it does not follow that it is so wholly

without the law that its legal activities may be pursued without proper qualifications and without court supervision. The interest of the public is not protected by the narrow specialization of an individual who lacks the perspective
and the orientation which comes only from a thorough knowledge and understanding of basic legal concepts, of legal processes, and of the interrelation of
the law in all its branches. Generally speaking, whenever, as incidental to
another transaction or calling, a layman, as part of his regular course of conduct, resolves legal questions for another — at the latter's request and for a
consideration — by giving him advice or by taking action for and in his behalf,
he is practicing law if difficult or doubtful legal questions are involved which,
to safeguard the public, reasonably demand the application of a trained legal
mind. What is a difficult or doubtful question of law is not to be measured by
the comprehension of a trained legal mind, but by the understanding thereof
which is possessed by a reasonably intelligent layman who is reasonably familiar with similar transactions. A criterion which designates the determination
of a difficult or complex question of law as law practice, and the application of
an elementary or simple legal principle as not, may indeed be criticized for
uncertainty if a rule of thumb is sought which can be applied with mechanical
precision to all cases. Any rule of law which purports to reflect the needs of the
public welfare in a changing society, by reason of its essential and inherent
flexibility, will, however, be as variable in operation as the particular facts to
which it is applied."

We are confirmed in our conclusion that the activities of the plaintiff which
we have detailed fall within the domain of the lawyer by a consideration of The
Statement of Principles Relating to Practice in the Field of Federal Income
Taxation, which was recommended by the National Conference of Lawyers and
Certified Public Accountants and approved by The Council of the American
Institute of Accountants May 8, 1951, wherein it is stated (pars. 3, 6, 8):

"3. *Ascertainment of probable tax effects of transactions.* * * * The ascertainment of probable tax effects of transactions frequently is within the
function of either a certified public accountant or a lawyer. However, in
many instances, problems arise which require the attention of a member
of one or the other profession, or members of both. When such ascertainment raises uncertainties as to the interpretation of law (both tax law and
general law), or uncertainties as to the application of law to the transaction involved, the certified public accountant should advise the taxpayer
to enlist the services of a lawyer. When such ascertainment involves
difficult questions of classifying and summarizing the transaction in a
significant manner and in terms of money, or interpreting the financial
results thereof, the lawyer should advise the taxpayer to enlist the services
of a certified public accountant. * * *

"6. *Representation of taxpayers before Treasury Department.* Under
Treasury Department regulations lawyers and certified public accountants are authorized, upon a showing of their professional status, and
subject to certain limitations as defined in the Treasury Rules, to
represent taxpayers in proceedings before that Department. If, in the
course of such proceedings, questions arise involving the application of
legal principles, a lawyer should be retained, and if, in the course of
such proceedings accounting questions arise, a certified public accountant should be retained. * * *

"8. *Claims for refund.* * * * Claims for refund may be prepared by lawyers or certified public accountants, provided, however, that where a controversial legal issue is involved or where the claim is to be made the basis of litigation, the services of a lawyer should be obtained." (37 A.B.A.J., 517, 536–537).

From what has been said, it appears that plaintiff undertook to determine the "tax effect" of defendant's transaction with Pritchard, the ascertainment of which involved uncertainties both as to the interpretation of the taxing statute as well as the application thereof to the transaction in question. It is likewise evident from the plaintiff's testimony that at the time of preparing the application for carry back adjustment and refund he realized that a "controversial legal issue" was involved with respect to which the Treasury Department might take a contrary view, for he assigned this as a reason why he could not then advise defendants as to what his fee in the matter would be. And when he finally submits his bill we find that, in detailing therein the services covered thereby, no mention is made of accounting work or that involved in the preparation of the returns, but rather he describes the same as consisting of "conferences with revenue agent(s)" and *"research of the problems involved and preparation of arguments to overcome"* the proposed additional assessments, the only basis for which could be the Treasury Department's claim that the Pritchard loss did not constitute a "net operating loss" under section [172]. Surely the solution of this "problem" did not involve or depend upon the application of accounting principles or procedure, but of legal principles and precedents. These were the subject of plaintiff's "research" and these alone could serve as the foundation for his "arguments" addressed to the representatives of the Treasury Department in resisting the "proposed assessments."

From what has been said, we would have but little hesitancy in concluding that the services rendered by plaintiff other than those involved in the preparation of the income tax returns and possibly others of an accounting character constitute the practice of law as that term has been judicially defined in this state. The more serious questions which present themselves, however, are (1) whether the controlling test of what constitutes the practice of law in the field of federal income taxation is dictated by federal legislation, congressional or administrative, and (2) the effect of the federal regulations which have been adopted in this field. Upon behalf of the plaintiff, it is urged by amicus curiae that an affirmative answer is required to the first inquiry and that, inasmuch as plaintiff was enrolled as an agent in the Treasury Department, and by virtue thereof licensed to practice before that department, all of his activities in the instant case were within the scope of such license, and any action by a state court which would interfere with or curtail the right so granted is not only unwarranted but unconstitutional.

By the Act of July 7, 1884, . . . Secretary of the Treasury is authorized to prescribe "regulations governing the recognition of agents . . . representing claimants before his Department . . ." Pursuant to this statutory authority, the secretary issued Circular 230, which insofar as material here reads as follows: "An agent enrolled before the Treasury Department shall have the same rights, powers and privileges and be subject to the same duties as an enrolled attorney: *Provided*, that an enrolled agent shall not have the privilege of drafting or preparing any written instrument by which title to real or personal property may be conveyed or transferred for the purpose of affecting Federal taxes, nor shall such enrolled agent advise a client as to the legal sufficiency of such an instrument or its legal effect upon the Federal taxes of such client; *And provided further*, That nothing in the regulations in this part shall be construed as authorizing persons not members of the bar to practice law.". . . [The last clause appears by itself today as Circular 230 § 10.32. The remainder of the earlier provision is no longer in Circular 230, which instead authorizes various categories of professionals to "practice before the Internal Revenue Service" (§ 10.3) and then defines such "practice" (§ 10.2(d)) in language somewhat more expansive than the language in the paragraph immediately below, but which nonetheless seems to imply that the activities in the first proviso above are not within the authority granted under Circular 230.]

"Practice before the Treasury Department shall be deemed to comprehend all matters connected with the presentation of a client's interests to the Treasury Department, including the preparation and filing of necessary written documents, and correspondence with the Treasury Department relative to such interests. Unless otherwise stated, the term 'Treasury Department,' as used in this paragraph and elsewhere in this part, includes any division, branch, bureau, office, or unit of the Treasury Department, whether in Washington or in the field, and any officer or employee of any such division, branch, bureau, office or unit."

[The court here mentions the fact that CPAs can be admitted to practice before the Tax Court, but does not seem to attach much importance to this fact.]

No case which we have been able to discover has undertaken to directly decide the precise question with which we are confronted, namely, whether the Treasury regulations referred to have the effect of declaring that services performed by an enrolled agent in connection with federal income tax matters do not constitute the practice of law in the sense that such practice is prohibited, by state law, when engaged in by other than members of the bar. We direct our attention, however, to such as have been cited as having more or less a bearing upon the question.

* * *

In re Lyon (1938), 301 Mass. 30, cited on behalf of plaintiff . . . is, we believe, factually distinguishable. Moreover, it must be viewed in the light of the discussion in the more recent decision of the same court — *Lowell Bar Assn.* v. *Loeb* (1943), 2[3]15 Mass. 176, wherein the court adverted to but did not undertake to determine the effect of the Treasury regulations previously referred to. The court there said: "Neither do we consider at this time whether the permission granted to certified public accountants and other persons not members of the bar to practice in tax matters by the rules of the United States Treasury Department and of the administrative tribunal . . . now called the Tax Court of the United States, can have the effect of granting by implication to holders of 'Treasury enrollment cards' a right to perform in this Commonwealth services in connection with Federal taxes which in their nature are comprised in the practice of law. It may deserve consideration whether the rules of a Federal administrative tribunal can legalize acts done in the States in matters not actually before the tribunal, though of a class that might eventually come before it."

Were we convinced that the effect of the Treasury Regulations is to declare that acts constituting the practice of law in the accepted sense could lawfully be performed by nonmembers of the bar, we would entertain the same doubts as those suggested by the Supreme Judicial Court of Massachusetts in the portion of the opinion quoted above. We do not, however, believe that the regulations in question were intended to or have the effect contended for on behalf of plaintiff. We regard as highly significant the concluding clause in section 10.2(f) "that nothing in the regulations in this part shall be construed as authorizing persons not members of the Bar to practice law." This statement must be read in context with the opening sentence of the section providing that "An agent enrolled before the Treasury Department shall have the same rights, powers and privileges . . . as an enrolled attorney" and as qualifying the same. As admittedly the Treasury Department is without authority to prescribe the rights and privileges to be exercised by persons except those appearing before it upon behalf of others, this provision could only have been intended as a disavowal of any intent upon the part of the Secretary of the Treasury to confer authority upon enrolled agents, not members of the bar, to perform acts upon behalf of others in connection with matters before the department which would otherwise constitute the practice of law. We cannot subscribe to the argument advanced upon behalf of the plaintiff that this provision was merely "a catch-all clause designed to prevent enrolled agents from holding themselves out as general attorneys" and "to limit the authority granted an enrolled agent to the precise field of Federal income taxation." Rather it suggests a recognition that "practice before the Treasury Department," while it may include acts which do not constitute the practice of law, and hence within the authority of enrolled agents, though not lawyers, to perform, also comprehends others of such character as to bring them within this classification.

In essence plaintiff's contention is that the effect of the Treasury regulations is to declare that an enrolled agent, though not a lawyer, may, in the representation of others in tax matters before the Treasury Department, lawfully perform all of the services which a member of the bar is authorized to perform except "the privilege of drafting or preparing any written instrument by which title to real or personal property may be conveyed or transferred for the purpose of affecting Federal taxes" or advising "a client as to the legal sufficiency of such an instrument or its legal effect upon the Federal taxes of such client." If this be true, we see no reason for the concluding proviso in 10.2(f), disavowing any intent to thereby authorize nonlawyers to perform acts in connection with tax matters before the Department which would constitute the practice of law.

Yet another consideration confirms us in the conclusion we have reached. We refer to the Statement of Principles previously adverted to which were approved by the American Institute of Accountants, wherein it is recognized that representation before the Treasury Department may involve the "application of legal principles" necessitating the retention of a lawyer. We can hardly believe that, if the conferees representing the certified public accountants who joined in recommending the adoption of the Statement and the Members of the Council of the American Institute of Accountants who approved it, were of the view that the effect of the Treasury regulations authorized an enrolled agent who was not a lawyer to perform any and all services on behalf of others before the

Treasury Department that might be performed by a lawyer, they would have given their adherence thereto.

Thus we conclude that, as indicated, the judgment in favor of plaintiff includes an award for services, which constituted the practice of law, for which, not being a member of the bar, he was not entitled to recover.

It is tempting to think that *Agran* is irrelevant because it is more than fifty years old and is clearly at odds with the modern business world. In fact, when one of the authors first read the opinion, his reaction was that it reflects the fact that much of the judiciary is clueless about business practices. If the full implications of *Agran* needed to be reflected in the way tax practice is handled, the law schools would have to produce thousands of new tax lawyers immediately. As two observers have commented as recently as 2004, under *Agran* "preparation of even a simple tax return might constitute the practice of law" and "tax planning [would appear to be] definitely the practice of law and should not be done by nonlawyers."[5] Since this decision is so clearly at odds with the normal practice of accounting firms throughout the country, perhaps we should ask why.

The bottom line is that there is comparatively little litigation of UPL cases in the tax area. Historically, some bar groups attempted to have nonlawyers (or persons other than lawyers and CPAs) enjoined from preparing tax returns or publishing and distributing pamphlets or other printed material discussing ways to reduce taxes and prepare returns, but these cases have met with only limited success.[6] *Agran*, however, is typical of a kind of unauthorized practice of law case involving tax services that is not likely to disappear. Such cases feature a client who has been provided services by one not a member of the local bar (usually an accountant or a lawyer licensed to practice in another jurisdiction) and has decided to resist paying for the services by arguing that the provider engaged in UPL. Without having undertaken an exhaustive review of the cases, it appears that the clients in these cases seem to have received competent assistance, which makes the willingness of the courts to deprive the service provider of the agreed compensation all the more remarkable. After all, the whole rationale for prohibiting UPL is to protect clients from incompetent counsel. Yet these cases rarely, if ever, involve incompetent counsel! Certainly, there are no equitable considerations supporting a decision like *Agran*.

---

[5] Katherine D. Black & Stephen T. Black, *A National Tax Bar: An End to the Attorney-Accountant Tax Turf War*, 36 St. Mary's L. J. 1, 27–28 (2004).

[6] *See, e.g.*, Groninger v. Fletcher Trust Co., 41 N.E.2d 140 (Ind. 1942) (trust company distributed pamphlets with information about reducing taxes and preparing returns to customers; held, not UPL); New York County Lawyers' Ass'n v. Dacey, 21 N.Y.S.2d 694 (N.Y. 1957) (publication of "how to" book not UPL). A United States District Court in Texas, however, enjoined the publication of the Quicken Family Lawyer software, which included many standard legal forms for documents such as wills and premarital agreements (both of which obviously have significant tax consequences), on the ground that the publication of the software constituted UPL. The injunction was reversed on appeal. Unauthorized Practice of Law Comm. v. Parsons Tech., 1999 U.S. Dist. LEXIS 813 (N.D. Tex. 1999), *vacated and remanded*, 179 F.3d 956 (5th Cir. 1999). The result in the district court case was rejected by the Texas legislature as well. *See* Tex. H. B. 1507, 76th Leg., Reg. Sess. (Feb. 16, 1999). *See generally* 7 Am. Jur. 2d, Attorneys at Law § 119 (2004).

State authorities, on the other hand, often shy away from UPL cases. One of the authors was told by a friend who was for many years a state Deputy Attorney General that the state in question would never consider pursuing a UPL charge unless a nonlawyer actually tried to represent a client in court. Utah, on the other hand, in 2004 limited the practice of law category by legislation to practice before a court.[7] At first blush, this (and more of the same confusion in other states) suggests a federal standard for who is authorized to do what in the tax field as a tempting solution to the problem — until the question of who can prepare *state* tax returns and give *state* tax advice is raised. Surely, federalization could never extend this far. Yet, for most taxpayers, federal and state tax return preparation and planning are inevitably intertwined. Indeed, in many states, the state income tax system, at least, piggybacks to one degree or another on the federal system.

Despite the inherent confusion about the status of tax practice by nonlawyers, or by out-of-state lawyers, the consequences of engaging in UPL can be serious. The practitioner may not be able to collect a contractual fee, although some courts seem willing to consider a recovery on a quantum meruit basis. If the practitioner is subject to the supervision of some professional or state regulatory authority, the practitioner may have her right to practice suspended or terminated, and may be subject to other penalties, depending on the jurisdiction. The practitioner may be enjoined from certain kinds of tax practice activities and, if a lawyer licensed in another jurisdiction, might have her opportunity to be admitted in the state in which the unauthorized practice took place either delayed or perhaps permanently lost. If the client thought confidentiality and privilege attached to communications with a practitioner thought to be a lawyer, perhaps because the practitioner was admitted to the bar in another jurisdiction, these protections might not apply.

Consider Problems 5-1 through 5-3 under state law, i.e., without considering Circular 230 or federal preemption principles (discussed *infra*).

PROBLEM 5-1

Josie prepares state and federal income tax returns for a variety of small business clients and individuals. She has no formal training and is not an enrolled agent, licensed return preparer under state law, CPA, accountant, or lawyer. Assume that there is no state statute either authorizing her to prepare returns or barring her from preparing returns. From time to time, when a difficult question arises, such as whether an individual can deduct a hobby loss or the expense of a home office, she does research in the local law school library.

a. Is Josie engaged in UPL? No hot unauthorized practice of law.

b. Same facts as (a), except that Josie is an enrolled agent, entitled to represent taxpayers before the Internal Revenue Service. Same as A

c. Same facts as (b), except that a client's return is under audit by state tax authorities and Josie is preparing a memorandum to the state tax authorities on behalf of her client. Bordering law approach depends on state laws constitution.

---

[7] *See* UTAH CODE ANN. § 78-9-102. Utah also expressly authorizes CPAs to prepare tax returns and give tax advice. UTAH CODE ANN. § 58-26a-102(9).

d. Same facts as (a), except that Josie is a public accountant but not a CPA. *No*

e. Same facts as (a), except that Josie is a CPA, thereby authorized under Circular 230 to represent taxpayers before the IRS. *No not UPL*

f. Same facts as (a) through (e), except that clients often call Josie before buying or selling investments or their homes to ask her what the federal and state tax consequences of the sales will be. Josie keeps a few tax resources in her office and tries to answer these questions to the best of her ability. *Stronger aroma of being law*

PROBLEM 5-2

No, advised clients to obtain legal counsel not UPL.

a. Ernesto works for AAAA Life Insurance Company as an agent. Ernesto's income is principally derived from commissions generated by the sale of life insurance, annuities and related products. In assisting his insureds, he has found it useful to become educated about financial planning for higher education, retirement alternatives and succession planning for family businesses. He often provides guidance to his insureds on these matters, sometimes with spread sheets and written memos about the tax consequences of various scenarios. While he strongly counsels his clients to consult with their lawyers on such matters, he knows that many of them do not. Is he engaged in UPL? *See* In re New Jersey Soc'y of Certified Public Accountants, 507 A.2d 717 (N.J. 1986).

No, not UPL, consider PLR. If a CPA notion will practice law. Better grounds as a CPA.

b. Same facts as (a), above, except that Ernesto happens to be a CPA. Would your answer differ if Ernesto did not routinely counsel his clients to consult attorneys? In any event, should that really matter?

PROBLEM 5-3

Yes, incorrectly as she should reference cases. she prevails only b/c did not cite.

Penny, a CPA, represented a taxpayer before the IRS in connection with a dispute about the taxpayer's accounting method. Penny researched accounting methods in the county law library, but did not cite any cases in her communications with the IRS. Did Penny engage in the practice of law? *See* Zelkin v. Caruso Discount Corp., 9 Cal. Rptr. 220 (Ct. App. 2d Dist. 1960) (distinguishing *Agran* on the ground that Zelkin neither read the law nor cited any cases, although he performed research in two law libraries).

III. CIRCULAR 230, TAX COURT RULES AND FEDERAL PREEMPTION

Circular §§ 10.2(a), 10.3 and 10.32
Tax Court Rule 200(a) (Appendix F)

Despite state UPL prohibitions or restrictions on the provision by nonlawyers of tax services to clients, federal law clearly permits nonlawyers to practice before the IRS and to represent clients in Tax Court proceedings. Furthermore, under Circular 230 § 10.2(a)(4), practice before the IRS includes "rendering written advice with respect to any entity, transaction, plan or arrangement, or other plan or arrangement having a potential for tax avoidance or evasion," a description that probably covers most estate planning for relatively well-to-do clients (other than the drafting of legal documents such as wills and trusts) and a host of other kinds of tax planning, unless the planning is not accompanied by written advice.[8] The interplay between this authority and the authority of the states to regulate the practice of law within their respective jurisdictions is a matter of considerable controversy. The leading case related to this interplay, *Sperry v. Florida*, involved practice before the United States Patent Office (now called the United States Patent and Trademark Office). Read the opinion and see if you can figure out how, if at all, it applies to tax professionals.

SPERRY v. FLORIDA
United States Supreme Court
373 U.S. 379 (1963)

Atty prevails. FL has no authority to impose, summons, subpoena, as no Patent office is the Law body.

MR. CHIEF JUSTICE WARREN delivered the opinion of the Court.

Petitioner is a practitioner registered to practice before the United States Patent Office. He has not been admitted to practice law before the Florida or any other bar. Alleging, among other things, that petitioner "is engaged in the unauthorized practice of law, in that although he is not a member of The Florida Bar, he nevertheless maintains an office * * * in Tampa, Florida, * * * holds himself out to the public as a Patent Attorney * * * represents Florida clients before the United States Patent Office, * * * has rendered opinions as to patentability, and * * * has prepared various legal instruments, including * * * applications and amendments to applications for letters patent, and filed same in the United States Patent Office in Washington, D. C.," the Florida Bar instituted these proceedings in the Supreme Court of Florida to enjoin the performance of these and other specified acts within the State. Petitioner filed an answer in which he admitted the above allegations but pleaded as a defense "that the work performed by him for Florida citizens is solely that work which is presented to the United States Patent Office and that he charges fees solely for his work of preparing and prosecuting patent applications and patent assignments and determinations incident to preparing and prosecuting patent applications and assignments." Thereupon, the court granted the Bar's motion for a summary decree and permanently enjoined the petitioner from pursuing the following activities in Florida until and unless he became a member of the State Bar:

"1. using the term 'patent attorney' or holding himself out to be an attorney at law in this state in any field or phase of the law (we recognize that the respondent according to the record before us has already voluntarily ceased the use of the word 'attorney');

"2. rendering legal opinions, including opinions as to patentability or infringement on patent rights;

"3. preparing, drafting and construing legal documents;

"4. holding himself out, in this state, as qualified to prepare and prosecute applications for letters patent, and amendments thereto;

---

[8] The language of Circular 230 § 10.2(a)(4) was taken directly from 31 U.S.C. § 330(d), enacted in 2004 to strengthen Treasury's arsenal of tools to combat tax shelters. This underlying statutory authority, however, does not tell us anything about where the line is drawn, or is permitted to be drawn under the Constitution, between federal authority and state authority in this area.

"5. preparation and prosecution of applications for letters patent, and amendments thereto, in this state; and

"6. otherwise engaging in the practice of law."

The Supreme Court of Florida concluded that petitioner's conduct constituted the unauthorized practice of law which the State, acting under its police power, could properly prohibit, and that neither federal statute nor the Constitution of the United States empowered any federal body to authorize such conduct in Florida.

In his petition for certiorari, petitioner attacked the injunction "only insofar as it prohibits him from engaging in the specific activities * * * [referred to above], covered by his federal license to practice before the Patent Office. He does not claim that he has any right otherwise to engage in activities that would be regarded as the practice of law." We granted certiorari to consider the significant, but narrow, questions thus presented.

We do not question the determination that under Florida law the preparation and prosecution of patent applications for others constitutes the practice of law. Such conduct inevitably requires the practitioner to consider and advise his clients as to the patentability of their inventions under the statutory criteria as well as to consider the advisability of relying upon alternative forms of protection which may be available under state law. It also involves his participation in the drafting of the specification and claims of the patent application And upon rejection of the application, the practitioner may also assist in the preparation of amendments which frequently requires written argument to establish the patentability of the claimed invention under the applicable rules of law and in light of the prior art. Nor do we doubt that Florida has a substantial interest in regulating the practice of law within the State and that, in the absence of federal legislation, it could validly prohibit nonlawyers from engaging in this circumscribed form of patent practice.

But "the law of the State, though enacted in the exercise of powers not controverted, must yield" when incompatible with federal legislation. Congress has provided that the Commissioner of Patents "may prescribe regulations governing the *recognition* and conduct *of agents*, attorneys, *or other persons* representing applicants or other parties before the Patent Office," 35 U. S. C. § 31, and the Commissioner, pursuant to § 31, has provided by regulation that "an applicant for patent * * * *may be represented by an* attorney or *agent* authorized to practice before the Patent Office in patent cases." 37 CFR § 1.31. (Emphasis added.) The current regulations establish two separate registers "on which are entered the names of all persons recognized as *entitled to represent applicants* before the Patent Office in the preparation and prosecution of applications for patent." (Emphasis added.) One register is for attorneys at law and the other is for nonlawyer "agents." A person may be admitted under either category only by establishing "that he is of good moral character and of good repute and possessed of the legal and scientific and technical qualifications necessary to enable him to render applicants for patents valuable service, and is otherwise competent to advise and assist them in the presentation and prosecution of their applications before the Patent Office." 37 CFR § 1.341 (c).

The statute thus expressly permits the Commissioner to authorize practice before the Patent Office by nonlawyers, and the Commissioner has explicitly granted such authority. If the authorization is unqualified, then, by virtue of the Supremacy Clause, Florida may not deny to those failing to meet its own qualifications the right to perform the functions within the scope of the federal authority. A State may not enforce licensing requirements which, though valid in the absence of federal regulation, give "the State's licensing board a virtual power of review over the federal determination" that a person or agency is qualified and entitled to perform certain functions, or which impose upon the performance of activity sanctioned by federal license additional conditions not contemplated by Congress.

Respondent argues, however, that we must read into the authorization conferred by the federal statute and regulations the condition that such practice not be inconsistent with state law, thus leaving registered practitioners with the unqualified right to practice only in the physical presence of the Patent Office and in the District of Columbia, where the Office is now located.

The only language in either the statute or regulations which affords any plausible support for this view is the provision in the regulations that "registration in the Patent Office * * * shall only entitle the persons registered to practice before the Patent Office." 37 CFR § 1.341. Respondent suggests that the meaning of this limitation is clarified by reference to the predecessor provision, which provided that registration "shall not be construed as authorizing persons not members of the bar to practice law." Yet the progression to the more circumscribed language without more tends to indicate that the provision was intended only to emphasize that registration in the Patent Office does not authorize the general practice of patent law, but sanctions only the performance of those services which are reasonably necessary and incident to the preparation and prosecution of patent applications. That no more was intended is further shown by the contrast with the regulations governing practice before the Patent Office in trademark cases, also issued by the Commissioner of Patents. These regulations now provide that "recognition of any person under this section is not to be construed as sanctioning or authorizing the performance of any acts regarded in the jurisdiction where performed as the unauthorized practice of law." 37 CFR § 2.12 (d). The comparison is perhaps sufficiently telling. But any possible uncertainty as to the intended meaning of the Commissioner must be dispelled by the fact that when the present regulations were amended in 1948, it was first proposed to add a provision similar to that appearing in the trademark regulations. After objection had been leveled against the revision on the ground that it "indicated that the office thinks that the states have the power to circumscribe and limit the rights of patent attorneys who are not lawyers," the more sweeping language was deleted and the wording modified to its present form.

* * *

Examination of the development of practice before the Patent Office and its governmental regulation reveals that: (1) nonlawyers have practiced before the Office from its inception, with the express approval of the Patent Office and to the knowledge of Congress; (2) during prolonged congressional study of unethical practices before the Patent Office, the right of nonlawyer agents to practice before the Office went unquestioned, and there was no suggestion that abuses might be curbed by state regulation; (3) despite protests of the bar, Congress in enacting the Administrative Procedure Act refused to limit the right to practice before the administrative agencies to lawyers; and (4) the Patent Office has defended the value of nonlawyer practitioners while taking steps to protect the interests which a State has in prohibiting unauthorized practice of law. We find implicit in this history congressional (and administrative) recognition that registration in the Patent Office confers a right to practice before the Office without regard to whether the State within which the practice is conducted would otherwise prohibit such conduct.

* * *

Moreover, the extent to which specialized lay practitioners should be allowed to practice before some 40-odd federal administrative agencies, including the Patent Office, received continuing attention both in and out of Congress during the period prior to 1952. . . . Although [the Administrative Procedure Act] disavows any intention to change the existing practice before any of the agencies, so that the right of nonlawyers to practice before each agency must be determined by reference to the statute and regulations applicable to the particular agency, the history of § 6 (a) contains further recognition of the power of agencies to admit nonlawyers, and again we see no suggestion that this power is in any way conditioned on the approval of the State.

* * *

Finally, regard to the underlying considerations renders it difficult to conclude that Congress would have permitted a State to prohibit patent agents from operating within its boundaries had it expressly directed its attention to the problem. The rights conferred by the issuance of letters patent are federal rights. . . . The Government, appearing as *amicus curiae*, informs the Court that of the 7,544 persons registered to practice before the Patent Office in November 1962, 1,801 were not lawyers and 1,687 others were not lawyers admitted to the bar of the State in which they were practicing. Hence, under the respondent's view, one-quarter of the present practitioners would be subject to disqualification or to relocation in the District of Columbia and another one-fourth, unless reciprocity provisions for admission to the bar of the State in which they are practicing are available to them, might be forced to relocate, apply for admission to the State's bar, or discontinue practice. The disruptive effect which this could have upon Patent Office proceedings cannot be ignored. On the other hand, the State is primarily concerned with protecting its citizens from unskilled and unethical practitioners, interests which, as we have seen, the Patent Office now safeguards by testing applicants for registration, and by insisting on the maintenance of high standards of integrity. Failure to comply with these standards may result in suspension or disbarment. . . . Moreover, since patent practitioners are authorized to practice only before the Patent Office, the State maintains control over the practice of law within its borders except to the limited extent necessary for the accomplishment of the federal objectives.[9]

---

[9] [47] Because of the breadth of the injunction issued in this case, we are not called upon to determine what functions are reasonably within the scope of the practice authorized by the Patent Office. The Commissioner has issued no regulations touching upon this point. We note, however, that a practitioner authorized to prepare patent applications must of course render opinions as to the patentability of the inventions brought to him, and that it is entirely reasonable for a practitioner to hold himself out as qualified to perform his specialized work, so long as he does not misrepresent the scope of his license.

Review the last part of the *Agran* opinion. Is it consistent with *Sperry*? *See* Grace v. Allen, 407 S.W.2d 321 (Tex. Civ. App. 1966) (applying *Sperry* to allow a CPA to collect his fee for handling a case on administrative appeal within the IRS).

PROBLEM 5-4

Reconsider Problems 5-1 and 5-2(b). In the cases where you concluded that Josie or Ernesto was engaged in the practice of law, could a state succeed in a UPL action against them? In Problem 5-1(f), does it matter whether the advice is oral or written? Is Circular 230 § 10.32 relevant to these questions? If not, what is its import?

[handwritten margin notes: No, not anticipated unless formal pro... no, does not matter. Practitioners cannot practice law, however law is intermingled in tax.]

PROBLEM 5-5

a. Molly is an enrolled agent who resides and has her office in Philadelphia.
   1. Can Molly represent clients whose residence (if individuals) or only place of business is located across the Delaware River in New Jersey before the IRS? *[handwritten: Yes pro-hac-vice for lmtd instances + authort/is Federal.]*
   2. Can Molly design a pension plan for such a client? *[handwritten: No, lawyers do this C+B. Any legal doc. Practitioners should be wary]*
   3. Can Molly provide such a client advice about the tax consequences of the client's divorce? Does it matter whether the client is represented in the divorce proceeding by a member of the New Jersey Bar? *[handwritten: Tax consequences allowed, consult legal counsel]*
   4. Can Molly do estate planning for such a client? For a client whose residence is in Pennsylvania? *[handwritten: Legal advice always rendered by an atty not a tax practicioner.]*
   5. Can Molly advise such a client on matters of New Jersey state tax law? *[handwritten: yes, wary of legal]*
   6. Can Molly represent such a client in a New Jersey state tax audit? *[handwritten: Yes + maybenot stronger legal aroma]*

b. Same facts as (a), above, except that Molly is admitted to the Pennsylvania Bar but not the New Jersey Bar. *[handwritten: should advise NJ counsel for NJ matters]*

c. Same facts as (b), above, except that Molly's membership in the Pennsylvania Bar has been suspended. *[handwritten: No state or federal matters UPL.]*

d. Same facts as (c), above, except that Molly is also a CPA in good standing in Pennsylvania. *[handwritten: May prepare PA returns + federal, should disclose]*

e. Same facts as (a), above, except the question is whether Molly can provide federal tax advice about a planned merger of a New Jersey corporation into a Pennsylvania corporation. The merger will be governed by Pennsylvania law. *[handwritten: Tax advice limited, legal advice no, Too much Tetering in Law almost immersed]*

f. Same facts as (e), above, except that the merger will be governed by New Jersey law. *[handwritten: Same as above]*

PROBLEM 5-6

Manuel is a CPA licensed to practice in Virginia. He has also been admitted to the Bar of the United States Tax Court. Manuel has represented a Virginia client in a particular tax matter before the IRS through both the audit and administrative appeals process. When the notice of deficiency is issued, can he recommend that the client file a petition in the Tax Court? Is the answer different if Manuel is instead a member of the Bar in North Carolina, but not Virginia? *See* Model Rule 1.7.

[handwritten: Yes may petition in tax ct, but should have legal counsel. no, cannot in NC, yes different procedures legally in different states]

IV. MULTIJURISDICTIONAL PRACTICE

Most of tax practice, of course, involves the provision of advice to clients about federal tax law. As federal law experts, tax lawyers tend to think they may freely advise clients throughout the country despite being admitted to the bar in only one or two jurisdictions. State bar associations and regulatory authorities as well as state courts, on the other hand, take a much less sanguine view of out-of-state tax experts counseling their citizens and businesses. While this surely results in part from a protectionist view of law practice within a state's borders, it is also true that an out-of-state tax lawyer — no matter how well-versed in federal tax law — may know very little about relevant state law principles that may be highly relevant or even control the tax result. The materials that follow address the principal MJP issues that tax lawyers may confront, but it cannot be overemphasized that local case law (if any) and state bar ethics rules must be consulted. There is considerable variation around the country. Furthermore, a tax lawyer whose tax expertise is sought by clients outside his own state of licensure should always be mindful of the fact that the underlying state law in another jurisdiction might be different from that at home. Associating with a local lawyer is often a wise course, even when not required by the local ethics rules.

A. What Constitutes the Practice of Law in a State?

BIRBROWER, MONTALBANO, CONDON & FRANK v. SUPERIOR COURT
California Supreme Court
949 P.2d 1 (1998)

CHIN, J.

Business and Professions Code section 6125 states: "No person shall practice law in California unless the person is an active member of the State Bar." We must decide whether an out-of-state law firm, not licensed to practice law in this state, violated section 6125 when it performed legal services in California for a California-based client under a fee agreement stipulating that California law would govern all matters in the representation.

Although we are aware of the interstate nature of modern law practice and mindful of the reality that large firms often conduct activities and serve clients in several states, we do not believe these facts excuse law firms from complying with section 6125. Contrary to the Court of Appeal, however, we do not believe the Legislature intended section 6125 to apply to those services an out-of-state firm renders in its home state. We therefore conclude that, to the extent defendant law firm Birbrower, Montalbano, Condon & Frank, P.C. (Birbrower), practiced law in California without a license, it engaged in the unauthorized practice of law in this state. (§ 6125.) We also conclude that Birbrower's fee agreement with real party in interest ESQ Business Services, Inc. (ESQ), is invalid to the extent it authorizes payment for the substantial legal services Birbrower performed in California. If, however, Birbrower can show it generated fees under its agreement for limited services it performed in New York, and it earned those fees under the otherwise invalid fee agreement, it may, on remand, present to the trial court evidence justifying its recovery of fees for those New York services. Conversely, ESQ will have an opportunity to produce contrary evidence.

I.　BACKGROUND

The facts with respect to the unauthorized practice of law question are essentially undisputed. Birbrower is a professional law corporation incorporated in New York, with its principal place of business in New York. During 1992 and 1993, Birbrower attorneys, defendants Kevin F. Hobbs and Thomas A. Condon (Hobbs and Condon), performed substantial work in California relating to the law firm's representation of ESQ. Neither Hobbs nor Condon has ever been licensed to practice law in California. None of Birbrower's attorneys were licensed to practice law in California during Birbrower's ESQ representation.

ESQ is a California corporation with its principal place of business in Santa Clara County. In July 1992, the parties negotiated and executed the fee agreement in New York, providing that Birbrower would perform legal services for ESQ, including "All matters pertaining to the investigation of and prosecution of all claims and causes of action against Tandem Computers Incorporated [Tandem]." The "claims and causes of action" against Tandem, a Delaware corporation with its principal place of business in Santa Clara County, California, related to a software development and marketing contract between Tandem and ESQ dated March 16, 1990 (Tandem Agreement). The Tandem Agreement stated that "The internal laws of the State of California (irrespective of its choice of law principles) shall govern the validity of this Agreement, the construction of its terms, and the interpretation and enforcement of the rights and duties of the parties hereto." Birbrower asserts, and ESQ disputes, that ESQ knew Birbrower was not licensed to practice law in California.

While representing ESQ, Hobbs and Condon traveled to California on several occasions. In August 1992, they met in California with ESQ and its accountants. During these meetings, Hobbs and Condon discussed various matters related to ESQ's dispute with Tandem and strategy for resolving the dispute. They made recommendations and gave advice. During this California trip, Hobbs and Condon also met with Tandem representatives on four or five occasions during a two-day period. At the meetings, Hobbs and Condon spoke on ESQ's behalf. Hobbs demanded that Tandem pay ESQ $ 15 million. Condon told Tandem he believed that damages would exceed $ 15 million if the parties litigated the dispute.

Around March or April 1993, Hobbs, Condon, and another Birbrower attorney visited California to interview potential arbitrators and to meet again with ESQ and its accountants. Birbrower had previously filed a demand for arbitration against Tandem with the San Francisco offices of the American Arbitration Association (AAA). In August 1993, Hobbs returned to California to assist ESQ in settling the Tandem matter. While in California, Hobbs met with ESQ and its accountants to discuss a proposed settlement agreement Tandem authored. Hobbs also met with Tandem representatives to discuss possible changes in the proposed agreement. Hobbs gave ESQ legal advice during this trip, including his opinion that ESQ should not settle with Tandem on the terms proposed.

ESQ eventually settled the Tandem dispute, and the matter never went to arbitration. But before the settlement, ESQ and Birbrower modified the contingency fee agreement. The modification changed the fee arrangement from contingency to fixed fee, providing that ESQ would pay Birbrower over $ 1 million. The original contingency fee arrangement had called for Birbrower to receive "one-third (1/3) of all sums received for the benefit of the Clients. . . whether obtained through settlement, motion practice, hearing, arbitration, or trial by way of judgment, award, settlement, or otherwise. . . ."

In January 1994, ESQ sued Birbrower for legal malpractice and related claims in Santa Clara County Superior Court. Birbrower removed the matter to federal court and filed a counterclaim, which included a claim for attorney fees for the work it performed in both California and New York. The matter was then remanded to the superior court. There ESQ moved for summary judgment and/or adjudication on the first through fourth causes of action of Birbrower's counterclaim, which asserted ESQ and its representatives breached the fee agreement. ESQ argued that by practicing law without a license in California and by failing to associate legal counsel while doing so, Birbrower violated section 6125, rendering the fee agreement unenforceable. Based on these undisputed facts, the Santa Clara Superior Court granted ESQ's motion for summary adjudication of the first through fourth causes of action in Birbrower's counterclaim. The court also granted summary adjudication in favor of ESQ's third and fourth causes of action in its second amended complaint, seeking declaratory relief as to the validity of the fee agreement and its modification. The court concluded that: (1) Birbrower was "not admitted to the practice of law in California"; (2) Birbrower "did not associate California counsel";[10] (3) Birbrower "provided legal services in this state"; and (4) "The law is clear that no one may recover compensation for services as an attorney in this state unless he or she was a member of the state bar at the time those services were performed."

Although the trial court's order stated that the fee agreements were unenforceable, at the hearing on the summary adjudication motion, the trial court also observed: "It seems to me that those are some of the issues that this Court has to struggle with, and then it becomes a question of if they aren't allowed to collect their attorney's fees here, I don't think that puts the attorneys in a position from being precluded from collecting all of their attorney's fees, only those fees probably that were generated by virtue of work that they performed in California and not that work that was performed in New York."

* * *

Birbrower petitioned the Court of Appeal for a writ of mandate directing the trial court to vacate the summary adjudication order. The Court of Appeal denied Birbrower's petition and affirmed the trial court's order, holding that Birbrower violated section 6125. The Court of Appeal also concluded that Birbrower's violation barred the firm from recovering its legal fees under the written fee agreement, including fees generated in New York by the attorneys when they were physically present in New York, because the agreement included payment for California or "local" services for a California client in

---

[10] [2] Contrary to the trial court's implied assumption, no statutory exception to section 6125 allows out-of-state attorneys to practice law in California as long as they associate local counsel in good standing with the State Bar.

California. The Court of Appeal agreed with the trial court, however, in deciding that Birbrower could pursue its remaining claims against ESQ, including its equitable claim for recovery of its fees in quantum meruit.

We granted review to determine whether Birbrower's actions and services performed while representing ESQ in California constituted the unauthorized practice of law under section 6125 and, if so, whether a section 6125 violation rendered the fee agreement wholly unenforceable.

II.   DISCUSSION

A.   The Unauthorized Practice of Law

The California Legislature enacted section 6125 in 1927 as part of the State Bar Act (the Act), a comprehensive scheme regulating the practice of law in the state. Since the Act's passage, the general rule has been that, although persons may represent themselves and their own interests regardless of State Bar membership, no one but an active member of the State Bar may practice law for another person in California. The prohibition against unauthorized law practice is within the state's police power and is designed to ensure that those performing legal services do so competently.

A violation of section 6125 is a misdemeanor. (§ 6126.) Moreover, "No one may recover compensation for services as an attorney at law in this state unless [the person] was at the time the services were performed a member of The State Bar."

Although the Act did not define the term "practice law," case law explained it as "'the doing and performing services in a court of justice in any matter depending therein throughout its various stages and in conformity with the adopted rules of procedure.'" (*People v. Merchants Protective Corp.* (1922) 189 Cal. 531, 535 [209 P. 363] (*Merchants*).) *Merchants* included in its definition legal advice and legal instrument and contract preparation, whether or not these subjects were rendered in the course of litigation.

In addition to not defining the term "practice law," the Act also did not define the meaning of "in California." In today's legal practice, questions often arise concerning whether the phrase refers to the nature of the legal services, or restricts the Act's application to those out-of-state attorneys who are physically present in the state.

Section 6125 has generated numerous opinions on the meaning of "practice law" but none on the meaning of "in California." In our view, the practice of law "in California" entails sufficient contact with the California client to render the nature of the legal service a clear legal representation. In addition to a quantitative analysis, we must consider the nature of the unlicensed lawyer's activities in the state. Mere fortuitous or attenuated contacts will not sustain a finding that the unlicensed lawyer practiced law "in California." The primary inquiry is whether the unlicensed lawyer engaged in sufficient activities in the state, or created a continuing relationship with the California client that included legal duties and obligations.

Our definition does not necessarily depend on or require the unlicensed lawyer's physical presence in the state. Physical presence here is one factor we may consider in deciding whether the unlicensed lawyer has violated section

6125, but it is by no means exclusive. For example, one may practice law in the state in violation of section 6125 although not physically present here by advising a California client on California law in connection with a California legal dispute by telephone, fax, computer, or other modern technological means. Conversely, although we decline to provide a comprehensive list of what activities constitute sufficient contact with the state, we do reject the notion that a person *automatically* practices law "in California" whenever that person practices California law anywhere, or "virtually" enters the state by telephone, fax, e-mail, or satellite. (See e.g., *Baron v. City of Los Angeles* (1970) 469 P.2d 353 (*Baron*) ["practice law" does not encompass all professional activities].) We must decide each case on its individual facts.

This interpretation acknowledges the tension that exists between interjurisdictional practice and the need to have a state-regulated bar. As stated in the American Bar Association Model Code of Professional Responsibility, Ethical Consideration EC 3–9, "Regulation of the practice of law is accomplished principally by the respective states. Authority to engage in the practice of law conferred in any jurisdiction is not per se a grant of the right to practice elsewhere, and it is improper for a lawyer to engage in practice where he is not permitted by law or by court order to do so. However, the demands of business and the mobility of our society pose distinct problems in the regulation of the practice of law by the states. In furtherance of the public interest, the legal profession should discourage regulation that unreasonably imposes territorial limitations upon the right of a lawyer to handle the legal affairs of his client or upon the opportunity of a client to obtain the services of a lawyer of his choice in all matters including the presentation of a contested matter in a tribunal before which the lawyer is not permanently admitted to practice." *Baron* implicitly agrees with this canon.

* * *

Exceptions to section 6125 do exist, but are generally limited to allowing out-of-state attorneys to make brief appearances before a state court or tribunal. They are narrowly drawn and strictly interpreted. For example, an out-of-state attorney not licensed to practice in California may be permitted, *by consent of a trial judge*, to appear in California in a particular pending action.

In addition, with the permission of the California court in which a particular cause is pending, out-of-state counsel may appear before a court as counsel pro hac vice. A court will approve a pro hac vice application only if the out-of-state attorney is a member in good standing of another state bar and is eligible to practice in any United States court or the highest court in another jurisdiction. The out-of-state attorney must also associate an active member of the California Bar as attorney of record and is subject to the Rules of Professional Conduct of the State Bar. (See Rules Prof. Conduct, rule 1-100(D)(2) [includes lawyers from other jurisdictions authorized to practice in this state].)

* * *

B.   The Present Case

The undisputed facts here show that neither *Baron*'s definition nor our "sufficient contact" definition of "practice law in California" would excuse Birbrower's extensive practice in this state. Nor would any of the limited statutory exceptions to section 6125 apply to Birbrower's California practice. As the Court of

Appeal observed, Birbrower engaged in unauthorized law practice *in California* on more than a limited basis, and no firm attorney engaged in that practice was an active member of the California State Bar. As noted, in 1992 and 1993, Birbrower attorneys traveled to California to discuss with ESQ and others various matters pertaining to the dispute between ESQ and Tandem. Hobbs and Condon discussed strategy for resolving the dispute and advised ESQ on this strategy. Furthermore, during California meetings with Tandem representatives in August 1992, Hobbs demanded Tandem pay $ 15 million, and Condon told Tandem he believed damages in the matter would exceed that amount if the parties proceeded to litigation. Also in California, Hobbs met with ESQ for the stated purpose of helping to reach a settlement agreement and to discuss the agreement that was eventually proposed. Birbrower attorneys also traveled to California to initiate arbitration proceedings before the matter was settled. As the Court of Appeal concluded, ". . . the Birbrower firm's in-state activities clearly constituted the [unauthorized] practice of law" *in California.*

Birbrower contends, however, that section 6125 is not meant to apply to *any* out-of-state *attorneys*. Instead, it argues that the statute is intended solely to prevent nonattorneys from practicing law. This contention is without merit because it contravenes the plain language of the statute. Section 6125 clearly states that *no person* shall practice law in California unless that person is a member of the State Bar. The statute does not differentiate between attorneys or nonattorneys, nor does it excuse a person who is a member of another state bar.

Birbrower next argues that we do not further the statute's intent and purpose — to protect California citizens from incompetent attorneys — by enforcing it against out-of-state attorneys. Birbrower argues that because out-of-state attorneys have been licensed to practice in other jurisdictions, they have already demonstrated sufficient competence to protect California clients. But Birbrower's argument overlooks the obvious fact that other states' laws may differ substantially from California law. Competence in one jurisdiction does not necessarily guarantee competence in another. By applying section 6125 to out-of-state attorneys who engage in the extensive practice of law in California without becoming licensed in our state, we serve the statute's goal of assuring the competence of all attorneys practicing law in this state.

California is not alone in regulating who practices law in its jurisdiction. Many states have substantially similar statutes that serve to protect their citizens from unlicensed attorneys who engage in unauthorized legal practice. Like section 6125, these other state statutes protect local citizens "against the dangers of legal representation and advice given by persons not trained, examined and licensed for such work, whether they be laymen or lawyers from other jurisdictions." (*Spivak v. Sachs* (1965) 16 N.Y.2d 163 [263 N.Y.S.2d 953, 211 N.E.2d 329, 331].) Whether an attorney is duly admitted in another state and is, in fact, competent to practice in California is irrelevant in the face of section 6125's language and purpose. Moreover, as the North Dakota Supreme Court pointed out in *Ranta* [*v. McCarney* (N.D. 1986) 391 N.W.2d 161]: "It may be that such an [out-of-state attorney] exception is warranted, but such a plea is more properly made to a legislative committee considering a bill enacting such an exception or to this court in its rule-making function than it is in a judicial decision." (*Id.* at p. 165.) Similarly, a decision to except out-of-state attorneys licensed in their own jurisdictions from section 6125 is more appropriately left to the California Legislature.

[The court then refused to create an arbitration exception to section 6125's prohibition of the unlicensed practice of law in the state.]

Although, as discussed, we recognize the need to acknowledge and, in certain cases, to accommodate the multistate nature of law practice, the facts here show that Birbrower's extensive activities within California amounted to considerably more than any of our state's recognized exceptions to section 6125 would allow. Accordingly, we reject Birbrower's suggestion that we except the firm from section 6125's rule under the circumstances here.

C.   Compensation for Legal Services

Because Birbrower violated section 6125 when it engaged in the unlawful practice of law in California, the Court of Appeal found its fee agreement with ESQ unenforceable in its entirety. Without crediting Birbrower for some services performed in New York, for which fees were generated under the fee agreement, the court reasoned that the agreement was void and unenforceable because it included payment for services rendered to a California client in the state by an unlicensed out-of-state lawyer. The court opined that "When New York counsel decided to accept [the] representation, it should have researched California law, including the law governing the practice of law in this state." The Court of Appeal let stand, however, the trial court's decision to allow Birbrower to pursue its fifth cause of action in quantum meruit.[11] We agree with the Court of Appeal to the extent it barred Birbrower from recovering fees generated under the fee agreement for the unauthorized legal services it performed in California. We disagree with the same court to the extent it implicitly barred Birbrower from recovering fees generated under the fee agreement for the limited legal services the firm performed in New York.

It is a general rule that an attorney is barred from recovering compensation for services rendered in another state where the attorney was not admitted to the bar. The general rule, however, has some recognized exceptions.

Initially, Birbrower seeks enforcement of the entire fee agreement, relying first on the federal court exception. This exception does not apply in this case; none of Birbrower's activities related to federal court practice.

A second exception on which Birbrower relies to enforce its entire fee agreement relates to "Services not involving courtroom appearance." California has implicitly rejected this broad exception through its comprehensive definition of what it means to "practice law." Thus, the exception Birbrower seeks for all services performed outside the courtroom in our state is too broad under section 6125.

Some jurisdictions have adopted a third exception to the general rule of non-recovery for in-state services, if an out-of-state attorney "makes a full disclosure to his client of his lack of local license and does not conceal or misrepresent

---

[11] [5] We observe that ESQ did not seek (and thus the court did not grant) summary adjudication on the Birbrower firm's quantum meruit claim for the reasonable value of services rendered. Birbrower thus still has a cause of action pending in quantum meruit.

the true facts." For example, in *Freeling v. Tucker* (1930) 49 Idaho 475 [289 P. 85], the court allowed an Oklahoma attorney to recover for services rendered in an Idaho probate court. Even though an Idaho statute prohibited the unlicensed practice of law, the court excused the Oklahoma attorney's unlicensed representation because he had not falsely represented himself nor deceptively held himself out to the client as qualified to practice in the jurisdiction. (*Id.* at p. 86.) In this case, Birbrower alleges that ESQ at all times knew that the firm was not licensed to practice law in California. Even assuming that is true, however, we reject the full disclosure exception for the same reasons we reject the argument that section 6125 is not meant to apply to nonattorneys. Recognizing these exceptions would contravene not only the plain language of section 6125 but the underlying policy of assuring the competence of those practicing law in California.

Therefore, as the Court of Appeal held, none of the exceptions to the general rule prohibiting recovery of fees generated by the unauthorized practice of law apply to Birbrower's activities in California. Because Birbrower practiced substantial law in this state in violation of section 6125, it cannot receive compensation under the fee agreement for any of the services it performed in California. Enforcing the fee agreement in its entirety would include payment for the unauthorized practice of law in California and would allow Birbrower to enforce an illegal contract.

Birbrower asserts that even if we agree with the Court of Appeal and find that none of the above exceptions allowing fees for unauthorized California services apply to the firm, it should be permitted to recover fees for those limited services it performed exclusively *in New York* under the agreement. In short, Birbrower seeks to recover under its contract for those services it performed for ESQ in New York that did not involve the practice of law in California, including fee contract negotiations and some corporate case research. Birbrower thus alternatively seeks reversal of the Court of Appeal's judgment to the extent it implicitly precluded the firm from seeking fees generated in New York under the fee agreement.

We agree with Birbrower that it may be able to recover fees under the fee agreement for the limited legal services it performed for ESQ in New York to the extent they did not constitute practicing law in California, even though those services were performed for a California client. Because section 6125 applies to the practice of law in California, it does not, in general, regulate law practice in other states. Thus, although the general rule against compensation to out-of-state attorneys precludes Birbrower's recovery under the fee agreement for its actions in California, the severability doctrine may allow it to receive its New York fees generated under the fee agreement, if we conclude the illegal portions of the agreement pertaining to the practice of law in California may be severed from those parts regarding services Birbrower performed in New York. (. . . see also *Ranta, supra*, 391 N.W.2d at p. 166 [remanding case to determine which fees related to practice locally and which related to attorney's work in state where he was licensed].)

* * *

The fee agreement between Birbrower and ESQ became illegal when Birbrower performed legal services in violation of section 6125. It is true that courts will not ordinarily aid in enforcing an agreement that is either illegal or against public policy. Illegal contracts, however, will be enforced under certain circumstances, such as when only a part of the consideration given for the contract involves illegality. In other words, notwithstanding an illegal consideration, courts may sever the illegal portion of the contract from the rest of the agreement. ""When the transaction is of such a nature that the good part of the consideration can be separated from that which is bad, the Courts will make the distinction, for the . . . law . . . [divides] according to common reason; and having made that void that is against law, lets the rest stand. . . ."" If the court is unable to distinguish between the lawful and unlawful parts of the agreement, "the illegality taints the entire contract, and the entire transaction is illegal and unenforceable."

* * *

In this case, the parties entered into a fee agreement. ESQ was to pay money to Birbrower in exchange for Birbrower's legal services. The object of their agreement may not have been entirely illegal, assuming ESQ was to pay Birbrower compensation based in part on work Birbrower performed in New York that did not amount to the practice of law in California. The illegality arises, instead, out of the amount to be paid to Birbrower, which, if paid fully, would include payment for services rendered in California in violation of section 6125.

Therefore, we conclude the Court of Appeal erred in determining that the fee agreement between the parties was entirely unenforceable because Birbrower violated section 6125's prohibition against the unauthorized practice of law in California. Birbrower's statutory violation may require exclusion of the portion of the fee attributable to the substantial illegal services, but that violation does not necessarily entirely preclude its recovery under the fee agreement for the limited services it performed outside California.

Thus, the portion of the fee agreement between Birbrower and ESQ that includes payment for services rendered in New York may be enforceable to the extent that the illegal compensation can be severed from the rest of the agreement. On remand, therefore, the trial court must first resolve the dispute surrounding the parties' fee agreement and determine whether their agreement conforms to California law. If the parties and the court resolve the fee dispute and determine that [the] fee agreement is operable and does not violate any state drafting rules, the court may sever the illegal portion of the consideration (the value of the California services) from the rest of the fee agreement. [If] the trial court finds the fee agreement to be valid, it will determine whether some amount is due under the valid agreement. The trial court must then determine, on evidence the parties present, how much of this sum is attributable to services Birbrower rendered in New York. The parties may then pursue their remaining claims.

III. Disposition

We conclude that Birbrower violated section 6125 by practicing law in California. To the extent the fee agreement allows payment for those illegal local services, it is void, and Birbrower is not entitled to recover fees under the agreement for those services. The fee agreement is enforceable, however, to the extent it is possible to sever the portions of the consideration attributable to Birbrower's services illegally rendered in California from those attributable to Birbrower's New York services. Accordingly, we affirm the Court of Appeal judgment to the extent it concluded that Birbrower's representation of ESQ in California violated

Convicted of UPL

section 6125, and that Birbrower is not entitled to recover fees under the fee agreement for its local services. We reverse the judgment to the extent the court did not allow Birbrower to argue in favor of a severance of the illegal portion of the consideration (for the California fees) from the rest of the fee agreement, and remand for further proceedings consistent with this decision.

KENNARD, J., DISSENTING.

In California, it is a misdemeanor to practice law when one is not a member of the State Bar. In this case, New York lawyers who were not members of the California Bar traveled to this state on several occasions, attempting to resolve a contract dispute between their clients and another corporation through negotiation and private arbitration. Their clients included a New York corporation and a sister corporation incorporated in California; the lawyers had in previous years represented the principal owners of these corporations. The majority holds that the New York lawyers' activities in California constituted the unauthorized practice of law. I disagree.

The majority focuses its attention on the question of whether the New York lawyers had engaged in the practice of law *in California*, giving scant consideration to a decisive preliminary inquiry: whether, through their activities here, the New York lawyers had engaged in the practice of law *at all*. In my view, the record does not show that they did. In reaching a contrary conclusion, the majority relies on an overbroad definition of the term "practice of law." I would adhere to this court's decision in *Baron v. City of Los Angeles* (1970) 2 Cal. 3d 535, more narrowly defining the practice of law as the representation of another in a judicial proceeding or an activity requiring the application of that degree of legal knowledge and technique possessed only by a trained legal mind. Under this definition, this case presents a triable issue of material fact as to whether the New York lawyers' California activities constituted the practice of law.

I

Defendant Birbrower, Montalbano, Condon & Frank, P.C. (hereafter Birbrower) is a New York law firm. Its lawyers are not licensed to practice law in California.

Kamal Sandhu was the sole shareholder of ESQ Business Services Inc., a New York corporation (hereafter ESQ-NY), of which his brother Iqbal Sandhu was the vice-president. Beginning in 1986, Birbrower lawyers represented the Sandhu family in various business matters. In 1990, Kamal Sandhu asked Birbrower lawyer Kevin Hobbs to review a proposed software development and marketing agreement between ESQ-NY and Tandem Computers Incorporated (hereafter Tandem). The agreement granted Tandem worldwide distribution rights to computer software created by ESQ-NY. The agreement also provided that it would be governed by California law and that, according to Birbrower's undisputed assertion, disputes were to be resolved by arbitration under the rules of the American Arbitration Association. ESQ-NY and Tandem signed the agreement.

Thereafter, a second corporation, also named ESQ Business Services, Inc. (hereafter ESQ-CAL), was incorporated in California, with Iqbal Sandhu as a principal shareholder. In 1991, ESQ-CAL consulted Birbrower lawyers concerning Tandem's performance under the agreement. In 1992, ESQ-NY and ESQ-CAL jointly hired Birbrower to resolve the dispute with Tandem, including the investigation and prosecution of claims against Tandem if necessary. ESQ-NY and ESQ-CAL entered into a contingency fee agreement with Birbrower; this agreement was executed in New York but was later modified to a fixed fee agreement in California.

The efforts of the Birbrower lawyers to resolve the dispute with Tandem included several brief trips to California. On these trips, Birbrower lawyers met with officers of both ESQ-NY and ESQ-CAL and with representatives of Tandem; they also interviewed arbitrators and participated in negotiating the settlement of the dispute with Tandem. On February 12, 1993, Birbrower initiated an arbitration proceeding against Tandem, on behalf of both ESQ-NY and ESQ-CAL, by filing a claim with the American Arbitration Association in San Francisco, California. Before an arbitration hearing was held, the dispute with Tandem was settled.

In January 1994, ESQ-CAL and Iqbal Sandhu, the principal shareholder, sued Birbrower for malpractice. Birbrower cross-complained to recover its fees under the fee agreement. Plaintiffs ESQ-CAL and Iqbal Sandhu thereafter amended their complaint to add ESQ-NY as a plaintiff. Plaintiffs moved for summary adjudication, asserting the fee agreement was unenforceable because the Birbrower lawyers had engaged in the unauthorized practice of law in California. The trial court agreed, and granted plaintiffs' motion. The Court of Appeal upheld the trial court's ruling, as does a majority of this court today.

II

Business and Professions Code section 6125 states: "No person shall practice law in California unless the person is an active member of the State Bar." The Legislature, however, has not defined what constitutes the practice of law.

Pursuant to its inherent authority to define and regulate the practice of law, this court in 1922 defined the practice of law as follows: "'[A]s the term is generally understood, the practice of the law is the doing and performing services in a court of justice in any matter depending therein throughout its various stages and in conformity with the adopted rules of procedure. But in a larger sense it includes legal advice and counsel and the preparation of legal instruments and contracts by which the legal rights are secured although such matter may or may not be depending [sic] in a court.'"

In 1970, in *Baron v. City of Los Angeles, supra*, 2 Cal. 3d 535, 542 (*Baron*), this court reiterated the *Merchants* court's definition of the term "practice of law." We were quick to point out in *Baron*, however, that "ascertaining whether a particular activity falls within this general definition may be a formidable endeavor." *Baron* emphasized "that it is not the whole spectrum of professional services of lawyers with which the State Bar Act is most concerned, but rather it is the smaller area of activities defined as the 'practice of law.'" It then observed: "In close cases, the courts have determined that the resolution of legal questions for another by advice and action is practicing law 'if difficult or doubtful legal questions are involved which, to safeguard the public, reasonably demand the application of a *trained legal mind*.'" *Baron* added that "if the application of legal knowledge and technique is *required*, the activity constitutes the practice of law. . . ." This definition is quite similar to that proposed by Cornell Law School Professor Charles Wolfram, the chief reporter for the American Law Institute's Restatement of the Law Governing Lawyers: "The correct form of the test [for the practice of law] should inquire whether the matter handled was of such complexity that only a person trained as a lawyer should be permitted to deal with it." (Wolfram, Modern Legal Ethics (1986) p. 836.)

The majority asserts that the definition of practice of law I have stated above misreads this court's opinion in *Baron*. But what the majority characterizes as "the dissent's fanciful interpretation of the [*Baron* court's] thoughtful guidelines" consists of language I have quoted directly from *Baron*.

The majority also charges that the narrowing construction of the term "practice of law" that this court adopted in *Baron* "effectively limit[s] section 6125's application to those cases in which nonlicensed out-of-state lawyers appeared in a California courtroom without permission." Fiddlesticks. Because the *Baron* definition encompasses all activities that "'reasonably demand application of a trained legal mind'", the majority's assertion would be true only if there were no activities, apart from court appearances, requiring application of a trained legal mind. Many attorneys would no doubt be surprised to learn that, for example, drafting testamentary documents for large estates, preparing merger agreements for multinational corporations, or researching complex legal issues are not activities that require a trained legal mind.

* * *

The majority, too, purports to apply the definition of the practice of law as articulated in *Baron*. The majority, however, focuses only on *Baron*'s quotation of the general definition of the practice of law set forth in *Merchants, supra*. The majority ignores both the ambiguity in the *Merchants* definition and the manner in which *Baron* resolved that ambiguity. The majority apparently views the practice of law as encompassing *any* "legal advice and legal instrument and contract preparation, whether or not these subjects were rendered in the course of litigation."

The majority's overbroad definition would affect a host of common commercial activities. On point here are comments that Professor Deborah Rhode made in a 1981 article published in the Stanford Law Review: "For many individuals, most obviously accountants, bankers, real estate brokers, and insurance agents, it would be impossible to give intelligent counsel without reference to legal concerns that such statutes reserve as the exclusive province of attorneys. As one [American Bar Association] official active in unauthorized practice areas recently acknowledged, there is growing recognition that 'all kinds of other professional people are practicing law almost out of necessity.' Moreover, since most legislation does not exempt gratuitous activity, much advice commonly imparted by friends, employers, political organizers, and newspaper commentators constitutes unauthorized practice. For example, although the organized bar has not yet evinced any inclination to drag [nationally syndicated advice columnist] Ann Landers through the courts, she is plainly fair game under extant statutes [proscribing the unauthorized practice of law]." (Rhode, *Policing the Professional Monopoly: A Constitutional and Empirical Analysis of Unauthorized Practice Prohibitions, supra*, 34 Stan. L. Rev. at p. 47, fns. omitted.)

Unlike the majority, I would for the reasons given above adhere to the more narrowly drawn definition of the practice of law that this court articulated in *Baron*: the representation of another in a judicial proceeding or an activity requiring the application of that degree of legal knowledge and technique possessed only by a trained legal mind. Applying that definition here, I conclude that the trial court should not have granted summary adjudication for plaintiffs based on the Birbrower lawyers' California activities.

* * *

Birbrower stunned the legal community. While the opinion focused on two primary issues: (1) what constitutes the practice of law and (2) when is such practice of law in California, the response to the opinion dealt with neither of these issues — so the doctrinal holdings of the opinion are largely intact in California and are likely to be influential elsewhere. For example, *Birbrower* was relied upon by the Hawaii Supreme Court in a case involving an Oregon lawyer representing an Oregon corporation, who consulted with Hawaii counsel on an appeal in Hawaii and did a variety of work for his client in Oregon in connection with the dispute in Hawaii. Fought & Co. v. Steel Eng'g & Erection, 87 Haw. 37, 951 P.2d 487 (1998). The Hawaii Court, however, disagreed with *Birbrower*'s expansive view of when an out-of-state lawyer is treated as practicing law within a jurisdiction (Hawaii), noting that the global economy offers "compelling reasons for refraining from adopting" a view "so broad" that an out-of-state law firm "may automatically be deemed to have practiced law within the jurisdiction by advising a client regarding the effect of Hawaii law or by 'virtually entering' the jurisdiction on behalf of a client via telephone, fax, computer or other modern technological means." 951 P.2d at 497.[12] *See also* ALI RESTATEMENT OF THE LAW GOVERNING LAWYERS § 3 Jurisdictional Scope of Practice of Law by Lawyer.

The response to *Birbrower* was swift. The California legislature enacted a temporary rule authorizing most arbitrators to permit appearances by out-of-state lawyers. Subsequently, in 2004, the California Supreme Court adopted the California Supreme Court Rules on MJP (reproduced in Appendix M). Rule 9.66 permits an out-of-state attorney to temporarily practice law in California as part of a "formal proceeding,"[13] which is defined to mean "litigation, arbitration, mediation or a legal action before an administrative decision-maker." The permission is subject to a lengthy list of requirements.

Of most interest to the tax world is the last category of formal proceeding, legal action before an administrative decisionmaker. This seems to clearly authorize an out-of-state lawyer to represent a California client before the IRS if all the requirements of the Rule are satisfied, but that was probably authorized by federal law anyway. Perhaps more surprising, assuming that all the requirements of the provision are met, is that an out-of-state lawyer may be permitted to represent a California client before the California Franchise Tax Board, although not permitted to provide the client tax advice more generally.

---

[12] It seems clear to the authors that *Fought* was distinguishable because the Oregon lawyer clearly worked with local Hawaii counsel.

[13] The caption for Rule 9.66 reads "Attorneys practicing law temporarily in California as part of *litigation*." (Emphasis added.) One wonders whether this misleading caption is intentional.

What the new Rules do not do is change the definition of practice of law under California law or change the definition of practice of law *in California*. The implications of *Birbrower*, therefore, remain substantial for out-of-state tax practitioners. Before looking into these implications in the context of some Problems that compare the California rules on MJP with Model Rule 5.5, however, there is one more decision that addresses another aspect of the practice of law *in California* issue. Again, this case is likely to be influential in other jurisdictions.

ESTATE OF CONDON v. MCHENRY
California Court of Appeal, First District
65 Cal. App. 4th 1138 (1998)

WALKER, J.

Michael R. Condon and his attorneys, Michael Katz and his firm (the Elrod firm), appeal an order of the probate court denying Katz attorney fees for services rendered to the estate of Evelyn J. Condon. Michael, Evelyn's son, was appointed co-executor of her will with his sister, Caroline M. McHenry, the respondent to this appeal. Michael lives in Colorado; Caroline lives in California, as did their mother. The Elrod firm, which Evelyn J. Condon had retained to prepare her will and other documents effectuating her estate plan, is in Colorado, where the will was prepared, and where Katz is licensed to practice law. Katz is not a member of the California State Bar.

Michael retained Katz and the Elrod firm to advise him as co-executor in the probate proceedings. Caroline retained counsel in California, James Cody and his firm (the Carr firm), to represent her as co-executor in the same proceedings. The record reflects that Katz did most of his work in Colorado, where Michael resides, communicating by telephone, mail, and fax with Cody and with other of the Condon siblings in California.[14] Michael also retained California counsel, Dominic Campisi and his firm (the Evans firm), to file papers and make appearances on his behalf in the probate court in San Mateo County.

In January 1996, fully three acrimonious years after the will was admitted to probate, the parties scheduled a hearing to approve the account, distribute the estate's assets, and award the fees owed the executors and their attorneys. Michael, through Campisi, filed a petition seeking compensation from the estate for Katz's ordinary and extraordinary legal services. Caroline challenged the petition, asserting that some of the work for which Katz sought payment was done for Michael and their brother, Eugene, individually, not for the estate. She also contended that the sums Katz claimed were unreasonable.

The probate judge never reached the issues Caroline raised. Once he determined that Katz was not a member of the California State Bar and had not applied to appear *pro hac vice*, he expressed his view that Katz was not an "attorney" within the meaning of Probate Code section 10810: "[A]s far as this

---

[14] [2] Generally the services rendered by the Elrod firm and Katz at issue here, included implementation of the buy/sell agreement concerning the business assets; resolution of litigation and disputes regarding the disposition of other estate assets, including settlement negotiations and the preparation of a written settlement agreement; resolution of threatened litigation and disputes regarding life insurance, trust issues and the preparation of accountings. The Elrod firm expended 315.8 billable hours for non-tax-related services, of which only 10 represented hours for services rendered while Katz was physically present in California.

court is concerned he's not a licensed legal practitioner. . . ." The judge adjourned the hearing, telling Campisi, "I will give you [two hours] to come up with some authority [for me] to order payment out of a California estate to a nonmember of the California bar for attorney's fees[.]"

When the hearing resumed, the judge denied Katz's hastily assembled application for leave to appear *pro hac vice*. After hearing argument, he concluded that, by serving as counsel for the co-executor of a will written for a California decedent, which devised California property, and was subject to California probate proceedings, Katz, a nonmember of the State Bar, had "practice[d] law in California" in violation of Business and Professions Code section 6125. The court therefore refused to authorize payment of his legal fees. Michael and the Elrod firm timely appealed.

In our June 25, 1997, opinion, we reversed the probate court's order, holding that California Probate Code section 8570 et seq. allowed for such fees and that section 6125 did not proscribe them. Following our denial of a petition for rehearing, the Supreme Court granted review and ordered action on the cause deferred until disposition of *Birbrower, Montalbano, Condon & Frank v. Superior Court* (1998) (*Birbrower*) then pending before it. Following its decision, the Supreme Court transferred review to us with directions to vacate our prior decision and to reconsider that case in light of *Birbrower*.

Following our review we conclude that Katz did not violate section 6125. He is therefore entitled under the Probate Code to ordinary statutory fees and to extraordinary fees in whatever amount the court deems reasonable for the services he rendered to Michael in his capacity as co-executor.

THE LEGAL QUESTION

* * *

We must decide whether an out-of-state law firm, not licensed to practice law in California, violated section 6125 when it performed legal services by either physically or virtually[15] entering California on behalf of a Colorado client who was an executor of a California estate.

ANALYSIS

1. *The Probate Code Allows the Payment of Attorney Fees to an Out-of-state Attorney Rendering Services on Behalf of a California Estate.*

The Probate Code makes specific allowance for a nonresident, such as Michael, to serve as executor of a will subject to probate in California, and our courts have made clear that "[t]he executor[] has the right to choose independent counsel to perform the necessary legal services on behalf of the estate." Here, Michael's choice was not only his to make, it was also reasonable; the Elrod firm did business where he lived and its principals had originally prepared his mother's estate plan.

---

[15] [6] We define virtual presence as used in our opinion as entry into the State of California by telephone, fax, e-mail, satellite or any other means of communication when a person outside of the State of California communicates with one within.

* * *

2. *Section 6125 Does Not Proscribe an Award of Attorney Fees to an Out-of-state Attorney for Services Rendered on Behalf of an Out-of-state Client Regardless of Whether the Attorney Is Either Physically or Virtually Present Within the State of California.*

* * *

In fleshing out the definition of the practice of law in California the Supreme Court in *Birbrower* states: "Our definition does not necessarily depend on or require the unlicensed lawyer's physical presence in the state. Physical presence here is one factor we may consider in deciding whether the unlicensed lawyer has violated section 6125, but it is by no means exclusive. For example, one may practice law in the state in violation of section 6125 although not physically present here by advising a *California client* on California law in connection with a California legal dispute by telephone, fax, computer, or other modern technological means. Conversely, although we decline to provide a comprehensive list of what activities constitute sufficient contact with the state, we do reject the notion that a person *automatically* practices law 'in California' whenever that person practices California law anywhere, or 'virtually' enters the state by telephone, fax, e-mail, or satellite."

Implicit in the court's formulation of the rule is the ingredient that the client is a "California client," one that either resides in or has its principal place of business in California. This conclusion is not only logical, it comports with the reason underlying the proscription of section 6125.

In the real world of 1998 we do not live or do business in isolation within strict geopolitical boundaries. Social interaction and the conduct of business transcends state and national boundaries; it is truly global. A tension is thus created between the right of a party to have counsel of his or her choice and the right of each geopolitical entity to control the activities of those who practice law within its borders. In resolving the issue of the applicability of section 6125 it is useful to look to the reason underlying the proscription of section 6125. *Birbrower* instructs that the rationale is to protect California citizens from incompetent attorneys stating: "California is not alone in regulating who practices law in its jurisdiction. Many states have substantially similar statutes that serve to *protect their citizens* from unlicensed attorneys who engage in unauthorized legal practice. Like section 6125, these other state statutes protect local citizens 'against the dangers of legal representation and advice given by persons not trained, examined and licensed for such work, whether they be laymen or lawyers from other jurisdictions.' Whether an attorney is duly admitted in another state and is, in fact, competent to practice in California is irrelevant in the face of section 6125's language and *purpose*."

It is therefore obvious that, given the facts before us, the client's residence or its principal place of business is determinative of the question of whether the practice is proscribed by section 6125. Clearly the State of California has no interest in disciplining an out-of-state attorney practicing law on behalf of a client residing in the lawyer's home state.[16]

---

[16] [7] This, of course, does not apply to attorneys physically coming into California to practice law in our courts.

3. *The Applicability of the Birbrower Guidelines to This Case.*

It is apparent that both the facts and the issues in *Birbrower* are distinguishable from those presented in this case. Most significantly Michael R. Condon was a resident of the State of Colorado. Thus, the issue was not "whether an out-of-state law firm, not licensed to practice law in this state, violated section 6125, when it performed legal services in California for a *California-based client . . .*" but whether an out-of-state law firm practicing law on behalf of a resident of the lawyer's home state violated section 6125 when that lawyer either physically or virtually entered the State of California and practiced law on behalf of that client. Adopting the premise, as articulated in *Birbrower*, that the goal of section 6125 is to protect California citizens from incompetent or unscrupulous practitioners of law we must conclude that section 6125 is simply not applicable to our case.

The Elrod firm was retained by Michael to represent him in his capacity as coexecutor of the estate of Evelyn J. Condon. The firm's primary representation involved the implementation of the buy/sell agreement which was part of an estate plan drafted by the firm in Colorado. Its services involved the negotiation, settlement and drafting of documents resolving the dispute among the heirs of the estate leading to the sale of the estate's principal asset, the family business. The negotiation and discussion with beneficiaries of the estate and their attorneys in California occurred for the most part by phone, fax and mail while the attorneys were physically located in Colorado. It appears that communication between Michael and the Elrod firm took place entirely within Colorado.

Under *Birbrower* one of the factors to be considered by the court in determining the applicability of section 6125 is whether the practitioner is plying "California law." Nevertheless, our Supreme Court instructs that a person does not automatically practice law "in California" whenever that person practices "California law" anywhere. In the matter before this court there is no record reflecting that Katz was practicing "California law." Furthermore, that factor is not relevant to our holding. If indeed the goal of the statute is to protect California citizens from the incompetent and unscrupulous practitioner (licensed or unlicensed), it simply should make no difference whether the out-of-state lawyer is practicing California law or some other breed since the impact of incompetence on the client is precisely the same.

Also, it would be presumptuous of this court to assume that in a multistate business transaction where parties are located in diverse states and represented by counsel in those states, the lawyers are practicing "California law." Furthermore, it is insular to assume that only California lawyers can be trained in California law. Surely the citizens of states outside of California should not have to retain California lawyers to advise them on California law. Finally, the fact that California law was not implicated in the Elrod firm's representation of Michael R. Condon provides us additional impetus to conclude that the policy of protecting California citizens from untrained and incompetent attorneys has not been breached.

For the reasons stated herein we hold that Katz and the Elrod firm (licensed to practice law in Colorado) did not practice law "in California" within the meaning of section 6125 when its members entered California either physically or virtually to practice law on behalf of Michael (a Colorado citizen).

In light of the foregoing, we conclude that appellants did not violate our Business and Professions Code. Katz and the Elrod firm are, therefore, entitled under the Probate Code to ordinary statutory fees and to extraordinary fees in whatever amount the court deems reasonable for any services he rendered to Michael in his capacity as co-executor.

———

Although *Birbrower* surprised many corporate lawyers at major firms who think that they are free to advise anyone in the country who calls them, *Estate of Condon* is perhaps more surprising in allowing an out-of-state client to send his own out-of-state lawyer to represent him. It is true that the out-of-state lawyer worked with California counsel who handled court appearances, but the court shows a surprising deference to the out-of-state client's choice of counsel.

Florida would have been unlikely to allow this in the past in a probate context, although new rules might permit such a result now. More generally, though, Florida has historically taken a much more aggressive view of when an out-of-state lawyer is engaged in UPL within the state. Perhaps the most aggressive published example of Florida's view was Florida Bar Staff Opinion 24894 (Sept. 3, 2003). This informal advisory opinion was the result of an inquiry by a Florida lawyer about how to respond to inquiries by letter and telephone from out-of-state lawyers with out-of-state clients who owned Florida real estate. The inquiries often included claims, arguments and interpretations of Florida documents and Florida law. The opinion confirmed the propriety of the inquiring lawyer's response to the effect that it was inappropriate for him to communicate with "unadmitted" attorneys about Florida law and Florida real estate documents and that such matters should be handled through a Florida-admitted attorney. The Florida Bar Ethics counsel further noted that such a response was consistent with the inquiring lawyer's ethical obligation not to assist an out-of-state lawyer in UPL. The opinion did not say this was the only way to respond to the inquiries. Nor is it clear whether the fact that Florida real estate was involved was crucial. Finally, it should be noted that the mere giving of advice to a client about the law of another jurisdiction is not likely to be regarded as the practice of law in the other jurisdiction as such. There must presumably be more of a nexus with the other jurisdiction. In any event, Florida subsequently adopted a version of Model Rule 5.5, discussed below.

B. When is Practice by an Out-of-State Lawyer Permitted?

Model Rules 5.5 and Comments, and 8.5 and Comments
California Supreme Court MJP Rules (Appendix M)

The broadest response to *Birbrower* was the adoption of Model Rule 5.5, which does several things. First, Model Rule 5.5(a) makes it a violation of a state's rules of licensure to practice law in another jurisdiction in violation of the other jurisdiction's rules or to assist someone else in doing so. If this rule had been in effect in New York at the time that the representation at issue in *Birbrower* occurred, the New York lawyers who provided legal services in California would have been subject to discipline in New York. (The New York rule at the time produced the same result. NY Code of Prof. Resp. DR 3–101(b), as in effect before April 1, 2009.) Furthermore, under Model Rule 8.5, New York would have been obligated to apply California ethical rules to the lawyers' conduct because the lawyers' conduct occurred in California. It is clearly the intent of Model Rule 8.5 to subject out-of-state practitioners, in appropriate cases, to discipline in both the state of licensure and the state where the practice of law takes place.

Second, Model Rule 5.5(b) generally prohibits an out-of-state lawyer from establishing an office or "other systematic and continuous presence" in the state for the practice of law or holding out to the public or otherwise representing that the lawyer is admitted to practice in the state. The same standards appear in the California MJP Rules, but California Rules 9.66 and 9.67 add several other requirements, and thus are considerably more onerous.

Third, Model Rules 5.5(c) and (d) provide several exceptions, describing situations in which MJP is permitted. Most of these, such as providing legal services to the lawyer's employer or its organizational affiliates[17] or providing temporary services in association with a lawyer who is admitted to practice in the state and who actively participates in the matter, are not controversial and simply codify existing prior practice. Model Rule 5.5(d)(2) permits the out-of-state lawyer to provide services that a lawyer is authorized to provide by federal law or the law of the state. This principle, in the case of federal authorization, has been well-established for some time, but as this chapter indicates, is difficult to apply clearly across the board.

Model Rule 5.5(c)(2) provides an exception for services provided by an out-of-state lawyer on a temporary basis that are "in or reasonably related to a pending or potential proceeding before a tribunal" (whether in state or not) "if the lawyer, or a person the lawyer is assisting, is authorized by law or order to appear in such proceeding or reasonably expects to be so authorized." Comment [9] indicates that this exception applies where the proceeding is before an administrative agency. So it would apply to an appearance before a state or municipal agency that hears tax appeals or to an appearance before the IRS. The exception also applies to subordinate lawyers who are associated with the lawyer who reasonably expects to be authorized to appear or is authorized to appear but who perform other services in support of the lawyer responsible for the "litigation."[18]

Model Rule 5.5(c)(3) provides a similar exception for temporary services in or reasonably related to a pending or potential alternative dispute resolution proceeding if the services arise out of or are reasonably related to the lawyer's practice where the lawyer is licensed and are not services for which pro hac vice admission is required. This exception would seem to be of limited relevance to tax lawyers.

---

[17] Comment [16] states that this provision does not "authorize the provision of personal legal services to the employer's officers or employees." This may be a problem for a tax lawyer working in the general counsel's office who is not a member of the local bar and is occasionally asked for personal advice by an officer or employee. Of course, the careful lawyer should avoid answering such inquiries because of possible conflicts of interest in many cases.

[18] Comment [11] uses the word "litigation" but it seems clear that it should be read to include any kind of proceeding that otherwise qualifies for the exception under the rule.

It is Model Rule 5.5(c)(4) that has generated the most controversy. The Rule itself, like other controversial Model Rules, is vague, leaving plenty of questions to be resolved in its implementation. The Rule allows an out-of-state lawyer to provide on a temporary basis services that are not covered by paragraphs (c)(2) or (3) if the services "arise out of or are reasonably related to the lawyer's practice in a jurisdiction in which the lawyer is admitted to practice." The Comments add to this vague language, first by stating, in Comment [13], that such services include "services that nonlawyers may perform but that are considered the practice of law when performed by lawyers." This sounds as if it might include the preparation of tax returns if the other standards of the exception are satisfied, i.e., the reasonable relationship test is met.

Comment [14] elaborates on the statutory language, mentioning various factors that one might expect to be relevant in applying the "reasonably related" standard (client previously represented, client resident in or with substantial contacts to jurisdiction of lawyer's admission, matter with a significant connection to jurisdiction of lawyer's admission, significant aspect of matter may involve law of jurisdiction of admission, multiple jurisdictions involved, etc.). The Comment then states:

> In addition, the services may draw on the lawyer's recognized expertise developed through the regular practice of law on behalf of clients in matters involving a particular body of federal, nationally uniform, foreign, or international law.

Thus, under Model Rule 5.5(c)(4), a tax lawyer who is an expert on federal corporate taxation and admitted to the New York bar apparently can provide federal corporate tax advice on a temporary basis to a client in any jurisdiction that has adopted Model Rule 5.5(c)(4) and the Comments as drafted.[19] Perhaps more interestingly, if the out-of-state lawyer is a leading expert on the state taxation of the gambling industry, the lawyer may be permitted under this Rule to provide services regarding the state tax laws applicable to the gambling industry, even if none of the relevant jurisdictions is one in which the lawyer is admitted to practice.

In working through the problems below, assume all states have adopted Model Rule 5.5. Then consider whether the results would be different if the state in which the services were provided was California.

PROBLEM 5-7

Generally can do + proceed w/o seperate council

Lawyer and her firm have a longstanding relationship with Client, a manufacturer with nationwide operations. Lawyer regularly advises Client on federal tax matters from Lawyer's office in Chicago, near client's headquarters;

---

[19] If the same out-of-state tax lawyer does this too often for clients in the same state, at some point she will cross the "temporary" line and be in violation of the state's rules, but as new as this Model Rule is it is hard to know where the line will be. The lawyer might then, of course, claim that the representation is authorized under federal law anyway, but the authors are not sure how this claim will fare. One of the authors believes that the situation described, i.e., providing federal tax advice on a regular basis to out-of-state clients is so commonplace as to be the accepted (and unquestioned) norm. The other author agrees that this may be the accepted norm among lawyers in major law firms, but is skeptical that state bars or state supreme courts would approve it.

[handwritten margin note: Atty should recommend seperate council b'each location.]

Lawyer is a member of the Illinois bar. In connection with planning for a new plant, Client has asked Lawyer for advice on property tax laws, exemptions and holidays in California, Texas, Michigan, and Connecticut. In rendering such advice, will Lawyer be engaged in UPL in any of these states? Does it matter whether lawyer travels to any of these states to meet with Client's employees, state officials or municipal officials on Client's behalf? Does it matter whether Lawyer's advice is given orally or in writing? Should it matter?

[handwritten margin note: No travel is note dependent factor oral or written advice is same]

PROBLEM 5-8

[handwritten margin note: client hire atty in another state. Know who is the client]

Attorney is an estate planner who is licensed and practices in California. Attorney is approached by a financial planner in California to review and prepare an estate plan for a client who lives in Oregon. The client occasionally (perhaps once a month) travels to California on business. Attorney is not licensed in Oregon. The client is high profile in Oregon and some of the estate planning issues are quite sensitive. Consequently, the client does not want to use Oregon counsel. Is attorney engaged in UPL in Oregon? If so, would it matter if Attorney never sent any documents to Oregon, by mail, fax or email? Do you see any other potential problems? *See* Model Rule 5.5, Comment [20]. Consider the result if Attorney hires competent counsel in Oregon. Must the client know that Oregon counsel has been hired? *See* Model Rule 1.4. Does it matter that the identity of the client is not disclosed to Oregon counsel?

[handwritten margin note: Yes UPL is initiated in few occurances allowed. No would not matter as legal advice constitutes.]

[handwritten note: Yes client should know. No identity need not be disclosed.]

PROBLEM 5-9

[handwritten margin note: Atty practicing in Georgia. No UPL]

Attorney has represented both owners of interrelated, but separate, business entities for years. Two of the entities operate in Georgia and three operate in Alabama. One owner resides in Georgia and the other in Alabama. Attorney is licensed only in Georgia. Company Y has made an offer to acquire all five (5) entities. Company Y is located in Massachusetts, as is its counsel. As part of the transaction, Attorney is asked to provide a legal opinion addressing the tax treatment of the transaction under both Georgia and Alabama law. It is not necessary for Attorney to travel outside of Georgia to complete the opinion. In which states is Attorney practicing law? Is any of this practice UPL?

PROBLEM 5-10

[handwritten margin note: Get an atty in the specific jurisdiction to handle the matters in that state.]

Attorney is a transactional lawyer in Illinois. For years, Attorney has represented Company X, which conducts business throughout the country but has its principal place of business in California. Attorney is hired by Company X to assist it in acquiring a business that has operations only in California. Completing this transaction is expected to take some time and will require Attorney to spend considerable time in California. Will Attorney be engaged in UPL in California? *See* Model Rule 5.5, Comment [6]. Would the result be different if Attorney's firm had an office in California, but no California attorneys worked on the matter? If Company X had its principal place of business in Illinois? If Company X had its principal place of business in Tennessee?

[handwritten margin note: No, should have atty licensed in that state. If in IL no issue. If TN issue exists — yes]

PROBLEM 5-11

a. Client A maintains a home in New York and has been using Attorney (licensed in New York) for many years on both personal and business matters. Client A now spends much of his time in Florida and has established residency there, principally for state tax purposes. Attorney is not licensed in Florida. Client A asks attorney to prepare a codicil to his will. Attorney prepares the codicil, which she mails to Client A in Florida for execution. Client A executes the codicil in triplicate, keeping two copies in Florida and sending one back to Attorney, who keeps it in her firm's vault. Has Attorney engaged in UPL in Florida? *Yes*

b. Suppose that in the course of representing Client A, Attorney is introduced to Client B, Client A's neighbor in Florida, who wants a similar estate plan to that of Client A. Client B has never used Attorney and has no contacts with New York. Advise Attorney on whether she can provide similar estate planning services to Client B and, if she does, what risks she could face — even if she never spends any time in Florida. Would the answer be different if she took the documents to Florida for execution? *No*
See RESTATEMENT (THIRD) OF THE LAW GOVERNING LAWYERS § 3 Jurisdictional Scope of Practice of Law by Lawyer, Illus. 5.

No

PROBLEM 5-12

Federal have govern here. ethical COI?

Attorney is a tax litigator who is licensed and practices in the State of *Not license to* Virginia. Attorney is retained by Company B to handle tax litigation that could *practice in SC* not be resolved at the IRS Office of Appeals. Company B has its principal place *so it go to dist.ct* of business in South Carolina, but has no operations or sales in Virginia. *but can represent* Attorney is not a member of the South Carolina bar but is admitted to practice *in tax ct.* before the Tax Court and the United States Court of Federal Claims. Is Attorney engaged in UPL in South Carolina? Do you see any other ethical issue that *May want to* Attorney should consider? *engage SC counsel.*

V.   ADVERTISING AND SOLICITATION

Model Rules 7.1, 7.2, 7.3, 7.4 and 7.5, and Comments
Circular 230 § 10.30

Lawyer advertising has been permitted for three decades since the United States Supreme Court decision in *Bates v. State Bar of Arizona*, 433 U.S. 350 (1977), which held that a broad prohibition on advertising by lawyers failed to pass muster under the First Amendment. Subsequently, a lawyer-CPA who was also a certified financial planner won the right to place the CPA and CFP credentials next to her name in her Yellow Pages listing (under "Attorneys") and on her business cards and stationery. Ibanez v. Fla. Dept. of Bus. & Prof. Reg'n, Bd. of Accountancy, 512 U.S. 136 (1994).[20] The Board of Accountancy had claimed that use of the designations amounted to "false, deceptive and misleading" advertising, assertions that the Court found "entirely insubstantial" (CPA) and "scarcely more persuasive" (CFP). *See also* Peel v. Attorney Registration & Disciplinary Comm'n of Ill., 496 U.S. 91 (1990) (lawyer's use of designation "Certified Civil Trial Specialist by the National Board of Trial Advocacy" was neither actually nor inherently misleading).

---

[20] This case is notable for the fact that Ms. Ibanez, basically a tax lawyer who had never appeared in the Supreme Court, argued her own case. Edward L. Birk, *Protecting Truthful Advertising by Attorney-CPAs*, 23 FLA. ST. U. L. REV. 77, 78 (1995).

Many state bar authorities continue to monitor lawyer advertising and limit it to the extent they think they can. Both the Model Rules (7.1 through 7.4) and Circular 230 § 10.30(a) and (c) have largely abandoned the effort to heavily regulate lawyer advertising, except where the advertising is false, misleading, fraudulent or deceptive. However, it takes serious thought at times to realize what might be viewed as problematic for one of these reasons. In any event, many states have much more rigorous, specific rules. *See, e.g.,* Texas Disc. Rule 7.02; Calif. Rule of Profess'l Conduct 1–400.

The Supreme Court has generally applied the same principles to advertising by lawyers and other professionals, such as CPAs. In the case of client solicitation, in person, by phone (or perhaps by fax or other forms of electronic communication), however, the Court's two leading cases, reproduced below, come to opposite conclusions for lawyers and CPAs. As you read the cases, consider whether this means that the accounting profession has an edge in soliciting new business in the tax field.

OHRALIK v. OHIO STATE BAR ASSOCIATION
United States Supreme Court
436 U.S. 447 (1978)

MR. JUSTICE POWELL delivered the opinion of the Court.

In *Bates* v. *State Bar of Arizona*, 433 U.S. 350 (1977), this Court held that truthful advertising of "routine" legal services is protected by the First and Fourteenth Amendments against blanket prohibition by a State. The Court expressly reserved the question of the permissible scope of regulation of "in-person solicitation of clients — at the hospital room or the accident site, or in any other situation that breeds undue influence — by attorneys or their agents or 'runners.'" Today we answer part of the question so reserved, and hold that the State — or the Bar acting with state authorization — constitutionally may discipline a lawyer for soliciting clients in person, for pecuniary gain, under circumstances likely to pose dangers that the State has a right to prevent.

I

Appellant, a member of the Ohio Bar, lives in Montville, Ohio. Until recently he practiced law in Montville and Cleveland. On February 13, 1974, while picking up his mail at the Montville Post Office, appellant learned from the postmaster's brother about an automobile accident that had taken place on February 2 in which Carol McClintock, a young woman with whom appellant was casually acquainted, had been injured. Appellant made a telephone call to Ms. McClintock's parents, who informed him that their daughter was in the hospital. Appellant suggested that he might visit Carol in the hospital. Mrs. McClintock assented to the idea, but requested that appellant first stop by at her home.

During appellant's visit with the McClintocks, they explained that their daughter had been driving the family automobile on a local road when she was hit by an uninsured motorist. Both Carol and her passenger, Wanda Lou Holbert, were injured and hospitalized. In response to the McClintocks' expression of apprehension that they might be sued by Holbert, appellant explained that Ohio's guest statute would preclude such a suit. When appellant suggested to the McClintocks that they hire a lawyer, Mrs. McClintock retorted that such a decision would be up to Carol, who was 18 years old and would be the beneficiary of a successful claim.

Appellant proceeded to the hospital, where he found Carol lying in traction in her room. After a brief conversation about her condition, appellant told Carol he would represent her and asked her to sign an agreement. Carol said she would have to discuss the matter with her parents. She did not sign the agreement, but asked appellant to have her parents come to see her.[21] Appellant also attempted to see Wanda Lou Holbert, but learned that she had just been released from the hospital. He then departed for another visit with the McClintocks.

On his way appellant detoured to the scene of the accident, where he took a set of photographs. He also picked up a tape recorder, which he concealed under his raincoat before arriving at the McClintocks' residence. Once there, he re-examined their automobile insurance policy, discussed with them the law applicable to passengers, and explained the consequences of the fact that the driver who struck Carol's car was an uninsured motorist. Appellant discovered that the McClintocks' insurance policy would provide benefits of up to $ 12,500 each for Carol and Wanda Lou under an uninsured-motorist clause. Mrs. McClintock acknowledged that both Carol and Wanda Lou could sue for their injuries, but recounted to appellant that "Wanda swore up and down she would not do it." The McClintocks also told appellant that Carol had phoned to say that appellant could "go ahead" with her representation. Two days later appellant returned to Carol's hospital room to have her sign a contract, which provided that he would receive one-third of her recovery.

In the meantime, appellant obtained Wanda Lou's name and address from the McClintocks after telling them he wanted to ask her some questions about the accident. He then visited Wanda Lou at her home, without having been invited. He again concealed his tape recorder and recorded most of the conversation with Wanda Lou. After a brief, unproductive inquiry about the facts of the accident, appellant told Wanda Lou that he was representing Carol and that he had a "little tip" for Wanda Lou: the McClintocks' insurance policy contained an uninsured-motorist clause which might provide her with a recovery of up to $ 12,500. The young woman, who was 18 years of age and not a high school graduate at the time, replied to appellant's query about whether she was going to file a claim by stating that she really did not understand what was going on. Appellant offered to represent her, also, for a contingent fee of one-third of any recovery, and Wanda Lou stated "O.K."[22]

Wanda's mother attempted to repudiate her daughter's oral assent the following day, when appellant called on the telephone to speak to Wanda. Mrs. Holbert informed appellant that she and her daughter did not want to sue anyone or to have appellant represent them, and that if they decided to sue they would consult their own lawyer. Appellant insisted that Wanda had entered into a binding agreement. A month later Wanda confirmed in writing

---

[21] [2] Despite the fact that appellant maintains that he did not secure an agreement to represent Carol while he was at the hospital, he waited for an opportunity when no visitors were present and then took photographs of Carol in traction.

[22] [4] Appellant told Wanda that she should indicate assent by stating "O.K.," which she did. Appellant later testified: "I would say that most of my clients have essentially that much of a communication. . . . I think most of my clients, that's the way I practice law".

that she wanted neither to sue nor to be represented by appellant. She requested that appellant notify the insurance company that he was not her lawyer, as the company would not release a check to her until he did so. Carol also eventually discharged appellant. Although another lawyer represented her in concluding a settlement with the insurance company, she paid appellant one-third of her recovery in settlement of his lawsuit against her for breach of contract.

Both Carol McClintock and Wanda Lou Holbert filed complaints against appellant with the Grievance Committee of the Geauga County Bar Association. The County Bar Association referred the grievance to appellee, which filed a formal complaint with the Board of Commissioners on Grievances and Discipline of the Supreme Court of Ohio. After a hearing, the Board found that appellant had violated Disciplinary Rules (DR) 2–103 (A) and 2–104 (A) of the Ohio Code of Professional Responsibility. The Board rejected appellant's defense that his conduct was protected under the First and Fourteenth Amendments. The Supreme Court of Ohio adopted the findings of the Board, reiterated that appellant's conduct was not constitutionally protected, and increased the sanction of a public reprimand recommended by the Board to indefinite suspension.

The decision in *Bates* was handed down after the conclusion of proceedings in the Ohio Supreme Court. We noted probable jurisdiction in this case to consider the scope of protection of a form of commercial speech, and an aspect of the State's authority to regulate and discipline members of the bar, not considered in *Bates*. We now affirm the judgment of the Supreme Court of Ohio.

II

The solicitation of business by a lawyer through direct, in-person communication with the prospective client has long been viewed as inconsistent with the profession's ideal of the attorney-client relationship and as posing a significant potential for harm to the prospective client. It has been proscribed by the organized Bar for many years. Last Term the Court ruled that the justifications for prohibiting truthful, "restrained" advertising concerning "the availability and terms of routine legal services" are insufficient to override society's interest, safeguarded by the First and Fourteenth Amendments, in assuring the free flow of commercial information. *Bates*, 433 U.S., at 384. The balance struck in *Bates* does not predetermine the outcome in this case. The entitlement of in-person solicitation of clients to the protection of the First Amendment differs from that of the kind of advertising approved in *Bates*, as does the strength of the State's countervailing interest in prohibition.

A

Appellant contends that his solicitation of the two young women as clients is indistinguishable, for purposes of constitutional analysis, from the advertisement in *Bates*. Like that advertisement, his meetings with the prospective clients apprised them of their legal rights and of the availability of a lawyer to pursue their claims. According to appellant, such conduct is "presumptively an exercise of his free speech rights" which cannot be curtailed in the absence of proof that it actually caused a specific harm that the State has a compelling interest in preventing. But in-person solicitation of professional employment by a lawyer does not stand on a par with truthful advertising about the availability and terms of routine legal services, let alone with forms of speech more traditionally within the concern of the First Amendment.

Expression concerning purely commercial transactions has come within the ambit of the Amendment's protection only recently. We have not discarded the "common-sense" distinction between speech proposing a commercial transaction, which occurs in an area traditionally subject to government regulation, and other varieties of speech. Rather than subject the First Amendment to such a devitalization, we instead have afforded commercial speech a limited measure of protection, commensurate with its subordinate position in the scale of First Amendment values, while allowing modes of regulation that might be impermissible in the realm of noncommercial expression.

* * *

In-person solicitation by a lawyer of remunerative employment is a business transaction in which speech is an essential but subordinate component. While this does not remove the speech from the protection of the First Amendment, it lowers the level of appropriate judicial scrutiny.

As applied in this case, the Disciplinary Rules are said to have limited the communication of two kinds of information. First, appellant's solicitation imparted to Carol McClintock and Wanda Lou Holbert certain information about his availability and the terms of his proposed legal services. In this respect, in-person solicitation serves much the same function as the advertisement at issue in *Bates*. But there are significant differences as well. Unlike a public advertisement, which simply provides information and leaves the recipient free to act upon it or not, in-person solicitation may exert pressure and often demands an immediate response, without providing an opportunity for comparison or reflection. The aim and effect of in-person solicitation may be to provide a one-sided presentation and to encourage speedy and perhaps uninformed decisionmaking; there is no opportunity for intervention or counter-education by agencies of the Bar, supervisory authorities, or persons close to the solicited individual. In-person solicitation is as likely as not to discourage persons needing counsel from engaging in a critical comparison of the "availability, nature, and prices" of legal services, cf. *Bates*, 433 U.S., at 364; it actually may disserve the individual and societal interest, identified in *Bates*, in facilitating "informed and reliable decisionmaking."

It also is argued that in-person solicitation may provide the solicited individual with information about his or her legal rights and remedies. In this case, appellant gave Wanda Lou a "tip" about the prospect of recovery based on the uninsured-motorist clause in the McClintocks' insurance policy, and he explained that clause and Ohio's guest statute to Carol McClintock's parents. But neither of the Disciplinary Rules here at issue prohibited appellant from communicating information to these young women about their legal rights and the prospects of obtaining a monetary recovery, or from recommending that they obtain counsel. DR 2–104 (A) merely prohibited him from using the information as bait with which to obtain an agreement to represent them for a fee. The Rule does not prohibit a lawyer from giving unsolicited legal advice; it proscribes the acceptance of employment resulting from such advice.

* * *

B

The state interests implicated in this case are particularly strong. In addition to its general interest in protecting consumers and regulating commercial transactions, the State bears a special responsibility for maintaining standards among members of the licensed professions. While lawyers act in part as "self-employed businessmen," they also act "as trusted agents of their clients, and as assistants to the court in search of a just solution to disputes." *Cohen* v. *Hurley*, 366 U.S. 117, 124 (1961).

. . . [I]t appears that the ban on solicitation by lawyers originated as a rule of professional etiquette rather than as a strictly ethical rule. But the fact that the original motivation behind the ban on solicitation today might be considered an insufficient justification for its perpetuation does not detract from the force of the other interests the ban continues to serve.

* * *

The substantive evils of solicitation have been stated over the years in sweeping terms: stirring up litigation, assertion of fraudulent claims, debasing the legal profession, and potential harm to the solicited client in the form of overreaching, overcharging, underrepresentation, and misrepresentation. The American Bar Association, as *amicus curiae*, defends the rule against solicitation primarily on three broad grounds: It is said that the prohibitions embodied in DR 2–103 (A) and 2–104 (A) serve to reduce the likelihood of overreaching and the exertion of undue influence on lay persons, to protect the privacy of individuals, and to avoid situations where the lawyer's exercise of judgment on behalf of the client will be clouded by his own pecuniary self-interest.

* * *

We agree that protection of the public from these aspects of solicitation is a legitimate and important state interest.

III

Appellant's concession that strong state interests justify regulation to prevent the evils he enumerates would end this case but for his insistence that none of those evils was found to be present in his acts of solicitation. He challenges what he characterizes as the "indiscriminate application" of the Rules to him and thus attacks the validity of DR 2–103 (A) and DR 2–104 (A) not facially, but as applied to his acts of solicitation. And because no allegations or findings were made of the specific wrongs appellant concedes would justify disciplinary action, appellant terms his solicitation "pure," meaning "soliciting and obtaining agreements from Carol McClintock and Wanda Lou Holbert to represent each of them," without more. Appellant therefore argues that we must decide whether a State may discipline him for solicitation *per se* without offending the First and Fourteenth Amendments.

We agree that the appropriate focus is on appellant's conduct. And, as appellant urges, we must undertake an independent review of the record to determine whether that conduct was constitutionally protected. But appellant errs in assuming that the constitutional validity of the judgment below depends on proof that his conduct constituted actual overreaching or inflicted some specific injury on Wanda Holbert or Carol McClintock. His assumption flows from the premise that nothing less than actual proved harm to the solicited individual would be a sufficiently important state interest to justify disciplining the attorney who solicits employment in person for pecuniary gain.

Appellant's argument misconceives the nature of the State's interest. The Rules prohibiting solicitation are prophylactic measures whose objective is the prevention of harm before it occurs. The Rules were applied in this case to discipline a lawyer for soliciting employment for pecuniary gain under circumstances likely to result in the adverse consequences the State seeks to avert. In such a situation, which is inherently conducive to overreaching and other forms of misconduct, the State has a strong interest in adopting and enforcing rules of conduct designed to protect the public from harmful solicitation by lawyers whom it has licensed.

The State's perception of the potential for harm in circumstances such as those presented in this case is well founded. The detrimental aspects of face-to-face selling even of ordinary consumer products have been recognized and addressed by the Federal Trade Commission, and it hardly need be said that the potential for overreaching is significantly greater when a lawyer, a professional trained in the art of persuasion, personally solicits an unsophisticated, injured, or distressed lay person. Such an individual may place his trust in a lawyer, regardless of the latter's qualifications or the individual's actual need for legal representation, simply in response to persuasion under circumstances conducive to uninformed acquiescence. Although it is argued that personal solicitation is valuable because it may apprise a victim of misfortune of his legal rights, the very plight of that person not only makes him more vulnerable to influence but also may make advice all the more intrusive. Thus, under these adverse conditions the overtures of an uninvited lawyer may distress the solicited individual simply because of their obtrusiveness and the invasion of the individual's privacy, even when no other harm materializes. Under such circumstances, it is not unreasonable for the State to presume that in-person solicitation by lawyers more often than not will be injurious to the person solicited.

The efficacy of the State's effort to prevent such harm to prospective clients would be substantially diminished if, having proved a solicitation in circumstances like those of this case, the State were required in addition to prove actual injury. Unlike the advertising in *Bates*, in-person solicitation is not visible or otherwise open to public scrutiny. Often there is no witness other than the lawyer and the lay person whom he has solicited, rendering it difficult or impossible to obtain reliable proof of what actually took place. This would be especially true if the lay person were so distressed at the time of the solicitation that he could not recall specific details at a later date. If appellant's view were sustained, in-person solicitation would be virtually immune to effective oversight and regulation by the State or by the legal profession, in contravention of the State's strong interest in regulating members of the Bar in an effective, objective, and self-enforcing manner. It therefore is not unreasonable, or violative of the Constitution, for a State to respond with what in effect is a prophylactic rule.

On the basis of the undisputed facts of record, we conclude that the Disciplinary Rules constitutionally could be applied to appellant. He approached two young accident victims at a time when they were especially incapable of making informed judgments or of assessing and protecting their own interests. He solicited Carol McClintock in a hospital room where she lay in traction and sought out Wanda Lou Holbert on the day she came home from the hospital, knowing from his prior inquiries that she had just been released. Appellant urged his services upon the young women and used the information he had obtained from the McClintocks, and the fact of his agreement with Carol, to induce Wanda to say "O.K." in response to his solicitation. He employed a concealed tape recorder, seemingly to insure that he would have evidence of Wanda's oral assent to the representation. He emphasized that his fee would come out of the recovery, thereby tempting the young women with what sounded like a cost-free and therefore irresistible offer. He refused to withdraw when Mrs. Holbert requested him to do so only a day after the initial meeting between appellant and Wanda Lou and continued to represent himself to the insurance company as Wanda Holbert's lawyer.

The court below did not hold that these or other facts were proof of actual harm to Wanda Holbert or Carol McClintock but rested on the conclusion that appellant had engaged in the general misconduct proscribed by the Disciplinary Rules. Under our view of the State's interest in averting harm by prohibiting solicitation in circumstances where it is likely to occur, the absence of explicit proof or findings of harm or injury is immaterial. The facts in this case present a striking example of the potential for overreaching that is inherent in a lawyer's in-person solicitation of professional employment. They also demonstrate the need for prophylactic regulation in furtherance of the State's interest in protecting the lay public. We hold that the application of DR 2–103 (A) and 2–104 (A) to appellant does not offend the Constitution.

Accordingly, the judgment of the Supreme Court of Ohio is affirmed.

EDENFIELD v. FANE
United States Supreme Court
507 U.S. 761 (1993)

JUSTICE KENNEDY delivered the opinion of the Court.

In previous cases we have considered the constitutionality of state laws prohibiting lawyers from engaging in direct, personal solicitation of prospective clients. See *Ohralik* v. *Ohio State Bar Assn.* In the case now before us, we consider a solicitation ban applicable to certified public accountants (CPA's) enacted by the State of Florida. We hold that, as applied to CPA solicitation in the business context, Florida's prohibition is inconsistent with the free speech guarantees of the First and Fourteenth Amendments.

I

Respondent Scott Fane is a CPA licensed to practice in the State of Florida by the Florida Board of Accountancy (Board). Before moving to Florida in 1985, Fane had his own accounting CPA practice in New Jersey, specializing in providing tax advice to small and medium-sized businesses. He often obtained business clients by making unsolicited telephone calls to their executives and arranging meetings to explain his services and expertise. This direct, personal, uninvited solicitation was permitted under New Jersey law.

When he moved to Florida, Fane wished to build a practice similar to his solo practice in New Jersey but was unable to do so because the Board of Accountancy had a comprehensive rule prohibiting CPA's from engaging in the direct, personal solicitation he had found most effective in the past. The Board's rules provide that a CPA "shall not by any direct, in-person, uninvited solicitation solicit an engagement to perform public accounting services . . . where the engagement would be for a person or entity not already a client of [the CPA], unless such person or entity has invited such a communication." Fla. Admin. Code § 21A-24.002(2)(c) (1992). "Direct, in-person, uninvited solicitation" means "any communication which directly or implicitly requests an immediate oral response from the recipient," which, under the Board's rules, includes all "uninvited in-person visits or conversations or telephone calls to a specific potential client." § 21A-24.002(3).

The rule, according to Fane's uncontradicted submissions, presented a serious obstacle, because most businesses are willing to rely for advice on the accountants or CPA's already serving them. In Fane's experience, persuading a business to sever its existing accounting relations or alter them to include a new CPA on particular assignments requires the new CPA to contact the business and explain the advantages of a change. This entails a detailed discussion of the client's needs and the CPA's expertise, services and fees.

Fane sued the Board in the United States District Court for the Northern District of Florida, seeking declaratory and injunctive relief on the ground that the Board's antisolicitation rule violated the First and Fourteenth Amendments. Fane alleged that but for the prohibition he would seek clients through personal solicitation and would offer fees below prevailing rates.

In response to Fane's submissions, the Board relied on the affidavit of Louis Dooner, one of its former chairmen. Dooner concluded that the solicitation ban was necessary to preserve the independence of CPA's performing the attest function, which involves the rendering of opinions on a firm's financial statements. His premise was that a CPA who solicits clients "is obviously in need of business and may be willing to bend the rules." In Dooner's view, "if [a CPA] has solicited the client he will be beholden to him." Dooner also suggested that the ban was needed to prevent "overreaching and vexatious conduct by the CPA."

The District Court gave summary judgment to Fane and enjoined enforcement of the rule "as it is applied to CPA's who seek clients through in-person, direct, uninvited solicitation in the business context." A divided panel of the Court of Appeals for the Eleventh Circuit affirmed. 945 F.2d 1514 (1991).

We granted certiorari and now affirm.

II

In soliciting potential clients, Fane seeks to communicate no more than truthful, nondeceptive information proposing a lawful commercial transaction. We need not parse Fane's proposed communications to see if some parts are entitled to greater protection than the solicitation itself. This case comes to us testing the solicitation, nothing more. That is what the State prohibits and Fane proposes.

Whatever ambiguities may exist at the margins of the category of commercial speech, it is clear that this type of personal solicitation is commercial expression to which the protections of the First Amendment apply. While we did uphold a ban on in-person solicitation by lawyers in *Ohralik* v. *Ohio State Bar Assn.*, that opinion did not hold that all personal solicitation is without First Amendment protection. There are, no doubt, detrimental aspects to personal commercial solicitation in certain circumstances but these detriments are not so inherent or ubiquitous that solicitation of this sort is removed from the ambit of First Amendment protection.

In the commercial context, solicitation may have considerable value. Unlike many other forms of commercial expression, solicitation allows direct and spontaneous communication between buyer and seller. A seller has a strong financial incentive to educate the market and stimulate demand for his product or service, so solicitation produces more personal interchange between buyer and seller than would occur if only buyers were permitted to initiate contact. Personal interchange enables a potential buyer to meet and evaluate the person offering the product or service and allows both parties to discuss and negotiate the desired form for the transaction or professional relation. Solicitation also enables the seller to direct his proposals toward those consumers who he has a reason to believe would be most interested in what he has to sell. For the buyer, it provides an opportunity to explore in detail the way in which a particular product or service compares to its alternatives in the market. In particular, with respect to nonstandard products like the professional services offered by CPA's, these benefits are significant.

In denying CPA's and their clients these advantages, Florida's law threatens societal interests in broad access to complete and accurate commercial information that First Amendment coverage of commercial speech is designed to safeguard. The commercial marketplace, like other spheres of our social and cultural life, provides a forum where ideas and information flourish. Some of the ideas and information are vital, some of slight worth. But the general rule is that the speaker and the audience, not the government, assess the value of the information presented. Thus, even a communication that does no more than propose a commercial transaction is entitled to the coverage of the First Amendment.

Commercial speech, however, is "linked inextricably" with the commercial arrangement that it proposes so the State's interest in regulating the underlying transaction may give it a concomitant interest in the expression itself. For this reason, laws restricting commercial speech, unlike laws burdening other forms of protected expression, need only be tailored in a reasonable manner to serve a substantial state interest in order to survive First Amendment scrutiny. *Central Hudson Gas & Electric Corp.*, 447 U.S., at 564. Even under this intermediate standard of review, however, Florida's blanket ban on direct, in-person, uninvited solicitation by CPA's cannot be sustained as applied to Fane's proposed speech.

III

To determine whether personal solicitation by CPA's may be proscribed under the test set forth in *Central Hudson* we must ask whether the State's interests in proscribing it are substantial, whether the challenged regulation advances these interests in a direct and material way, and whether the extent of the restriction on protected speech is in reasonable proportion to the interests served. Though we conclude that the Board's asserted interests are substantial, the Board has failed to demonstrate that its solicitation ban advances those interests.

A

* * *

To justify its ban on personal solicitation by CPA's, the Board proffers two interests. First, the Board asserts an interest in protecting consumers from fraud or overreaching by CPA's. Second, the Board claims that its ban is necessary to maintain both the fact and appearance of CPA independence in auditing a business and attesting to its financial statements.

The State's first interest encompasses two distinct purposes: to prevent fraud and other forms of deception, and to protect privacy. As to the first purpose, we have said that "the First Amendment . . . does not prohibit the State from insuring that the stream of commercial information flow[s] cleanly as well as freely," and our cases make clear that the State may ban commercial expression that is fraudulent or deceptive without further justification. But where, as with the blanket ban involved here, truthful and nonmisleading expression will be snared along with fraudulent or deceptive commercial speech, the State must satisfy the remainder of the *Central Hudson* test by demonstrating that its restriction serves a substantial state interest and is designed in a reasonable way to accomplish that end. For purposes of that test, there is no question that Florida's interest in ensuring the accuracy of commercial information in the market-place is substantial.

Likewise, the protection of potential clients' privacy is a substantial state interest. Even solicitation that is neither fraudulent nor deceptive may be pressed with such frequency or vehemence as to intimidate, vex, or harass the recipient. In *Ohralik*, we made explicit that "protection of the public from these aspects of solicitation is a legitimate and important state interest."

The Board's second justification for its ban — the need to maintain the fact and appearance of CPA independence and to guard against conflicts of interest — is related to the audit and attest functions of a CPA. In the course of rendering these professional services, a CPA reviews financial statements and attests that they have been prepared in accordance with generally accepted accounting principles and present a fair and accurate picture of the firm's financial condition. In the Board's view, solicitation compromises the independence necessary to perform the audit and attest functions, because a CPA who needs business enough to solicit clients will be prone to ethical lapses. The Board claims that even if actual misconduct does not occur, the public perception of CPA independence will be undermined if CPA's behave like ordinary commercial actors.

We have given consistent recognition to the State's important interests in maintaining standards of ethical conduct in the licensed professions. See, e.g., *Ohralik*. With regard to CPA's, we have observed that they must "maintain total independence" and act with "complete fidelity to the public trust" when serving as independent auditors. Although the State's interest in obscuring the commercial nature of public accounting practice is open to doubt, the Board's asserted interest in maintaining CPA independence and ensuring against conflicts of interest is not. We acknowledge that this interest is substantial.

B

That the Board's asserted interests are substantial in the abstract does not mean, however, that its blanket prohibition on solicitation serves them. The penultimate prong of the *Central Hudson* test requires that a regulation impinging upon commercial expression "directly advance the state interest involved; the regulation may not be sustained if it provides only ineffective or remote support for the government's purpose." We agree with the Court of Appeals that the Board's ban on CPA solicitation as applied to the solicitation of business clients fails to satisfy this requirement.

* * *

The Board has not demonstrated that, as applied in the business context, the ban on CPA solicitation advances its asserted interests in any direct and material way. It presents no studies that suggest personal solicitation of prospective business clients by CPA's creates the dangers of fraud, overreaching, or compromised independence that the Board claims to fear. The record does not disclose any anecdotal evidence, either from Florida or another State, that validates the Board's suppositions. This is so even though 21 States place no specific restrictions of any kind on solicitation by CPA's, and only 3 States besides Florida have enacted a categorical ban. Not even Fane's own conduct suggests that the Board's concerns are justified. Cf. *Ohralik*. The only suggestion that a ban on solicitation might help prevent fraud and overreaching or preserve CPA independence is the affidavit of Louis Dooner, which contains nothing more than a series of conclusory statements that add little if anything to the Board's original statement of its justifications.

The Board directs the Court's attention to a report on CPA solicitation prepared by the American Institute of Certified Public Accountants in 1981. See AICPA, Report of the Special Committee on Solicitation (1981), App. 29. The Report contradicts, rather than strengthens, the Board's submissions. The AICPA Committee stated that it was "unaware of the existence of any empirical data supporting the theories that CPAs (a) are not independent of clients obtained by direct uninvited solicitation, or (b) do not maintain their independence in mental attitude toward those clients subjected to direct uninvited solicitation by another CPA." Louis Dooner's suggestion that solicitation of new accounts signals the need for work and invites an improper approach from the client ignores the fact that most CPA firms desire new clients. The AICPA Report discloses no reason to suspect that CPA's who engage in personal solicitation are more desperate for work, or would be any more inclined to compromise their professional standards, than CPA's who do not solicit, or who solicit only by mail or advertisement. With respect to the prospect of harassment or overreaching by CPA's, the report again acknowledges an "absence of persuasive evidence that direct uninvited solicitation by CPAs is likely to lead to false or misleading claims or oppressive conduct."

Other evidence concerning personal solicitation by CPA's also belies the Board's concerns. In contrast to the Board's anxiety over uninvited solicitation, the literature on the accounting profession suggests that the main dangers of compromised independence occur when a CPA firm is too dependent upon, or involved with, a longstanding client. It appears from the literature that a business executive who wishes to obtain a favorable but unjustified audit opinion from a CPA would be less likely to turn to a stranger who has solicited him than to pressure his existing CPA, with whom he has an ongoing, personal relation and over whom he may also have some financial leverage.

* * *

C

Relying on *Ohralik*, the Board seeks to justify its solicitation ban as a prophylactic rule. It acknowledges that Fane's solicitations may not involve any misconduct but argues that all personal solicitation by CPA's must be banned, because this contact most often occurs in private offices and is difficult to regulate or monitor.

We reject the Board's argument and hold that, as applied in this context, the solicitation ban cannot be justified as a prophylactic rule. *Ohralik* does not stand for the proposition that blanket bans on personal solicitation by all types of professionals are constitutional in all circumstances. Because "the distinctions, historical and functional, between professions, may require consideration of quite different factors," the constitutionality of a ban on personal solicitation will depend upon the identity of the parties and the precise circumstances of the solicitation. Later cases have made this clear, explaining that *Ohralik*'s holding was narrow and depended upon certain "unique features of in-person solicitation by lawyers" that were present in the circumstances of that case.

Ohralik was a challenge to the application of Ohio's ban on attorney solicitation and held only that a State Bar "constitutionally may discipline a lawyer for soliciting clients in person, for pecuniary gain, under circumstances likely to pose dangers that the State has a right to prevent." While *Ohralik* discusses the generic hazards of personal solicitation, the opinion made clear that a preventative rule was justified only in situations "inherently conducive to overreaching and other forms of misconduct." The Court in *Ohralik* explained why the case before it met this standard:

> "[T]he potential for overreaching is significantly greater when a lawyer, a professional trained in the art of persuasion, personally solicits an unsophisticated, injured, or distressed lay person. Such an individual may place his trust in a lawyer, regardless of the latter's qualifications or the individual's actual need for legal representation, simply in response to persuasion under circumstances conducive to uninformed acquiescence. Although it is argued that personal solicitation is valuable because it may apprise a victim of misfortune of his legal rights, the very plight of that person not only makes him more vulnerable to influence but also may make advice all the more intrusive. Thus, under these adverse conditions the overtures of an uninvited lawyer may distress the solicited individual simply because of their obtrusiveness and the invasion of the individual's privacy, even when no other harm materializes. Under such circumstances, it is not unreasonable for the State to presume that in-person solicitation by lawyers more often than not will be injurious to the person solicited." 436 U.S. at 465–466.

The solicitation here poses none of the same dangers. Unlike a lawyer, a CPA is not "a professional trained in the art of persuasion." A CPA's training emphasizes independence and objectivity, not advocacy. The typical client of a CPA is far less susceptible to manipulation than the young accident victim in *Ohralik*. Fane's prospective clients are sophisticated and experienced business executives who understand well the services that a CPA offers. In general, the prospective client has an existing professional relation with an accountant and so has an independent basis for evaluating the claims of a new CPA seeking professional work.

The manner in which a CPA like Fane solicits business is conducive to rational and considered decisionmaking by the prospective client, in sharp contrast to the "uninformed acquiescence" to which the accident victims in *Ohralik* were prone. While the clients in *Ohralik* were approached at a moment of high stress and vulnerability, the clients Fane wishes to solicit meet him in their own offices at a time of their choosing. If they are unreceptive to his initial telephone solicitation, they need only terminate the call. Invasion of privacy is not a significant concern.

If a prospective client does decide to meet with Fane, there is no expectation or pressure to retain Fane on the spot; instead, he or she most often exercises caution, checking references and deliberating before deciding to hire a new CPA. Because a CPA has access to a business firm's most sensitive financial records and internal documents, retaining a new accountant is not a casual decision. The engagements Fane seeks are also long term in nature; to the extent he engages in unpleasant, high pressure sales tactics, he can impair rather than improve his chances of obtaining an engagement or establishing a satisfactory professional relation. The importance of repeat business and referrals gives the CPA a strong incentive to act in a responsible and decorous manner when soliciting business. In contrast with *Ohralik*, it cannot be said that under these circumstances, personal solicitation by CPA's "more often than not will be injurious to the person solicited."

The Board's reliance on *Ohralik* is misplaced for yet another reason: The Board misunderstands what *Ohralik* meant when it approved the use of a prophylactic rule. The ban on attorney solicitation in *Ohralik* was prophylactic in the sense that it prohibited conduct conducive to fraud or overreaching at the outset, rather than punishing the misconduct after it occurred. But *Ohralik* in no way relieves the State of the obligation to demonstrate that it is regulating speech in order to address what is in fact a serious problem and that the preventative measure it proposes will contribute in a material way to solving that problem.

Were we to read *Ohralik* in the manner the Board proposes, the protection afforded commercial speech would be reduced almost to nothing; comprehensive bans on certain categories of commercial speech would be permitted as a matter of course. That would be inconsistent with the results reached in a number of our prior cases. It would also be inconsistent with this Court's general approach to the use of preventative rules in the First Amendment context. . . . Even under the First Amendment's somewhat more forgiving standards for restrictions on commercial speech, a State may not curb protected expression without advancing a substantial governmental interest. Here, the ends sought by the State are not advanced by the speech restriction, and legitimate commercial speech is suppressed. For this reason, the Board's rule infringes upon Fane's right to speak, as guaranteed by the Constitution.

The judgment of the Court of Appeals is affirmed.

JUSTICE O'CONNOR, dissenting.

* * *

But even if I agreed that the States may target only professional speech that directly harms the listener, I still would dissent in this case. *Ohralik* v. *Ohio State Bar Assn.* held that an attorney could be sanctioned for the in-person solicitation of two particularly vulnerable potential clients, because of the inherent risk under such circumstances that the attorney's speech would be directly harmful, and because a simple prohibition on fraud or overreaching would be difficult to enforce in the context of in-person solicitation.

* * *

I see no constitutional difference between a rule prohibiting in-person solicitation by attorneys, and a rule prohibiting in-person solicitation by certified public accountants (CPA's). The attorney's rhetorical power derives not only from his specific training in the art of persuasion but more generally from his *professional expertise*. His certified status as an expert in a complex subject matter — the law — empowers the attorney to overawe inexpert clients. CPA's have an analogous power. The drafters of Fla. Admin. Code § 21A-24.002(2)(c) (1992) reasonably could have envisioned circumstances analogous to those in *Ohralik*, where there is a substantial risk that the CPA will use his professional expertise to mislead or coerce a naive potential client.

* * *

The majority also relies on the fact that petitioners were enjoined only from enforcing the rule in the "business context." Yet this narrowing of focus, without more, does not salvage the District Court's remedy. I fail to see why § 21A-24.002(2)(c) should be valid overall, but not "in the business context." Small businesses constitute the vast majority of business establishments in the United States. The drafters of Florida's rule reasonably could have believed that the average small businessman is no more sophisticated than the average individual who is wealthy enough to hire a CPA for his personal affairs.

* * *

With regard to telephone solicitation by lawyers, see *Texans Against Censorship v. State Bar of Texas*, 888 F. Supp. 1328 (E.D. Tex. 1995) (Texas ban on telephone solicitation by lawyers upheld), *aff'd*, 100 F.3d 953 (5th Cir. 1996). *See also* Falanga v. State Bar, 150 F.3d 1333 (11th Cir. 1998) (Georgia ban on in-person solicitation by lawyers upheld).

VI. SPECIALIZATION CERTIFICATION

Model Rule 7.4 and Comment [3]

Lawyers often want to advertise that they have expertise in a particular field of law. This is particularly true of tax lawyers and estate planners, many of whom specialize in these fields. Ethics rules permit a lawyer to advertise that her practice is limited to a particular area of law, to mention that the lawyer has an advanced degree such as an LL.M. in Taxation or an M.S. in Taxation, and to mention experience with a state or federal revenue agency such as the IRS or the California Franchise Tax Board, but the state bars view general statements about "expertise" and "specialization" with suspicion because terms like these, in the abstract, are easily misunderstood and difficult for the public to evaluate.

Model Rule 7.4(d) reflects a compromise with respect to specialization. The Rule permits a lawyer to state that he is certified as a specialist in a particular field of law only if the lawyer has been certified as a specialist by an organization that has been approved by an appropriate state authority or that has been accredited by the ABA ("or another organization, such as a state bar association, that has been approved by the state authority to accredit organizations that certify lawyers as specialists"),[23] and if the name of the certifying organization is clearly identified in the communication. The rationale is that this standard

---

[23] The parenthetical language appears only in Comment [3], but not in the Rule itself.

assures that the certification means the lawyer possesses an advanced degree of knowledge and experience in the specialty area that has met objective standards and is "greater than is suggested by general licensure to practice law." Rule 7.4 Comment [3]. Some state variations are considerably more complex.[24]

Each state's rules for certification programs are different. However, some basic requirements are found in nearly all of the programs: bar membership in good standing, passing a written exam, providing peer references, showing a significant commitment of time (sometimes measured as a percentage of practice time) to the specialty area of law for at least five years, and meeting CLE requirements. Certification usually expires after five years (seven years in some cases), but can be renewed by filing a renewal application. At this writing, only a handful of states have approved standards for certification as a specialist in Taxation Law.[25] All of these programs are state programs. The high standards required for certification are indicated by California's practice and educational requirements, which appear in Appendix M. It is important to understand that the educational and practice requirements are separate — both must be satisfied.

Nearly all the states have certification programs in Estate Planning, some private, some state and in three states there are both state and private programs. A list of Estate Planning programs and the current requirements at this writing for some sample Estate Planning certification programs appear in Appendix L.

PROBLEM 5-13

Which of the following terms or statements is permitted to be included in an advertisement by a tax lawyer or an estate planner? (Some of these might refer to return preparation, but many lawyers prepare tax returns.)

(a) 15 years of experience with the IRS. *yes*

(b) Put a highly qualified tax lawyer to work when the IRS questions your return. *Maybe misleading*

(c) LL.M. in Taxation. *See* ABA Informal Op. 1131 (1970). *yes* *not clear for state b, ok for Federal*

(d) Maximum refund or it's free. *contingency fee*

(e) California taxes welcome. (In Nevada Yellow pages!)

(f) Experienced tax lawyer. *See* Spencer v. Honorable Justices of Supreme Court, 579 F. Supp. 880 (E.D. Pa. 1984). *not good what qualifies as experienced*

(g) Refunds in a flash.

(h) Masters in Tax Law. *yes*

(i) Minimize the effect of probate! Plan now! *Borderline less problematic*

(j) Listed in the Bar Register of Preeminent Lawyers. *who's the preeminent*

(k) Listed in "Top 100 New Jersey Super Lawyers." *See* N.J.R. Prof'l Conduct 7.1(a)(3) (effective Nov. 2, 2009).

---

[24] *See, e.g.,* Texas Disc. Rule 7.04(b)(2) and (o); N.Y.R. Prof'l Cond. 7.4(c) (requiring a statement that certification is not required to practice law and does not indicate greater competence than other attorneys experienced in the particular field of law). The required New York disclaimer is remarkable in that it is directly conflicts with the underlying rationale for certification programs.

[25] Arizona, California, Florida, Louisiana, New Mexico, Ohio, South Carolina and Texas.

(l)   All tax problems resolved. Eliminate or reduce all tax debt. *misleading*

(m)   U.S. Naval Aviator L.C.D.R. (Ret.) (stated under lawyer's name in ad for estate planning practice) *not misleading*

PROBLEM 5-14

Reconsider Problem 5-13, except where the word "lawyer" appears, substi- *Cannot have* tute "CPA" or "enrolled agent." Are the answers different? *direct solicitation*

PROBLEM 5-15

Silvia Ibanez was an attorney, a CPA and a certified financial planner. Suppose she was only a certified financial planner and an attorney subject to the Model Rules, and had been hired to do financial planning for a client (Raoul) who wanted to invest $100,000 inherited from an uncle in order to provide for his children's college educations. She does this work. Later that year, she calls Raoul to explain to him what she can provide him in the way of estate planning. Is Silvia permitted to make that telephone call?

PROBLEM 5-16

a.   If Smith is a tax lawyer from New Jersey who moves to Florida and *Not as a lawyer* attempts to solicit new business in exactly the same way that Fane did, *Fallowed* can the Florida Bar successfully discipline Smith for in-person or live telephone solicitation of prospective clients? Why? Is this sensible? Fair? What is the impact of Circular 230 § 10.30(a)(2) in this context?

b.   Suppose that Smith is both a tax lawyer and a CPA. How can he solicit *disallowed* business in Florida without being subject to discipline?

PROBLEM 5-17

Mary has a seven year old son, Herb. Mary is an attorney specializing in *if a CPA* tax and estate planning, as well as the design of pension plans. Herb is in *may do legal* second grade and plays soccer for hours on the weekends. Mary sits in the *work* stands watching Herb play soccer, chatting mostly about nothing in particular with the other soccer moms and dads. Last week, a new kid, Sven, arrived for *if a case,* soccer, along with his mother, Gertrude. Gertrude is a resident physician at *personal* the local hospital. She and Mary talk about their kids and other matters. *relationship* Gertrude, in response to Mary's inquiry about what kind of work she does, explains that she is planning to open her own pediatric practice when her residency is completed. What can Mary do under the legal ethical rules to explain to Gertrude that Mary can help Gertrude set up her practice in a tax-sensible way, designing a pension plan, working through the use of other tax-saving fringe benefits, not to speak of helping Gertrude with estate planning, which is essential for a young doctor with a seven-year-old soccer playing son? Is there something wrong with rules that even make this a subject that needs to be discussed?

PROBLEM 5-18

Know at 15 yrs, not a problem

Jacob and Scott belong to the same synagogue. Both have been members for 15 years. They have served on committees together over the years and chat casually when they run into each other before or after a service. They have never discussed professional or financial matters before. Jacob, a tax attorney, hears "through the grapevine" that Scott just won two million dollars in the state lottery. Would it be ethically permissible for Jacob to offer to assist Scott with tax issues arising from his bonanza? *Personal relationship already exists*

PROBLEM 5-19

Can Tax Lawyer enter into a referral agreement with CPA pursuant to which Tax Lawyer agrees to refer any of Tax Lawyer's clients in need of accounting work to CPA and CPA agrees to refer any of CPA's clients in need of legal work to Tax Lawyer? If not, what kind of referral agreement can the two enter into? *See* Model Rule 7.2, Comment [8]; Model Rule 1.7.

should have an exclusion agreement + have said referrals

Chapter 6

MALPRACTICE AND OTHER CIVIL LIABILITY

I. IN GENERAL

Lawyers and other tax professionals may be liable for professional negligence to clients or nonclients to whom they owe a duty of care. In the case of lawyers, the duty of care requires that one exercise the competence and diligence "normally exercised by lawyers in similar circumstances."[1] While a violation of an ethical rule (or even a statutory rule regulating the conduct of lawyers or other tax professionals) does not itself give rise to a cause of action, evidence of violation of the rule or statute may be relevant in establishing breach of a duty to the client in civil litigation.[2] In general, then, a tax professional who fails to adhere to any of the standards of practice discussed in this book and, as a result, injures a client is potentially liable to the client for damages resulting from the injury. The spectrum of tax malpractice litigation is vast.[3] The discussion herein is designed to highlight principal issues of concern.

Actions for tax malpractice are generally based on tort (usually negligence) or contract theories. The tax professional, whether an accountant or a lawyer,[4] is held to essentially the same standard of care under both theories. *Horne v. Peckham*, excerpted below, is a seminal case in the area and illustrates the application of the standard of care in the tax field.

HORNE v. PECKHAM

California Court of Appeal, Third District
97 Cal. App. 3d 404 (1979)

PARAS, ACTING P.J.

Defendant, an attorney, appeals from a judgment entered after a jury awarded damages of $64,983.31 against him for legal malpractice in connection with the drafting of a "Clifford Trust" for plaintiffs Roy C. Horne (Horne) and Doris G. Horne, husband and wife. He contends that the judgment should be reversed or in the alternative that another attorney, Thomas J. McIntosh, upon whom he relied for advice, should indemnify him.

In 1960, Horne obtained a patent for processing low grade wood into defect-free material known as "Perfect Plank Plus." In 1962, he founded a business called "Perfect Plank," and in 1967 began to produce the patented

---

[1] *See* RESTATEMENT (THIRD) OF LAW GOVERNING LAWYERS §§ 48, 50, 51, 52; *see also* Ventura County Humane Society v. Holloway, 115 Cal. Rptr. 464 (1974).

[2] RESTATEMENT, *supra* at § 52(2); Model Rules, Scope [20].

[3] *See generally* Jacob L. Todres, *Malpractice and the Tax Practitioner: An Analysis of the Areas in Which Malpractice Occurs*, 48 EMORY L.J. 547 (1999); Jacob L. Todres, *Tax Malpractice: Areas in Which It Occurs and the Measure of Damages—an Update*, 78 ST. JOHN'S L. REV. 1011 (2004).

[4] Presumably, an enrolled agent or pension consultant could also be sued for malpractice under certain circumstances.

product. The business was incorporated in 1965, with the Hornes as sole share-holders. Horne anticipated that production of the product might generate substantial income, so he became interested when he read in a newsletter of the tax advantages of a so-called "Clifford Trust." On July 18, 1967, on the recommendation of Herbert McClanahan, his accountant, he went to defendant and asked him to prepare such a trust, Horne's three sons to be its beneficiaries.

Defendant testified he told Horne ". . . that I had no knowledge of tax matters. I had no expertise in tax matters; that if somebody else could figure out what needed to be done, I could draft the documents." He said that McClanahan had provided him with ". . . a couple of pages of translucencies . . . governing Clifford Trusts," and he also consulted the two-volume annual set of American Jurisprudence on federal taxation, which included a discussion of Clifford Trusts; he otherwise relied on McClanahan's judgment.

The original plan was to put the patent, which had 10 more years of life, into the trust. However, on October 11, 1967, Horne told defendant he no longer desired this and asked ". . . if it wouldn't be just as good to put in a [nonexclusive] [l]icense . . ." of the patent rights. Horne testified that he preferred not to put the patent itself into the trust, because the substantial royalties from it would result in more money that should properly be given to his sons.

Defendant testified he told Horne that ". . . I didn't know whether . . . [a license] would be just as good or not, but that we were having a high-priced tax expert come up here — like the following day — who was undoubtedly going to charge plenty of money for the consultation, and that we should ask him on that point." The tax expert to whom defendant referred was McIntosh, an attorney from Albany, California, who had been recommended by McClanahan as an expert in deferred compensation and profit-sharing plans. Such plans for Horne's company were to be discussed at a meeting with McIntosh arranged by McClanahan and scheduled for the next day, October 12. Unknown to defendant, McIntosh had been licensed to practice law less than a year, although he was also a certified public accountant and had worked for two and one-half or three years as a tax accountant.

The meeting of October 12 was attended by Horne, his wife, one son, McClanahan, defendant, and McIntosh. Defendant testified that he asked McIntosh whether it would be just as effective to transfer a license agreement into the contemplated trust as the patent itself, and received an affirmative answer. He further testified that Horne had been talking of a nonexclusive license during the meeting, thus McIntosh should have been aware that such a license was contemplated. However, defendant also testified that no one told McIntosh that the contemplated license would have a five year duration.

Horne testified that he thought the subject of license versus patent arose at that meeting, but he had no independent recollection of it. McIntosh testified that even though at his deposition he thought he recalled such a discussion, he did not recall it at trial.

Sometime after the meeting, defendant drafted the final documents and sent them to McClanahan for approval. He had no further discussions or correspondence with McIntosh. The documents were signed in November 1967, although dated February 1, 1967, the date production of the product began. The first document was an irrevocable trust agreement between the Hornes as trustors and McClanahan, defendant, and one Bill Ryan as trustees for the Horne's three sons, to terminate in twelve years (1979). The second was a license agreement between Horne and Perfect Plank, granting the corporation a license to produce the patented product for two years with an option to renew for an additional three years, in return for royalty payments determined by production; inter alia, the agreement stated "This license is not exclusive. Licensor retains the right to issue other licenses of the same patent to any other parties whatsoever." The third document was an assignment to the trustees by Horne of Horne's rights under the license agreement thus furnishing the trust with a corpus.

The license royalties were paid into the trust until 1970 when the Internal Revenue Service (IRS) audited Horne's tax returns. Horne was notified of the audit by mail sometime prior to March 18, 1970, and knew within a few days thereafter of a challenge to the favorable tax aspect of the trust. In August 1970, the IRS assessed a deficiency on the ground that the trust did not transfer tax liability for the licensor's income to the beneficiaries. Horne hired McIntosh to contest the assessment.

After losing at the first administrative level, Horne conceded his tax liability rather than contest it further. On May 12, 1972, he sued defendant for damages for malpractice. On June 18, 1973, defendant filed a cross-complaint for indemnity against McIntosh and his law partnership. After a jury trial, judgment was entered against defendant on the complaint, and in favor of McIntosh on the cross-complaint.

I

Defendant's first argument on appeal is that "It is not legal malpractice (negligence) on the part of an attorney general practitioner to draw documents without doing research on a point of law on which there is no appellate decision or statute in point."

The argument has two parts; first, that the trust documents were in fact valid as a tax shelter, second, that even if invalid, their invalidity is so debatable that he should not be liable for making an error regarding a matter about which reasonable attorneys can disagree. He is wrong on both points. The documents are invalid for their intended purpose, and the invalidity is rather obvious. To demonstrate this, one need go no further than the original *Clifford* case, from which the name "Clifford Trust" is derived, and the legislation it brought about.

In *Helvering v. Clifford* (1940) 309 U.S. 331), the taxpayer had established an irrevocable five-year trust, with himself as trustee and his wife as beneficiary. The trust corpus consisted of securities owned by the taxpayer. The income was payable to the wife, and the corpus reverted to the taxpayer at the end of five years. The Supreme Court ruled that ". . . the short duration of the trust, the fact that the wife was the beneficiary, and the retention of control over the corpus by [the taxpayer] all lead irresistably *[sic]* to the conclusion that [the taxpayer] continued to be the owner for purposes of § 22(a) [now § 61(a), defining gross income]."

On the issue of control, the *Clifford* court made the following observations, which are directly applicable to this case: "So far as his dominion and control were concerned it seems clear that the trust did not effect any substantial change. In substance his control over the corpus was in all essential respects the same after the trust was created, as before. The wide powers which he retained included for all practical purposes most of the control which he as an individual would have. There were, we may assume, exceptions, such as his disability to make a gift of the corpus to others during the term of the trust and to make loans to himself. But this dilution in his control would seem to be insignificant and immaterial, since control over investment remained."

In the present case, the Hornes, by control of the patent and the licensee corporation, also controlled the license. They not only retained the absolute power to control the income from the license agreement by increasing or reducing production of the patented product; they could also cease production entirely, form a new corporation, license it under the patent, and individually receive all future royalties. This would effectively work a termination or revocation of the sole income generating asset of the trust.

Following the *Clifford* decision, the IRS adopted regulations to implement it, and these formed the basis for sections 671–678 of the Internal Revenue Code's 1954 revision. Directly applicable to the present case is section 675, which provides: "The grantor shall be treated as the owner of any portion of a trust in respect of which —

> "(4) ... A power of administration is exercisable in a nonfiduciary capacity by any person without the approval or consent of any person in a fiduciary capacity. For purposes of this paragraph, the term 'power of administration' means any one or more of the following powers: (A) a power to vote or direct the voting of stock or other securities of a corporation in which the holdings of the grantor and the trust are significant from the viewpoint of voting control; . . ."

Since the Hornes have always owned all the stock of the licensee corporation, and since Horne was the sole owner of the patent, clearly the "holdings of the grantor (who holds all of the stock) and the trust (which holds none of the stock) are *significant* from the viewpoint of voting control" where the sole asset of the trust is a license agreement entirely dependent for royalties (the income to be given favorable tax treatment) upon production of the patented product by the grantor's corporation. As we have seen, this arrangement permitted the Hornes at any time to render the trust valueless and to divert any income from production of the patented product to themselves or others.

If the *Clifford* decision and section 675 were to be deemed insufficient authority, *Commissioner v. Sunnen* (1948) 333 U.S. 591, cited by defendant himself, provides (and provided in 1967) further authority to establish the trust's invalidity as a Clifford Trust. [The opinion contains an extensive discussion of *Sunnen* and concludes that:]

In light of the foregoing, it is apparent that there is no merit to defendant's contention that there was "no appellate decision or statute in point." Internal Revenue Code section 675 and the *Sunnen* case were very much in point.

II

Defendant's second contention is that "An attorney in general practice does not have a duty to refer his client to a 'specialist' or to recommend the 'assistance of a specialist' or be guilty of malpractice."

The court gave a jury instruction which states: "It is the duty of an attorney who is a general practitioner to refer his client to a specialist or recommend the assistance of a specialist if under the circumstances a reasonably careful and skillful practitioner would do so.

"If he fails to perform that duty and undertakes to perform professional services without the aid of a specialist, it is his further duty to have the knowledge and skill ordinarily possessed, and exercise the care and skill ordinarily used by specialists in good standing in the same or similar locality and under the same circumstances.

"A failure to perform any such duty is negligence."

This instruction is based upon California's Book of Approved Jury Instructions (BAJI), instruction No. 6.04, which is found in that work's section on medical malpractice. Its applicability to legal malpractice presents an issue of first impression. Defendant points out that legal specialties were not officially recognized in California until 1973, and therefore contends that he could not have had a duty in 1967 to refer his client to a specialist or to meet the standard of care of a specialist.

We cannot accept this contention. A California survey in 1968 revealed that two-thirds of the attorneys in the state at that time limited their practice to a very few areas, frequently to one only. Thus, in the words of a leading treatise, the recent debate over *official* recognition of specialists must be considered "academic," for "[the] reality is that many attorneys have become specialists." (Mallen & Levitt, Legal Malpractice (1977) § 114, p. 172.) Moreover, "[in] those jurisdictions which recognize specialties or permit the attorney to make such a designation, taxation is one of the areas of law most commonly acknowledged." Taxation also was one of the three specialties initially recognized in California.

Defendant himself recognized the existence of tax specialists in 1967 when he advised Horne in 1967 that he was not a tax expert, and that such experts existed. Of course, the fact that the specialty exists does not mean that every tax case must be referred to a specialist. Many tax matters are so generally known that they can well be handled by general practitioners. But defendant himself acknowledged his need for expert assistance throughout his testimony, insisting he had no opinion of his own as to the tax consequences of the trust. Under the circumstances he cannot argue persuasively that it was error for the court to give the above quoted instruction.

III

Defendant's next contention is that the question of law involved here was one upon which reasonable doubt may be entertained by well-informed lawyers, and therefore he should not be found liable for committing error. He relies upon *Lucas v. Hamm* (1961) 56 Cal.2d 58, which held that "the rule against perpetuities poses such complex and difficult problems for the draftsman that even careful and competent attorneys occasionally fall prey to its trap."

But *Lucas v. Hamm* did not condone failure to do research, and *Smith v. Lewis* makes it clear that an attorney's obligation is not satisfied by simply determining that the law on a particular subject is doubtful or debatable:

"[Even] with respect to an unsettled area of the law, . . . an attorney assumes an obligation to his client to undertake reasonable research in an effort to ascertain relevant legal principles and to make an informed decision as to a course of conduct based upon an intelligent assessment of the problem." In other words, an attorney has a duty to *avoid* involving his client in murky areas of the law if research reveals alternative courses of conduct. At least he should inform his client of uncertainties and let the client make the decision.

* * *

V

Defendant argues that plaintiffs cannot maintain their cause of action in the absence of a prior legal determination of the validity of the trust in a court of competent jurisdiction, citing *Westlake Community Hosp. v. Superior Court* (1976) 17 Cal.3d 465. The *Westlake* case does not assist defendant. It is nothing more than a variation of the firmly ingrained legal doctrine of exhaustion of administrative remedies.

It is always true of course that a wrongdoer is not required to compensate an injured party for damages which are avoidable by reasonable effort. The jury here was instructed on mitigation of damages. But the mitigation doctrine does not require the injured party to take measures which are unreasonable or impractical, or which involve expenditures disproportionate to the loss sought to be avoided, or which may lie beyond his financial means. In light of our expressed opinion regarding the trust's invalidity to supply a tax benefit, we cannot say as a matter of law that plaintiffs acted unreasonably in abandoning further legal efforts to gain a favorable tax ruling.

* * *

The judgment is affirmed.

———————

Although earlier cases, like *Horne v. Peckham*, were usually based on one of the two traditional malpractice theories, more recent cases have included numerous other possible grounds for recovery. A recent Fifth Circuit decision, for example, originated with RICO claims (based on violations of the Racketeer Influenced and Corrupt Organization Act, 18 U.S.C. §§ 1961–1968) and included, as well, claims for breach of fiduciary duty, fraud, negligent misrepresentation, breach of contract, civil conspiracy, and unfair trade practices.[5] Other cases have involved allegations of securities law violations, false and deceptive trade practices, intentional misrepresentation, breach of covenant of good faith and fair dealing, intentional or negligent infliction of emotional distress, and breach of fiduciary duty.[6] These various theories are often included in allegations not so much because the overall standard of care varies, but because of differences among the theories as to statutes of limitations, the measure of damages, the

———————

[5] Ducote Jax Holdings v. Bradley, 335 Fed. Appx. 392, 2009 U.S. App. LEXIS 13445 (5th Cir. 2009).

[6] *See* Jacob L. Todres, *Tax Malpractice Damages: A Comprehensive Review of the Elements and the Issues,* 61 TAX LAW. 705, 710 (2008).

ability to recover legal fees, to whom liability extends and perhaps other matters.[7] The bottom line, however, is to determine when the professional has a duty to a client that could lead to any civil liability.

The problems below raise important tax malpractice related issues, not all of which have clear answers.

PROBLEM 6-1

Lawyer prepared an estate plan for client that involves a revocable trust and a will designed to maximize the benefits of the marital deduction for the estates of both Client and Client's Spouse. Absent the tax law, Client would have preferred to leave all of his property outright to his spouse. One year after Client executed all of the relevant documents, Congress repeals the estate tax.

[handwritten: Do not have to notify client something max not be feasible]

a. Does Lawyer have a duty to advise Client of the legislative change and its effect on Client's will, trust and related matter? Would it matter if Lawyer had an ongoing professional relationship with Client (e.g., representing Client in business matters) or if Lawyer's preparation of the will and trust instead represented a one-time engagement with Client?

b. Same facts as (a), above, except that Client called Lawyer when Client heard that estate tax repeal was being considered and Lawyer said "I'll let you know if anything important happens".

[handwritten: Now maybe vulnerable.]

c. If you think Lawyer has a duty to advise Client of the estate tax repeal in (a) or (b), above, how should Lawyer advise the client? *[handwritten: if significant administrative burden]*

d. Assume Lawyer had a duty to advise Client of the change in the law in any of parts (a) through (c) and did not do so. Client dies a year later and part of Client's estate ends up in a marital trust in which Client's Spouse has only a life estate. Is Lawyer potentially liable for failing to advise Client of the change in law? If so, to whom? If so, what would the measure of damages be? *[handwritten: depending on amt proving damage or suffering hardship. Potential to be sued.]*

e. In any of parts (a) through (c), what should Lawyer have done to avoid having a duty to update Client about changes in the law affecting Client's estate plan? *[handwritten: Tax law Disclaimer, object to change. Include in retainer ltr.]*

[handwritten: Disengagement ltr is appropriate, however may not be best as it good could discourage client.]

PROBLEM 6-2

Lawyer is engaged by Client to provide tax planning advice. The general area of tax law in which Lawyer's advice is sought is known as one in which there are some patents on tax planning strategies. *[handwritten: No patents on further Tax strategies allowed.]*

a. Does Lawyer have a duty to advise Client that a patent search should be undertaken before choosing to implement a strategy that might be affected by a patent? *[handwritten: Disclosure is Pivotal]*

b. Does Lawyer have a duty, in connection with vetting possible strategies to propose to Client, to search for patents before proposing any course of action to Client?

---

[7] *Id.* at 708–09; *see also Ducote Jax Holdings.*

c. If Lawyer finds a patent that covers the planning strategy that Lawyer wants to recommend to Client, does Lawyer have a duty to discuss the patent with Client before proceeding? *Yes*

d. Same facts as (c), above. If Lawyer reasonably believes the patent would be declared invalid if the matter were litigated, does Lawyer have a duty to tell this to Client? *Yes*

Anything atty does not do, actually has the risk of malpractice.

e. Lawyer informed Client of an existing patent that the plan for Client would infringe, but Lawyer reasonably believed that the patent would be invalidated. Lawyer did not discuss with Client how the patent might be invalidated. Client agreed to proceed with the plan and is subsequently sued for infringement by the patent holder. Client discovers that defending against infringement will cost $1,000,000 and agrees to settle the case by agreeing to pay a $200,000 license fee to patent holder. Is Lawyer potentially liable to Client for malpractice to Client? Does it matter that Client would have ultimately prevailed in the infringement litigation?

PROBLEM 6-3

Neither atty/acct is liable not malpractice

In connection with the filing of a tax return, Client retains Lawyer to provide a written opinion supporting a Client favorable position on an uncertain issue on the return. Lawyer provides a substantial authority opinion, which clearly explains what "substantial authority" means. Client does not read the opinion, but takes the position Lawyer advises on her return. Client is audited and the IRS disagrees with the position taken on the return. Following an unsuccessful administrative appeal and the filing of a petition in Tax Court, Client settles the case for the tax deficiency asserted plus interest. No penalty is imposed by the IRS. Is Lawyer liable to Client for malpractice? If so, what is the measure of damages?

PROBLEM 6-4

Law firm not held negligent.

would be held liable

Two years ago, on the advice of defendant Law Firm, Plaintiff invested in a transaction that was later identified by the IRS as a tax shelter. The IRS disallowed all of the deductions generated by the investment. Plaintiff sued Law Firm for malpractice alleging, *inter alia,* that the firm had been negligent in rendering a written opinion that the deductions would be sustained. What result? *See DuPont v. Brady,* 646 F. Supp. 1067, 1075 (S.D.N.Y. 1986) (finding that a law firm's opinion was honestly held, based on the materials, information and legal authority that were available at the time the opinion was rendered): "Under these circumstances, where a 'lawyer errs on a question not elementary or conclusively set by authority, that error is one of judgment for which he is not liable.'"

PROBLEM 6-5

 In the mail this week, CPA received a short memo from a business acquaintance, outlining the details of an oil and gas drilling partnership designed to produce generous tax deductions for limited partner investors. CPA approached Client, a drummer who had made a fortune playing in a rock band, with the proposal. When Client expressed interest, CPA recommended that Client ask Lawyer for legal advice about the tax consequences of the transaction. Lawyer provided an oral more likely than not opinion in the circumstances described below.

> Lawyer asked Client if Client expected to make money on the investment before taking taxes into account. Client said, "Sure. CPA told me I could make a lot of money on this deal if everything goes right. He showed me some impressive projections." Lawyer did not ask to see or review the projections, but discussed the transaction generally with Client, pointing out that the transaction met the technical requirements of the Code for the desired tax treatment, but that any investments that generate large tax deductions could be subject to challenge on economic substance grounds, especially if Client did not reasonably believe he could make a before-tax profit. Client then said, "Yes. I understand." Lawyer responded, "If you intend to make, and do make, a healthy before-tax profit, in my opinion, you are more likely than not to get the tax treatment you want even if the IRS challenges you."

[handwritten: No]

b. Client is audited by the IRS, receives a notice of deficiency, goes to Tax Court and loses on the ground that the transaction lacked economic substance. Is Lawyer liable to client in malpractice? *[handwritten: If lawyer engaged, expected some level of due diligence they're being negligent.]*

c. Same facts as (a), above, except that Lawyer's opinion is in writing and appears to satisfy all of the rules for written advice in Circular 230 § 10.35. *[handwritten: derelict in their duties]*

d. Same facts as (c), above, but the written opinion does not satisfy the rules in Circular 230 § 10.35 because Lawyer's opinion is that Client has substantial authority for taking the deductions generated by the partnership. Assume that Lawyer's conclusion that there was substantial authority was correct as a matter of law and that Lawyer explained to Client what substantial authority means. *[handwritten: under C. 694 should render more likely than not opinion vulnerable]*

II. DAMAGES

In a negligence-based action to recover damages for legal malpractice,[8] the plaintiff must prove that (1) the attorney was negligent, (2) the attorney's negligence was the proximate cause of the loss sustained, and (3) the plaintiff sustained *actual* damages as a result of the attorney's negligence.

<u>Negligence</u>. As noted earlier, "[n]egligence or malpractice exists where the attorney failed to exercise that degree of skill commonly exercised by an ordinary member of the legal community." Estate of Nevelson v. Carro, Spanbock, Kaster & Cuiffo, 259 A.D.2d 282, 283 (NY Sup. Ct. App. Div. 1999).[9]

---

[8] This brief discussion of legal malpractice damages issues is based largely on New York law. Attorneys should, of course, consult the laws of their own states.

[9] The malpractice action in *Nevelson* was filed after the IRS assessed millions of dollars in estate taxes against the estate of sculptor Louise Nevelson, as well as gift taxes against her son and the executor of her estate. The defendant law firm had advised Ms. Nevelson to organize a wholly owned corporation in an attempt to cause her artwork and the income from it to pass outside of her taxable estate. The crux of the claim was that the estate plan could not have survived IRS scrutiny and that the law firm never advised the plaintiffs of any risks of potential estate or gift tax liability that could arise based on the level of compensation that the corporation paid to Ms. Nevelson.

Proximate Cause. The plaintiff must demonstrate that "but for" the attorney's alleged negligence or malpractice, the plaintiff would not have sustained any actual damages. *Estate of Nevelson*, 259 A.D.2d at 284; DuPont v. Brady, 646 F. Supp. 1067, 1076 (S.D.N.Y. 1986), *rev'd on other grounds*, 828 F.2d 75 (2d Cir. 1987).

Damages. Damages claimed in a legal malpractice action must be actual and ascertainable. *Estate of Nevelson*, 259 A.D.2d at 284. There are several possible types of damages that can be recovered. The rules and precedents among the states vary. For a comprehensive study of this subject, see Todres, *supra* note 6.

1.   Back taxes. In New York, for example, a plaintiff may not recover for back taxes. Alpert v. Shea Gould Climenko & Casey, 559 N.Y.S.2d 312 (NY Sup. Ct. App. Div. 1990). The rationale is that a victim of fraud may not recover the benefit of an alternative agreement that might have been overlooked in favor of a fraudulent one. In other words, a plaintiff may not recover the difference between back taxes that she was required to pay and the taxes that she would have paid had she picked another (legitimate) investment.

2.   Interest. States are divided on the recoverability of interest. Some states, like New York, do not permit recovery of interest. *Alpert*; *Estate of Nevelson*. The rationale is that interest is a payment to the IRS for the use of money, not damages suffered by the plaintiff. Moreover, plaintiffs should not get the benefit both of having used the tax money for several years (between the year in which the tax should have been paid and the year in which it was paid) and recovering interest thereon. This New York rule appears, however, to be the minority view. *See* Todres, *supra* note 6, at 724 (text accompanying note 111).

Other states, probably the majority, permit recovery of interest because the plaintiff would never have had to pay interest to the IRS if the tax professional had advised properly in the first instance. Thus, awarding interest accords with the traditional view that damages should return the plaintiff to the position in which she would have found herself but for the defendant's tortious conduct. Finally, a few states allow recovery of interest "only to the extent it exceeds the interest actually earned by the plaintiff on the underpaid taxes" Todres, *supra* note 6, at 724. *See generally* Todres, *supra* note 6, at 722–731; Caroline Rule, *What and When Can a Taxpayer Recover From a Negligent Tax Advisor?*, 92 J. Tax'n 176, 176–79 (Mar. 2000).

3.   Taxpayer Penalties. Penalties should be recoverable. *See, e.g.,* King v. Neal, 19 P.3d 899 (Okla. Ct. Civ. App. 2001) (upholding jury award that included tax penalties); *see* Todres, *supra* note 6, at 731–33.

4.   Legal fees incurred in contesting the underlying tax liability with the IRS. Professional fees incurred in contesting the underlying tax liability should be recoverable. *See, e.g.*, Sorenson v. Fio Rito, 413 N.E.2d 47 (Ill. App. Ct. 1980). See also Proskauer Rose Goetz & Mendelsohn v. Munao, 704 N.Y.S.2d 590, 592 (App. Div. 2000), where the court held:

> The extent to which defendants incurred taxes and related expenses they would not otherwise have incurred but for plaintiff's advice, and the extent to which defendants realized any offsetting profits as a result of that advice, are not apparent on the face of the complaint, and go to the issue of defendants' damages, if any, not the sufficiency of

their pleading, which gives ample notice of identifiable losses allegedly *taxes would be owed anyway cannot sue for damages*
sustained as a direct result of plaintiff's advice.

PROBLEM 6-6

A tax professional carelessly fails to report on the taxpayer's return dividend and interest income totaling nearly $34,000 from one Form 1099. As a result of this discrepancy, the return is audited and a questionable deduction of $30,000 in business expenses, mostly for travel and entertainment, is disallowed. Similar expenses had never been questioned in prior years. Is the tax professional liable to the taxpayer for the additional taxes, interest and penalties paid to the IRS as a result of the inclusion of the interest and dividend income in gross income and the denial of the deductions? *See* Todres, *supra* note 6, at 756–58.

PROBLEM 6-7

Taxpayer's warehouse was condemned to make way for a new freeway. Taxpayer received $4,000,000 for the warehouse. Taxpayer's adjusted basis in the warehouse was $1,000,000. Because of the size of the gain, Taxpayer consulted Lawyer about how to reduce the state and federal taxes on the gain. Lawyer incorrectly advised taxpayer that if he reinvested the gain on the condemnation ($3,000,000), the entire gain could be deferred under Section 1033. Taxpayer bought a replacement property for $3,100,000 and filed the return for the year deferring the entire gain. The IRS discovered the error when auditing the return and the taxpayer was required to pay additional tax, and interest on the tax, on $900,000 of capital gain. Additional tax and interest were also paid to the state. Is Lawyer liable in malpractice to Taxpayer. If so, what is the measure of damages?

Appendix A

TREASURY DEPARTMENT CIRCULAR NO. 230

Treasury Department Circular No. 230 (Rev. 4-2008)
Cat. Num. 16586R
www.irs.gov

Regulations Governing the Practice of Attorneys, Certified Public Accountants, Enrolled Agents, Enrolled Actuaries, Enrolled Retirement Plan Agents, and Appraisers before the Internal Revenue Service

Department of the Treasury

Title 31 Code of Federal Regulations, Subtitle A, Part 10, published September 26, 2007

Internal Revenue Service

Table of Contents

Table of Contents (cont'd)

Paragraph 1. The authority citation for 31 CFR, part 10 continues to read as follows:
Authority: Sec. 3, 23 Stat. 258, secs. 2-12, 60 Stat. 237 et seq.; 5 U.S.C. 301, 500, 551-559; 31 U.S.C. 321; 31 U.S.C. 330; Reorg. Plan No. 26 of 1950, 15 FR 4935, 64 Stat. 1280, 3 CFR, 1949-1953 Comp., p. 1017.

§ 10.0 Scope of part.

This part contains rules governing the recognition of attorneys, certified public accountants, enrolled agents, and other persons representing taxpayers before the Internal Revenue Service. Subpart A of this part sets forth rules relating to the authority to practice before the Internal Revenue Service; Subpart B of this part prescribes the duties and restrictions relating to such practice; Subpart C of this part prescribes the sanctions for violating the regulations; Subpart D of this part contains the rules applicable to disciplinary proceedings; and Subpart E of this part contains general provisions including provisions relating to the availability of official records.

Subpart A — Rules Governing Authority to Practice

§ 10.1 Director of the Office of Professional Responsibility.

(a) *Establishment of office.* The Office of Professional Responsibility is established in the Internal Revenue Service. The Director of the Office of Professional Responsibility is appointed by the Secretary of the Treasury, or delegate.

(b) *Duties.* The Director of the Office of Professional Responsibility acts on applications for enrollment to practice before the Internal Revenue Service; makes inquiries with respect to matters under the Director's jurisdiction; institutes and provides for the conduct of disciplinary proceedings relating to practitioners (and employers, firms or other entities, if applicable) and appraisers; and performs other duties as are necessary or appropriate to carry out the functions under this part or as are otherwise prescribed by the Secre-

tary of the Treasury, or delegate.

(c) *Acting Director of the Office of Professional Responsibility.* The Secretary of the Treasury, or delegate, will designate an officer or employee of the Treasury Department to act as Director of the Office of Professional Responsibility in the absence of the Director or during a vacancy in that office.

(d) *Effective/applicability date.* This section is applicable on September 26, 2007.

§ 10.2 Definitions.

(a) As used in this part, except where the text provides otherwise —

(1) *Attorney* means any person who is a member in good standing of the bar of the highest court of any state, territory, or possession of the United States, including a Commonwealth, or the District of Columbia.

(2) *Certified public accountant* means any person who is duly qualified to practice as a certified public accountant in any state, territory, or possession of the United States, including a Commonwealth, or the District of Columbia.

(3) *Commissioner* refers to the Commissioner of Internal Revenue.

(4) *Practice before the Internal Revenue Service* comprehends all matters connected with a presentation to the Internal Revenue Service or any of its officers or employees relating to a taxpayer's rights, privileges, or liabilities under laws or regulations administered by the Internal Revenue Service. Such presentations include, but are not limited to, preparing and filing documents, corresponding and communicating with the Internal Revenue Service, rendering written advice with respect to any entity, transaction, plan or arrangement, or other plan or arrangement having a potential for tax avoidance or evasion, and representing a client at conferences, hearings and meetings.

(5) *Practitioner* means any individual described in paragraphs (a), (b), (c), (d) or (e) of §10.3.

(6) A *tax return* includes an amended tax return and a claim for refund.

(7) *Service* means the Internal Revenue Service.

(b) *Effective/applicability date.* This section is applicable on September 26, 2007.

§ 10.3 Who may practice.

(a) *Attorneys.* Any attorney who is not currently under suspension or disbarment from practice before the Internal Revenue Service may practice before the Internal Revenue Service by filing with the Internal Revenue Service a written declaration that the attorney is currently qualified as an attorney and is authorized to represent the party or parties. Notwithstanding the preceding sentence, attorneys who are not currently under suspension or disbarment from practice before the Internal Revenue Service are not required to file a written declaration with the IRS before rendering written advice covered under §10.35 or §10.37, but their rendering of this advice is practice before the Internal Revenue Service.

(b) *Certified public accountants.* Any certified public accountant who is not currently under suspension or disbarment from practice before the Internal Revenue Service may practice before the Internal Revenue Service by filing with the Internal Revenue Service a written declaration that the certified public accountant is currently qualified as a certified public accountant and is authorized to represent the party or parties. Notwithstanding the preceding sentence, certified public accountants who are not currently under suspension or disbarment from practice before the Internal Revenue Service are not required to file a written declaration with the IRS before rendering written advice covered under §10.35 or §10.37, but their rendering of this advice is practice before the Internal Revenue Service.

(c) *Enrolled agents.* Any individual enrolled as an agent pursuant to this part who is not currently under suspension or disbarment from practice before the Internal Revenue Service may practice before the Internal Revenue Service.

(d) *Enrolled actuaries.*

(1) Any individual who is enrolled as an actuary by the Joint Board for the Enrollment of Actuaries pursuant to 29 U.S.C. 1242 who is not currently under suspension or disbarment from practice before the Internal Revenue Service may practice before the Internal Revenue Service by filing with the Internal Revenue Service a written declaration stating that he or she is currently qualified as an enrolled actuary and is authorized to represent the party or parties on whose behalf he or she acts.

(2) Practice as an enrolled actuary is limited to representation with respect to issues involving the following statutory provisions in title 26 of the United States Code: sections 401 (relating to qualification of employee plans), 403(a) (relating to whether an annuity plan meets the requirements of section 404(a) (2)), 404 (relating to deductibility of employer contributions), 405 (relating to qualification of bond purchase plans), 412 (relating to funding requirements for certain employee plans), 413 (relating to application of qualification requirements to collectively bargained plans and to plans maintained by more than one employer), 414 (relating to definitions and special rules with respect to the employee plan area), 419 (relating to treatment of funded welfare benefits), 419A (relating to qualified asset accounts), 420 (relating to transfers of excess pension assets to retiree health accounts), 4971 (relating to excise taxes payable as a result of an accumulated funding deficiency under section 412), 4972 (relating to tax on nondeductible contributions to qualified employer plans), 4976 (relating to taxes with respect to funded welfare benefit plans), 4980 (relating to tax on reversion of qualified plan assets to employer), 6057 (relating to annual registration of plans), 6058 (relating to information required in connection with certain plans of deferred compensation), 6059 (relating to periodic report of actuary), 6652(e) (relating to the failure to file annual registration and other notifications by pension plan), 6652(f) (relating to the failure to file information required in connection with certain plans of deferred compensation), 6692 (relating to the failure to file actuarial report), 7805(b) (relating to the extent to which an Internal Revenue Service ruling or determination letter coming under the statutory provisions listed here will be applied without retroactive effect); and 29 U.S.C. § 1083 (relating to the waiver of funding for nonqualified plans).

(3) An individual who practices before the Inter-

Page 5

nal Revenue Service pursuant to paragraph (d)(1) of this section is subject to the provisions of this part in the same manner as attorneys, certified public accountants and enrolled agents.

(e) *Enrolled retirement plan agents —*

(1) Any individual enrolled as a retirement plan agent pursuant to this part who is not currently under suspension or disbarment from practice before the Internal Revenue Service may practice before the Internal Revenue Service.

(2) Practice as an enrolled retirement plan agent is limited to representation with respect to issues involving the following programs: Employee Plans Determination Letter program; Employee Plans Compliance Resolution System; and Employee Plans Master and Prototype and Volume Submitter program. In addition, enrolled retirement plan agents are generally permitted to represent taxpayers with respect to IRS forms under the 5300 and 5500 series which are filed by retirement plans and plan sponsors, but not with respect to actuarial forms or schedules.

(3) An individual who practices before the Internal Revenue Service pursuant to paragraph (e)(1) of this section is subject to the provisions of this part in the same manner as attorneys, certified public accountants and enrolled agents.

(f) *Others.* Any individual qualifying under paragraph §10.5(d) or §10.7 is eligible to practice before the Internal Revenue Service to the extent provided in those sections.

(g) *Government officers and employees, and others.* An individual, who is an officer or employee of the executive, legislative, or judicial branch of the United States Government; an officer or employee of the District of Columbia; a Member of Congress; or a Resident Commissioner may not practice before the Internal Revenue Service if such practice violates 18 U.S.C. §§ 203 or 205.

(h) *State officers and employees.* No officer or employee of any State, or subdivision of any State, whose duties require him or her to pass upon, investigate, or deal with tax matters for such State or subdivision, may practice before the Internal Revenue Service, if such employment may disclose facts or information applicable to Federal tax matters.

Page 6

(i) *Effective/applicability date.* This section is applicable on September 26, 2007.

§ 10.4 Eligibility for enrollment as an enrolled agent or enrolled retirement plan agent.

(a) *Enrollment as an enrolled agent upon examination.* The Director of the Office of Professional Responsibility may grant enrollment as an enrolled agent to an applicant who demonstrates special competence in tax matters by written examination administered by, or administered under the oversight of, the Director of the Office of Professional Responsibility and who has not engaged in any conduct that would justify the censure, suspension, or disbarment of any practitioner under the provisions of this part.

(b) *Enrollment as a retirement plan agent upon examination.* The Director of the Office of Professional Responsibility may grant enrollment as an enrolled retirement plan agent to an applicant who demonstrates special competence in qualified retirement plan matters by written examination administered by, or administered under the oversight of, the Director of the Office of Professional Responsibility and who has not engaged in any conduct that would justify the censure, suspension, or disbarment of any practitioner under the provisions of this part.

(c) *Enrollment of former Internal Revenue Service employees.* The Director of the Office of Professional Responsibility may grant enrollment as an enrolled agent or enrolled retirement plan agent to an applicant who, by virtue of past service and technical experience in the Internal Revenue Service, has qualified for such enrollment and who has not engaged in any conduct that would justify the censure, suspension, or disbarment of any practitioner under the provisions of this part, under the following circumstances —

(1) The former employee applies for enrollment to the Director of the Office of Professional Responsibility on a form supplied by the Director of the Office of Professional Responsibility and supplies the information requested on the form and such other information regarding the experience and training of the applicant as may be relevant.

(2) An appropriate office of the Internal Revenue Service, at the request of the Director of the Office of Professional Responsibility, will provide the Director of the Office of Professional Responsibility with a detailed report of the nature and rating of the applicant's work while employed by the Internal Revenue Service and a recommendation whether such employment qualifies the applicant technically or otherwise for the desired authorization.

(3) Enrollment as an enrolled agent based on an applicant's former employment with the Internal Revenue Service may be of unlimited scope or it may be limited to permit the presentation of matters only of the particular class or only before the particular unit or division of the Internal Revenue Service for which the applicant's former employment has qualified the applicant. Enrollment as an enrolled retirement plan agent based on an applicant's former employment with the Internal Revenue Service will be limited to permit the presentation of matters only with respect to qualified retirement plan matters.

(4) Application for enrollment as an enrolled agent or enrolled retirement plan agent based on an applicant's former employment with the Internal Revenue Service must be made within 3 years from the date of separation from such employment.

(5) An applicant for enrollment as an enrolled agent who is requesting such enrollment based on former employment with the Internal Revenue Service must have had a minimum of 5 years continuous employment with the Internal Revenue Service during which the applicant must have been regularly engaged in applying and interpreting the provisions of the Internal Revenue Code and the regulations relating to income, estate, gift, employment, or excise taxes.

(6) An applicant for enrollment as an enrolled retirement plan agent who is requesting such enrollment based on former employment with the Internal Revenue Service must have had a minimum of 5 years continuous employment with the Internal Revenue Service during which the applicant must have been regularly engaged in applying and interpreting the provisions of the Internal Revenue Code and the regulations relating to qualified retirement plan matters.

(7) For the purposes of paragraphs (b)(5) and (b)(6) of this section, an aggregate of 10 or more years of employment in positions involving the application and interpretation of the provisions of the Internal Revenue Code, at least 3 of which occurred within the 5 years preceding the date of application, is the equivalent of 5 years continuous employment.

(d) *Natural persons.* Enrollment to practice may be granted only to natural persons.

(e) *Effective/applicability date.* This section is applicable on September 26, 2007.

§ 10.5 Application for enrollment as an enrolled agent or enrolled retirement plan agent.

(a) *Form; address.* An applicant for enrollment as an enrolled agent or enrolled retirement plan agent must apply as required by forms or procedures established and published by the Office of Professional Responsibility, including proper execution of required forms under oath or affirmation. The address on the application will be the address under which a successful applicant is enrolled and is the address to which all correspondence concerning enrollment will be sent.

(b) *Fee.* A reasonable nonrefundable fee will be charged for each application for enrollment as an enrolled agent filed with the Director of the Office of Professional Responsibility in accordance with *26 CFR 300.5*. A reasonable nonrefundable fee will be charged for each application for enrollment as an enrolled retirement plan agent filed with the Director of the Office of Professional Responsibility.

(c) *Additional information; examination.* The Director of the Office of Professional Responsibility, as a condition to consideration of an application for enrollment, may require the applicant to file additional information and to submit to any written or oral examination under oath or otherwise. The Director of the Office of Professional Responsibility will, on written request filed by an applicant, afford such applicant the opportunity to be heard with respect to his or her application for enrollment.

(d) *Temporary recognition.* On receipt of a properly executed application, the Director of the Office of Professional Responsibility may grant the applicant temporary recognition to practice pending a determination as to whether enrollment to practice should be granted. Temporary recognition will be granted only in unusual circumstances and it will not be granted, in any circumstance, if the application is not regular on its face, if the information stated in the application, if true, is not sufficient to warrant enrollment to practice, or if there is any information before the Director of the Office of Professional Responsibility indicating that the statements in the application are untrue or that the applicant would not otherwise qualify for enrollment. Issuance of temporary recognition does not constitute enrollment to practice or a finding of eligibility for enrollment, and the temporary recognition may be withdrawn at any time by the Director of the Office of Professional Responsibility.

(e) *Appeal from denial of application.* The Director of the Office of Professional Responsibility must inform the applicant as to the reason(s) for any denial of an application for enrollment. The applicant may, within 30 days after receipt of the notice of denial of enrollment, file a written appeal of the denial of enrollment with the Secretary of the Treasury or his or her delegate. A decision on the appeal will be rendered by the Secretary of the Treasury, or his or her delegate, as soon as practicable.

(f) *Effective/applicability date.* This section is applicable to enrollment applications received on or after September 26, 2007.

§ 10.6 Enrollment as an enrolled agent or enrolled retirement plan agent.

(a) *Term of enrollment.* Each individual enrolled to practice before the Internal Revenue Service will be accorded active enrollment status subject to his or her renewal of enrollment as provided in this part.

(b) *Enrollment card.* The Director of the Office of Professional Responsibility will issue an enrollment card to each individual whose application for enrollment to practice before the Internal Revenue Service is approved after July 26, 2002. Each enrollment card

Page 8

will be valid for the period stated on the enrollment card. An individual is not eligible to practice before the Internal Revenue Service if his or her enrollment card is not valid.

(c) *Change of address.* An enrolled agent or enrolled retirement plan agent must send notification of any change of address to the address specified by the Director of the Office of Professional Responsibility. This notification must include the enrolled agent's or enrolled retirement plan agent's name, prior address, new address, social security number or tax identification number and the date.

(d) *Renewal of enrollment.* To maintain active enrollment to practice before the Internal Revenue Service, each individual is required to have the enrollment renewed. Failure to receive notification from the Director of the Office of Professional Responsibility of the renewal requirement will not be justification for the individual's failure to satisfy this requirement.

(1) All individuals licensed to practice before the Internal Revenue Service who have a social security number or tax identification number that ends with the numbers 0, 1, 2, or 3, except for those individuals who received their initial enrollment after November 1, 2003, must apply for renewal between November 1, 2003, and January 31, 2004. The renewal will be effective April 1, 2004.

(2) All individuals licensed to practice before the Internal Revenue Service who have a social security number or tax identification number that ends with the numbers 4, 5, or 6, except for those individuals who received their initial enrollment after November 1, 2004, must apply for renewal between November 1, 2004, and January 31, 2005. The renewal will be effective April 1, 2005.

(3) All individuals licensed to practice before the Internal Revenue Service who have a social security number or tax identification number that ends with the numbers 7, 8, or 9, except for those individuals who received their initial enrollment after November 1, 2005, must apply for renewal between November 1, 2005, and January 31, 2006. The renewal will be effective April 1, 2006.

(4) Thereafter, applications for renewal as an

enrolled agent will be required between November 1 and January 31 of every subsequent third year as specified in paragraphs (d)(1),(2) or (3) of this section according to the last number of the individual's social security number or tax identification number. Those individuals who receive initial enrollment as an enrolled agent after November 1 and before April 2 of the applicable renewal period will not be required to renew their enrollment before the first full renewal period following the receipt of their initial enrollment. Applications for renewal as an enrolled retirement plan agent will be required of all enrolled retirement plan agents between April 1 and June 30 of every third year period subsequent to their initial enrollment.

(5) The Director of the Office of Professional Responsibility will notify the individual of the renewal of enrollment and will issue the individual a card evidencing enrollment.

(6) A reasonable nonrefundable fee will be charged for each application for renewal of enrollment as an enrolled agent filed with the Director of the Office of Professional Responsibility in accordance with *26 CFR 300.6*. A reasonable nonrefundable fee will be charged for each application for renewal of enrollment as an enrolled retirement plan agent filed with the Director of the Office of Professional Responsibility.

(7) Forms required for renewal may be obtained by sending a written request to the Director of the Office of Professional Responsibility, Internal Revenue Service, 1111 Constitution Avenue, NW., Washington, DC 20224 or from such other source as the Director of the Office of Professional Responsibility will publish in the Internal Revenue Bulletin (see *26 CFR 601.601(d)(2)(ii)(b)*) and on the Internal Revenue Service Web page (*http://www.irs.gov*).

(e) *Condition for renewal: Continuing professional education.* In order to qualify for renewal of enrollment, an individual enrolled to practice before the Internal Revenue Service must certify, on the application for renewal form prescribed by the Director of the Office of Professional Responsibility, that he or she has satisfied the following continuing professional education requirements.

(1) *Definitions.* For purposes of this section —

(i) *Enrollment year* means January 1 to December 31 of each year of an enrollment cycle.

(ii) *Enrollment cycle* means the three successive enrollment years preceding the effective date of renewal.

(iii) The *effective date of renewal* is the first day of the fourth month following the close of the period for renewal described in paragraph (d) of this section.

(2) *For renewed enrollment effective after December 31, 2006* —

(i) *Requirements for enrollment cycle.* A minimum of 72 hours of continuing education credit must be completed during each enrollment cycle.

(ii) *Requirements for enrollment year.* A minimum of 16 hours of continuing education credit, including 2 hours of ethics or professional conduct, must be completed during each enrollment year of an enrollment cycle.

(iii) *Enrollment during enrollment cycle.* —

(A) *In general.* Subject to paragraph (e)(2)(iii) (B) of this section, an individual who receives initial enrollment during an enrollment cycle must complete 2 hours of qualifying continuing education credit for each month enrolled during the enrollment cycle. Enrollment for any part of a month is considered enrollment for the entire month.

(B) *Ethics.* An individual who receives initial enrollment during an enrollment cycle must complete 2 hours of ethics or professional conduct for each enrollment year during the enrollment cycle. Enrollment for any part of an enrollment year is considered enrollment for the entire year.

(f) *Qualifying continuing education* —

(1) *General* —

(i) *Enrolled agents.* To qualify for continuing education credit for an enrolled agent, a course of learning must —

(A) Be a qualifying program designed to enhance professional knowledge in Federal taxation or Federal tax related matters (programs comprised of current subject matter in Federal taxation or Federal tax related matters, including accounting, tax preparation software and taxation or ethics);

Page 9

(B) Be a qualifying program consistent with the Internal Revenue Code and effective tax administration; and

(C) Be sponsored by a qualifying sponsor.

(ii) *Enrolled retirement plan agents.* To qualify for continuing education credit for an enrolled retirement plan agent, a course of learning must —

(i) Be a qualifying program designed to enhance professional knowledge in qualified retirement plan matters;

(ii) Be a qualifying program consistent with the Internal Revenue Code and effective tax administration; and

(iii) Be sponsored by a qualifying sponsor.

(2) *Qualifying programs* —

(i) *Formal programs.* A formal program qualifies as continuing education programs if it —

(A) Requires attendance. Additionally, the program sponsor must provide each attendee with a certificate of attendance; and

(B) Requires that the program be conducted by a qualified instructor, discussion leader, or speaker, i.e., a person whose background, training, education and experience is appropriate for instructing or leading a discussion on the subject matter of the particular program; and

(C) Provides or requires a written outline, textbook, or suitable electronic educational materials.

(ii) *Correspondence or individual study programs (including taped programs).* Qualifying continuing education programs include correspondence or individual study programs that are conducted by qualifying sponsors and completed on an individual basis by the enrolled individual. The allowable credit hours for such programs will be measured on a basis comparable to the measurement of a seminar or course for credit in an accredited educational institution. Such programs qualify as continuing education programs if they —

(A) Require registration of the participants by the sponsor;

(B) Provide a means for measuring completion by the participants (e.g., a written examination), including the issuance of a certificate of completion by the sponsor; and

(C) Provide a written outline, textbook, or suitable electronic educational materials.

(iii) *Serving as an instructor, discussion leader or speaker.*

(A) One hour of continuing education credit will be awarded for each contact hour completed as an instructor, discussion leader, or speaker at an educational program that meets the continuing education requirements of paragraph (f) of this section.

(B) Two hours of continuing education credit will be awarded for actual subject preparation time for each contact hour completed as an instructor, discussion leader, or speaker at such programs. It is the responsibility of the individual claiming such credit to maintain records to verify preparation time.

(C) The maximum credit for instruction and preparation may not exceed 50 percent of the continuing education requirement for an enrollment cycle.

(D) An instructor, discussion leader, or speaker who makes more than one presentation on the same subject matter during an enrollment cycle, will receive continuing education credit for only one such presentation for the enrollment cycle.

(iv) *Credit for published articles, books, etc.*

(A) For enrolled agents, continuing education credit will be awarded for publications on Federal taxation or Federal tax related matters, including accounting, tax preparation software, and taxation or ethics, provided the content of such publications is current and designed for the enhancement of the professional knowledge of an individual enrolled to practice before the Internal Revenue Service. The publication must be consistent with the Internal Revenue Code and effective tax administration. For enrolled retirement plan agents, continuing education credit will be awarded for publications on qualified retirement plan matters, provided the content of such publications is current and designed for the enhancement of the professional knowledge of an individual enrolled to practice as an enrolled retirement plan agent before the Internal Revenue Service. The publication must be consistent with the Internal Revenue Code and effective tax administration.

(B) The credit allowed will be on the basis

of one hour credit for each hour of preparation time for the material. It is the responsibility of the person claiming the credit to maintain records to verify preparation time.

(C) The maximum credit for publications may not exceed 25 percent of the continuing education requirement of any enrollment cycle.

(3) *Periodic examination.*

(i) Individuals may establish eligibility for renewal of enrollment for any enrollment cycle by —

(A) Achieving a passing score on each part of the Special Enrollment Examination administered under this part during the three year period prior to renewal; and

(B) Completing a minimum of 16 hours of qualifying continuing education during the last year of an enrollment cycle.

(ii) Courses designed to help an applicant prepare for the examination specified in paragraph (a) of §10.4 are considered basic in nature and are not qualifying continuing education.

(g) *Sponsors.*

(1) Sponsors are those responsible for presenting programs.

(2) To qualify as a sponsor, a program presenter must —

(i) Be an accredited educational institution;

(ii) Be recognized for continuing education purposes by the licensing body of any State, territory, or possession of the United States, including a Commonwealth, or the District of Columbia.

(iii) Be recognized by the Director of the Office of Professional Responsibility as a professional organization or society whose programs include offering continuing professional education opportunities in subject matters within the scope of paragraph (f)(1)(i) of this section; or

(iv) File a sponsor agreement with the Director of the Office of Professional Responsibility and obtain approval of the program as a qualified continuing education program.

(3) A qualifying sponsor must ensure the program complies with the following requirements —

(i) Programs must be developed by individual(s) qualified in the subject matter;

(ii) Program subject matter must be current;

(iii) Instructors, discussion leaders, and speakers must be qualified with respect to program content;

(iv) Programs must include some means for evaluation of technical content and presentation;

(v) Certificates of completion must be provided to the participants who successfully complete the program; and

(vi) Records must be maintained by the sponsor to verify the participants who attended and completed the program for a period of three years following completion of the program. In the case of continuous conferences, conventions, and the like, records must be maintained to verify completion of the program and attendance by each participant at each segment of the program.

(4) Professional organizations or societies wishing to be considered as qualified sponsors must request this status from the Director of the Office of Professional Responsibility and furnish information in support of the request together with any further information deemed necessary by the Director of the Office of Professional Responsibility.

(5) *Sponsor renewal.*

(i) *In general.* A sponsor maintains its status as a qualified sponsor during the sponsor enrollment cycle.

(ii) *Renewal Period.* Each sponsor must file an application to renew its status as a qualified sponsor between May 1 and July 31, 2008. Thereafter, applications for renewal will be required between May 1 and July 31 of every subsequent third year.

(iii) *Effective date of renewal.* The effective date of renewal is the first day of the third month following the close of the renewal period.

(iv) *Sponsor enrollment cycle.* The sponsor enrollment cycle is the three successive calendar years preceding the effective date of renewal.

(h) *Measurement of continuing education coursework.*

(1) All continuing education programs will be measured in terms of contact hours. The shortest recognized program will be one contact hour.

(2) A contact hour is 50 minutes of continuous

participation in a program. Credit is granted only for a full contact hour, i.e., 50 minutes or multiples thereof. For example, a program lasting more than 50 minutes but less than 100 minutes will count as one contact hour.

(3) Individual segments at continuous conferences, conventions and the like will be considered one total program. For example, two 90-minute segments (180 minutes) at a continuous conference will count as three contact hours.

(4) For university or college courses, each semester hour credit will equal 15 contact hours and a quarter hour credit will equal 10 contact hours.

(i) *Recordkeeping requirements.*

(1) Each individual applying for renewal must retain for a period of three years following the date of renewal of enrollment the information required with regard to qualifying continuing professional education credit hours. Such information includes —

(i) The name of the sponsoring organization;

(ii) The location of the program;

(iii) The title of the program and description of its content;

(iv) Written outlines, course syllabi, textbook, and/or electronic materials provided or required for the course;

(v) The dates attended;

(vi) The credit hours claimed;

(vii) The name(s) of the instructor(s), discussion leader(s), or speaker(s), if appropriate; and

(viii) The certificate of completion and/or signed statement of the hours of attendance obtained from the sponsor.

(2) To receive continuing education credit for service completed as an instructor, discussion leader, or speaker, the following information must be maintained for a period of three years following the date of renewal of enrollment —

(i) The name of the sponsoring organization;

(ii) The location of the program;

(iii) The title of the program and description of its content;

(iv) The dates of the program; and

(v) The credit hours claimed.

(3) To receive continuing education credit for

publications, the following information must be maintained for a period of three years following the date of renewal of enrollment —

(i) The publisher;

(ii) The title of the publication;

(iii) A copy of the publication;

(iv) The date of publication; and

(v) Records that substantiate the hours worked on the publication.

(j) *Waivers.*

(1) Waiver from the continuing education requirements for a given period may be granted by the Director of the Office of Professional Responsibility for the following reasons —

(i) Health, which prevented compliance with the continuing education requirements;

(ii) Extended active military duty;

(iii) Absence from the United States for an extended period of time due to employment or other reasons, provided the individual does not practice before the Internal Revenue Service during such absence; and

(iv) Other compelling reasons, which will be considered on a case-by-case basis.

(2) A request for waiver must be accompanied by appropriate documentation. The individual is required to furnish any additional documentation or explanation deemed necessary by the Director of the Office of Professional Responsibility. Examples of appropriate documentation could be a medical certificate or military orders.

(3) A request for waiver must be filed no later than the last day of the renewal application period.

(4) If a request for waiver is not approved, the individual will be placed in inactive status, so notified by the Director of the Office of Professional Responsibility, and placed on a roster of inactive enrolled individuals.

(5) If a request for waiver is approved, the individual will be notified and issued a card evidencing renewal.

(6) Those who are granted waivers are required to file timely applications for renewal of enrollment.

(k) *Failure to comply.*

(1) Compliance by an individual with the re-

quirements of this part is determined by the Director of the Office of Professional Responsibility. An individual who fails to meet the requirements of eligibility for renewal of enrollment will be notified by the Director of the Office of Professional Responsibility at his or her enrollment address by first class mail. The notice will state the basis for the determination of noncompliance and will provide the individual an opportunity to furnish information in writing relating to the matter within 60 days of the date of the notice. Such information will be considered by the Director of the Office of Professional Responsibility in making a final determination as to eligibility for renewal of enrollment.

(2) The Director of the Office of Professional Responsibility may require any individual, by notice sent by first class mail to his or her enrollment address, to provide copies of any records required to be maintained under this part. The Director of the Office of Professional Responsibility may disallow any continuing professional education hours claimed if the individual fails to comply with this requirement.

(3) An individual who has not filed a timely application for renewal of enrollment, who has not made a timely response to the notice of noncompliance with the renewal requirements, or who has not satisfied the requirements of eligibility for renewal will be placed on a roster of inactive enrolled individuals. During this time, the individual will be ineligible to practice before the Internal Revenue Service.

(4) Individuals placed in inactive enrollment status and individuals ineligible to practice before the Internal Revenue Service may not state or imply that they are enrolled to practice before the Internal Revenue Service, or use the terms enrolled agent or enrolled retirement plan agent, the designations "EA" or "ERPA" or other form of reference to eligibility to practice before the Internal Revenue Service.

(5) An individual placed in an inactive status may be reinstated to an active enrollment status by filing an application for renewal of enrollment and providing evidence of the completion of all required continuing professional education hours for the enrollment cycle. Continuing education credit under this paragraph (k)(5) may not be used to satisfy the requirements of the enrollment cycle in which the individual has been placed back on the active roster.

(6) An individual placed in an inactive status must file an application for renewal of enrollment and satisfy the requirements for renewal as set forth in this section within three years of being placed in an inactive status. The name of such individual otherwise will be removed from the inactive enrollment roster and his or her enrollment will terminate. Eligibility for enrollment must then be reestablished by the individual as provided in this section.

(7) Inactive enrollment status is not available to an individual who is the subject of a disciplinary matter in the Office of Professional Responsibility.

(l) *Inactive retirement status.* An individual who no longer practices before the Internal Revenue Service may request being placed in an inactive retirement status at any time and such individual will be placed in an inactive retirement status. The individual will be ineligible to practice before the Internal Revenue Service. Such individual must file a timely application for renewal of enrollment at each applicable renewal or enrollment period as provided in this section. An individual who is placed in an inactive retirement status may be reinstated to an active enrollment status by filing an application for renewal of enrollment and providing evidence of the completion of the required continuing professional education hours for the enrollment cycle. Inactive retirement status is not available to an individual who is the subject of a disciplinary matter in the Office of Professional Responsibility.

(m) *Renewal while under suspension or disbarment.* An individual who is ineligible to practice before the Internal Revenue Service by virtue of disciplinary action is required to be in conformance with the requirements for renewal of enrollment before his or her eligibility is restored.

(n) *Verification.* The Director of the Office of Professional Responsibility may review the continuing education records of an enrolled individual and/or qualified sponsor in a manner deemed appropriate to determine compliance with the requirements and standards for renewal of enrollment as provided in paragraph (f) of this section.

Page 13

(o) *Enrolled Actuaries.* The enrollment and the re-newal of enrollment of actuaries authorized to prac-tice under paragraph (d) of §10.3 are governed by the regulations of the Joint Board for the Enrollment of Actuaries at 20 CFR 901.1 through 901.71.

(p) *Effective/applicability date.* This section is ap-plicable to enrollment effective on or after Septem-ber 26, 2007.

(Approved by the Office of Management and Budget under Control No. 1545-0946 and 1545-1726)

§ 10.7 Representing oneself; participating in rulemaking; limited practice; special appearances; and return preparation.

(a) *Representing oneself.* Individuals may appear on their own behalf before the Internal Revenue Service provided they present satisfactory identification.

(b) *Participating in rulemaking.* Individuals may participate in rulemaking as provided by the Admin-istrative Procedure Act. See 5 U.S.C. § 553.

(c) *Limited practice* —

(1) *In general.* Subject to the limitations in para-graph (c)(2) of this section, an individual who is not a practitioner may represent a taxpayer before the Internal Revenue Service in the circumstances de-scribed in this paragraph (c)(1), even if the taxpayer is not present, provided the individual presents satis-factory identification and proof of his or her author-ity to represent the taxpayer. The circumstances de-scribed in this paragraph (c)(1) are as follows:

(i) An individual may represent a member of his or her immediate family.

(ii) A regular full-time employee of an individ-ual employer may represent the employer.

(iii) A general partner or a regular full-time em-ployee of a partnership may represent the partner-ship.

(iv) A bona fide officer or a regular full-time employee of a corporation (including a parent, sub-sidiary, or other affiliated corporation), association, or organized group may represent the corporation, association, or organized group.

(v) A regular full-time employee of a trust, re-

ceivership, guardianship, or estate may represent the trust, receivership, guardianship, or estate.

(vi) An officer or a regular employee of a gov-ernmental unit, agency, or authority may represent the governmental unit, agency, or authority in the course of his or her official duties.

(vii) An individual may represent any individu-al or entity, who is outside the United States, before personnel of the Internal Revenue Service when such representation takes place outside the United States.

(viii) An individual who prepares and signs a taxpayer's tax return as the preparer, or who prepares a tax return but is not required (by the instructions to the tax return or regulations) to sign the tax return, may represent the taxpayer before revenue agents, customer service representatives or similar officers and employees of the Internal Revenue Service during an examination of the taxable year or period covered by that tax return, but, unless otherwise prescribed by regulation or notice, this right does not permit such individual to represent the taxpayer, regardless of the circumstances requiring representation, before appeals officers, revenue officers, Counsel or similar officers or employees of the Internal Revenue Ser-vice or the Department of Treasury.

(2) *Limitations.*

(i) An individual who is under suspension or disbarment from practice before the Internal Rev-enue Service may not engage in limited practice be-fore the Internal Revenue Service under paragraph (c)(1) of this section.

(ii) The Director, after notice and opportunity for a conference, may deny eligibility to engage in limited practice before the Internal Revenue Service under paragraph (c)(1) of this section to any individ-ual who has engaged in conduct that would justify a sanction under §10.50.

(iii) An individual who represents a taxpayer under the authority of paragraph (c)(1) of this section is subject, to the extent of his or her authority, to such rules of general applicability regarding standards of conduct and other matters as the Director of the Of-fice of Professional Responsibility prescribes.

(d) *Special appearances.* The Director of the Office of Professional Responsibility may, subject to such conditions as he or she deems appropriate, authorize an individual who is not otherwise eligible to practice before the Internal Revenue Service to represent another person in a particular matter.

(e) *Preparing tax returns and furnishing information.* Any individual may prepare a tax return, appear as a witness for the taxpayer before the Internal Revenue Service, or furnish information at the request of the Internal Revenue Service or any of its officers or employees.

(f) *Fiduciaries.* For purposes of this part, a fiduciary (i.e., a trustee, receiver, guardian, personal representative, administrator, or executor) is considered to be the taxpayer and not a representative of the taxpayer.

(g) *Effective/applicability date.* This section is applicable on September 26, 2007.

§ 10.8 Customhouse brokers.

Nothing contained in the regulations in this part will affect or limit the right of a customhouse broker, licensed as such by the Commissioner of Customs in accordance with the regulations prescribed therefore, in any customs district in which he or she is so licensed, at a relevant local office of the Internal Revenue Service or before the National Office of the Internal Revenue Service, to act as a representative in respect to any matters relating specifically to the importation or exportation of merchandise under the customs or internal revenue laws, for any person for whom he or she has acted as a customhouse broker.

(g) Effective/applicability date. This section is applicable on September 26, 2007.

Subpart B — Duties and Restrictions Relating to Practice Before the Internal Revenue Service

§ 10.20 Information to be furnished.

(a) *To the Internal Revenue Service.*

(1) A practitioner must, on a proper and lawful request by a duly authorized officer or employee of the Internal Revenue Service, promptly submit records or information in any matter before the Internal Rev-

enue Service unless the practitioner believes in good faith and on reasonable grounds that the records or information are privileged.

(2) Where the requested records or information are not in the possession of, or subject to the control of, the practitioner or the practitioner's client, the practitioner must promptly notify the requesting Internal Revenue Service officer or employee and the practitioner must provide any information that the practitioner has regarding the identity of any person who the practitioner believes may have possession or control of the requested records or information. The practitioner must make reasonable inquiry of his or her client regarding the identity of any person who may have possession or control of the requested records or information, but the practitioner is not required to make inquiry of any other person or independently verify any information provided by the practitioner's client regarding the identity of such persons.

(b) *To the Director of the Office of Professional Responsibility.* When a proper and lawful request is made by the Director of the Office of Professional Responsibility, a practitioner must provide the Director of the Office of Professional Responsibility with any information the practitioner has concerning an inquiry by the Director of the Office of Professional Responsibility into an alleged violation of the regulations in this part by any person, and to testify regarding this information in any proceeding instituted under this part, unless the practitioner believes in good faith and on reasonable grounds that the information is privileged.

(c) *Interference with a proper and lawful request for records or information.* A practitioner may not interfere, or attempt to interfere, with any proper and lawful effort by the Internal Revenue Service, its officers or employees, or the Director of the Office of Professional Responsibility, or his or her employees, to obtain any record or information unless the practitioner believes in good faith and on reasonable grounds that the record or information is privileged.

§ 10.21 Knowledge of client's omission.

A practitioner who, having been retained by a client with respect to a matter administered by the Internal Revenue Service, knows that the client has not complied with the revenue laws of the United States or has made an error in or omission from any return, document, affidavit, or other paper which the client submitted or executed under the revenue laws of the United States, must advise the client promptly of the fact of such noncompliance, error, or omission. The practitioner must advise the client of the consequences as provided under the Code and regulations of such noncompliance, error, or omission.

§ 10.22 Diligence as to accuracy.

(a) *In general.* A practitioner must exercise due diligence —

(1) In preparing or assisting in the preparation of, approving, and filing tax returns, documents, affidavits, and other papers relating to Internal Revenue Service matters;

(2) In determining the correctness of oral or written representations made by the practitioner to the Department of the Treasury; and

(3) In determining the correctness of oral or written representations made by the practitioner to clients with reference to any matter administered by the Internal Revenue Service.

(b) *Reliance on others.* Except as provided in §§ 10.34, 10.35 and 10.37, a practitioner will be presumed to have exercised due diligence for purposes of this section if the practitioner relies on the work product of another person and the practitioner used reasonable care in engaging, supervising, training, and evaluating the person, taking proper account of the nature of the relationship between the practitioner and the person.

(c) *Effective/applicability date.* This section is applicable on September 26, 2007.

§ 10.23 Prompt disposition of pending matters.

A practitioner may not unreasonably delay the
Page 16

prompt disposition of any matter before the Internal Revenue Service.

§ 10.24 Assistance from or to disbarred or suspended persons and former Internal Revenue Service employees.

A practitioner may not, knowingly and directly or indirectly:

(a) Accept assistance from or assist any person who is under disbarment or suspension from practice before the Internal Revenue Service if the assistance relates to a matter or matters constituting practice before the Internal Revenue Service.

(b) Accept assistance from any former government employee where the provisions of § 10.25 or any Federal law would be violated.

§10.25 Practice by former government employees, their partners and their associates.

(a) *Definitions.* For purposes of this section —

(1) *Assist* means to act in such a way as to advise, furnish information to, or otherwise aid another person, directly, or indirectly.

(2) *Government employee* is an officer or employee of the United States or any agency of the United States, including a special Government employee as defined in *18 U.S.C. 202(a)*, or of the District of Columbia, or of any State, or a member of Congress or of any State legislature.

(3) *Member of a firm* is a sole practitioner or an employee or associate thereof, or a partner, stockholder, associate, affiliate or employee of a partnership, joint venture, corporation, professional association or other affiliation of two or more practitioners who represent nongovernmental parties.

(4) *Particular matter involving specific parties* is defined at 5 CFR 2637.201(c), or superseding post-employment regulations issued by the U.S. Office of Government Ethics.

(5) *Rule* includes Treasury regulations, whether issued or under preparation for issuance as notices of proposed rulemaking or as Treasury decisions, revenue rulings, and revenue procedures pub-

lished in the Internal Revenue Bulletin (see *26 CFR 601.601(d)(2)(ii)(b)*).

(b) *General rules* —

(1) No former Government employee may, subsequent to Government employment, represent anyone in any matter administered by the Internal Revenue Service if the representation would violate *18 U.S.C. 207* or any other laws of the United States.

(2) No former Government employee who personally and substantially participated in a particular matter involving specific parties may, subsequent to Government employment, represent or knowingly assist, in that particular matter, any person who is or was a specific party to that particular matter.

(3) A former Government employee who within a period of one year prior to the termination of Government employment had official responsibility for a particular matter involving specific parties may not, within two years after Government employment is ended, represent in that particular matter any person who is or was a specific party to that particular matter.

(4) No former Government employee may, within one year after Government employment is ended, communicate with or appear before, with the intent to influence, any employee of the Treasury Department in connection with the publication, withdrawal, amendment, modification, or interpretation of a rule the development of which the former Government employee participated in, or for which, within a period of one year prior to the termination of Government employment, the former government employee had official responsibility. This paragraph (b)(4) does not, however, preclude any former employee from appearing on one's own behalf or from representing a taxpayer before the Internal Revenue Service in connection with a particular matter involving specific parties involving the application or interpretation of a rule with respect to that particular matter, provided that the representation is otherwise consistent with the other provisions of this section and the former employee does not utilize or disclose any confidential information acquired by the former employee in the development of the rule.

(c) *Firm representation* —

(1) No member of a firm of which a former Government employee is a member may represent or knowingly assist a person who was or is a specific party in any particular matter with respect to which the restrictions of paragraph (b)(2) of this section apply to the former Government employee, in that particular matter, unless the firm isolates the former Government employee in such a way to ensure that the former Government employee cannot assist in the representation.

(2) When isolation of a former Government employee is required under paragraph (c)(1) of this section, a statement affirming the fact of such isolation must be executed under oath by the former Government employee and by another member of the firm acting on behalf of the firm. The statement must clearly identify the firm, the former Government employee, and the particular matter(s) requiring isolation. The statement must be retained by the firm and, upon request, provided to the Director of the Office of Professional Responsibility.

(d) *Pending representation.* The provisions of this regulation will govern practice by former Government employees, their partners and associates with respect to representation in particular matters involving specific parties where actual representation commenced before the effective date of this regulation.

(e) *Effective/applicability date.* This section is applicable on September 26, 2007.

§ 10.26 Notaries.

A practitioner may not take acknowledgments, administer oaths, certify papers, or perform any official act as a notary public with respect to any matter administered by the Internal Revenue Service and for which he or she is employed as counsel, attorney, or agent, or in which he or she may be in any way interested.

§ 10.27 Fees.

(a) *In general.* A practitioner may not charge an unconscionable fee in connection with any matter before the Internal Revenue Service.

Page 17

(b) *Contingent fees —*

(1) Except as provided in paragraphs (b)(2), (3), and (4) of this section, a practitioner may not charge a contingent fee for services rendered in connection with any matter before the Internal Revenue Service.

(2) A practitioner may charge a contingent fee for services rendered in connection with the Service's examination of, or challenge to —

(i) An original tax return; or

(ii) An amended return or claim for refund or credit where the amended return or claim for refund or credit was filed within 120 days of the taxpayer receiving a written notice of the examination of, or a written challenge to the original tax return.

(3) A practitioner may charge a contingent fee for services rendered in connection with a claim for credit or refund filed solely in connection with the determination of statutory interest or penalties assessed by the Internal Revenue Service.

(4) A practitioner may charge a contingent fee for services rendered in connection with any judicial proceeding arising under the Internal Revenue Code.

(c) *Definitions.* For purposes of this section —

(1) *Contingent fee* is any fee that is based, in whole or in part, on whether or not a position taken on a tax return or other filing avoids challenge by the Internal Revenue Service or is sustained either by the Internal Revenue Service or in litigation. A contingent fee includes a fee that is based on a percentage of the refund reported on a return, that is based on a percentage of the taxes saved, or that otherwise depends on the specific result attained. A contingent fee also includes any fee arrangement in which the practitioner will reimburse the client for all or a portion of the client's fee in the event that a position taken on a tax return or other filing is challenged by the Internal Revenue Service or is not sustained, whether pursuant to an indemnity agreement, a guarantee, rescission rights, or any other arrangement with a similar effect.

(2) *Matter before the Internal Revenue Service* includes tax planning and advice, preparing or filing or assisting in preparing or filing returns or claims for refund or credit, and all matters connected with a

presentation to the Internal Revenue Service or any of its officers or employees relating to a taxpayer's rights, privileges, or liabilities under laws or regulations administered by the Internal Revenue Service. Such presentations include, but are not limited to, preparing and filing documents, corresponding and communicating with the Internal Revenue Service, rendering written advice with respect to any entity, transaction, plan or arrangement, and representing a client at conferences, hearings, and meetings.

(d) *Effective/applicability date.* This section is applicable for fee arrangements entered into after March 26, 2008.

§ 10.28 Return of client's records.

(a) In general, a practitioner must, at the request of a client, promptly return any and all records of the client that are necessary for the client to comply with his or her Federal tax obligations. The practitioner may retain copies of the records returned to a client. The existence of a dispute over fees generally does not relieve the practitioner of his or her responsibility under this section. Nevertheless, if applicable state law allows or permits the retention of a client's records by a practitioner in the case of a dispute over fees for services rendered, the practitioner need only return those records that must be attached to the taxpayer's return. The practitioner, however, must provide the client with reasonable access to review and copy any additional records of the client retained by the practitioner under state law that are necessary for the client to comply with his or her Federal tax obligations.

(b) For purposes of this section — Records of the client include all documents or written or electronic materials provided to the practitioner, or obtained by the practitioner in the course of the practitioner's representation of the client, that preexisted the retention of the practitioner by the client. The term also includes materials that were prepared by the client or a third party (not including an employee or agent of the practitioner) at any time and provided to the practitioner with respect to the subject matter of the representation. The term also includes any return, claim for refund, schedule, affidavit, appraisal or any other document prepared by the practitioner, or his or her employee or agent, that was presented to the client with respect to a prior representation if such document is necessary for the taxpayer to comply with his or her current Federal tax obligations. The term does not include any return, claim for refund, schedule, affidavit, appraisal or any other document prepared by the practitioner or the practitioner's firm, employees or agents if the practitioner is withholding such document pending the client's performance of its contractual obligation to pay fees with respect to such document.

§ 10.29 Conflicting interests.

(a) Except as provided by paragraph (b) of this section, a practitioner shall not represent a client before the Internal Revenue Service if the representation involves a conflict of interest. A conflict of interest exists if —

(1) The representation of one client will be directly adverse to another client; or

(2) There is a significant risk that the representation of one or more clients will be materially limited by the practitioner's responsibilities to another client, a former client or a third person, or by a personal interest of the practitioner.

(b) Notwithstanding the existence of a conflict of interest under paragraph (a) of this section, the practitioner may represent a client if —

(1) The practitioner reasonably believes that the practitioner will be able to provide competent and diligent representation to each affected client;

(2) The representation is not prohibited by law; and

(3) Each affected client waives the conflict of interest and gives informed consent, confirmed in writing by each affected client, at the time the existence of the conflict of interest is known by the practitioner. The confirmation may be made within a reasonable period of time after the informed consent, but in no event later than 30 days.

(c) Copies of the written consents must be retained by the practitioner for at least 36 months from the date of the conclusion of the representation of the affected clients, and the written consents must be provided to any officer or employee of the Internal Revenue Service on request.

(d) *Effective/applicability date.* This section is applicable on September 26, 2007.

§ 10.30 Solicitation.

(a) *Advertising and solicitation restrictions.*

(1) A practitioner may not, with respect to any Internal Revenue Service matter, in any way use or participate in the use of any form of public communication or private solicitation containing a false, fraudulent, or coercive statement or claim; or a misleading or deceptive statement or claim. Enrolled agents or enrolled retirement plan agents, in describing their professional designation, may not utilize the term of art "certified" or imply an employer/employee relationship with the Internal Revenue Service. Examples of acceptable descriptions for enrolled agents are "enrolled to represent taxpayers before the Internal Revenue Service," "enrolled to practice before the Internal Revenue Service," and "admitted to practice before the Internal Revenue Service." Similarly, examples of acceptable descriptions for enrolled retirement plan agents are "enrolled to represent taxpayers before the Internal Revenue Service as a retirement plan agent" and "enrolled to practice before the Internal Revenue Service as a retirement plan agent."

(2) A practitioner may not make, directly or indirectly, an uninvited written or oral solicitation of employment in matters related to the Internal Revenue Service if the solicitation violates Federal or State law or other applicable rule, e.g., attorneys are precluded from making a solicitation that is prohibited by conduct rules applicable to all attorneys in their State(s) of licensure. Any lawful solicitation made by or on behalf of a practitioner eligible to practice before the Internal Revenue Service must, nevertheless, clearly identify the solicitation as such and, if applicable, identify the source of the information used in choosing the recipient.

(b) *Fee information.*

Page 19

(1)(i) A practitioner may publish the availability of a written schedule of fees and disseminate the following fee information —

 (A) Fixed fees for specific routine services.

 (B) Hourly rates.

 (C) Range of fees for particular services.

 (D) Fee charged for an initial consultation.

 (ii) Any statement of fee information concerning matters in which costs may be incurred must include a statement disclosing whether clients will be responsible for such costs.

(2) A practitioner may charge no more than the rate(s) published under paragraph (b)(1) of this section for at least 30 calendar days after the last date on which the schedule of fees was published.

(c) *Communication of fee information.* Fee information may be communicated in professional lists, telephone directories, print media, mailings, and electronic mail, facsimile, hand delivered flyers, radio, television, and any other method. The method chosen, however, must not cause the communication to become untruthful, deceptive, or otherwise in violation of this part. A practitioner may not persist in attempting to contact a prospective client if the prospective client has made it known to the practitioner that he or she does not desire to be solicited. In the case of radio and television broadcasting, the broadcast must be recorded and the practitioner must retain a recording of the actual transmission. In the case of direct mail and e-commerce communications, the practitioner must retain a copy of the actual communication, along with a list or other description of persons to whom the communication was mailed or otherwise distributed. The copy must be retained by the practitioner for a period of at least 36 months from the date of the last transmission or use.

(d) *Improper associations.* A practitioner may not, in matters related to the Internal Revenue Service, assist, or accept assistance from, any person or entity who, to the knowledge of the practitioner, obtains clients or otherwise practices in a manner forbidden under this section.

(e) *Effective/applicability date.* This section is applicable on September 26, 2007.

(Approved by the Office of Management and Budget under Control No. 1545-1726)

§ 10.31 Negotiation of taxpayer checks.

A practitioner who prepares tax returns may not endorse or otherwise negotiate any check issued to a client by the government in respect of a Federal tax liability.

§ 10.32 Practice of law.

Nothing in the regulations in this part may be construed as authorizing persons not members of the bar to practice law.

§ 10.33 Best practices for tax advisors.

(a) *Best practices.* Tax advisors should provide clients with the highest quality representation concerning Federal tax issues by adhering to best practices in providing advice and in preparing or assisting in the preparation of a submission to the Internal Revenue Service. In addition to compliance with the standards of practice provided elsewhere in this part, best practices include the following:

(1) Communicating clearly with the client regarding the terms of the engagement. For example, the advisor should determine the client's expected purpose for and use of the advice and should have a clear understanding with the client regarding the form and scope of the advice or assistance to be rendered.

(2) Establishing the facts, determining which facts are relevant, evaluating the reasonableness of any assumptions or representations, relating the applicable law (including potentially applicable judicial doctrines) to the relevant facts, and arriving at a conclusion supported by the law and the facts.

(3) Advising the client regarding the import of the conclusions reached, including, for example, whether a taxpayer may avoid accuracy-related penalties under the Internal Revenue Code if a taxpayer acts in reliance on the advice.

(4) Acting fairly and with integrity in practice be-

fore the Internal Revenue Service.

(b) *Procedures to ensure best practices for tax advisors.* Tax advisors with responsibility for overseeing a firm's practice of providing advice concerning Federal tax issues or of preparing or assisting in the preparation of submissions to the Internal Revenue Service should take reasonable steps to ensure that the firm's procedures for all members, associates, and employees are consistent with the best practices set forth in paragraph (a) of this section.

(c) *Applicability date.* This section is effective after June 20, 2005.

§ 10.34 Standards with respect to tax returns and documents, affidavits and other papers.

(a) [Reserved]

(b) *Documents, affidavits and other papers* —

(1) A practitioner may not advise a client to take a position on a document, affidavit or other paper submitted to the Internal Revenue Service unless the position is not frivolous.

(2) A practitioner may not advise a client to submit a document, affidavit or other paper to the Internal Revenue Service —

(i) The purpose of which is to delay or impede the administration of the Federal tax laws;

(ii) That is frivolous; or

(iii) That contains or omits information in a manner that demonstrates an intentional disregard of a rule or regulation unless the practitioner also advises the client to submit a document that evidences a good faith challenge to the rule or regulation.

(c) *Advising clients on potential penalties* —

(1) A practitioner must inform a client of any penalties that are reasonably likely to apply to the client with respect to —

(i) A position taken on a tax return if —

(A) The practitioner advised the client with respect to the position; or

(B) The practitioner prepared or signed the tax return; and

(ii) Any document, affidavit or other paper submitted to the Internal Revenue Service.

(2) The practitioner also must inform the client

of any opportunity to avoid any such penalties by disclosure, if relevant, and of the requirements for adequate disclosure.

(3) This paragraph (c) applies even if the practitioner is not subject to a penalty under the Internal Revenue Code with respect to the position or with respect to the document, affidavit or other paper submitted.

(d) *Relying on information furnished by clients.* A practitioner advising a client to take a position on a tax return, document, affidavit or other paper submitted to the Internal Revenue Service, or preparing or signing a tax return as a preparer, generally may rely in good faith without verification upon information furnished by the client. The practitioner may not, however, ignore the implications of information furnished to, or actually known by, the practitioner, and must make reasonable inquiries if the information as furnished appears to be incorrect, inconsistent with an important fact or another factual assumption, or incomplete.

(e) [Reserved]

(f) *Effective/applicability date.* Section 10.34 is applicable to tax returns, documents, affidavits, and other papers filed on or after September 26, 2007.

§ 10.35 Requirements for covered opinions.

(a) A practitioner who provides a covered opinion shall comply with the standards of practice in this section.

(b) *Definitions.* For purposes of this subpart —

(1) *A practitioner* includes any individual described in §10.2(a)(5).

(2) *Covered opinion* —

(i) *In general.* A *covered opinion* is written advice (including electronic communications) by a practitioner concerning one or more Federal tax issues arising from —

(A) A transaction that is the same as or substantially similar to a transaction that, at the time the advice is rendered, the Internal Revenue Service has determined to be a tax avoidance transaction and identified by published guidance as a listed transaction under 26 CFR 1.6011-4(b)(2);

Page 21

(B) Any partnership or other entity, any investment plan or arrangement, or any other plan or arrangement, the principal purpose of which is the avoidance or evasion of any tax imposed by the Internal Revenue Code; or

(C) Any partnership or other entity, any investment plan or arrangement, or any other plan or arrangement, a significant purpose of which is the avoidance or evasion of any tax imposed by the Internal Revenue Code if the written advice —

(1) Is a *reliance opinion*;

(2) Is a *marketed opinion*;

(3) Is subject to *conditions of confidentiality*; or

(4) Is subject to *contractual protection*.

(ii) *Excluded advice.* A *covered opinion* does not include —

(A) Written advice provided to a client during the course of an engagement if a practitioner is reasonably expected to provide subsequent written advice to the client that satisfies the requirements of this section;

(B) Written advice, other than advice described in paragraph (b)(2)(i)(A) of this section (concerning listed transactions) or paragraph (b)(2)(i)(B) of this section (concerning the principal purpose of avoidance or evasion) that —

(1) Concerns the qualification of a qualified plan;

(2) Is a *State or local bond opinion*; or

(3) Is included in documents required to be filed with the Securities and Exchange Commission.

(C) Written advice prepared for and provided to a taxpayer, solely for use by that taxpayer, after the taxpayer has filed a tax return with the Internal Revenue Service reflecting the tax benefits of the transaction. The preceding sentence does not apply if the practitioner knows or has reason to know that the written advice will be relied upon by the taxpayer to take a position on a tax return (including for these purposes an amended return that claims tax benefits not reported on a previously filed return) filed after the date on which the advice is provided to the taxpayer;

(D) Written advice provided to an employer

by a practitioner in that practitioner's capacity as an employee of that employer solely for purposes of determining the tax liability of the employer; or

(E) Written advice that does not resolve a Federal tax issue in the taxpayer's favor, unless the advice reaches a conclusion favorable to the taxpayer at any confidence level (e.g., not frivolous, realistic possibility of success, reasonable basis or substantial authority) with respect to that issue. If written advice concerns more than one Federal tax issue, the advice must comply with the requirements of paragraph (c) of this section with respect to any Federal tax issue not described in the preceding sentence.

(3) *A Federal tax issue* is a question concerning the Federal tax treatment of an item of income, gain, loss, deduction, or credit, the existence or absence of a taxable transfer of property, or the value of property for Federal tax purposes. For purposes of this subpart, a *Federal tax issue* is significant if the Internal Revenue Service has a reasonable basis for a successful challenge and its resolution could have a significant impact, whether beneficial or adverse and under any reasonably foreseeable circumstance, on the overall Federal tax treatment of the transaction(s) or matter(s) addressed in the opinion.

(4) *Reliance opinion* —

(i) Written advice is a *reliance opinion* if the advice concludes at a confidence level of at least more likely than not (a greater than 50 percent likelihood) that one or more significant Federal tax issues would be resolved in the taxpayer's favor.

(ii) For purposes of this section, written advice, other than advice described in paragraph (b)(2)(i)(A) of this section (concerning listed transactions) or paragraph (b)(2)(i)(B) of this section (concerning the principal purpose of avoidance or evasion), is not treated as a *reliance opinion* if the practitioner prominently discloses in the written advice that it was not intended or written by the practitioner to be used, and that it cannot be used by the taxpayer, for the purpose of avoiding penalties that may be imposed on the taxpayer.

(5) *Marketed opinion* —

(i) Written advice is a *marketed opinion* if the practitioner knows or has reason to know that the written advice will be used or referred to by a person other than the practitioner (or a person who is a member of, associated with, or employed by the practitioner's firm) in promoting, marketing or recommending a partnership or other entity, investment plan or arrangement to one or more taxpayer(s).

(ii) For purposes of this section, written advice, other than advice described in paragraph (b)(2)(i)(A) of this section (concerning listed transactions) or paragraph (b)(2)(i)(B) of this section (concerning the principal purpose of avoidance or evasion), is not treated as a *marketed opinion* if the practitioner prominently discloses in the written advice that —

(A) The advice was not intended or written by the practitioner to be used, and that it cannot be used by any taxpayer, for the purpose of avoiding penalties that may be imposed on the taxpayer;

(B) The advice was written to support the promotion or marketing of the transaction(s) or matter(s) addressed by the written advice; and

(C) The taxpayer should seek advice based on the taxpayer's particular circumstances from an independent tax advisor.

(6) *Conditions of confidentiality.* Written advice is subject to *conditions of confidentiality* if the practitioner imposes on one or more recipients of the written advice a limitation on disclosure of the tax treatment or tax structure of the transaction and the limitation on disclosure protects the confidentiality of that practitioner's tax strategies, regardless of whether the limitation on disclosure is legally binding. A claim that a transaction is proprietary or exclusive is not a limitation on disclosure if the practitioner confirms to all recipients of the written advice that there is no limitation on disclosure of the tax treatment or tax structure of the transaction that is the subject of the written advice.

(7) *Contractual protection.* Written advice is subject to *contractual protection* if the taxpayer has the right to a full or partial refund of fees paid to the practitioner (or a person who is a member of, associated with, or employed by the practitioner's firm) if all or a part of the intended tax consequences from the matters addressed in the written advice are not sustained, or if the fees paid to the practitioner (or

a person who is a member of, associated with, or employed by the practitioner's firm) are contingent on the taxpayer's realization of tax benefits from the transaction. All the facts and circumstances relating to the matters addressed in the written advice will be considered when determining whether a fee is refundable or contingent, including the right to reimbursements of amounts that the parties to a transaction have not designated as fees or any agreement to provide services without reasonable compensation.

(8) *Prominently disclosed.* An item is *prominently disclosed* if it is readily apparent to a reader of the written advice. Whether an item is readily apparent will depend on the facts and circumstances surrounding the written advice including, but not limited to, the sophistication of the taxpayer and the length of the written advice. At a minimum, to be prominently disclosed an item must be set forth in a separate section (and not in a footnote) in a typeface that is the same size or larger than the typeface of any discussion of the facts or law in the written advice.

(9) *State or local bond opinion.* A *State or local bond opinion* is written advice with respect to a *Federal tax issue* included in any materials delivered to a purchaser of a State or local bond in connection with the issuance of the bond in a public or private offering, including an official statement (if one is prepared), that concerns only the excludability of interest on a State or local bond from gross income under section 103 of the Internal Revenue Code, the application of section 55 of the Internal Revenue Code to a State or local bond, the status of a State or local bond as a qualified tax-exempt obligation under section 265 (b)(3) of the Internal Revenue Code, the status of a State or local bond as a qualified zone academy bond under section 1397E of the Internal Revenue Code, or any combination of the above.

(10) *The principal purpose.* For purposes of this section, the principal purpose of a partnership or other entity, investment plan or arrangement, or other plan or arrangement is the avoidance or evasion of any tax imposed by the Internal Revenue Code if that purpose exceeds any other purpose. The principal purpose of a partnership or other entity, investment plan or arrangement, or other plan or arrangement is

not to avoid or evade Federal tax if that partnership, entity, plan or arrangement has as its purpose the claiming of tax benefits in a manner consistent with the statute and Congressional purpose. A partnership, entity, plan or arrangement may have a significant purpose of avoidance or evasion even though it does not have the principal purpose of avoidance or evasion under this paragraph (b)(10).

(c) *Requirements for covered opinions.* A practitioner providing a *covered opinion* must comply with each of the following requirements.

(1) *Factual matters.*

(i) The practitioner must use reasonable efforts to identify and ascertain the facts, which may relate to future events if a transaction is prospective or proposed, and to determine which facts are relevant. The opinion must identify and consider all facts that the practitioner determines to be relevant.

(ii) The practitioner must not base the opinion on any unreasonable factual assumptions (including assumptions as to future events). An unreasonable factual assumption includes a factual assumption that the practitioner knows or should know is incorrect or incomplete. For example, it is unreasonable to assume that a transaction has a business purpose or that a transaction is potentially profitable apart from tax benefits. A factual assumption includes reliance on a projection, financial forecast or appraisal. It is unreasonable for a practitioner to rely on a projection, financial forecast or appraisal if the practitioner knows or should know that the projection, financial forecast or appraisal is incorrect or incomplete or was prepared by a person lacking the skills or qualifications necessary to prepare such projection, financial forecast or appraisal. The opinion must identify in a separate section all factual assumptions relied upon by the practitioner.

(iii) The practitioner must not base the opinion on any unreasonable factual representations, statements or findings or of the taxpayer or any other person. An unreasonable factual representation includes a factual representation that the practitioner knows or should know is incorrect or incomplete. For example, a practitioner may not rely on a factual representation that a transaction has a business purpose if the

representation does not include a specific description of the business purpose or the practitioner knows or should know that the representation is incorrect or incomplete. The opinion must identify in a separate section all factual representations, statements or finds of the taxpayer relied upon by the practitioner.

(2) *Relate law to facts.*

(i) The opinion must relate the applicable law (including potentially applicable judicial doctrines) to the relevant facts.

(ii) The practitioner must not assume the favorable resolution of any significant Federal tax issue except as provided in paragraphs (c)(3)(v) and (d) of this section, or otherwise base an opinion on any unreasonable legal assumptions, representations, or conclusions.

(iii) The opinion must not contain internally inconsistent legal analyses or conclusions.

(3) *Evaluation of significant Federal tax issues*
—

(i) *In general.* The opinion must consider all significant Federal tax issues except as provided in paragraphs (c)(3)(v) and (d) of this section.

(ii) *Conclusion as to each significant Federal tax issues.* The opinion must provide the practitioner's conclusion as to the likelihood that the taxpayer will prevail on the merits with respect to each significant Federal tax issue considered in the opinion. If the practitioner is unable to reach a conclusion with respect to one or more of those issues, the opinion must state that the practitioner is unable to reach a conclusion with respect to those issues. The opinion must describe the reasons for the conclusions, including the facts and analysis supporting the conclusions, or describe the reasons that the practitioner is unable to reach a conclusion as to one or more issues. If the practitioner fails to reach a conclusion at the confidence level of at least more likely than not with respect to one or more significant Federal tax issues considered, the opinion must include the appropriate disclosure(s) required under paragraph (e) of this section.

(iii) *Evaluation based on chances of success on the merits.* In evaluating the significant Federal tax issues addressed in the opinion, the practitioner must not take into account the possibility that a tax return will not be audited, that an issue will not be raised on audit, or that an issue will be resolved through settlement if raised.

(iv) *Marketed opinions.* In the case of a *marketed opinion*, the opinion must provide the practitioner's conclusion that the taxpayer will prevail on the merits at a confidence level of at least more likely than not with respect to each significant Federal tax issue. If the practitioner is unable to reach a more likely than not conclusion with respect to each significant Federal tax issue, the practitioner must not provide the marketed opinion, but may provide written advice that satisfies the requirements in paragraph (b)(5)(ii) of this section.

(v) *Limited scope opinions.* (A) The practitioner may provide an opinion that considers less than all of the significant Federal tax issues if —

(1) The practitioner and the taxpayer agree that the scope of the opinion and the taxpayer's potential reliance on the opinion for purposes of avoiding penalties that may be imposed on the taxpayer are limited to the Federal tax issue(s) addressed in the opinion;

(2) The opinion is not advice described in paragraph (b)(2)(i)(A) of this section (concerning listed transactions), paragraph (b)(2)(i)(B) of this section (concerning the principal purpose of avoidance or evasion) or paragraph (b)(5) of this section (a *marketed opinion*); and

(3) The opinion includes the appropriate disclosure(s) required under paragraph (e) of this section.

(B) A practitioner may make reasonable assumptions regarding the favorable resolution of a Federal tax issue (as assumed issue) for purposes of providing an opinion on less than all of the significant Federal tax issues as provided in this paragraph (c)(3)(v). The opinion must identify in a separate section all issues for which the practitioner assumed a favorable resolution.

(4) *Overall conclusion.*

(i) The opinion must provide the practitioner's overall conclusion as to the likelihood that the Federal tax treatment of the transaction or matter that is the subject of the opinion is the proper treatment and the reasons for that conclusion. If the practitioner is unable to reach an overall conclusion, the opinion must state that the practitioner is unable to reach and overall conclusion and describe the reasons for the practitioner's inability to reach a conclusion.

(ii) In the case of a *marketed opinion*, the opinion must provide the practitioner's overall conclusion that the Federal tax treatment of the transaction or matter that is the subject of the opinion is the proper treatment at a confidence level of at least more likely than not.

(d) *Competence to provide opinion; reliance on opinions of others.*

(1) The practitioner must be knowledgeable in all of the aspects of Federal tax law relevant to the opinion being rendered, except that the practitioner may rely on the opinion of another practitioner with respect to one or more significant Federal tax issues, unless the practitioner knows or should know that the opinion of the other practitioner should not be relied on. If a practitioner relies on the opinion of another practitioner, the relying practitioner's opinion must identify the other opinion and set forth the conclusions reached in the other opinion.

(2) The practitioner must be satisfied that the combined analysis of the opinions, taken as a whole, and the overall conclusion, if any, satisfy the requirements of this section.

(e) *Required disclosures.* A covered opinion must contain all of the following disclosures that apply —

(1) *Relationship between promoter and practitioner.* An opinion must prominently disclose the existence of —

(i) Any compensation arrangement, such as a referral fee or a fee-sharing arrangement, between the practitioner (or the practitioner's firm or any person who is a member of, associated with, or employed by the practitioner's firm) and any person (other than the client for whom the opinion is prepared) with respect to promoting, marketing or recommending the entity, plan, or arrangement (or a substantially similar arrangement) that is the subject of the opinion; or

(ii) Any referral agreement between the practitioner (or the practitioner's firm or any person who is a member of, associated with, or employed by the practitioner's firm) and a person (other than the client for whom the opinion is prepared) engaged in promoting, marketing or recommending the entity, plan, or arrangement (or a substantially similar arrangement) that is the subject of the opinion.

(2) *Marketed opinions.* A *marketed opinion* must prominently disclose that —

(i) The opinion was written to support the promotion or marketing of the transaction(s) or matter(s) addressed in the opinion; and

(ii) The taxpayer should seek advice based on the taxpayer's particular circumstances from an independent tax advisor.

(3) *Limited scope opinions.* A limited scope opinion must prominently disclose that —

(i) The opinion is limited to the one or more Federal tax issues addressed in the opinion;

(ii) Additional issues may exist that could affect the Federal tax treatment of the transaction or matter that is the subject of the opinion and the opinion does not consider or provide a conclusion with respect to any additional issues; and

(iii) With respect to any significant Federal tax issues outside the limited scope of the opinion, the opinion was not written, and cannot be used by the taxpayer, for the purpose of avoiding penalties that may be imposed on the taxpayer.

(4) *Opinions that fail to reach a more likely than not conclusion.* An opinion that does not reach a conclusion at a confidence level of at least more likely than not with respect to a significant Federal tax issue must prominently disclose that —

(i) The opinion does not reach a conclusion at a confidence level of at least more likely than not with respect to one or more significant Federal tax issues addressed by the opinion; and

(ii) With respect to those significant Federal tax issues, the opinion was not written, and cannot be used by the taxpayer, for the purpose of avoiding penalties that may be imposed on the taxpayer.

(5) *Advice regarding required disclosures.* In the case of any disclosure required under this section, the practitioner may not provide advice to any person

that is contrary to or inconsistent with the required disclosure.

(f) *Effect of opinion that meets these standards* —

(1) *In general.* An opinion that meets the requirements of this section satisfies the practitioner's responsibilities under this section, but the persuasiveness of the opinion with regard to the tax issues in question and the taxpayer's good faith reliance on the opinion will be determined separately under applicable provisions of the law and regulations.

(2) *Standards for other written advice.* A practitioner who provides written advice that is not a covered opinion for purposes of this section is subject to the requirements of §10.37.

(g) *Effective date.* This section applies to written advice that is rendered after June 20, 2005.

§ 10.36 Procedures to ensure compliance.

(a) *Requirements for covered opinions.* Any practitioner who has (or practitioners who have or share) principal authority and responsibility for overseeing a firm's practice of providing advice concerning Federal tax issues must take reasonable steps to ensure that the firm has adequate procedures in effect for all members, associates, and employees for purposes of complying with §10.35. Any such practitioner will be subject to discipline for failing to comply with the requirements of this paragraph if —

(1) The practitioner through willfulness, recklessness, or gross incompetence does not take reasonable steps to ensure that the firm has adequate procedures to comply with §10.35, and one or more individuals who are members of, associated with, or employed by, the firm are, or have engaged in a pattern or practice, in connection with their practice with the firm, of failing to comply with §10.35; or

(2) The practitioner knows or should know that one or more individuals who are members of, associated with, or employed by, the firm are, or have, engaged in a pattern or practice, in connection with their practice with the firm, that does not comply with §10.35 and the practitioner, through willfulness, recklessness, or gross incompetence, fails to take prompt action to correct the noncompliance.

(b) *Effective date.* This section is applicable after June 20, 2005.

§ 10.37 Requirements for other written advice.

(a) *Requirements.* A practitioner must not give written advice (including electronic communications) concerning one or more Federal tax issues if the practitioner bases the written advice on unreasonable factual or legal assumptions (including assumptions as to future events), unreasonably relies upon representations, statements, findings or agreements of the taxpayer or any other person, does not consider all relevant facts that the practitioner knows or should know, or, in evaluating a Federal tax issue, takes into account the possibility that a tax return will not be audited, that an issue will not be raised on audit, or that an issue will be resolved through settlement if raised. All facts and circumstances, including the scope of the engagement and the type and specificity of the advice sought by the client will be considered in determining whether a practitioner has failed to comply with this section. In the case of an opinion the practitioner knows or has reason to know will be used or referred to by a person other than the practitioner (or a person who is a member of, associated with, or employed by the practitioner's firm) in promoting, marketing or recommending to one or more taxpayers a partnership or other entity, investment plan or arrangement a significant purpose of which is the avoidance or evasion of any tax imposed by the Internal Revenue Code, the determination of whether a practitioner has failed to comply with this section will be made on the basis of a heightened standard of care because of the greater risk caused by the practitioner's lack of knowledge of the taxpayer's particular circumstances.

(b) *Effective date.* This section applies to written advice that is rendered after June 20, 2005.

§ 10.38 Establishment of advisory committees.

(a) *Advisory committees.* To promote and maintain the public's confidence in tax advisors, the Director of the Office of Professional Responsibility is autho-

rized to establish one or more advisory committees composed of at least five individuals authorized to practice before the Internal Revenue Service. The Director should ensure that membership of an advisory committee is balanced among those who practice as attorneys, accountants, and enrolled agents. Under procedures prescribed by the Director, an advisory committee may review and make general recommendations regarding professional standards or best practices for tax advisors, including whether hypothetical conduct would give rise to a violation of §§ 10.35 or 10.36.

(b) *Effective date.* This section applies after December 20, 2004.

Subpart C — Sanctions for Violation of the Regulations

§ 10.50 Sanctions.

(a) *Authority to censure, suspend, or disbar.* The Secretary of the Treasury, or delegate, after notice and an opportunity for a proceeding, may censure, suspend, or disbar any practitioner from practice before the Internal Revenue Service if the practitioner is shown to be incompetent or disreputable (within the meaning of §10.51), fails to comply with any regulation in this part (under the prohibited conduct standards of §10.52), or with intent to defraud, willfully and knowingly misleads or threatens a client or prospective client. Censure is a public reprimand.

(b) *Authority to disqualify.* The Secretary of the Treasury, or delegate, after due notice and opportunity for hearing, may disqualify any appraiser for a violation of these rules as applicable to appraisers.

(1) If any appraiser is disqualified pursuant to this subpart C, the appraiser is barred from presenting evidence or testimony in any administrative proceeding before the Department of the Treasury or the Internal Revenue Service, unless and until authorized to do so by the Director of the Office of Professional Responsibility pursuant to §10.81, regardless of whether the evidence or testimony would pertain to an appraisal made prior to or after the effective date of disqualification.

Page 27

(2) Any appraisal made by a disqualified appraiser after the effective date of disqualification will not have any probative effect in any administrative proceeding before the Department of the Treasury or the Internal Revenue Service. An appraisal otherwise barred from admission into evidence pursuant to this section may be admitted into evidence solely for the purpose of determining the taxpayer's reliance in good faith on such appraisal.

(c) *Authority to impose monetary penalty—*

(1) *In general.*

(i) The Secretary of the Treasury, or delegate, after notice and an opportunity for a proceeding, may impose a monetary penalty on any practitioner who engages in conduct subject to sanction under paragraph (a) of this section.

(ii) If the practitioner described in paragraph (c)(1)(i) of this section was acting on behalf of an employer or any firm or other entity in connection with the conduct giving rise to the penalty, the Secretary of the Treasury, or delegate, may impose a monetary penalty on the employer, firm, or entity if it knew, or reasonably should have known of such conduct.

(2) *Amount of penalty.* The amount of the penalty shall not exceed the gross income derived (or to be derived) from the conduct giving rise to the penalty.

(3) *Coordination with other sanctions.* Subject to paragraph (c)(2) of this section —

(i) Any monetary penalty imposed on a practitioner under this paragraph (c) may be in addition to or in lieu of any suspension, disbarment or censure and may be in addition to a penalty imposed on an employer, firm or other entity under paragraph (c)(1)(ii) of this section.

(ii) Any monetary penalty imposed on an employer, firm or other entity may be in addition to or in lieu of penalties imposed under paragraph (c)(1)(i) of this section.

(d) *Sanctions to be imposed.* The sanctions imposed by this section shall take into account all relevant facts and circumstances.

(e) *Effective/applicability date.* This section is applicable to conduct occurring on or after September 26, 2007, except paragraph (c) which applies to prohibited conduct that occurs after October 22, 2004.

Page 28

§ 10.51 Incompetence and disreputable conduct.

(a) *Incompetence and disreputable conduct.* Incompetence and disreputable conduct for which a practitioner may be sanctioned under §10.50 includes, but is not limited to —

(1) Conviction of any criminal offense under the Federal tax laws.

(2) Conviction of any criminal offense involving dishonesty or breach of trust.

(3) Conviction of any felony under Federal or State law for which the conduct involved renders the practitioner unfit to practice before the Internal Revenue Service.

(4) Giving false or misleading information, or participating in any way in the giving of false or misleading information to the Department of the Treasury or any officer or employee thereof, or to any tribunal authorized to pass upon Federal tax matters, in connection with any matter pending or likely to be pending before them, knowing the information to be false or misleading. Facts or other matters contained in testimony, Federal tax returns, financial statements, applications for enrollment, affidavits, declarations, and any other document or statement, written or oral, are included in the term "information."

(5) Solicitation of employment as prohibited under §10.30, the use of false or misleading representations with intent to deceive a client or prospective client in order to procure employment, or intimating that the practitioner is able improperly to obtain special consideration or action from the Internal Revenue Service or any officer or employee thereof.

(6) Willfully failing to make a Federal tax return in violation of the Federal tax laws, or willfully evading, attempting to evade, or participating in any way in evading or attempting to evade any assessment or payment of any Federal tax.

(7) Willfully assisting, counseling, encouraging a client or prospective client in violating, or suggesting to a client or prospective client to violate, any Federal tax law, or knowingly counseling or suggesting to a client or prospective client an illegal plan to evade Federal taxes or payment thereof.

(8) Misappropriation of, or failure properly or

promptly to remit, funds received from a client for the purpose of payment of taxes or other obligations due the United States.

(9) Directly or indirectly attempting to influence, or offering or agreeing to attempt to influence, the official action of any officer or employee of the Internal Revenue Service by the use of threats, false accusations, duress or coercion, by the offer of any special inducement or promise of an advantage or by the bestowing of any gift, favor or thing of value.

(10) Disbarment or suspension from practice as an attorney, certified public accountant, public accountant, or actuary by any duly constituted authority of any State, territory, or possession of the United States, including a Commonwealth, or the District of Columbia, any Federal court of record or any Federal agency, body or board.

(11) Knowingly aiding and abetting another person to practice before the Internal Revenue Service during a period of suspension, disbarment or ineligibility of such other person.

(12) Contemptuous conduct in connection with practice before the Internal Revenue Service, including the use of abusive language, making false accusations or statements, knowing them to be false, or circulating or publishing malicious or libelous matter.

(13) Giving a false opinion, knowingly, recklessly, or through gross incompetence, including an opinion which is intentionally or recklessly misleading, or engaging in a pattern of providing incompetent opinions on questions arising under the Federal tax laws. False opinions described in this paragraph (a)(13) include those which reflect or result from a knowing misstatement of fact or law, from an assertion of a position known to be unwarranted under existing law, from counseling or assisting in conduct known to be illegal or fraudulent, from concealing matters required by law to be revealed, or from consciously disregarding information indicating that material facts expressed in the opinion or offering material are false or misleading. For purposes of this paragraph (a)(13), reckless conduct is a highly unreasonable omission or misrepresentation involving an extreme departure from the standards of ordinary

care that a practitioner should observe under the circumstances. A pattern of conduct is a factor that will be taken into account in determining whether a practitioner acted knowingly, recklessly, or through gross incompetence. Gross incompetence includes conduct that reflects gross indifference, preparation which is grossly inadequate under the circumstances, and a consistent failure to perform obligations to the client.

(14) Willfully failing to sign a tax return prepared by the practitioner when the practitioner's signature is required by Federal tax laws unless the failure is due to reasonable cause and not due to willful neglect.

(15) Willfully disclosing or otherwise using a tax return or tax return information in a manner not authorized by the Internal Revenue Code, contrary to the order of a court of competent jurisdiction, or contrary to the order of an administrative law judge in a proceeding instituted under §10.60.

(b) *Effective/applicability date.* This section is applicable to conduct occurring on or after September 26, 2007.

§ 10.52 Violations subject to sanction.

(a) A practitioner may be sanctioned under §10.50 if the practitioner —

(1) Willfully violates any of the regulations (other than §10.33) contained in this part; or

(2) Recklessly or through gross incompetence (within the meaning of §10.51(a)(13)) violates §§ 10.34, 10.35, 10.36 or 10.37.

(b) *Effective/applicability date.* This section is applicable to conduct occurring on or after September 26, 2007.

§ 10.53 Receipt of information concerning practitioner.

(a) *Officer or employee of the Internal Revenue Service.* If an officer or employee of the Internal Revenue Service has reason to believe that a practitioner has violated any provision of this part, the officer or employee will promptly make a written report to the

Director of the Office of Professional Responsibility of the suspected violation. The report will explain the facts and reasons upon which the officer's or employee's belief rests.

(b) *Other persons.* Any person other than an officer or employee of the Internal Revenue Service having information of a violation of any provision of this part may make an oral or written report of the alleged violation to the Director of the Office of Professional Responsibility or any officer or employee of the Internal Revenue Service. If the report is made to an officer or employee of the Internal Revenue Service, the officer or employee will make a written report of the suspected violation to the Director of the Office of Professional Responsibility.

(c) *Destruction of report.* No report made under paragraph (a) or (b) of this section shall be maintained by the Director of the Office of Professional Responsibility unless retention of the report is permissible under the applicable records control schedule as approved by the National Archives and Records Administration and designated in the Internal Revenue Manual. The Director of the Office of Professional Responsibility must destroy the reports as soon as permissible under the applicable records control schedule.

(d) *Effect on proceedings under subpart D.* The destruction of any report will not bar any proceeding under subpart D of this part, but will preclude the Director of the Office of Professional Responsibility's use of a copy of the report in a proceeding under subpart D of this part.

(e) *Effective/applicability date.* This section is applicable on September 26, 2007.

Subpart D — Rules Applicable to Disciplinary Proceedings

§ 10.60 Institution of proceeding.

(a) Whenever the Director of the Office of Professional Responsibility determines that a practitioner (or employer, firm or other entity, if applicable) violated any provision of the laws governing practice before the Internal Revenue Service or the regula-

tions in this part, the Director of the Office of Professional Responsibility may reprimand the practitioner or, in accordance with §10.62, institute a proceeding for a sanction described in §10.50. A proceeding is instituted by the filing of a complaint, the contents of which are more fully described in §10.62.

(b) Whenever the Director of the Office of Professional Responsibility is advised or becomes aware that a penalty has been assessed against an appraiser under section 6701(a) of the Internal Revenue Code, the Director of the Office of Professional Responsibility may reprimand the appraiser or, in accordance with §10.62, institute a proceeding for disqualification of the appraiser. A proceeding for disqualification of an appraiser is instituted by the filing of a complaint, the contents of which are more fully described in §10.62.

(c) Except as provided in §10.82, a proceeding will not be instituted under this section unless the proposed respondent previously has been advised in writing of the law, facts and conduct warranting such action and has been accorded an opportunity to dispute facts, assert additional facts, and make arguments (including an explanation or description of mitigating circumstances).

(d) *Effective/applicability date.* This section is applicable on September 26, 2007.

§ 10.61 Conferences.

(a) *In general.* The Director of the Office of Professional Responsibility may confer with a practitioner, employer, firm or other entity, or an appraiser concerning allegations of misconduct irrespective of whether a proceeding has been instituted. If the conference results in a stipulation in connection with an ongoing proceeding in which the practitioner, employer, firm or other entity, or appraiser is the respondent, the stipulation may be entered in the record by either party to the proceeding.

(b) *Voluntary sanction* —

(1) *In general.* In lieu of a proceeding being instituted or continued under §10.60(a), a practitioner or appraiser (or employer, firm or other entity, if ap-

plicable) may offer a consent to be sanctioned under §10.50.

(2) *Discretion; acceptance or declination.* The Director of the Office of Professional Responsibility may, in his or her discretion, accept or decline the offer described in paragraph (b)(1) of this section. In any declination, the Director of the Office of Professional Responsibility may state that he or she would accept the offer described in paragraph (b)(1) of this section if it contained different terms. The Director of the Office of Professional Responsibility may, in his or her discretion, accept or reject a revised offer submitted in response to the declination or may counteroffer and act upon any accepted counteroffer.

(c) *Effective/applicability date.* This section is applicable on September 26, 2007.

§ 10.62 Contents of complaint.

(a) *Charges.* A complaint must name the respondent, provide a clear and concise description of the facts and law that constitute the basis for the proceeding, and be signed by the Director of Office of Professional Responsibility or a person representing the Director of the Office of Professional Responsibility under §10.69(a)(1). A complaint is sufficient if it fairly informs the respondent of the charges brought so that the respondent is able to prepare a defense.

(b) *Specification of sanction.* The complaint must specify the sanction sought by the Director of the Office of Professional Responsibility against the practitioner or appraiser. If the sanction sought is a suspension, the duration of the suspension sought must be specified.

(c) *Demand for answer.* The Director of the Office of Professional Responsibility must, in the complaint or in a separate paper attached to the complaint, notify the respondent of the time for answering the complaint, which may not be less than 30 days from the date of service of the complaint, the name and address of the Administrative Law Judge with whom the answer must be filed, the name and address of the person representing the Director of the Office of Professional Responsibility to whom a copy of the answer must be served, and that a decision by default

may be rendered against the respondent in the event an answer is not filed as required.

(d) *Effective/ applicability date.* This section is applicable to complaints brought on or after September 26, 2007.

§ 10.63 Service of complaint; service of other papers; service of evidence in support of complaint; filing of papers.

(a) *Service of complaint.*

(1) *In general.* The complaint or a copy of the complaint must be served on the respondent by any manner described in paragraphs (a) (2) or (3) of this section.

(2) *Service by certified or first class mail.*

(i) Service of the complaint may be made on the respondent by mailing the complaint by certified mail to the last known address (as determined under section 6212 of the Internal Revenue Code and the regulations thereunder) of the respondent. Where service is by certified mail, the returned post office receipt duly signed by the respondent will be proof of service.

(ii) If the certified mail is not claimed or accepted by the respondent, or is returned undelivered, service may be made on the respondent, by mailing the complaint to the respondent by first class mail. Service by this method will be considered complete upon mailing, provided the complaint is addressed to the respondent at the respondent's last known address as determined under section 6212 of the Internal Revenue Code and the regulations thereunder.

(3) *Service by other than certified or first class mail.*

(i) Service of the complaint may be made on the respondent by delivery by a private delivery service designated pursuant to section 7502(f) of the Internal Revenue Code to the last known address (as determined under section 6212 of the Internal Revenue Code and the regulations there under) of the respondent. Service by this method will be considered complete, provided the complaint is addressed to the respondent at the respondent's last known address as determined under section 6212 of the Internal Revenue Code and the regulations thereunder.

(ii) Service of the complaint may be made in person on, or by leaving the complaint at the office or place of business of, the respondent. Service by this method will be considered complete and proof of service will be a written statement, sworn or affirmed by the person who served the complaint, identifying the manner of service, including the recipient, relationship of recipient to respondent, place, date and time of service.

(iii) Service may be made by any other means agreed to by the respondent. Proof of service will be a written statement, sworn or affirmed by the person who served the complaint, identifying the manner of service, including the recipient, relationship of recipient to respondent, place, date and time of service.

(4) For purposes of this section, *respondent* means the practitioner, employer, firm or other entity, or appraiser named in the complaint or any other person having the authority to accept mail on behalf of the practitioner, employer, firm or other entity or appraiser.

(b) *Service of papers other than complaint.* Any paper other than the complaint may be served on the respondent, or his or her authorized representative under §10.69(a)(2) by:

(1) mailing the paper by first class mail to the last known address (as determined under section 6212 of the Internal Revenue Code and the regulations thereunder) of the respondent or the respondent's authorized representative,

(2) delivery by a private delivery service designated pursuant to section 7502(f) of the Internal Revenue Code to the last known address (as determined under section 6212 of the Internal Revenue Code and the regulations thereunder) of the respondent or the respondent's authorized representative, or

(3) as provided in paragraphs (a)(3)(ii) and (a)(3)(iii) of this section.

(c) *Service of papers on the Director of the Office of Professional Responsibility.* Whenever a paper is required or permitted to be served on the Director of the Office of Professional Responsibility in connection with a proceeding under this part, the paper will be served on the Director of the Office of Professional Responsibility's authorized representative under §10.69(a)(1) at the address designated in the complaint, or at an address provided in a notice of appearance. If no address is designated in the complaint or provided in a notice of appearance, service will be made on the Director of the Office of Professional Responsibility, Internal Revenue Service, 1111 Constitution Avenue, NW, Washington, DC 20224.

(d) *Service of evidence in support of complaint.* Within 10 days of serving the complaint, copies of the evidence in support of the complaint must be served on the respondent in any manner described in paragraphs (a)(2) and (3) of this section.

(e) *Filing of papers.* Whenever the filing of a paper is required or permitted in connection with a proceeding under this part, the original paper, plus one additional copy, must be filed with the Administrative Law Judge at the address specified in the complaint or at an address otherwise specified by the Administrative Law Judge. All papers filed in connection with a proceeding under this part must be served on the other party, unless the Administrative Law Judge directs otherwise. A certificate evidencing such must be attached to the original paper filed with the Administrative Law Judge.

(f) *Effective/applicability date.* This section is applicable to complaints brought on or after September 26, 2007.

§ 10.64 Answer; default.

(a) *Filing.* The respondent's answer must be filed with the Administrative Law Judge, and served on the Director of the Office of Professional Responsibility, within the time specified in the complaint unless, on request or application of the respondent, the time is extended by the Administrative Law Judge.

(b) *Contents.* The answer must be written and contain a statement of facts that constitute the respondent's grounds of defense. General denials are not permitted. The respondent must specifically admit or deny each allegation set forth in the complaint, except that the respondent may state that the respondent is without sufficient information to admit or deny a specific allegation. The respondent, nevertheless, may not deny a material allegation in the complaint that the respondent knows to be true, or state that the respondent is without sufficient information to form a belief, when the respondent possesses the required information. The respondent also must state affirmatively any special matters of defense on which he or she relies.

(c) *Failure to deny or answer allegations in the complaint.* Every allegation in the complaint that is not denied in the answer is deemed admitted and will be considered proved; no further evidence in respect of such allegation need be adduced at a hearing.

(d) *Default.* Failure to file an answer within the time prescribed (or within the time for answer as extended by the Administrative Law Judge), constitutes an admission of the allegations of the complaint and a waiver of hearing, and the Administrative Law Judge may make the decision by default without a hearing or further procedure. A decision by default constitutes a decision under §10.76.

(e) *Signature.* The answer must be signed by the respondent or the respondent's authorized representative under §10.69(a)(2) and must include a statement directly above the signature acknowledging that the statements made in the answer are true and correct and that knowing and willful false statements may be punishable under 18 U.S.C. §1001.

§ 10.65 Supplemental charges.

(a) *In general.* The Director of the Office of Professional Responsibility may file supplemental charges, by amending the complaint with the permission of the Administrative Law Judge, against the respondent, if, for example —

(1) It appears that the respondent, in the answer, falsely and in bad faith, denies a material allegation of fact in the complaint or states that the respondent has insufficient knowledge to form a belief, when the respondent possesses such information; or

(2) It appears that the respondent has knowingly introduced false testimony during proceedings against the respondent.

(b) *Hearing.* The supplemental charges may be heard with other charges in the case, provided the re-

spondent is given due notice of the charges and is afforded a reasonable opportunity to prepare a defense to the supplemental charges.

(c) *Effective/applicability date.* This section is applicable on September 26, 2007.

§ 10.66 Reply to answer.

The Director of the Office of Professional Responsibility may file a reply to the respondent's answer, but unless otherwise ordered by the Administrative Law Judge, no reply to the respondent's answer is required. If a reply is not filed, new matter in the answer is deemed denied.

§ 10.67 Proof; variance; amendment of pleadings.

In the case of a variance between the allegations in pleadings and the evidence adduced in support of the pleadings, the Administrative Law Judge, at any time before decision, may order or authorize amendment of the pleadings to conform to the evidence. The party who would otherwise be prejudiced by the amendment must be given a reasonable opportunity to address the allegations of the pleadings as amended and the Administrative Law Judge must make findings on any issue presented by the pleadings as amended.

§ 10.68 Motions and requests.

(a) *Motions —*

(1) *In general.* At any time after the filing of the complaint, any party may file a motion with the Administrative Law Judge. Unless otherwise ordered by the Administrative Law Judge, motions must be in writing and must be served on the opposing party as provided in §10.63(b). A motion must concisely specify its grounds and the relief sought, and, if appropriate, must contain a memorandum of facts and law in support.

(2) *Summary adjudication.* Either party may move for a summary adjudication upon all or any part of the legal issues in controversy. If the non-moving party opposes summary adjudication in the moving party's favor, the non-moving party must file a writ-

ten response within 30 days unless ordered otherwise by the Administrative Law Judge.

(3) *Good Faith.* A party filing a motion for extension of time, a motion for postponement of a hearing, or any other non-dispositive or procedural motion must first contact the other party to determine whether there is any objection to the motion, and must state in the motion whether the other party has an objection.

(b) *Response.* Unless otherwise ordered by the Administrative Law Judge, the nonmoving party is not required to file a response to a motion. If the Administrative Law Judge does not order the nonmoving party to file a response, and the nonmoving party files no response, the nonmoving party is deemed to oppose the motion. If a nonmoving party does not respond within 30 days of the filing of a motion for decision by default for failure to file a timely answer or for failure to prosecute, the nonmoving party is deemed not to oppose the motion.

(c) *Oral motions; oral argument —*

(1) The Administrative Law Judge may, for good cause and with notice to the parties, permit oral motions and oral opposition to motions.

(2) The Administrative Law Judge may, within his or her discretion, permit oral argument on any motion.

(d) *Orders.* The Administrative Law Judge should issue written orders disposing of any motion or request and any response thereto.

(e) *Effective/applicability date.* This section is applicable on September 26, 2007.

§ 10.69 Representation; ex parte communication.

(a) *Representation.*

(1) The Director of the Office of Professional Responsibility may be represented in proceedings under this part by an attorney or other employee of the Internal Revenue Service. An attorney or an employee of the Internal Revenue Service representing the Director of the Office of Professional Responsibility in a proceeding under this part may sign the complaint or any document required to be filed in the proceeding on behalf of the Director of the Office of

Professional Responsibility.

(2) A respondent may appear in person, be represented by a practitioner, or be represented by an attorney who has not filed a declaration with the Internal Revenue Service pursuant to §10.3. A practitioner or an attorney representing a respondent or proposed respondent may sign the answer or any document required to be filed in the proceeding on behalf of the respondent.

(b) *Ex parte communication.*
The Director of the Office of Professional Responsibility, the respondent, and any representatives of either party, may not attempt to initiate or participate in ex parte discussions concerning a proceeding or potential proceeding with the Administrative Law Judge (or any person who is likely to advise the Administrative Law Judge on a ruling or decision) in the proceeding before or during the pendency of the proceeding. Any memorandum, letter or other communication concerning the merits of the proceeding, addressed to the Administrative Law Judge, by or on behalf of any party shall be regarded as an argument in the proceeding and shall be served on the other party.

§ 10.70 Administrative Law Judge.

(a) *Appointment.* Proceedings on complaints for the sanction (as described in §10.50) of a practitioner, employer, firm or other entity, or appraiser will be conducted by an Administrative Law Judge appointed as provided by *5 U.S.C. 3105.*

(b) *Powers of the Administrative Law Judge.* The Administrative Law Judge, among other powers, has the authority, in connection with any proceeding under §10.60 assigned or referred to him or her, to do the following:

(1) Administer oaths and affirmations;

(2) Make rulings on motions and requests, which rulings may not be appealed prior to the close of a hearing except in extraordinary circumstances and at the discretion of the Administrative Law Judge;

(3) Determine the time and place of hearing and regulate its course and conduct;

(4) Adopt rules of procedure and modify the same

from time to time as needed for the orderly disposition of proceedings;

(5) Rule on offers of proof, receive relevant evidence, and examine witnesses;

(6) Take or authorize the taking of depositions or answers to requests for admission;

(7) Receive and consider oral or written argument on facts or law;

(8) Hold or provide for the holding of conferences for the settlement or simplification of the issues with the consent of the parties;

(9) Perform such acts and take such measures as are necessary or appropriate to the efficient conduct of any proceeding; and

(10) Make decisions.

(c) *Effective/applicability date.* This section is applicable on September 26, 2007.

§ 10.71 Discovery.

(a) *In general.* Discovery may be permitted, at the discretion of the Administrative Law Judge, only upon written motion demonstrating the relevance, materiality and reasonableness of the requested discovery and subject to the requirements of §10.72(d)(2) and (3). Within 10 days of receipt of the answer, the Administrative Law Judge will notify the parties of the right to request discovery and the timeframe for filing a request. A request for discovery, and objections, must be filed in accordance with §10.68. In response to a request for discovery, the Administrative Law Judge may order —

(1) Depositions upon oral examination; or

(2) Answers to requests for admission.

(b) *Depositions upon oral examination* —

(1) A deposition must be taken before an officer duly authorized to administer an oath for general purposes or before an officer or employee of the Internal Revenue Service who is authorized to administer an oath in Federal tax law matters.

(2) In ordering a deposition, the Administrative Law Judge will require reasonable notice to the opposing party as to the time and place of the deposition. The opposing party, if attending, will be provided the opportunity for full examination and cross-examination of any witness.

(3) Expenses in the reporting of depositions shall be borne by the party at whose instance the deposition is taken. Travel expenses of the deponent shall be borne by the party requesting the deposition, unless otherwise authorized by Federal law or regulation.

(c) *Requests for admission.* Any party may serve on any other party a written request for admission of the truth of any matters which are not privileged and are relevant to the subject matter of this proceeding. Requests for admission shall not exceed a total of 30 (including any subparts within a specific request) without the approval from the Administrative Law Judge.

(d) *Limitations.* Discovery shall not be authorized if —

(1) The request fails to meet any requirement set forth in paragraph (a) of this section;

(2) It will unduly delay the proceeding;

(3) It will place an undue burden on the party required to produce the discovery sought;

(4) It is frivolous or abusive;

(5) It is cumulative or duplicative;

(6) The material sought is privileged or otherwise protected from disclosure by law;

(7) The material sought relates to mental impressions, conclusions, of legal theories of any party, attorney, or other representative, or a party prepared in the anticipation of a proceeding; or

(8) The material sought is available generally to the public, equally to the parties, or to the party seeking the discovery through another source.

(e) *Failure to comply.* Where a party fails to comply with an order of the Administrative Law Judge under this section, the Administrative Law Judge may, among other things, infer that the information would be adverse to the party failing to provide it, exclude the information from evidence or issue a decision by default.

(f) *Other discovery.* No discovery other than that specifically provided for in this section is permitted.

(g) *Effective/applicability date.* This section is applicable to proceedings initiated on or after September 26, 2007.

§ 10.72 Hearings.

(a) *In general* —

(1) *Presiding officer.* An Administrative Law Judge will preside at the hearing on a complaint filed under §10.60 for the sanction of a practitioner, employer, firm or other entity, or appraiser.

(2) *Time for hearing.* Absent a determination by the Administrative Law Judge that, in the interest of justice, a hearing must be held at a later time, the Administrative Law Judge should, on notice sufficient to allow proper preparation, schedule the hearing to occur no later than 180 days after the time for filing the answer.

(3) *Procedural requirements.*

(i) Hearings will be stenographically recorded and transcribed and the testimony of witnesses will be taken under oath or affirmation.

(ii) Hearings will be conducted pursuant to 5 *U.S.C. 556.*

(iii) A hearing in a proceeding requested under §10.82(g) will be conducted de novo.

(iv) An evidentiary hearing must be held in all proceedings prior to the issuance of a decision by the Administrative Law Judge unless —

(A) The Director of the Office of Professional Responsibility withdraws the complaint;

(B) A decision is issued by default pursuant to §10.64(d);

(C) A decision is issued under §10.82 (e);

(D) The respondent requests a decision on the written record without a hearing; or

(E) The Administrative Law Judge issues a decision under §10.68(d) or rules on another motion that disposes of the case prior to the hearing.

(b) *Cross-examination.* A party is entitled to present his or her case or defense by oral or documentary evidence, to submit rebuttal evidence, and to conduct cross-examination, in the presence of the Administrative Law Judge, as may be required for a full and true disclosure of the facts. This paragraph (b) does not limit a party from presenting evidence contained within a deposition when the Administrative Law Judge determines that the deposition has been obtained in compliance with the rules of this subpart D.

Page 36

(c) *Prehearing memorandum.* Unless otherwise ordered by the Administrative Law Judge, each party shall file, and serve on the opposing party or the opposing party's representative, prior to any hearing, a prehearing memorandum containing —

(1) A list (together with a copy) of all proposed exhibits to be used in the party's case in chief;

(2) A list of proposed witnesses, including a synopsis of their expected testimony, or a statement that no witnesses will be called;

(3) Identification of any proposed expert witnesses, including a synopsis of their expected testimony and a copy of any report prepared by the expert or at his or her direction; and

(4) A list of undisputed facts.

(d) *Publicity* —

(1) *In general.* All reports and decisions of the Secretary of the Treasury, or delegate, including any reports and decisions of the Administrative Law Judge, under this Subpart D are, subject to the protective measures in paragraph (d)(4) of this section, public and open to inspection within 30 days after the agency's decision becomes final.

(2) *Request for additional publicity.* The Administrative Law Judge may grant a request by a practitioner or appraiser that all the pleadings and evidence of the disciplinary proceeding be made available for inspection where the parties stipulate in advance to adopt the protective measures in paragraph (d)(4) of this section.

(3) *Returns and return information* —

(i) *Disclosure to practitioner or appraiser.* Pursuant to *section 6103(l)(4) of the Internal Revenue Code,* the Secretary of the Treasury, or delegate, may disclose returns and return information to any practitioner or appraiser, or to the authorized representative of the practitioner or appraiser, whose rights are or may be affected by an administrative action or proceeding under this subpart D, but solely for use in the action or proceeding and only to the extent that the Secretary of the Treasury, or delegate, determines that the returns or return information are or may be relevant and material to the action or proceeding.

(ii) *Disclosure to officers and employees of the Department of the Treasury.* Pursuant to *sec-*

tion 6103(l)(4)(B) of the Internal Revenue Code the Secretary of the Treasury, or delegate, may disclose returns and return information to officers and employees of the Department of the Treasury for use in any action or proceeding under this subpart D, to the extent necessary to advance or protect the interests of the United States.

(iii) *Use of returns and return information.* Recipients of returns and return information under this paragraph (d)(3) may use the returns or return information solely in the action or proceeding, or in preparation for the action or proceeding, with respect to which the disclosure was made.

(iv) *Procedures for disclosure of returns and return information.* When providing returns or return information to the practitioner or appraiser, or authorized representative, the Secretary of the Treasury, or delegate, will —

(A) Redact identifying information of any third party taxpayers and replace it with a code;

(B) Provide a key to the coded information; and

(C) Notify the practitioner or appraiser, or authorized representative, of the restrictions on the use and disclosure of the returns and return information, the applicable damages remedy under *section 7431 of the Internal Revenue Code*, and that unauthorized disclosure of information provided by the Internal Revenue Service under this paragraph (d)(3) is also a violation of this part.

(4) *Protective measures —*

(i) *Mandatory protection order.* If redaction of names, addresses, and other identifying information of third party taxpayers may still permit indirect identification of any third party taxpayer, the Administrative Law Judge will issue a protective order to ensure that the identifying information is available to the parties and the Administrative Law Judge for purposes of the proceeding, but is not disclosed to, or open to inspection by, the public.

(ii) *Authorized orders.*

(A) Upon motion by a party or any other affected person, and for good cause shown, the Administrative Law Judge may make any order which justice requires to protect any person in the event

disclosure of information is prohibited by law, privileged, confidential, or sensitive in some other way, including, but not limited to, one or more of the following —

(1) That disclosure of information be made only on specified terms and conditions, including a designation of the time or place;

(2) That a trade secret or other information not be disclosed, or be disclosed only in a designated way.

(iii) *Denials.* If a motion for a protective order is denied in whole or in part, the Administrative Law Judge may, on such terms or conditions as the Administrative Law Judge deems just, order any party or person to comply with, or respond in accordance with, the procedure involved.

(iv) *Public inspection of documents.* The Secretary of the Treasury, or delegate, shall ensure that all names, addresses or other identifying details of third party taxpayers are redacted and replaced with the code assigned to the corresponding taxpayer in all documents prior to public inspection of such documents.

(e) *Location.* The location of the hearing will be determined by the agreement of the parties with the approval of the Administrative Law Judge, but, in the absence of such agreement and approval, the hearing will be held in Washington, D.C.

(f) *Failure to appear.* If either party to the proceeding fails to appear at the hearing, after notice of the proceeding has been sent to him or her, the party will be deemed to have waived the right to a hearing and the Administrative Law Judge may make his or her decision against the absent party by default.

(g) *Effective/applicability date.* This section is applicable on September 26, 2007.

§ 10.73 Evidence.

(a) *In general.* The rules of evidence prevailing in courts of law and equity are not controlling in hearings or proceedings conducted under this part. The Administrative Law Judge may, however, exclude evidence that is irrelevant, immaterial, or unduly repetitious.

(b) *Depositions.* The deposition of any witness taken pursuant to §10.71 may be admitted into evidence in any proceeding instituted under §10.60.

(c) *Requests for admission.* Any matter admitted in response to a request for admission under §10.71 is conclusively established unless the Administrative Law Judge on motion permits withdrawal or modification of the admission. Any admission made by a party is for the purposes of the pending action only and is not an admission by a party for any other purpose, nor may it be used against a party in any other proceeding.

(d) *Proof of documents.* Official documents, records, and papers of the Internal Revenue Service and the Office of Professional Responsibility are admissible in evidence without the production of an officer or employee to authenticate them. Any documents, records, and papers may be evidenced by a copy attested to or identified by an officer or employee of the Internal Revenue Service or the Treasury Department, as the case may be.

(e) *Withdrawal of exhibits.* If any document, record, or other paper is introduced in evidence as an exhibit, the Administrative Law Judge may authorize the withdrawal of the exhibit subject to any conditions that he or she deems proper.

(f) *Objections.* Objections to evidence are to be made in short form, stating the grounds for the objection. Except as ordered by the Administrative Law Judge, argument on objections will not be recorded or transcribed. Rulings on objections are to be a part of the record, but no exception to a ruling is necessary to preserve the rights of the parties.

(g) *Effective/applicability date.* This section is applicable on September 26, 2007.

§ 10.74 Transcript.

In cases where the hearing is stenographically reported by a Government contract reporter, copies of the transcript may be obtained from the reporter at rates not to exceed the maximum rates fixed by contract between the Government and the reporter. Where the hearing is stenographically reported by a regular employee of the Internal Revenue Service, a copy will

Page 38

be supplied to the respondent either without charge or upon the payment of a reasonable fee. Copies of exhibits introduced at the hearing or at the taking of depositions will be supplied to the parties upon the payment of a reasonable fee (Sec. 501, Public Law 82-137)(65 Stat. 290)(31 U.S.C. § 483a).

§ 10.75 Proposed findings and conclusions.

Except in cases where the respondent has failed to answer the complaint or where a party has failed to appear at the hearing, the parties must be afforded a reasonable opportunity to submit proposed findings and conclusions and their supporting reasons to the Administrative Law Judge.

§ 10.76 Decision of Administrative Law Judge.

(a) *In general* —

(1) *Hearings.* Within 180 days after the conclusion of a hearing and the receipt of any proposed findings and conclusions timely submitted by the parties, the Administrative Law Judge should enter a decision in the case. The decision must include a statement of findings and conclusions, as well as the reasons or basis for making such findings and conclusions, and an order of censure, suspension, disbarment, monetary penalty, disqualification, or dismissal of the complaint.

(2) *Summary adjudication.* In the event that a motion for summary adjudication is filed, the Administrative Law Judge should rule on the motion for summary adjudication within 60 days after the party in opposition files a written response, or if no written response if filed, within 90 days after the motion for summary adjudication is filed. A decision shall thereafter be rendered if the pleadings, depositions, admissions, and any other admissible evidence show that there is no genuine issue of material fact and that a decision may be rendered as a matter of law. The decision must include a statement of conclusions, as well as the reasons or basis for making such conclusions, and an order of censure, suspension, disbarment, monetary penalty, disqualification, or dismissal of the complaint.

Treasury Dept. Circular 230

(3) *Returns and return information.* In the decision, the Administrative Law Judge should use the code assigned to third party taxpayers (described in §10.72(d)).

(b) *Standard of proof.* If the sanction is censure or a suspension of less than six months' duration, the Administrative Law Judge, in rendering findings and conclusions, will consider an allegation of fact to be proven if it is established by the party who is alleging the fact by a preponderance of the evidence in the record. If the sanction is a monetary penalty, disbarment or a suspension of six months or longer duration, an allegation of fact that is necessary for a finding against the practitioner must be proven by clear and convincing evidence in the record. An allegation of fact that is necessary for a finding of disqualification against an appraiser must be proved by clear and convincing evidence in the record.

(c) *Copy of decision.* The Administrative Law Judge will provide the decision to the Director of the Office of Professional Responsibility, with a copy to the Director's authorized representative, and a copy of the decision to the respondent or the respondent's authorized representative.

(d) *When final.* In the absence of an appeal to the Secretary of the Treasury or delegate, the decision of the Administrative Law Judge will, without further proceedings, become the decision of the agency 30 days after the date of the Administrative Law Judge's decision.

(e) *Effective/applicability date.* This section is applicable to proceedings initiated on or after September 26, 2007.

§ 10.77 Appeal of decision of Administrative Law Judge.

(a) *Appeal.* Any party to the proceeding under this subpart D may file an appeal of the decision of the Administrative Law Judge with the Secretary of the Treasury, or delegate. The appeal must include a brief that states exceptions to the decision of the Administrative Law Judge and supporting reasons for such exceptions.

(b) *Time and place for filing of appeal.* The appeal and brief must be filed, in duplicate, with the Director of the Office of Professional Responsibility within 30 days of the date that the decision of the Administrative Law Judge is served on the parties. The Director of the Office of Professional Responsibility will immediately furnish a copy of the appeal to the Secretary of the Treasury or delegate who decides appeals. A copy of the appeal for review must be sent to any non-appealing party. If the Director of the Office of Professional Responsibility files an appeal, he or she will provide a copy of the appeal and certify to the respondent that the appeal has been filed.

(c) *Effective/applicability date.* This section is applicable on September 26, 2007.

§ 10.78 Decision on review.

(a) *Decision on review.* On appeal from or review of the decision of the Administrative Law Judge, the Secretary of the Treasury, or delegate, will make the agency decision. The Secretary of the Treasury, or delegate, should make the agency decision within 180 days after receipt of the appeal

(b) *Standard of review.* The decision of the Administrative Law Judge will not be reversed unless the appellant establishes that the decision is clearly erroneous in light of the evidence in the record and applicable law. Issues that are exclusively matters of law will be reviewed de novo. In the event that the Secretary of the Treasury, or delegate, determines that there are unresolved issues raised by the record, the case may be remanded to the Administrative Law Judge to elicit additional testimony or evidence.

(c) *Copy of decision on review.* The Secretary of the Treasury, or delegate, will provide copies of the agency decision to the Director of the Office of Professional Responsibility and the respondent or the respondent's authorized representative.

(d) *Effective/applicability date.* This section is applicable on September 26, 2007.

§ 10.79 Effect of disbarment, suspension, or censure.

(a) *Disbarment.* When the final decision in a case is against the respondent (or the respondent has offered his or her consent and such consent has been accepted by the Director of the Office of Professional Responsibility) and such decision is for disbarment, the respondent will not be permitted to practice before the Internal Revenue Service unless and until authorized to do so by the Director of the Office of Professional Responsibility pursuant to §10.81.

(b) *Suspension.* When the final decision in a case is against the respondent (or the respondent has offered his or her consent and such consent has been accepted by the Director of the Office of Professional Responsibility) and such decision is for suspension, the respondent will not be permitted to practice before the Internal Revenue Service during the period of suspension. For periods after the suspension, the practitioner's future representations may be subject to conditions as authorized by paragraph (d) of this section.

(c) *Censure.* When the final decision in the case is against the respondent (or the respondent has offered his or her consent and such consent has been accepted by the Director of the Office of Professional Responsibility) and such decision is for censure, the respondent will be permitted to practice before the Internal Revenue Service, but the respondent's future representations may be subject to conditions as authorized by paragraph (d) of this section.

(d) *Conditions.* After being subject to the sanction of either suspension or censure, the future representations of a practitioner so sanctioned shall be subject to conditions prescribed by the Director of the Office of Professional Responsibility designed to promote high standards of conduct. These conditions can be imposed for a reasonable period in light of the gravity of the practitioner's violations. For example, where a practitioner is censured because he or she failed to advise his or her clients about a potential conflict of interest or failed to obtain the clients' written consents, the Director of the Office of Professional Responsibility may require the practitioner

to provide the Director of the Office of Professional Responsibility or another Internal Revenue Service official with a copy of all consents obtained by the practitioner for an appropriate period following censure, whether or not such consents are specifically requested.

§ 10.80 Notice of disbarment, suspension, censure, or disqualification.

On the issuance of a final order censuring, suspending, or disbarring a practitioner or a final order disqualifying an appraiser, the Director of the Office of Professional Responsibility may give notice of the censure, suspension, disbarment, or disqualification to appropriate officers and employees of the Internal Revenue Service and to interested departments and agencies of the Federal government. The Director of the Office of Professional Responsibility may determine the manner of giving notice to the proper authorities of the State by which the censured, suspended, or disbarred person was licensed to practice.

§ 10.81 Petition for reinstatement.

The Director of the Office of Professional Responsibility may entertain a petition for reinstatement from any person disbarred from practice before the Internal Revenue Service or any disqualified appraiser after the expiration of 5 years following such disbarment or disqualification. Reinstatement may not be granted unless the Director of the Office of Professional Responsibility is satisfied that the petitioner, thereafter, is not likely to conduct himself contrary to the regulations in this part, and that granting such reinstatement would not be contrary to the public interest.

§ 10.82 Expedited suspension.

(a) *When applicable.* Whenever the Director of the Office of Professional Responsibility determines that a practitioner is described in paragraph (b) of this section, the Director of the Office of Professional Responsibility may institute a proceeding under this section to suspend the practitioner from practice before the Internal Revenue Service.

(b) *To whom applicable.* This section applies to any practitioner who, within 5 years of the date a complaint instituting a proceeding under this section is served:

(1) Has had a license to practice as an attorney, certified public accountant, or actuary suspended or revoked for cause (not including a failure to pay a professional licensing fee) by any authority or court, agency, body, or board described in §10.51(a)(10).

(2) Has, irrespective of whether an appeal has been taken, been convicted of any crime under title 26 of the United States Code, any crime involving dishonesty or breach of trust, or any felony for which the conduct involved renders the practitioner unfit to practice before the Internal Revenue Service.

(3) Has violated conditions imposed on the practitioner pursuant to §10.79(d).

(4) Has been sanctioned by a court of competent jurisdiction, whether in a civil or criminal proceeding (including suits for injunctive relief), relating to any taxpayer's tax liability or relating to the practitioner's own tax liability, for —

(i) Instituting or maintaining proceedings primarily for delay;

(ii) Advancing frivolous or groundless arguments; or

(iii) Failing to pursue available administrative remedies.

(c) *Instituting a proceeding.* A proceeding under this section will be instituted by a complaint that names the respondent, is signed by the Director of the Office of Professional Responsibility or a person representing the Director of the Office of Professional Responsibility under §10.69(a)(1), is filed in the Director of the Office of Professional Responsibility's office, and is served according to the rules set forth in paragraph (a) of §10.63. The complaint must give a plain and concise description of the allegations that constitute the basis for the proceeding. The complaint must notify the respondent —

(1) Of the place and due date for filing an answer;

(2) That a decision by default may be rendered if the respondent fails to file an answer as required;

(3) That the respondent may request a conference with the Director of the Office of Professional Responsibility to address the merits of the complaint and that any such request must be made in the answer; and

(4) That the respondent may be suspended either immediately following the expiration of the period within which an answer must be filed or, if a conference is requested, immediately following the conference.

(d) *Answer.* The answer to a complaint described in this section must be filed no later than 30 calendar days following the date the complaint is served, unless the Director of the Office of Professional Responsibility extends the time for filing. The answer must be filed in accordance with the rules set forth in §10.64, except as otherwise provided in this section. A respondent is entitled to a conference with the Director of the Office of Professional Responsibility only if the conference is requested in a timely filed answer. If a request for a conference is not made in the answer or the answer is not timely filed, the respondent will be deemed to have waived his or her right to a conference and the Director of the Office of Professional Responsibility may suspend such respondent at any time following the date on which the answer was due.

(e) *Conference.* The Director of the Office of Professional Responsibility or his or her designee will preside at a conference described in this section. The conference will be held at a place and time selected by the Director of the Office of Professional Responsibility, but no sooner than 14 calendar days after the date by which the answer must be filed with the Director of the Office of Professional Responsibility, unless the respondent agrees to an earlier date. An authorized representative may represent the respondent at the conference. Following the conference, upon a finding that the respondent is described in paragraph (b) of this section, or upon the respondent's failure to appear at the conference either personally or through an authorized representative, the Director of the Office of Professional Responsibility may immediately suspend the respondent from practice before the Internal Revenue Service.

(f) *Duration of suspension.* A suspension under this section will commence on the date that written notice of the suspension is issued. A practitioner's suspension will remain effective until the earlier of the following —

(1) The Director of the Office of Professional Responsibility lifts the suspension after determining that the practitioner is no longer described in paragraph (b) of this section or for any other reason; or

(2) The suspension is lifted by an Administrative Law Judge or the Secretary of the Treasury in a proceeding referred to in paragraph (g) of this section and instituted under §10.60.

(g) *Proceeding instituted under §10.60.* If the Director of the Office of Professional Responsibility suspends a practitioner under this section, the practitioner may ask the Director of the Office of Professional Responsibility to issue a complaint under §10.60. The request must be made in writing within 2 years from the date on which the practitioner's suspension commences. The Director of the Office of Professional Responsibility must issue a complaint requested under this paragraph within 30 calendar days of receiving the request.

(h) *Effective/applicability date.* This section is applicable on September 26, 2007.

Subpart E — General Provisions

§ 10.90 Records.

(a) *Roster.* The Director of the Office of Professional Responsibility will maintain, and may make available for public inspection in the time and manner prescribed by the Secretary of the Treasury, or delegate, rosters of —

(1) Enrolled agents, including individuals —

(i) Granted active enrollment to practice;

(ii) Whose enrollment has been placed in inactive status for failure to meet the requirements for renewal of enrollment;

(iii) Whose enrollment has been placed in inactive retirement status; and

(iv) Whose offer of consent to resign from enrollment has been accepted by the Director of the Office of Professional Responsibility under §10.61;

(2) Individuals (and employers, firms or other entities, if applicable) censured, suspended or disbarred from practice before the Internal Revenue Service or upon whom a monetary penalty was imposed;

(3) Disqualified appraisers; and

(4) Enrolled retirement plan agents, including individuals —

(i) Granted active enrollment to practice;

(ii) Whose enrollment has been placed in inactive status for failure to meet the requirements for renewal of enrollment;

(iii) Whose enrollment has been placed in inactive retirement status; and

(iv) Whose offer of consent to resign from enrollment has been accepted by the Director of the Office of Professional Responsibility under §10.61;

(b) *Other records.* Other records of the Director of the Office of Professional Responsibility may be disclosed upon specific request, in accordance with the applicable law.

(c) *Effective/applicability date.* This section is applicable on September 26, 2007.

§ 10.91 Saving provision.

Any proceeding instituted under this part prior to July 26, 2002, for which a final decision has not been reached or for which judicial review is still available will not be affected by these revisions. Any proceeding under this part based on conduct engaged in prior to September 26, 2007, which is instituted after that date, will apply subpart D and E or this part as revised, but the conduct engaged in prior to the effective date of these revisions will be judged by the regulations in effect at the time the conduct occurred.

§ 10.92 Special orders.

The Secretary of the Treasury reserves the power to issue such special orders as he or she deems proper in any cases within the purview of this part.

§ 10.93 Effective date.

Except as otherwise provided in each section and Subject to §10.91, Part 10 is applicable on July 26, 2002.

Linda E. Stiff,
Acting Deputy Commissioner for Services and Enforcement

Approved: September 19, 2007
Robert Hoyt, General Counsel, Office of the Secretary

[FR Doc. E7-18918 Filed 9-25-07; 8:45 am]

Addendum to Treasury Department Circular No. 230, Selected Sections (Rev. 4-2008)

Selected sections are the 2002 version of Subparts B and C, unless otherwise indicated.

§10.22 Diligence as to accuracy.

(a) *In general.* A practitioner must exercise due diligence —
(1) In preparing or assisting in the preparation of, approving, and filing tax returns, documents, affidavits, and other papers relating to Internal Revenue Service matters;
(2) In determining the correctness of oral or written representations made by the practitioner to the Department of the Treasury; and
(3) In determining the correctness of oral or written representations made by the practitioner to clients with reference to any matter administered by the Internal Revenue Service.
(b) *Reliance on others.* Except as provided in §§ 10.33 and 10.34, a practitioner will be presumed to have exercised due diligence for purposes of this section if the practitioner relies on the work product of another person and the practitioner used reasonable care in engaging, supervising, training, and evaluating the person, taking proper account of the nature of the relationship between the practitioner and the person.

§10.25 Practice by former Government employees, their partners and their associates.

(a) *Definitions.* For purposes of this section —
(1) *Assist* means to act in such a way as to advise, furnish information to, or otherwise aid another person, directly or indirectly.
(2) *Government employee* is an officer or employee of the United States or any agency of the United States, including a *special government employee* as defined in 18 U.S.C. 202(a), or of the District of Columbia, or of any State, or a member of Congress or of any State legislature.
(3) *Member of a firm* is a sole practitioner or an employee or associate thereof, or a partner, stockholder, associate, affiliate or employee of a partnership, joint venture, corporation, professional association or other affiliation of two or more practitioners who represent nongovernmental parties.

(4) *Practitioner* includes any individual described in paragraph (f) of §10.2.

(5) *Official responsibility* means the direct administrative or operating authority, whether intermediate or final, and either exercisable alone or with others, and either personally or through subordinates, to approve, disapprove, or otherwise direct Government action, with or without knowledge of the action.

(6) *Participate or participation* means substantial involvement as a Government employee by making decisions, or preparing or reviewing documents with or without the right to exercise a judgment of approval or disapproval, or participating in conferences or investigations, or rendering advice of a substantial nature.

(7) *Rule* includes Treasury Regulations, whether issued or under preparation for issuance as Notices of Proposed Rule Making or as Treasury Decisions; revenue rulings; and revenue procedures published in the Internal Revenue Bulletin. *Rule* does not include a *transaction* as defined in paragraph (a)(8) of this section.

(8) *Transaction* means any decision, determination, finding, letter ruling, technical advice, Chief Counsel advice, or contract or the approval or disapproval thereof, relating to a particular factual situation or situations involving a specific party or parties whose rights, privileges, or liabilities under laws or regulations administered by the Internal Revenue Service, or other legal rights, are determined or immediately affected therein and to which the United States is a party or in which it has a direct and substantial interest, whether or not the same taxable periods are involved. *Transaction* does not include *rule* as defined in paragraph (a)(7) of this section.

(b) *General rules.*

(1) No former Government employee may, subsequent to his or her Government employment, represent anyone in any matter administered by the Internal Revenue Service if the representation would violate 18 U.S.C. 207 or any other laws of the United States.

(2) No former Government employee who participated in a transaction may, subsequent to his or her Government employment, represent or knowingly assist, in that transaction, any person who is or was a specific party to that transaction.

(3) A former Government employee who within a period of one year prior to the termination of Government employment had official responsibility for a transaction may not, within two years after his or

her Government employment is ended, represent or knowingly assist in that transaction any person who is or was a specific party to that transaction.

(4) No former Government employee may, within one year after his or her Government employment is ended, appear before any employee of the Treasury Department in connection with the publication, withdrawal, amendment, modification, or interpretation of a rule in the development of which the former Government employee participated or for which, within a period of one year prior to the termination of his or her Government employment, he or she had official responsibility. This paragraph (b)(4) does not, however, preclude such former employee from appearing on his or her own behalf or from representing a taxpayer before the Internal Revenue Service in connection with a transaction involving the application or interpretation of such a rule with respect to that transaction, provided that such former employee does not utilize or disclose any confidential information acquired by the former employee in the development of the rule.

(c) *Firm representation.*

(1) No member of a firm of which a former Government employee is a member may represent or knowingly assist a person who was or is a specific party in any transaction with respect to which the restrictions of paragraph (b)(2) or (3) of this section apply to the former Government employee, in that transaction, unless the firm isolates the former Government employee in such a way to ensure that the former Government employee cannot assist in the representation.

(2) When isolation of a former Government employee is required under paragraph (c)(1) of this section, a statement affirming the fact of such isolation must be executed under oath by the former Government employee and by another member of the firm acting on behalf of the firm. The statement must clearly identify the firm, the former Government employee, and the transaction(s) requiring isolation and it must be filed with the Director of Practice (and at such other place(s) directed by the Director of Practice) and in such other place and in the manner prescribed by rule or regulation.

(d) *Pending representation.* Practice by former Government employees, their partners and associates with respect to representation in specific matters where actual representation commenced before July 26, 2002, is governed by the regulations set forth at 31 CFR Part 10 revised as of July 1, 2002. The burden of showing that representation commenced before July 26, 2002, lies with the former Government employees, and their partners and associates.

§10.27 Fees.

(a) *Generally.* A practitioner may not charge an unconscionable fee for representing a client in a matter before the Internal Revenue Service.

(b) *Contingent fees.*

(1) For purposes of this section, a contingent fee is any fee that is based, in whole or in part, on whether or not a position taken on a tax return or other filing avoids challenge by the Internal Revenue Service or is sustained either by the Internal Revenue Service or in litigation. A contingent fee includes any fee arrangement in which the practitioner will reimburse the client for all or a portion of the client's fee in the event that a position taken on a tax return or other filing is challenged by the Internal Revenue Service or is not sustained, whether pursuant to an indemnity agreement, a guarantee, rescission rights, or any other arrangement with a similar effect.

(2) A practitioner may not charge a contingent fee for preparing an original tax return or for any advice rendered in connection with a position taken or to be taken on an original tax return.

(3) A contingent fee may be charged for preparation of or advice in connection with an amended tax return or a claim for refund (other than a claim for refund made on an original tax return), but only if the practitioner reasonably anticipates at the time the fee arrangement is entered into that the amended tax return or refund claim will receive substantive review by the Internal Revenue Service.

§10.29 Conflicting interests.

(a) Except as provided by paragraph (b) of this section, a practitioner shall not represent a client in his or her practice before the Internal Revenue Service if the representation involves a conflict of interest. A conflict of interest exists if:

(1) The representation of one client will be directly adverse to another client; or

(2) There is a significant risk that the representation of one or more clients will be materially limited by the practitioner's responsibilities to another client, a former client or a third person or by a personal interest of the practitioner.

(b) Notwithstanding the existence of a conflict of interest under paragraph (a) of this section, the practitioner may represent a client if:

(1) The practitioner reasonably believes that the practitioner will be able to provide competent and diligent representation to each affected client;

(2) The representation is not prohibited by law;

(3) Each affected client gives informed consent, confirmed in writing.

(c) Copies of the written consents must be retained by the practitioner for at least 36 months from the date of the conclusion of the representation of the affected clients and the written consents must be provided to any officer or employee of the Internal Revenue Service on request.

(Approved by the Office of Management and Budget under Control No. 1545-1726)

§10.30 Solicitation.

(a) *Advertising and solicitation restrictions.*

(1) A practitioner may not, with respect to any Internal Revenue Service matter, in any way use or participate in the use of any form of public communication or private solicitation containing a false, fraudulent, or coercive statement or claim; or a misleading or deceptive statement or claim. Enrolled agents, in describing their professional designation, may not utilize the term of art "certified" or imply an employer/employee relationship with the Internal Revenue Service. Examples of acceptable descriptions are "enrolled to represent taxpayers before the Internal Revenue Service," "enrolled to practice before the Internal Revenue Service," and "admitted to practice before the Internal Revenue Service."

(2) A practitioner may not make, directly or indirectly, an uninvited written or oral solicitation of employment in matters related to the Internal Revenue Service if the solicitation violates Federal or State law or other applicable rule, e.g., attorneys are precluded from making a solicitation that is prohibited by conduct rules applicable to all attorneys in their State(s) of licensure. Any lawful solicitation made by or on behalf of a practitioner eligible to practice before the Internal Revenue Service must, nevertheless, clearly identify the solicitation as such and, if applicable, identify the source of the information used in choosing the recipient.

(b) *Fee information.*

(1)(i) A practitioner may publish the availability of a written schedule of fees and disseminate the following fee information —

(A) Fixed fees for specific routine services.

(B) Hourly rates.

(C) Range of fees for particular services.

(D) Fee charged for an initial consultation.

(ii) Any statement of fee information concerning matters in which costs may be incurred must include a statement disclosing whether clients will be responsible for such costs.

(2) A practitioner may charge no more than the rate(s) published under paragraph (b)(1) of this section for at least 30 calendar days after the last date on which the schedule of fees was published.

(c) *Communication of fee information.* Fee information may be communicated in professional lists, telephone directories, print media, mailings, and electronic mail, facsimile, hand delivered flyers, radio, television, and any other method. The method chosen, however, must not cause the communication to become untruthful, deceptive, or otherwise in violation of this part. A practitioner may not persist in attempting to contact a prospective client if the prospective client has made it known to the practitioner that he or she does not desire to be solicited. In the case of radio and television broadcasting, the broadcast must be recorded and the practitioner must retain a recording of the actual transmission. In the case of direct mail and e-commerce communications, the practitioner must retain a copy of the actual communication, along with a list or other description of persons to whom the communication was mailed or otherwise distributed. The copy must be retained by the practitioner for a period of at least 36 months from the date of the last transmission or use.

(d) *Improper associations.* A practitioner may not, in matters related to the Internal Revenue Service, assist, or accept assistance from, any person or entity who, to the knowledge of the practitioner, obtains clients or otherwise practices in a manner forbidden under this section.

(Approved by the Office of Management and Budget under Control No. 1545-1726)

§10.34 Standards for advising with respect to tax return positions and for preparing or signing returns.

(a) *Realistic possibility standard.* A practitioner may not sign a tax return as a preparer if the practitioner determines that the tax return contains a position that does not have a realistic possibility of being sustained on its merits (the realistic possibility standard) unless the position is not frivolous and is adequately disclosed to the Internal Revenue Service. A practitioner may not advise a client to take a position on a tax return, or prepare the portion of a tax return on which a position is taken, unless —

(1) The practitioner determines that the position satisfies the realistic possibility standard; or

(2) The position is not frivolous and the practitioner advises the client of any opportunity to avoid the accuracy-related penalty in section 6662 of the Internal Revenue Code by adequately disclosing the position and of the requirements for adequate disclosure.

(b) *Advising clients on potential penalties.* A practitioner advising a client to take a position on a tax return, or preparing or signing a tax return as a preparer, must inform the client of the penalties reasonably likely to apply to the client with respect to the position advised, prepared, or reported. The practitioner also must inform the client of any opportunity to avoid any such penalty by disclosure, if relevant, and of the requirements for adequate disclosure. This paragraph (b) applies even if the practitioner is not subject to a penalty with respect to the position.

(c) *Relying on information furnished by clients.* A practitioner advising a client to take a position on a tax return, or preparing or signing a tax return as a preparer, generally may rely in good faith without verification upon information furnished by the client. The practitioner may not, however, ignore the implications of information furnished to, or actually known by, the practitioner, and must make reasonable inquiries if the information as furnished appears to be incorrect, inconsistent with an important fact or another factual assumption, or incomplete.

(d) *Definitions.* For purposes of this section —

(1) *Realistic possibility.* A position is considered to have a realistic possibility of being sustained on its merits if a reasonable and well informed analysis of the law and the facts by a person knowledgeable in the tax law would lead such a person to conclude that the position has approximately a one in three, or greater, likelihood of being sustained on its merits. The authorities described in 26 CFR 1.6662-4(d)(3)(iii), or any successor provision, of the substantial understatement penalty regulations may be taken into account for purposes of this analysis. The possibility that a tax return will not be audited, that an issue will not be raised on audit, or that an issue will be settled may not be taken into account.

(2) *Frivolous.* A position is frivolous if it is patently improper.

Subpart C — Sanctions for Violation of the Regulations

§10.50 Sanctions.

(a) *Authority to censure, suspend, or disbar.* The Secretary of the Treasury, or his or her delegate, after notice and an opportunity for a proceeding, may censure, suspend or disbar any practitioner from practice before the Internal Revenue Service if the practitioner is shown to be incompetent or disreputable, fails to comply with any regulation in this part, or with intent to defraud, willfully and knowingly misleads or threatens a client or prospective client. Censure is a public reprimand.

(b) *Authority to disqualify.* The Secretary of the Treasury, or his or her delegate, after due notice and opportunity for hearing, may disqualify any appraiser with respect to whom a penalty has been assessed under section 6701(a) of the Internal Revenue Code.

(1) If any appraiser is disqualified pursuant to this subpart C, such appraiser is barred from presenting evidence or testimony in any administrative proceeding before the Department of Treasury or the Internal Revenue Service, unless and until authorized to do so by the Director of Practice pursuant to §10.81, regardless of whether such evidence or testimony would pertain to an appraisal made prior to or after such date.

(2) Any appraisal made by a disqualified appraiser after the effective date of disqualification will not have any probative effect in any administrative proceeding before the Department of the Treasury or the Internal Revenue Service. An appraisal otherwise barred from admission into evidence pursuant to this section may be admitted into evidence solely for the purpose of determining the taxpayer's reliance in good faith on such appraisal.

§10.51 Incompetence and disreputable conduct.

Incompetence and disreputable conduct for which a practitioner may be censured, suspended or disbarred from practice before the Internal Revenue Service includes, but is not limited to —

(a) Conviction of any criminal offense under the revenue laws of the United States;

(b) Conviction of any criminal offense involving dishonesty or breach of trust;

(c) Conviction of any felony under Federal or State law for which the conduct involved renders the practitioner unfit to practice before the Internal Revenue

Service;

(d) Giving false or misleading information, or participating in any way in the giving of false or misleading information to the Department of the Treasury or any officer or employee thereof, or to any tribunal authorized to pass upon Federal tax matters, in connection with any matter pending or likely to be pending before them, knowing such information to be false or misleading. Facts or other matters contained in testimony, Federal tax returns, financial statements, applications for enrollment, affidavits, declarations, or any other document or statement, written or oral, are included in the term *information.*

(e) Solicitation of employment as prohibited under §10.30, the use of false or misleading representations with intent to deceive a client or prospective client in order to procure employment, or intimating that the practitioner is able improperly to obtain special consideration or action from the Internal Revenue Service or officer or employee thereof.

(f) Willfully failing to make a Federal tax return in violation of the revenue laws of the United States, willfully evading, attempting to evade, or participating in any way in evading or attempting to evade any assessment or payment of any Federal tax, or knowingly counseling or suggesting to a client or prospective client an illegal plan to evade Federal taxes or payment thereof.

(g) Misappropriation of, or failure properly and promptly to remit funds received from a client for the purpose of payment of taxes or other obligations due the United States.

(h) Directly or indirectly attempting to influence, or offering or agreeing to attempt to influence, the official action of any officer or employee of the Internal Revenue Service by the use of threats, false accusations, duress or coercion, by the offer of any special inducement or promise of advantage or by the bestowing of any gift, favor or thing of value.

(i) Disbarment or suspension from practice as an attorney, certified public accountant, public accountant, or actuary by any duly constituted authority of any State, territory, possession of the United States, including a Commonwealth, or the District of Columbia, any Federal court of record or any Federal agency, body or board.

(j) Knowingly aiding and abetting another person to practice before the Internal Revenue Service during a period of suspension, disbarment, or ineligibility of such other person.

(k) Contemptuous conduct in connection with practice before the Internal Revenue Service, including the use of abusive language, making false accusations and statements, knowing them to be false, or circulating or publishing malicious or libelous matter.

(l) Giving a false opinion, knowingly, recklessly, or through gross incompetence, including an opinion which is intentionally or recklessly misleading, or engaging in a pattern of providing incompetent opinions on questions arising under the Federal tax laws. False opinions described in this paragraph (l) include those which reflect or result from a knowing misstatement of fact or law, from an assertion of a position known to be unwarranted under existing law, from counseling or assisting in conduct known to be illegal or fraudulent, from concealing matters required by law to be revealed, or from consciously disregarding information indicating that material facts expressed in the tax opinion or offering material are false or misleading. For purposes of this paragraph (l), reckless conduct is a highly unreasonable omission or misrepresentation involving an extreme departure from the standards of ordinary care that a practitioner should observe under the circumstances. A pattern of conduct is a factor that will be taken into account in determining whether a practitioner acted knowingly, recklessly, or through gross incompetence. Gross incompetence includes conduct that reflects gross indifference, preparation which is grossly inadequate under the circumstances, and a consistent failure to perform obligations to the client.

§10.52 Violation of regulations.

A practitioner may be censured, suspended or disbarred from practice before the Internal Revenue Service for any of the following:

(a) Willfully violating any of the regulations contained in this part.

(b) Recklessly or through gross incompetence (within the meaning of §10.51(l)) violating §10.33 or 10.34.

§10.53 Receipt of information concerning practitioner *(June 2005)*.

(a) *Officer or employee of the Internal Revenue Service.* If an officer or employee of the Internal Revenue Service has reason to believe that a practitioner has violated any provision of this part, the officer or employee will promptly make a written report to the Director of Practice of the suspected violation. The report will explain the facts and reasons upon which the officer's or employee's belief rests.

(b) *Other persons.* Any person other than an officer or employee of the Internal Revenue Service having information of a violation of any provision of this part may make an oral or written report of the alleged violation to the Director of Practice or any officer or employee of the Internal Revenue Service. If the report is made to an officer or employee of the Internal Revenue Service, the officer or employee will make a written report of the suspected violation to the Director of Practice.

(c) *Destruction of report.* No report made under paragraph (a) or (b) of this section shall be maintained by the Director of Practice unless retention of such record is permissible under the applicable records control schedule as approved by the National Archives and Records Administration and designated in the Internal Revenue Manual. The Director of Practice must destroy such reports as soon as permissible under the applicable records control schedule.

(d) *Effect on proceedings under subpart D.* The destruction of any report will not bar any proceeding under subpart D of this part, but precludes the Director of Practice's use of a copy of such report in a proceeding under subpart D of this part.

Appendix B

ABA FORMAL OPINION 85-352

ABA FORMAL OPINION 85-352
(July 7, 1986)[1]

A lawyer may advise reporting a position on a tax return so long as the lawyer believes in good faith that the position is warranted in existing law or can be supported by a good faith argument for an extension, modification or reversal of existing law and there is some realistic possibility of success if the matter is litigated.

The Committee has been requested by the Section of Taxation of the American Bar Association to reconsider the "reasonable basis" standard in the Committee's Formal Opinion 314 governing the position a lawyer may advise a client to take on a tax return.

Opinion 314 (April 27, 1965) was issued in response to a number of specific inquiries regarding the ethical relationship between the Internal Revenue Service and lawyers practicing before it. The opinion formulated general principles governing this relationship, including the following:

> [A] lawyer who is asked to advise his client in the course of the preparation of the client's tax returns may freely urge the statement of positions most favorable to the client just as long as there is a *reasonable basis* for this position. (Emphasis supplied).

The Committee is informed that the standard of "reasonable basis" has been construed by many lawyers to support the use of any colorable claim on a tax return to justify exploitation of the lottery of the tax return audit selection process.[2] This view is not universally held, and the Committee does not believe that the reasonable basis standard, properly interpreted and applied, permits this construction.

However, the Committee is persuaded that as a result of serious controversy over this standard and its persistent criticism by distinguished members of the tax bar, IRS officials and members of Congress, sufficient doubt has been created regarding the validity of the standard so as to erode its effectiveness as an ethical guideline. For this reason, the Committee has concluded that it should be restated. Another reason for restating the standard is that since

---

[1] Formal Opinion 85-352 © 1985 by the American Bar Association. Reprinted with permission. Copies of ABA Formal Ethics Opinions are available from Service Center, American Bar Association, 321 North Clark Street, Chicago, IL 60654, 1-800-285-2221. All rights reserved. This information or any portion thereof may not be copied or disseminated in any form or by any means or stored in an electronic database or retrieval system without the express written consent of the American Bar Association.

[2] [1] This criticism has been expressed by the Section of Taxation and also by the U.S. Department of the Treasury and some legal writers. See, e.g., Robert H. Mundheim, *Speech as General Counsel to Treasury Department, reprinted in* HOW TO PREPARE AND DEFEND TAX SHELTER OPINIONS: RISKS AND REALITIES FOR LAWYERS AND ACCOUNTANTS (Law and Business, Inc. 1981); Rowen, *When May a Lawyer Advise a Client That He May Take a Position on a Tax Return?* 29 TAX LAWYER 237 (1976).

publication of Opinion 314, the ABA has adopted in succession the Model Code of Professional Responsibility (1969, revised 1980) and the Model Rules of Professional Conduct (1983). Both the Model Code and the Model Rules directly address the duty of a lawyer in presenting or arguing positions for a client in language that does not refer to "reasonable basis." It is therefore appropriate to conform the standard of Opinion 314 to the language of the new rules.

This opinion reconsiders and revises only that part of Opinion 314 that relates to the lawyer's duty in advising a client of positions that can be taken on a tax return. It does not deal with a lawyer's opinion on tax shelter investment offerings, which is specifically addressed by this Committee's Formal Opinion 346 (Revised), and which involves very different considerations, including third party reliance.

The ethical standards governing the conduct of a lawyer in advising a client on positions that can be taken in a tax return are no different from those governing a lawyer's conduct in advising or taking positions for a client in other civil matters. Although the Model Rules distinguish between the roles of advisor and advocate,[3] both roles are involved here, and the ethical standards applicable to them provide relevant guidance. In many cases a lawyer must realistically anticipate that the filing of the tax return may be the first step in a process that may result in an adversary relationship between the client and the IRS. This normally occurs in situations when a lawyer advises an aggressive position on a tax return, not when the position taken is a safe or conservative one that is unlikely to be challenged by the IRS.

Rule 3.1 of the Model Rules, which is in essence a restatement of DR 7- 102(A)(2) of the Model Code,[4] states in pertinent part:

> A lawyer shall not bring or defend a proceeding, or assert or controvert an issue therein, unless there is a basis for doing so that is not frivolous, which includes a good faith argument for an extension, modification or reversal of existing law.

Rule 1.2(d), which applies to representation generally, states:

> A lawyer shall not counsel a client to engage, or assist a client, in conduct that the lawyer knows is criminal or fraudulent, but a lawyer may discuss the legal consequences of any proposed course of conduct with a client and may counsel or assist a client to make a good faith effort to determine the validity, scope, meaning or application of the law.

On the basis of these rules and analogous provisions of the Model Code, a lawyer, in representing a client in the course of the preparation of the client's tax return, may advise the statement of positions most favorable to the client if the lawyer has a good faith belief that those positions are warranted in

---

[3] [2] See, e.g., Model Rules 2.1 and 3.1.

[4] [3] DR 7-102(A)(2) states:

In his representation of a client, a lawyer shall not:

. . .

(2) Knowingly advance a claim or defense that is unwarranted under existing law, except that he may advance such claim or defense if it can be supported by good faith argument for an extension, modification or reversal of existing law.

existing law or can be supported by a good faith argument for an extension, modification or reversal of existing law. A lawyer can have a good faith belief in this context even if the lawyer believes the client's position probably will not prevail.[5] However, good faith requires that there be some realistic possibility of success if the matter is litigated.

This formulation of the lawyer's duty in the situation addressed by this opinion is consistent with the basic duty of the lawyer to a client, recognized in ethical standards since the ABA Canons of Professional Ethics, and in the opinions of this Committee: zealously and loyally to represent the interests of the client within the bounds of the law.

Thus, where a lawyer has a good faith belief in the validity of a position in accordance with the standard stated above that a particular transaction does not result in taxable income or that certain expenditures are properly deductible as expenses, the lawyer has no duty to require as a condition of his or her continued representation that riders be attached to the client's tax return explaining the circumstances surrounding the transaction or the expenditures.

In the role of advisor, the lawyer should counsel the client as to whether the position is likely to be sustained by a court if challenged by the IRS, as well as of the potential penalty consequences to the client if the position is taken on the tax return without disclosure. Section 6661 of the Internal Revenue Code imposes a penalty for substantial understatement of tax liability which can be avoided if the facts are adequately disclosed or if there is or was substantial authority for the position taken by the taxpayer. Competent representation of the client would require the lawyer to advise the client fully as to whether there is or was substantial authority for the position taken in the tax return. If the lawyer is unable to conclude that the position is supported by substantial authority, the lawyer should advise the client of the penalty the client may suffer and of the opportunity to avoid such penalty by adequately disclosing the facts in the return or in a statement attached to the return. If after receiving such advice the client decides to risk the penalty by making no disclosure and to take the position initially advised by the lawyer in accordance with the standard stated above, the lawyer has met his or her ethical responsibility with respect to the advice.

In all cases, however, with regard both to the preparation of returns and negotiating administrative settlements, the lawyer is under a duty not to mislead the Internal Revenue Service deliberately, either by misstatements or by silence or by permitting the client to mislead. Rules 4.1 and 8.4(c); DRs 1- 102(A)(4), 7-102(A)(3) and (5).

In summary, a lawyer may advise reporting a position on a return even where the lawyer believes the position probably will not prevail, there is no 'substantial authority' in support of the position, and there will be no disclosure of the position in the return. However, the position to be asserted must be one which the lawyer in good faith believes is warranted in existing law or can be supported by a good faith argument for an extension, modification or reversal of existing law. This requires that there is some realistic possibility of success if the matter is litigated. In addition, in his role as advisor, the lawyer should refer to potential penalties and other legal consequences should the client take the position advised.

---

[5] [4] Comment to Rule 3.11; see also Model Code EC 7-4.

Appendix C

STATEMENTS ON STANDARDS FOR TAX SERVICES[1]

Statements on Standards for Tax Services

Issued by the Tax Executive Committee

November 2009

1-7

Statement on Standards for Tax Services No. 1,
Tax Return Positions

Statement on Standards for Tax Services No. 2,
Answers to Questions on Returns

Statement on Standards for Tax Services No. 3,
Certain Procedural Aspects of Preparing Returns

Statement on Standards for Tax Services No. 4,
Use of Estimates

Statement on Standards for Tax Services No. 5,
Departure From a Position Previously Concluded in an Administrative Proceeding or Court Decision

Statement on Standards for Tax Services No. 6,
Knowledge of Error: Return Preparation and Administrative Proceedings

Statement on Standards for Tax Services No. 7,
Form and Content of Advice to Taxpayers

(Supersedes Statement on Standards for Tax Services Nos. 1–8 effective January 1, 2010.)

AMERICAN INSTITUTE OF CERTIFIED PUBLIC ACCOUNTANTS

Contents of Statements

Preface

1. Standards are the foundation of a profession. The AICPA aids its members in fulfilling their ethical responsibilities by instituting and maintaining standards against which their professional performance can be measured. Compliance with professional standards of tax practice also reaffirms the public's awareness of the professionalism that is associated with CPAs as well as the AICPA.

2. This publication sets forth enforceable tax practice standards for members of the AICPA, Statements on Standards for Tax Services (SSTSs or statements). These statements apply to all members providing tax services regardless of the jurisdictions in which they practice. Interpretations of these statements may be issued as guidance to assist in understanding and applying the statements. The SSTSs and their interpretations are intended to complement other standards of tax practice, such as Treasury Department Circular No. 230, *Regulations Governing the Practice of Attorneys, Certified Public Accountants, Enrolled Agents, Enrolled Actuaries, Enrolled Retirement Plan Agents, and Appraisers before the Internal Revenue Service;* penalty provisions of the Internal Revenue Code; and state boards of accountancy rules.

3. The SSTSs are written in as simple and objective a manner as possible. However, by their nature, practice standards provide for an appropriate range of behavior and need to be interpreted to address a broad range of personal and professional situations. The SSTSs recognize this need by, in some sections, providing relatively subjective rules and by leaving certain terms undefined. These terms are generally rooted in tax concepts and, therefore, should be readily understood by tax practitioners. Accordingly, enforcement of these rules, as part of the AICPA's Code of Professional Conduct Rule 201, *General Standards*, and Rule 202, *Compliance With Standards* (AICPA, *Professional Standards*, vol. 2, ET sec. 201 par. .01 and ET sec. 202 par. .01), will be undertaken on a case-by-case basis. Members are expected to comply with them.

6　Statement on Standards for Tax Services Nos. 1–7

History

4. The SSTSs have their origin in the Statements on Responsibilities in Tax Practice (SRTPs), which provided a body of advisory opinions on good tax practice. The guidelines as originally set forth in the SRTPs became more important than many members had anticipated when the guidelines were issued. The courts, the IRS, state accountancy boards, and other professional organizations recognized and relied on the SRTPs as the appropriate articulation of professional conduct in a CPA's tax practice. The SRTPs became *de facto* enforceable standards of professional practice, because state disciplinary organizations and courts regularly held CPAs accountable for failure to follow the guidelines set forth in the SRTPs.

5. The AICPA's Tax Executive Committee concluded it was appropriate to issue tax practice standards that would become a part of the AICPA's *Professional Standards*. At its July 1999 meeting, the AICPA Board of Directors approved support of the executive committee's initiative and placed the matter on the agenda of the October 1999 meeting of the AICPA's governing Council. On October 19, 1999, Council approved designating the Tax Executive Committee as a standard-setting body, thus authorizing that committee to promulgate standards of tax practice. As a result, the original SSTSs, largely mirroring the SRTPs, were issued in August 2000.

6. The SRTPs were originally issued between 1964 and 1977. The first nine SRTPs and the introduction were promulgated in 1976; the tenth SRTP was issued in 1977. The original SRTPs concerning the CPA's responsibility to sign the tax return (SRTP No. 1, *Signature of Preparers*, and No. 2, *Signature of Reviewer: Assumption of Preparer's Responsibility*) were withdrawn in 1982 after Treasury Department regulations were issued adopting substantially the same standards for all tax return preparers. The sixth and seventh SRTPs, concerning the responsibility of a CPA who becomes aware of an error, were revised in 1991. The first interpretation of the SRTPs, Interpretation No. 1-1, "Realistic Possibility Standard," was approved in December 1990. The SSTSs and Interpretation No. 1-1, "Realistic Possibility Standard," of SSTS No. 1, *Tax Return Positions*, superseded and replaced the SRTPs and their Interpretation No. 1-1, effective October 31, 2000. Although the number and names of the SSTSs, and the substance of the rules contained in each of them, remained the same as in the SRTPs, the language was revised to both clarify and reflect the enforceable nature of the SSTSs. In addition, because the applicability of these standards is not limited to federal income tax practice (as was the case with the SRTPs), the language was changed to indicate the broader scope. In 2003, in connection with the tax shelter debate, SSTS Interpretation No. 1-2, "Tax Planning," of SSTS No. 1 was issued to clarify a member's responsibilities in connection with tax planning; that interpretation became effective December 31, 2003.

7. When the original SSTSs were issued, an effort was made to keep to a minimum any changes in the language of the SSTSs from that of the predecessor SRTPs. This was done to alleviate concerns regarding the enforceability of standards that differed from the SRTPs under which members had been practicing. Since the issuance of the original SSTSs, members have asked for clarification on certain matters, such as the duplication of the language in SSTS No. 6, *Knowledge of Error: Return Preparation*, and No. 7, *Knowledge of Error: Administrative Proceedings*. Also, certain changes in federal and state tax laws have raised concerns regarding the need to revise SSTS No. 1. As a result, in 2008, the original SSTS Nos. 1–8 were updated, effective January 1, 2010. The original SSTS Nos. 6–7 were combined into the revised SSTS No. 6, *Knowledge of Error: Return Preparation and Administrative Proceedings*. The original SSTS No. 8, *Form and Content of Advice to Taxpayers*, was renumbered SSTS No. 7. In addition, various revisions were made to the language of the original SSTSs.

Ongoing Process

8. The following SSTSs and any interpretations issued thereunder reflect the AICPA's standards of tax practice and delineate members' responsibilities to taxpayers, the public, the government, and the profession. The statements are intended to be part of an ongoing process of articulating standards of tax practice for members. These standards are subject to change as necessary or appropriate to address changes in the tax law or other developments in the tax practice environment.

9. Members are encouraged to assess the adequacy of their practices and procedures for providing tax services in conformity with these standards. This process will vary according to the size of the practice and the nature of tax services performed.

10. The Tax Executive Committee promulgates the SSTSs and their interpretations. Acknowledgment is also due to the many members who have devoted their time and efforts over the years to developing and revising the AICPA's standards.

Statement on Standards for Tax Services No. 1, *Tax Return Positions*

Introduction

1. This statement sets forth the applicable standards for members when recommending tax return positions, or preparing or signing tax returns (including amended returns, claims for refund, and information returns) filed with any taxing authority. For purposes of these standards

a. a *tax return position* is (i) a position reflected on a tax return on which a member has specifically advised a taxpayer or (ii) a position about which a member has knowledge of all material facts and, on the basis of those facts, has concluded whether the position is appropriate.

b. a *taxpayer* is a client, a member's employer, or any other third-party recipient of tax services.

2. This statement also addresses a member's obligation to advise a taxpayer of relevant tax return disclosure responsibilities and potential penalties.

3. In addition to the AICPA, various taxing authorities, at the federal, state, and local levels, may impose specific reporting and disclosure standards with regard to recommending tax return positions or preparing or signing tax returns.[1] These standards can vary between taxing authorities and by type of tax.

---

[1] A member should refer to the current version of Internal Revenue Code Section 6694, Understatement of taxpayer's liability by tax return preparer, and other relevant federal, state, and jurisdictional authorities to determine the reporting and disclosure standards that are applicable to preparers of tax returns.

Statement

4.   A member should determine and comply with the standards, if any, that are imposed by the applicable taxing authority with respect to recommending a tax return position, or preparing or signing a tax return.

5.   If the applicable taxing authority has no written standards with respect to recommending a tax return position or preparing or signing a tax return, or if its standards are lower than the standards set forth in this paragraph, the following standards will apply:

    a.   A member should not recommend a tax return position or prepare or sign a tax return taking a position unless the member has a good-faith belief that the position has at least a realistic possibility of being sustained administratively or judicially on its merits if challenged.

    b.   Notwithstanding paragraph 5(a), a member may *recommend a tax return position* if the member (i) concludes that there is a reasonable basis for the position and (ii) advises the taxpayer to appropriately disclose that position. Notwithstanding paragraph 5(a), a member may *prepare or sign a tax return* that reflects a position if (i) the member concludes there is a reasonable basis for the position and (ii) the position is appropriately disclosed.

6.   When recommending a tax return position or when preparing or signing a tax return on which a position is taken, a member should, when relevant, advise the taxpayer regarding potential penalty consequences of such tax return position and the opportunity, if any, to avoid such penalties through disclosure.

7.   A member should not recommend a tax return position or prepare or sign a tax return reflecting a position that the member knows

    a.   exploits the audit selection process of a taxing authority, or

    b.   serves as a mere arguing position advanced solely to obtain leverage in a negotiation with a taxing authority.

8.   When recommending a tax return position, a member has both the right and the responsibility to be an advocate for the taxpayer with respect to any position satisfying the aforementioned standards.

Explanation

9. The AICPA and various taxing authorities impose specific reporting and disclosure standards with respect to tax return positions and preparing or signing tax returns. In a given situation, the standards, if any, imposed by the applicable taxing authority may be higher or lower than the standards set forth in paragraph 5. A member is to comply with the standards, if any, of the applicable taxing authority; if the applicable taxing authority has no standards or if its standards are lower than the standards set forth in paragraph 5, the standards set forth in paragraph 5 will apply.

10. Our self-assessment tax system can function effectively only if taxpayers file tax returns that are true, correct, and complete. A tax return is prepared based on a taxpayer's representation of facts, and the taxpayer has the final responsibility for positions taken on the return. The standards that apply to a taxpayer may differ from those that apply to a member.

11. In addition to a duty to the taxpayer, a member has a duty to the tax system. However, it is well established that the taxpayer has no obligation to pay more taxes than are legally owed, and a member has a duty to the taxpayer to assist in achieving that result. The standards contained in paragraphs 4–8 recognize a member's responsibilities to both the taxpayer and the tax system.

12. In reaching a conclusion concerning whether a given standard in paragraph 4 or 5 has been satisfied, a member may consider a well-reasoned construction of the applicable statute, well-reasoned articles or treatises, or pronouncements issued by the applicable taxing authority, regardless of whether such sources would be treated as *authority* under Internal Revenue Code Section 6662, *Imposition of accuracy-related penalty on underpayments*, and the regulations thereunder. A position would not fail to meet these standards merely because it is later abandoned for practical or procedural considerations during an administrative hearing or in the litigation process.

13. If a member has a good-faith belief that more than one tax return position meets the standards set forth in paragraphs 4–5, a member's advice concerning alternative acceptable positions may include a discussion of the likelihood that each such position might or might not cause the taxpayer's tax return to be examined and whether the position would be challenged in an examination. In such circumstances, such advice is not a violation of paragraph 7.

14. A member's determination of whether information is appropriately disclosed by the taxpayer should be based on the facts and circumstances of the particular case and the disclosure requirements of the applicable taxing authority. If a member recommending a position, but not engaged to prepare or sign the related tax return, advises the taxpayer concerning appropriate disclosure of the position, then the member shall be deemed to meet the disclosure requirements of these standards.

15. If particular facts and circumstances lead a member to believe that a taxpayer penalty might be asserted, the member should so advise the taxpayer and should discuss with the taxpayer the opportunity, if any, to avoid such penalty by disclosing the position on the tax return. Although a member should advise the taxpayer with respect to disclosure, it is the taxpayer's responsibility to decide whether and how to disclose.

16. For purposes of this statement, preparation of a tax return includes giving advice on events that have occurred at the time the advice is given if the advice is directly relevant to determining the existence, character, or amount of a schedule, entry, or other portion of a tax return.

Statement on Standards for Tax Services No. 2, Answers to Questions on Returns

Introduction

1.   This statement sets forth the applicable standards for members when signing the preparer's declaration on a tax return if one or more questions on the return have not been answered. The term *questions* includes requests for information on the return, in the instructions, or in the regulations, whether or not stated in the form of a question.

Statement

2.   A member should make a reasonable effort to obtain from the taxpayer the information necessary to provide appropriate answers to all questions on a tax return before signing as preparer.

Explanation

3.   It is recognized that the questions on tax returns are not of uniform importance, and often they are not applicable to the particular taxpayer. Nevertheless, there are at least three reasons why a member should be satisfied that a reasonable effort has been made to obtain information to provide appropriate answers to the questions on the return that are applicable to a taxpayer:

   a.   A question may be of importance in determining taxable income or loss, or the tax liability shown on the return, in which circumstance an omission may detract from the quality of the return.

   b.   A request for information may require a disclosure necessary for a complete return or to avoid penalties.

   c.   A member often must sign a preparer's declaration stating that the return is true, correct, and complete.

4.   Reasonable grounds may exist for omitting an answer to a question applicable to a taxpayer. For example, reasonable grounds may include the following:

    a.   The information is not readily available and the answer is not significant in terms of taxable income or loss, or the tax liability shown on the return.

    b.   Genuine uncertainty exists regarding the meaning of the question in relation to the particular return.

    c.   The answer to the question is voluminous; in such cases, a statement should be made on the return that the data will be supplied upon examination.

5.   A member should not omit an answer merely because it might prove disadvantageous to a taxpayer.

6.   A member should consider whether the omission of an answer to a question may cause the return to be deemed incomplete or result in penalties.

7.   If reasonable grounds exist for omission of an answer to an applicable question, a taxpayer is not required to provide on the return an explanation of the reason for the omission.

Statement on Standards for Tax Services No. 3, *Certain Procedural Aspects of Preparing Returns*

Introduction

1.   This statement sets forth the applicable standards for members concerning the obligation to examine or verify certain supporting data or to consider information related to another taxpayer when preparing a taxpayer's tax return.

Statement

2.   In preparing or signing a return, a member may in good faith rely, without verification, on information furnished by the taxpayer or by third parties. However, a member should not ignore the implications of information furnished and should make reasonable inquiries if the information furnished appears to be incorrect, incomplete, or inconsistent either on its face or on the basis of other facts known to the member. Further, a member should refer to the taxpayer's returns for one or more prior years whenever feasible.

3.   If the tax law or regulations impose a condition with respect to deductibility or other tax treatment of an item, such as taxpayer maintenance of books and records or substantiating documentation to support the reported deduction or tax treatment, a member should make appropriate inquiries to determine to the member's satisfaction whether such condition has been met.

4.   When preparing a tax return, a member should consider information actually known to that member from the tax return of another taxpayer if the information is relevant to that tax return and its consideration is necessary to properly prepare that tax return. In using such information, a member should consider any limitations imposed by any law or rule relating to confidentiality.

Explanation

5. The preparer's declaration on a tax return often states that the information contained therein is true, correct, and complete to the best of the preparer's knowledge and belief based on all information known by the preparer. This type of reference should be understood to include information furnished by the taxpayer or by third parties to a member in connection with the preparation of the return.

6. The preparer's declaration does not require a member to examine or verify supporting data; a member may rely on information furnished by the taxpayer unless it appears to be incorrect, incomplete, or inconsistent. However, there is a need to determine by inquiry that a specifically required condition, such as maintaining books and records or substantiating documentation, has been satisfied and to obtain information when the material furnished appears to be incorrect, incomplete, or inconsistent. Although a member has certain responsibilities in exercising due diligence in preparing a return, the taxpayer has the ultimate responsibility for the contents of the return. Thus, if the taxpayer presents unsupported data in the form of lists of tax information, such as dividends and interest received, charitable contributions, and medical expenses, such information may be used in the preparation of a tax return without verification unless it appears to be incorrect, incomplete, or inconsistent either on its face or on the basis of other facts known to a member.

7. Even though there is no requirement to examine underlying documentation, a member should encourage the taxpayer to provide supporting data where appropriate. For example, a member should encourage the taxpayer to submit underlying documents for use in tax return preparation to permit full consideration of income and deductions arising from security transactions and from pass-through entities, such as estates, trusts, partnerships, and S corporations.

8. The source of information provided to a member by a taxpayer for use in preparing the return is often a pass-through entity, such as a limited partnership, in which the taxpayer has an interest but is not involved in management. A member may accept the information provided by the pass-through entity without further inquiry, unless there is reason to believe it is incorrect, incomplete, or inconsistent, either on its face or on the basis of other facts known to the member. In some instances, it may be appropriate for a member to advise the taxpayer to ascertain the nature and amount of possible exposure to tax deficiencies, interest, and penalties by taxpayer contact with management of the pass-through entity.

9. A member should make use of a taxpayer's returns for one or more prior years in preparing the current return whenever feasible. Reference to prior returns and discussion of prior-year tax determinations with the taxpayer should provide information to determine the taxpayer's general tax status, avoid the omission or duplication of items, and afford a basis for the treatment of similar or related transactions. As with the examination of information supplied for the current year's return, the extent of comparison of the details of income and deduction between years depends on the particular circumstances.

Statement on Standards for Tax Services No. 4, *Use of Estimates*

Introduction

1.   This statement sets forth the applicable standards for members when using the taxpayer's estimates in the preparation of a tax return. A member may advise on estimates used in the preparation of a tax return, but the taxpayer has the responsibility to provide the estimated data. Appraisals or valuations are not considered estimates for purposes of this statement.

Statement

2.   Unless prohibited by statute or by rule, a member may use the taxpayer's estimates in the preparation of a tax return if it is not practical to obtain exact data and if the member determines that the estimates are reasonable based on the facts and circumstances known to the member. The taxpayer's estimates should be presented in a manner that does not imply greater accuracy than exists.

Explanation

3.   Accounting requires the exercise of professional judgment and, in many instances, the use of approximations based on judgment. The application of such accounting judgments, as long as not in conflict with methods set forth by a taxing authority, is acceptable. These judgments are not estimates within the purview of this statement. For example, a federal income tax regulation provides that if all other conditions for accrual are met, the exact amount of income or expense need not be known or ascertained at year end if the amount can be determined with reasonable accuracy.

4.   When the taxpayer's records do not accurately reflect information related to small expenditures, accuracy in recording some data may be difficult to achieve. Therefore, the use of estimates by a tax-

payer in determining the amount to be deducted for such items may be appropriate.

5.   When records are missing or precise information about a transaction is not available at the time the return must be filed, a member may prepare a tax return using a taxpayer's estimates of the missing data.

6.   Estimated amounts should not be presented in a manner that provides a misleading impression about the degree of factual accuracy.

7.   Specific disclosure that an estimate is used for an item in the return is not generally required; however, such disclosure should be made in unusual circumstances where nondisclosure might mislead the taxing authority regarding the degree of accuracy of the return as a whole. Some examples of unusual circumstances include the following:

a. A taxpayer has died or is ill at the time the return must be filed.

b. A taxpayer has not received a Schedule K-1 for a pass-through entity at the time the tax return is to be filed.

c. There is litigation pending (for example, a bankruptcy proceeding) that bears on the return.

d. Fire, computer failure, or natural disaster has destroyed the relevant records.

Statement on Standards for Tax Services No. 5, Departure From a Position Previously Concluded in an Administrative Proceeding or Court Decision

Introduction

1. This statement sets forth the applicable standards for members in recommending a tax return position that departs from the position determined in an administrative proceeding or in a court decision with respect to the taxpayer's prior return.

2. For purposes of this statement, *administrative proceeding* includes an examination by a taxing authority or an appeals conference relating to a return or a claim for refund.

3. For purposes of this statement, *court decision* means a decision by any court having jurisdiction over tax matters.

Statement

4. The tax return position with respect to an item as determined in an administrative proceeding or court decision does not restrict a member from recommending a different tax position in a later year's return, unless the taxpayer is bound to a specified treatment in the later year, such as by a formal closing agreement. Therefore, the member may recommend a tax return position or prepare or sign a tax return that departs from the treatment of an item as concluded in an administrative proceeding or court decision with respect to a prior return of the taxpayer provided the requirements of Statement on Standards for Tax Services (SSTS) No. 1, *Tax Return Positions*, are satisfied.

Explanation

5.   If an administrative proceeding or court decision has resulted in a determination concerning a specific tax treatment of an item in a prior year's return, a member will usually recommend this same tax treatment in subsequent years. However, departures from consistent treatment may be justified under such circumstances as the following:

a. Taxing authorities tend to act consistently in the disposition of an item that was the subject of a prior administrative proceeding but generally are not bound to do so. Similarly, a taxpayer is not bound to follow the tax treatment of an item as consented to in an earlier administrative proceeding.

b. The determination in the administrative proceeding or the court's decision may have been caused by a lack of documentation. Supporting data for the later year may be appropriate.

c. A taxpayer may have yielded in the administrative proceeding for settlement purposes or not appealed the court decision, even though the position met the standards in SSTS No. 1.

d. Court decisions, rulings, or other authorities that are more favorable to a taxpayer's current position may have developed since the prior administrative proceeding was concluded or the prior court decision was rendered.

6.   The consent in an earlier administrative proceeding and the existence of an unfavorable court decision are factors that the member should consider in evaluating whether the standards in SSTS No. 1 are met.

Statement on Standards for Tax Services No. 6, *Knowledge of Error: Return Preparation and Administrative Proceedings*

Introduction

1.   This statement sets forth the applicable standards for a member who becomes aware of (*a*) an error in a taxpayer's previously filed tax return; (*b*) an error in a return that is the subject of an administrative proceeding, such as an examination by a taxing authority or an appeals conference; or (*c*) a taxpayer's failure to file a required tax return. As used herein, the term *error* includes any position, omission, or method of accounting that, at the time the return is filed, fails to meet the standards set out in Statement on Standards for Tax Services (SSTS) No. 1, *Tax Return Positions*. The term *error* also includes a position taken on a prior year's return that no longer meets these standards due to legislation, judicial decisions, or administrative pronouncements having retroactive effect. However, an error does not include an item that has an insignificant effect on the taxpayer's tax liability. The term *administrative proceeding* does not include a criminal proceeding.

2.   This statement applies whether or not the member prepared or signed the return that contains the error.

3.   Special considerations may apply when a member has been engaged by legal counsel to provide assistance in a matter relating to the counsel's client.

Statement

4.   A member should inform the taxpayer promptly upon becoming aware of an error in a previously filed return, an error in a return that is the subject of an administrative proceeding, or a taxpayer's failure to file a required return. A member also should advise the taxpayer of the potential consequences of the error and recommend the correc-

tive measures to be taken. Such advice and recommendation may be given orally. The member is not allowed to inform the taxing authority without the taxpayer's permission, except when required by law.

5.   If a member is requested to prepare the current year's return and the taxpayer has not taken appropriate action to correct an error in a prior year's return, the member should consider whether to withdraw from preparing the return and whether to continue a professional or employment relationship with the taxpayer. If the member does prepare such current year's return, the member should take reasonable steps to ensure that the error is not repeated.

6.   If a member is representing a taxpayer in an administrative proceeding with respect to a return that contains an error of which the member is aware, the member should request the taxpayer's agreement to disclose the error to the taxing authority. Lacking such agreement, the member should consider whether to withdraw from representing the taxpayer in the administrative proceeding and whether to continue a professional or employment relationship with the taxpayer.

Explanation

7.   While performing services for a taxpayer, a member may become aware of an error in a previously filed return or may become aware that the taxpayer failed to file a required return. The member should advise the taxpayer of the error and the potential consequences, and recommend the measures to be taken. Similarly, when representing the taxpayer before a taxing authority in an administrative proceeding with respect to a return containing an error of which the member is aware, the member should advise the taxpayer to disclose the error to the taxing authority and of the potential consequences of not disclosing the error. Such advice and recommendation may be given orally.

8.   It is the taxpayer's responsibility to decide whether to correct the error. If the taxpayer does not correct an error, a member should consider whether to withdraw from the engagement and whether to continue a professional or employment relationship with the taxpayer. Although recognizing that the taxpayer may not be required by statute to correct an error by filing an amended return, a member should consider whether a taxpayer's decision not to file an amended return

or otherwise correct an error may predict future behavior that might require termination of the relationship.

9.   Once the member has obtained the taxpayer's consent to disclose an error in an administrative proceeding, the disclosure should not be delayed to such a degree that the taxpayer or member might be considered to have failed to act in good faith or to have, in effect, provided misleading information. In any event, disclosure should be made before the conclusion of the administrative proceeding.

10. A conflict between the member's interests and those of the taxpayer may be created by, for example, the potential for violating Code of Professional Conduct Rule 301, *Confidential Client Information* (AICPA, *Professional Standards*, vol. 2, ET sec. 301 par. .01) (relating to the member's confidential client relationship); the tax law and regulations; or laws on privileged communications, as well as by the potential adverse impact on a taxpayer of a member's withdrawal. Therefore, a member should consider consulting with his or her own legal counsel before deciding upon recommendations to the taxpayer and whether to continue a professional or employment relationship with the taxpayer.

11. If a member believes that a taxpayer may face possible exposure to allegations of fraud or other criminal misconduct, the member should advise the taxpayer to consult with an attorney before the taxpayer takes any action.

12. If a member decides to continue a professional or employment relationship with the taxpayer and is requested to prepare a tax return for a year subsequent to that in which the error occurred, the member should take reasonable steps to ensure that the error is not repeated. If the subsequent year's tax return cannot be prepared without perpetuating the error, the member should consider withdrawal from the return preparation. If a member learns that the taxpayer is using an erroneous method of accounting and it is past the due date to request permission to change to a method meeting the standards of SSTS No. 1, the member may sign a tax return for the current year, providing the tax return includes appropriate disclosure of the use of the erroneous method.

13. Whether an error has no more than an insignificant effect on the taxpayer's tax liability is left to the professional judgment of the member based on all the facts and circumstances known to the mem-

ber. In judging whether an erroneous method of accounting has more than an insignificant effect, a member should consider the method's cumulative effect, as well as its effect on the current year's tax return or the tax return that is the subject of the administrative proceeding.

14. If a member becomes aware of the error while performing services for a taxpayer that do not involve tax return preparation or representation in an administrative proceeding, the member's responsibility is to advise the taxpayer of the existence of the error and to recommend that the error be discussed with the taxpayer's tax return preparer. Such recommendation may be given orally.

Statement on Standards for Tax Services No. 7, Form and Content of Advice to Taxpayers

Introduction

1.   This statement sets forth the applicable standards for members concerning certain aspects of providing advice to a taxpayer and considers the circumstances in which a member has a responsibility to communicate with a taxpayer when subsequent developments affect advice previously provided. The statement does not, however, cover a member's responsibilities when the expectation is that the advice rendered is likely to be relied on by parties other than the taxpayer.

Statement

2.   A member should use professional judgment to ensure that tax advice provided to a taxpayer reflects competence and appropriately serves the taxpayer's needs. When communicating tax advice to a taxpayer in writing, a member should comply with relevant taxing authorities' standards, if any, applicable to written tax advice. A member should use professional judgment about any need to document oral advice. A member is not required to follow a standard format when communicating or documenting oral advice.

3.   A member should assume that tax advice provided to a taxpayer will affect the manner in which the matters or transactions considered would be reported or disclosed on the taxpayer's tax returns. Therefore, for tax advice given to a taxpayer, a member should consider, when relevant (*a*) return reporting and disclosure standards applicable to the related tax return position and (*b*) the potential penalty consequences of the return position. In ascertaining applicable return reporting and disclosure standards, a member should follow the standards in Statement on Standards for Tax Services No. 1, *Tax Return Positions*.

4.   A member has no obligation to communicate with a taxpayer when subsequent developments affect advice previously provided

with respect to significant matters, except while assisting a taxpayer in implementing procedures or plans associated with the advice provided or when a member undertakes this obligation by specific agreement.

Explanation

5. Tax advice is recognized as a valuable service provided by members. The form of advice may be oral or written and the subject matter may range from routine to complex. Because the range of advice is so extensive and because advice should meet the specific needs of a taxpayer, neither a standard format nor guidelines for communicating or documenting advice to the taxpayer can be established to cover all situations.

6. Although oral advice may serve a taxpayer's needs appropriately in routine matters or in well-defined areas, written communications are recommended in important, unusual, substantial dollar value, or complicated transactions. The member may use professional judgment about whether, subsequently, to document oral advice.

7. In deciding on the form of advice provided to a taxpayer, a member should exercise professional judgment and should consider such factors as the following:

a. The importance of the transaction and amounts involved

b. The specific or general nature of the taxpayer's inquiry

c. The time available for development and submission of the advice

d. The technical complexity involved

e. The existence of authorities and precedents

f. The tax sophistication of the taxpayer

g. The need to seek other professional advice

h. The type of transaction and whether it is subject to heightened reporting or disclosure requirements

i. The potential penalty consequences of the tax return position for which the advice is rendered

j. Whether any potential applicable penalties can be avoided through disclosure *k.* Whether the member intends for the taxpayer to rely upon the advice to avoid potential penalties

    8. A member may assist a taxpayer in implementing procedures or plans associated with the advice offered. When providing such assistance, the member should review and revise such advice as warranted by new developments and factors affecting the transaction.

    9. Sometimes a member is requested to provide tax advice but does not assist in implementing the plans adopted. Although such developments as legislative or administrative changes or future judicial interpretations may affect the advice previously provided, a member cannot be expected to communicate subsequent developments that affect such advice unless the member undertakes this obligation by specific agreement with the taxpayer.

    10. Taxpayers should be informed that (*a*) the advice reflects professional judgment based upon the member's understanding of the facts, and the law existing as of the date the advice is rendered and (*b*) subsequent developments could affect previously rendered professional advice. Members may use precautionary language to the effect that their advice is based on facts as stated and authorities that are subject to change.

    11. In providing tax advice, a member should be cognizant of applicable confidentiality privileges.

30

These Statements on Standards for Tax Services were unanimously adopted by the assenting votes of the 17 members of the 18-member Tax Executive Committee who participated in the August 6, 2009, Tax Executive Committee meeting.

Tax Executive Committee (2008–2009)

Alan R. Einhorn, *Chair*
Jeffrey R. Hoops, *Immediate Past Chair*
Diane Cornwell
Eve Elgin
Andrew D. Gibson
Cherie J. Hennig
Lawrence W. McKoy
T. Chris Muirhead
Gregory A. Porcaro

Jeffrey A Porter
Roby Sawyers
Christopher J. Sokolowski
Norman S. Solomon
Patricia Thompson
Christine Turgeon
Mark Van Deveer
Richard P. Weber
Brian T. Whitlock

Tax Practice Responsibilities Committee (2008–2009)

Arthur J. Kip Dellinger, Jr., *Chair*
Gregory M. Fowler, *Vice Chair*
Harvey Coustan
Todd C. Craft
Diane D. Fuller
Jan D. Hayden
Andrew M. Mattson

Douglas Milford
Trenton S. Olmstead
Gerald W. Padwe
James W. Sansone
James H. Schlesser
Lisa G. Workman

SSTS Revisions Task Force

Conrad M. Davis, *Cochair*
Jay M. Levine, *Cochair*
Timothy J. Burke, Jr.
Arthur J. Kip Dellinger, Jr.
Eve Elgin
Jeffrey Frishman

Gregory M. Fowler
John C. Gardner
Keith R. Lee
Mark N. Schneider
Gerard H. Schreiber, Jr.
J. Edward Swails

AICPA Staff

Thomas P. Ochsenschlager
Vice President—Taxation
Tax Division

Edward S. Karl
Director
Tax Division

Jean E. Trompeter
Technical Manager
Tax Division

Note: *Statements on Standards for Tax Services are issued by the Tax Executive Committee, the senior technical body of the AICPA designated to promulgate standards of tax practice. Rule 201, General Standards, and Rule 202, Compliance With Standards, of the Code of Professional Conduct (AICPA, Professional Standards, vol. 2, ET sec. 201 par. .01 and ET sec. 202 par. .01), require compliance with these standards.*

AICPA Member and
Public Information:
aicpa.org

AICPA Online Store:
cpa2biz.com

065015PDF

Appendix D

INTERPRETATION NO. 1-2, "TAX PLANNING," OF SSTSs NO. 1, *TAX RETURN POSITIONS*[1]

October 2003

Statement on Standards for Tax Services

Issued by the Tax Executive Committee

Interpretation No. 1-2, "Tax Planning," of Statement on Standards for Tax Services No. 1, *Tax Return Positions*

Notice to Readers

The Statements on Standards for Tax Services (SSTSs) and Interpretations, promulgated by the Tax Executive Committee, reflect the AICPA's standards of tax practice and delineate members' responsibilities to taxpayers, the public, the government, and the profession. The Statements are intended to be part of an ongoing process that may require changes to and Interpretations of current SSTSs in recognition of the accelerating rate of change in tax laws and the continued importance of tax practice to members. Interpretation No. 1-2 was approved by the Tax Executive Committee on August 21, 2003; its effective date is December 31, 2003.

The SSTSs have been written in as simple and objective a manner as possible. However, by their nature, ethical standards provide for an appropriate range of behavior that recognizes the need for Interpretations to meet a broad range of personal and professional situations. The SSTSs recognize this need by, in some sections, providing relatively subjective rules and by leaving certain terms undefined. These terms and concepts are generally rooted in tax concepts, and therefore should be readily understood by tax practitioners. It is, therefore, recognized that the enforcement of these rules, as part of the AICPA's Code of Professional Conduct Rule 201, *General Standards*, and Rule 202, *Compliance With Standards*, will be undertaken with flexibility in mind and handled on a case-by-case basis. Members are expected to comply with them.

Contents

Background

1.   Statements on Standards for Tax Services (SSTSs) are enforceable standards that govern the conduct of members of the AICPA in tax practice. A significant area of many members' tax practices involves assisting taxpayers in tax planning. Two of the eight SSTSs issued as of the date of this Interpretation's release directly set forth standards that affect the most common activities in tax planning. Several other SSTSs set forth standards related to specific factual situations that may arise while a member is assisting a taxpayer in tax planning. The two SSTSs that are most typically relevant to tax planning are SSTS No. 1, *Tax Return Positions* (AICPA, *Professional Standards*, vol. 2, TS sec. 100), including Interpretation No. 1-1, "Realistic Possibility Standard" (AICPA, *Professional Standards*, vol. 2, TS sec. 9100), and SSTS No. 8, *Form and Content of Advice to Taxpayers* (AICPA, *Professional Standards*, vol. 2, TS sec. 800).

2.   Taxing authorities, courts, the AICPA, and other professional organizations have struggled with defining and regulating *tax shelters* and *abusive transactions*. Crucial to the debate is the difficulty of clearly distinguishing between transactions that are abusive and transactions that are legitimate. At the same time, it must be recognized that taxpayers have a legitimate interest in arranging their affairs so as to pay no more than the taxes they owe. It must be recognized that tax professionals, including members, have a role to play in advancing these efforts.

3.   This Interpretation is part of the AICPA's continuing efforts at self-regulation of its members in tax practice. It has its origins in the AICPA's desire to provide adequate guidance to its members when providing services in connection with tax planning. The Interpretation does not change or elevate any level of conduct prescribed by any standard. Its goal is to clarify existing standards. It was determined that there was a compelling need for a comprehensive Interpretation of a member's responsibilities in connection with *tax planning*, with the recognition that such guidance would clarify how those standards would apply across the spectrum of tax planning, including those situations involving *tax shelters*, regardless of how that term is defined.

General Interpretation

4.   The realistic possibility standard (see SSTS No. 1, TS sec. 100.02(a), and Interpretation No. 1-1) applies to a member when providing professional services that involve *tax planning*. A member may still recommend a nonfrivolous position provided that the member recommends appropriate disclosure (see SSTS No. 1, TS sec. 100.02(c)).

5.   For purposes of this Interpretation, *tax planning* includes, both with respect to prospective and completed transactions, recommending or expressing an opinion (whether written or oral) on (*a*) a tax return position or (*b*) a specific tax plan developed by the member, the taxpayer, or a third party.

6.   When issuing an opinion to reflect the results of the tax planning service, a member should do all of the following:

- Establish the relevant background facts.
- Consider the reasonableness of the assumptions and representations.
- Apply the pertinent authorities to the relevant facts.
- Consider the business purpose and economic substance of the transaction, if relevant to the tax consequences of the transaction.
- Arrive at a conclusion supported by the authorities.

7.   In assisting a taxpayer in a tax planning transaction in which the taxpayer has obtained an opinion from a third party, and the taxpayer is looking to the member for an evaluation of the opinion, the member should be satisfied as to the source, relevance, and persuasiveness of the opinion, which would include considering whether the opinion indicates the third party did all of the following:

- Established the relevant background facts
- Considered the reasonableness of the assumptions and representations
- Applied the pertinent authorities to the relevant facts
- Considered the business purpose and economic substance of the transaction, if relevant to the tax consequences of the transaction
- Arrived at a conclusion supported by the authorities

8.   In conducting the due diligence necessary to establish the relevant background facts, the member should consider whether it is appropriate to rely on an assumption concerning facts in lieu of either other procedures to support the advice or a representation from the taxpayer or another person. A member should also consider whether the member's tax advice will be communicated to third parties, particularly if those third parties may not be knowledgeable or may not be receiving independent tax advice with respect to a transaction.

9.   In tax planning, members often rely on assumptions and representations. Although such reliance is often necessary, the member must take care to assess whether such assumptions and representations are reasonable. In deciding whether an assumption or representation is reasonable, the member should consider its source and consistency with other information known to the member. For example, depending on the circumstances, it may be reasonable for a member to rely on a representation made by the taxpayer, but not on a representation made by a person who is selling or otherwise promoting the transaction to the taxpayer.

10.   When engaged in tax planning, the member should understand the business purpose and economic substance of the transaction when relevant to the tax consequences. If a transaction has been proposed by a party other than the taxpayer, the member should consider whether the assumptions made by the third party are consistent with the facts of the taxpayer's situation. If written advice is to be rendered concerning a transaction, the business purpose for the transaction generally should be described. If the business reasons are relevant to the tax consequences, it is insufficient to merely assume that a transaction is entered into for valid business reasons without specifying what those reasons are.

11.   The scope of the engagement should be appropriately determined. A member should be diligent in applying such procedures as are appropriate under the circumstances to understand and evaluate the entire transaction. The specific procedures to be performed in this regard will vary with the circumstances and the scope of the engagement.

Specific Illustrations

12.   The following illustrations address general fact patterns. Accordingly, the application of the guidance discussed in the "General Interpretation" section to variations in such general facts or

to particular facts or circumstances may lead to different conclusions. In each illustration, there is no authority other than that indicated.

13.   *Illustration 1*. The relevant tax code imposes penalties on substantial underpayments that are not associated with tax shelters as defined in such code unless the associated positions are supported by substantial authority.

14.   *Conclusion*. In assisting the taxpayer in tax planning in which any associated underpayment would be substantial, the member should inform the taxpayer of the penalty risks associated with the tax return position recommended with respect to any plan under consideration that satisfies the realistic possibility of success standard, but does not possess sufficient authority to satisfy the substantial authority standard.

15.   *Illustration 2*. The relevant tax code imposes penalties on tax shelters, as defined in such code, unless the taxpayer concludes that a position taken on a tax return associated with such a tax shelter is, more likely than not, the correct position.

16.   *Conclusion*. In assisting the taxpayer in tax planning, the member should inform the taxpayer of the penalty risks associated with the tax return position recommended with respect to any plan under consideration that satisfies the realistic possibility of success standard, but does not possess sufficient authority to satisfy the more likely than not standard.

17. *Illustration 3*. The relevant tax regulation provides that the details of (or certain information regarding) a specific transaction are required to be attached to the tax return, regardless of the support for the associated tax return position (for example, even if there is substantial authority or a higher level of comfort for the position). While preparing the taxpayer's return for the year, the member is aware that an attachment is required.

18. *Conclusion*. In general, if the taxpayer agrees to include the attachment required by the regulation, the member may sign the return if the member concludes the associated tax return position satisfies the realistic possibility standard. However, if the taxpayer refuses to include the attachment, the member should not sign the return, unless the member concludes the associated tax return position satisfies the realistic possibility standard and there are reasonable grounds for the taxpayer's position with respect to the attachment. In

this regard, the member should consider SSTS No. 2, *Answers to Questions on Returns* (AICPA, *Professional Standards*, vol. 2, TS sec. 200.01 and .05), which provides that the term *questions*, as used in the standard, "includes requests for information on the return, in the instructions, or in the regulations, whether or not stated in the form of a question," and that a "member should not omit an answer merely because it might prove disadvantageous to a taxpayer."

19. *Illustration 4.* The relevant tax regulations provide that the details of certain potentially abusive transactions that are designated as "listed transactions" are required to be disclosed in attachments to tax returns, regardless of the support for the associated tax return position (for example, even if there is substantial authority or a higher level of support for the position). Under the regulations, if a listed transaction is not disclosed as required, the taxpayer will have additional penalty risks. While researching the tax consequences of a proposed transaction, a member concludes that the transaction is a listed transaction.

20. *Conclusion.* Notwithstanding the member's conclusion that the transaction is a listed transaction, the member may still recommend a tax return position with respect to the transaction if he or she concludes that the proposed tax return position satisfies the realistic possibility standard. However, the member should inform the taxpayer of the enhanced disclosure requirements of listed transactions and the additional penalty risks for nondisclosure.

21. *Illustration 5.* The same regulations apply as in Illustration 4. The member first becomes aware that a taxpayer entered into a transaction while preparing the taxpayer's return for the year of the transaction. While researching the tax consequences of the transaction, the member concludes that the taxpayer's transaction is a listed transaction.

22. *Conclusion.* The member should inform the taxpayer of the enhanced disclosure requirement and the additional penalty risks for nondisclosure. If the taxpayer agrees to make the disclosure required by the regulation, the member may sign the return if the member concludes the associated tax return position satisfies the realistic possibility standard. Reasonable grounds for nondisclosure (see the conclusion to Illustration 3) generally are not present for a listed transaction. The member should not sign the return if the transaction is not disclosed. If the member is a nonsigning preparer of the return, the member should recommend that the taxpayer disclose the transaction.

23. *Illustration 6.* The same regulations apply as in Illustration 4. The member first becomes aware that a taxpayer entered into a transaction while preparing the taxpayer's return for the year of the transaction. While researching the tax consequences of the transaction, the member concludes that there is uncertainty about whether the taxpayer's transaction is a listed transaction.

24. *Conclusion.* The member should inform the taxpayer of the enhanced disclosure requirement and the additional penalty risks for nondisclosure. If the taxpayer agrees to make the disclosure required by the relevant regulation, the member may sign the return if the member concludes the associated tax return position satisfies the realistic possibility standard. If the taxpayer does not want to disclose the transaction because of the uncertainty about whether it is a listed transaction, the member may sign the return if the member concludes the associated tax return position satisfies the realistic possibility standard and there are reasonable grounds for the taxpayer's position with regard to nondisclosure. In this regard, the member should consider SSTS No. 2, TS sec. 200.04, which indicates that the degree of uncertainty regarding the meaning of a question on a return may affect whether there are reasonable grounds for not responding to the question.

25. *Illustration 7.* A member advises a taxpayer concerning the tax consequences of a transaction involving a loan from a U.S. bank. In the process of reviewing documents associated with the proposed transaction, the member uncovers a reference to a deposit that a wholly owned foreign subsidiary of the taxpayer will make with an overseas branch of the U.S. bank. The transaction documents appear to indicate that this deposit is linked to the U.S. bank's issuance of the loan.

26. *Conclusion.* The member should consider the effect, if any, of the deposit in advising the taxpayer about the tax consequences of the proposed transaction.

27. *Illustration 8.* Under the relevant tax law, the tax consequences of a leasing transaction depend on whether the property to be leased is reasonably expected to have a residual value of 15 percent of its value at the beginning of the lease. The member has relied on a taxpayer's instruction to use a particular assumption concerning the residual value.

28. *Conclusion.* Such reliance on the taxpayer's instructions may be appropriate if the assumption is supported by the expertise of the taxpayer, by the member's review of information provided by

the taxpayer or a third party, or through the member's own knowledge or analysis.

29. *Illustration 9.* A member is assisting a taxpayer with evaluating a proposed equipment leasing transaction in which the estimated residual value of the equipment at the end of the lease term is critical to the tax consequences of the lease. The broker arranging the leasing transaction has prepared an analysis that sets out an explicit assumption concerning the equipment's estimated residual value.

30. *Conclusion.* The member should consider whether it is appropriate to rely on the broker's assumption concerning the estimated residual value of the equipment instead of obtaining a representation from the broker concerning estimated residual value or performing other procedures to validate the amount to be used as an estimate of residual value in connection with the member's advice. In considering the appropriateness of the broker's assumption, the member should consider, for example, factors such as the broker's experience in the area, the broker's methodology, and whether alternative sources of information are reasonably available.

31. *Illustration 10.* The tax consequences of a particular reorganization depend, in part, on the majority shareholder of a corporation not disposing of any stock received in the reorganization pursuant to a prearranged agreement to dispose of the stock.

32. *Conclusion.* The member should consider whether it is appropriate in rendering tax advice to assume that such a disposition will not occur or whether, under the circumstances, it is appropriate to request a written representation of the shareholder's intent concerning disposition as a condition to issuing an opinion on the reorganization.

33. *Illustration 11.* A taxpayer is considering a proposed transaction. The taxpayer and the taxpayer's attorney advise the member that the member is responsible for advising the taxpayer on the tax consequences of the transaction.

34. *Conclusion.* In addition to complying with the requirements of paragraph 6, the member generally should review all relevant draft transaction documents in formulating the member's tax advice relating to the transaction.

35. *Illustration 12.* A member is responsible for advising a taxpayer on the tax consequences of the taxpayer's estate plan.

36. *Conclusion*. Under the circumstances, the member should review the will and all other relevant documents to assess whether there appear to be any tax issues raised by the formulation or implementation of the estate plan.

37. *Illustration 13*. A member is assisting a taxpayer in connection with a proposed transaction that has been recommended by an investment bank. To support its recommendation, the investment bank offers a law firm's opinion on the tax consequences. The member reads the opinion, and notes that it is based on a hypothetical statement of facts rather than the taxpayer's facts.

38. *Conclusion*. The member may rely on the law firm's opinion when determining whether the realistic possibility standard has been satisfied with respect to the tax consequences of the hypothetical transaction if the member is satisfied about the source, relevance, and persuasiveness of the opinion. However, the member should be diligent in taking such steps as are appropriate under the circumstances to understand and evaluate the transaction as it applies to the taxpayer's specific situation by:

- Establishing the relevant background facts
- Considering the reasonableness of the assumptions and representations
- Applying the pertinent authorities to the relevant facts
- Considering the business purpose and economic substance of the transaction, if relevant to the tax consequences of the transaction (Mere reliance on a representation that there is business purpose or economic substance is generally insufficient.)
- Arriving at a conclusion supported by the authorities

39. *Illustration 14*. The facts are the same as in Illustration 13 except the member also notes that the law firm that prepared the opinion is one that has a reputation as being knowledgeable about the tax issues associated with the proposed transaction.

40. *Conclusion*. The conclusion is the same as the conclusion to Illustration 13, notwithstanding the expertise of the law firm.

41. *Illustration 15*. A member is assisting a taxpayer in connection with a proposed transaction that has been recommended by an investment bank. To support that recommendation, the investment bank offers a law firm's opinion about the tax consequences. The member

reads the opinion, and notes that (unlike the opinions described in Illustrations 13 and 14), it is carefully tailored to the taxpayer's facts.

42. *Conclusion*. The member may rely on the opinion when determining whether the realistic possibility standard has been met with respect to the taxpayer's participation in the transaction if the member is satisfied about the source, relevance, and persuasiveness of the opinion. In making that determination, the member should consider whether the opinion indicates the law firm did all of the following:

- Established the relevant background facts
- Considered the reasonableness of the assumptions and representations
- Applied the pertinent authorities to the relevant facts
- Considered the business purpose and economic substance of the transaction, if relevant to the tax consequences of the transaction (Mere reliance on a representation that there is business purpose or economic substance is generally insufficient.)
- Arrived at a conclusion supported by the authorities

43. *Illustration 16*. The facts are the same as in Illustration 15, except the member also notes that the law firm that prepared the opinion is one that has a reputation of being knowledgeable about the tax issues associated with the proposed transaction.

44. *Conclusion*. The conclusion is the same as the conclusion to Illustration 15, notwithstanding the expertise of the law firm.

45. *Illustration 17*. A member is assisting a taxpayer with year-end planning in connection with the taxpayer's proposed contribution of stock in a closely held corporation to a charitable organization. The taxpayer instructs the member to calculate the anticipated tax liability assuming a contribution of 10,000 shares to a tax-exempt organization assuming the stock has a fair market value of $100 per share. The member is aware that on the taxpayer's gift tax returns for the prior year, the taxpayer indicated that her stock in the corporation was worth $50 per share.

46. *Conclusion*. The member's calculation of the anticipated tax liability is subject to the general interpretations described in paragraphs 8 and 9. Accordingly, even though this potentially may be a case in which the value of the stock substantially appreciated during the year, the member should consider the reasonableness of the

assumption and consistency with other information known to the member in connection with preparing the projection. The member should consider whether to document discussions concerning the increase in value of the stock with the taxpayer.

47. *Illustration 18.* The tax consequences to Target Corporation's shareholders of an acquisition turn in part on Acquiring Corporation's continuance of the trade or business of Target Corporation for some time after the acquisition. The member is preparing a tax opinion addressed to Target's shareholders. A colleague has drafted a tax opinion for the member's review. That opinion makes an explicit assumption that Acquiring will continue Target's business for two years following the acquisition.

48. *Conclusion.* In conducting the due diligence necessary to establish the relevant background facts, the member should consider whether it is appropriate to rely on an assumption concerning facts in lieu of a representation from another person. In this case, the member should make reasonable efforts to obtain a representation from Acquiring Corporation concerning its plan to continue Target's business and further consider whether to request a written representation to that effect.

49. *Illustration 19.* The member receives a telephone call from a taxpayer who is the sole shareholder of a corporation. The taxpayer indicates that he is thinking about exchanging his stock in the corporation for stock in a publicly traded business. During the call, the member explains how the transaction should be structured so it will qualify as a tax-free acquisition.

50. *Conclusion.* Although oral advice may serve a taxpayer's needs appropriately in routine matters or in well-defined areas, written communications are recommended in important, unusual, or complicated transactions. The member should use professional judgment about the need to document oral advice.

51. *Illustration 20.* The member receives a telephone call from a taxpayer who wants to know whether he or she should lease or purchase a car. During the call, the member explains how the arrangement should be structured so as to help achieve the taxpayer's objectives.

52. *Conclusion.* In this situation, the member's response is in conformity with this Interpretation in view of the routine nature of the inquiry and the well-defined tax issues. However, the member should evaluate whether other considerations, such as avoiding misunderstanding with the taxpayer, suggest that the conversation should be documented.

This Interpretation was adopted by the assenting votes of the eighteen voting members of the nineteen-member Tax Executive Committee.

Tax Executive Committee (2002-2003)

Robert A. Zarzar, *Chair*
Pamela J. Pecarich, *IP Chair*
Steven K. Bentley
Barbara A. Bond
Mark H. Ely
Lisa C. Germano
Ronald B. Hegt
Kenneth H. Heller
Jeffrey R. Hoops
Nancy K. Hyde

Annette Nellen
Thomas P. Ochsenschlager
Robert A. Petersen
Thomas J. Purcell, III
James W. Sansone
C. Clinton Stretch
Judyth A. Swingen
William A. Tate
James P. Whitson

Tax Practice Responsibilities Committee (2002-2003)

Dan L. Mendelson, *Chair*
J. Edward Swails, *Vice Chair*
Lawrence H. Carleton
Conrad M. Davis
Alan R. Einhorn
Eve Elgin
John C. Gardner

Stuart Kessler
Dori Laskin
Robin C. Makar
Christine K. Peterson
Michael J. Predhomme
Joseph F. Scutellaro
Thomas G. Tierney

SSTS Tax Shelter Task Force

Michael E. Mares, *Chair*
Eve Elgin
John C. Gardner
Ronald S. Katch

William C. Potter
J. Edward Swails
Claude R. Wilson, Jr.

AICPA Staff

Gerald W. Padwe
Vice President
Taxation

Edward S. Karl
Director
Taxation

Benson S. Goldstein
Technical Manager
Taxation

Note: *Statements on Standards for Tax Services are issued by the Tax Executive Committee, the senior technical body of the Institute designated to promulgate standards of tax practice. Rules 201 and 202 of the Institute's Code of Professional Conduct require compliance with these standards.*

Appendix E

OFFICE OF PROFESSIONAL RESPONSIBILITY GUIDE TO SANCTIONS

INTRODUCTION

This Guide to Sanctions is included as an Exhibit to Internal Revenue Manual _____. The Guide represents violations of 31 C.F.R. Part 10, revised as of September 26, 2007, (Circular 230), and a range of suggested reasonable sanctions. It is not intended to be an exhaustive listing of all offenses. The facts and circumstances of each case must be considered. Progressive suspension terms, up to and including disbarment, are based on individual mitigating and/ or aggravating factors. The sanctions are graduated based upon these factors as set forth below, the number of violations, and current fitness to practice.

SANCTION AUTHORITY

Under 31 U.S.C. § 330, the Secretary of the Treasury may . . .

regulate the practice of representatives of persons before the Department of the Treasury; and . . .

after notice and opportunity for a proceeding, the Secretary may suspend or disbar from practice before the Department, or censure, a representative who—

    (1)   is incompetent;

    (2)   is disreputable;

    (3)   violates regulations prescribed under this section; or

    (4)   with intent to defraud, willfully and knowingly misleads or threatens the person being represented or a prospective person to be represented.

The sanction authority is designed to correct misconduct. The proposed remedial sanction in each case must be fair, equitable, impartial, and should not be to punish but to correct and motivate the individual to adhere to his duties under Circular 230.

CHOOSING AN APPROPRIATE SANCTION UNDER THESE GUIDELINES

In considering whether corrective sanction is warranted, OPR will review and analyze all the evidence of record.

Choosing a corrective sanction that is reasonable and appropriate for the circumstances involved is extremely important. All relevant factors must be given careful consideration. This document serves as a guide for determining the proper corrective sanction, and is not intended to establish a rigid standard or to imply that a greater or lesser corrective sanction is inappropriate.

A corrective sanction that is below the range indicated could be appropriate where there are compelling mitigating factors.

A corrective sanction that is above the range indicated could be appropriate for particularly egregious misconduct or for cases where there are significant aggravating factors. Even for offenses where disbarment is not listed, disbarment for a first offense is not precluded.

This guide may be deviated from depending on the individual circumstances that may be involved. Each case will be considered individually and dealt with on its merits. Deviations from the guideline will be documented in the file. Mitigating factors, set forth below, must be considered when proposing and deciding disciplinary and adverse sanctions. Multiple offenses, offenses which violate more than one section of Circular 230 and repeated offenses normally will be grounds for a more severe sanction than is warranted for a single offense.

In general, a reprimand or censure is appropriate where that sanction is all that is necessary to correct the behavior. Where the determination of suspension is 6 months or less, reprimand or censure may be appropriate. Suspensions up to 24 months are appropriate where a suspension is necessary to bring home to the practitioner the severity of his or her violation of Circular 230. Suspensions in excess of 24 months are appropriate where the misconduct indicates that the practitioner may be perpetrating an on-going harm to the taxpaying community or where the misconduct, for instance, multiple instances of violations, indicates a current lack of fitness to practice that would not be rectified by a shorter suspension. The suggested suspensions are for each individual violation. Disbarment will be sought for any violation where the determination of suspension is at least 5 years.

These Guidelines are effective for settlements occurring after OPR has finalized its investigation.

MITIGATING AND AGGRAVATING FACTORS FOR DETERMINING THE APPROPRIATE SANCTION

- Not all of the following factors apply in every case and not all factors will be given equal weight. Before deciding upon a corrective sanction, OPR will consider the relevant factors, given the circumstances of each individual case, and strike an appropriate balance. The list of factors is neither meant to be exhaustive nor intended to be applied mechanically, and will be viewed in the context of the nature and severity of the violation at issue.

Mitigating Factors

1. For tax non-compliance cases, correction of the violation before contact with the IRS.
2. For tax non-compliance cases, correction of the violation before contact with OPR.
3. For tax non-compliance cases, correction initiated within a reasonably short period after contact by OPR.
4. Illness, incapacitation, or personal hardships directly correlating to the action or inaction violating Circular 230.
5. Illness, incapacitation or personal hardships of the family or others close to the practitioner directly correlating to the action or inaction violating Circular 230.

6. Personal or professional financial distress correlating to non-payment of taxes, but not non-payment of form 941 employment tax obligations.

7. Extrinsic circumstances such as natural disasters directly correlating to the action or inaction violating Circular 230

8. Recognition of action or inaction violating Circular 230 and commitment to future compliance.

9. For firms, commitment to establishing internal controls to prevent recurrences of the violation.

10. Preventative measures in effect prior to the misconduct and/ or measures put into place after the misconduct to prevent future violations.

11. Age of allegations.

Aggravating Factors

1. Failure to respond to OPR contact.

2. For tax non-compliance cases, failure to correct the issue after contact from the IRS.

3. For tax non-compliance cases, failure to correct after contact by OPR.

4. For tax non-compliance cases, multiple tax issues related to noncompliance on multiple types of forms in the same tax period, including penalties.

5. For tax non-compliance cases, sum of money at issue.

6. Motive, especially those indicating personal gain.

7. Pattern of action or inaction violating Circular 230.

8. Assertion of legal arguments previously ruled frivolous by courts of law.

9. Confrontational behavior outside the bounds of zealous defense.

10. Previous incidents of violation of Circular 230.

11. The number of offenses (See Note).

12. Failure to understand or recognize that actions constituted a violation of Circular 230.

13. Negative effect on tax administration.

OFFENSE	CIRCULAR 230 OFFENSE	RANGE OF SUSPENSION
If a form 1040 is late filed at time of OPR contact	Section 10.51(a)(6)	Then 2 to 4 months for each form 1040. If a form 1040 has or had a balance past due and/or penalties then 4 months for each form late filed 1040 with a past due balance, but no increase where financial hardship has affected the ability to pay.
If a form 1040 is non-filed at time of OPR contact	Section 10.51(a)(6)	Then 4 to 6 months for each non-filed form 1040. If a form 1040 has or had a balance past due and/or penalties then 6 months for each non-filed form 1040 with a balance, but no increase where financial hardship has affected ability to pay.
If a form 941 is filed late at time of contact	Section 10.51(a)(6)	Then 2 months to 4 months for each form 941 late filed. If a late filed form 941 has or had a balance past due and/or penalties then 4 months for each form 941 late filed, BUT NO consideration is made of financial hardship or ability to pay.
If a form 941 is non-filed at time of OPR contact	Section 10.51(a)(6)	Then 4 to 6 months for each form 941 non-filed. If a non-filed form 941 has or had a balance past due and/or penalties then 6 months for each form 941 non-filed, BUT NO consideration is made of financial hardship or ability to pay.
If a form 940 is late-filed at time of OPR contact	Section 10.51(a)(6)	Then 1 month to 2 months for each form 940 late-filed. If a form 940 has or had a balance due then 2 months for each late-filed form 940, but no increase where financial hardship has affected ability to pay.
If a form 940 is non-filed at time of OPR contact	Section 10.51(a)(6)	Then 2 months to 4 months for each form 940 non-filed. If a form 940 has or had a balance due then 4 months for each late-filed form 940, but no increase where financial hardship has affected the ability to pay.

Note: For late filed or non-filed form 1040's or form 940's, if 4 or more years are involved, multiply the base determination for those late filed or non-filed 1040's or 940's by 2. It is within the discretion of the enforcement attorney to not apply the multiplier where there is mitigation directly correlating to charged years.

For late filed or non-filed form 941's, if 8 or more quarters are involved, multiply the base determination for those late filed or non-filed 941's by 2. It is within the discretion of the enforcement attorney to not apply the multiplier where there is mitigation for each of the charged years.

Examples:

1. H, a CPA, has a practice which consists of preparation of returns for individuals and businesses. H filed her 2004 and 2005 form 1040's one year past the filing deadline and requested no extensions. Because she does not represent before the Service, OPR will close as lacking jurisdiction as she is not a Circular 230 practitioner; however, OPR may make a referral to IRS Examination.

2. Q is a Circular 230 Practitioner. Q has a practice which includes preparation of returns and representation before the Service for individuals. Q filed his 2004 and 2005 form 1040's one year past the filing deadline and requested no extension. Q made all payments on all taxes due and is due a refund. Q responded promptly to OPR's inquiry but offered no explanations for his lapses. Q has never been sanctioned by OPR before.

   For late filed 1040 returns at the time of OPR contact, the suggested sanction range is 2–4 months. As there are no mitigating or aggravating factors, the suggested sanction falls in the middle at 3 months. Thus, for 2 late filed form 1040's the total suggested suspension is 6 months (3 months × 2 years late filing). Note — the evidentiary standard at hearing for suspensions of less than 6 months is "preponderance of the evidence." For suspensions of 6 months or more, the standard is "clear and convincing evidence." See Cir. 230 § 10.76.

3. X is a Circular 230 Practitioner. X has a practice which includes tax planning and representation before the Service for individuals and businesses. Although X received extensions for 2004, 2005, and 2006, X filed his form 1040's for those three years one year past the extension and has not filed his first two quarters of his 941's due in 2005. X did make payments on all taxes due and is due a refund. X responded promptly to the OPR inquiry and indicated that in early 2005 X's wife filed for divorce and they underwent a contentious custody dispute. X also submits substantiating medical documentation that in early 2006 he ruptured a disc in his back that required surgery had a long recuperation. X has never been sanctioned by OPR.

   X has offered mitigating personal and health circumstances for the late-filing of his 2004 and 2005 form 1040's and for the first two quarters of form 941's due in 2005. The range for a 1040 late-filed at time of OPR contact is 2–4 months. Due to the mitigating factor of personal and health circumstances, 2 months is the appropriate range for the late filings for 2004 and 2005 each. For the 2006 late filed form 1040, there are no mitigating or aggravating factors, so the suggested suspension falls in the middle range of 3 months. Thus, for the late filed form 1040's the suggested total sanction is 7 months (2 months × 2 years late filing with mitigating factors + 3 months × 1 year late filing with no mitigating or aggravating factors). For the two 941's the range of sanctions for non-filed 941's at time of OPR contact is 4–6 months for each violation. Due to the mitigating factor of personal circumstances, 4 months is the appropriate sanction. The suggested suspension for the non-filed 941's is 8 months (4 months × 2 quarters of non-filing with mitigating factors). The total recommended sanction is 15 months.

4. Z is a Circular 230 Practitioner. Z has a practice which includes preparation of individual tax returns and representation before the Service. Although Z received extensions for 2005, 2006, and 2007, she has failed to file her form 1040's for those three years and has not filed her first two quarters of her 941s due in 2006. Z did make payments on all taxes due and is due a refund. Z has never been sanctioned by OPR. Upon contact by OPR, Z becomes is confrontational beyond the bounds of an appropriate defense and asserts that OPR has no authority over her. Z states that she was so busy with her booming business that she had no time to attend to her own tax matters. She states that she will get the filings done when she gets to them.

    Z's booming business is not a mitigating factor for the non-filings. In fact, Z's conduct indicates that she fails to understand or recognize that her actions constituted a violation of Circular 230. As such it is an aggravating factor. The suggested range for nonfiled 1040's at the time of contact is 4–6 months. The suggested sanction for Z's non-filed 1040's is 18 months (6 months × 3 years non-filing with aggravating factors). The suggested range for nonfiled 941's is 4–6 months; accordingly, the suggested sanction for Z's non-filed 941's is 12 months (6 months × 2 quarters non-filing with aggravating factors). The total suggested sanction is 30 months suspension.

5. Y is a Circular 230 Practitioner. Y has a practice which includes preparation of individual and entity tax returns, tax planning and representation before the Service for individuals and businesses. Although Y received extensions for her 2005 and 2006 1040's, she filed 2005 in January 2007 and had not filed 2006 until OPR contacted her, whereupon she immediately filed. Y responded promptly to the OPR inquiry and indicated that in September 2006, while she was already on extension, a local river flooded her basement office. She has provided insurance documentation verifying the flood. She was unable to recreate her documents in time to meet the extension deadline but filed as soon as she could. Moreover, she has always paid her taxes timely and has never been the subject of an OPR investigation. Y does not address the circumstances behind the late filing of her 2006 form 1040.

    Y has offered mitigating circumstances for the late filing of her 2005 return that is sufficient to allow OPR to go below the minimum suggested guideline of 2 months for a form 1040 late filed at time of OPR contact, and impose no suspension for that late filing. X has not provided sufficient mitigating evidence for the late filed 2006 return. The range for a 1040 non-filed at time of contact is 4–6 months. The recommended sanction would be 4 months suspension as she filed promptly upon contact (4 months × one year non-filing with mitigating factors.)

Appendix F

UNITED STATES TAX COURT RULES 200, 201, AND 202

TITLE XX

PRACTICE BEFORE THE COURT

RULE 200. ADMISSION TO PRACTICE AND PERIODIC REGISTRATION FEE[1]

(a) Qualifications: (1) *General:* An applicant for admission to practice before the Court must establish to the satisfaction of the Court that the applicant is of good moral and professional character and possesses the requisite qualifications to provide competent representation before the Court. In addition, the applicant must satisfy the other requirements of this Rule. If the applicant fails to satisfy the requirements of this Rule, then the Court may deny such applicant admission to practice before the Court.

(2) *Attorney Applicants:* An applicant who is an attorney at law must, as a condition of being admitted to practice, file with the Admissions Clerk at the address listed in paragraph (b) of this Rule a completed application accompanied by a fee to be established by the Court, see Appendix II, and a current certificate from the Clerk of the appropriate court, showing that the applicant has been admitted to practice before and is a member in good standing of the Bar of the Supreme Court of the United States, or of the highest or appropriate court of any State or of the District of Columbia, or any commonwealth, territory, or possession of the United States. A current court certificate is one executed within 90 calendar days preceding the date of the filing of the application.

(3) *Nonattorney Applicants:* An applicant who is not an attorney at law must, as a condition of being admitted to practice, file with the Admissions Clerk at the address listed in paragraph (b) of this Rule, a completed application accompanied by a fee to be established by the Court. See Appendix II. In addition, such an applicant must, as a condition of being admitted to practice, satisfy the Court, by means of a written examination given by the Court, that the applicant possesses the requisite qualifications to provide competent representation before the Court. Written examinations for applicants who are not attorneys at

---

[1] The amendments are effective as of September 20, 2005.

343

law will be held no less often than every 2 years. By public announcement at least 6 months prior to the date of each examination, the Court will announce the date and the time of such examination. The Court will notify each applicant, whose application for admission is in order, of the time and the place at which the applicant is to be present for such examination, and the applicant must present that notice to the examiner as authority for taking such examination.

(b) Applications for Admission: An application for admission to practice before the Court must be on the form provided by the Court. Application forms and other necessary information will be furnished upon request addressed to the Admissions Clerk, United States Tax Court, 400 Second St., N.W., Washington, D.C. 20217. As to forms of payment for application fees, see Rule 11.

(c) Sponsorship: An applicant for admission by examination must be sponsored by at least two persons theretofore admitted to practice before this Court, and each sponsor must send a letter of recommendation directly to the Admissions Clerk at the address listed in paragraph (b) of this Rule, where it will be treated as a confidential communication. The sponsor shall send this letter promptly after the applicant has been notified that he or she has passed the written examination required by paragraph (a)(3) of this Rule. The sponsor shall state fully and frankly the extent of the sponsor's acquaintance with the applicant, the sponsor's opinion of the moral character and repute of the applicant, and the sponsor's opinion of the qualifications of the applicant to practice before this Court. The Court may in its discretion accept such an applicant with less than two such sponsors.

(d) Admission: Upon the Court's approval of an application for admission in which an applicant has subscribed to the oath or affirmation and upon an applicant's satisfaction of the other applicable requirements of this Rule, such applicant will be admitted to practice before the Court and be entitled to a certificate of admission.

(e) Change of Address: Each person admitted to practice before the Court shall promptly notify the Admissions Clerk at the address listed in paragraph (b) of this Rule of any change in office address for mailing purposes. See also

Rule 21(b)(4) regarding the filing of a separate notice of change of address for each docket number in which such person has entered an appearance.

(f) Corporations and Firms Not Eligible: Corporations and firms will not be admitted to practice or recognized before the Court.

(g) Periodic Registration Fee: (1) Each person admitted to practice before the Court shall pay a periodic registration fee. The frequency and the amount of such fee shall be determined by the Court, except that such amount shall not exceed $30 per calendar year. The Clerk shall maintain an Ineligible List containing the names of all persons admitted to practice before the Court who have failed to comply with the provisions of this paragraph (g)(1). No such person shall be permitted to commence a case in the Court or enter an appearance in a pending case while on the Ineligible List. The name of any person appearing on the Ineligible List shall not be removed from the List until the currently due registration fee has been paid and arrearages have been made current. Each person admitted to practice before the Court, whether or not engaged in private practice, must pay the periodic registration fee. As to forms of payment, see Rule 11.

(2) The fees described in paragraph (g)(1) of this Rule shall be used by the Court to compensate independent counsel appointed by the Court to assist it with respect to disciplinary matters. See Rule 202(f).

RULE 201. CONDUCT OF PRACTICE BEFORE THE COURT

(a) General: Practitioners before the Court shall carry on their practice in accordance with the letter and spirit of the Model Rules of Professional Conduct of the American Bar Association.

(b) Statement of Employment: The Court may require any practitioner before it to furnish a statement, under oath, of the terms and circumstances of his or her employment in any case.

RULE 202.   DISCIPLINARY MATTERS [1]

(a)   General: A member of the Bar of this Court may be disciplined by this Court as a result of:

(1)   Conviction in any court of the United States, or of the District of Columbia, or of any State, territory, commonwealth, or possession of the United States of any felony or of any lesser crime involving false swearing, misrepresentation, fraud, criminal violation of any provision of the Internal Revenue Code, bribery, extortion, misappropriation, theft, or moral turpitude;

(2)   Imposition of discipline by any other court of whose bar an attorney is a member, or an attorney's disbarment or suspension by consent or resignation from the bar of such court while an investigation into allegations of misconduct is pending;

(3)   Conduct with respect to the Court which violates the letter and spirit of the Model Rules of Professional Conduct of the American Bar Association, the Rules of the Court, or orders or other instructions of the Court; or

(4)   Any other conduct unbecoming a member of the Bar of the Court.

(b)   Disciplinary Actions: Discipline may consist of disbarment, suspension from practice before the Court, reprimand, admonition, or any other sanction that the Court may deem appropriate. The Court may, in the exercise of its discretion, immediately suspend a practitioner from practice before the Court until further order of the Court. However, no person shall be suspended for more than 60 days or disbarred until such person has been afforded an opportunity to be heard. A Judge of the Court may immediately suspend any person for not more than 60 days for contempt or misconduct during the course of any trial or hearing.

(c)   Disciplinary Proceedings: Upon the occurrence or allegation of any event described in paragraph (a)(1) through (a)(4), except for any suspension imposed for 60 days or less pursuant to paragraph (b), the Court shall issue to the practitioner an order to show cause why the practitioner should not be disciplined or shall otherwise take appropriate action. The order to show cause shall direct that a written response be filed within such period as the Court may direct and shall

---

[1] The amendments are effective as of September 20, 2005.

set a prompt hearing on the matter before one or more Judges of the Court. If the disciplinary proceeding is predicated upon the complaint of a Judge of the Court, the hearing shall be conducted before a panel of three other Judges of the Court.

(d) Reinstatement: (1) A practitioner suspended for 60 days or less pursuant to paragraph (b) shall be automatically reinstated at the end of the period of suspension.

(2) A practitioner suspended for more than 60 days or disbarred pursuant to this Rule may not resume practice before the Court until reinstated by order of the Court.

(A) A disbarred practitioner or a practitioner suspended for more than 60 days who wishes to be reinstated to practice before the Court must file a petition for reinstatement. Upon receipt of the petition for reinstatement, the Court may set the matter for prompt hearing before one or more Judges of the Court. If the disbarment or suspension for more than 60 days was predicated upon the complaint of a Judge of the Court, any such hearing shall be conducted before a panel of three other Judges of the Court.

(B) In order to be reinstated before the Court, the practitioner must demonstrate by clear and convincing evidence in the petition for reinstatement and at any hearing that such practitioner's reinstatement will not be detrimental to the integrity and standing of the Court's Bar or to the administration of justice, or subversive of the public interest.

(C) No petition for reinstatement under this Rule shall be filed within 1 year following an adverse decision upon a petition for reinstatement filed by or on behalf of the same person.

(e) Right to Counsel: In all proceedings conducted under the provisions of this Rule, the practitioner shall have the right to be represented by counsel.

(f) Appointment of Court Counsel: The Court, in its discretion, may appoint counsel to the Court to assist it with respect to any disciplinary matters.

(g) Jurisdiction: Nothing contained in this Rule shall be construed to deny to the Court such powers as are necessary for the Court to maintain control over proceedings conducted before it, such as proceedings for contempt under Code section 7456 or for costs under Code section 6673(a)(2).

Appendix G

UNITED STATES TAX COURT RULE 24(g)

RULE 24. APPEARANCE AND REPUTATION

(g) Conflict of Interest: If any counsel of record (1) was involved in planning or promoting a transaction or operating an entity that is connected to any issue in a case, (2) represents more than one person with differing interests with respect to any issue in a case, or (3) is a potential witness in a case, then such counsel must either secure the informed consent of the client (but only as to items (1) and (2)); withdraw from the case; or take whatever other steps are necessary to obviate a conflict of interest or other violation of the ABA Model Rules of Professional Conduct, and particularly Rules 1.7, 1.8, and 3.7 thereof. The Court may inquire into the circumstances of counsel's employment in order to deter such violations. See Rule 201.

Appendix H

AICPA CODE OF PROFESSIONAL CONDUCT ET § 102.01 AND INTERPRETATION 102-2[1]

ET SECTION 102—INTEGRITY AND OBJECTIVITY

.01   Rule 102—Integrity and objectivity.

In the performance of any professional service, a member shall maintain objectivity and integrity, shall be free of conflicts of interest, and shall not knowingly misrepresent facts or subordinate his or her judgment to others.

Interpretations under Rule 102

. . .

.03   102-2—Conflicts of interest.

A conflict of interest may occur if a member performs a professional service for a client or employer and the member or his or her firm has a relationship with another person, entity, product, or service that could, in the member's professional judgment, be viewed by the client, employer, or other appropriate parties as impairing the member's objectivity. If the member believes that the professional service can be performed with objectivity, and the relationship is disclosed to and consent is obtained from such client, employer, or other appropriate parties, the rule shall not operate to prohibit the performance of the professional service. When making the disclosure, the member should consider Rule 301, *Confidential Client Information* [ET section 301.01].

Certain professional engagements, such as audits, reviews, and other attest services, require independence. Independence impairments under rule 101 [ET section 101.01], its interpretations, and rulings cannot be eliminated by such disclosure and consent.

The following are examples, not all-inclusive, of situations that should cause a member to consider whether or not the client, employer, or other appropriate parties could view the relationship as impairing the member's objectivity:

- A member has been asked to perform litigation services for the plaintiff in connection with a lawsuit filed against a client of the member's firm.
- A member has provided tax or personal financial planning (PFP) services for a married couple who are undergoing a divorce, and the member has been asked to provide the services for both parties during the divorce proceedings.

- In connection with a PFP engagement, a member plans to suggest that the client invest in a business in which he or she has a financial interest.
- A member provides tax or PFP services for several members of a family who may have opposing interests.
- A member has a significant financial interest, is a member of management, or is in a position of influence in a company that is a major competitor of a client for which the member performs management consulting services.
- A member serves on a city's board of tax appeals, which considers matters involving several of the member's tax clients.
- A member has been approached to provide services in connection with the purchase of real estate from a client of the member's firm.
- A member refers a PFP or tax client to an insurance broker or other service provider, which refers clients to the member under an exclusive arrangement to do so.
- A member recommends or refers a client to a service bureau in which the member or partner(s) in the member's firm hold material financial interest(s).

The above examples are not intended to be all-inclusive.

Appendix I

INTERNAL REVENUE MANUAL ¶ 4.11.55.4.2 (Last revised 1-15-2005)

4.11.55.4.2 Referral to the Office of Professional Responsibility

1. A referral to the Office of Professional Responsibility (OPR) is a consideration to institute disciplinary action against a practitioner. If OPR has reason to believe that a provision of the law or regulations governing practice before the IRS has been violated based on the referral, OPR may reprimand or institute proceedings for disbarment or suspension. Each referral should describe and document the practitioner's actions in order to support disciplinary action.

2. Announcements of censures, disbarments and suspensions normally are published in the Internal Revenue Bulletin. As long as the preparer's name appears on the list, he/she is not permitted to appear before the examiner as an advocate with or without the taxpayer, but only as a witness for the taxpayer under Rev. Proc. 68-29. Additional information is provided in *See IRM 4.11.55.1.2.2.*

4.11.55.4.2.1 Practitioners under the Office of Professional Responsibility's Authority

1. The Office of Professional Responsibility exercises jurisdiction over Attorneys, CPAs, Enrolled Agents, Enrolled Actuaries, and Appraisers.

2. Unenrolled Preparers are under the jurisdiction of the Area Director.

4.11.55.4.2.2 When Should a Referral Be Made to OPR?

1. Examiners are to exercise discretion in making referrals of specific cases to the Director of the OPR.

2. In matters involving non-willful conduct, a referral should only be made when it can be established that the preparer has a pattern of failing to meet the required standards of Circular 230.

3. An isolated instance in which a penalty may apply should not, in and of itself, require a referral unless willful conduct is involved. Accordingly, the imposition of penalties under IRC 6694(a), and IRC 6695(a) through (e) should not automatically generate a referral to the Director of the OPR.

4.11.55.4.2.2.1 Situations Requiring a Mandatory Referral

1. When the following penalties are asserted against a practitioner a mandatory referral should be prepared:

A. Understatements due to unrealistic positions (IRC § 6694(a)) - when closed agreed, sustained in Appeals, or closed unagreed without Appeals contact.

B. Willful or reckless conduct (IRC § 6694(b)) - when closed agreed, sustained in Appeals, or closed unagreed without Appeals contact.

C. Negotiation of check (IRC § 6695(f)).

D. Aiding and abetting penalties (IRC § 6701) - The assessment of an aiding and abetting penalty against a tax practitioner or appraiser should mandate an automatic referral. In addition, referrals should be considered in those situations in which the aiding and abetting penalty was considered but not imposed.

E. Promoting abusive tax shelters (IRC § 6700) - The assessment of an IRC § 6700 penalty against an attorney, CPA or enrolled agent.

F. Action to enjoin promoters of abusive tax shelters (IRC §§ 7407 and 7408)

G. Injunctive action under IRC § 7408 taken against an attorney, CPA or enrolled agent.

Note:

The Deficit Reduction Act of 1984 expanded IRC § 7408 to include conduct subject to the penalty under IRC § 6701.

4.11.55.4.2.2.2   Situations Which May Warrant A Referral

1. The following situations **may** warrant a referral to the Office of Professional Responsibility:

A. Return preparer referrals made to Criminal Investigation under IRC § 7206.

B. An appraiser who aids or assists in the preparation or presentation of an appraisal in connection with the tax laws will be subject to disciplinary action if the appraiser knows that the appraisal will be used in connection with the tax laws and will result in an understatement of the tax liability of another person.

C. A by-pass of representative letter was issued to a tax practitioner.

D. Disreputable conduct or incompetence described in Circular 230, Section 10.51.

E. The implication of a tax practitioner in a frivolous tax return matter (IRC 6702) should result in a referral.

F. The accuracy-related penalty under IRC 6662(d) for a substantial understatement is asserted and the facts of the case suggest the practitioner did not exercise due diligence in the preparation of the return.

Note:

IRM 20.1.5.8 provides that whenever IRC 6662(d) is not asserted because the taxpayer has met the "advice" standard under the reasonable cause exception, contact with the preparer is mandatory before the case is closed from the group. A comment should be made on Form 4318, Penalties, as to consideration of a referral to the Office of Professional Responsibility.

G. The Office of Professional Responsibility should receive referrals in instances where a practitioner fails to comply with the tax shelter registration requirement or characterizes the registration as an IRS endorsement of the shelter under IRC 6111 and IRC 6112 and takes a position on a tax return which reflects the endorsement.

H. Opinions rendered by tax practitioners and used or referred to in the marketing of tax shelters (abusive or otherwise) issued after May 23, 1984. Tax shelter opinions which violate Circular 230 will be referred to the Office of Professional Responsibility.

I. Examination report of any tax return of an attorney, CPA, or enrolled agent, or of a return prepared by an attorney, CPA or enrolled agent where a Pre-filing Notification Letter was issued in connection with the tax shelter and the loss and/or credit from the promotion was nevertheless claimed on the tax return.

4.11.55.4.2.3   Referral to OPR Procedures

1. Once it has been determined that a referral is necessary, a referral package to the Office of Professional Responsibility must be prepared and closed separately from the related case. Include in the referral package:

   A. Completed Form 8484, *Penalty Information Report* to Office of Professional Responsibility, including status of the case (agreed, unagreed).

   B. A complete copy of the tax return.

   C. A complete copy of the RAR (including explanation of items and workpapers).

   D. Letters, Memoranda, copies of Form 2311 (Affidavit) or similar attested document, and Form 2797, *Referral Report for Potential Fraud Cases*, if applicable.

   E. Penalty summary from RGS.

   F. Form 2848, Power of Attorney, if available.

   G. Explanatory memorandum, which details all the pertinent facts. The actions of the return preparer must be described and documented in sufficient detail to develop a substantial position for disciplinary action. Include documentation and exhibits from the income tax file. Include a statement regarding the preparer's appearance before the Service (a record of contacts and activity of the preparer).

   H. Document the preparer's position, whether an appeal will be made, and the extent the preparer practices before the Service.

   I. The name and TIN of the related case(s) should be noted in the referral package.

2. The Form 4318/4700A for the related income tax case should note the referral was prepared and forwarded to the Return Preparer Coordinator.

3. In cases in which a referral is not prepared but was considered, a comment should be made on Form 4318/4700 explaining why the referral was not made.

4.11.55.4.2.4 Routing of Referral to OPR

1. The routing of the referral package depends upon the purpose of the referral. The referral requesting disciplinary action under Circular 230 is routed differently than a referral for information purposes.

2. *Circular 230 Action*: Examiners will send referrals for Circular 230 action to the Office of Professional Responsibility on Form 8484, Penalty Information Report. It is routed through the Return Preparer Coordinator in PSP who forwards it to the Area Director.

3. *Informational Purposes*: If the referral is for information and NOT for Circular 230 action, examiners will route Form 8484 through the Return Preparer Coordinator (RPC) who will send it directly to the Director of the OPR.

Appendix J

AICPA CODE OF PROFESSIONAL CONDUCT
ET § 302.01 AND INTERPRETATION 302-1[1]

ET SECTION 302—CONTINGENT FEES

.01   Rule 302—Contingent fees.

A member in public practice shall not

(1) Perform for a contingent fee any professional services for, or receive such a fee from a client for whom the member or the member's firm performs,

   (a) an audit or review of a financial statement; or

   (b) a compilation of a financial statement when the member expects, or reasonably might expect, that a third party will use the financial statement and the member's compilation report does not disclose a lack of independence; or

   (c) an examination of prospective financial information; or

(2) Prepare an original or amended tax return or claim for a tax refund for a contingent fee for any client.

The prohibition in (1) above applies during the period in which the member or the member's firm is engaged to perform any of the services listed above and the period covered by any historical financial statements involved in any such listed services.

Except as stated in the next sentence, a contingent fee is a fee established for the performance of any service pursuant to an arrangement in which no fee will be charged unless a specified finding or result is attained, or in which the amount of the fee is otherwise dependent upon the finding or result of such service. Solely for purposes of this rule, fees are not regarded as being contingent if fixed by courts or other public authorities, or, in tax matters, if determined based on the results of judicial proceedings or the findings of governmental agencies.

A member's fees may vary depending, for example, on the complexity of services rendered.

Interpretation under Rule 302

—Contingent Fees

.02   302-1—Contingent fees in tax matters.

This interpretation defines certain terms in rule 302 [ET section 302.01] and provides examples of the application of the rule.

Definition of Terms

(a) Preparation of an original or amended tax return or claim for tax refund includes giving advice on events which have occurred at the time the advice is given if such advice is directly relevant to determining the existence, character, or amount of a schedule, entry, or other portion of a return or claim for refund.

(b) A fee is considered determined based on the findings of governmental agencies if the member can demonstrate a reasonable expectation, at the time of a fee arrangement, of substantive consideration by an agency with respect to the member's client. Such an expectation is deemed not reasonable in the case of preparation of original tax returns.

Examples

The following are examples, not all-inclusive, of circumstances where a contingent fee would be permitted:

1. Representing a client in an examination by a revenue agent of the client's federal or state income tax return.
2. Filing an amended federal or state income tax return claiming a tax refund based on a tax issue that is either the subject of a test case (involving a different taxpayer) or with respect to which the taxing authority is developing a position.
3. Filing an amended federal or state income tax return (or refund claim) claiming a tax refund in an amount greater than the threshold for review by the Joint Committee on Internal Revenue Taxation ($1 million at March 1991) or state taxing authority.
4. Requesting a refund of either overpayments of interest or penalties charged to a client's account or deposits of taxes improperly accounted for by the federal or state taxing authority in circumstances where the taxing authority has established procedures for the substantive review of such refund requests.
5. Requesting, by means of "protest" or similar document, consideration by the state or local taxing authority of a reduction in the "assessed value" of property under an established taxing authority review process for hearing all taxpayer arguments relating to assessed value.
6. Representing a client in connection with obtaining a private letter ruling or influencing the drafting of a regulation or statute.

The following is an example of a circumstance where a contingent fee would not be permitted:

1. Preparing an amended federal or state income tax return for a client claiming a refund of taxes because a deduction was inadvertently omitted from the return originally filed. There is no question as to the propriety of the deduction; rather the claim is filed to correct an omission.

Appendix K

AICPA CODE OF PROFESSIONAL CONDUCT
ET § 301.01[1]

ET SECTION 301—CONTINGENT FEES

.01 Rule 301—Confidential client information.

A member in public practice shall not disclose any confidential client information without the specific consent of the client.

This rule shall not be construed (1) to relieve a member of his or her professional obligations under rules 202 [ET section 202.01] and 203 [ET section 203.01], (2) to affect in any way the member's obligation to comply with a validly issued and enforceable subpoena or summons, or to prohibit a member's compliance with applicable laws and government regulations, (3) to prohibit review of a member's professional practice under AICPA or state CPA society or Board of Accountancy authorization, or (4) to preclude a member from initiating a complaint with, or responding to any inquiry made by, the professional ethics division or trial board of the Institute or a duly constituted investigative or disciplinary body of a state CPA society or Board of Accountancy.

Members of any of the bodies identified in (4) above and members involved with professional practice reviews identified in (3) above shall not use to their own advantage or disclose any member's confidential client information that comes to their attention in carrying out those activities. This prohibition shall not restrict members' exchange of information in connection with the investigative or disciplinary proceedings described in (4) above or the professional practice reviews described in (3) above.

Appendix L

SELECTED INFORMATION ON TAXATION LAW AND ESTATE PLANNING SPECIALIZATION PROGRAMS

ESTATE PLANNING CERTIFICATION REQUIREMENTS

California (as of 5/16/2008):[1]

1. Member of the State Bar in good standing
2. Pass a written exam
3. Pay fees
4. Favorably evaluated by other attorneys and judges familiar with the attorney's work
5. Experience/Practice in the area of certification: Maintain a minimum of 25 percent of the time the attorney has spent in occupational endeavors during the previous five (5) years.
6. Practice in the area of certification: within five years immediately preceding submission of the written application, applicant must make a prima facie showing of substantial involvement in the area of estate planning, trust and probate law that includes the performance of any two of the following:
    a. Thirty (30) tax planning matters for at least 20 separate clients;
    b. Fifty (50) estate and incapacity plans, at least 20 of which must include tax issues;
    c. Forty (40) administration procedures for at least 20 separate clients;
    d. Completed transfers, by administration or otherwise, of a decedent's assets upon deaths of forty (40) persons; or
    e. Twenty (20) litigated matters or contested hearings for at least 10 separate clients.

7. Continuing education requirement: An applicant must show that, within the three (3) years immediately preceding the application for certification, he or she has completed not less than forty-five (45) hours of educational activities specifically approved for estate planning, trust and probate law.

Arizona (as of 2002):[2]

1. Member of the State Bar in good standing
2. Pass written exam
3. Pay fees

---

[1] California State Bar, http://www.calbar.ca.gov.
2 Arizona State Bar, http://www.myazbar.org.

4. Completed application

5. Recommendation by the Advisory Commission. An applicant shall be recommended to the BLS for certification as a lawyer specializing in estate and trust law when the applicant is found to have complied with the applicable standards by not less than five members of the Estate and Trust Advisory Commission.

6. Required Period of Law Practice. Applicants must be admitted to the practice of law for a minimum of five (5) years, of which a minimum of two (2) years immediately preceding the application must have been in the practice of law within the State of Arizona and after such admission shall have engaged in legal service equivalent to at least 50 percent of a full-time law practice.

7. Substantial involvement in the field of estate and trust law during at least four (4) of the preceding six (6) years, including the year immediately preceding the application.

8. An applicant must demonstrate honesty, integrity, professionalism, and a high degree of competence in the practice of estate and trust law.

9. Provide the names of at least five (5) Arizona attorneys who practice in the field or judges before whom the applicant appears, familiar with the applicant's practice, and not including current partners or associates.

10. Continuing Education Requirements. Continuing legal education requirements for attorneys certified as estate and trust law specialists shall be 12 hours per year in one or more approved seminar and, in addition, three (3) hours in professional responsibility.

Ohio (as of 11/05/2006):[3]

1. Member of the State Bar in good standing

2. Pass written exam

3. Pay fees

4. Completed application

5. Demonstrate substantial and continuing involvement in the specialty

6. Provide references regarding competency

7. Earned a minimum of 36 CLE credits in the specialty during three (3) years immediately preceding application

8. Be in good standing with the Supreme Court

9. Prove financial responsibility through specific minimum professional liability coverage

Florida (as of 4/13/2007):[4]

1. Member of the State Bar in good standing.

2. Pass written exam.

3. Pay fees.

---

[3] Ohio State Bar, http://www.sconet.state.oh.us.
[4] Florida State Bar, http://www.floridabar.org.

4. Completed application.

5. Required Period of Law Practice. The 5-year practice of law requirement may be completed after application filing, but no later than November 30 of the year in which application is made.

6. References: Each applicant shall submit names of lawyers and judges who can attest to the applicant's special competence and substantial involvement in the practice of law in which certification is sought, as well as the applicant's character, ethics, and reputation for professionalism, in accordance with the area standards.

7. Continuing Education Requirements. Certain continuing legal education requirements may be completed after application filing, if satisfactory proof of completion of the educational program is furnished to the BLSE prior to the application filing deadline or to an extended deadline as approved by BLSE.

8. Record of professional competence and ethics.

9. Substantial involvement: applicants must clearly demonstrate 40 percent of their practice has consisted of matters governed by Florida law during each of the two years immediately preceding application.

ESTATE PLANNING CERTIFICATION RENEWAL REQUIREMENTS

California (as of 5/16/2008):[5]

An applicant for recertification must show that, during the current five (5) year certification period, he or she has completed not less than sixty (60) hours of educational activities specifically approved for estate planning, trust and probate law specialists in at least three (3) of the following five (5) areas:

1. Incapacity planning and administrative procedures including conservatorships, guardianships, special needs trusts, public benefit planning and procedures, powers of attorney for asset management, advanced health care directives, and elder abuse;

2. Estate planning including preparation of wills and revocable and irrevocable trusts, business entities, charitable trusts and giving, life insurance trusts, marital property issues, retirement planning issues, marital deductions, qualified domestic trusts, generation-skipping tax issues, and recent developments;

3. Estate and gift tax return preparation and audit, valuation analysis and issues, business entity tax elections, stock redemptions for estate taxes, installment and hardship extensions, special use valuation;

4. Administration of decedents' estates, probate and summary proceedings, funding administration and termination of trusts, joint tenancy terminations, trust accounting and procedures;

5. Adversarial and litigated proceedings regarding any of the above areas.

---

[5] California State Bar, http://www.calbar.ca.gov.

Arizona (as of 2002):[6]

A renewal application is required every five (5) years. For the purposes of re-certification, the lawyer shall demonstrate continued substantial involvement in the area of estate and trust law. These services shall be detailed on an application form, showing the nature of the legal services in which the applicant has been engaged in the past five years, and identifying the types of issues of estate and trust law with which the applicant has dealt and the frequency of involvement. Such demonstration shall be made upon re-certification through the completing by the applicant of a form of questionnaire approved by the BLS. Formal written examination for recertification shall not be required where there has been no break in certification.

Ohio (as of 11/05/2006):[7]

The period of certification shall be set by the Applicant but shall be not less than three (3) nor more than seven (7) years, after which time lawyers who have been certified must apply for recertification. Recertification shall satisfy the minimum standards set forth in Gov. Bar R. XIV Section 6 and shall require similar evidence of competence as that required for initial certification in the areas of substantial involvement, peer review, education experience, and evidence of good standing. The Applicant shall have in existence or be in the process of developing a plan for periodic recertification at the time of application for accreditation.

Florida (as of 4/13/2007):[8]

Applicant must have adopted a plan for recertification of all lawyers previously certified. Certification or recertification shall be valid for 5 years. While no examination shall be required for recertification, each certified lawyer must show continued competence in the specialty field in accordance with standards comparable to, but no less than, those required for recertification under the Florida plan and, where the same or similar specialty area exists under the Florida plan, applicant shall require no less than the standards set forth for that specialty area. In addition, each applicant must submit the names of three (3) references who are active in Wills, Trusts and Estates and are familiar with the applicant's practice.

CALIFORNIA TASK AND EDUCATIONAL REQUIREMENTS FOR TAXATION LAW CERTIFICATION

2.0 TASK REQUIREMENT FOR CERTIFICATION

2.1 An applicant must demonstrate that within the five (5) years immediately preceding the initial application, he or she has been substantially involved in the practice of taxation law, which shall include handling matters in one or more of the following areas:

---

[6] Arizona State Bar, http://www.myazbar.org.

[7] Ohio State Bar, http://www.sconet.state.oh.us.

[8] Florida State Bar, http://www.floridabar.org.

2.1.1 Individual Income Tax;

2.1.2 Corporate Income Tax;

2.1.3 Partnership Income Tax;

2.1.4 Real Estate Income Tax;

2.1.5 Tax Procedures;

2.1.6 Compensation and Benefit Tax;

2.1.7 California Taxes;

2.1.8 Estate and Gift Tax and Estate Planning;

2.1.9 Tax Exempt Organizations; and

2.1.10 International Tax.

2.2 A prima facie showing of substantial involvement in the area of taxation law is made by performance of the following activities:

2.2.1 Principal author of not less than ten (10) written tax opinions, memoranda, advice letters to clients or similar documents concerning substantive tax issues;

2.2.2 Active participation in not less than five (5) administrative tax examinations, ruling requests, determination letters or similar matters; and

2.2.3 Active participation in not less than five (5) tax litigation proceedings at any level, including appearances before the Appeals division of the IRS or state or local tax agency or revenue authority.

3.0 EDUCATIONAL REQUIREMENT FOR CERTIFICATION

An applicant must show that, within the three (3) years immediately preceding the application for certification, he or she has completed not less than forty-five (45) hours of educational activities specifically approved for taxation law. Such education shall be in at least four (4) of the areas of taxation law specified below, with no fewer than four (4) hours in any of the four (4) areas, nor more than twenty (20) hours in any one area, or by receiving, within the five (5) years immediately preceding application, an LL.M. degree in taxation law from a law school accredited by the American Bar Association or a degree determined to be equivalent by the Advisory Commission:

3.1 Individual Income Tax - Federal and California tax law relating to individual business tax matters including forms of business entities, real estate and other investments; and federal and California tax law relating to individual personal taxes, including family matters and foreign tax matters;

3.2 Corporate Income Tax - Federal and California tax law relating to the formation, operation, reorganization and liquidation of corporations, and the tax status of particular kinds of corporate entities;

3.3 Partnership Income Tax - Federal and California tax law relating to the formation, operation, reorganization and liquidation of partnerships and the tax status of particular kinds of partnership entities;

3.4 Real Estate Income Tax - Federal and California tax law relating to the acquisition, development, operation and disposition of real estate;

3.5 Tax Procedures - Federal and California income, estate and gift tax law relating to the preparation of returns, elections, audits, appeals, and litigation in civil and criminal matters;

3.6 Compensation and Benefits Tax - Federal and California income, estate and gift tax law relating to employee compensation, including stock options and other payments in kind; employee benefit plans, including ERISA and other qualified and nonqualified retirement and fringe benefit matters;

3.7 California Taxes - California personal and corporate income, property, sales and use and other local taxes;

3.8 Estate, Gift Tax and Estate Planning - Federal and California tax law relating to disposition of property including estate planning;

3.9 Tax Exempt Organizations - Federal and California tax law relating to tax exempt organizations;

3.10 Current Developments - Federal and California income, estate and gift tax law relating to current developments in any of the other areas of the tax law curriculum, of the kind covered by annual tax seminars, institutes and similar programs;

3.11 International Tax - Federal and California tax law relating to the taxation of non-resident aliens, foreign entities and foreign related transactions; and

3.12 Ethics of Tax Practice. Courses covering the ethical considerations of tax practice, including tax opinions, Circular 230, conflicts of interest, penalties and related matters.

STATE CERTIFICATION PROGRAMS IN TAXATION LAW AND ESTATE PLANNING

States with Certification, as a State Program, in Taxation[9]

1. Arizona
2. California
3. Florida
4. Louisiana
5. New Mexico
6. Ohio
7. South Carolina
8. Texas

States with Certification, as a State or Private Program, in Estate Planning[10]

1. Alabama (Private)
2. Alaska (Private)
3. Arizona (State)

---

[9] Data extracted from Table 1.0 below. The American Bar Association, http://www.abanet.org/legalservices/specialization/directory. **[I don't see where Table 1.0 is...]**

[10] *Id.*

4. Arkansas (Private)
5. California (State and Private)
6. Delaware (Private)
7. Florida (State)
8. Georgia (Private)
9. Hawaii (Private)
10. Idaho (Private)
11. Illinois (Private)
12. Kansas (Private)
13. Kentucky (Private)
14. Louisiana (State)
15. Maine (Private)
16. Maryland (Private)
17. Massachusetts (Private)
18. Michigan (Private)
19. Mississippi (Private)
20. Missouri (Private)
21. Montana (Private)
22. Nebraska (Private)
23. Nevada (Private)
24. New Hampshire (Private)
25. New Jersey (Private)
26. New Mexico (State and Private)
27. New York (Private)
28. North Carolina (State and Private)
29. North Dakota (Private)
30. Ohio (Private)
31. Oklahoma (Private)
32. Oregon (Private)
33. Pennsylvania (Private)
34. Rhode Island (Private)
35. South Carolina (State and Private)
36. South Dakota (Private)
37. Tennessee (State)
38. Texas (State)
39. Utah (Private)
40. Vermont (Private)
41. Virginia (Private)
42. Washington (Private)
43. West Virginia (Private)
44. Wisconsin (Private)
45. Wyoming (Private)

However, less than half of the states' certification programs are accredited by the American Bar Association.

List of States' Certification Programs Accredited by the ABA[11]

1. Alabama
2. Alaska
3. Arkansas
4. California
5. Delaware
6. Hawaii
7. Idaho
8. Maine
9. Mississippi
10. Montana
11. Nebraska
12. Nevada
13. New Hampshire
14. New Jersey
15. New York
16. North Carolina
17. North Dakota
18. South Carolina
19. South Dakota
20. Tennessee
21. Vermont
22. Wisconsin

CALIFORNIA'S MINIMUM CERTIFICATION REQUIREMENTS[12]

4.06 – Certification Requirements – An Applicant shall require for certification of lawyers as specialists, as a minimum, the following:

(A) Substantial Involvement – Substantial involvement in the specialty area throughout the three-year period immediately preceding application to the certifying organization. Substantial involvement is measured by the type and number of cases or matters handled and the amount of time spent practicing in the specialty area, and require that the time spent in practicing the specialty be no less than twenty-five percent (25%) of the total practice of a lawyer engaged in a normal full-time practice.

---

[11] Id.

[12] The American Bar Association, http://www.abanet.org/legalservices/specialization/standard.html#46.

(B) Peer Review – A minimum of five references, a majority of which are from attorneys or judges who are knowledgeable regarding the practice area and are familiar with the competence of the lawyer, and none of which are from persons related to or engaged in legal practice with the lawyer.

    (1) Type of References – The certification requirements shall allow lawyers seeking certification to list persons to whom reference forms could be sent, but shall also provide that the Applicant organization send out all reference forms. In addition, the organization may seek and consider reference forms from persons of the organization's own choosing.

    (2) Content of Reference Forms – The reference forms shall inquire into the respondent's areas of practice, the respondent's familiarity with both the specialty area and with the lawyer seeking certification, and the length of time that the respondent has been practicing law and has known the applicant. The form shall inquire about the qualifications of the lawyer seeking certification in various aspects of the practice and, as appropriate, the lawyer's dealings with judges and opposing counsel.

(C) Written Examination – An evaluation of the lawyer's knowledge of the substantive and procedural law in the specialty area, determined by written examination of suitable length and complexity. The examination shall include professional responsibility and ethics as it relates to the particular specialty.

(D) Educational Experience – A minimum of 36 hours of participation in continuing legal education in the specialty area in the three-year period preceding the lawyer's application for certification. This requirement may be met through any of the following means:

    (1) Attending programs of continuing legal education or courses offered by Association accredited law schools in the specialty area;

    (2) Teaching courses or seminars in the specialty area;

    (3) Participating as panelist, speaker or workshop leader at educational or professional conferences covering the specialty area; or

    (4) Writing published books or articles concerning the specialty area.

(E) Good Standing – A lawyer seeking certification is admitted to practice and is a member in good standing in one or more states or territories of the United States or the District of Columbia.

Appendix M

CALIFORNIA SUPREME COURT MULTIJURISDICTIONAL PRACTICE RULES[1]

Title 9. Rules On Law Practice, Attorneys, And Judges
Division 4. Appearances and Practice by Individuals Who Are
Not Members of the State Bar of California

Rule 9.43. Out-of-state attorney arbitration counsel

(a) Definition

An "out-of-state attorney arbitration counsel" is an attorney who is:

(1) Not a member of the State Bar of California but who is a member in good standing of and eligible to practice before the bar of any United States court or the highest court in any state, territory, or insular possession of the United States, and who has been retained to appear in the course of, or in connection with, an arbitration proceeding in this state;

(2) Has served a certificate in accordance with the requirements of Code of Civil Procedure section 1282.4 on the arbitrator, the arbitrators, or the arbitral forum, the State Bar of California, and all other parties and counsel in the arbitration whose addresses are known to the attorney; and

(3) Whose appearance has been approved by the arbitrator, the arbitrators, or the arbitral forum.

(Subd (a) amended effective January 1, 2007.)

(b) State Bar Out-of-State Attorney Arbitration Counsel Program

The State Bar of California must establish and administer a program to implement the State Bar of California's responsibilities under Code of Civil Procedure section 1282.4. The State Bar of California's program may be operative only as long as the applicable provisions of Code of Civil Procedure section 1282.4 remain in effect.

(Subd (b) amended effective January 1, 2007.)

(c) Eligibility to appear as an out-of-state attorney arbitration counsel

To be eligible to appear as an out-of-state attorney arbitration counsel, an attorney must comply with all of the applicable provisions of Code of Civil Procedure section 1282.4 and the requirements of this rule and the related rules and regulations adopted by the State Bar of California.

(Subd (c) amended effective January 1, 2007.)

(d) Discipline

An out-of-state attorney arbitration counsel who files a certificate containing false information or who otherwise fails to comply with the standards of professional conduct required of members of the State Bar of California is subject to the disciplinary jurisdiction of the State Bar with respect to any of his or her acts occurring in the course of the arbitration.

(Subd (d) amended effective January 1, 2007.)

(e) Disqualification

Failure to timely file and serve a certificate or, absent special circumstances, appearances in multiple separate arbitration matters are grounds for disqualification from serving in the arbitration in which the certificate was filed.

(Subd (e) amended effective January 1, 2007.)

(f) Fee

Out-of-state attorney arbitration counsel must pay a reasonable fee not exceeding $50 to the State Bar of California with the copy of the certificate that is served on the State Bar.

(Subd (f) amended effective January 1, 2007.)

(g) Inherent power of Supreme Court

Nothing in these rules may be construed as affecting the power of the Supreme Court to exercise its inherent jurisdiction over the practice of law in California.

(Subd (g) amended effective January 1, 2007.)

Rule 9.43 amended and renumbered effective January 1, 2007; adopted as rule 983.4 by the Supreme Court effective July 1, 1999.

Rule 9.44. Registered foreign legal consultant

(a) Definition

A "registered foreign legal consultant" is a person who:

(1) Is admitted to practice and is in good standing as an attorney or counselor-at-law or the equivalent in a foreign country; and

(2) Has a currently effective certificate of registration as a registered foreign legal consultant from the State Bar.

(Subd (a) amended effective January 1, 2007.)

(b) State Bar Registered Foreign Legal Consultant Program

The State Bar must establish and administer a program for registering foreign attorneys or counselors-at-law or the equivalent under rules adopted by the Board of Governors of the State Bar.

(Subd (b) amended effective January 1, 2007.)

(c) Eligibility for certification

To be eligible to become a registered foreign legal consultant, an applicant must:

(1) Present satisfactory proof that the applicant has been admitted to practice and has been in good standing as an attorney or counselor-at-law or the equivalent in a foreign country for at least four of the six years immediately preceding the application and, while so admitted, has actually practiced the law of that country;

(2) Present satisfactory proof that the applicant possesses the good moral character requisite for a person to be licensed as a member of the State Bar of California;

(3) Agree to comply with the provisions of the rules adopted by the Board of Governors of the State Bar relating to security for claims against a foreign legal consultant by his or her clients;

(4) Agree to comply with the provisions of the rules adopted by the Board of Governors of the State Bar relating to maintaining an address of record for State Bar purposes;

(5) Agree to notify the State Bar of any change in his or her status in any jurisdiction where he or she is admitted to practice or of any discipline with respect to such admission;

(6) Agree to be subject to the jurisdiction of the courts of this state with respect to the laws of the State of California governing the conduct of attorneys, to the same extent as a member of the State Bar of California;

(7) Agree to become familiar with and comply with the standards of professional conduct required of members of the State Bar of California;

(8) Agree to be subject to the disciplinary jurisdiction of the State Bar of California;

(9) Agree to be subject to the rights and obligations with respect to attorney client privilege, work-product privilege, and other professional privileges, to the same extent as attorneys admitted to practice law in California; and

(10) Agree to comply with the laws of the State of California, the rules and regulations of the State Bar of California, and these rules.

(Subd (c) amended effective January 1, 2007.)

(d) Authority to practice law

Subject to all applicable rules, regulations, and statutes, a registered foreign legal consultant may render legal services in California, except that he or she may not:

(1) Appear for a person other than himself or herself as attorney in any court, or before any magistrate or other judicial officer, in this state or prepare pleadings or any other papers or issue subpoenas in any action or proceeding brought in any court or before any judicial officer;

(2) Prepare any deed, mortgage, assignment, discharge, lease, or any other instrument affecting title to real estate located in the United States;

(3) Prepare any will or trust instrument affecting the disposition on death of any property located in the United States and owned by a resident or any instrument relating to the administration of a decedent's estate in the United States;

(4) Prepare any instrument in respect of the marital relations, rights, or duties of a resident of the United States, or the custody or care of the children of a resident; or

(5) Otherwise render professional legal advice on the law of the State of California, any other state of the United States, the District of Columbia, the United States, or of any jurisdiction other than the jurisdiction named in satisfying the requirements of (c) of this rule, whether rendered incident to preparation of legal instruments or otherwise.

(Subd (d) amended effective January 1, 2007.)

(e) Failure to comply with program

A registered foreign legal consultant who fails to comply with the requirements of the State Bar Registered Foreign Legal Consultant Program will have her or his certification suspended or revoked under rules adopted by the Board of Governors of the State Bar.

(Subd (e) amended effective January 1, 2007.)

(f) Fee and penalty

The State Bar has the authority to set and collect appropriate fees and penalties for this program.

(Subd (f) amended effective January 1, 2007.)

(g) Inherent power of Supreme Court

Nothing in these rules may be construed as affecting the power of the Supreme Court to exercise its inherent jurisdiction over the practice of law in California.

(Subd (g) amended effective January 1, 2007.)

Rule 9.44 amended and renumbered effective January 1, 2007; adopted as rule 988 effective December 1, 1993.

Rule 9.45. Registered legal services attorneys

(a) Definitions

The following definitions apply in this rule:

(1) "Qualifying legal services provider" means either of the following, provided that the qualifying legal services provider follows quality-control procedures approved by the State Bar of California:

(A) A nonprofit entity incorporated and operated exclusively in California that as its primary purpose and function provides legal services without charge in civil matters to indigent persons, especially underserved client groups, such as the elderly, persons with disabilities, juveniles, and non-English-speaking persons; or

(B) A program operated exclusively in California by a nonprofit law school approved by the American Bar Association or accredited by the State Bar of California that has operated for at least two years at a cost of at least $20,000 per year as an identifiable law school unit with a primary purpose and function of providing legal services without charge to indigent persons.

(2) "Active member in good standing of the bar of a United States state, jurisdiction, possession, territory, or dependency" means an attorney who:

(A) Is a member in good standing of the entity governing the practice of law in each jurisdiction in which the member is licensed to practice law;

(B) Remains an active member in good standing of the entity governing the practice of law in at least one United States state, jurisdiction, possession, territory, or dependency other than California while practicing law as a registered legal services attorney in California; and

(C) Has not been disbarred, has not resigned with charges pending, or is not suspended from practicing law in any other jurisdiction.

(Subd (a) relettered effective January 1, 2007; adopted as subd (j) effective November 15, 2004.)

(b) Scope of practice

Subject to all applicable rules, regulations, and statutes, an attorney practicing law under this rule may practice law in California only while working, with or without pay, at a qualifying legal services provider, as defined in this rule, and, at that institution and only on behalf of its clients, may engage, under supervision, in all forms of legal practice that are permissible for a member of the State Bar of California.

(Subd (b) amended and relettered effective January 1, 2007; adopted as subd (a) effective November 15, 2004.)

(c) Requirements

For an attorney to practice law under this rule, the attorney must:

(1) Be an active member in good standing of the bar of a United States state, jurisdiction, possession, territory, or dependency;

(2) Register with the State Bar of California and file an Application for Determination of Moral Character;

(3) Meet all of the requirements for admission to the State Bar of California, except that the attorney:

(A) Need not take the California bar examination or the Multistate Professional Responsibility Examination; and

(B) May practice law while awaiting the result of his or her Application for Determinat ion of Moral Character;

(4) Comply with the rules adopted by the Board of Governors relating to the State Bar Registered Legal Services Attorney Program;

(5) Practice law exclusively for a single qualifying legal services provider, except that, if so qualified, an attorney may, while practicing under this rule, simultaneously practice law as registered in-house counsel;

(6) Practice law under the supervision of an attorney who is employed by the qualifying legal services provider and who is a member in good standing of the State Bar of California;

(7) Abide by all of the laws and rules that govern members of the State Bar of California, including the Minimum Continuing Legal Education (MCLE) requirements;

(8) Satisfy in his or her first year of practice under this rule all of the MCLE requirements, including ethics education, that members of the State Bar of California must complete every three years; and

(9) Not have taken and failed the California bar examination within five years immediately preceding application to register under this rule.

(Subd (c) relettered effective January 1, 2007; adopted as subd (b) effective November 15, 2004.)

(d) Application

To qualify to practice law as a registered legal services attorney, the attorney must:

(1) Register as an attorney applicant and file an Application for Determination of Moral Character with the Committee of Bar Examiners;

(2) Submit to the State Bar of California a declaration signed by the attorney agreeing that he or she will be subject to the disciplinary authority of the Supreme Court of California and the State Bar of California and attesting that he or she will not practice law in California other than under supervision at a qualifying legal services provider during the time he or she practices law as a registered legal services attorney in California, except that, if so qualified, the attorney may, while practicing under this rule, simultaneously practice law as registered in-house counsel; and

(3) Submit to the State Bar of California a declaration signed by a qualifying supervisor on behalf of the qualifying legal services provider in California attesting that the applicant will work, with or without pay, as an attorney for the organization; that the applicant will be supervised as specified in this rule; and that the qualifying legal services provider and the supervising attorney assume professional responsibility for any work performed by the applicant under this rule.

(Subd (d) relettered effective January 1, 2007; adopted as subd (c) effective November 15, 2004.)

(e) Duration of practice

An attorney may practice for no more than a total of three years under this rule.

(Subd (e) relettered effective January 1, 2007; adopted as subd (d) effective November 15, 2004.)

(f) Application and registration fees

The State Bar of California may set appropriate application fees and initial and annual registration fees to be paid by registered legal services attorneys.

(Subd (f) amended and relettered effective January 1, 2007; adopted as subd (e) effective November 15, 2004.)

(g) State Bar Registered Legal Services Attorney Program

The State Bar may establish and administer a program for registering California legal services attorneys under rules adopted by the Board of Governors of the State Bar.

(Subd (g) relettered effective January 1, 2007; adopted as subd (f) effective November 15, 2004.)

(h) Supervision

To meet the requirements of this rule, an attorney supervising a registered legal services attorney:

(1) Must be an active member in good standing of the State Bar of California;

(2) Must have actively practiced law in California and been a member in good standing of the State Bar of California for at least the two years immediately preceding the time of supervision;

(3) Must have practiced law as a full-time occupation for at least four years;

(4) Must not supervise more than two registered legal services attorneys concurrently;

(5) Must assume professional responsibility for any work that the registered legal services attorney performs under the supervising attorney's supervision;

(6) Must assist, counsel, and provide direct supervision of the registered legal services attorney in the activities authorized by this rule and review such activities with the supervised attorney, to the extent required for the protection of the client;

(7) Must read, approve, and personally sign any pleadings, briefs, or other similar documents prepared by the registered legal services attorney before their filing, and must read and approve any documents prepared by the registered legal services attorney for execution by any person who is not a member of the State Bar of California before their submission for execution; and

(8) May, in his or her absence, designate another attorney meeting the requirements of (1) through (7) to provide the supervision required under this rule.

(Subd (h) relettered effective January 1, 2007; adopted as subd (g) effective November 15, 2004.)

(i) Inherent power of Supreme Court

Nothing in this rule may be construed as affecting the power of the Supreme Court of California to exercise its inherent jurisdiction over the practice of law in California.

(Subd (i) amended and relettered effective January 1, 2007; adopted as subd (h) effective November 15, 2004.)

(j) Effect of rule on multijurisdictional practice

Nothing in this rule limits the scope of activities permissible under existing law by attorneys who are not members of the State Bar of California.

(Subd (j) relettered effective January 1, 2007; adopted as subd (i) effective November 15, 2004.)

Rule 9.45 amended and renumbered effective January 1, 2007; adopted as rule 964 by the Supreme Court effective November 15, 2004.

Rule 9.46.   Registered in-house counsel

(a) Definitions

The following definitions apply to terms used in this rule:

(1) "Qualifying institution" means a corporation, a partnership, an association, or other legal entity, including its subsidiaries and organizational affiliates. Neither a governmental entity nor an entity that provides legal services to others can be a qualifying institution for purposes of this rule. A qualifying institution must:

(A) Employ at least 10 employees full time in California; or
(B) Employ in California an attorney who is an active member in good standing of the State Bar of California.

(2) "Active member in good standing of the bar of a United States state, jurisdiction, possession, territory, or dependency" means an attorney who meets all of the following criteria:

(A) Is a member in good standing of the entity governing the practice of law in each jurisdiction in which the member is licensed to practice law;
(B) Remains an active member in good standing of the entity governing the practice of law in at least one United States state, jurisdiction, possession, territory, or dependency, other than California, while practicing law as registered in-house counsel in California; and
(C) Has not been disbarred, has not resigned with charges pending, or is not suspended from practicing law in any other jurisdiction.

(Subd (a) relettered effective January 1, 2007; adopted as subd (j) effective November 15, 2004.)

(b) Scope of practice

Subject to all applicable rules, regulations, and statutes, an attorney practicing law under this rule is:

(1) Permitted to provide legal services in California only to the qualifying institution that employs him or her;

(2) Not permitted to make court appearances in California state courts or to engage in any other activities for which *pro hac vice* admission is required if they are performed in California by an attorney who is not a member of the State Bar of California; and

(3) Not permitted to provide personal or individual representation to any customers, shareholders, owners, partners, officers, employees, servants, or agents of the qualifying institution.

(Subd (b) amended and relettered effective January 1, 2007; adopted as subd (a) effective November 15, 2004.)

(c) Requirements

For an attorney to practice law under this rule, the attorney must:

(1) Be an active member in good standing of the bar of a United States state, jurisdiction, possession, territory, or dependency;

(2) Register with the State Bar of California and file an Application for Determination of Moral Character;

(3) Meet all of the requirements for admission to the State Bar of California, except that the attorney:

    (A) Need not take the California bar examination or the Multistate Professional Responsibility Examination; and

    (B) May practice law while awaiting the result of his or her Application for Determination of Moral Character;

(4) Comply with the rules adopted by the Board of Governors relating to the State Bar Registered In-House Counsel Program;

(5) Practice law exclusively for a single qualifying institution, except that, while practicing under this rule, the attorney may, if so qualified, simultaneously practice law as a registered legal services attorney;

(6) Abide by all of the laws and rules that govern members of the State Bar of California, including the Minimum Continuing Legal Education (MCLE) requirements;

(7) Satisfy in his or her first year of practice under this rule all of the MCLE requirements, including ethics education, that members of the State Bar of California must complete every three years and, thereafter, satisfy the MCLE requirements applicable to all members of the State Bar; and

(8) Reside in California.

(Subd (c) relettered effective January 1, 2007; adopted as subd (b) effective November 15, 2004.)

(d) Application

To qualify to practice law as registered in-house counsel, an attorney must:

(1) Register as an attorney applicant and file an Application for Determination of Moral Character with the Committee of Bar Examiners;

(2) Submit to the State Bar of California a declaration signed by the attorney agreeing that he or she will be subject to the disciplinary authority of the Supreme Court of California and the State Bar of California and attesting that he or she will not practice law in California other than on behalf of the qualifying institution during the time he or she is registered in-house counsel in California, except that if so qualified, the attorney may, while practicing under this rule, simultaneously practice law as a registered legal services attorney; and

(3) Submit to the State Bar of California a declaration signed by an officer, a director, or a general counsel of the applicant's employer, on behalf of the applicant's employer, attesting that the applicant is employed as an attorney for the employer, that the nature of the employment conforms to the requirements of this rule, that the employer will notify the State Bar of California within 30 days of the cessation of the applicant's employment in California, and that the person signing the declaration believes, to the best of his or her knowledge after reasonable inquiry, that the applicant qualifies for registration under this rule and is an individual of good moral character.

(Subd (d) relettered effective January 1, 2007; adopted as subd (c) effective November 15, 2004.)

(e) Duration of practice

A registered in-house counsel must renew his or her registration annually. There is no limitation on the number of years in-house counsel may register under this rule. Registered in-house counsel may practice law under this rule only for as long as he or she remains employed by the same qualifying institution that provided the declaration in support of his or her application. If an attorney practicing law as registered in-house counsel leaves the employment of his or her employer or changes employers, he or she must notify the State Bar of California within 30 days. If an attorney wishes to practice law under this rule for a new employer, he or she must first register as in-house counsel for that employer.

(Subd (e) amended and relettered effective January 1, 2007; adopted as subd (d) effective November 15, 2004.)

(f) Eligibility

An application to register under this rule may not be denied because:

(1) The attorney applicant has practiced law in California as in-house counsel before the effective date of this rule.

(2) The attorney applicant is practicing law as in-house counsel at or after the effective date of this rule, provided that the attorney applies under this rule within six months of its effective date.

(Subd (f) amended and relettered effective January 1, 2007; adopted as subd (e) effective November 15, 2004.)

(g) Application and registration fees

The State Bar of California may set appropriate application fees and initial and annual registration fees to be paid by registered in-house counsel.

(Subd (g) amended and relettered effective January 1, 2007; adopted as subd (f) effective November 15, 2004.)

(h) State Bar Registered In-House Counsel Program

The State Bar must establish and administer a program for registering California in-house counsel under rules adopted by the Board of Governors.

(Subd (h) amended and relettered effective January 1, 2007; adopted as subd (g) effective November 15, 2004.)

(i) Inherent power of Supreme Court

Nothing in this rule may be construed as affecting the power of the Supreme Court of California to exercise its inherent jurisdiction over the practice of law in California.

(Subd (i) amended and relettered effective January 1, 2007; adopted as subd (h) effective November 15, 2004.)

(j) Effect of rule on multijurisdictional practice

Nothing in this rule limits the scope of activities permissible under existing law by attorneys who are not members of the State Bar of California.

(Subd (j) relettered effective January 1, 2007; adopted as subd (i) effective November 15, 2004.)

Rule 9.46 amended and renumbered effective January 1, 2007; adopted as rule 965 by the Supreme Court effective November 15, 2004.

Rule 9.47. Attorneys practicing law temporarily in California as part of litigation

(a) Definitions

The following definitions apply to the terms used in this rule:

(1) "A formal legal proceeding" means litigation, arbitration, mediation, or a legal action before an administrative decision-maker.

(2) "Authorized to appear" means the attorney is permitted to appear in the proceeding by the rules of the jurisdiction in which the formal legal proceeding is taking place or will be taking place.

(3) "Active member in good standing of the bar of a United States state, jurisdiction, possession, territory, or dependency" means an attorney who meets all of the following criteria:

(A) Is a member in good standing of the entity governing the practice of law in each jurisdiction in which the member is licensed to practice law;

(B) Remains an active member in good standing of the entity governing the practice of law in at least one United States state, jurisdiction, possession, territory, or dependency while practicing law under this rule; and

(C) Has not been disbarred, has not resigned with charges pending, or is not suspended from practicing law in any other jurisdiction.

(Subd (a) relettered effective January 1, 2007; adopted as subd (g) effective November 15, 2004.)

(b) Requirements

For an attorney to practice law under this rule, the attorney must:

(1) Maintain an office in a United States jurisdiction other than California and in which the attorney is licensed to practice law;

(2) Already be retained by a client in the matter for which the attorney is providing legal services in California, except that the attorney may provide legal advice to a potential client, at the potential client's request, to assist the client in deciding whether to retain the attorney;

(3) Indicate on any Web site or other advertisement that is accessible in California either that the attorney is not a member of the State Bar of California or that the attorney is admitted to practice law only in the states listed; and

(4) Be an active member in good standing of the bar of a United States state, jurisdiction, possession, territory, or dependency.

(Subd (b) relettered effective January 1, 2007; adopted as subd (a) effective November 15, 2004.)

(c) Permissible activities

An attorney meeting the requirements of this rule, who complies with all applicable rules, regulations, and statutes, is not engaging in the unauthorized practice of law in California if the attorney's services are part of:

(1) A formal legal proceeding that is pending in another jurisdiction and in which the attorney is authorized to appear;

(2) A formal legal proceeding that is anticipated but is not yet pending in California and in which the attorney reasonably expects to be authorized to appear;

(3) A formal legal proceeding that is anticipated but is not yet pending in another jurisdiction and in which the attorney reasonably expects to be authorized to appear; or

(4) A formal legal proceeding that is anticipated or pending and in which the attorney's supervisor is authorized to appear or reasonably expects to be authorized to appear.

The attorney whose anticipated authorization to appear in a formal legal proceeding serves as the basis for practice under this rule must seek that authorization promptly after it becomes possible to do so. Failure to seek that authorization promptly, or denial of that authorization, ends eligibility to practice under this rule.

(Subd (c) relettered effective January 1, 2007; adopted as subd (b) effective November 15, 2004.)

(d) Restrictions

To qualify to practice law in California under this rule, an attorney must not:

(1) Hold out to the public or otherwise represent that he or she is admitted to practice law in California;

(2) Establish or maintain a resident office or other systematic or continuous presence in California for the practice of law;

(3) Be a resident of California;

(4) Be regularly employed in California;

(5) Regularly engage in substantial business or professional activities in California; or

(6) Have been disbarred, have resigned with charges pending, or be suspended from practicing law in any other jurisdiction.

(Subd (d) relettered effective January 1, 2007; adopted as subd (c) effective November 15, 2004.)

(e) Conditions

By practicing law in California under this rule, an attorney agrees that he or she is providing legal services in California subject to:

(1) The jurisdiction of the State Bar of California;

(2) The jurisdiction of the courts of this state to the same extent as is a member of the State Bar of California; and

(3) The laws of the State of California relating to the practice of law, the State Bar Rules of Professional Conduct, the rules and regulations of the State Bar of California, and these rules.

(Subd (e) relettered effective January 1, 2007; adopted as subd (d) effective November 15, 2004.)

(f) Inherent power of Supreme Court

Nothing in this rule may be construed as affecting the power of the Supreme Court of California to exercise its inherent jurisdiction over the practice of law in California.

(Subd (f) amended and relettered effective January 1, 2007; adopted as subd (e) effective November 15, 2004.)

(g) Effect of rule on multijurisdictional practice

Nothing in this rule limits the scope of activities permissible under existing law by attorneys who are not members of the State Bar of California.

(Subd (g) relettered effective January 1, 2007; adopted as subd (f) effective November 15, 2004.)

Rule 9.47 amended and renumbered effective January 1, 2007; adopted as rule 966 by the Supreme Court effective November 15, 2004.

Rule 9.48. Nonlitigating attorneys temporarily in California to provide legal services

(a) Definitions

The following definitions apply to terms used in this rule:

(1) "A transaction or other nonlitigation matter" includes any legal matter other than litigation, arbitration, mediation, or a legal action before an administrative decision-maker.

(2) "Active member in good standing of the bar of a United States state, jurisdiction, possession, territory, or dependency" means an attorney who meets all of the following criteria:

(A) Is a member in good standing of the entity governing the practice of law in each jurisdiction in which the member is licensed to practice law;

(B) Remains an active member in good standing of the entity governing the practice of law in at least one United States state, jurisdiction, possession, territory, or dependency other than California while practicing law under this rule; and

(C) Has not been disbarred, has not resigned with charges pending, or is not suspended from practicing law in any other jurisdiction.

(Subd (a) relettered effective January 1, 2007; adopted as subd (h) effective November 15, 2004.)

(b) Requirements

For an attorney to practice law under this rule, the attorney must:

(1) Maintain an office in a United States jurisdiction other than California and in which the attorney is licensed to practice law;

(2) Already be retained by a client in the matter for which the attorney is providing legal services in California, except that the attorney may provide legal advice to a potential client, at the potential client's request, to assist the client in deciding whether to retain the attorney;

(3) Indicate on any Web site or other advertisement that is accessible in California either that the attorney is not a member of the State Bar of California or that the attorney is admitted to practice law only in the states listed; and

(4) Be an active member in good standing of the bar of a United States state, jurisdiction, possession, territory, or dependency.

(Subd (b) relettered effective January 1, 2007; adopted as subd (a) effective November 15, 2004.)

(c) Permissible activities

An attorney who meets the requirements of this rule and who complies with all applicable rules, regulations, and statutes is not engaging in the unauthorized practice of law in California if the attorney:

(1) Provides legal assistance or legal advice in California to a client concerning a transaction or other nonlitigation matter, a material

aspect of which is taking place in a jurisdiction other than California and in which the attorney is licensed to provide legal services;

(2) Provides legal assistance or legal advice in California on an issue of federal law or of the law of a jurisdiction other than California to attorneys licensed to practice law in California; or

(3) Is an employee of a client and provides legal assistance or legal advice in California to the client or to the client's subsidiaries or organizational affiliates.

(Subd (c) relettered effective January 1, 2007; adopted as subd (b) effective November 15, 2004.)

(d) Restrictions

To qualify to practice law in California under this rule, an attorney must not:

(1) Hold out to the public or otherwise represent that he or she is admitted to practice law in California;

(2) Establish or maintain a resident office or other systematic or continuous presence in California for the practice of law;

(3) Be a resident of California;

(4) Be regularly employed in California;

(5) Regularly engage in substantial business or professional activities in California; or

(6) Have been disbarred, have resigned with charges pending, or be suspended from practicing law in any other jurisdiction.

(Subd (d) amended and relettered effective January 1, 2007; adopted as subd (c) effective November 15, 2004.)

(e) Conditions

By practicing law in California under this rule, an attorney agrees that he or she is providing legal services in California subject to:

(1) The jurisdiction of the State Bar of California;

(2) The jurisdiction of the courts of this state to the same extent as is a member of the State Bar of California; and

(3) The laws of the State of California relating to the practice of law, the State Bar Rules of Professional Conduct, the rules and regulations of the State Bar of California, and these rules.

(Subd (e) amended and relettered effective January 1, 2007; adopted as subd (d) effective November 15, 2004.)

(f) Scope of practice

An attorney is permitted by this rule to provide legal assistance or legal services concerning only a transaction or other nonlitigation matter.

(Subd (f) relettered effective January 1, 2007; adopted as subd (e) effective November 15, 2004.)

(g) Inherent power of Supreme Court

Nothing in this rule may be construed as affecting the power of the Supreme Court of California to exercise its inherent jurisdiction over the practice of law in California.

(Subd (g) amended and relettered effective January 1, 2007; adopted as subd (f) effective November 15, 2004.)

(h) Effect of rule on multijurisdictional practice

Nothing in this rule limits the scope of activities permissible under existing law by attorneys who are not members of the State Bar of California.

(Subd (h) relettered effective January 1,2007; adopted as subd (g) effective November 15, 2004.)

Rule 9.48 amended and renumbered effective January 1, 2007; adopted as rule 967 by the Supreme Court effective November 15, 2004.

TABLE OF CASES

[References are to page numbers.]

TABLE OF STATUTES

[References are to page numbers.]

RACKETEER INFLUENCED AND CORRUPT ORGANIZATION ACT (RICO)

REVENUE ACT OF 1978

Section

SMALL BUSINESS AND WORK OPPORTUNITY TAX ACT OF 2007

TAX EXTENDERS AND ALTERNATIVE MINIMUM TAX RELIEF ACT OF 2008

TAX REFORM ACT OF 1976

TREASURY REGULATIONS

Section

UNITED STATES CODE (U.S.C.)

TABLE OF SECONDARY AUTHORITIES

[References are to page numbers.]

AMERICAN BAR ASSOCIATION (ABA) SECTION OF TAXATION COMMITTEE ON STANDARDS OF TAX PRACTICE, STANDARDS OF TAX PRACTICE STATEMENT

Statement

AMERICAN INSTITUTE OF CERTIFIED PUBLIC ACCOUNTANTS (AICPA) CODE OF PROFESSIONAL CONDUCT

ET Section

Interpretation

Rule

AMERICAN INSTITUTE OF CERTIFIED PUBLIC ACCOUNTANTS (AICPA) STATEMENTS ON RESPONSIBILITIES IN TAX PRACTICE (SRTPS)

AMERICAN INSTITUTE OF CERTIFIED PUBLIC ACCOUNTANTS (AICPA) STATEMENTS ON STANDARDS FOR TAX SERVICES (SSTSs)

BOOKS

FEDERAL REGISTER

FEDERAL RULES OF CIVIL PROCEDURE

I.R.S. FORMS

I.R.S. NOTICES

LAW REVIEW/LAW JOURNAL ARTICLES

TAXATION DETERMINATIONS (T.D.)

TAX COURT RULES

INDEX